TANTRA IN PRACTICE

PRINCETON READINGS IN RELIGIONS

Donald S. Lopez, Jr., Editor

TITLES IN THE SERIES

Religions of India in Practice edited by Donald S. Lopez, Jr.

Buddhism in Practice edited by Donald S. Lopez, Jr.

Religions of China in Practice edited by Donald S. Lopez, Jr.

Religions of Tibet in Practice edited by Donald S. Lopez, Jr.

Religions of Japan in Practice edited by George J. Tanabe, Jr.

Asian Religions in Practice: An Introduction edited by Donald S. Lopez, Jr.

Religions of Late Antiquity in Practice edited by Richard Valantasis

Tantra in Practice edited by David Gordon White

TANTRA

IN PRACTICE

David Gordon White, Editor

PRINCETON READINGS IN RELIGIONS

PRINCETON UNIVERSITY PRESS

PRINCETON AND OXFORD

Published by Princeton University Press, 41 William Street,
Princeton, New Jersey 08540
In the United Kingdom: Princeton University Press, 3 Market Place, Woodstock,
Oxfordshire OX20 ISY

Library of Congress Cataloging-in-Publication Data

Tantra in practice / David Gordon White, editor.
p. cm. — (Princeton readings in religions)
Includes bibliographical references and index.
ISBN 0-691-05778-8 (cloth: alk.paper) — ISBN 0-691-05779-6 (paper: alk.paper)
1. Tantrism. 2. Tantric Buddhism. I. White, David Gordon. II. Series.
BL1283.84 .T36 2000
294.5'95—dc21 00-022890

This book has been composed in Berkeley

The paper used in this publication meets the minimum requirements
of ANSI/NISO Z39.48-1992 (R 1997) (*Permanence of Paper*)

www.pup.princeton.edu

Printed in the United States of America

1 3 5 7 9 10 8 6 4 2

1 3 5 7 9 10 8 6 4 2
(Pbk.)

PRINCETON READINGS IN RELIGIONS

Princeton Readings in Religions is a new series of anthologies on the religions of the world, representing the significant advances that have been made in the study of religions in the last thirty years. The sourcebooks used by previous generations of students, whether for Judaism and Christianity or for the religions of Asia and the Middle East, placed a heavy emphasis on "canonical works." Princeton Readings in Religions provides a different configuration of texts in an attempt better to represent the range of religious practices, placing particular emphasis on the ways in which texts have been used in diverse contexts. The volumes in this series therefore include ritual manuals, hagiographical and autobiographical works, popular commentaries, and folktales, as well as some ethnographic material. Many works are drawn from vernacular sources. The readings in the series are new in two senses. First, very few of the works contained in the volumes have ever been made available in an anthology before; in the case of the volumes on Asia, few have even been translated into a Western language. Second, the readings are new in the sense that each volume provides new ways to read and understand the religions of the world, breaking down the sometimes misleading stereotypes inherited from the past in an effort to provide both more expansive and more focused perspectives on the richness and diversity of religious expressions. The series is designed for use by a wide range of readers, with key terms translated and technical notes omitted. Each volume also contains a substantial introduction by a distinguished scholar in which the histories of the traditions are outlined and the significance of each of the works is explored.

Tantra in Practice is the eighth volume of Princeton Readings in Religions and the first substantial anthology of Tantric works ever to appear in English. The thirty-nine contributors, drawn from around the world, are leading scholars of Tantra. Each contributor has provided a translation of a key work, in most cases translated here for the first time. Each chapter in the volume begins with an introduction in which the translator discusses the history and influence of the work, identifying points of particular difficulty or interest. David White has provided a general introduction to the volume that serves as an ideal guide to the riches contained between the covers of this book. He has organized the volume thematically, providing fascinating juxtapositions of works from different regions, periods, and traditions. Two additional tables of contents are provided, organizing the works by tradition and by country of origin.

The range of works represented here is remarkable, spanning the continent of Asia and the traditions of Hinduism, Buddhism, Jainism, and Islam over more than a millennium. With the publication of this volume, the long disparaged and neglected Tantric traditions of Asia receive the attention they so rightly deserve. This is a groundbreaking work.

Donald S. Lopez, Jr.
Series Editor

NOTE ON TRANSLITERATION

The works in this volume are translated from many Indic languages, as well as from the Chinese, Japanese, and Tibetan languages. In the case of the Indic languages, the translators have, in general, adhered to the standard transliteration system for each of the languages. Certain common place names, proper names, and selected terms that have entered into English usage on the Indian subcontinent are shown without diacritical marks. Chinese terms appear in Pinyin. Japanese terms appear in Hepburn transliteration. Tibetan terms are rendered in a phonetic equivalent by the translator, after which the term is provided in Wylie transliteration. Modern place-names and names of modern authors and editors are transliterated without diacriticals.

CONTENTS

Traditions in Transition and Conflict

Tantric Paths

Rites and Techniques

Yoga and Meditation

CONTENTS BY TRADITION

Buddhist Tantra

Hindu Tantra

Jain Tantra

Tantra and Islam in South Asia

CONTENTS BY COUNTRY

China

India

Japan

Nepal

Tibet

CONTRIBUTORS

Yael Bentor teaches in the Department of Indian Studies at the Hebrew University of Jerusalem.

Bronwen Bledsoe is a graduate student in the Department of South Asian Studies at the University of Chicago.

William Bodiford teaches in the Department of East Asian Languages and Cultures at the University of California, Los Angeles.

Douglas Renfrew Brooks teaches in the Department of Religion and Classics at University of Rochester.

Gudrun Bühnemann teaches in the Department of South Asian Studies at the University of Wisconsin, Madison.

John E. Cort teaches in the Department of Religion at Denison University.

Richard H. Davis teaches in the Department of Religion at Bard College.

Paul Dundas teaches in the Department of Sanskrit at the University of Edinburgh.

Kathleen M. Erndl teaches in the Department of Religion at Florida State University.

Bernard Faure teaches in the Department of Religion at Stanford University.

Gavin Flood teaches in the Department of Theology and Religious Studies at the University of Wales, Lampeter.

David L. Gardiner teaches in the Department of Religion at Colorado College.

David Germano teaches in the Department of Religious Studies at the University of Virginia.

Teun Goudriaan is Professor Emeritus at the University of Utrecht.

Allan G. Grapard teaches in the Department of Religious Studies at the University of California, Santa Barbara.

Sanjukta Gupta teaches in the Faculty of Oriental Studies, Oxford University.

Janet Gyatso teaches in the Department of Religion at Amherst College.

Glen A. Hayes teaches in the Department of Religious Studies at Bloomfield College.

D. Dennis Hudson teaches in the Department of Religion at Smith College.

Matthew T. Kapstein teaches in the Department of South Asian Studies at the University of Chicago.

Dominique-Sila Khan is a Research Fellow at the Institute of Rajasthan Studies, Jaipur, India.

Anne Carolyn Klein teaches in the Department of Religious Studies at Rice University.

Donald S. Lopez, Jr. teaches in the Department of Asian Languages and Cultures at the University of Michigan.

David N. Lorenzen teaches in the Centro de Estudios de Asia y Africa at El Colegio de Mexico.

June McDaniel teaches in the Department of Philosophy and Religion at the College of Charleston.

Rachel Fell McDermott teaches in the Department of Asian and Middle Eastern Cultures at Barnard College.

Paul E. Muller-Ortega teaches in the Department of Religion and Classics at the University of Rochester.

John Newman teaches in the Division of the Humanities at the New College of the University of South Florida.

Giacomella Orofino teaches at the Istituto Universitario Orientale, Naples.

Charles D. Orzech teaches in the Department of Religious Studies at the University of North Carolina, Greensboro.

André Padoux is a Directeur de Recherche at the Centre National de la Recherche Scientifique, Paris.

Richard K. Payne is Director of the Institute of Buddhist Studies, San Francisco.

Olle Qvarnström teaches in the Department of Theological and Religious Studies at Lund University.

Michael D. Rabe teaches in the Art Department of Saint Xavier University, Chicago.

Fabio Rambelli teaches in the Department of Culture Studies at Sapporo University.

Robin Rinehart teaches in the Department of Religion at Lafayette College.

James H. Sanford teaches in the Department of Religious Studies at the University of North Carolina, Chapel Hill.

Tony K. Stewart teaches in the Department of Philosophy and Religion at North Carolina State University.

Michael Walter is a Research Fellow at the Lumbini Research Center, Lumbini, Nepal.

David Gordon White teaches in the Department of Religious Studies at the University of California, Santa Barbara.

TANTRA IN PRACTICE

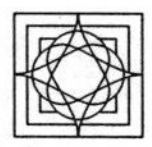

INTRODUCTION

Tantra in Practice: Mapping a Tradition

David Gordon White

As with all the books in this series, the present volume has the word "practice" in its title. Practice is impossible without agents of practice, that is, practitioners, and the first four sections of this volume comprise those contributions that focus on Tantric practitioners or actors. These include Tantric preceptors (*gurus*) and their followers; kings and priests; and devotees and the Tantric gods they worship (for the gods too are Tantric actors). These relationships were not static, however, and the fourth section contains accounts of traditions in transition and conflict. The last three sections of the volume are devoted to the practices themselves. Those contributions which describe the broad general practice of an entire tradition or region of the Tantric world make up the fifth section. A wide gamut of types or elements of Tantric practice, both external rites and their internal correlates, is explored in sections six and seven.

It may be that the ideal medium for a presentation of Tantric practice (or any practice, for that matter) would be a video or CD-ROM, in which one could actually view Tantric practitioners practicing their Tantra. This is impossible for a number of reasons—Tantric secrecy, the fact that many of the practices detailed here disappeared centuries ago, the practical limitations of scholarly publishing—so the reader is presented with a thick book. But books have their advantages as well, and the Tantras themselves (which are texts) clearly state that scripture is the necessary complement to the oral teachings one receives from the mouth of one's guru. Furthermore, "pure" practice without interpretive theory is like a map without a legend: if you don't know what the various elements of the practice mean, then it is nothing but empty gestures. The reader should therefore not be susprised to find that this volume on Tantric practice contains a significant amount of material on Tantric theory. Very often, this is built into the structure of the Tantric texts themselves: instructions for practice are contextualized in the theories—of man, the universe, and everything—that undergird them. Yet these theories can be as impenetrable as the practices themselves, especially in such esoteric traditions as these. Therefore, a second level of interpretation is in order, and this is the invaluable contribution of the thirty-nine scholars whose chapters are presented here, for not only have they translated the many languages of the Tantras into English but they have also translated the multifaceted Tantric worldview into comprehensible language in their introductory essays.

I have attempted to do the same in this general introduction, and the reader will find that my analysis is based in no small part on the work of these same scholars, whose publications I cite. In this introduction, names in [square brackets] refer to contributions found in this volume; references in (parentheses) refer to works found in the bibliography to this essay.

Can Tantra Be Mapped?

The contributions brought together in this volume all treat of Tantra, a body of religious practice that has long defied scholarly attempts at definition. There are many who maintain that Tantra or "Tantrism" is a Western category, imposed upon Asian traditions in much the same way that the term "Hinduism" was applied, some centuries ago, to a wide swath of mainstream religious beliefs and practices found on the Indian subcontinent. As Gertrude Stein did for the city of Oakland, such persons assert on the subject of Tantra that there is no "there" there. One could make the same claim regarding much of the terminology we live with, of course: the categories of "religion," "democracy," and "art," for example, prove to be quite nebulous when exposed to the glare of critical scrutiny. Others would maintain that the Indian parable of the blind men and the elephant is applicable to Tantra. Depending on which part of the elephant (which specific Tantric tradition) a given blind man (scholar) is touching (studying), his account of the animal (Tantra) will vary widely from that of his fellow blind man. The scholar examining the fine hard tusk of pure Buddhist esotericism in modern-day Japan would find herself hard pressed to recognize that the deeply furrowed hide of the medieval Indian Kāpālika's (Skull-Bearer's) practice [Lorenzen] is a part of the same Tantric organism.

Then there are the Western dilettantes, the self-proclaimed Tantric entrepreneurs, who have hitched their elephant-wagons to the New Age star to peddle a dubious product called Tantric Sex, which they (and their clientele) assume to be all there ever was to Tantra. It is certainly the case that the earliest accounts of Tantra to reach the West were colonial descriptions from India, penned by missionaries or administrators who presented its practices as particularly abominable excrescences of South Asian superstition. Their descriptions often included shocking images of wholesale orgy in which every taboo was broken and all human propriety perverted. Over the past two hundred years, there have been three sorts of reactions to these distorted images. The first of these is that of India itself: colonial and postcolonial Indians simply deny that such has ever existed; or if it has, that it has had anything to do with Hinduism (another term that defies categorization). The second is that of Tantric scholar-practitioners, both Asian and Western, who, in an attempt to rehabilitate this image of Tantra, have emphasized the refined ("right-handed") philosophical speculation that grew out of preexisting ("left-handed") Tantric practices—some of which were of a sexual or transgressive nature—while generally denying the foundational importance of transgressivity or sexuality to the traditions themselves. The third, already mentioned, is that of the for-profit purveyors of Tantric Sex, who have no compunctions about appropriating a misguided nineteenth-century polemic to peddle their shoddy wares.

All three interpretive strategies may be viewed as legacies of the original "text" of colonial misrepresentations of Tantra in India. All three tend to imagine Tantra as a timeless, unalterable essence or excrescence that did not undergo any changes either prior to or since its nineteenth-century "coming out," and that remained constant as it was carried outward from India into every part of Asia. As the variety of contributions to this volume show, neither the sensationalist colonial representations nor the unsatisfactory monothetic responses to them, either "for" or "against," stand up against the empirical data. The picture that emerges is rather one of a complex array of ritual, theoretical, and narrative strategies that are specific to their various religious, cultural, sociopolitical, geographical, and historical contexts. Yet for all this, there nonetheless exists a grouping of common denominators that should permit us to classify these as so many varieties of a single tradition, the "there" of Tantra.

In the pages that follow, I attempt to tease out the parameters and lineaments of this thing called Tantra from a number of perspectives. The first of these is thematic or phenomenological. This is mainly a comparative endeavor, in which the common elements of many types of Tantric theory and practice are juxtaposed and synthesized. This sort of outsider's assessment of Tantra is an etic one: made from a variety of perspectives, it will tend to characterize Tantra in ways not necessarily recognizable to Tantric practitioners themselves. The Tantric insider's or emic view must of necessity also be incorporated into our description. These two perspectives, when juxtaposed with one another, ought to provide us with a Tantric "ideology"—that is, a set of categorical "lenses" through which Tantric practitioners have made sense of their practice within their broader worldview (their ontology) and understandings of power in the world (their religious polity), and human salvation in or beyond this world (their soteriology). Systems of practice that are incompatible with or unadaptable to lived experience on the one hand, and to an imagined ontology, polity, and soteriology on the other, will not persist through time. Perhaps unbeknownst to themselves, practitioners are constantly testing their traditions against lived reality, and although religious change is notoriously slow, it is nonetheless inexorable. Therefore, if there is still something called Tantra that has persisted since its origins in the middle of the first millennium of the common era down to the present day—and I contend that there is—its architectonics should be discernable through its emic categories. Our approach, then, will consist of an inductive linking of the most salient features of Tantric practice to specific and general Tantric precepts.

The second perspective adopted here is historical. It is the case that every South and East Asian religious tradition has had a Tantric phase or component, and many of these continue down to the present day. However, none of these have continued unchanged since the original Tantric impetus, and it is for this reason that our account of Tantra must be historical. No synchronic taxonomy of the salient features of Tantric theory and practice will suffice; only through a diachronic or evolutionary overview of the various schools, sects, scriptures, bodies of practice, and lines of transmission that have comprised Tantra will we be able to make sense of this tradition. Such a historical accounting must not, moreover, be limited to a simple history of ideas. It must engage as well with ground-level practice, imagery, institutions, political realities, and the interface between public and private religion.

Third, our approach must attend to the human agents or actors in the dissemination and transformation of Tantric doctrines and practices. Here the following questions must be addressed. Which Tantric practitioners have practiced for themselves, and which have practiced for others as Tantric specialists? What have been the social and religious backgrounds of the latter? Who have constituted their clienteles? What have been their clients' motives for engaging them to perform their functions? When a king or other potentate is a Tantric practitioner, what impact does his patronage have on religious institutions and the religious and political life of his subjects? What has been the nature of the interface between "popular" and "elite" forms of practice? How do theory and practice change when practice becomes individual as opposed to collective?

Finally, a word about the scope of this endeavor. Because this is a comparative enterprise (in which different forms of Tantra, from different historical periods, religious traditions, and sociopolitical contexts are being compared), the question of parameters arises: where does one draw the line between "Tantra" and "not-Tantra"? In other words, if we are attempting to delimit Tantra from other forms of religious practice in Asia, what are our criteria to be for determining Tantra's specificity? What is it that has made Tantra stand out from the mainstream (or in some cases, *as* the mainstream) as a body of practice to live for—and sometimes to fight for, to kill for, or to die for? Throughout the fifteen hundred years of its history, Tantra has rarely left people indifferent, and this has been precisely due to the fact that it has been viewed as something *different*.

Our definition of Tantra must therefore attend to Tantra's difference, but here as well we must tread with caution. We may speak in terms of a "hard core" and a "soft core" of Tantra. The former, composed solely of those elements of Tantric doctrine and practice that are not found anywhere else in the Asian religious traditions under study, would provide us with a sharply defined but very limited account of Tantra—and one that would, moreover, probably exclude many of the doctrines and practices that practitioners have themselves deemed to be Tantric. A more inclusive, "soft core," definition tends to break down, however, because its parameters will encompass doctrines and practices found in nearly all forms of the various Asian traditions, from the Vedas and early teachings of the Buddha and Mahāvīra down through conventional forms of Hinduism, Jainism,

Buddhism, Daoism, and Shintō, as well as in many nonelite forms of Asian religious practice. For example, much of mainstream Hindu devotional ritual—preliminary purifications, the use of mantras for honoring the deity, forms of worship, and so on—has its origins in the scriptures of the "soft core" of Hindu Tantra, the Śaiva Āgamas. Elsewhere, the Tantric dictum that the human being (as opposed to an animal or a deity) is the creature best suited to salvation or liberation through Tantric practice differs little from anthropocentric doctrines of the broader Hindu, Buddhist, or Jain mainstream. The danger here is that everything becomes Tantra, and our category loses its specificity.

Yet, at the same time, if we were to deny that this "soft core" is authentically Tantric, we would fly in the face of the emic understandings of householders and ritual specialists from the modern-day Tantric mainstream, including Hindu Śrīvidyā practitioners in India and Nepal, Buddhist Gelugpa practitioners in Tibet and the Tibetan diaspora, and practitioners of pure Buddhist esotericism (*mikkyō*, from the Chinese *mijiao*, "esoteric teaching") in Japan. If these practitioners consider their daily religious observances as well as their life-cycle rites and postmortem rituals to be Tantric, who are we to say they are wrong?

A Working Definition

Tantra has persisted and often thrived throughout Asian history since the middle of the first millennium of the common era. Its practitioners have lived in India, China, Japan, Tibet, Nepal, Bhutan, Pakistan, Sri Lanka, Korea, and Mongolia, as well as in the "Greater India" of medieval Southeast Asia: Cambodia, Burma, and Indonesia. No form of medieval Hinduism, Buddhism, or Jainism [Dundas] has been without a Tantric component; and some South Asian Islamic traditions have, as well, borne a Tantric stamp [Khan]. In Hindu India, the Pāñcarātra [Flood], Gauḍīya Vaiṣṇava, Sahajiyā, Pāśupata, Kāpālika, Śaiva Siddhānta, Siddha Kaula, Yoginī Kaula, Krama, Trika, Śrīvidyā, Paścimāmnāya, Nāth Siddha, Aghori, Bengali Śākta-Vaiṣṇava and Bāul traditions, and Tamil Nāyaṉār and Āḻvār traditions [Hudson], have all been Tantric or heavily colored by Tantra.

Although Buddhism disappeared from India in the thirteenth century, India was the source of the Buddhist Mahāsiddha tradition [Kapstein] and the cradle of Buddhist Tantra in its Mahāyāna, Mantrayāna, and Vajrayāna (including Kālacakra [Newman]) forms. In Java, the layout of the massive Borobadur monument, begun in the eighth century, is that of a massive cosmogram, perhaps the dharmadhātu-maṇḍala, a Buddhist Tantric rendering of the enlightened universe. The late tenth-century author of the Buddhist *Kālacakra Tantra*, although he may have been born in Java (Newman 1985: 85), probably composed his work, which contains a number of references to Islam, in what is now central Pakistan (Orofino 1997). Tibetan Buddhism is by definition a Tantric tradition: this applies to the four major orders (the Nyingmapas, Kagyupas, Sakyapas, and Gelugpas), as well as to the Dzogchen [Klein] and other syncretistic traditions. Much of the ritual of the medieval Chinese state was Tantric, and it was from China that nearly all of the Buddhist Tantric traditions of Japan were transmitted. In China, Tantra has survived since the twelfth century C.E. within Daoist ritual practice, and it has been said that Daoism is the most enduring Chinese monument to Tantric Buddhism (Strickmann 1996: 49). Elsewhere, the Chinese Chan (a Sinicization of Sanskrit *dhyāna*, "meditation") school lives on in Japan as Zen Buddhism [Bodiford]. In Burma, the Zawgyis, Theravāda monk-alchemists, have for centuries combined elements of Theravāda Buddhism, Daoism, and Tantric alchemy in their practice. Cambodian inscriptions indicate the presence of Hindu tāntrikas (practitioners of Tantra) there in the medieval period. Present-day Balinese Hinduism betrays its medieval Indian Tantric origins, and Sri Lankan cults of the "demonic" beings known as *yakkhas* (*yakṣas* in Sanskrit) and of Kataragama (the equivalent of Skanda/Mañjuśrī) contain elements that may be qualified as Tantric. In Japan, all of the eight schools of Buddhism have a Tantric pedigree, although Shingon and Tendai have been Japan's most sucessful exponents of "Pure Buddhist Esotericism."

Finally, the constitutional monarchies of Nepal and Bhutan are the world's sole surviving "Tantric kingdoms"; their state ceremonial comprises Hindu Tantric liturgies and rituals, and nearly all of their deities are Tantric. One of these, Bhairava, is a Tantric god found in every part of Asia, and worshiped in a Tantric mode by Hindus, Jains, and Buddhists alike. Similarly, the goddesses and gods Tārā, Ambikā, Akṣobhya, Mahākāla, Gaṇeśa, Avalokiteśvara-Lokeśvara-Guanyin-Kannon, and Skanda-Mañjuśrī, as well as numerous groups of multiple Tantric deities, are found throughout much of Asia. It is the pan-Asian existence of deities such as these that supports an argument that medieval and precolonial Asian religions, rather than having been discrete Tantric Hindu, Buddhist, and Jain traditions, were, to a great extent, Hindu, Buddhist, and Jain varieties of an overarching tradition called "Tantra."

On what theoretical basis or bases may we term all of these medieval, precolonial, or modern traditions "Tantric"? I will begin by borrowing a definition proposed by Madeleine Biardeau and broadened by André Padoux. Padoux (1986: 273), citing Biardeau, begins by saying that the doctrinal aspect of Tantra is "an attempt to place *kāma*, desire, in every sense of the word, in the service of liberation . . . not to sacrifice this world for liberation's sake, but to reinstate it, in varying ways, within the perspective of salvation. This use of *kāma* and of all aspects of this world to gain both worldly and supernatural enjoyments (*bhukti*) and powers (*siddhis*), and to obtain liberation in this life (*jīvanmukti*), implies a particular attitude on the part of the Tantric adept toward the cosmos, whereby he feels integrated within an all-embracing system of micro-macrocosmic correlations."

This definition concentrates on the goals of Tantric practice (*sādhana*). Here, I wish to add a consideration of the nature of Tantric practice itself. Tantric practice is an effort to gain access to and appropriate the energy or enlightened consciousness of the absolute godhead that courses through the universe, giving its creatures life and the potential for salvation. Humans in particular are empowered to realize this goal through strategies of embodiment—that is, of causing that divine energy to become concentrated in one or another sort of template, grid, or mesocosm—prior to its internalization in or identification with the individual microcosm. With this, I offer the following working definition of Tantra:

> Tantra is that Asian body of beliefs and practices which, working from the principle that the universe we experience is nothing other than the concrete manifestation of the divine energy of the godhead that creates and maintains that universe, seeks to ritually appropriate and channel that energy, within the human microcosm, in creative and emancipatory ways.

This definition, however, must be modified according to its contexts, given that it would probably be rejected out of hand by many Tantric practitioners, who would find it at variance with their own particular doctrines and perspectives. Buddhists, for example, would be inclined to replace the term "energy" with "teaching" or "enlightened consciousness," whereas a village-level practitioner would, if asked, probably feel more comfortable with the term "beings." However, when this definition is shown to be applicable to major forms of Tantric practice across the gamut of its regional and vernacular Hindu, Buddhist, and Jain forms in Asia, it becomes a valuable organizing principle.

The Tantric Maṇḍala

The key to understanding Tantric practice is the maṇḍala, the energy grid that represents the constant flow of divine and demonic, human and animal impulses in the universe, as they interact in both constructive and destructive patterns. Like the Vedic sacrificial altar of which it is a streamlined form, the maṇḍala is a mesocosm, mediating between the great and small (the universal macrocosm and the individual microcosm), as well as between the mundane and the sublime (the protocosm of the visible world of human experience and the transcendent-yet-immanent metacosm that is its invisible fount). This grid is three dimensional, in the sense that it locates the supreme deity (god, goddess, celestial buddha, bodhisattva, or enlightened tīrthaṅkara), the source of that energy and ground of the grid itself, at the center and apex of a hierarchized cosmos. All other beings, including the practitioner, will be situated at lower levels of energy/consciousness/being, radiating downward and outward from the maṇḍala's elevated center point.

Because the deity is both transcendent and immanent, all of the beings located at the various energy levels on the grid participate in the outward flow of the godhead, and are in some way emanations or hypostases of the deity himself (or herself). For Hindu Tantra, this means that the world is real and not an illusion; this is an important distinguishing feature of Hindu Tantric doctrine. Rather than attempting to see through or transcend the world, the practioner comes to recognize "that" (the world) as "I" (the supreme egoity of the godhead): in other words, s/he gains a "god's eye view" of the universe, and recognizes it to be nothing other than herself/himself. For East Asian Buddhist Tantra in particular, this means that the totality of the cosmos is a "realm of Dharma," sharing an underlying common principle (the teachings of the buddhas), if not a common material substance [Rambelli]. More generally, this means that buddhahood is virtual within all creatures. In the words of the *Hevajra Tantra* (2.4.70, 75), "All beings are buddhas" and "there is no being that is not enlightened, if it but knows its own true nature." To render this blissful Buddha nature manifest is the purpose of Tantric practice—whether externalized in rites or internalized in yoga (Kværne 1975: 128)—and the body is "the indispensable organ for contact with the absolute" (Faure 1998: 61). Rather than being impediments, the world and the human body become channels to salvation.

At popular levels of practice throughout Asia, this means that the world of everyday life can only be negotiated by transacting with myriad beings extending from the spirit world of the recently deceased to the fierce protector deities that are the lower emanations or simply the servants of the high gods at the center of the elite maṇḍalas. Here, embodying the divine is less a goal than a ritual technique (inducing a state of possession) for combatting demons. We will turn to the nonelite Tantric practice of the maṇḍala in Part Two of this essay; here, we concentrate on elite theory and practice.

The energy levels of the Tantric universe are generally represented as a set of concentric circles (*cakras*) of hypostasized forms of the divine energy which, in addition to appearing as an array of divine, enlightened, perfected, demonic, human, or animal beings, also manifest themselves on an acoustic level, as garlands or piled-up aggregates of phonemes (*mantras*); on a graphic level, as the written characters of the hieratic alphabets; and as the hierarchized cakras of the yogic body. These same configurations constitute the flow charts of Tantric lineages, with the flow of divine energy (but also the fluid, acoustic, or photic essence of the godhead; or the teachings of enlightened buddhas) streaming downward and outward through a succession of male and female deities and demigods—the latter often portrayed in an animal or demonic mode—into "superhuman" gurus [Padoux] and their human disciples.

In every case, one detects "fractal" patterns, in which the original bipolar dyad of the godhead in essence and manifestation (usually male and female) proliferates into increasing orders of multiplicity. Unity in multiplicity is a hallmark of Tantra, and in this respect, it is an extension of earlier, less complex, Asian metaphysical systems. There is, in Tantra, an exponential explosion of all preexisting pantheons of deities, and together with these, an expansion of every sort of category—family, number, color, direction, aspect, and so on—into an intricate cosmic calculus. With its perfect geometric forms and elaborately interwoven lines, the maṇḍala is the ideal conceptual tool for plotting the multi-leveled and polyvalent interrelationships between these categories. As such it can, and often does, become self-referential, a transcendent and ideal "utopia," entirely abstracted from the "real world" of which it is the invisible, theoretical ground. Perhaps the best-known maṇḍala-cum-plotting device in the Tantric universe is the Śrī Cakra or Śrī Yantra of Hindu Tantric practice, a perfectly balanced three-dimensional geometric diagram comprising of a series of eleven interlocking and embedded triangles (also called cakras) radiating downward and outward from a center point, and enclosed by a circle and a square. The maṇḍalas of Buddhist and Jain Tantric practice follow similar structural and dynamic principles.

Even at this level of abstraction, the Tantric maṇḍala remains a template through which humans may interact with the divine, and thereby come to experience reality from a superhuman perspective. The practice of the maṇḍala generally involves a meditative or performative projection of both the metacosmic godhead and the protocosmic self into its vortex, followed by an implosion of the entire grid into its center point. Here, the underlying assumption is that this implosion is a reversal of the original cosmogony—that is, of a primal impulse or flow (*saṃsāra*) into manifest existence—back into the source of energies mapped on the grid. One's self-projection into the maṇḍala and gradual return to the center is therefore a return to the source of one's being; at each level, one is gnoseologically transformed into a higher, more divine, more enlightened being, until one becomes the god or buddha at the center (except in some dualist forms of Tantra). As we will show, there is an implicit notion of biological succession here, from the supreme godhead down through a guru-disciple lineage, which makes initiation and consecration central features of Tantric theory and practice.

Although the name, attributes, and entourage of the deity located at the center of the maṇḍala vary from one tradition to another, nearly all Tantric practice of the maṇḍala has this same goal, of transacting with and eventually identifying with that deity. In this practice, movement toward the center, effected through a combination of external ritual and internal meditative practices, entails harmonizing one's own energy or consciousness level with that of the (deities of the) circle in which one finds oneself. First encountered as obstacles, these divine, demonic, or animal impulses are eventually overcome, that is, transformed into positive sources of energy that carry one closer and closer to the deity at the center. Alternatively, one may, having overcome them, also coerce those same potentially destructive lower-level beings to do one's bidding through various ritual technologies, about which more below. Here, the true sense of the term *yantra* (as in the Śrī Yantra) is brought to the fore: a yantra is a mesocosmic device or machine for controlling (from the Sanskrit root *yam*) one's conceptual reality [Rabe].

It is the nature of this grid or template, together with the chosen medium—that is, the mediating substance—of this process of divine embodiment that, more than anything else, differentiates one form of Tantra from another. When the template is the body of a naked maiden and the medium her sexual or menstrual discharge, we are in the presence of the Tantra of the old Hindu "clans" (the Kula or Kaula) and their inner and East Asian Buddhist Tantric homologues. Once we leave these traditions behind, however, the template will more often be a body of sound, of organized space, or of a deity—either in the form of a concrete or abstract worship support, a buddha's "pleasure body" (*sambhogakāya*), one's own subtle body, the person of the Tantric guru or lama, or the empty sky.

Often, templates and media will be combined. By far the most prevalent and most important example of this is the practice of identifying the deity with his or her "seed mantra" (*bīja-mantra*): this notion, that the sound shape of a mantra exactly renders a given deity's energy level, is the basis for mantric practice across all Tantric traditions. Elsewhere, maṇḍalas will have mantras inscribed on them; mantras infused into water will transform it into nectar and other fluids worthy of the gods; configurations or positions of the practitioner's hands or body (*mudrās*) will represent a deity's energies; maṇḍalas will be projected onto the subtle body, while the practitioner identifies with the deity at the center (as in Buddhist "deity yoga" [Lopez]); using mantras, deities will be transferred from the subtle body into a concrete image for worship; or maṇḍalas with their arrays of deities will be reproduced by human participants in ritual choreographies (Brooks 1992: 418–28; Samuel 1993: 266). Much of Tantric yogic practice combines nearly all of these elements, embodying the energy of the godhead on the grid of the subtle body through solid, fluid, acoustic, and photic media.

Generally speaking, the more subtle the medium (sound and light), the more internal, meditative, and sublimated the practice; conversely, concrete (fluid and solid) media imply external and more body-related practice, including sexual ritual, alchemy, and haṭha yoga. Internal practice, although it may incorporate the lower demonic and animal forms of divine energy, will tend to focus on the deity in sublime, even abstract, ways; external practice, which often implies sacrificial offerings, possessed states, and ritual technologies, will more often focus on fierce forms or hypostases of the deity, which it seeks to coerce and control. Much of the "soft core" of mainstream Tantric practice combines external ritual manipulations with internal meditiative practice, through the templates of maṇḍala, mantra, and mudrā, and often in a devotional mode [Gupta].

One might characterize the range of Tantric uses of these templates and media as a continuum extending from "doing" to "knowing." At one extreme, we find the concrete external utilization of blood offerings, human bones, bodily fluids, sexual intercourse, and so on, that characterize the mortuary practices—or at least the imagery thereof—of the early Hindu Kaula, early Jain Tantra, and the Buddhist Tantras of Supreme Yoga. At the other, we find a meditative ritual construction and mental enactment of generally less horrific or erotic practices, which Douglas Brooks has referred to as the "prescriptive imagination," and Glen Hayes the "imaginative structuring of experience." We also find a correlation between these bodies of practice, with their variable media and templates, and their goals. Practitioners who "do" their Tantra will emphasize the somatic goals of bodily immortality (*jīvanmukti*), pleasure (*bhukti*), and power (or "powers," *siddhis*) in the world. Those who "know" their practice will tend to focus on self-deification at a more cognitive or psychological level: the transformation of human consciousness into divine consciousness [Muller-Ortega] or the perfection of wisdom and realization of one's own inherent Buddha nature. Here, ritual practice mainly serves as a catalyst for a spiritual breakthrough, a transformation of consciousness; the Zen koan is a well-known case in point. In Buddhist Tantra—and in this it differs from Hinduism or Jainism—the ultimate goal of both those who "do" and who "know" their practice will be to enlighten and thereby liberate all other creatures from suffering existence. This ethical parameter is by and large absent from Hindu Tantra (Samuel 1993: 243). Finally, the goals of "soft-core" Tantric householders will differ little from those of their "non-Tantric" counterparts: liberation into the godhead, the extinction of suffering, purification, health, wealth, long life, and a strong family unit.

What is important to remember here is that the basic structure and dynamics of the maṇḍala itself remain constant, regardless of variations in the media that flow through it or the names and iconographies of the deities found within its boundaries. Although it is mainly on the basis of these important details that various Tantric lineages, sects, and traditions distinguish themselves from one another, it is their common use of the maṇḍala, more than any other feature of their practice, that makes them Tantric. Viewed in this way, the varieties of Tantric practice exhibit a certain uniformity. Practitioners located outside or at the margins of the mesocosmic energy grid project themselves into the maṇḍala and work their way back to the deity at the center, with whom they identify (in nondualist Tantric systems) or with whom they enter into immediate proximity or contact (in such dualist systems as Śaiva Siddhānta, which maintained that one could never become Śiva; at best, one could become a "second Śiva," and experience the world in the same way as god). Now, it is true that all of these media (with the possible exception of sexual fluids) may also be found in non-Tantric forms of practice throughout Asia, ranging from mainstream devotional traditions to the "ritual technologies" of shamans and other nonelite religious specialists. The ritual use of these media, however, in combination with the maṇḍala as matrix for the energy flow between the protocosmic and metacosmic levels of cosmic reality is, I would argue, specific to Tantra.

Tantric Initiation

The theory and practice of the Tantric maṇḍala operates on a mesocosmic level, that is, on the level of a mediating template between protocosm and metacosm as well as between macrocosm and microcosm. Quite often, Tantric practitioners will project the maṇḍala upon the internal grid of the "heart," the subtle or yogic body, or a body that has been modified to embody enlightenment. This process of internalization generally begins with initiation, which plays two complementary roles. On the one hand, it transforms a biologically given individual into a vessel capable of receiving, channeling, or actualizing the divine energy of the godhead; on the other, it initiates her or him into a particular Tantric lineage and body of teachings that extend back, through the guru or lama and his predecessors, to the godhead itself. Initiation is effected by the teacher, who has been previously transformed and empowered through his own initiation (*dīkṣā*) and consecration (*abhiṣeka*), who plants in the initiate's body a "seed" or "seme" of the essence of the godhead. This seed takes a number of forms, ranging from a drop of bodily or sexual fluid to a mantra, a photic image, or a drop or seed of consciousness or the bodhisattva's "thought of enlightenment" (*bodhicitta*). Vital breath (*prāṇa*) is generally the dynamic element in this transfer, just as it is in the animation of external images for worship and the internal practices of yoga. Through this "insemination" process, the guru or lama makes the initiate a part of the flow chart of the Tantric lineage, which radiates outward in maṇḍala fashion from the godhead or buddhahood that is its center and source. In many Tantric traditions, this process involves a transfer of the guru or lama's feminine energy (*śakti*) or wisdom (*prajñā*) into his disciple. The form that that transfer takes, ranging from the actual participation of a female consort in ritual sex to more sublimated transfers effected through food (yogurt, for example), mantras, or other media, varies according to tradition. The pivotal and transformative role of the guru in initiation has led to an equation in most Tantric traditions between guru and godhead, and meditation will often involve visualizing the guru as god at the center of the maṇḍala.

This very concrete notion of lineage is so fundamental to Tantra in the Tibetan tradition that two similar terms (both pronounced *gyṛ*) are used for "teaching linege," "genealogical lineage," and "Tantra" in the Tibetan language. Similarly, in Indian Hindu and Buddhist Tantra, the term *kula* ("family," "clan") is applied to the entire maṇḍala [Brooks]: initiation into the maṇḍala is initiation into the divine family of Śiva, Vajradhara, and so on, and the maṇḍala of the monastery constitutes a sort of microcosmic household (Samuel 1993: 150–51). This intimate relationship between spiritual lineage and biological lineage is based in no small part in socioreligious reality; very often, one is initiated into a Tantric tradition by one's biological father. The same rule often applies at the state level; lineages of princes and kings are initiated by parallel lineages of royal Tantric gurus, with the lineage god or goddess of both king and priest—that is, the deity at the heart of the maṇḍala—being the same for both. In cases of theocratic government, as in Tibet, the interpenetration of biological, spiritual, and royal lines become more pronounced.

Yoga and Tantra

Crucial to the initiation process is the notion that within the gross body of the human microcosm or protocosm there is a subtle, yogic body that is the mesocosmic replica of the divine, universal macrocosm or metacosm. As such, yoga constitutes a vital component of Hindu, Buddhist, and Jain [Qvarnström] Tantric theory and practice. This body, which comprises energy channels (*nāḍīs*) and centers (*cakras*), drops, and winds, is itself a maṇḍala. If it were to be viewed from above, the vertical central channel of the subtle body, which mediates the bipolar (and sexually gendered) internal dynamic of the godhead, would appear as the center point of the maṇḍala, with the various cakras aligned along that channel appearing as so many concentric circles, wheels, or lotuses radiating outward from that center. Often, each of the spokes or petals of these cakras will have male and female deities, as well as Sanskrit phonemes and graphemes, assigned to it. As such, initiation and all forms of yogic practice involve, once again, an effort on the part of the practitioner to return to the elevated center point of the emanated maṇḍala. Once the practitioner has succeeded in centering all of the energies coursing through his subtle body—energies that flow through the myriad subtle channels in the form of fluids, phonemes, and graphemes—the final phase of his practice will effect the reimplosion of feminine energy into (a usually) masculine essence or pure consciousness. This final phase is often portrayed as the merging of the inner female energy—called Kuṇḍalinī (the coiled serpent energy, in Hinduism) or Avadhūtī or Cāṇḍālī (in Buddhism)—situated in the lower half of the body, with a masculine principle (Śiva in Hinduism, Upāya in Buddhism) located in the cranial vault. This union is represented in terms not only of energies but of sexual fluids, as well. In Hindu practice, the sanguinary Kuṇḍalinī rises to join the seminal Śiva in the cranial vault, with the "nectar" produced from their union optimally being held there by the practitioner, as a means to becoming a Siddha, a "self-made god" (White 1996: 320)

Buddhist yogic imagery is similar to that of the Hindus. A number of early Vajrayāna works speak of red and white sexual fluids being united into the thought of enlightenment in the central channel; one of these texts, the *Hevajra Tantra* (1.32), portrays the internal feminine energy as the Cāṇḍālī ("Outcaste Woman") who blazes upward into the cranial vault. The male "moon" residing there is made to melt by her heat, and their conjoined fluid—now the bodhicitta—flows down through the cakras, suffusing the practitioner as it does with the bliss of their union. Later Buddhist traditions more closely follow the dynamic of Hindu haṭha yogic practice, with feminine energy being made to rise through the cakras to the "Lotus of Great Bliss" in the head (Kværne 1975: 120–21). The Completion Phase of Supreme Yoga visualization [Bentor]—in which the maṇḍala is incorporated into the subtle body—is rife with the imagery of both sexuality and death; however, as in all of Buddhist practice, these transformative experiences are but means to the higher end of enlightenment and buddhahood.

"Tantric Sex"

Both historically and conceptually, yoga is in many ways an internalization of sexual intecourse between a man and a woman [Hayes], which brings us back to the vexed matter of Tantric sex. Tantric art abounds in representations of couples (and sometimes larger groups) engaged in all manner of sexual intercourse (*maithuna*, *yab-yum*, and so on), and most Tantric scriptures include extended discussions of sexual practice. Śiva and Vajrasattva, the high gods of Śaiva Hindu Tantra and Buddhist Vajrayāna, are themselves depicted as engaging in endless sexual marathons with their consorts, when they (and a number of other supernatural beings) are not portrayed as actually dwelling inside the female organ itself. If the Tantric practitioner's goal is to replace mundane human thought with enlightened god-consciousness, and if sexuality is the divine path to enlightenment, then the practitioner's imitatio dei should, quite reasonably, be enacted in a sexual mode. Yet, over the centuries, the debate has raged as to whether Tantric sexual imagery is to be taken literally or simply as so much figurative symbolization of exalted, dispassionate, even disembodied, states of consciousness.

This debate, both pro and con, may be somewhat misplaced, when one considers the possible origins of "Tantric sex." In early Hindu Tantra, sexual intercourse was often simply the practical means for generating the sexual fluids that constituted the preferred offering of the Tantric deities. Elsewhere, there can be no doubt that an early and persistent form of Tantric initiation and practice involved transactions in sexual fluids between a male initiate and a female consort—termed yoginī, dūtī (the female "messenger"), or śakti ("energy") for Hindus; and ḍākinī, prajñā ("wisdom"), or mudrā (the "seal") for their Buddhist counterparts. Here, the male initiate was physically inseminated or insanguinated with the sexual emissions of the female consort (sometimes together with the semen of the male guru or lama), as a means of transforming him, reproductively as it were, into a son of the clan (*kula-putra*, in Hindu Tantra). Here, the role of the female consort is vital, because the clan fluid (*kula-dravya*) or clan nectar (*kulāmṛta*), vulval essence (*yoni-tattva*), or thought of enlightenment (*bodhicitta*) is understood to flow naturally through her womb. Because she is herself the embodiment of the energy of the godhead (or Wisdom, the complement to male Skill in Means), her sexual or menstrual discharge is considered to be the germ plasm of the godhead or enlightened consciousness itself. Human males, through whom this divine fluid does not naturally flow, can only gain access to it through the conduit of the female sexual organ (White 1998). As such, "Tantric sex" would originally have been a matter of generating, offering, and ingesting transformative sexual fluids. It was only later that bliss itself would come to take center stage, replacing the notion of sexual orgasm as a means to an end with a more psychologized understanding of the same as an end in itself—a blissful expansion of consciousness (Sanderson 1988: 679–80).

Transactions in and the consumption of sexual fluids also served as means for affirming the doctrine of identity in difference, or the identity of saṃsāra and nirvāṇa, in Hindu and Buddhist Tantra. In tenth- to eleventh-century Hindu Tantra in Kashmir, for example, a recognition of the consciousness-expanding effects of orgasm was accompanied by an understanding of the psychological effects of the oral consumption of such an impure—and thereby powerful and dangerous—substance as female discharge (sexual emissions and menstrual blood), as well as the other prohibited substances: the five makāras, the five nectars, and so on. Here, in a socioreligious system in which "you are what you eat," the potentially self-destructive act of ingesting such substances was deemed sufficient to effect a breakthrough from limited conventional thought to expanded, enlightened god-consciousness (Sanderson 1995: 85–87). The Siddhas and "crazy yogis" of Vajrayāna tradition are legendary for having resorted to alimentary and sexual transgression as means of teaching the identity of saṃsāra and nirvāṇa. One of these, the Bhutanese Drukpa Kunley, made a career of converting demonesses to Buddhism with his "flaming thunderbolt of wisdom," that is, his penis, about which he then sang songs in public meetings. For those who had eyes to see and ears to hear, this would no doubt have been a consciousness-raising experience (Dowman 1980).

Erotico-mystical practices such as these were not present in every form of early Tantra, and most Tantric traditions have, over time, refined them into more sublimated forms of practice, on a mantric, mandalic, ritual, or yogic level; some traditions have played down their importance or eschewed them as too dangerous for all but the supremely qualified. Many later Hindu and Buddhist Tantric schools have valued visualization of the Tantric consort over actual intercourse with her; and in spite of explicit references to emission of the bodhicitta in most Supreme Yoga Tantra consecrations, Buddhist Tantra has generally emphasized seminal retention and the reversal of sexual energy within the body of the male practitioner (Kværne 1975: 108). In fact, the great bulk of Buddhist Tantric discourse on sexuality—as well as on alchemy, which is the union of male and female reagents—has long since been internalized into descriptions of the yogic union of female Wisdom with male Skill in Means, within the subtle body.

Yet the sexual referent has nearly always remained present in even the most "cosmeticized" or "semanticized" forms of Tantric discourse (Sanderson 1995: 79). If Michel Strickmann (1996: 203) is correct when he asserts that Tantric art *is* Tantric ritual, and that Buddhist Tantric ritual is [sexual] union with an icon, then there is little to Tantric practice that has not borne some occult or explicit sexual valence. This is as it should be. The soteriological value of passion or desire itself has always been a watchword of Tantra: on this basis alone, "salvific sexuality" ought to lie at the heart of Tantric practice. However, the extent to which precept has been reproduced in practice varies from one Tantric tradition to another, and has changed over time within every one of those traditions.

Here, a general statement on the place of the feminine in Tantra is in order. Many if not most Tantric traditions emphasize the role of women and (or as) goddesses on a number of levels. One of the distinguishing features of Tantra is, in fact, its proliferation of goddesses—sometimes benign like the compassionate Guanyin, or ambiguous like the hunchbacked Kubjikā [Goudriaan], but most often fierce, like the terrible black Kālī [McDermott]. In such traditions, the hypostases or energies of the male (or sometimes female, in "pure Śākta" forms of Hindu Tantra) godhead are generally female, as are the inner energies of the subtle body, the body of the Tantric consort, Buddhist Wisdom (*prajñā*), and the sacred geography of the world itself. In the Hindu Tantric worldview, the world is the body of the goddess, and its myriad religious landscapes her many physical features. This understanding lies at the heart of the networks of the goddess's pīṭhas ("benches") in South Asia (Sircar 1973; Dyczkowski 1999), as well as of the many "womb-caves" of the Tantric goddesses that dot the Tibetan and inner Asian Buddhist landscape (Stein 1988). Elsewhere, exceptional women have risen to prominence in certain Tantric traditions—the Tibetan Yoginī Ma gcig Lab sgron being a case in point [Orofino]—and women have been praised and often worshiped as goddesses in many Tantric scriptures.

It would, however, be incorrect to say that all Tantric traditions have placed this stress on the power of the feminine. Japanese Tantra generally identifies the "six elements" of our world as the body of the male buddha Vairocana, and Japanese sacred mountains are generally male. Elsewhere, a number of early "clerical" Tantric traditions, discussed below (especially Hindu Śaiva Siddhānta and the Buddhist Tantras of Action and Observance), portray the expansion of the godhead into the world as a predominantly masculine affair. Furthermore, it would be hasty to conclude, on the basis of the general Tantric exaltation of feminine energy, that female practitioners have ever dominated the religious or political Tantric sphere. Even in her transformative initiatory role, the Tantric consort has remained instrumental to the requirements of the male practitioners she transforms.

Historical Parameters

As Geoffrey Samuel (1993: 7–10) has argued for Tibetan Buddhist society, the body of doctrines and practices that are grouped under the heading of Tantra all draw, to varying degrees, upon two types of sources. These are the "shamanic" magical practices or ritual technologies of nonelite religious specialists and their clienteles; and the speculative and scholasticist productions of often state-sponsored religious elites (which Samuel terms "clerical"). The history of Tantra is the history of the interaction between these two strands of practice and practitioners, whose clienteles, comprising commoners and political elites, have nearly always overlapped. There can be no doubt that the relationships among Indian kings and the Tantric specialists they chose over other alternatives (generally Vedic) are key to understanding the origins and history of this interaction. These specialists would probably have included professional priests of emerging temples of Tantric deities; royal chaplains seeking enhanced religious protection for their royal clients; court astrologers, physicians, and magicians; "shamanic" itinerant Siddhas and their female consorts or śaktis (Gupta-Hoens-Goudriaan 1979: 29–35); and the leaders of important monastic orders.

Apart from the fact of its Indian provenance, the "origin" of Tantra will not be treated here. Depending on whether one's criteria are text- or iconography-based or grounded in practice, deities, lineages, or sociopolitical contexts, one's dating and account of Tantra's origins will vary significantly. Here, we limit ourselves to stating that Tantra was an orthogenic development out of prior mainstream (but not necessarily elite) traditions, that nonetheless also drew on both foreign (adstratal) and popular (substratal) sources. So, for example, the homa (fire) rites common to most Tantric traditions are direct heirs of the Vedic homa sacrifices (an orthogenic development), whereas certain elements of Tibetan Buddhist Tantra clearly draw on both Iranian (adstratal) and indigenous (substratal) traditions. In Japan, the sanrinjin (literally, "three bodies with discs") theory, which divided the Buddha's appearances in the phenomenal world into three types, was an explicit means for incorporating the (adstratal) Indian deities of Hinduism into the Buddhist fold as "propagators of Buddhism" (a strategy introduced in India), as well as for Buddhicizing (substratal) indigenous Japanese kami deities (Matsunaga 1987: 52). The question nonetheless remains as to when and by what means these deities and the rituals and beliefs associated with them became "Tantric," as opposed to "Vedic," "non-Tantric Buddhist," "non-Tantric Jain," "popular Indian," "popular Chinese," "popular Japanese," and so on.

When subjected to close scrutiny, these sorts of distinctions nearly always break down. We may take as an example the multiple goddesses—called yoginīs, ḍākinīs, "vixen" spirits, and so on—that are found in nearly every Tantric tradition. In the Indian context out of which so much of Tantra arose, cults of multiple goddesses were already present, prior to the common era, in the apsarasas (nymphs), yakṣinīs (female dryads), mātṛs (Mothers), and grahaṇīs (female seizers), who were generally propitiated with animal sacrifices and early forms of devotional worship. Although it is true that such powerful and petulant beings (devouring when ignored, but nurturing when honored) were rarely if ever qualified as high gods by the Hindu, Buddhist, or Jain elites, nevertheless, whenever any woman—whether the wife of a brahman, king, or commoner—was about to give birth, an image of one or more of these female deities would have been painted on the walls of the birthing chamber. That these goddesses were mainstream is further attested by the fact that such Mothers or female seizers as Ṣaṣṭhī and Hārītī were depicted on Kushan and Gupta-age coinage and sculpture throughout greater India. Moreover, groups of goddesses of this type figure prominently among the "export deities" that took root and flourished in foreign soil, in Inner and East Asia—making theirs a truly cosmopolitan cult.

When persons from every level of Asian society were worshiping these multiple female deities, is it proper to call this a "folk" or "popular" cult? And where does one draw the line between "indigenous" and "foreign"? Often the sole changes that have historically occurred in the cults of these groups have been their group name and the use to which they have been put in religious practice. Thus Pūtanā, one of the multiple Mothers or female seizers of Hindu epic tradition, is later listed as a yoginī in the Hindu Purāṇas and Tantras. The name Pūtanā also appears as the name of a class of disease demonesses in such Buddhist sources as the early Mahāyāna *Lotus of the True Law* (Filliozat 1937: 160) and the early seventh-century Chinese version of *Collection of the Dhāraṇī Teachings* (Strickmann 1996: 156). In these later developments, Pūtanā the Hindu yoginī or Pūtanā the Buddhist ḍākinī is no longer merely propitiated as a means of preventing miscarriage or childhood diseases; she has now become a part of the "enshrinement and employment of demigods as instruments of power" (Sutherland 1991: 146) that was and remains one of the hallmarks of Tantric practice. One calls her and her dangerous host down upon oneself, and through ritual manipulation, compels them to do one's bidding.

This ritual strategy forms the core of the so-called Buddhist dhāraṇī texts (Matsunaga 1987: 47–48), collections of spells and ritual techniques that, composed in India in the second to sixth centuries C.E., were in the centuries that followed the calling cards of the Tantric masters who became the most powerful and prestigious ritualists of the Chinese imperial court (Strickmann 1996: 30). In Japan, a Shingon legend concerning Kamatari, the seventh-century founder of the Fujiwara lineage, relates that he was, in his youth, abducted by a vixen that was a manifestation of a deity named Dakini. After having had sexual relations with the vixen, he received from her the magic formula and the insignia of power (*kama*) that became part of his name (Faure 1998: 262). In modern-day rural Japan, certain types of vixens, termed "witch animals," are brought under the control of solitary male ascetics through a rite formerly known as the Daten or Dagini rite (Blacker 1975: 51–55)—this latter term clearly being a Japanese rendering of the Sanskrit *ḍākinī*. If it were possible to determine the precise dates of appropriations such as this into an explicitly Tantric classification schema and body of practice, one could, perhaps, pinpoint the century of the "origins" of this element of Tantra. As this is impossible, however, I will close this digression by simply stating that Tantra emerged out of the South Asian elite and popular mainstream some time in the middle of the first millennium C.E.

The origins of Tantra are, from both emic and etic perspectives, Indian. All authentic Tantric lineages—of deities, scriptures, oral teachings, and teachers—claim to extend back to Indian sources. Perhaps the earliest reference to sects that have subsequently come to be classified as Tantric is a passage from a fourth-century C.E. portion of the great Hindu epic, the *Mahābhārata* (12.335.40), which names the (Śaiva) Pāśupatas and the (Vaiṣṇava) Pāñcarātras as "non-Vedic." The founders of every major Tantric tradition, school, or sect either trace their guru-disciple lineages back to an Indian source or are considered to be incarnations of bodhisattvas of Indian "origin." The exploded pantheon of Tantra—its principal multiheaded and multiarmed deities and their burgeoning families or clans—are generally Indian, or at least traceable to Indian prototypes. The same holds for scriptural traditions: all Asian Tantric traditions are explicit concerning the Indian origins of their teachings, and the transmission of their teachings from India; this includes the Tibetan Treasure—*gter ma*, pronounced "terma"—traditions which, while "discovered" in Tibet, were nonetheless "hidden" there by the Indian teachers Vimalamitra and Padmasambhava [Germano-Gyatso]. Much of Tantric legend concerns the Indian "shamanic culture heroes" (Samuel 1993: 19) known as Siddhas or Mahāsiddhas. The hieratic language of Tantra generally remains the Sanskrit of medieval Indian Hinduism and Buddhism. That is, for any lineage-based Tantric body of practice (*sādhana*) to be legitimate in Chinese, Japanese, or Tibetan Tantric traditions, its translated root text must be traceable back to a Sanskrit original. In these translated sources, mantras—whose efficacy resides in their sound shape—will not be translated but rather frozen (at least in theory) in the original Sanskrit. Furthermore, Indic characters form the basis of the hieratic Siddhaṃ script employed in Chinese and Japanese Tantric maṇḍalas and texts. The yogic practice that is so central to Tantra is also of Indian origin (albeit influenced by Daoist techniques)—and the list goes on.

As for the history of Tantra, it may be approached from both emic and etic perspectives. By way of presenting the problems of Tantric historiography, I begin by presenting an emic dilemma in Japan. Here, of course, we are in the presence of "export" Tantra, in this case Mahāyāna traditions brought to greater Asia from India by monks and other religious specialists from the fifth century C.E. onward. What we find, in fact, is that the historical time frame in which the transmission (to China, Tibet, Korea, Japan, Southeast Asia) of various Indian Tantric paradigms occurred has invariably proven definitive for the structure and content of the "export" Tantric tradition in question. It is as if the original revelation remained fossilized, like an insect in a block of amber, in the export tradition. This is manifestly the case, for example, with Japanese Shingon—founded by Kūkai (774–835 C.E.)—whose core revelations are the seventh-century C.E. *Mahāvairocana-sūtra* and the *Tattvasaṃgraha-sūtra*. It was precisely these two south Indian Mahāyāna texts—brought to China by Śubhakarasiṁha (637–735 C.E.) for the *Mahāvairocana*, and Vajrabodhi (671–741 C.E.) and Amoghavajra (eighth century C.E.), for the *Tattvasaṃgraha*, and taught to him in China by Amoghavajra's disciple Huiguo—that formed the core of Kūkai's Shingon teachings. Shingon practice remains, in many respects, a preserved specimen of those enshrined in seventh-century Indian paradigms, but with a Japanese overlay. Following this eighth-century watershed, subsequent Indian developments in Tantra had limited or no impact on Shingon for four centuries (Matsunaga 1987: 50–52; Yamasaki 1988: 3–12, 19–20). Similarly, Tibetan Buddhism, with its preponderance of Vajrayāna practice based on revelations found in what would later be classified as the Tantras of Yoga and Supreme Yoga, preserves the Tantric status quo of eighth-century India, from which it was introduced into Tibet by the legendary Vimalamitra and Padmasambhava.

Shingon is one of the two most important mainstream forms of Japanese Tantra, the other being Tendai, founded by Saichō (767–822 C.E.). Together, Shingon and Tendai are widely considered to constitute mikkyō, the "esoteric Buddhism" or "pure esotericism" of Japan. Here, mikkyō is held to be "pure" in contradistinction to the "mixed esotericism" of Tantra, of which two medieval movements were termed *jakyō* (heresies) (Faure 1998: 126). One of these, injected into Shingon from Tibet via Chinese Daoism, was the Tachikawa-ryū [Faure]. In Tachikawa—which equated sexual bliss with Kūkai's doctrine of "bodily buddhahood"—Tantric practice took a new (for Shingon) highly sexualized coloring, typical of Supreme Yoga Tantra consecrations (described in Snellgrove 1987: 257–61). Here, "Skull Ritual" initiations—real or imagined—that involved the union of (male) Skill in Means and (female) Wisdom, enacted through sexual intercourse and the subsequent collection of sexual fluids, were very close in style to *Hevajra* and *Caṇḍamahāroṣaṇa Tantra*-based consecrations that had, in the tenth and eleventh centuries, been incorporated into the Tibetan Tantric "clerical" mainstream. By the mid-thirteenth century, the doctrines of this school had become so popular as to necessitate an orthodox Shingon backlash against the "Tachikawa heresy," which culminated in its effective suppression by the late fifteenth century (Sanford 1991: 1–4, 9–18; Strickmann 1996: 245).

Yet, as Bernard Faure has indicated, Japanese mikkyō, like Indo-Tibetan Vajrayāna, feminized a number of Buddhist deities; and ritual sex with them (or their human substitutes) was part of the ritual. In the same vein, the *Bizei betsu* (Particular Notes on the Abhiṣeka) of Jien, an "orthodox" twelfth- to thirteenth-century Tendai text, describes a cognate rite of sexual union between the emperor and his consort, in the role of Tantric adepts (Faure 1998: 126). In spite of the historical presence, within their own traditions, of these elements of Indo-Tibetan Tantric practice, Shingon and Tendai apologists have for centuries tried to distance themselves from—if not deny the existence of—the darker magical (and in particular sexual) components of Tachikawa-ryū and other Tantric "heresies." How can their emic claims to purity prevail against the etic historical data presented here?

Here, let us turn to a set of emic categories that, although they originated in India, have been used widely to classify all the Buddhist Tantric sects and schools. These are the categories of the Tantras of Action (Kriyā Tantras), Tantras of Observance (Caryā Tantras), Tantras of Yoga (Yoga Tantras), and Tantras of Supreme Yoga (Anuttarayoga Tantras). These categories are used in reference to bodies of revealed texts, ritual practice, and especially to types of consecration, with the latter two being far more esoteric than the former two forms of Buddhist Tantric practice. Within more esoteric Buddhist traditions, this means that Yoga and Supreme Yoga consecrations follow or are "higher" than those of Action and Observance. In the more conventional or exoteric Buddhist Tantric schools, these Yoga and Supreme Yoga texts, rituals, and consecrations are simply omitted.

This emic hierarchy or ordering does not, however, necessarily imply a historical evolution. As Geoffrey Samuel (1993: 411–12) has argued, the Tantras of Action and Observance, which grew up as extensions of ritual, yogic, and devotional tendencies already present within earlier Mahāyāna traditions, were probably well ensconced within Indian Buddhist monastic communities by the eighth and ninth centuries. As for the more esoteric and antinomian Tantras of Yoga and Supreme Yoga—the core of Vajrayāna Buddhism (so-called for its "diamond," that is, vajra, families of deities)—their origins were probably coeval with if not prior to those of the Tantras of Action and Observance. However, these remained the preserve of the more independent and solitary "shamanic" Siddha-type practitioners until the tenth and eleventh centuries. For this reason, there are relatively few texts of the Yoga and Supreme Yoga variety prior to their insertion, as "higher" or more esoteric initiations, into "clerical" Tantric traditions. Whatever the case, the patterns of development of these hierarchized revelations appear to fall into lockstep with similar evolutions taking place within the Hindu Tantric schools in India; this parallel evolution has been clearly delineated by Alexis Sanderson (1988: 678–79) as follows:

> By the eighth century C.E. the Buddhists had accumulated a hierarchy of Tantric revelations roughly parallel in its organisation and character to that of the [Hindu] Mantramārga [whose textual canon comprises the *Śiva-Āgamas* and *Rudra-Āgamas* of the Śaiva Siddhānta and the *Bhairava-Āgamas* of Kāpālika Śaivism]. Their literature

> was divided in order of ascending esotericism into the Tantras of Action (*kriyā-tantras*), of Observance (*caryā-tantras*), of Yoga (*yoga-tantras*), and Supreme Yoga (*yogānuttara-tantras*). . . .
>
> [W]e can compare the relatively orthodox cult of the mild Vairocana Buddha in the Tantras of Observance (*Mahāvairocanasūtra*, etc.) and Yoga (*Tattvasamgraha, Paramādya*, etc.) with the Śaiva Siddhānta cult of Sadāśiva, and the more esoteric and heteropractic traditions of the Higher Yoga (*Guhyasamāja*, etc.), and Supreme Yoga (*Abhidhānottara, Hevajra, Ḍākiṇīvajrapañjara*, etc.) with the [more orthoprax male-deity-oriented] Mantrapīṭha and [the heteroprax female-deity-oriented] Vidyāpīṭha of the Tantras of Bhairava. Just as the Svacchandabhairava cult of the Mantrapīṭha is transitional between the more exoteric Śaiva Siddhānta and the Kāpālika Vidyāpīṭha, so that of Akṣobhya in the Higher Yoga stands bridging the gap between the Vairocana cult and the feminised and Kāpālika-like cults of Heruka, Vajravarāhī and the other *khaṭvāṅga* (skull-rattle)-bearing deities of the Supreme Yoga.
>
> At the lower levels of the Buddhist Tantric canon, there is certainly the influence of the general character and liturgical methods of the Śaiva and Pāñcarātra-Vaiṣṇava Tantric traditions. But at the final (and latest) level the dependence is much more profound and detailed. As in the Vidyāpīṭha cults these Buddhist deities are Kāpālika in an iconic form. They wear the five bone-ornaments and are smeared with ashes (the six seals [*mudrās*] of the Kāpālikas). They drink blood from skull-bowls (*kapāla*), have the Śaiva third eye, stand on the prostrate bodies of lesser deities, wear Śiva's sickle moon in their massed and matted hair (*jaṭā*). And, just as in the Vidyāpīṭha, their cults are set in that of the Yoginīs. Those who are initiated by introduction into the *maṇḍalas* of these Yoginī-encircled Buddhist deities are adorned with bone-ornaments and given the Kāpālika's *khaṭvāṅga* and skull-bowl to hold.

Sanderson goes on to argue that it was the Buddhists who borrowed from the Hindus in these forms of Tantric practice, an argument that has been expanded by Robert Mayer (1996: 102–32) with specific reference to Tibetan Buddhism. This is not the place to discuss the issue of who borrowed from whom; the point is that Tantra was a body of religious practice that evolved through similar phases both within India and throughout its expansion into greater Asia. For any given period, there has been a certain uniformity to Tantric practice that would have been identifiable as "Tantra," both within India and across Asia.

Within India, we may take the example of an early tenth-century Jain Tantra entitled the *Jvālinī Kalpa*. This text—which features yakṣiṇīs as consorts of the tīrthaṅkaras; Tantric sorcery (*ṣaṭkriyā*); yoga and alchemy; erotic practice involving the use of a female partner's sexual fluids as power substances (*caṇḍālī vijjā*); use of maṇḍalas, mudrās, and mantras; nyāsa (imposition of the deity's body on the practitioner's); and cult of the Eight Mothers (Nandi, 1973: 147–67)—is in nearly every respect identical to Hindu and Buddhist Tantric sources of the same period. Nothing but the names of the deities invoked, visualized, or manipulated in these practices is specifically Jain; all the features, however, are specific to tenth-century Indian Tantra, whether Hindu, Buddhist, or Jain. Most of these "hard core" practices disappeared from Jain Tantra in the centuries that followed, just as they did from Hindu and Buddhist Tantra; however, in this tenth-century stratum, Jain, Hindu, and Buddhist Tantra were largely identical.

Outside of India, we may return to the emic conundrum of the Japanese proponents of mikkyō, who have had to grapple with (or who more often simply deny) the problem of the presence, within the historical development of their own tradition, of elements of the Tachikawa "heresy." The same principle that applies within Indo-Tibetan Buddhism also applies to "export" Tantra. Both the exoteric Mahāyāna form of Tantra that was central to the formation of Shingon in the eighth century and the esoteric Vajrayāna form of Tantra central to Tachikawa practice were forms of Tantric practice that were normative for their respective times. In the light of this, the Shingon emic category of mikkyō as well as the broader Tantric emic category of the four types of revelation (encompassing both Shingon as "pure esotericism" and the Tachikawa "heresy") that fell within the purview of some twelfth-century Shingon practices are both admissable, when viewed through the etic lens of historical development.

Tantric Actors

Tantric actors, who include Siddhas, gurus or lamas, monks and nuns, yogins, sorcerers, witches, rulers, royal preceptors and chaplains, spirit mediums, visionary bards, oracles, astrologers, healers, and lay- or householder-practitioners, may be classified into three main groups: Tantric specialists who have received initiation into a textual, teaching lineage and their generally elite clients; Tantric specialists lacking in formal initiation, whose training tends to be through oral transmission (or divine possession) alone, and their generally nonelite clients; and householder or lay nonspecialists whose personal practice may be qualified as Tantric. Although the third category is numerically the largest, lay or householder Tantric practice is generally "soft core," and will therefore not enter significantly into our discussion. There is overlap among these groups, of course, with householder practitioners, for example, calling upon one or another type of specialist for teachings, guidance, and ritual expertise and practice. The purview of the Tantric actor par excellence, the Tantric ruler—usually a king or emperor but, in the case of Tibet, a head of the monastic theocracy—covers all three of these categories. Apart from the kings of Nepal and Bhutan, there are no Tantric rulers remaining in the world, and it is perhaps for this reason that most twentieth-century scholarly and popular accounts of Tantra tend to view it either as little more than popular superstition or "sympathetic magic," on the one hand, or as a sublime theoretical edifice on the other, without seeking to describe the relationship between these types of practice and their practitioners. In this final section, I argue that the person and office of the Tantric ruler is the glue that holds together all three levels or types of Tantric practice, without whom an integrated understanding of Tantra cannot be gained. As before, the Tantric maṇḍala will serve to map the tradition.

The View from the Center

In our working definition of Tantra, we identified the maṇḍala as the hallmark of Tantric theory and practice, the mesocosmic template through which the Tantric practitioner transacts with and appropriates the myriad energies that course through every level of the cosmos. Here, it is important to note that the maṇḍala was, in its origins, directly related to royal power. The notion of the king as cakravartin—as both he who turns (*vartayati*) the wheel (*cakra*) of his kingdom or empire from its center and he whose chariot wheel has rolled around its perimeter without obstruction—is one that goes back to the late Vedic period in India. A cognate ideology of the emperor, the "son of Heaven," as center was already in place in China in the same period. Basic to these constructions of kingship is the notion that the king, standing at the center of his kingdom (from which he also rules over the periphery) mirrors the godhead at the center of his realm, his divine or celestial kingdom. However, whereas the godhead's heavenly kingdom is unchanging and eternal, the terrestrial ruler's kingdom is only made so through the "utopia" of the maṇḍala. As such, the idealized "constructed kingdom" of the maṇḍala is the mesocosmic template between real landscapes, both geographical and political (the protocosm) and the heavenly kingdom of the godhead (metacosm), with the person of the king as god on earth constituting the idealized microcosm. Ruling from his capital at the conceptual center of the universe, the king is strategically located at the base of the prime channel of communication between upper and lower worlds, which he keeps "open" through the mediation of his religious specialists.

This royal ideology of "galactic polity" (Tambiah 1976: 102–31) or the "exemplary center" comprising the king, his deity, and the capital city, has been mediated by the maṇḍala in nearly every premodern Asian political system. In India, the practice of the maṇḍala is tantamount to the royal conquest of the four directions (*digvijaya*) which, beginning with a fire sacrifice (*homa*), has the king process through the four compass points, around the theoretical perimeter of his realm, before returning to his point of origin, which has now been transformed into the royal capital and center of the earth (Sax 1990: 143, 145). This last detail is an important one, because it highlights the king's dual role as pivot between heaven and earth. On the one hand, he is the microcosmic godhead incarnate, ruling from the center; on the other, he is the protocosmic representative of Everyman, struggling against myriad hostile forces that threaten him from the periphery. It is here that, in terms of the maṇḍala and Tantric practice in general, the king constitutes the link that binds together elite and nonelite practitioners and traditions.

In reality, the king's hold on the maṇḍala of his realm has often been more utopian than real. Conversely, given the intrinsically utopian (belonging to "no-place") nature of the maṇḍala, Tantric practitioners have often flourished, or at least survived, in situations of political anarchy or oppression; that is, in the absence of a religiously sanctioned ruler. In this latter case, religious power, when forced to operate on a clandestine level, controls the invisible forces of the universe from the hidden "center" of the tāntrika's "peripheral" shrine, monastery, or lodge. It is not for nothing that in India, the abbot of a powerful monastery or leader of a religious order continues to be addressed, in the present day, as gururāja, "preceptor-king."

In this sense, the Tantric practitioner is a crypto-potentate, transacting like a king with the boundless energy of the godhead that flows from the elevated center of his worship maṇḍala. The early history of the Gauḍīya Vaiṣṇavas, arguably a Tantric sect in its origins, is a remarkable example of this strategy. Finding themselves in a world without a Vaiṣṇava king following the fall of the Gajapati dynasty in Orissa in 1568 C.E., the Gauḍīya Vaiṣṇavas created a ritually ordered cosmos for themselves in which the cultic centers of Nabadwip and Vrindaban came to be identified, through the architectonics of the maṇḍala, with the descent of the celestial realm (*dhāman*) of the royal god Viṣṇu/Kṛṣṇa. Since that time, Gauḍīya Vaiṣṇava practitioners have visualized themselves at the center of a utopian kingdom, meditatively envisioning the power relationship between features of these cult centers' natural landscape and the divine realm of Kṛṣṇa's Goloka heaven (Stewart, 1995: 5).

Here, then, we see that the utopia of the Tantric maṇḍala may serve both to ground legitimate royal authority and power when the king is a Tantric practitioner, and to subvert illegitimate power or create a covert nexus of power when the wrong king or no king is on the throne. This is precisely the strategy of the present Dalai Lama's government in exile vis-à-vis the occupation of Tibet by the People's Republic of China. The role of the lama in Tibetan Buddhist religious polity stands out as a unique case in the history of Tantra inasmuch as the lamas have actually exercised temporal power, governing, protecting, and working for the enlightenment of their country and its people. This is a pattern that began in the thirteenth century with the establishment of a relationship between the Sakyapa order and the Mongol emperors, whereby the former became the Tantric initiators of the latter. In terms of religious ideology, however, this pattern goes back to the twelfth century, at which time certain Nyingmapa "Treasure" scriptures had begun to portray the seventh-century Tibetan monarch Song-tsen Gampo as a Tantric manifestation of Avalokiteśvara, and created an elaborate national mythos around this theme (Kapstein 1992: 79–93). This was institutionalized (also with Mongol support) with the establishment of the fifth Dalai Lama as the temporal and spiritual ruler of Tibet in 1642; for the next 308 years, the Gelugpa Dalai Lama, the incarnation of the celestial bodhisattva Avalokiteśvara, "ruled" Tibet from his Potala palace (Samuel 1993: 488, 527, 544). Since 1950, the maṇḍala of the Dalai Lama's rule has once more become a utopian one.

In the entire history of Tantra, the Tibetan theocracy alone has succeeded in collapsing the three types of Tantric practitioners mentioned at the beginning of this section—as well as the dual (spiritual and temporal) role of the Tantric ruler—into the single person of the lama. In the remainder of the Tantric world, the division of labor outlined above has remained the rule, with the royal courts of Hindu and Buddhist kings constituting the privileged clienteles of Tantric specialists. This symbiotic relationship between Tantric "power brokers" and their power-wielding royal patrons is particularly apparent in Tantric rituals of initiation (*dīkṣā*), and consecration or empowerment (*abhiṣeka*). Tantric consecration has long been the special prerogative of Asian rulers. In fact, royal participation in Tantric ritual colors the totality of Tantric literature; and "it is no mystery that central ritual of Tantra—consecration—was modeled on the ancient Indian ritual of royal investiture, [which] not only transformed monks into Tantric kings, but also kings into Tantric masters" (Strickmann 1996: 40).

In fact, abhiṣeka itself may well have had a sexual connotation, from the time of the royal consecrations of the Vedic period. As Per Kværne has argued, the verbal root of this term is *sic*, which means "sprinkle," "wet," "soak," and the original sense of consecration was one of a hieros gamos, a sacred marriage between king and earth. As such, the distant origins of this core element of Tantric practice may lie in a notion that the sex act and the ritual act were in some way equivalent (Kværne 1975: 102–9). The practices of the Tachikawa-ryū that so shocked the Shingon mainstream in Japan should also be viewed in this light: the sexual symbolism of the imperial accession ceremony was the same as that of the Tachikawa ritual, although it is not clear which influenced the other. These cult practices may also have had a pre-Tantric precedent in Japan, in which the ancient enthronement ceremony included a secret rite wherein an imitation of the hierogamy between the emperor and a goddess may have been enacted with a sacred prostitute (Faure 1998: 125–29, 169–70).

In India as well, the role of the person of the queen—and of her sexual emission—as the source of her husband's energy is one that predates the emergence of Tantra by several centuries. A particularly evocative description of such is found in a ca. 100–300 C.E. Tamil poem, the *Neṭunalvāṭai*, which has been summarized and interpreted by Dennis Hudson (1993: 133–34) as follows:

> Inside the house of the Pāṇḍya king there stood another "house," in which *aṇaṅku*, the sexual and sacred power of the *ūr*, the territory of his kingdom as a person, was present. This house, called the *karu* ("embryo")—like the inner sanctum, the "womb house" (*garbha-gṛha*) of the Hindu temple—was a bedroom into which the sole male that entered was the king himself. In the place of the temple altar was a large round bed replete with symbols of marital and fertile power. On the bed sat the queen, naked save for her wedding necklace, awaiting her king who had gone into battle. One of her maidservants prayed to the Mother goddess for his victory.
>
> The round bed is the round Vedic fire altar that symbolizes the earth and the queen the Vedic fire, awaiting the oblation of soma-semen from her husband. Known as "The Goddess Who Founds the Family" (*kula-mutaltevi*), she embodies the

> "Mother" to whom the maidservant prays for victory, and the *aṇaṅku* that pervades the fortress. That *aṇaṅku*, transmitted by her to the king each time they have sexual intercourse (*kūṭal*), is carried inside of him as the *śakti*, the energy, that wins him victory in battle.

Yet the king must exile himself to the periphery of his kingdom, to the borderlands where the battleline is constantly being drawn, to protect the center.

The View from the Periphery

As we have noted, the role of the king in the practice of the Tantric maṇḍala is a dual one. In Chinese parlance, the emperor is the "son of Heaven" when he rules from the center of his palace in the heart of the middle kingdom; at the same time, he is the representative of Everyman, battling to protect the periphery of his realm against eruptions of barbarian demons, monsters, epidemics, and so on. Here, it may be helpful to introduce the typology of the "transcendental" and "pragmatic" aspects of religion. This typology, first proposed in the 1960s by the anthropologist David Mandelbaum (1966) in relation to village-level religious practice in India, should help us to understand the dual role of the Tantric king, and serve as a theoretical bridge between what appear today to be two distinct types of Tantric specialists and their clients, and two distinct and generally disconnected types of Tantric practice in Asia.

When practitioners pay homage to the great gods of their tradition in the controlled atmosphere of a religious festival or periodical ritual observance, this is an example of a "transcendental" religion. When, however, an uncontrolled epidemic breaks out in their village or territory, and the local or regional deity of the disease in question is worshiped to protect and save them from their affliction, this is an example of "pragmatic" religion. Tantric elites—kings and their priestly specialists, householder practitioners, and so on—will generally take a "transcendental" approach to their religion, transacting with high gods through the controlled template of the maṇḍala. On the other hand, Tantric specialists from lower levels of society—healers, exorcists, spirit-mediums, and so on—will generally be called upon by their clients for their "pragmatic" abilities to transact with a malevolent spirit world that has already erupted into their lives, far away from the maṇḍala's quiet center. By and large, the transcendental approach is proactive, while the pragmatic approach is reactive.

From the transcendent perspective, the maṇḍala is a utopia ("no-place") as geometrically perfect as the Hindu Śrī Yantras or Tibetan Buddhist sand maṇḍalas. But real life always occurs "someplace," and it is here, at the pragmatic fringes, that the world of the maṇḍala becomes somewhat messier. More than any other Tantric actor, the king is obliged to adopt both transcendental and pragmatic strategies in his transactions through the maṇḍala. We have already outlined the transcendental side of his practice: in the latter role, he is Everyman, not only because he is the representative and protector of every one of his people, but also because he is himself his own person, subject to many of the same trammels of existence as everyone else in his realm. Like them, he has a home and a family, a body that is prey to disease and death, and deceased relations who come to visit him in his dreams. In this respect, he must transact with the same gods, ghosts, and ancestors as have most Asian individuals from time immemorial—beings which, because they are closer to the human world than are the high gods, are generally viewed as having a more immediate impact on human life.

Most pragmatic religious life in Asia revolves around family gods, that is, those deceased family members, distant or recent, who have died untimely or unusual deaths. Such a death has barred their path to the protected world of the ancestors—the happy dead—and as such, these unhappy and unsettled spirits find themselves condemned to a marginal and dangerous existence. Because these spirits inhabit the world between the living and the dead, they are most readily encountered in the places at which they departed from this world: graveyards and charnel- and cremation- grounds [McDaniel]. As such, these sites become the privileged venues of certain types of pragmatic Tantric practice (exorcism, subjugation, killing, and so on), and are described in gruesome detail in Tantric literature and graphically illustrated on the lower portions or borders of Buddhist maṇḍala art, in particular.

In their unhappy situation, these beings will often seek to avenge themselves against their family, clan, or village, and so become malevolent ghosts, the bhūt-prets of India or kuei of China. The semantic field of this latter term is particularly telling, extending as it does to not only the mesocosm of the household and the malevolent deities that threaten it but also to that of the empire, and the barbarian-monsters (*kuei*) that would overrun the center were the king's armies not vigilantly patrolling the periphery. The protean horde of these lesser deities form or hem in the outermost fringes of the great maṇḍala that the king, as an incarnation of the godhead, rules from the center. Yet it is one and the same maṇḍala, the same mesocosm of interpenetrating energies; all that changes is the perspective from which it is viewed.

Over the past two millennia, Asian traditions have generated a remarkably unified taxonomy of these malevolent deities, based for the most part on origin, form, and function. They are a highly volatile and capricious group, by turns hostile and friendly, terrible and benign, semidemonic and semidivine, with changes in demeanor corresponding directly to the ritual attention given them by humans. Capable of changing bodily containers—that is, of possessing the bodies of both the living and dead—their host fills the sky, earth, waters, stones, and trees, as well as the bodies of every type of living creature. Their names are legion, as are their forms and functions. In South Asia alone, one encounters—across Hindu, Buddhist, Jain, and Muslim traditions alike—cults of and practices relating to female yoginīs, ḍākinīs, śaktis, Mothers, yakṣiṇīs, rākṣasīs, piśācinīs, and vidyārājñīs; and male bhairavas, Siddhas, vīras, gaṇas, bhūtas, pretas, vetālas, rākṣasas, piśācas, māras, and vidyārājas. Many of these classes of beings were carried from India, in the first wave of export Tantric literature and liturgies, into Inner and East Asia, where they came to jostle and often merge with already existing indigenous pantheons. They continue to be found in myriad regional and vernacular forms throughout all of Asia. Yet, as has already been stated, we must not conclude from this that Asian belief systems and practices concerning these hosts of beings constitute the "origins" of Tantra. They have always been with the Asian peoples: when their cults became "Tantric"—or when "Tantra" emerged out of their cult practices—is a chicken/egg question that is impossible to resolve.

At the pragmatic outer fringes of the maṇḍala, possession, exorcism, divination, and healing have historically been the most pervasive forms of Tantric practice [Erndl], and it has been in their roles as ritual healers, "psychoanalysts," clairvoyants, and ground-level problem solvers [Walter] that nonelite Tantric specialists—whether they be called Ojhas or Bhopas in India, Gcod-pas (pronounced "chöpa") in Tibet, or even Daoists in China, or Shintō priests in Japan—first established and have continued to maintain their closest ties with every level of Asian society. The dark counterpart to these practices is ritual sorcery or black magic, the manipulation of the same low-level deities or demons to strike down enemies with the same afflictions as those they are called upon to placate or eliminate. Most often, practitioners gain access to and control over these malevolent deities by entering into a possessed state or mediumistic trance, and it must be allowed that at this level, Tantric specialists rarely make explicit use of the maṇḍala. Nonetheless, it informs their practice, since they know themselves to be transacting with deities that are in some way the emanations, sons, daughters, or servants of the transcendent godhead at the distant center. This is the case, for example, with the multiple Bhairavas of popular Hindu traditions in South Asia. In Jain Tantric practice, these beings are termed "unliberated deities," as opposed to the enlightened and liberated tīrthaṇkaras [Cort]; in Buddhist Tantra, they are conceived as ordinary worldly deities who have vowed to protect the Dharma, as opposed to enlightened buddhas or bodhisattvas.

We should bear in mind here that the transcendent/pragmatic religion typology is just that: an ideal construct employed to classify types of Tantric practice. In fact, the world of Tantric practice is a continuum that draws on both the transcendent and the pragmatic approaches. This is the strategy of the Tibetan lamas, who are both teachers of the Dharma and protectors of their people from malevolent deities. Lay practitioners too will often combine the two approaches, appealing directly to semidivine intermediaries for protection and succor in their daily lives while focusing their meditative practice on the godhead at the center of the maṇḍala. An example of such a combinatory practice is the preliminary Tantric ritual process known as bhūtaśuddhi, the "cleansing of the five elements" but also "the purging of the demonic beings." Prior to meditatively constructing the god at the center of the worship maṇḍala, and then identifying it with their own subtle bodies, practitioners must first purge their bodies of these lower elements/malevolent beings (*bhūtas*). In some Hindu practice, this process culminates in the dramatic expulsion of a black "Sin Man" (*pāpapuruṣa*)—a condensation of all the malevolent beings inhabiting the mandalic mesocosm of his body—through the practitioner's left nostril.

What differentiates elite Tantric specialists from their nonelite counterparts is not the basic structure of the maṇḍala as transactional mesocosm, but rather the name and attributes of the deities with whom they transact. Elite practitioners—by virtue of their higher Tantric empowerments, textual lineages, and formal instruction—are able to transact with the supreme transcendent-yet-immanent deity of the Tantric universe at the center to control all of the beings of the maṇḍala—divine, semidivine, and demonic—for the protection the king, his court, and the state as a whole. The principal deity with whom the nonelite specialist or practitioner will interact—some low-level "lord of spirits"—will not be absent from the elite maṇḍala; rather, he or she will be relegated to a zone nearer to the periphery of that maṇḍala, as a fierce protector deity guarding the maṇḍala of the king's (and supreme deity's) utopian realm from incursions by malevolent spirits from the outside, that is, enemies.

In this, his protective role, the ruler will call upon his elite Tantric specialists to perform rituals generally considered to fall within the purview of their nonelite counterparts (or, in some cases, simply call upon the latter to perform them). "Binding the directions" (*dig-bandhana*) to fence out demons from the maṇḍala, a standard preliminary to nearly every type of Tantric ritual, is a practice that betrays this concern with the dangerous boundary between inside and outside, "us" and "them" [Gardiner]. Yet this is but one of a body of ritual technologies—for driving away, immobilizing, confusing, and annihilating "demonic" enemies of the state—that elite Tantric specialists have marshaled on behalf of their royal clients for over a millennium. From this royal perspective as well, the fierce and heavily armed deities pictured at the borders and gates of the Tantric maṇḍalas are recognized as protectors of the realm. Very often, those fierce deities have been female—circles of wild animal- or bird-headed goddesses—a reminder once again that the activated energy that flows through the Tantric maṇḍala is nearly always feminine.

Contributions to this volume amply illustrate this intimate relationship between various types of Tantric specialists, their royal clients, and the protection of the state throughout Asia, including Tang China [Orzech-Sanford], Heian Japan [Grapard], Malla Nepal [Bledsoe], and Kalacuri central India [Davis]. Here, elite ritual technologies have been backed up by military force: as in the West, fighting monastic orders have long been a part of the Asian landscape, and the orders in question, in both South and East Asia, have generally been Tantric (Strickmann 1996: 41; Lorenzen 1978: 61–75). In South Asia, tāntrikas were power brokers throughout the medieval period, and one may even see in the presence, in the early 1990s, of the Nāth Siddha leader Avaidyanāth on the ruling council of the Hindu-nationalist organization known as the Viśva Hindu Pariṣad, an attempt to reclaim that role in postcolonial India (White 1996: 304–13; 342–49).

Where is the Mainstream?

Throughout this essay, I have made ambiguous use of the term "mainstream," sometimes referring to the "Tantric mainstream" and at others contrasting Tantric with non-Tantric "mainstream" practices, albeit with the mitigating heuristic device of "hard-core" and "soft-core" Tantra. This ambiguity is one that flows (to stay with a fluid metaphor) from the ambiguity of the Tantric maṇḍala itself. As has been argued, the Tantric maṇḍala becomes "utopian" when there is no temporal ruler to be identified with the godhead at the center. In such cases, Tantra is outside the mainstream, potentially subversive and antinomian, the province of the practitioner as crypto-potentate. When, however, the ruler is himself a Tantric practitioner/client, then the maṇḍala takes on a real-world referent, and stands as the mesocosmic template between politicoreligious realities and their metacosmic prototype, the realm of the divine. In the first instance, the Tantric maṇḍala is covert and occulted; in the latter, it is overt and hegemonic. The anonymous author of the *Āgama Prakāśa* [Rinehart-Stewart] states this aphoristically: "Every city has one-fourth part of its population as Śāktas [that is, tāntrikas]—and the ceremonies are performed very secretly in the middle of the night; if a king be a supporter, they are also observed publicly."

It is this bivalency of the portable Tantric maṇḍala that has both ensured the survival of Tantra in times of religious and political subjugation and rendered an accounting of it so difficult for the scholar. When the king is a Tantric practitioner, Tantra is a protective bulwark of the state, and its specialists are power-brokering bearers of religious authority. Geoffrey Samuel (1993: 34) sums up this situation in the following terms: "[A] practitioner can relate directly to the sources of power and authority, by contacting the Tantric 'deities' and other central 'culture-heroes.' Once the practitioner becomes a lama, this direct contact with power legitimates a social role that can as easily extend into the political sphere." When, however, there is no ruler, or when the "wrong king" is on the throne, the Tantric specialist becomes a covert operative, an occult cosmocrat, controlling a universe in which he is, through his identity with the god at the center of the maṇḍala, the creator, preserver, and destroyer. This latter state of affairs is, of course, threatening to the "wrong king" in question, and Siddha mythology is replete with accounts of the triumph of Tantric masters over wrong-headed temporal rulers. There are, however, other possible scenarios, giving rise to other strategies on the part of Tantric actors, which need to be explored. These concern relationships among power elites—Tantric specialists and their royal or aristocratic clients—in which the former, whether they consider their royal client to be legitimate or not, seek to find ways by which to assert their authority over the latter. These are the strategies of secrecy and dissimulation.

Until recent times, Tantric ritual constituted a bulwark for the state in the Indianized and Sanskritized monarchies of Asia, from Nepal to Bali (Strickmann 1996: 348). Reciprocally, it has especially been through royal support (protection, land grants, tax-exempt status, and so on) that the various Tantric orders have been empowered both to propagate their sectarian teachings and to consolidate their socioeconomic position in the realm. In this symbiotic relationship, Tantric lineages—of families, teaching traditions, and royal, priestly, and monastic succession—have often been closely intertwined. It is particularly in Nepal—where the royal preceptor (*rāj guru*) has, since the thirteenth century, been the king's chief religious advisor, initiating his royal client into the circles of deities that comprise and energize the nepāla-maṇḍala (Toffin 1989: 24–25)—that the relationship between the tāntrika and his king has remained in force down to the present day.

This modern-day survival of a medieval Tantric legacy has been the subject of the important research of Mark Dyczkowski, the fruits of which will appear shortly in the context of a forthcoming massive study of the Kubjikā Tantras. According to Dyczkowski's analysis, control of the cult of the great royal goddess Taleju (whose secret worship and liturgies are based on those of the Tantric Hindu goddess Kubjikā) lies at the heart of the power relationship between that goddess's Newar priesthood and the royal family of Nepal. After reviewing the cults of the gods of the Newars' public religion, the gods of the "civic space" or "mesocosm" (Levy 1992), Dyczkowski (2000: 2–3) presents the following scenario:

> But there is an inner secret domain which is the Newars' "microcosm." This does not form a part of the sacred geography of the Newar *civis*, although, from the initiate's point of view, it is the source and reason for much of it. The deities that populate this "inner space" and their rites are closely guarded secrets and, often, they are the secret identity of the public deities known only to initiates. The two domains complement each other. The outer is dominantly male. It is the domain of the attendants and protectors of both the civic space and the inner expanse, which is dominantly female. In the public domain . . . the male dominates the female, while the secret lineage deities of the higher castes [of the elite Tantric specialists] are invariably female accompanied by male consorts. . . . The inner domain is layered and graded in hierarchies of deepening and more elevated esotericism that ranges from the individual to the family group, clan, caste, and out through the complex interrelationships that make up Newar society. Thus the interplay between the inner and outer domains is maintained both by the secrecy in which it is grounded and one of the most characteristic features of Newar Tantrism as a whole, namely, its close relationship to the Newar caste system.

The outer domain is that of the pragmatic boundary of the maṇḍala, discussed earlier; here, the multiple Bhairabs (Bhairavas) who guard the boundaries of villages, fields, and the entire Kathmandu Valley itself are so many hypostases of the great Bhairabs of the royal cultus: Kāl Bhairab, Ākāś Bhairab, and so on. As we have noted, however, it is only by transacting with the transcendent deity at the heart of the maṇḍala that one gains and maintains supreme power. Here secrecy becomes a prime strategy. The Taleju brahmans offer Bhairava initiations to the king as the maintainer of the outer, public state cultus; however, it is only among themselves that they offer initiations and empowerments specific to their lineage goddess—and it is precisely through these secret initiations and empowerments that they maintain their elevated status vis-à-vis all the other castes in the Kathmandu Valley, including that of their principal client, the king himself. Because the goddess at the center of that maṇḍala is their lineage goddess, and theirs alone, and because her higher initiations are their secret prerogative, the

Newar priesthood is able to "control" the king and the nepāla-maṇḍala as a whole. Higher levels of initiation into the Kubjikā Tantras, accessible only to these elite tāntrikas, afford them hegemony over the religious life of the kingdom, which translates into an occult control of the Nepal royal administration—the political edifice that protects the kingdom from all malevolent spirits, both internal and external—which in turn enhances their social status and economic situation. A comparison with the world of espionage is perhaps useful: only those of the privileged inner circle (heart of the Tantric maṇḍala) have the highest security clearance (Tantric initiations) and access to the most secret codes (Tantric mantras) and classified documents (Tantric scriptures). The Taleju brahmans of Kathmandu, tāntrikas to the king, are the "intelligence community" of the kingdom, and their secret knowledge affords them a symbolic and real power greater than that of the king himself. In this way, the political power that the Newars lost through the eighteenth-century invasion of the Kathmandu Valley by the founder of the Shah dynasty has been recovered through their control of the goddess at the heart of the royal maṇḍala and their control of the administration of the kingdom.

When one looks at the strategy of secrecy employed by the Taleju brahmans of Nepal to exert occult control over a kingdom whose political power they lost over two centuries ago, one is not far from the practice of dissimulation, of pretending to be someone other than who one is. Dissimulation is a particular strategy for maintaining secrecy that is most often employed when the "wrong king" is on the throne, and practitioners are forced "underground." Basically the same aphorism, found in both Hindu and Buddhist Tantric traditions, expresses this strategy: "outwardly Vedic, a Śaiva at home, secretly a Śākta [that is, a tāntrika]"; "externally a Hīnayāna, internally a Mahayāna, secretly a Vajrayāna," in the Buddhist version. This strategy is altogether comprehensible in a situation of political or religious oppression. Curiously, or not so curiously, it is a strategy employed in times of relative freedom, as well. This is the stuff secret societies are made of the world over. The question of why one would wish to dissemble when fear of oppression is not one's principal motivation may again be approached by borrowing terminology from the world of espionage. Dissimulation allows for covert operatives to possess a double (or triple) identity, and to inhabit more than one world at the same time. It is also a means for "insiders" to recognize one another without being recognized by "outsiders," through the use of secret signs (mudrās), language (mantras), codes (forms of mantric encryption), and so on. It is a means for creating an elite, even if its eliteness is known to none but the insider community.

The Broken World of Tantra

The Tantric ruler is the Tantric actor par excellence, with galactic polity operating on the level of maṇḍalas of deities as well as that of agglomerations of peoples, clans, and territorial units. The royal palace is located at the center of a maṇḍala that is the master grid controlling and encompassing all the beings—human, subhuman, and superhuman—within its purview; at the same time, the king polices and protects the boundaries of his royal maṇḍala from outside incursions. As such, the office and person of the king have constituted the vital link between elite and nonelite forms of Tantric practice. Without him, the center is missing, and the phenomenon that is Tantra becomes cloven into two bodies of practice—the one transcendent and quietistic and the other pragmatic and "shamanistic"—that appear to have little or no relationship to one another. Yet, as we have noted, with the possible exceptions of Bhutan, Nepal (now a constitutional monarchy), and Tibet (a theocracy in exile), there are no Tantric systems of galactic polity remaining on the planet.

What effect has this loss of the center had on Tantra? Generally speaking, it has apparently split Tantra into two bodies of practice whose connections are barely recognizable to either practitioners or scholars. On the one hand, the powerful Tantric rites of subjugation, immobilization, annihilation, and so on—the "Six Practices" or "Six Rites of Magic" (*ṣaṭkarmāṇi*) [Bühnemann]—have become the sole province of individuals practicing for their own prestige and profit, or on behalf of other individuals on a for-cash basis. In the absence of state patronage, deployment of these ritual technologies often amounts to little more than black magic. When no longer employed in the service of the state, what had previously been a coherent body of practice for the state's protection can appear to be little other than a massive "protection racket" against supernatural thugs. It is in this context that many Hindus in India today deny the relevance of Tantra to their tradition, past or present, and identify what they call "tantra-mantra" as so much mumbo-jumbo.

The second body of practice that has emerged from this loss of a political center generally involves Tantric elites. When there no longer is a royal client to support them, many of those elite specialists who had been royal chaplains or preceptors have tended to turn their energies toward "perfecting" the rituals and liturgies for which a performance arena no longer exists. Closed into monasteries or other conventicles, these specialists have tended to scholasticize Tantric theory and internalize, sublimate, or semanticize external Tantric practice. Taken to its extreme, this scholasticizing tendency has removed Tantra from its this-worldly concerns and transformed it into an idealized and intellectualized inner exercise generally reserved for an elite group of insiders. Minutely categorizing every facet of the universe of experience and practice is the mark of scholasticist Tantra, and a great number of the passages translated in this volume betray that mindset. This tendency has been further catalyzed by a gradual loss of touch with the original clan lineage-based ground for Tantric ritual (Gupta-Hoens-Goudriaan 1979: 124; White 1998: 192–95).

There have been two major upshots of these developments. On the one hand, much of Tantra has become highly philosophical, and many of the most brilliant Tantric summa have been the work of "pure theoreticians." Even when the language of such forms of Tantra remains antinomian, this is a purely ritual or philosophical antinomianism, one cut off from the outside world, that is being espoused. On the other, as we have already noted, Tantric specialists have often, in the absence of politically powerful patrons, adopted the strategy of dissimulation, of hiding their "true" Tantric identity behind a façade of conventional behavior in the public sphere. In this context, elite "Tantra has moved towards the doctrinally orthodox and politically unobjectionable. . . . The magical and shamanic powers have lost their importance, the 'disreputable' sexual practices are avoided, and Tantric ritual has become little more than a supplement to the ordinary Brahmanic cult. Much the same . . . appears to be true for Buddhist Tantra among the Newars of the Kathmandu Valley, and in Japan, and for both Buddhist and Hindu Tantra in Bali" (Samuel 1993: 432).

These two strategies, of appropriating Tantric ritual technologies as means to self-promotion, and of dissimulation combined with scholasticist theorization, only appear to be the legacy of two different traditions. In fact, they are two sides of the same coin; however, the coin is one that no longer bears a royal head or device on its face. Such is the broken world of Tantra at the dawn of the new millennium.

Works Cited

Blacker, Carmen (1975). *The Catalpa Bow, A Study of Shamanistic Practices in Japan*. London: George Allen and Unwin.

Brooks, Douglas Renfrew (1992). "Encountering the Hindu 'Other': Tantrism and the Brahmans of South India," *Journal of the American Academy of Religion* 60.3 (Fall): 405–36.

Dowman, Keith (1980). *The Divine Madman: The Sublime Life and Songs of Drukpa Kunley*. London: Rider).

Dyczkowski, Mark (1999). "The Sacred Geography of the Kubjikā Tantras with Reference to the Bhairava and Kaula Tantras." *Nepal Research Center Journal*.

——— (2000). "Kubjikā, Kālī, Tripurā, and Trika." Manuscript.

Faure, Bernard (1998). *The Red Thread: Buddhist Approaches to Sexuality*. Princeton: Princeton University Press).

Filliozat, Jean (1937). *Le Kumāratantra de Rāvaṇa et les textes parallèles indiens tibétains, chinois, cambodgien et arabe*. Cahiers de la Société Asiatique, 1st series, vol. 4. Paris: Imprimerie Nationale.

Gupta, Sanjukta, Dirk Jan Hoens, and Teun Goudriaan (1979). *Hindu Tāntrism*. Leiden: E. J. Brill.

Hudson, Dennis (1993). "Madurai: The City as Goddess." In *Urban Form and Meaning in South Asia: The Shaping of Cities from Prehistoric to Precolonial Times*, edited by Howard Spodek and Doris Meth Srinivasan. Washington, D.C.: National Gallery of Art, pp. 125–42.

Kapstein, Matthew (1992). "Remarks on the Maṇi bka'-'bum and the Cult of Avalokiteśvara in Tibet." *Tibetan Buddhism: Reason and Revelation*, edited by Steven D. Goodman and Ronald M. Davidson. Albany: State University of New York Press, pp. 79–93.

Kværne, Per (1975). "On the Concept of Sahaja in Indian Buddhist Tantric Literature." *Temenos* 11, pp. 88–135.

Levy, Robert (1992). *Mesocosm: Hinduism and the Organization of a Traditional Newar City in Nepal*. Delhi: Motilal Banarsidass.

Lorenzen, David (1978). "Warrior Ascetics in Indian History." *Journal of the American Oriental Society* 98 (January-March) 61–75.

Mandelbaum, David (1966). "Transcendental and Pragmatic Aspects of Religion." *American Anthropologist* 68 (October): 1,175–91.

Matsunaga, Yukei (1987). "From Indian Tantric Buddhism to Japanese Buddhism." In *Japanese Buddhism: Its Tradition, New Religions and Interaction with Christianity*, edited by Minoru Kiyota. Tokyo: Buddhist Books International, pp. 47–54.

Mayer, Robert (1996). *A Scripture of the Ancient Tantra Collection, The Phur-pa bcu-gnyis*. Oxford: Kiscadale Publications.

Nandi, Ramendra Nath (1973). *Religious Institutions and Cults in the Deccan*. Delhi: Motilal Banarsidass.

Newman, John (1985). "A Brief History of Kālacakra." In *The Wheel of Time: The Kālacakra in Context*, edited by Beth Simon. Madison, Wisc.: Deer Park Books, pp. 51–90.

Orofino, Giacomella (1997). "Apropos of Some Foreign Elements in the Kālacakratantra." In *Tibetan Studies: Proceedings of the 7th Seminar of the International Association for Tibetan Studies, Graz, 1995*, edited by H. Krasser, M. T. Much, E. Steinkellner, and H. Tauscher. Vienna: Österreichische Akademie der Wissenschaften. Vol. 2, pp. 717–24.

Padoux, André (1986). "Tantrism." In *Encyclopedia of Religions*, edited by Mircea Eliade. New York: Macmillan. Vol. 14, pp. 272–76.

Samuel, Geoffrey (1993). *Civilized Shamans, Buddhism in Tibetan Societies*. Washington, D.C.: Smithsonian Institution Press.

Sanderson, Alexis (1988). "Śaivism and the Tantric Tradition." In *The World's Religions*, edited by Stewart Sutherland et al. London: Routledge & Kegan Paul, pp. 660–704.

——— (1995). "Meaning in Tantric Ritual." In *Essais sur le rituel, III* (Colloque du Centenaire de la Section des Sciences Religieuses de l'Ecole Pratique des Hautes Etudes), edited by Anne-Marie Blondeau and Kristofer Schipper. Louvain-Paris: Peeters, pp. 15–95.

Sanford, James H. (1991). "The Abominable Tachikawa Skull Ritual." *Monumenta Nipponica* 46.1 (Spring), pp. 1–20.

Sax, William S. (1990). "The Ramnagar Ramlila: Text, Performance, Pilgrimage." *History of Religions* 30.4 (November): 129–53.

Sircar, Dinesh Chandra (1973). *The Śākta Pīṭhas*. Delhi: Motilal Banarsidass.

Snellgrove, David (1987). *Indo-Tibetan Buddhism: Indian Buddhists and Their Tibetan Successors*. Vol. 1. Boston: Shambhala.

Stein, R. A. (1988). *Grottes-matrices et lieux saints de la déesse en Asie orientale*. Paris: Ecole Française d'Extrême Orient.

Stewart, Tony (1995). "Maṇḍala and Utopia in Gauḍīya Vaiṣṇavism," Paper read at the University of Virginia, March 1995.

Strickmann, Michel (1996). *Mantras et mandarins. Le bouddhisme tantrique en Chine*. Paris: Gallimard.

Sutherland, Gail Hinich (1991). *The Disguises of the Demon: The Development of the Yakṣa in Hinduism and Buddhism*. Albany, N.Y.: State University of New York Press.

Tambiah, Stanley (1976). *World Conquerer and World Renouncer: A Study of Buddhism and Polity in Thailand against a Historical Background*. Cambridge: Cambridge University Press.

Toffin, Gérard (1989). "La Voie des «héros»: Tantrisme et héritage védique chez les brâhmanes rājopādhyāya du Népal." In *Prêtrise, Pouvoirs et Autorité en Himalaya (Puruṣārtha 12)*, edited by Véronique Bouillier and Gérard Toffin. Paris: Editions de l'EHESS, pp. 19–40.

White, David Gordon (1996). *The Alchemical Body: Siddha Traditions in Medieval India*. Chicago: University of Chicago Press.

——— (1998). "Transformations in the Art of Love: Kāmakalā Practices in Hindu Tantric and Kaula Traditions." *History of Religions* 38.4 (November): 172–98.

Yamasaki, Taiko (1988). *Shingon: Japanese Esoteric Buddhism*. Boston: Shambhala.

Gurus and Adepts

—1—

The Tantric Guru

André Padoux

The importance accorded to the spiritual master, the guru or ācārya, was a general characteristic of Indian culture from very early times, and the trait was developed and intensified in Tantric Hinduism and Buddhism. It goes back to the Vedic period and is still visible in India today.

A reason for the guru's importance may lie in the fact that Indian traditions always gave precedence to the oral/aural/verbal, rather than to the written, form of religious or spiritual teachings. The Vedic Revelation is not scripture. It is śruti, that which has been heard and which is transmitted by word of mouth. The Buddha and the Jina taught orally, and their teaching was long committed to memory only. The various Tantric doctrines, though they seem to have been written down early (by the fifth or sixth century C.E., perhaps, for Hindu Tantras, earlier for the Buddhist ones), were also deemed to have been revealed—that is, told, orally expressed—by a deity to a first master and then transmitted in the same oral fashion to initiates alone, through a succession of masters (*gurupāraṃparya*), to succeeding generations of believers or adepts. Tantric texts that embody this sort of teaching in writing are therefore often couched in the form of a dialogue between a deity and a mortal, or between two deities speaking in mythical times—one asking to be taught, the other revealing orally his/her teaching.

In this Indian context, the highest wisdom, liberating truth, can issue only from the mouth of the master: *gurumukhād eva*. All such teaching, moreover, is necessarily esoteric. It is given, orally, only to those whom the guru considers worthy of receiving it and capable of keeping it secret. The esoteric transmission of doctrine by the guru to his chosen disciple includes the (necessarily oral) transmission of a mantra that is believed to be all-powerful, superhuman in nature: only someone endowed with superhuman powers can have access to and transmit such a power. This is a further reason why the Tantric guru is regarded as divine.

Tantric texts often do not expressly state that the guru is divine. They take it for granted, so obvious is such a notion to them. This identification with the deity goes so far that in some cases it is not clear whether the Tantra refers to the master or to the deity. For example, there is a passage in the *Yoginīhṛdaya* (a Śaiva text dating probably from the tenth or eleventh century C.E., but still read and used in Śrīvidyā circles today) which exhorts the adept to invoke and perceive mentally in one of the centers (*cakras*) of his "subtle" imaginary body the presence of the "footprints or sandals of the Master" (*gurupādukās*); these, says the text, "pervade the universe and fill it with celestial ambrosia," that is, with bliss. Now, the commentary explains this pādukā to be that of the guru, but it goes on to quote a stanza that mentions only the deity, while alluding further on to the pādukā of "the guru whose nature is that of the supreme Śiva." To realize mystically the supreme nature of the gurupādukā, says the *Yoginīhṛdaya*, is also to realize one's total identity with the supreme deity. What the adept is to experience is thus both the spiritual presence in his heart of his guru and the presence of the deity: they are both there but as one and the same, both transcendant and immanent reality. As appears in the translation given below of excerpts from the *Kulārṇavatantra*, this is what is generally implied by the term *pādukā*.

Admittedly, the *Yoginīhṛdaya* belongs doctrinally to the nondualistic form of Śaivism for which the supreme godhead forms the essence and omnipresent substrate of the cosmos, a divine essence that pervades the guru as well. However, it goes further than that. For this Tantric text (as for many others) there is a real, active, all-powerful and grace-bestowing presence of the deity existing in, or rather as, the guru. He has to be divine because in spiritual matters one gives not so much what one has as what one is.

The reverence and respect paid to the guru are reflected in the fact that Tantric ritual worship usually begins by an invocation of the guru (*gurusmaraṇa*) by which the worshiper places him/herself mentally within his/her own tradition: rather than one's own guru, it is the succession of the gurus of one's tradition, the gurupāraṃparya or gurupaṅkti, which is thus made spiritually present.

In the Śaiva Kaula traditions, this gurupaṅkti is sometimes described as consisting of a threefold succession or "flow" (*ogha*) of masters, the first group being "divine" (*divya*), the second "accomplished" (*siddha*) and the last "human" (*mānava*). If not historically then at least mythically, this flow links all the succeding gurus to the supreme godhead by whom the tradition is supposed to have been originally revealed. In this threefold succession (sometimes considered to correspond to the yugas, the succeeding ages of the world), the gurus are progressively less perfect as they pass from a divine to a mere human condition. However, even human gurus are incarnations of the godhead and are to be worshiped as such by their disciples.

Tantric traditions are not alone in viewing the guru as divine. It could be said that Indian gurus of whatever persuasion, and whether living in the past or the present, are regarded by their disciples as divine. A well-known and remarkable non-Tantric instance of such divinization is that of Caitanya, who came to be regarded as an androgynous incarnation of Rādhā and Kṛṣṇa. It is well known that Ananda Moyi, who died a few years ago, used to be worshiped in Varanasi as an incarnation of the goddess Durgā. More curious is the case of Śobha Mā, who lives in Varanasi now, and who is considered by her disciples as a manifestation of the (Tantric) goddess Kālī. But once a year, she is worshiped by them as an incarnation of the non-Tantric god Kṛṣṇa. One is also tempted to refer to the famous Bengali guru Rāmakṛṣṇa, who came from a Tantric milieu, was a priest of Kālī, and was initiated by two Tantric ascetics. But he stopped halfway, lacking the will to act as a real tāntrika. Such instances (and many others could be quoted) are clearly due to the diffusion, throughout India, of the Tantric conception of the guru. As a well-known stanza from the *Kulārṇavatantra* (12.45) puts it, "Whoever regards the guru as a human being, the mantra as mere letters, and the images [of deities] as stone, goes to hell." The proper attitude toward the guru is summarized by another oft-quoted stanza from the same text (12.49): "The guru is the father, the guru is the mother, the guru is God, the supreme Lord. When Śiva is angry, the guru saves [from his wrath]. When the guru is angry, nobody [can help]." Many such quotations could be cited. The *Tantrarājatantra* (The King of All Tantras), an undated—perhaps seventeenth-century—text belonging to the Śrīvidyā tradition, includes in its first chapter a brief hymn to the guru, identifying him with different aspects of the deity or of the cosmos; the human condition appears to be utterly transcended.

A richer and more detailed description of the Tantric guru is that of the twelfth chapter (*ullāsa*), "concerning the footprints [of the guru]," of the *Kulārṇavatantra*. This Śaiva Tantra is an important text of the Kaula tradition, and one of the best known. Its date is unknown, but it is certainly earlier than the fifteenth century. It was edited by Arthur Avalon and commented upon by him. The chapter in question, 129 stanzas in length, is too long to be translated here in its entirety. But the excerpts below show how far the extolling of the guru can go. Excessive praise is of course an ancient Indian literary practice, and it was never to be taken literally. But in its excess the *Kulārṇavatantra* expresses a widespread, typically Tantric perception of the spiritual master. The eulogy is reinforced in the following chapter of the same text, all 133 stanzas of which deal with the qualities, good or bad, of the guru and of the disciple. It describes especially the traits a disciple must exhibit in order for him to be chosen and then to serve his master properly: absolute devotion and submission are the rule.

Considered to be divine, deserving of praise, and treated as a deity, the Tantric guru is naturally a figure to be worshiped. Indeed, a gurupūjā, ritual worship of the guru, is sometimes prescribed. It is to be carried out by the newly initiated disciple for the master who has initiated him, and by the newly consecrated ācārya for the master who has consecrated him and whom he is to succeed. The pūjā may consist of a mere recitation (*japa*) of the gurumantra, which is sometimes a long formula, and sometimes simply *Oṃ Oṃ śrī gurave namaḥ*. Whether short or long, the gurumantra, when its japa is completed, is to be "offered" by the performer of the rite and symbolically placed in the guru's right hand. This is prescribed in all Tantric cults for the final japa of the deity's mantra. This rite is interesting as a symbolic offering both of one's prayer and of oneself to the godhead—or to the guru.

The gurupūjā may also be a complete ritual program during which the guru, seated on a throne (*āsana*) that symbolizes the whole cosmos (which he is thus deemed to transcend), is worshiped "with his mantras" and with the same offerings as those made to a deity, with the remainder of the offered drinks or food then being consumed (as in any pūjā) by the disciple, who must also worship the "wheel of power" (*śakticakra*) presumed to encircle the guru. If all this is not done, it is said, the whole initiation ritual would be void and without effect.

Such being the divine nature ascribed to the Tantric guru and the worship shown him, we would expect him to appear mysteriously, as a supernatural being spontaneously endowed with all manner of perfections and uncommon powers. But in fact only the founding masters of Tantric traditions, Hindu or Buddhist, are ever described in such a way. This is often the case with the Siddhas. Well-known examples are those of Matsyendranātha and Gorakṣanātha, the mythical founders of the Nātha tradition. On the other hand, whenever human rather than mythical gurus are concerned, Tantric texts carefully describe and emphasize the necessity of their ritual initiation (*dīkṣā*) or consecration (*abhiṣeka*). The guru, though essentially divine, is a human person who in fact becomes divine only after a ritual empowerment by which his master transmits to him his own supernatural excellence, together with his spiritual powers and ritual qualifications. There is such a thing as the "making of a master" (*ācāryakaraṇam*).

As a rule the ācārya- (or guru-) dīkṣā or abhiṣeka is the highest in a series of initiations and is therefore given only to persons who have already received lesser initiations. To become a guru one must, in addition, have a number of social, physical, and mental qualities. These vary according to the doctrines, preferences, or prejudices of the different Tantric traditions. They concern caste (often the guru must be a brahman, he must at least be of good family, a kulin), gender (usually only males can be gurus), family (a guru is normally married), knowledge of the scriptures (the Śāstras) and the ability to explain them, and so forth. Texts often insist on the beauty, majestic appearance, deep voice, and other physical traits a guru ought to possess. Some Tantras say a good guru cannot come from certain parts of India. The thirteenth chapter of the *Kulārṇavatantra* mentions different kinds of guru, with different capacities and different ways of teaching and practicing different rituals. It lists the particular subjects with which a guru ought to be conversant. It also mentions and warns against bad gurus. Only the sadguru, the real guru, the embodiment of absolute truth, saves and is to be worshiped. All of this goes to show that though extolled as divine, the Tantric guru is also viewed a mere mortal who is not above human frailties. A point worth noting is that the guru takes over his office and his powers from the master, who initiates him and thereby transfers and relinquishes to him his own role and authority. According to the *Mṛgendrāgama*, the initiating master says to his successor: "The power and authority I resign to you now, you will henceforth wield until you transmit them to another." The rule is that there are never two masters officially active at the same time in the same gurupāraṃparya.

The importance thus attributed to ritual notions and practices should not come as a surprise. The Tantric world is permeated and fundamentally characterized by ritual. Contrary to what some believe, tāntrikas are not antiritualists or transgressive mystical seekers of supernatural powers and liberation. They are first and foremost super-ritualists, "specialists in intensified ritual." Ritual, however, cannot be separated from the doctrine that accompanies and justifies it: in the case of Hindu Tantra, the prevailing ideology is that of the pervasive presence of divine power, śakti, a power conceived of differently in different Tantric systems, but one that can be mastered and deployed ritually to gain mundane or supramundane ends. These two aspects of the Tantric reality come together in the ācaryābhiṣeka, in which the guru is spiritually consecrated and is invested (thanks to the mantras he ritually receives) with supernatural powers, powers of such intensity that he is divinized.

Some Tantric traditions, notably the dualist Śaiva Siddhānta whose scriptures are the Sanskrit Āgamas, insist on the absolute and total efficacy of ritual. Such is also the position of the Vaiṣṇava tradition of the Pāñcarātra, despite the importance given there to devotion to the Lord. Others, notably the nondualist Śaivas, consider that the principal element in the making of a guru is not the ritual of the dīkṣā, but rather the divine influx of power: the grace of God (*anugraha*) or the "descent of power" (*śaktipāta*).

Thus, the Kashmiri philosopher Abhinavagupta (tenth to eleventh century) contrasts the ritually initiated, "fabricated" (*kalpita*) gurus with those who are "not fabricated" (*akalpita*) but spontaneously and directly illuminated (and hence initiated) by Śiva's grace. This is a position, Abhinavagupta says, that was already held by such earlier Tantras as the *Brahmayāmala* and even of Āgamas such as the *Kiraṇāgama*. The highest guru, according to him, is the one called "spontaneous" (*svayambhu*) because he is spontaneously and divinely schooled in all the traditional sciences. Such a master is absolutely perfect (*sāṃsiddhika*), omniscient, and divine; he destroys ignorance and spreads bliss by his mere presence. Illuminated by the light of intuitive knowledge (*prātibhaṃ jñānam*), he is sometimes called prātibhaguru. This guru, Abhinavagupta explains, is in fact initiated by the "goddesses of his own consciousness" (*svasaṃvittidevībhir dīkṣitaḥ*). This is interesting, since it identifies the powers and movements that sustain and animate a person's spiritual, mental, and physical life with divine entities. This perception of one's powers as identical with, or reflecting, a set of deities (the Kālīs), this conception of these "goddesses as the blissful, uncontracted awareness which is within and behind one's individuality" (to quote Alexis Sanderson), was taken over by Abhinavagupta from the Kashmiri form of the ancient Śaiva Krama tradition.

An akalpitaguru, according to him, may also be ritually initiated, in particular so as to learn (and be able to teach) certain doctrines or practices. He is then said to be an akalpitakalpita ("fabricated and not-fabricated") guru. Such a master, says Abhinavagupta, is really the god Bhairava. Continually deepening his perfect knowledge of all the Tantras and religious treatises, following the teaching of his own Master but also remaining constantly immersed in the light of divine Consciousness, he reaches such a degree of plenitude (*pūrṇatā*) that he is identified with Bhairava, that fearsome form of Śiva. The *Brahmayāmalatantra* further teaches that a person can be initiated and enlightened (that is, liberated) thanks only to the effulgence or power (*sphurattā*) of a mantra. By means of this method, says the Tantra, one may become an ācārya in a month. This may be taken as yet another example of the power ascribed to mantras in Tantric Hinduism. But the Tantra explains that this sort of direct mantric initiation is obtained while one performs a particular ritual of worship of the goddess Raktā: "Raktādevī initiates progressively through the japa of her mantras. This however can be done only if one has found such a guru as can transmit the mantra." Even divine action sometimes needs the help of human power. Here, however, the idea is to exclude the possibility of obtaining a mantra by finding it for oneself in a text: a written mantra, as is well known, is powerless.

Emphasis on the divinity of the guru is proper to Hindu Tantric traditions. The Buddhist Tantric conception is naturally different. Buddhist Tantric spiritual masters are also regarded as superhuman. But there seems to be more emphasis on the strangeness or eccentricity, as well as the supernatural origins and extraordinary feats and powers, of these "accomplished" beings (called Siddhas or Mahāsiddhas), than on their divine nature. In Tibetan Buddhism, they may be sprulsku, incarnate lamas, which also places them on a higher plane than that of ordinary people. Their disciples as well must obey and serve them slavishly. The sufferings and acts of self-denial of such disciples form part of the biographies of the great spiritual masters (especially the Tibetan ones). The trials endured by Milarepa as the disciple of Marpa, or of Naropa as the disciple of Tilopa are well known. The tales are largely imaginary or allegorical, but their raison d'être is to underline the supernatural nature and powers of these exceptional, quasi-divine beings. The Tantric guru is always held to be superhuman.

The *Kulārṇavatantra*, edited by Arthur Avalon [Sir John Woodroffe] (Madras: Ganesh, 1965) includes a long introduction, two chapters of which provide a partial translation and commentary on chapters 12 and 13 of that work. The two sections of verses translated below are based on that edition, from chapters 12 and 13, respectively.

Further Reading

Chapters 13 and 14 of Sriyukta Shiva Chandra Vidyarnava Bhattacharya, *The Principles of Tantra*, edited by Arthur Avalon (Madras: Ganesh, 1914, 1952) treat of the guru and his selection, and quote from a number of Tantras. On the case of Rāmakṛṣṇa, see Jeffrey Kripal's interesting book, *Kālī's Child: The Mystical and the Erotic in the Life and Teaching of Rāmakrishna* (Chicago: University of Chicago Press, 1995). Those with a reading knowledge of French should consult the excellent study of Śobha Mā by Catherine Clémentin-Ojha, *La divinité conquise* (Nanterre: Société d'Ethnographie, 1990). On the Buddhist Tantric guru, one may usefully read Herbert V. Guenther, *The Life and Teaching of Naropa* (Oxford: Oxford University Press, 1963; reprint Boston: Shambala, 1995).

On the Pādukā of the Guru

2. Listen, O Goddess, to what you wish me to tell you and which, when heard, quickly fosters devotion.

4. Better than millions of gifts, millions of ritual observances, millions of the greatest sacrifices is the mere invocation of the holy pādukā [of the guru].

5. Superior to millions of mantras, millions of bathings at pilgrimage places, superior even to the worshiping of millions of deities is the mere evocation of the holy pādukā.

6. The pādukā, when called to mind in time of distress, protects against all evil and all calamity; it dispels the greatest fear as well as all harm or illnesses.

7. The pādukā, when remembered, dispels difficulty in thinking, moving, speaking, intercourse, communication, or action. Indeed, memory, knowledge, wishing, or giving are done by him alone who ever keeps the holy pādukā on the tip of his tongue.

8. O Goddess! he who, full of devotion, freed of all evil, does the japa of the holy pādukā reaches immediately the supreme state of being.

10. Immediately, O Goddess! he who devotedly does the japa of the holy pādukā attains effortlessly the [four aims of life:] religious merit, wealth, pleasure, and liberation.

11. In whatever direction shine the lotus feet of the Lord, thereto one must bow every day, O Dear One!

12. There is no mantra higher than the pādukā, no god superior to the holy guru, no [valid] initiation other than that of śakti, no merit higher than that accruing from Kaula worship.

13–14. The form of the guru is the root of meditation (*dhyāna*), at the root of worship are the feet of the guru, the root of mantra is the word of the guru, the root of liberation is the compassion of the guru. All actions in this world are rooted in the guru, O Mistress of the Kula! The guru therefore is constantly to be served with all marks of devotion.

15. Fear, distress, grief, perplexity, delusion, error, and so forth exist only as long as one does not take refuge in reverent devotion to the guru.

16. So long as they have no devotion to a perfect master (*sadguru*), human beings wander in saṃsāra, suffering from all forms of pain and delusion.

17. The glorious mantra that bestows the fruits of all accomplishments is rooted in the grace of the guru. It leads to the supreme Reality.

18. Just as the boon-conferring guru, satisfied and happy, gives the mantra, so one must please him with devotion, even by offering him one's own life.

19. When the best of gurus (*deśikottama*) gives himself to the disciple, the latter is liberated. He will not be born again.

20. The disciple should strive to satisfy and honor his guru so that he may always be pleased. For when the guru is pleased the sins of the disciple are destroyed.

21. Yogins, sages, gods such as Brahmā, Viṣṇu, and Śiva bestow their grace when the guru is pleased. No doubt about it!

22. The disciple, directed by the compassionate guru who is pleased with his devotion, is liberated from [the fetters of] action and gains liberation as well as other rewards (*bhuktimukti*).

32. He who devotedly recalls "My guru is Śiva in the form of the Master, who grants rewards as well as liberation," for him perfection is not far away.

38. Why such exertions as those of pilgrimage, wherefore observances that emaciate the body, when the pure service of and devotion to the guru [afford the same fruit]?

46. Never regard the guru as a mere mortal, for to one who thinks so neither mantras nor the worship of gods will ever give any boon.

47. Those who associate the holy guru with ordinary [people] either in their remembrance or in their talk—even their good actions will turn into evil, O Dear One!

48. Parents, being the cause of one's birth, are to be honored with great care. Still more particularly is to be honored the guru, for he makes known what is and what is not the sociocosmic Order (*dharmādharma*).

49. The guru is the father, the guru is the mother, the guru is God, the supreme Lord. When Śiva is angry, the guru saves [from his wrath], but when the guru is angry, nobody [can help].

50. By mind, by speech, by action, do what is helpful to the guru. By doing what is bad for him, O Goddess, one becomes a prey to calamity.

51. Those who do not act properly toward the holy guru in body, wealth, or vital power will certainly become worms or insects [in a future life].

52. Death results from the forsaking of one's mantra, misery from forsaking one's guru. To forsake both guru and mantra leads to hell.

53. The body must be borne for the guru's sake. For him alone should one acquire wealth. One must exert oneself in the service of the guru regardless of one's life.

56. When the guru is there, no austerity (*tapas*) is to be practiced, nor fasting, pilgrimage, purifying bath, or anything else.

59. He who worships someone else when his guru is present, O Ambikā, will go to a frightful hell; and such worship would be useless.

60. To hold on one's head the lotus feet of the guru is not to bear a burden. One must act as he commands, for the guru is command (*ājñā*).

78. Destruction results from the anger of the guru, harm from treachery to him, and evil death from criticism of the guru, and the greatest ill from his displeasure.

79. A man may survive after entering a fire, or after drinking poison, or falling into the hands of death, but not one who has sinned against his master.

80. Where the holy guru is criticized, one must turn away one's ear, O Ambikā, and leave that place immediately, so that no such thing can be heard. One must then invoke the name of the guru so as to counteract what has been heard.

81. One must love those whom the guru befriends and respect his spouse and family. His practice must never be criticized, be it Vedic, Śāstric or Āgamic.

82. The holy pādukā is the [disciple's] ornament. To remember his name is japa. To do what he commands is ritual action. To attend obediently on him is indeed to worship the guru.

Guru and Disciple

51–52. Śiva is all-pervading, subtle, transcending the mind, without attributes, imperishable, space-like, unborn, infinite: how could he be worshiped, O Dear One? This is why Śiva takes on the visible form of the guru who, [when] worshiped with devotion, grants liberation and rewards.

53. I am Śiva without any form, O Goddess, imperceptible to the human senses. This is why the virtuous disciples can worship [Me] in the form of the guru.

54. The guru is the the supreme Śiva himself, manifestly perceptible as enclosed in human skin. Remaining thus concealed, he bestows grace (*anugraha*) on the good disciple.

55–56. It is to protect and help his devotees that Śiva, though formless, takes on form and, full of compassion, appears in this world as if he were part of the cosmic flow (*saṃsāra*). Concealing his third eye, the crescent moon [on his head], his energies, and two of his arms, he appears on this earth in the form of the guru.

57. Śiva without his three eyes, Viṣṇu without his four arms, Brahmā without his four faces, such indeed is what is called a guru, O Dear One!

60–61. The guru is none other than the Eternal Śiva. This is the truth. No doubt about it. The guru is Śiva himself . Who, otherwise, would bestow liberation as well as other rewards? There is no difference, O Pārvatī, between the guru and the god Sadāśiva. He who distinguishes between them is sinful.

99. Difficult to find is the guru who, when pleased, immediately affords the treasure of liberation, thus saving from the cosmic flow.

104. Many are the gurus who shine [feebly] like lamps in a house. Difficult to obtain is the guru who, like the sun, illuminates everything.

105. Many are the gurus well versed in the Veda, the Śāstras, and so forth. Difficult to find is the guru who has mastered the supreme Truth (*paratattva*).

107. Many are the gurus who know bad mantras and medicinal herbs, but a guru who knows the mantras given in the Tantric and Vedic traditions (*āgamanigama*) and in the Śāstras is difficult to find on this earth.

108. Many are the gurus who despoil their disciples of their wealth. Difficult to find, O Goddess, is the guru who destroys the sufferings of the disciple.

109. Many on earth are [the gurus] who follow the rules of caste and stage of life (*varṇāśramadharma*) and who know the kula practice (*kulācāra*), but the guru whose mind is free of all discursive thought is not easy to find.

110. A guru is one whose mere contact brings about supreme bliss. Such a guru the wise man choses, not another one. Verily, by the mere sight of him one gains liberation.

114. As blades of grass are blown away by a great wind, so the sins of the disciple are destroyed by the gaze of the guru.

115. As a lighted fire burns away all fuel, moist or dry, so by the compassion of the guru are all sins destroyed.

116. As darkness is dispelled at the sight of a lamp, so the mere sight of the perfect master (*sadguru*) destroys ignorance.

117. He who has all the proper characteristics, who knows all the precepts of the Veda and the Śāstras as well as the rules governing the ways [to liberation] (*upāya*), he indeed is a guru.

121. Even [a guru] who does not have all the [proper] qualities is still a guru [if he] knows the supreme Truth, for only one who knows the Truth is liberated and can liberate [others].

After having enumerated different kinds of gurus, the chapter ends as follows:

129. Though gurus are numerous, only one who performs the full consecration (*pūrṇābhiṣeka*) is to be worshiped. No doubt about it!

130–32. Having found a holy guru endowed with all the proper qualities, one who destroys all doubts and bestows knowledge, O Goddess, one should not stay with another one. If, however, one happens to have a guru who has no real knowledge and who causes doubts, no harm would be incurred by leaving him. Indeed, as the bee eager for honey flies from flower to flower, so the disciple eager for knowledge goes from master to master.

133. Thus have I told you briefly the qualities of the guru and of the disciple, O Mistress of the Kula. What else do you wish to hear?

—2—

King Kuñji's Banquet

Matthew T. Kapstein

The traditions concerning the Indian Tantric adepts known as the Siddhas ("perfected ones") have long fascinated scholars of the Tantric religions. This reflects the great popularity of these traditions in the arts and literature of India, Nepal, and Tibet, and the fact that several of the living Tantric communities, both Śaivite and Buddhist, trace themselves back to the inspiration of the Siddhas.

Although some of the Siddhas were no doubt purely mythical personages, many were famed teachers and adepts who lived in India during the last centuries of the first millennium C.E. and the first centuries of the second. The tales concerning the lives of all of them, however, are entwined in sacred legend, so that in most cases it is very difficult to arrive at precise historical conclusions about these figures. Several traditions speak of a collective grouping of eighty-four Mahāsiddhas ("Great Siddhas"), and though the precise enumeration of the eighty-four differs somewhat from one lineage to another, a Buddhist version of the *Lives of the Eighty-four Mahāsiddhas,* as compiled by the Indian adept Abhayadatta and preserved in a Tibetan translation done close to the year 1100, has become the most widely known source for the legendary accounts of their lives.

The *Lives* is itself only one part of a larger collection of Buddhist literature relating to the Mahāsiddhas that was introduced into Tibet during the same period. Also important is a short verse collection, the *Anthology of the Essential Realizations of the Eighty-four Siddhas,* compiled initially by an Indian teacher named Vīraprabha. This work parallels the *Lives* and has an extensive commentary recording the oral commentary of Abhayadatta upon it. The three works just mentioned, however, do not yet constitute the totality of the collection. Unnoticed by scholars so far is a peculiar text called the *Garland of Gems,* translated for the first time below, which is also accompanied by a commentary attributed to the collaboration of Abhayadatta and his Tangut disciple Möndrup Sherap (Smon-grub-shes-rab). This work, like the commentary on the anthology of songs, was certainly written in Tibetan, possibly on the basis of the Indian master Abhayadatta's instructions, but it is not the direct translation of an Indian text.

The *Garland of Gems* presents itself as a summary of the systems of Tantric yoga and meditation taught by the eighty-four Siddhas, though the commentary in fact only mentions some of the eighty-four by name. According to the legend of its origin, the *Garland of Gems* was first taught on behalf of a yakṣiṇī, a type of female spirit who in this case is said to have haunted a cremation ground. The efficacy of its teachings is accentuated by this tale, for it is claimed that by practicing them a tormented, inhuman creature achieved in the end a state of physical and psychic well-being. The text was first promulgated among ordinary human beings after the strange banquet hosted by a certain King Kuñji, as recounted in the first extract translated below. The actual content of the *Garland of Gems* is consistent with later Tibetan Tantric accounts of the teaching of the Mahāsiddhas, and accordingly emphasizes instructions concerning the ultimate nature of mind, often referred to elsewhere as the "Great Seal" *(mahāmudrā),* and the major techniques of Buddhist Tantric yoga called the "six doctrines": the Inner Heat, or Wild Woman, whereby one masters the subtle physical energies of the body; Apparition, through which the illusion-like nature of ordinary experience becomes known; Dream, in which one achieves the ability to explore consciously and to transform the dream experience; Radiant Light, referring to the luminous dimension of the mind; Transference, the means to cause one's consciousness to leave the body abruptly at the moment of death, and to seek rebirth in a pure realm; and the Liminal Passage *(bardo* in Tibetan), which here refers primarily to the state of consciousness in the course of migration between death and rebirth. The first four enable one to attain enlightenment swiftly during this very lifetime, the last two to achieve it at death.

The most widely known part of the Buddhist Siddha literature, however, has been Abhayadatta's *Lives,* which consists of an exotic collection of stories, not exactly fairy tales, speaking of strange and eccentric saints. As an example, we may summarize the first episode, which recounts the life of Lūipa, the "eater of fish guts." In this case, as in many others, the "name" of the Siddha is actually a sobriquet, referring to an outstanding characteristic or, as in the case of Tantipa, the weaver, the Siddha's occupation. "Pa," which is affixed to the names of many of the Siddhas, is ultimately derived from the Sanskrit word for "foot" *(pāda)* and in this context means "venerable," that is, one whose feet are worthy of veneration.

Lūipa, it is said, was a Sri Lankan prince, and the reluctant heir to his father's throne. After several failed efforts to flee the palace he succeeded at last, and became a wandering ascetic in India. By chance one day, while begging, he encountered a prostitute who was in fact a ḍākinī, a woman embodying enlightened wisdom, and she, being clairvoyant, detected that despite his outward saintly deportment, there was still a smidgen of pride in his heart. She poured some vile slop into his begging bowl and he, disgusted, threw it out. At this the ḍākinī exclaimed, "how are you ever going to get enlightened, if you're still such a picky eater?" Lūipa, recognizing that indeed he was covertly preoccupied with mundane judgments, resolved to uproot the last of his attachments, and dwelling near a fishermen's settlement on the banks of the Ganges, he practiced austerities for twelve years while living on the entrails and other refuse discarded after the catch. So it was that he eventually freed himself from all mundane patterns of thought, and was able to transmute even the foulest matter into the deathless nectar of gnosis.

As we have seen above, the collection of which the *Lives* is one part also includes various songs and teachings attributed to the Siddhas. The relationship, in any given case, between a Siddha's life, song, and teaching is not always straightforward, but the verses attributed to Lūipa do seem to correlate with his story, and so may be taken to exemplify those cases in which such a correspondence is to be found. At the beginning of Vīraprabha's anthology he sings:

> When honey's smeared on the snout of a wild, mad dog,
> it eats whatever it meets.
> Likewise, when the guru bestows precepts on a luckless fool,
> his spirit is scorched.
> But the fortunate, who realize the unborn in whatever appears
> thereby destroy common thought.
> They become like mad battle elephants, swords tied to their trunks,
> demolishing enemy legions.

And the particular teaching attributed to Lūipa in the *The Garland of Gems,* translated below, is called the "the instruction that applies to all appearances you meet." All of this seems to fit neatly together with the tale of his overcoming his finicky tastes by adopting a diet of rubbish.

Much of the modern scholarship concerning the lives of the Siddhas has focused either upon the quasi-historical dimensions of these traditions or upon allegorical readings of them. Both approaches, to be sure, were in some sense sanctioned by the traditional Buddhist schools in which the collection was known. One author has gone so far as to tabulate a "lineage tree," arranging the eighty-four Siddhas into a single complex geneology. This tendency to historicization continues to inform Western interpretation, despite the observation, clearly articulated a half century ago by Shashibhushan Dasgupta, that eighty-four is a mystical number and that the grouping of eighty-four Siddhas is "complete" only in the sense that it fills out this mystical number. Accordingly, in Dasgupta's words, there is justifiable "doubt about the historical nature of the tradition of the eighty-four Siddhas." Dasgupta also provided a long and suggestive list of classifications that use the number eighty-four in Indian religious traditions; I add here only that, from a numerological point of view, the number eighty-four has the interesting property of being the product of the sum and the product of three and four:

$$(3 + 4) \times (3 \times 4) = 84$$

Thus, symbolically it encompasses the range of possible relationships obtaining among the innumerable magical and natural categories involving threes and fours.

That the number eighty-four is entirely arbitrary from a historical perspective is further underscored when the various traditional lists of Mahāsiddhas are compared, even if we restrict ourselves to the lists found within only the Buddhist tradition; for there are a great many significant discrepancies among them.

If the tales and traditions of the Siddhas are to be regarded not as historical but as constituting a mythic collection, then just what is this a myth of? Despite the tendency to incorporate the traditions of the Siddhas into those sanctioned by the mainstream monastic orders of Tibetan Buddhism, it is clear that marginality and idiosyncracy are powerful themes; this, indeed, accounts for the appeal these tales have had in the contemporary Western religious counterculture. The quasi-canonical status of the tradition, the often enigmatic language of its poetry, the eccentricities of the iconography associated with it, its apparently strong connections with other medieval Indian religious traditions that arose outside the bounds of high-status society, and similarly with such Tibetan Buddhist traditions as the Kagyü (Bka'-brgyud) yogic lineages—all of this seems to reinforce the view that this is a myth of freedom from convention, of the rejection of rigid norms. But this interpretation is clearly simplistic, for the force of tradition has been to normalize the apparently rebellious Siddhas, and to incorporate them and their teachings within a program of well-ordered religious discipline. The tale of King Kuñji's banquet seems to underwrite just such a perspective, by freezing the Siddhas in the form of statues worshiped by a royal patron. Perhaps we can speak, then, of the institutionalization of idiosyncracy through the cooperation of myth and normative practice. In other words, in the case of the Siddhas, a myth of idiosyncratic freedom undergirds an enduring ethos of order.

The Tibetan texts translated below are found in the great nineteenth-century encyclopedia of Tibetan esoterica: 'Jam mgon Kong sprul Blo gros mtha' yas, *Gdams ngag mdzod: A Treasury of Instructions and Techniques for Spiritual Realization* (Delhi: N. Lungtok and N. Gyaltsan, 1971), vol. 11, pp. 9–11 ("King Kuñji's Banquet) and 92–143 ("The Garland of Gems"). Because the cryptic style of the original does not lend itself to literal English translation, I provide a rather free rendition of the verse text of the *Garland of Gems*. In the case of the commentary accompanying the verses, I supply here an abridged restatement of the Tibetan original, supplemented by my own occasional remarks intended to clarify the meaning of the verses. For further clarification of the text as a whole, I have added a topical outline.

Further Reading

Abhayadatta's *Lives of the Siddhas* is available in an English translation in James B. Robinson, tr., *Buddha's Lions: The Lives of the Eighty-four Siddhas* (Berkeley: Dharma Publishing, 1979). The same work, with Vīraprabha's *Songs*, is also translated in Keith Dowman, *Masters of Mahamudra: Songs and Histories of the Eighty-*

four Buddhist Siddhas (Albany: State University of New York Press, 1985). The Indian Buddhist Tantric background for the Siddha traditions is surveyed in David Snellgrove, *Indo-Tibetan Buddhism: Indian Buddhists & Their Tibetan Successors* (Boston: Shambhala, 1987), vol. 1, chapter 3, "Tantric Buddhism." The song literature attributed to the Siddhas is very extensive, and there have been several useful translations and studies, including Shashibhusan Dasgupta, *Obscure Religious Cults* (Calcutta: University of Calcutta, 1946), part 1, "The Buddhist Sahajiyā Cult and Literature"; Herbert V. Guenther, *The Royal Song of Saraha: A Study in the History of Buddhist Thought* (Seattle: University of Washington Press, 1968); Per Kværne, *An Anthology of Buddhist Tantric Songs: A Study of the Caryāgīti* (Oslo: Universitetsforlaget, 1977); and David Snellgrove, "The Tantras," in Edward Conze, ed., *Buddhist Texts through the Ages* (New York: Philosophical Library, 1954), pp. 219–68. There is also a large body of indigenous Tibetan literature devoted to the lives, teachings, and songs of various Indian Siddhas, whether included in the lists of the eighty-four or not; for instance: Herbert V. Guenther, *The Life and Teaching of Nāropa* (Oxford: Clarendon Press, 1963); Dudjom Rinpoche and Jikdrel Yeshe Dorje, *The Nyingma School of Tibetan Buddhism: Its Fundamentals and History,* translated by Gyurme Dorje and Matthew Kapstein (London: Wisdom Publications, 1991), vol. 1, pp. 443–504; David Templeman, tr., *The Seven Instruction Lineages* (Dharamsala: Library of Tibetan Works and Archives, 1983); *Tibetan Religions in Practice,* edited by Donald S. Lopez, Jr. (Princeton: Princeton University Press, 1997), chapters 8–9. On the representation of the Siddhas in Tibetan painting, see Toni Schmid, *The Eighty-five Siddhas* (Stockholm: Statens Etnografiska Museum, 1958). For the teachings of the Siddhas in the Hindu Śaivite traditions, refer to David Gordon White, *The Alchemical Body* (Chicago: University of Chicago Press, 1996). Those who wish to learn more of the yoga of the transference of consciousness, mentioned toward the close of *The Garland of Gems,* may consult my "A Tibetan Festival of Rebirth Reborn: The 1992 Revival of the Drigung Powa Chenmo," in Melvyn C. Goldstein and Matthew T. Kapstein, eds., *Buddhism in Contemporary Tibet: Religious Revival and Cultural Identity* (Berkeley and Los Angeles: University of California Press, 1998).

King Kuñji's Banquet

In the western part of India, in Kantamara, a district in Saurastra [modern Gujarat], the religious king Kuñji governed his realm righteously. At some point his mother took ill and was fast approaching death. The king lovingly asked her, "Now it seems you will not live for long, Ma. For your benefit in future lives, I will do whatever you command and will offer donations for the worship of the community of monks, the brahmans, and the temples, and for charity and so forth."

His mother replied, "You needn't bother with the other virtues on my behalf. Just host a Tantric banquet for the eighty-four yogins and yoginīs who have

Figure 2.1. Two Mahāsiddhas as depicted in a Tibetan woodblock print. To the left, Saraha straightens the arrow of mind. Tilopa, on the right, plays the hand drum (*ḍamaru*) of awakening with his right hand, and in his left holds a skull-cup (*kapāla*) overflowing with the nectar of attainment. He wears a meditation belt, used for support during long periods of yogic practice.

become Siddhas, and pray to them for my sake!" With these last words, she died.

The king then thought, "Those past Siddhas are no longer seen among men, so how can I invite them? But I cannot violate mother's dying wish. Because the Mahāsiddhas are compassionate, all I can think to do is to pray." He prayed one-pointedly, and the two gnostic ḍākinīs, Kokali and Dharmaviśva ["Dhamadhuma" in the *Garland of Gems*], became visibly manifest and said, "We two will help you! Let's invite the Siddhas and prepare a banquet hall!" The king arranged a great hall for the Tantric feast, while the two ḍākinīs, through their miraculous abilities, journeyed to the various sacred lands in an instant to invite the Siddhas. Lūipa was the first to arrive, and the other Siddhas also arrived momentarily, in their appointed order, and took their seats. The king generously served up the delights of the banquet, and they remained assembled in the Tantric feast for a long time. In the end, although the king asked the Siddhas to remain for a while so that he could continue to worship them, they would not permit this. Instead, each Siddha sang for the king one of his or her own vajra-songs, called dohas, and then vanished into the unknown. The king constructed images to represent each of the Siddhas, before which each one's song was written, and there he worshiped them.

At the same time, a scholar named Vīraprabha, who was traveling far away to the east, heard that the eighty-four Siddhas had actually come to be worshiped by King Kuñji, and he made haste to come there, but arrived a week after the Siddhas had left. He grew disconsolate and prayed fervently for seven days, whereupon the two ḍākinīs visibly appeared, and transmitted to him the *Garland of Gems*, the very songs that had been sung at the royal feast, and other teachings, together with the tales of the eighty-four. He meditated upon their significance and thereby gained special realization, becoming himself a lord among Siddhas. He also authored a book in which the various dohas were collected together, and later he transmitted these teachings to the brahman scholar Kamala. The latter taught them to the Siddha and hermit Jamāri, and he to the scholar from Magadha, Abhayadatta, who composed the collection of the tales of the eighty-four Siddhas and the commentary on the dohas. All of texts mentioned above were brought together and translated here in Tibet by that same scholar and his disciple, the Tangut translator Möndrup Sherap.

The Garland of Gems

In the Indian Language: *Ratnamālā* [*-nāma*]
In the Tibetan Language: *Rin chen phreng ba zhes bya ba*

According to Tibetan custom, in order for future generations to recall the efforts of past translators and scholars, the title must be given in both Sanskrit and Tibetan. In this case, it is explained that because each of the teachings of the Siddhas has many precious facets, they are like gems *(ratnas),* and because many such teachings are strung together here, they form a garland *(mālā).*

Salutations to the Transcendent Lord of Speech [the bodhisattva Mañjuśrī]!

Mañjuśrī, the bodhisattva of wisdom, is invoked before the beginning of the verse text in order to remove obstacles to the understanding of the text as a whole.

Introductory Verses

1. Your black hair is piled in a topknot,
Your eyes deep blue like the blue lotus
Your body is convulsed in your terrible roar—
To you, Acala, I bow in homage.

Acala is one of the foremost divinities of Tantric Buddhism, and is depicted in many forms, usually ferocious or wrathful, and wielding a sword. In later Buddhist Tantrism he became particularly popular in Nepal and in Japan, where he is often seen as a temple protector and is called Fudō.

2. I will not set down here all that was seen and heard
At the assembly of eighty-four Siddhas
In the heaven of manifest delight,

That then was well practiced by Dhamadhuma;
But I shall explain the *Garland of Gems*
That was given as an instruction to the yakṣiṇī.

Because those fortunate enough to encounter or even hear of the assembly of the Siddhas become delighted by it, that assembly is known as the "heaven of manifest delight." The ḍākinī Dhamadhuma thoroughly mastered a great many teachings that the Siddhas bestowed there, but here only the *Garland of Gems,* which was taught on behalf of a yakṣiṇī, will be discussed. What, then, is the story of that teaching?

Once upon a time, in the cremation ground called Sama Grove *(sa-ma'i tshal),* there lived a yakṣiṇī who was condemned by her own misdeeds to dwell there feeding on carrion. In the northeastern quarter of the cremation ground there was a great hollow tree, inhabited by a family of seven bears. A huge rhinocerous-demon went to sleep there and fell over, crushing the tree and killing its inhabitants. At that point the yakṣiṇī arrived, killed the rhinocerous-demon, and found the flesh of the dead brood of bears. An ogre, however, was attracted by the odor of flesh and blood, and seeing that the yakṣiṇī had reached the feast first, became greatly enraged at her. Flying above, he poured molten copper upon her, so that she was horribly burned and suffered terribly. This was karmic retribution for the suffering she herself had caused other beings during her previous lives. Two ḍākinīs, named Kokila and Dharmadevī [the "Dhamadhuma" mentioned above], took pity upon her and healed her wounds with mantras, except for one place where she had been burned right through to the bone. However, the two were the disciples of the eighty-four Mahāsiddhas, who at that very time were gathered together in the pure land of manifest delight, where they recognized the yakṣiṇī to be receptive to the Buddha's teaching. They therefore composed a short text, the *Garland of Gems,* epitomizing their own religious instructions, and transmitted it to the two ḍākinīs, who in turn taught it to the yakṣiṇī. [In the commentary, however, the text is presented as a teaching given in direct dialogue with the yakṣiṇī.] By the power of this teaching she finally came to be fully healed in both body and spirit, and went on to become a great ḍākinī in her own right, named Sumati.

Lūipa's Teaching: "The Instruction That Applies to All Appearances"

The foregoing remarks serve as an introduction. The actual teaching of the *Garland of Gems* begins with an instruction of Lūipa, "The Instruction That Applies to All Appearances You Meet," which was delivered to benefit the ailing yakṣiṇī.

When she requested this teaching, he said to her,

"Your fault is not knowing your own nature. If you know that, you'll be freed from appearances, not to speak of bodily appearances alone."

"What's it to know your own nature?"

"It is a luminous gnosis, in which the continuum of mundane reality comes to an end."

When she replied that she still didn't get the point, he said:

3. In what is insubstantial and incessant,
Without boundary or center, and thus pervasive,
The fact of the matter is really profound,
Like the fire of Malaya Mountain.

Here "insubstantial" means that in the nature of things there is no substantial being. For instance, though one may speak of a "sky-flower," nevertheless, no such thing really exists, above and beyond the naming of it. Therefore, neither it, nor its supposed attributes, such as color and form, can be said to exist substantially. It is when the entire continuum of the attributions of existence, appearance, emptiness, idea, mind, and thought comes to an end that we speak of "luminous gnosis." Like the radiance of a precious gem, it is "incessant," and for this reason is characterized as "without boundary or center, and thus pervasive." Like uncompounded space, it embraces everything, from the highest heavens to the depths of hell. And because the yakṣiṇī has the potential to realize her pain, her mental activity, and her apprehension of appearances to be in fact that luminous gnosis, "the fact of the matter is really profound." It is "like the fire of Malaya Mountain" that incinerates all it encounters.

The yakṣiṇī, however, did not understand this, and so asked the Siddha Līlapa for clarification. He responded:

4. You are as one born from the ocean of things,
Longing to rest in the mire of things;
But what is experienced in the absence
Of the bee, nectar and flower?

The second couplet refers to the conditions for realization. Just as a sweet taste occurs when a flower, its nectar, and a bee come together, but not so long as they remain apart, so too, so long as you have not yet realized gnosis and remain clinging to bodily apprehensions, unable to detach yourself from objects, you will not experience the blissful taste of your inherent nature. And until you experience that taste, you will not be free of your pain.

The Siddha Kokala then taught her how that understanding becomes firm:

5. Like Brahmā to the external world and its inner inhabitants,
Like timely warmth and yogurt culture,
And like oil in mustard seed,
If you really realize it, you'll be certain of it.

Just as the creator-god Brahmā knows the entire universe and all its inhabitants, similarly the luminous gnosis, which is the nature of mind as taught by the guru, pervades all that you may know. But once it is known, how is that knowledge to grow firm? This is explained by the three examples that follow. "Timely warmth" refers to the warmth that occurs in the spring, which spreads throughout the natural world; so too, the individual who knows the radiant light of mind finds that it spreads through the range of experience. And just as a small amount of "yogurt culture" completely transforms a large quantity of milk, without ever getting rid of the milk, in the same way radiant light transforms mundane conceptual activity, without actually abandoning it. Similarly, as oil is present in a "mustard seed," and only needs to be brought out, but not newly created, you come to realize that the mind in its natural state is pervaded by its radiant light.

But what is the fruit of such realization? To answer this question, the Siddha Camaripa was the next to speak:

6ab. In that which is inevident, invisible, and clear,
That space itself is revealed.

This refers to the body of reality, the dharmakāya, which is like space, and so "inevident, invisible, and clear." Thus, it is not to be thought of as an entity or a nonentity, or as intellect, mind, or thought. But just as space, though not itself shaped or colored, provides a clearing in which sun, moon, and stars, as well as clouds, mists, rainbows, and more become manifest, so too in the invisible space of the dharmakāya, there is an incessant outpouring of compassion, taking form as the Buddha's bodies of rapture and emanation.

To this Saraha added these verses:

6cd. The body apprehended by no one is most beautiful,
Like a treasure-vase, a wishing gem, or a jewel.

It is in fact the nature of mind, free from the conceptions of apprehended object and apprehending subject, that is here described as "most beautiful."

Virūpa's Teaching: "The Empty City"

Then master Virūpa sang of an instruction entitled "The Empty City":

7. As for the city that is entirely empty,
Ask your self: who is the creator
Of body and speech in the three realms, the three spheres?
The self-nature of the self is nothing;
It rests within no bounds whatsoever.

The "city" refers outwardly to the three realms, or three spheres of the world, and inwardly to the three spheres of body, speech, and mind, as well as to past, present, and future. As all of this depends upon a concatenation of causes, and does not exist independently, the entire city, whatever we conceive it to be, is empty. To establish this, review its possible causes in turn, and ask your self who its creator might be. You must ask your self, for you must also examine the reality of that self: it, too, is empty, devoid of self-nature. Perhaps you will conclude that all there is *is* emptiness, but that is not so. In the final analysis, one can speak neither of emptiness, nor nonemptiness, nor both, nor neither—"it rests within no bounds whatsoever."

To affirm the meaning of this, Ḍombipa sang:

8. In the city that is emptied of everything
Where is any substantially existing thing?

This may be understood without further comment. Gorakṣa added:

9. In the city of appearance, sound, and thought,
Owing to apprehended objects, or to the apprehending of them,
The unhappy silkworm is ensnared in its own saliva.
You'll find happiness when, without apprehending, you let go.

The appearances and sounds of the world are imputed through conceptual activity—in truth, nothing goes beyond conceptual activity, so that this is a "city of thought." As you bind yourself therein, it may be exemplified by a silkworm, wrapping itself up in its own saliva. But if you let go, and abide in the natural condition of reality, you'll find happiness. Tantipa then said:

10. Without renunciation, without possession,
If you come to know, you'll not enter the city.
But like Nanda and the gemstone light,
You'll find the city to be supreme bliss.

When you have abandoned both acceptance and rejection, and become free of bewilderment, you no longer enter the city of bewilderment, but neither do you hold to not entering it as if that were a hard fact. Instead, bewilderment itself discloses the nature of reality, so that it becomes the city of supreme bliss. Then, like Nanda, the king of the serpents (*nāgas*), who perceives the wish-granting gem that is invisible to all others, you will see that the city of thought *is* the city of bliss.

Saraha's Teaching: "Remembrance Alone"

Following Virūpa's instruction on the blissful city, Saraha again sang to the yakṣiṇī:

11. When someone speaks of any phenomenon,
That speech is an act of remembrance.
So is it not also the faculty of remembrance
That speaks even of nirvāṇa?

This is the teaching of the great brahman Saraha's "Instruction on Remembrance Alone": all acts of speech are bound up in remembrance. This is the case whether one speaks of saṃsāra or nirvāṇa, tranquillity or insight, meditative equipoise or what follows after meditation, appearance or emptiness, and so on. But what follows from that?

12. Whatever appears—earth, water, fire, or wind—
    Simultaneously occurs within emptiness.
    The splendid appearance of gnosis
    Occurs in remembrance alone.

Although all those phenomena are bound up in remembrance, at the moment of their appearance they are simultaneously innately empty. Thus, all appearance is the appearance of the gnosis of emptiness. In this way, there is no independent phenomenon of remembrance, but it is, rather, indivisible from the appearance of gnosis. Being indivisible, they are one: this is what is meant by "remembrance alone."

The Siddha Śabari then sang:

13. If you do not know the conjunction of sun and moon,
    Things are as many as waves in the sea.
    When just that which is unique occurs,
    It is not possible to find division here.

Here, the sun symbolizes appearance, or method, and the moon emptiness, or discernment. If you do not understand the conjunction of these, things appear as multiplicity, like waves in the sea: despite the underlying union, conceptual acts of remembrance become manifold. But when the essential nature of remembrance, which is unique, and no different from the natural state, occurs, then "it is not possible to find division here."

To this Caurāṅgi added:

14. There is not even a particle of fault here.
    It does not arise through composition.

That is to say that the natural state of reality is entirely free from all independent acts of remembrance, which are bound up with conceptual activity. The realization of "remembrance alone" is not a conditioned phenomenon, dependent upon causal composition.

Then Vīnapa, too, sang:

15. The mountain of conceptual thought
    Sinks into the sea of nonconceptualization.
    As the subject is an appearance in the sphere of reality,
    Where can there be objective conceptualizations?

The remembrance of reality becomes like a vast ocean, into which all independent acts of remembrance dissolve. When the appearance of the subject is known to be just reality, there is no conceptualization of objects as real entities.

Mīnapa's Teaching: "Elemental Food and Clothing"

Following Saraha's instruction, master Mīnapa conferred an instruction on feeding and clothing oneself with the elements:

16. The bodily vessel becomes elemental light,
A melting stream of divine ambrosia above.
In the mass of reality's light,
Conceptions of the six aggregates are exhausted.

Primarily, this refers to the creative visualization of the deity. At the start of such meditation, the bodily mansion becomes like a vase, filled with the light of the elements: from the seed-syallable *yaṃ* comes fire-wind, like a solar orb, red in color and half a mile in diameter. Owing to its agitation there appears the red *raṃ,* from which fire radiates to the extent of the wind. From this steam and mist arise, red in color: this is the fire-water, but it is contemplated as being of the nature of light. From its condensation there appears the yellow syllable *su,* from which is projected fire-earth, to the same extent as those mentioned above.

Atop that mansion of elemental light, you then contemplate a white *hūṃ* which is in its nature a divinity embodying the essence of mind, radiating light, and from which there is a melting stream of ambrosia. It dissolves into the elements, intermingling thus with the bodily vase. Mind itself, in essence a divinity, of the nature of the elements, now dissolves into light, having emanated in the form of a hūṃ. Present as the mass of reality in the vase of light, it is like the self-luminous orb of the sun—concentrate upon this. The conceptual activity of the sensory fields reaches cessation herein, and if you examine the senses themselves, they are realized to be like lamps within a vase of light. The sign of contemplative success is an experience of outer warmth, and in this way one is clothed by the elements, while inner awareness is nourished by this contemplation, so that one is thus fed.

The yakṣiṇī, however, was unable to achieve this contemplation of elemental food and clothing, at which point the exalted Nāgārjuna sang to her:

17. The varied conceptions of the six classes of beings
Have arisen through the accumulated power of errant desire.
Through the power of knowledge which turns that around
You awaken as Buddha, so that all desires are fulfilled.

The beings who inhabit the three realms of the world may be embodied in any way whatsoever, according to the diversity of their conceptual activity, and through the accumulated power of their perverse desires and thirsts. Thus, the yakṣiṇī experienced her body and its pains as she did, but this would certainly be changed to bliss if she had the power to realize the nature of mind to be a mass of light, a solar orb.

To this master Śāntipa added his instruction on the "six views, outer and inner, which turn ephemeral cognitions around":

18. The appearance of objective conditions is ceaseless,
    Just like bubbles in water.
    This is reversed by the antidote that follows meditation,
    That is just like a staff in the water.

Sensory objects belonging to the six fields of sight, sound, taste, odor, bodily feeling, and thought arise incessantly. These ephemeral objects continue to arise, like bubbles in water, and so long as ephemeral appearances thus continue to arise they won't be stopped by the mounted spear-bearing cavalry of ephemeral cognitions (which, however forceful and impressive, have no power to stop them). Such is the view of the six outer objects.

To grasp the six objects, however, as independently existing things is an erroneous view, which is reversed by a cognition following meditation, which recognizes ephemeral occurrences to be of the nature of reality. That cognition, which cuts through all sensations, is like a staff that passes through water. This antidote, indeed, becomes gnosis, and is referred to as the "inner six views" (for it applies to the same six fields of experience and cognition mentioned above).

In the first instance, the ephemeral states are afflictions that should be renounced. Then they are renounced by gnosis, the antidote following meditation, which moves like a knife through the water. Finally, owing to that, what is to be renounced and its renunciation are realized to be no different—there is gnosis alone, known here as the "inner six views."

The Teaching of the Two Ḍākinīs

After that, the two ḍākinīs encouraged the yakṣiṇī to seek the attainments of the Tantric divinities through five practices which they asked the Siddhas to impart to her: master Khagarbha's abbreviated rites of Lord Acala; Kanaripa's rites of the Mother of Wisdom; Ḍombipa's rites which combine the tantric divinities Cakrasaṃvara and Hevajra; Caloka's rites of Amitāyus, the buddha of longevity; and Nāropa's instructions on the hundred-syllable mantra of purification and repentance. The yakṣiṇī practiced these instructions, but desired quick results and so seized on object and subject as real. When the longed-for attainments were not, therefore, forthcoming, she complained that there were no such attainments to be realized, that the divinities were nonexistent, and that to persist in reciting mantras really pissed her off.

The two ḍākinīs replied, "All those who have gone before have realized the attainments. If you have not, it's only because you've failed to purify your own continuum of being."

"I still don't understand what this 'continuum of being' business is about."

To explain it, they said:

19. That which possesses the seed of beauteous youth
    Abides pervading all beings.

This is grasped where the best faculties appear,
In the appearance of a unique act of gnosis.

20. This is the shifting shape of clouds in the sky,
The reflection appearing in a mirror.
When you examine this, just so,
No purpose is gained by the appearance of obscuration.
It is enjoyed through the power of secrets.

These two verses teach two topics, called "the little nail of the creative visualization of the deity" and "the methodical precept of symbolic significance." Concerning the first, "beauteous youth" characterizes the visualized deity whose body is not of the coarse elements and is therefore free from the aging process. Because there are no flaws owing to false imputations, the deity is beautiful. "That which possesses its seed" is that which resembles it, has the potential to engender it, that is to say, all beings of the six classes, who are thus pervaded by it, without regard to class or status. Those of "best faculties," in this context, are those who recognize the various forms of the deities to be the magical projection of mind, the unique appearance of gnosis, but not an independently existing god. The deity, pictured in the mind, is the body of rapture, whereas the unfabricated mind itself is the body of reality. The two bodies of rapture and emanation, appearances of that single gnosis, may appear as anything, ceaselessly. If you know this, the creative visualization of the deity is mastered.

Verse 20 then treats the second topic, "the methodical precept of symbolic significance." Here, the sky and the mirror are symbols for the body of reality, while clouds and reflections are indicative of the bodies of rapture and emanation. Obscuration, or ignorance, serves no purpose with respect to the appearance of these two bodies of the Buddha. To dispel such obscuration, the individual who is cultivating the path must adhere to the appropriate Tantric vows, and thus the result may be "enjoyed through the power of secrets."

The Teachings of Tilopa

The foregoing teachings hammer home the little nail of the creative visualization of the deity, so that now the essential instructions, the little nail of the subtle channels and vital energies, may be taught. The ḍākinīs gave many instructions on the channels and energies to the yakṣinī, but however much she practiced, though her past pain was at once relieved, she became disturbed because she could not achieve bliss. She then turned to Tilopa for further instruction.

On the Vital Energies

Tilopa's first teaching to her was this:

21. The seal which clarifies gnosis

Is solely impressed on the vital points of the body.
That apparitional machine
Develops the force of the faculties.

In respect to the clarification of gnosis, these paths are taught in the way of secret mantras: there is the path which transforms the ground, so that by realizing conceptual activity to be of the nature of gods and goddesses, the modalites of gnosis are clarified in visualization practice; and there is the path of passion, which is dissimilar in that it relies upon the seals, or vital points, of the body, and so focuses upon the realization of the body's subtle channels and vital energies. Then there is the path of liberation, which determines gnosis to be mere apparition, and the great path of liberation, which determines that gnosis itself is not and that this is no further gnosis, and that there are no afflictions or conceptualizations and that this too is no further gnosis—it is like a flower in space.

Now, then, what is "the seal which clarifies gnosis"? In this verse, this refers to the Wild Woman, the inner heat that rises below the navel, relying upon which the significance of gnosis comes clear. In cultivating it through exercises that make use of the body's channels and energies, the body becomes like an apparitional mechanism, developing the force of the sensory faculties. Tilopa added this example:

22. Like a banana tree,
 But with flesh, bone and marrow,
 Its growth is generated
 Just so by the channels and winds.

Just as a banana tree, depending upon the growth of its roots, trunk, and so on, finally produces its fruit, so in this case, it is the channels and energies within a body of flesh and bone that give rise to the appearance of gnosis, the triple body of enlightenment. Because that is the goal of the instruction on the body's vital channels and energies, Tilopa then conferred his precepts on the ultimate view and meditation upon it.

On the Ultimate View

He sang:

23. In that which is causeless and without result,
 All is clearly revealed.
 There is no example, no designation.
 In what is without separation, what clarification is needed?
 It is not generated by errancy or detour;
 Not straying, it is opposed to unmoving passivity.

Natural, luminous gnosis is the final significance of the view. It is the skylike body of reality, which is not engendered by any cause, and is therefore without any result. Nevertheless, though not a causally compounded result, in its ceaselessness the two resultant bodies of rapture and emanation are "clearly revealed." And in its essential nature, the skylike radiant light of mind can neither be exemplified nor designated.

So, then, can no experience be cultivated of it?

There is an experienceless cultivation of experience, meditationless meditation, incessant absorption, a result that is never to be attained, but from which one is never separated. Hence, "in what is without separation, what clarification is needed"? It does not drift off in errancy, or wander into any detour, or stray into apathy, or remain fixed should you seek to freeze it in immobility.

On Integrating Radiant Light with the Apparitional Body

The foregoing teaches the ultimate view of luminous gnosis. Its meditative cultivation, so that its realization becomes inseparable, is taught in the remainder of the text. Here, the view is that mind is radiant light, body is apparition, their connection is revealed in dream and in the liminal passage from death to rebirth, and the samādhi taught here is the transference of consciousness and the "penetration of the city." The following verses emphasize these teachings, discussing them in relation to five topics: liminal states, types of embodiment, potential disclosure, intermingling of the teachings, and their relevant connections. The first concerns the realization of radiant light during the liminal state between birth and death, that is to say, during this lifetime.

24. During the liminal passage from birth until death,
With respect to conceptions of the body of karmic maturation,
Desire is purified in luminousness—
This is the amazing instruction of the guru.

The liminal passage from birth to death is the period during which all sorts of conceptions become concretely manifest, so that one is embodied in the "body of karmic maturation." But conceptual activity may be disclosed as luminous in nature, and this luminosity in turn may be intermingled with the emotions and passions, purifying them. How so? On the path of transformation one holds the conceptions to be gods and goddesses, while on the path of desire one engenders bliss while relying upon the subtle channels and fluids, and on the path of liberation engenders bliss relying upon the Wild Woman; but here, on the path of great liberation, one does not hanker after those sorts of bliss at all, but realizes them to be luminous and so intermingles luminousness with passion. Owing to what relevant connection may these teachings be realized? *This is the amazing instruction of the guru!*

On the Yogas of Dream and the Liminal Passage

The yoga of the dream is to be mastered during this lifetime. It is summarized as follows:

25. There are the preliminaries and the main practice:
[The latter includes] apprehension and refinement,
Training in apparition, until one abandons fear,
And meditation that does not step beyond the nature of reality.

As for the preliminaries, the individual who embarks upon this path must not be lacking in karmic propensities, or have violated the Tantric vows, or be without merit, or be disrespectful to the guru; otherwise, he or she will not succeed in grasping his or her dreams. For this reason, the preliminary practices are those of repentance and purification, such as the hundred-syllable mantra, and devotion and worship directed to the guru and the Three Precious Jewels.

The main practice then has four parts: "apprehension," in which you learn to grasp your dreams, to become aware when you are dreaming; "refinement," whereby you learn to transform your dreams, and to travel freely within them; "training in apparition," through which you realize the truthlessness of dreams, and so come to abandon all fears; and, finally, knowing that dreams are the bewildering projections of mind, you apply your guru's instruction to whatever thoughts arise, and so cultivate "meditation that does not step beyond the nature of reality."

This is to be practiced during this life, and pertains to the liminal passage of the dream, which is described in this way:

26. In the liminal passage of the transformations of consciousness,
One is impelled by the body of latent dispositions.
The relevant preparation is actualized dreaming,
Wherein ignorance is dissolved in radiant light.
One applies oneself with fervent devotion.

Of the five topics mentioned earlier [verse 24], the liminal passage is here that of the dream, the body is that of latent dispositions, that which is to be disclosed is the potentiality of dreaming, which is to be intermingled primarily with the obscuration of ignorance as its antidote, while the relevant connection is formed through mindfulness and fervent devotion. In sleep itself one comes to realize the luminous nature of mind, so that sleep partakes of the essence of bliss and emptiness, giving rise to the experience of radiant light.

The liminal passage between death and rebirth, then, is taught in the following verse:

27. When this body of karmic ripening is destroyed,
[There remains] the mental body, with its latent dispositions,
Desire should be disclosed as radiant light,
And attachment to parents should be abandoned.

Here, the liminal passage is the liminal passage of the possibilities of existence; the body is the mental body; radiant light is to be disclosed and then intermingled with the obscuration of aversion; and the relevant connection is formed by the potential parents who are thus abodes for rebirth, for which reason "attachment to parents should be abandoned."

The mental body, between death and rebirth, unhampered by the physical body, is propelled by its confused dispositions. Those who have accumulated positive dispositions through meritorious action may nevertheless recollect the divine, or recall the true nature of things, and so be freed from the path of evil destinies. As in the yoga of the dream, one should not be bewildered by incessant apparitions, but attain instead the luminous body of reality.

The Transference of Consciousness

The foregoing verses have summarized the yogas of the dream, the liminal passage, apparition, and radiant light. Tilopa's final teachings concern samādhi, the transference of consciousness and the "penetration of the city." In order to realize these, one must cultivate mastery of the vital energies and radiant light, as indicated below:

28. Time, bodily exercise, and object of concentration—
These are the first application.
The essential point of the Wild Woman is said to be the four vital winds,
And these are explained as four radiant lights.

At appropriate times, when the vital winds circulate through the central channel, one adopts the vajra posture as a bodily exercise, and concentrates upon the movement of the energies in relation to the four cakras at the crown, throat, heart and navel. The essential teaching of the inner heat, or the Wild Woman, then stresses the fourfold control of the breath. When proficiency in the inner heat is achieved by day, radiant light is grasped in four ways by night: there is the natural radiant light, which is the purity of all phenomena; the meditational radiant light, arising in the contemplative experience of the yogin in union with his consort; the radiant light of sleep, when coarse mental activity comes to a halt in deep sleep; and the radiant light of death, arising when, during the liminal passage, the bodily elements are deceased.

29. In general, the transference of consciousness, a special form of yogic exercise, is said to cause the consciousness of the dying individual to depart suddenly from the body through a forced opening at the crown of the skull, and to travel immediately to a pure land, often the Sukhāvatī [the "Pure" or "Happy Land"] realm of the Buddha Amitābha, in which enlightenment can then be swiftly attained. The "penetration of the city" is an especially high-powered version of this, permitting one to project one's consciousness into the recently deceased corpse of another. The yakṣiṇī to whom Tilopa taught this technique soon achieved mastery of it, taking possession in this way of the body of the yoginī Sumati. According to Tibetan tradition, the actual technique was lost not long after it was

transmitted in Tibet during the eleventh century, and it has not been successfully practiced since. The yoga of the transference of consciousness, however, remains a fundamental practice of Tibetan Buddhism, and is widely practiced in connection with Tibetan funeral rites.

The verses in passage 29 in which *The Garland of Gems* discusses these techniques are, unfortunately, almost indecipherable and even the commentary fails to clarify the text at this point. For this reason these verses are left untranslated here. Perhaps one who prays earnestly to the eighty-four Siddhas will once again encounter the two ḍākinīs, and so come to recover this passage from the heaven of manifest delight.

Concluding Dedication

30. May the full realization of the entire teaching,
    Bestowed for the sake of the yakṣiṇī,
    And well practiced by Dhamadhuma,
    Bring all creatures to the stage of perfection!

The small text of the instructions of *The Garland of Gems* is now concluded.

—3—

Interviews with a Tantric Kālī Priest: Feeding Skulls in the Town of Sacrifice

June McDaniel

Skulls are widely used in Bengali folk Tantra. They empower buildings and grounds, like the relics in early and medieval churches. They are buried in temples, under the altar or in a corner, and they turn the building into sacred ground. They are also buried at the foot of sacred trees, and they make ordinary ground into an empowered meditation seat.

Although skulls and images of death are normally inauspicious in Hinduism, certain skulls bring luck and fortune in meditation. Skulls give protective energy (*śakti*) and support the sādhu in his efforts. They are often painted red, to show that they are alive and auspicious, and to protect them from mold and the Bengali weather. They are ironic images, which represent death yet encourage the spiritual rebirth of the holy man or sādhu. Skulls are not old bones, but relics that mediate the supernatural (*alaukika*) world, calling down the goddess Kālī to help the practitioner. Skulls are really not dead but alive, companions and friends of the sādhus. They are inhabited by earth-bound entities who seek spiritual knowledge rather than pleasure, but were never educated in this field during their lives.

Skulls give their power, and this is the sādhu's offering: he may become guru to the dead. He can teach them the way to the heavens, and initiate them with empowered mantras, the keys to the kingdom. Spirits are said to cluster around meditating sādhus, but the sādhu will only give mantras to those spirits who bring their skulls to him. They travel through the midnight air, carrying their skulls to offer, and the ones he accepts belong to the spirits who will be initiated. The sādhu takes the power from the skulls. This strengthens him in his own quest for infinite wisdom (*brahmajñāna*), for one needs power (*śakti*) to hold brahmajñāna. Without enough power, the Tantric sādhu could go insane, or he may have only glimpses of his goal but be unable to maintain the state.

Sādhana (spiritual practice) with skulls is rarely seen today, but it is associated with certain locales, especially those with a background of death and sacrifice. The town of Bolpur in Birbhum (West Bengal) was named for the large number of sacrifices performed by one of its kings. According to the legend, centuries ago the great king Rājā Surat had a vision of the goddess Kālī. She asked him to sacrifice one hundred thousand goats to her (some versions say it was buffaloes), and if he did this, his dreams would be fulfilled. He did indeed sacrifice these goats, and gave the town its name (*bali-pur*, "town of sacrifice"). Since that time, there has been temple worship of Kālī in the town.

There are several Kālī temples in Bolpur, and one of them is on the edge of town, near the woods, with a large cremation ground nearby. This is the Kālī Temple of the Dry Lake, a temple is dedicated to Dakṣiṇā Kālī, who is a benevolent form of the goddess worshiped by householders. She is also called Bhairavī Vaiṣṇavī, showing that she is a Tantric goddess with such Vaiṣṇava qualities as compassion and the ability to bestow happiness. Within the temple, there is a large statue of Dakṣiṇā Kālī, with black skin and a smiling face, with her two assistants, Ḍākinī and Yoginī, flanking her. There are also statues of the Śākta Siddhas (perfected beings) Vāmakṣepā, Rāmakṛṣṇa Paramahaṃsa, and his wife Śārada Mā. Behind the statues on the altar is a row of human skulls, painted red.

Dakṣiṇā Kālī is merciful to her devotees. Renouncers and sādhus worship more powerful forms of Kālī, called Śmaśanā Kālī (Goddess of the Burning Ground) and Vāma Kālī (Kālī of the Left Side, or Kālī of the Forbidden). They offer her meat and wine, flesh and blood, placed in a skull. At this temple, offerings of meat and wine are made to Kālī's assistants, Ḍākinī and Yoginī, but these are only offered outside the temple.

The priest or purohit of this temple is Tapan Goswami, whose Vaiṣṇava name reflects honors shown to his ancestors. He is a practicing Śākta, who worships Kālī and meditates upon her. His practice, however, includes many older elements.

Tapan was born in small village about twenty kilometers from Bolpur, where his grandfather was a respected temple priest and Tantric sādhu. He came from a Śākta family.

> My family's goddess in the village was Uluicandi. She came from the earth, in the form of a stone. She was found a thousand years ago. When there was no rain in the village, my ancestors would bathe the stone in the pond, and rain would come. They worshiped her under a *neem* tree, and she had a small shrine there. She was originally a house goddess, but then her worship was opened to the village. Later my ancestors had a statue (*mūrti*) made, and it was immersed each year, and a new statue made. They worshiped her every day except for the [festival] time of Kālī Pūjā, when a pitcher (*ghaṭ*) was worshiped instead.

However, village life is primarily agricultural, and during his childhood a drought came and brought famine. All of the crops failed. The family then moved to Bolpur, which at that time was surrounded by forests. In those days, the temple was not easily accessible to visitors. As Tapan states:

> I came to Bolpur when I was six years old, and my father began to work as the priest of this temple. At the age of about ten or eleven years, I began to visit the temple at night, secretly. I was kept from going there in the daytime. But I could get the keys to the temple, and I went there at night, even though often I was afraid. I felt that the Goddess looked with favor upon me.
>
> Here, we believe that on the new-moon night, people should offer incense and candles to the Goddess. When I opened the temple door one new moon night, I found that many types of offerings (*prasād*) were there. I ate them, because I was hungry, but then I was afraid that people would be angry at me, and I thought of not returning. But I had such a great longing to return, that I could not stay away, and after a few days I came back again.

He spent his childhood attracted to the Goddess but fearful of her power. One night, when there were visitors to the temple, he saw a cake suddenly materialize, rise in the air, and fly toward him. He took this as a sign of the Goddess's power and her gift to him, and he became more and more curious about her.

As he grew older, he began to visit many renunciant sādhus and sannyāsis, especially those performing Tantra sādhana. He asked them many questions about ritual practice, and about the nature of Kālī. When he was twenty-one years old, he met a sādhu who taught him about Tantra sādhana; however, he was not initiated. He wandered to different places in West Bengal; he studied for a while at the Ramakrishna Ashram in Suri, then spent time in a village, then attended Vishvabharati University in Shantiniketan. During his years at Vishvabharati, he spent his spare time doing ritual practices to the Goddess. After he graduated, he worked in Dubrajpur, but the job did not interest him, and he spent his spare time with the sādhus meditating on a sacred hill nearby. He left and returned to his own village; his father taught him techniques of ritual temple worship, and he learned to awaken the Goddess in the statue with rice and durva grass, and to line her eyes with black eyeliner (*kajal*). His father told him to work at the Kālī temple in Bolpur.

His relationship with the Goddess was not an easy one. He was angry at Kālī because she allowed many difficulties and uncertainties in his life, and would not solve his financial and family problems. However, in the end they made peace, and the Goddess was willing to help him. He said: "When I used to do the evening ritual, I would feel a cold wind blowing behind me, and it would extinguish the candles. I would shiver and my hair would stand on end. I would hear the wind, and know that there was power (*śakti*) in it. I felt it was the Goddess's presence."

She would visit him many times, even though he argued with her. When he came into the temple one night with his left arm broken (due to family fighting), the Goddess was there. Though they disagreed, his arm was miraculously healed, and it no longer looked twisted.

His major religious teacher was his grandfather, Ratneshvara Goswami, who helped him during his childhood. He is still in awe of his grandfather's power, and told a story about him:

> An interesting incident happened many years ago. When my father was just a child, he was very ill, and he was finally declared dead by the doctor. My grandfather took him into the forest. There were hundreds of jackals and vultures surrounding him, but no animal came near or tried to attack him. My grandfather went into a meditative trance, and was full of devotion for the Goddess. After three or four days, my father began to move, and he regained his life and his strength. The Goddess saves people in her many forms—Durgā, Kālī, Tārā—but it is my belief that my father was saved by the intervention of Kālī.

Tapan said that his grandfather was a powerful tāntrika, who could cure people from deadly diseases and snakebite. The grandfather had practiced Tantric rituals alone in the mountains, and had practiced the pañcamakāra rituals (the five Tantric "sacraments," all of which are words beginning with the letter M) with a temporary wife. He had a guru who guided him, and he had great devotion to the Goddess, which has continued in the family.

After his grandfather's death, Tapan continued to communicate with him. The spirit of his grandfather would come to visit Tapan in his dreams and visions, instructing him in ritual and relationships with the spirits. He says that his grandfather's spirit has chosen to dwell in his favorite meditation place, his ritual seat, which is placed over five buried skulls at the foot of a large tree in the woods near the temple. His grandfather created this "five-skull seat" (*pañcamuṇḍī āsana*) and spent much time there during his life. When Tapan wishes to communicate with his grandfather's spirit, he sits on this ritual seat and meditates there.

Tapan has been possessed by his grandfather. In Indian tradition, the guru is like a god, and being possessed by a god is a desirable situation. Tapan knows when he is coming:

> He comes to me like the wind, and I can hear the sound of his wooden shoes. Once, I was sitting here before the Goddess, and I heard the shoes and felt the wind at my back. It put out the candle. It was my grandfather's spirit, and he entered my body and I felt great joy (*ānanda*). I found myself chanting many mantras. I stayed conscious, and could see everything, but he was there too. He had told me that he would come that evening. The mantras made me feel full of power, and his presence was a powerful thing entering me. Once some people came and had cigarettes with some drug in them, and I felt myself becoming unconscious. I called on my grandfather for help, and he came to me and possessed me.

Visitors have been a problem: "Many people have come here and tried to meet my grandfather in his subtle body. He was annoyed when some tāntrikas wanted spiritual powers (*siddhi*s), and built their own pañcamuṇḍī āsana. There should never be more than one at a sacred site (*pīṭha*) at a time. I speak with him often, but he would not speak with those people."

Although Tapan was close to his grandfather, he was not as close to his own father, who only taught him formal ritual worship (*pūjā*). He had to learn spiritual practice on his own, by studying with the various sādhus he could find, and was never officially initiated. He learned on the road, and in his travels. He performed Tantra sādhana in the mountains, as his grandfather had done, but after he married and became a temple priest he limited his practice to more traditional worship, which he called Vedic sādhana. He felt that safeguarding his grandfather's property allowed him to fulfill his grandfather's "unspoken dreams," so he left his Tantric practices in the mountains.

> I began to meditate seriously, perfecting my knowledge and ritual practice. As I did this, I saw that I began to gain new power (*śakti*). I realized the power of sādhana, and that if any person could do it properly, he could gain perfection (*siddhi*). But it is difficult in daily life to balance family and spiritual practice. Families do not tend to encourage and inspire sādhana, and neighbors don't understand it; they look down on people who perform pūjā. This discourages practice. They are only interested in the Goddess when they are sick or in need: then they will worship. Otherwise, they stay aloof. They only want immediate gains and blessings. I think that true sādhana can only be done in isolation, away in the mountains.

However, he did retain one one Tantric-style ritual, the feeding of skulls, as taught to him by his grandfather. Behind the Kālī statue in his temple is a long line of bright red skulls, who are given offerings. He describes the ritual as follows:

> The Goddess is normally invisible before us, but through sādhana, we can see her. One ritual that I perform here is the feeding of skulls (*muṇḍake khāoyā nāo*). Generally, skulls like puffed rice, though some like fried lentils, curries, or wine. After performing a sacrifice (*bali*), I feed them with raw meat [in this case, "feeding" means offering a plate of food before each skull]. The feeding is accompanied by a ritual fire (*homa*) and sacrifice (*yajña*). After the feeding, I bathe them in ghee, yogurt, milk, and honey, and then I arrange them for worship. Sometimes I do this when I need more mental balance or physical strength.
>
> Skulls are useful, because the person's soul often stays with the skull. The soul can predict the future, and help the sādhu. People used to do the corpse ritual (*śava-sādhana*) and sit on the dead body of a virgin girl. She would then become Kālī, and the body would come back to life and talk. My grandfather did śava-sādhana, but people today are afraid of it—if you make one mistake, you die or go insane. This sādhu in orange that you see roaming around here in the burning ground did śava-sādhana wrongly, and he was made insane by it. But he will return to sanity one of these days.
>
> I feed the skulls on the altar, and they help me. I learned the skull-feeding ritual from my grandfather. When the skulls are fed, they are pacified and they become protectors. Then they are strong enough to fight off the evil souls (*ātmas*) who wish to distract or harm the sādhu. When negative spirits (*bhūtas* and *pretas*) try to disturb the sādhu's meditation, then the good souls fight the bad souls and keep the sādhu

on the right path. Sādhus often have helpers. Sometimes śava-sādhana is performed with a woman, who is called the uttarā sādhikā. She has great skill (*adhikārī*) and helps the male through meditation if he is distracted by evil spirits. When the sādhu draws a circle around himself to protect him from these spirits, she is within the circle. Sometimes the sādhu may invite his guru in subtle form to watch over him and help him.

Today, it is widely believed that there are no ghosts, but really there are souls who do not die. They are always around us. Sometimes they may enter into our physical bodies, and cause problems or even tragedies. It is only by sādhana, by dedication to the Goddess, that we gain control over them. Then they can work for our benefit. We become immune to fear, hate, and intense desire with their help. I show them loyalty, and they guard me.

The skulls in this temple mostly come from people who died in epidemics, especially cholera epidemics. Large numbers of people used to die, and there was no effective system of cremation at that time. Corpses would lie on the roadside or in the forests.

Under the altar (*vedi*) of this temple there are 108 skulls buried. Some altars have 1,008 skulls. Skulls awaken the Goddess, and make her present here. Male gods have stones (*śilas*) or liṅgas [of Śiva], but goddesses have skulls. Some skulls are used for pañcamuṇḍī āsana [a ritual in which the practitioner sits on a seat in the midst of five skulls, generally of different types of animals and persons]. People use the skulls of a low-caste man, a jackal, a tiger, a snake, and a virgin girl (*kumārī*). They must be young, and die suddenly by violence. Nobody wants the skulls of people who died of disease or old age. Some tāntrikas have a special relationship with the Ḍoms [low-caste people who traditionally burn the dead and deal with corpses] who work in hospitals. These Ḍoms notify them of appropriate deaths.

Tapan compares the skull-feeding ritual with the corpse ritual (*śava-sādhana*) because in both cases a dead object becomes a vessel for a living presence through ritual. The souls from the skulls are also like the Tantric consort or uttarā sādhikā in that they assist in ritual practice. Although the female consort can help the Tantric practitioner overcome the power of instinct by the use of mantra and mudrā at the correct times, the souls can help the practitioner battle evil spirits and temptations in his meditative visions.

The Goddess is more powerful than the souls, and comes to visit and help more rarely. Tapan calls the Goddess "Mā" (Mother).

Mā has given me many favors. I remember once at night, I dreamt of a little girl (whom I believe was Mā) who came to help me. At that time I had little money and was renting a very small room. The girl came to me and took me to a new house for rent in my neighborhood. I awoke the next morning, and followed the path that we had taken in the dream-vision. I saw a house that looked exactly like the one I had seen. There did turn out to be a room for rent there, a spacious room that I could afford. So I believe she really did help me. Once she appeared as an old woman,

> perhaps eighty years old, and she patted my head, which was on her lap. At that time I was under much stress—my sādhana was not smooth, and I was disturbed by many bad events, which frightened me. But Mā saved me, and she gave me her blessings.

She can also help at death, as can the guru.

> The Goddess gives blessings during life, and after death she can also help. She does not help directly, for such things are determined by karma. Those who did evil on earth are kept in hell (*pātāla*) in the forms of jackals or snakes, and they cannot leave immediately. If they didn't do much evil, they may move about their past family and friends in nonphysical (*aprākṛta*) form.
>
> But if the person dying had a true guru, then he could act as a mediator for the person to reach heaven (*svarga*) or Kailāsa [the mountain abode of Śiva], and Kālī can help to show the way. If one wishes to reach the kingdom of the gods and goddesses, it is necessary to worship them.
>
> It is difficult to describe. You see, in this world everything is both difficult and easy. It depends upon how you approach it. If a person has a proper guide, if he is given much instruction and experience, if his guru watches him closely, then nothing is difficult to attain. But the qualities (*guṇas*) inherited from previous lives are also important. Without the proper qualities, one cannot perform sādhana. If a person was educated in this area in his previous life, then he could guide himself automatically, and would not need anybody else.

Tapan has worshiped Kālī in a variety of ways.

> There are many forms of Tantric sādhana. There are three major styles (*bhāvas*): the sāttvika, rājasika and tāmasika bhāvas. The sāttvika bhāva is devotion (*bhakti*), and that is the best path to follow. The tāmasika bhāva can give one the presence of the Goddess, but it does not last long. It stays for a little while, and then it ceases. It is very brief, and very fickle. Devotion lasts longer. One cannot get really close to the Goddess without devotional love. Only bhakti justifies Tantra.
>
> I have practiced both Vedic and Tantric sādhana. But I do not call myself a tāntrika—I don't take liquor, bhāṅg, gañjikā [hashish] and that sort of thing. Tantra is a dangerous path—there is much possiblity of insanity and brain damage. The Tantric path to liberation is fast and easy (*sahaja*), but it always has risks. The Vedic path is longer, but the risks are fewer. I think that the feeding of skulls is the first stage of practice, where one learns to control ghosts and ghouls (*bhūtas* and *pretas*), and one gains immunity to snakebites, and dedication to the Goddess. Then the Goddess comes to protect her devotee, and vision comes, as well as telepathy and the ability to know the future.

He does not call himself a tāntrika because tāntrikas have a bad reputation in West Bengal. They are popularly portrayed as madmen, perverts, cannibals, drug addicts, and alcoholics. However, his practice does have a heavy Tantric flavor, which he renames as Vedic and devotional. He justifies this by saying that his ultimate goal is devotional, so his practice can be called devotional. Tantra is only a stage of worship.

Tapan has dedicated himself to his life as a priest and Śākta devotee:

> I inherited this temple and burning ground, and now they are my property. I have given my village land and shares in the lakes to my brothers. I want to fulfill the wishes of both my father and grandfather. I have been here since 1979, for fifteen years. Mā developed the temple, and I have been her mediator. I have also been inspired by a woman renouncer, a sannyāsinī named Sangadevī, a distant relative of Rabindranath Tagore. I will be forever obliged to her. She was a great help to me. I hope that the temple will grow, and that more people will come to worship the Goddess.

However, he finds it a hard life, and does not want his son to follow in his footsteps. He wants him to work in an office in the city.

> Really, śakti sādhana is becoming obsolete today because nobody teaches it. I do not want my own son to be a Śākta sādhu. I will teach others, but I will not teach him. I want him to work in an office. I had to go through much suffering in this practice, and I want to spare my son. Learning about śakti sādhana is predetermined; if it is his karma, he will learn it somehow. If it is in his blood he will do it, and find a guru of his own. I want him to do worship, but not sādhana. It is a difficult life, and much suffering is involved. I had only my grandfather to help me.

His comments about Tantric goddess worship (*śakti sādhana)* becoming obsolete are quite accurate, according to my observations. Very few people are willing to admit that they even practice, let alone teach it. As families are becoming more nuclear, the importance of the ancestors and grandparents decreases; as communism and Westernization spread through the villages, traditional religious beliefs die away. What remains are Vedānta, traditionally the province of the higher and more educated castes, and devotional bhakti, which is understandable to the Christians who possess money and can provide jobs. These approaches have not yet been subject to attack. Tapan states, "Now the atmosphere here is against tantra sādhana, and people are afraid, because sometimes people who do ritual practice are beaten by goondas [bullies or criminals, often hired by political groups]. Maybe tāntrikas can manage in a deserted forests or cremation grounds, but if anybody knows about the practice, there is trouble."

It seems that these attackers harass the sādhus as part of an organized attempt to rid West Bengal of people viewed as social parasites and troublemakers. Practitioners from several areas of West Bengal have described the harassment that they have suffered from the Communist "Anti-Superstition Clubs" in the elementary and high schools, and from other groups whose affiliations are not advertised. However, the worship of the Goddess in Tantric style continues sub rosa: "But people believe in śakti, even with communism. Many Communist leaders go to tāntrikas and astrologers to find out what the results of an election will be. I have had Communists come here to this cremation ground, though they tell their followers not to come here, that it is superstition. They tell them this because they are afraid that the illiterate people will get power from the Goddess, and take it away from them. They want to keep the power for themselves." Such a situation makes him wonder about the future of Tantric practice. Tapan states: "I think that worship of Kālī will survive, but there will be fewer members. I think that in fifty years there will be no gurus left, and the practices will all turn shallower and more superficial." Tapan's own long-term goal is universal and devotional: "What I want to do is stay at the beck and call of Mā, lay down before her feet, give her offerings and serve her, and also run my family and know about the outside world. Then my vision of her will be clear instead of fuzzy, and I can perform service to the world."

Maintaining the older Tantric traditions in the face of hostility from the forces of communism and Westernization is difficult for tāntrikas, and many have gone into hiding. Others have claimed to be devotees, bhaktas, or Vedic scholars, as a way of protecting themselves from attack. Few tāntrikas are wandering sādhus today; most have some job and status and perform Tantric sādhana privately. The Nababharata Press has published a number of Tantras in Sanskrit with Bengali translation, so that non-Sanskritists (usually meaning non-brahmans) can practice the rituals. There are also small Tantric circles, in which people study texts, and other small underground groups that practice rituals.

For virtually all the tāntrikas I interviewed, however, the dimension of Tantra that focuses on the conquest of death and transcendence of this world is more important than the sexual aspects that have been emphasized by many Western writers on Tantra. It may be that such a focus is regional, and that West Bengal is one of the few Tantric regions that has emphasized death and its symbolism as the major path to the Goddess's paradise. With the focus on death rituals, it is appropriate that the Tantric aides to transcendence are ghosts, who become helpers and protectors on the paths to Kālī's heaven.

Research for this article comes from fieldwork in West Bengal, from 1993–1994, on a Senior Scholar Fulbright Research Grant. The data in this biography come from visits to the Bolpur Kālī temple and to Tapan Goswami's house. The interviews were conducted in Bengali, as Tapan spoke no English.

Further Reading

For further information on Śākta Tantra in Bengal, see Narendranath Bhattacharyya, *History of the Tantric Religion* (New Delhi: Manohar, 1982); and June McDaniel, *The Madness of the Saints* (Chicago: University of Chicago Press, 1989).

—4—

A Parody of the Kāpālikas in the *Mattavilāsa*

David N. Lorenzen

The *Mattavilāsa* is a one-act comic farce written in Sanskrit and Prakrit and attributed to a Pallava ruler of south India named Mahendra-varman, who ruled from his capital at Kanchi from about 600 to 630 C.E. The principal character in the play is a drunken Kāpālika adept named Satyasoma.

The Kāpālikas or Kapālins are one of the earliest mentioned sectarian groups of Tantric adepts. Unfortunately no texts survive that can unambiguously be assigned to Kāpālika authors. We have, instead, many texts written by their opponents who criticize or parody Kāpālika beliefs and practices, and a few inscriptions that record donations to or from Kāpālika adepts.

The *Mattavilāsa* is one of the oldest works that features a Kāpālika adept. As such, it has undoubtedly influenced many later portraits. One cannot, however, assume that the Kāpālikas found in Sanskrit literature are simply fictional stereotypes. The inscriptions prove that the Kāpālikas really did exist, and many elements of their literary portraits correspond to what we know about Tantric religion from other sources. Reading between the lines of parodies such as the *Mattavilāsa*, then, we can arrive at a plausible picture of the nature of Kāpālika beliefs and practices.

A central feature of Kāpālika practice was their Great Vow or Mahāvrata. To fulfill this vow, the male adept would obtain his livelihood by begging for alms with a skull bowl. Since the Sanskrit word for skull is *kapāla*, this made him a Kāpālika or Kapālin, while the performance of the Mahāvrata made him a Mahāvratin. The rationale for this Great Vow is found in a myth about the gods Śiva and Brahmā. Although the details vary in different versions, the key episode is a quarrel between the two gods about who is the most powerful. Śiva, in his anger, cuts off the fifth head of Brahmā. Since Brahmā is the archetypal representative of the social class of the brahmans, this means that Śiva has committed the major crime of killing a brahman (*brahma-hatyā*). To atone for this crime, Śiva has to wander about as a Kapālin for twelve years, using Brahmā's skull as his begging bowl.

In the *Mattavilāsa*, the action centers around the Kāpālika's attempts to find his lost skull bowl. When he falsely accuses a Buddhist monk of having stolen it, the monk displays his own bowl, which has a quite different shape and color. The Kāpālika's female companion, Devasomā, laments that their skull—which was once "endowed with all the auspicious marks and was as holy as the skull of Brahmā"—has become black and ugly. The Kāpālika consoles her with the thought that his penance, like that of Śiva, can make it pure again: "Our master Śiva, who wears the crescent moon, was freed of the sin that arose when he cut off the head of Brahmā through undertaking this Great Vow."

We have no information about how the human Kāpālikas obtained their skulls, but it is most likely that they found them in cremation grounds. In a few sources, however, Kāpālikas are said to engage in human sacrifice. This seems unlikely, but the Kāpālikas' association with cremation grounds and other inauspicious places is in keeping with the ritual practices of more extreme Tantric ascetics. The basic aim of wandering about in such places was to overcome the duality of pure and impure, and the fear of death, by constant contact with impure places and things such as cremation grounds and corpses. This constant association with impurity would also force the adepts to learn to endure the scorn and disgust of persons who were still tied to the rules of proper social behavior.

Other social rules that the Kāpālikas and other Tantric adepts purposely transgressed concern sex and food. In literary works such as the *Mattavilāsa*, the Kāpālikas are often described as hedonists addicted to sexual play with beautiful female companions and to drinking liquor and eating meat. In the *Mattavilāsa*, the Kāpālika Satyasoma's lovely companion Devasomā is presumed to be his sexual partner and also attracts the lustful glances of the Buddhist monk and the Pāśupata ascetic. Together Satyasoma and Devasomā also enjoy the meat kabobs that they receive as alms in the skull bowl and the liquor that they drink from the same vessel.

From what we know about Tantric religion, it is unlikely the Kāpālikas were simple hedonists. Some Tantric adepts did engage in extramarital sexual intercourse and the consumption of foods prohibited to upper-caste Hindus, such as meat and liquor. Such behavior was, however, displayed in the context of a controlled ritual, not as simple hedonistic enjoyment. In the best-known ritual, the adept took the five prohibited things whose names begin with the letter M: liquor, meat, fish, parched grain, and sexual intercourse (*madya, māṃsa, matsya, mudrā, maithuna*). The female partner in the act of sexual intercourse is usually described as a low-caste woman who is not the male adept's own wife. The basic aim of all this, as in the case of the association with cremation grounds and corpses, was to rise above the duality of the pure and the impure through the transgression of the rules of proper social conduct.

One other aspect of the ritual act of sexual intercourse is often suggested in Tantric sources. The ritual is regarded as a reenactment of the sexual intercourse between Śiva and his wife, the goddess called Pārvatī or Umā. The bliss of this union is compared to the bliss of liberation or mokṣa, and the Tantric adepts were expected to recreate this divine bliss in their own acts of ritual intercourse.

The theological system of the Kāpālikas is often called Soma-siddhānta, the doctrine of Soma. Several commentaries on another Sanskrit drama with a Kāpālika character gloss the Soma of Soma-siddhānta as implying "Śiva united with Umā" (*sa-Umā = soma*). In fact, we have no way of knowing the nature of the doctrines of Soma-siddhānta, but the name appears both in literary texts and in inscriptions. In many sources, Soma-siddhāntin, like Mahāvratin, is another title given to the Kāpālikas. In the *Mattavilāsa*, the word *soma* appears in the names of both Satyasoma and Devasomā. It is also barely possible that the name also suggests some sort of connection with the ancient Brahmanical worship of the intoxicating sacred drink called soma.

The physical appearance of Kāpālika adepts is only hinted at in the *Mattavilāsa*, but other sources give more detailed descriptions. One of the most interesting is from an inscription from Andhra Pradesh dated about 1050 C.E. It records a donation by a Brahman (*vipra*) named Somi-bhaṭṭaraka who was the abbot of a local Śaṅkareśvara (Śiva) temple. The inscription calls him an expert in Soma-siddhānta and a Mahāvratin. He is described as "sprinkled with ashes; adorned with the six insignia; and holding a khaṭvāṅga club, a skull (*kapāla*), ḍamaru and mṛdaṅga drums, and a trumpet." The six insignia are not listed, but the south Indian Vaiṣṇava theologians Yāmunācārya and Rāmānuja identify the six insignia of the Kāpālikas as two different kinds of earrings, a necklace, a jeweled crest, ashes, and the sacred thread. They add the skull and khaṭvāṅga as secondary insignia. The khaṭvāṅga consists of a pole about fifty to seventy-five centimeters (twenty to thirty inches) in length, on which a complete skull is impaled.

It is impossible to know how the Kāpālikas were organized as a religious group, but their association with a specific vow, a specific doctrine, and a special dress code suggests some definite institutional tradition. By the thirteenth or fourteenth centuries, however, whatever organization they once may have had apparently had already disappeared. The Kāpālikas survived mainly in the literary and religious texts of their opponents as stereotypical villains, buffoons, or heretics.

The translation given below follows the text, *Mattavilāsaprahasana*, edited by T. Ganapati Sastri (Trivandrum: Government Press, 1917). More recent editions are available, but all seem to be based on this one. Here and there, I have added a short phrase or extra stage direction to explain things that might not be immediately obvious to readers. The translations of the numbered verses use English rhymes and/or meters to mark them off from the prose text. In the original, the women, the Buddhist, and the madman all speak in different varieties of Prakrit rather than in Sanskrit.

One additional point concerns two somewhat confusing references to the Kāpālika that appear in the text shortly after verse 20. He is called first a Great Brahman (*mahābrāhmaṇa*) and then a Great Pāśupata (*mahāpāśupata*). At least one translator has assumed that these terms should refer to the Pāśupata and not to the Kāpālika. In fact, the term Great Brahman is commonly used to refer to the untouchables who help officiate during the highly polluting rite of cremation. The term Great Pāśupata is evidently a similar ironic title.

Another point easily missed is the confusion of myths and legends in the madman's speech just before verse 19. Such mixed allusions will be lost on most modern readers, but they must have amused the cultured audience of Mahendravarman's court.

Further Reading

A general work on the Kāpālikas is David N. Lorenzen, *The Kāpālikas and Kālāmukhas,* 2nd ed. (Delhi: Motilal Banarsidass, 1991). This also contains a chapter on the Pāśupatas. The discussion of Somi-bhaṭṭaraka's inscription is in Appendix A of the book. For another recent English translation of the *Mattavilāsa*, one that includes the Sanskrit text, see *Mattavilāsa Prahasana ('The Farce of Drunken Sport'),* edited and translated by Michael Lockwood and A. Vishnu Bhat (Chennai: Christian Literature Society, 1981).

Mattavilāsa or Drunken Games

Cast:

Director
Actress
Kāpālika named Satyasoma
Kāpālika's female companion named Devasomā
Buddhist monk named Nāgasena
Pāśupata named Babhrukalpa
Madman

After the verse of blessing, the Director *enters.*

Director:

The god who carries a skull, the divine Kapālin,
Whose languages, costumes, forms, and actions are many,
Whose dance reveals beauty through intense emotion,
Whose power moves the cosmos, of infinite wisdom,
Who is also the silent spectator watching the show,
May he grant you fame that fills the entire earth. (1)

Ah, at last I have found a suitable way to please my older wife, who has been out of sorts ever since I appointed myself a younger wife. Today the royal assembly finally appointed us to put on a public show. I must go tell her the news. [*looking behind the scenes*]. My dear, please come here.

Actress: [*entering, angrily*] Have you at last come to play the drunken games of adolescents?

Director: It is as you say.

Actress: Then you should go play with her to whom you wish to make love.

Director: I want to perform it with you.
Actress: Were you told to do this?
Director: Yes, I was. What's more, if you join us you will be well paid.
Actress: You must be really pleased about this.
Director: My dear, aren't you pleased as well? If the assembly is satisfied by your performance, it will reward you generously.
Actress: [*happily*] Have I really won the honorable gentlemen's favor?
Director: I'm sure you've won it.
Actress: In that case, what favor can I offer to you?
Director: What's all this talk about favors?

My sweet love, your bright smile,
Curving eyebrow, and downy cheek,
Once I've seen your perfect face
What more is there for me to seek? (2)

Actress: What play are you about to present?
Director: The one you just mentioned, the farce called "Drunken Games."
Actress: It seems that my anger has spoken for me in this matter. Sir, who is the poet who has composed this work?
Director: Listen, my dear. In the lands ruled by the Pallava family there was the mighty scion Siṁhaviṣṇu-varman. Using many different tactics, he won a wide circle of vassals. In courage, he was the equal of Indra. In generosity, he outdid even the god of wealth. The author is his son, King Mahendra-vikrama-varman, a man who has conquered all personal vices and is dedicated to providing for the welfare of others.

Now, when the Kali Age is here,
And lofty virtues disappear,
Wisdom, compassion, and honesty,
Art, generosity, truth, and beauty,
Dignity, firmness, and modesty,
Seek refuge with this virtuous king.
As, when the universe began,
The countless fragments of creation
Sought refuge with the Primal Man. (3)

His eloquence is a mine
Of priceless gems, a presence
That brings praise to songs
Of good but lesser talents. (4)

Actress: What are we waiting for? Let the premier performance be begun.
Director:

By adding to this illustrous poet's fame,
My own humble songs have been put to shame.

[*From behind the scenes.*] My love, Devasomā!

Director:

And so, the Kāpālika, with lovely wench and skull,
Finds shame under the spell of alcohol. (5)

[*The two exit. The Kāpālika then enters with his female companion.*]

Kāpālika: [*acting drunk*] Devasomā, my love, it's true. The power of changing form at will is won by means of penance. The proper performance of the Great Vow has made you irresistibly beautiful:

Your soft laughter and gentle sighs,
Your falling garlands and flowing hair,
Your playful smiles and dancing eyes,
Your moist cheeks and lazy stare. (6)

Devasomā: My lord, you seem to be saying that it's I who am drunk.
Kāpālika: What did you say?
Devasomā: I'm not saying anything.
Kāpālika: Is it possible that I'm drunk?
Devasomā: My lord, the earth is spinning all around. I think I'm falling. Please hold me up.
Kāpālika: I've got you, my love. [*trying to support her and falling*] Somadevā, my love, are you angry at me? Every time I try to hold you up, you move away.
Devasomā: Hah! It must be this Somadevā who gets angry and moves away, even when you bow and scrape before her.
Kāpālika: Aren't you Somadevā? [*thinking*] No, you're Devasomā.
Devasomā: If you love this Somadevā so much, you shouldn't call her by my name.
Kāpālika: My dear, this was just a simple slip of the tongue. I'm drunk. No offense to you was intended.
Devasomā: How convenient that it's not you who's to blame.
Kāpālika: How can I let vile drink get control over me? All right. All right. Starting from today, I will stop being a slave of alcohol.
Devasomā: My lord, please don't interrupt your penance by breaking your holy vow because of me. [*falls at his feet*]
Kāpālika: [*happily raising her up and embracing her*] *Dhṛrṇa dhṛrṇa*, homage to Śiva. My love,

Drink up until intoxication,
Look deep into your lover's eyes,
Wear fancy clothes from every nation:
Long life to the god who found
So fine a path for our salvation. (7)

Devasomā: Is it proper to speak in this way? The Jain saints describe the path to salvation in quite another way.

Kāpālika: Dear, their views are completely mistaken.

The Jains argue that each effect
Resembles the cause from which it came.
But against this they also expect
That the bliss of our eternal salvation
Comes from penance and its pain.
These fools defeat this curious claim
With their own logical argumentation. (8)

Devasomā: May their sins be ended.

Kāpālika: May their sins be ended. There is no point even to revile these sinners. They torment living beings by making them remain celibate, tear out their hair, refuse to bathe, eat only at certain hours, and wear dirty clothes. Even mentioning them makes me now want to wash out my mouth with liquor.

Devasomā: Then let's go off to another liquor shop.

Kāpālika: My love, let's do it.

[*Both walk about.*]

Kāpālika: Ah, the city of Kanchi is incredibly beautiful. The sounds of drums mix with thunder from the clouds that sit on the top of the tall palaces; the flower markets create their own spring season; the rustle of young girls moving about announces the immanent victory of the God of Love. Likewise,

The infinite, incomparable bliss
That wise sages first discovered
Is now as close as one could wish.
For we have added a special measure,
No need to abandon the life of a lover
This bliss includes all sensual pleasure. (9)

Devasomā: My lord, just like the goddess of liquor, Kanchi is irreproachably sweet.

Kāpālika: My love, just look. This liquor shop equals the majesty of the sacrificial enclosure. Here the flag pole equals the sacrificial post; the liquor equals the soma; the drinkers, the priests; the liquor glasses, the soma cups; the snacks such as meat kabobs, the various oblations; the drunken chatter, the sacrificial formulas; the songs, the sacrificial hymns; the liquor vats, the sacrificial ladles; the thirst of the drinkers, the sacrificial fire; and the owner of the shop, the sponsor of the sacrifice.

Devasomā: And the alms we get here will be the offering to Rudra.

Kāpālika: Ah, the dances of these drunken games create such a beautiful, confused uproar. The dancers move to the rhythm of the drums, gesture, shout, flirt, lift up their shirts with one hand, and lose the beat for a second as they hike up their falling garments.

Devasomā: Ah, my teacher is a true connoisseur.

Kāpālika: When poured into glasses, the goddess of liquor puts jewels to shame, reconciles angry lovers, and gives courage to youth. She is the very soul of pleasure. What more can I say?

It's just not true what they claim
About the way the fiery ray
From Śiva's eye burned to ashes
The body of our god of love.
What really happened I prefer to think
Is that Śiva's penance was so intense
The heat produced could not be controlled,
So when love came too near to the flame
He melted like wax, and ever since
Has fueled the fire of our desire. (10)

Devasomā: This is true, my lord. Śiva is devoted to the world's welfare and would never destroy it.

[*Both drum on their own cheeks.*]

Kāpālika: Madam, please give us alms.

[*From behind the scenes.*] My lord, here are some alms. Please accept them.

Kāpālika: I accept them. My love, where is my skull bowl?

Devasomā: I don't see it anywhere.

Kāpālika: [*thinking*] Hm, I guess maybe I forgot it in the liquor shop? Oh well, we'll have to go back and see.

Devasomā: My lord, it is against our rule to not accept alms that have been offered with respect. What do we do now?

Kāpālika: We will have to resort to the rule for emergencies and accept them in this cow horn.

Devasomā: So be it. [*He accepts the alms.*]

[*Both then walk about looking for the skull bowl.*]

Kāpālika: How can it be that even here we cannot find it? [*acting depressed*] Listen, all you Māheśvaras, have any of you here seen our alms bowl? What did you say? You haven't seen it? Ay, I'm ruined. My penance is broken. How can I still remain a Kāpālika? Alas,

My spotless skull was a very dear friend.
With it in my hand I drank and was fed
And used it at night to pillow my head.
Its loss is a hurt that just won't mend. (11)

[*Falls and beats his head on the ground.*]

Let it be. The skull is merely a symbol. I can still keep the title of a Kāpālika. [*stands up*]

Devasomā: My lord, who could have grabbed the skull?

Kāpālika: My love, I suspect that it was stolen by a dog or by a Buddhist monk for the meat kabobs that were in it.

Devasomā: To find it, then, we're going to have to search the whole city of Kanchi.

Kāpālika: So we will, my love.

[*Both walk about. Then a Buddhist monk enters with a bowl in his hand.*]

Buddhist: Ah, the house of the lay devotee and merchant Dhanadāsa provides the most magnificent charity. There I obtained these abundant morsels of all sorts of rich smelling, tasty fish and meat. Now I'm going off to the royal monastery.

[*walking about, he says to himself*] The compassionate Lord Buddha gratified the community of monks with teachings that instruct them to live in mansions, to sleep on well-constructed beds, to eat in the morning, to take well-flavored drinks in the afternoon, to chew betel leaves mixed with five perfumes, and to wear comfortable clothes. But what I haven't seen are the rules for taking a wife or drinking liquor. Is it possible that the Omniscient One did not envision this? I suspect that these tired, evil Buddhist elders removed the rules about women and liquor from the holy books out of their jealousy of us young folk. Where can I find an unmodified original text? If I find it, I will gratify the community by making known to all the complete words of the Buddha.

[*He walks about.*]

Devasomā: My lord, look. Look at that fellow in the red robe scurrying about in the middle of this royal road filled with crowds of happy people. He is all hunched over, looking this way and that, and moving as if he's scared of something.

Kāpālika: My love, you're quite right. And his hand is inside his robe as if he is hiding something.

Devasomā: My lord, let's go and grab him and find out.

Kāpālika: So be it. [*approaching*] Hey, monk. Stop!

Buddhist: Who's calling me? [*turning and looking*] Ay, it's the evil Kāpālika who lives at the temple of Ekāmranātha. Well, I have no intention of being the target of his drunken violence. [*goes off in haste*]

Kāpālika: Aha. My love, we've found our skull. Did you see him run away in fear when he saw me? This is clear evidence that he is the thief. [*Quickly cutting him off, the Kāpālika stops him.*] Hah! Where will you go now, you bastard?

Buddhist: Kāpālika, please don't. What's this? [*aside*] Hm, this female devotee is really beautiful.

Kāpālika: Listen, monk. Show me right now. I want to see what you have in the hand hidden beneath your robe.

Buddhist: What is there to see? It is only a begging bowl.

Kāpālika: That's precisely what I want to see.

Buddhist: No, Kāpālika, please don't. It is proper that this bowl should be kept hidden.

Kāpālika: Aha, then it was for the sake of hiding things that the Buddha first taught you to wear such ample robes.

Buddhist: This is true.

Kāpālika: This is the relative truth. But I want to hear the absolute truth.

Buddhist: Enough of this mockery! The hours for begging are over. I have to go. [*He sets off.*]

Kāpālika: Ha, bastard, where are you going? Give me the skull.

[*He grabs the end of the monk's robe.*]

Buddhist: Hail to the Buddha!

Kāpālika: What you should say is "Hail to Kharapaṭa!" He's the one who wrote the sacred book of thieves. Or was the Buddha even more an expert in this topic than even Kharapaṭa? Why's this?

> The ideas he stole, that thieving Tathāgata,
> From the Upaniṣads and *Mahābhārata,*
> He brazenly claimed as original thinking,
> While foolish brahmans stood there blinking. (12)

Buddhist: May your sins be ended.

Kāpālika: How is it possible that the sins of a well-behaved ascetic like myself not be ended?

Devasomā: My lord, you look tired. This cherished skull is not going to be easy to obtain. You should drink some liquor from this cow horn in order to recover your strength before you get into a fight with him.

[*Devasomā gives some liquor to the Kāpālika.*]

Kāpālika: [*drinks*] My love, you too should remove your fatigue.

Devasomā: Thank you, my lord. [*drinks*]

Kāpālika: This Buddhist has offended us. But sharing is the chief thing in our own doctrine. Let this teacher have the rest.

Devasomā: Whatever my lord commands. Take this, Sir.

Buddhist: [*aside*] Ha, how easy it was to get a good result. But this is so sinful, and a big merchant might see me. [*aloud*] No, no, madam. This is not proper for us. [*licks the corners of his mouth*]

Devasomā: Go to hell! What makes you so smug?

Kāpālika: My love, his mouth is watering so much that his words, so opposed to his desire, can barely be understood.

Buddhist: You still have no compassion.
Kāpālika: If I had compassion, how could I be an ascetic free of passion?
Buddhist: One who is free of passion should also be free of anger.
Kāpālika: I'll be free of anger if you give me what belongs to me.
Buddhist: And what's that?
Kāpālika: My skull!
Buddhist: How your skull?
Kāpālika: "How your skull?" he says. But this is quite appropriate.

> If you are really a son of the Buddha,
> Who wrongly tried to insist
> That visible things, huge and imposing,
> Do not in fact exist,
> Even earth, mountains, rivers, and ocean,
> What could stop you from denying
> The skull you hold in your fist? (13)

Devasomā: My lord, He'll never give it back with such gentle treatment. Let's just go and grab it from his hand.
Kāpālika: Let's do it, my love. [*They do their best to grab it.*]
Buddhist: Go to hell, you evil Kāpālika! [*He pushes him with his hand and kicks him with his foot.*]
Kāpālika: How's this? I've fallen.
Devasomā: [*to Buddhist*] You're a dead man, son of a slave girl! [*She tries to grab him by the hair, but since he has none, she falls.*]
Buddhist: [*aside*] How wise was the Buddha when he foresaw the need to have a shaven head. [*aloud*] Get up, sister, get up. [*He helps Devasomā to get up.*]
Kāpālika: Look at this, Māheśvaras. This evil monk named Nāgasena is grabbing the hand of my sweetheart.
Buddhist: No, brother, I'm not. Our rule is to help those fallen into distress.
Kāpālika: Is this yet another rule of the Omniscient One? Wasn't I the first one to fall? But let it be. It doesn't matter. Now your head is about to become my skull bowl.

[*All of them make a big uproar.*]

Buddhist: Help, help!
Kāpālika: Look, Māheśvaras. This evil so-called monk first robs me of my skull bowl, and then *he* calls for help. Let it be. I too can make a scandal. Sacrilege, sacrilege!

[*A Pāśupata then enters.*]

Pāśupata: Satyasoma, why are you calling for help?
Kāpālika: Ah, Babhrukalpa, this evil so-called monk Nāgasena has stolen my skull bowl and doesn't want to give it back.
Pāśupata: [*aside*] In this matter I should act like the Gandharvas and try to get the girl for myself.

The barber's wench who I quite fancy
This Buddhist rogue has lured his way
Offering her coins from beneath his robe,
As if tempting a cow with a fist of hay. (14)

But I will now defeat my rival by inciting this pimp against him. [*aloud*] Nāgasena, is it true what he said?

Buddhist: My lord, How can you say this? It is a Buddhist precept that one should abstain from taking what is not given. It is a precept that one should abstain from false speech. It is a precept that one should abstain from sexual intercourse. It is a precept that one should abstain from taking a life. It is a precept that one should abstain from eating at inappropriate times. I take my refuge in the religion of the Buddha.

Pāśupata: Satyasoma, such is their moral code. What can you reply?

Kāpālika: Well, our code is that one should not tell lies.

Pāśupata: Both these codes are quite appropriate. But how can we decide the case?

Buddhist: What possible motive can there be for one who takes the Buddha's word as his authority to grab a bowl full of liquor?

Pāśupata: A disputant cannot win a case by mere affirmation.

Kāpālika: When we have direct evidence, what is the point of disputation?

Pāśupata: What sort of direct evidence?

Devasomā: My lord, he has the skull in his hand hidden inside his monk's robe.

Pāśupata: You heard what she said.

Buddhist: This so-called skull doesn't belong to anyone else.

Kāpālika: Let us see it then.

Buddhist: There! [*He shows it.*]

Kāpālika: [*sarcastically*] Look, Māheśvaras. Look at the injustice perpetrated by the Kāpālika and the excellent conduct of this Buddhist monk.

Buddhist: It is a Buddhist precept that one should abstain from taking what is not given. [*He again recites the precepts.*]

[*Both the Kāpālika and Devasomā dance.*]

Buddhist: What's this? When he should be ashamed, he dances instead.

Kāpālika: Hah, who's dancing? [*looking all around*] He thinks he sees dancing in the display of my delight, like a flower swaying in the wind, at once again seeing my lost skull bowl.

Buddhist: My lord, why don't you take a closer look at this bowl. Tell me, what color is it?

Kāpālika: What do you want me to say? Do you think I can't see? This skull is blacker than a crow.

Buddhist: Then you yourself admit that this is mine and not yours.

Kāpālika: What I really admit is that you know how to change its color. Look . . .

Once your robe was as white as chalk,
As bright as the silk of a lotus stalk,
And didn't you slyly make it one
With a tint as red as the rising sun? (15)

And besides . . .

Since you are stained, inside and out,
With a blood-red hue,
How could my skull not acquire
The same stain too? (16)

Devasomā: Ay, I'm ruined! How terrible! How did this skull get such a changed condition by coming into contact with stained cloth? Endowed with all the auspicious marks, it was as holy as the skull of Brahmā. It shone like the full moon and was always full of liquor. [*She weeps.*]

Kāpālika: My love, don't cry. It will become pure once again. The sacred scriptures say that great beings have their faults removed through penance.

Our Master Śiva, the god of the crescent moon,
Once undertook the vow called Mahāvrata
To free himself from the heavy sin that befell,
When he cut off one of the heads of the god of creation.
Likewise, Indra, king of the thirty gods,
Once killed the three-headed son of mighty Tvaṣṭar
But managed to get the burden of his sin removed
Through the merit of a hundred sacrifices. (17)

Babhrukalpa, is this not so?

Pāśupata: This is what the sacred Āgamas declare.

Buddhist: Sir, if I changed its color, who made it this shape and size?

Kāpālika: Did you Buddhists not spring from the lineage of Māyā?

Buddhist: For how long do I have to curse you? Here, you take it.

Kāpālika: Did not the Buddha himself perfect the supreme virtue of generosity?

Buddhist: Now that this is over, where will I find refuge?

Kāpālika: Isn't your refuge the Buddha, the Dharma, and the Saṅgha?

Pāśupata: I am unable to decide this case. We will have to take it to the court.

Devasomā: My lord, if we do this, it's goodbye to the skull.

Pāśupata: What do you mean?

Devasomā: This Buddhist has behind him the wealth of many monasteries. He can fill the mouths of the officials of the court at will. But we are servants of the poor Kāpālika, whose wealth is merely a snake skin and ashes. With what wealth do we enter the court?

Pāśupata: This isn't so.

The law, like the palace, has strong foundations,
Upright, solid, polished, and firm,
The one good pillars, the other good persons. (18)

Kāpālika: Enough of this! A person who obeys the law need not fear anything.
Buddhist: [*to the Pāśupata*] My Lord, you should lead the way.
Pāśupata: So be it.

[*All of them walk about. Then a madman enters.*]

Madman: This evil dog! You've grabbed the skull full of meat kabobs and run away with it. Son of a slave girl, where are you going to go? Now, he's dropped the skull and is coming running to bite me. [*looking in all directions*] I'll break his teeth with this stone. Why have you left the skull and run away? Crazy, evil dog, do you dare to get angry even with someone as brave as me? The ocean has mounted the boar of the village and flown up to the sky. It has conquered Rāvaṇa and has seized by force Indra's son Timiṅgala. Ay, castor oil tree, what did you say? "It's not true. It's not true." Is not this cloud, with its hands as long and wide as a club, my witness? But why should a person like me, whose bravery is renowned throughout the three worlds, need any witnesses? This is what I'm going to do. I'll eat the leftover morsel of meat that the dog bit into. [*He eats and then looks confused.*] Ay, ay, I've been killed by tears. [*He weeps and looks.*] Who is this who's beating me? [*He looks.*] Evil dog, I am the nephew of someone important, as Ghaṭotkaca was the nephew of Bhīmasena. Besides . . .

My belly is full of a hundred demons
In many guises, shapes, and sizes,
And from my mouth come flying out
Giant snakes and a hundred lions. (19)

Why are they harassing me? Be kind, be kind to me, my young lords. Don't harass me because of this morsel of meat. [*He looks ahead.*] This must be my teacher Śūranandin. I'll go up to him. [*He runs.*]
Pāśupata: Ay, this madman is coming toward me.

His robe is tattered and secondhand,
His hair a wild and tangled mess,
Around his neck a withered garland,
His body covered with dust and ash.
Above his head are crows and hawks,
ready to scavenge whatever they can
It looks as though before us walks
A garbage heap in the form of a man. (20)

Madman: I'll approach this one. [*He approaches.*] My lord, please accept this skull obtained from an excellent dog belonging to a Caṇḍāla.

Pāśupata: [*looking with disdain*] Let this be accepted by a more worthy person.

Madman: Great Brahman [*approaching the Buddhist*], please do me this favor.

Buddhist: [*indicating the Kāpālika*] This Great Pāśupata is more worthy.

Madman: [*Approaching the Kāpālika, he places the skull on the ground, circumambulates, and falls at his feet.*] Great saint, please do me this favor. This homage is for you.

Kāpālika: My skull!

Devasomā: So it is!

Kāpālika: By the grace of god I have again become a true Kāpālika.

Madman: You son of a slave girl, may you eat poison. [*He grabs the skull and goes off.*]

Kāpālika: [*chasing after him*] This servant of Death is stealing my life itself! Help me you two!

Both: As you wish. We'll be your helpers.

[*All try to stop the madman.*]

Kāpālika: Stop you, stop!

Madman: Why are they stopping me?

Kāpālika: Give me my skull and be gone.

Madman: You fool, can't you see that this is a gold bowl?

Kāpālika: Who would ever make a gold bowl like this?

Madman: I tell you, this is a gold bowl made by the bastard of a goldsmith who wears golden clothes.

Buddhist: What are you saying?

Madman: It's a gold bowl.

Buddhist: Is he a madman?

Madman: "Madman. . ." I keep hearing that word. Take this and show me the madman. [*He hands the skull to the Kāpālika.*]

Kāpālika: [*grabbing the skull*] He's over there hidden behind that wall. Go quickly and follow him.

Madman: You have been most kind.

[*The madman hastily exits.*]

Buddhist: It's a miracle! I have been saved by the success of my opponent.

Kāpālika: [*hugging the skull*]

> Unbroken penance for years I suffered,
> And devotion to Śiva alone I offered.
> Now the madman has gone away
> And you, my skull, are back, hooray! (21)

Devasomā: My lord, when I see you today, looking like the evening reunited with the moon, my very eyes rejoice.

Pāśupata: How lucky you are.
Kāpālika: Is this not a good result for all of you?
Pāśupata: [*aside*] What's true is that those who have no fault need not fear. Today this monk escaped from the mouth of the tiger. [*aloud*] Now that I have been made happy by the success of my friend, I will go and wait for the evening worship at the eastern temple of the Lord. And starting from today. . .

> May the quarrel that once bound you two together
> Now become the source of mutual love
> As once it was when Kirāta fought with Arjuna. (22)

[*The Pāśupata exits.*]

Kāpālika: Honorable Nāgasena, if I have done you any offense, I hope you will forgive me.
Buddhist: Need you even ask? What can I do for you?
Kāpālika: If I have your forgiveness, what thing better than that can I request?
Buddhist: It is time for me to go.
Kāpālika: I hope I will see you again.
Buddhist: May it be so. [*He exits.*]
Kāpālika: Devasomā, my love, let us go also.

[*Epilogue*]

> May the sacred fires always lift up to heaven
> Oblations offered on the people's behalf.
> May the brahmans serve the Vedas and cows give milk,
> May the people be happy, each intent on his dharma.
> May King Mahendra subdue his enemies' power
> And rule for as long as the sun and moon exist. (23)

[*Both exit.*]

Here ends the farce entitled *Drunken Games*

— 5 —

A Trance Healing Session with Mātājī

Kathleen M. Erndl

Bimlā Devī, or Passū Mātājī (Respected Mother from village Passu) as she is called by her clients and devotees, is a female trance healer living in a village near Dharamsala, Kangra district, Himachal Pradesh. She is regularly possessed by the Hindu Goddess Vaiṣṇo Devī. Mātājī maintains a small temple attached to her home, where three days a week she goes into trance and, as the Goddess Vaiṣṇo Devī, answers questions and offers cures for people. Those who come, mostly women, consult her for a variety of problems including mental and physical health, family relationships, employment, and spiritual concerns.

Possession by many types of deities and spirits, benevolent and malevolent, is widespread among women and men throughout South Asia. Divine possession by goddesses, primarily among women, is prevalent in the northwest part of India, which includes Kangra, as well as in some other areas. The śakti or divine power of the goddess enters into (or "plays," *kheltī hai*) and temporarily blots out the consciousness of the human medium. While in this possession trance, the medium speaks with the voice of the goddess. Afterward, most people, like Mātājī, have no memory of what they said in trance, and they return to their "normal" state of consciousness. By word of mouth, these women begin to attract followers who come to them for help with problems and address them as Mātājī, a term that not only means "mother" in the ordinary sense, but also "goddess." There is a transformation that takes place through repeated possession, such that the woman becomes more and more "goddess-like," more and more divinized. Some of these Mātājīs have adopted a renunciant lifestyle and have become gurus in a broader sense, teaching meditation to their devotees, building ashrams, and giving discourses on bhakti (devotion) and other spiritual paths.

I learned the details of Passū Mātājī's life, a sketch of which I give here, from her and some of her devotees. She was born around the time of Indian independence (1947), the youngest of six children to an impoverished family of the Giraths, a low-caste cultivating community of Kangra. She has no formal education and has never learned to read or write. As a child, she never played with other village children but only with another little girl who was always with her, but whom only she could see. When she told her mother about this little girl, her mother became concerned and brought her to a healer, a harijan (untouchable caste member) who made "tantra-mantra" on her and gave her holy water and cardamon. After that, she "went crazy," and a wandering holy man came by her house, saying that the Goddess had wanted to come there, but that it was contaminated. Her parents arranged a marriage for her when she was very young and tried to send her off to her husband's home at about age twelve. When she was placed in the palanquin, the Goddess entered into her and said, "don't go there. Stay here and build a temple for me." She followed the Goddess's order and some years later, again ordered by the Goddess, moved her temple and residence to its present location in another village. She never married again, and characterizes herself as "not a householder," though she does maintain a household and has brought up several relatives' children. She is also active in the local women's organization.

In practical terms, Tantra has as much to do with the fulfillment of mundane desires as with soteriological aims. The powers gained through Tantric practice can be used for both worldly *(bhukti)* and spiritual (*mukti*) purposes. In the non-dualist ontology of Tantra, these two are part of the same reality. Mātājī and her devotees are part of a broadly based grassroots religious expression, a kind of "folk Tantra" that connects the more formal textual and esoteric Tantric traditions with exoteric village religion.

I present below a transcription, with a few explanatory comments, of a trance session I recorded during field work in 1997. The original language was primarily Hindi with some Punjabi and the local Kangri dialect, with an occasional English word thrown in. I have not attempted to show this mix of languages in my translation. Indian languages allow for a much greater degree of ellipsis than is possible in English. Indirect constructions, omission of subjects and/or objects, gender-neutral pronouns, interchangeability of singular and plural in colloquial speech, all contribute to a discourse of vagueness that is highly appropriate to a trance session in which information of a personal and often delicate nature is being conveyed to devotees in a public arena where it can be overheard by everyone present. In my translation, I have preserved as much of this ambiguity as English usage will allow. Mātājī's linguistic register is at times highly colloquial, at times highly formal. In order to give some sense of the flow of language in the performance context, I have purposely not deleted the frequent repetition of stock phrases and formulas in Mātājī's trance speech. Typically, she will describe the problem, tell the cause, prescribe a remedy, and predict the outcome. Mātājī, like other healers in the area, focuses on a personal object, such as an item of clothing or jewelry, that belongs to the person seeking help and that is placed in front of her at the start of the session. The reader will note that Mātājī's diagnoses fall into several categories, including sorcery (*jadū ṭonā, oparī*), the evil eye *(nazar)*, and astrological influences (*graha)* such as that of the inauspicious planet Saturn (Śani), whose day, as in the West, falls on Saturday. In the case of sorcery, she will never pinpoint the evildoer by name but will answer questions concerning gender, caste, place of residence, and status within the family. The three most common cures are cardamon seeds, holy water, and threads of three, five, or seven colors (or sometimes plain black). When eaten or worn, these simple blessed items carry the Goddess's śakti (power) and function as amulets to neutralize negative forces and protect against further harm. Other cures include making donations, offerings to a deity, or the performance of specific rituals.

Further Reading

For background on the Goddess cult in Mātājī's geographic region and further discussion of divine possession in that context, see my *Victory to the Mother: The Hindu Goddess of Northwest India in Myth, Ritual, and Symbol* (New York: Oxford University Press, 1993) and "Śerānvālī: The Mother Who Possesses," in *Devī: Goddesses of India*, edited by Donna Wulff and John Stratton Hawley (Berkeley and Los Angeles, University of California Press, 1996), pp. 173–94. For attention to gender issues, see my "The Goddess and Women's Power: A Hindu Case Study," in *Women and Goddess Traditions in Antiquity and Today*, edited by Karen L. King with an introduction by Karen Jo Torjesen, (Minneapolis: Fortress Press, 1997), pp. 17–38. For more about Mātājī and other women like her, see my forthcoming *Playing with the Mother: Women, Goddess Possession, and Power in Kangra Hinduism*. An excellent general survey is Elisabeth Schoembucher, "Gods, Ghosts, and Demons: Possession in South Asia," in *Flags of Fame: Studies in South Asian Folk Culture,* edited by Heidrun Brüchner, Lothar Lutze, and Aditya Malik (New Delhi: Manohar, 1993), pp. 239–267. June McDaniel makes connections between divine possession and Tantra in *The Madness of the Saints: Ecstatic Religon in Bengal* (Chicago: University of Chicago Press, 1989). For a comprehensive study of Śāktism, which includes extensive discussions of the categories "folk Tantra" and "folk Śāktism," see June McDaniel, *Offering Flowers and Feeding Skulls: Varieties of Popular Shaktism in West Bengal,* forthcoming.

A Trance Healing Session with Mātājī

It was a chilly Sunday morning in February 1997. By eleven o'clock, about a dozen people were seated on the veranda outside the temple. This number would gradually swell to over fifty, as people continued to drift in. Because it was a holiday, there were more men present than there would have been on a weekday, about one-third of the total, and more school-age children. The devotees ranged from Dharamsala professionals to landless laborers from neighboring villages. The temple door was open, exposing the red-clad and garland-bedecked image of goddess Vaiṣṇo Devī. As devotees arrived, they would wash their hands at the nearby tap, approach the Goddess with folded hands, and bow in front of her. After a few minutes, Mātājī emerged from an adjacent building, wearing an orange-red flowered *salwar-kameez*, red shawl, and a red stocking cap on her head. She greeted me, as well as a middle-aged man who went inside with her. She called me in a few minutes later to sit next to her. She said something about a tape recorder. I had been there several times before without recording anything and asked if this time I could use it. Both she and the man readily agreed. I said that if anyone objected, I would turn it off. The man said no one minded. But I said that since people were asking personal things, that if someone objected, I would turn it off while that person was there. Mātājī agreed, but, in fact, no one seemed to mind. The people outside, who had been sitting in a line along the wall, turned and sat lined up in rows facing the temple. Mātājī started out by leading a devotional song to the Goddess, after asking someone outside to bring the *dholak* (a drum) and *chaine* (a tong-like percussion instrument) from inside the house. People from the congregation had already placed their "question" items and offerings of money on the floor in front of her. Those who came later entered the temple, touched her feet, placed their things in front of her, and took a seat outside. The congregation sang several devotional songs, a few of which are translated below, for about half an hour, after which Mātājī gradually went into trance, her head and body shaking to the beat of the music.

Song (*repeated many times)*

Give us darśan, Vaiṣṇo Mātā
The whole congregation has come
With cries of "Victory," we have come
Give us *darśan*, Vaiṣṇo Mātā

Mātājī begins "playing," her body shaking in time with the music, her hair flying around her face, her eyes glazed over. The devotees sing a new song, welcoming the appearance of the Goddess.

Song (*repeated many times)*

Riding on a yellow lion,
Look, the Mother-Queen has come.
O, Mother we've built a temple for you
We wave the chowrie before you.
Look, the Mother-Queen has come
The Lion-rider has come
The Gracious One has come.
The five Pāṇḍavas built a temple

Arjuna waved a chowrie
Look, the Lion-rider has come
Riding on a yellow lion, the Mother-Queen has come.
Body decorated with a beautiful gown, O Mother
A saffron mark adorning her brow
Look, the Mother-Queen has come
Riding on a yellow lion, the Queen-Mother has come
The Flame One has come.
O Mother, we offer betel leaf and nut, flags, coconuts, and songs.
Look, the Mother-Queen has come
The Gracious One has come
My Mother has come.

Song (*repeated many times*)

Now she's come, the Lion-rider
Now she's come, the Lion-rider
Now she's come, the Gracious One
Now she's come, the Gracious One
Get *darśan* now, devotees
Now she's come, the Lion-rider
Now she's come, the Lion-rider
Say: Victory to the true court!

Mātājī, still in trance, stops shaking and begins to speak. The singing stops immediately. She is now fully possessed by the Goddess and signals her presence by saying something that sounds like *jay kareś, jay kārakand,*" a phrase that no one, including her close devotees and Mātājī herself, could decode beyond the word *jay*, which means victory and is part of such slogans as "victory to the Mother." I have translated this utterance, which punctuates all of Mātājī's trance-talk simply as "victory." She will point out one by one the items devotees have placed in front of her, make the diagnosis, and prescribe the remedy, until all the questions have been answered. Each devotee approaches Mātājī in turn when her or his item has been selected, touches her feet, engages in a brief verbal exchange, then steps away. Each will return at the end of the session to receive the blessed articles that Mātājī has prescribed as remedies. The middle-aged man, referred to below as her "Helper" steps in from time to time to pick up the items and call devotees inside.

QUESTION ONE

Mātājī: Victory! Victory! Devotees, for I have come. Victory! The one with the red cloth is here to ask . . .

Helper: Whose red cloth is this?

Woman: It's mine, Jī.

Mātājī: Victory! Victory! Victory! Devotees, you want to ask about your distress.

Woman: Yes, Jī.

Mātājī: Victory! Because you want to ask, "Why is there this distress; what is the matter?"

Woman: Yes, Jī.

Mātājī: Innocent daughter, you have already been to doctors. Even so, there has been no improvement. Therefore, you want to ask, "Why is it like this? What is the reason? Is it my own fault or is it someone else's doing?"

Woman: Yes, Jī.

Mātājī: Victory, victory, O devotees, victory! There's pain in your head. Victory! Pain in your stomach. Victory! Your body feels as though someone has beaten it. You don't feel like eating. You don't even feel like talking to anyone. You think, "I should leave everything and go off somewhere. I should just go and sit somewhere alone." For this reason, you want to ask, "Why is this? What's the reason? Is it my own fault, or is it someone else's doing?"

Woman: Yes, Jī.

Mātājī: Victory! Innocent daughter, this is a mighty enemy's doing. Because of this, you have already wasted your time in so many doctors' houses. Even so, there has been no cure. For this, take a five-colored string, cardamon, and holy water. It's the enemy's might! It was fed to you in your food. The one who fed you is a widow. Victory! Next question . . .

QUESTION 2

Mātājī: Victory! The cloth in the middle . . .

Helper: This one? [*picking up one of several pieces of clothing*]

Mātājī: In front of it; the second one you lifted up.

Helper: This one? Whose is this? [*A man steps forward and touches Mātājī's feet.*]

Mātājī: Victory! Have you come to ask about your distress?

Man: Yes, Jī.

Mātājī: Innocent son, how much distress have you borne for three years? Innocent son, you have already wasted time in so many doctors' houses. There is pain in your chest. Victory! It is also as if a load has fallen on your mind. You don't ever feel like talking with anyone. You don't even feel like eating your food. Your heart says, "I should leave everything and go off somewhere and sit alone." For this reason, you want to ask, "Why is this? What is the reason? Is it my own fault or someone else's doing?" Innocent son, there had also been a quarrel over property.

Man: How many years ago, Mā?

Mātājī: Victory! Victory! Innocent son, five years have passed.

Man: Five years?

Mātājī: Why not? Victory! For this, innocent son . . . Victory! The one who did it is a woman. The one who made and brought it is a man. This deed has been done by those of low caste. For this take cardamon, holy water, and a seven-colored thread.

Man: All right, but how much longer will the illness last now?

Mātājī: Victory! Innocent son, if you keep devotion, then within a year there will be benefit. . . . Next question; the yellow cloth over there . . .

QUESTION 3

Mātājī: Victory! Victory! Innocent son, you want to ask about your health.

Man: Yes, Jī, Mātājī.

Mātājī: Innocent son, you want to ask why you are having difficulty with your health.

Man: Yes, Jī.

Mātājī: Innocent son, the reason is . . . Victory! It's because the one who did it has put you through an ordeal.

Man: Is the one who did it one of us [a relative] or an outsider?

Mātājī: Victory! It's an outsider, not a relative.

Man: Is it someone from here or from back there?

Mātājī: Victory! Someone from back there, not from here.

Man: What's the cure, now?

Mātājī: Innocent son, for this, take some cardamon, and you can drink holy water.

Man: Mātājī, will there be any happy outcome from this?

Mātājī: Innocent son, why not? But you must first reap some impure fruit.

Man: All right, Mātājī, whatever has happened to me, has it born fruit yet?

Mātājī: Innocent son, it is best.

Man: Mātājī, will there be good fortune?

Mātājī: Why not? After this is over, you will definitely benefit. Victory! Victory! Next question . . . The handkerchief . . .

QUESTION 4

Helper: Whose handkerchief is this?

Mātājī: The one you started to pick up . . . Victory! Victory! Victory! Have you come to ask about your health?

Woman: Mātājī, it's not myself I'm asking about.

Mātājī: You're asking about someone else. You've come asking about health and work. Why are you troubled?

Woman: Mātājī, it's about my child. It's about his studies.

Mātājī: Why are you troubled? What is the matter?

Woman: He can't focus his mind.

Mātājī: Innocent daughter, I am Kanyākumārī, the Virgin Goddess. I can figure it out for myself. Victory! How much trouble he's gotten into! Innocent daughter, he embraces knowledge then breaks away from it. Now he doesn't even want to look at it.

Woman: Yes, Mātājī, it's just like that.

Mātājī: Victory! Sometimes he feels like this: "I'll leave everyone and go and sit alone."

Woman: Yes, that's it, Mātājī.

Mātājī: Darkness has come over his eyes. So, you want to ask, "Why is this happening? Is it our fault, or is it someone else's doing?" Victory!

Woman: Victory to the Mother!

Mātājī: Innocent daughter, the reason for this is the action of a mighty enemy.

Woman: Mātājī, he's quarrelsome . . .

Mātājī: He's been uprooted from knowledge. For this, give him cardamon, holy water, and a three-color thread. And, innocent daughter, make a book donation on Tuesday.

Woman: To whom, Mātājī?

Mātājī: To anyone.

Another Woman: To anyone. Give a book to a child or to a poor person on a Tuesday during the month of Jyeṣṭhā [May-June] or any Tuesday.

Mātājī: Any Tuesday of any month. Victory! Take a three-color thread, cardamon, and holy water. Victory!

Woman: All right, Mātājī, very well.

Mātājī: Next question, there's a watch in the back. Victory! In the back, one with a gold chain.

QUESTION 5

Helper: Whose is this?

Mātājī: Victory, victory, victory! Do you want to ask about your health?

Woman: Yes, Jī, Mātājī.

Mātājī: Innocent daughter, your legs are numb and as if lifeless.

Woman: Yes, Jī, Mātājī.

Mātājī: Sometimes you can't even tell if they're on the ground or in the sky. Because of this, you want to ask, "Why does this happen? What's the matter?"

Woman: Mātājī, the pain is terrible.

Mātājī: Victory! Sometimes when you put your foot on the ground, it feels as is your leg is breaking, the right leg.

Woman: Yes, Mātājī.

Mātājī: Victory, victory! Below the knee, there is a lot of pain. Innocent daughter, the reason is the bonds of karma pressing down on you. For this, take a black-colored thread. You'll get happiness.

Woman: Mātājī, will my legs get better?

Mātājī: Take some pure oil, put on the thread, then after eight days, apply the oil.

Woman: All right, Mātājī.
Mātājī: Victory! Victory! In front there is a white-stoned ring.

QUESTION 6

Mātājī: Victory! You want to ask about your child's distress. She also wants to know why he's experiencing this distress. How much trouble there has been within the last two months! Innocent daughter, he doesn't even feel like eating. Victory! Sometimes his body feels as though someone has beaten it. Innocent daughter, someone who was learning is the one who perpetrated this. Innocent daughter, for this take a three-colored thread, cardamon, and holy water and give them to him immediately. He will definitely recover. . . . There's a striped handkerchief . . .
Helper: This one?
Mātājī: The one farthest in front, on this side.

QUESTION 7

Mātājī: Victory! This is a question about a man.
Woman: Yes, Jī.
Mātājī: You want to ask about your man's distress. And you want to ask, "Why is this distress occurring? What is the matter? Is it our fault or someone else's doing?" Victory! Innocent daughter, victory! Because it has gotten to the point that he doesn't even feel comfortable at home.
Woman: Yes, Jī.
Mātājī: When he comes into the house, it's obvious that he wants to go away. And it's as if the people at home are enemies. But he'll sit and talk with outsiders in a friendly way, as though they were family. Therefore, you want to ask, "Why is this happening? Is it one's own fault or someone else's doing?" Innocent daughter, this is a mighty enemy's doing. For this, take some cardamon. Victory! In the back, there is a cloth . . .

QUESTION 8

Mātājī: Victory! It's a question about a boy. You want to ask about his future.
Man: Yes, Jī, Mātājī. He doesn't focus his mind on his studies.
Mātājī: Victory! Innocent son, with him it's, "If it's to be done today, then I'll do it tomorrow. If it's to be done tomorrow, then the following morning." That's the way it is with him these days. Therefore, you want to ask, "Why is this going on with him? What is the reason? Is it one's own fault, or is it someone else's doing?" Innocent son, the reason for this is that it's a mighty enemy's doing.
Man: Where is he from?
Mātājī: Innocent son, someone has passed his hand over the boy's head. The one who has passed his hand lives nearby and is of a different caste. For

this, take a black-colored thread, holy water, and cardamon. The next question is a white handkerchief in the back.

QUESTION 9

Mātājī: Victory! Innocent son, you want to ask about work.
Man: Definitely.
Mātājī: Victory! You want to ask whether you will get what you want or not.
Man: No, I have already gotten it.
Mātājī: Innocent son, however far you advance, you find yourself falling behind the same distance.
Man: Yes, Jī.
Mātājī: Victory! Therefore you want to ask, "Now I'm running forward; will I reach my goal or not?" Innocent son, the influence of Saturn [Śani] has come over you. An astrological influence has come over you. For Śani you should donate something black, however much you can afford without difficulty, and innocent son, within eleven months you'll reach your goal.
Man: Within eleven months? What should I donate, Mātājī?
Mātājī: Make a black donation. Black beans. . . . Next question: a ring is lying there.

QUESTION 10

Mātājī: Victory! This is question about a woman. Innocent son, you want to ask why your woman is experiencing distress. Victory! Innocent son, her stomach hurts; her waist hurts. Victory! Innocent son, she doesn't feel like talking. She doesn't feel like eating her food. Sometimes her heart tells her, "I'll leave everything and go off somewhere. I'll sit alone." Therefore you want to ask, "Why is this happening? What is the reason? Is it one's own fault, or is it someone else's doing?" Innocent son, she went into the garden to pick some flowers. Innocent son, someone put something into her food, into her corn bread and wheat bread. For this, definitely give her cardamon and holy water. . . . A torn handkerchief in front . . .
Helper: Whose handkerchief is this?

QUESTION 11

[*An adolescent girl steps forward.*]

Mātājī: Victory! You want to ask about your future. You also want to ask . . . Victory . . . if in the future your karma will be bright or not and if you'll be rid of obstacles or not. Victory! Innocent daughter, it will take some time, but you will have good fortune. Victory! Definitely offer a libation to the Sun of water mixed with red sandalwood paste. Innocent daughter, your mind is fixed less on knowledge, and more on useless things. It's the plight brought on by the astrological influence of the Sun. Offer a libation to the Sun, along with sesame, rice, and red sandalwood.

Girl: Has the enemy's influence ended?

Mātājī: Innocent daughter, why not? Now there is some change from your previous state.

Girl: Now it is time for exams, and I can't focus my mind on studying.

Mātājī: Innocent daughter, you will have good fortune, but you have to keep discipline for some days. . . . Now the next question . . . in front there is a red-stoned ring . . .

QUESTION 12

Mātājī: Victory! You want to ask about your health. You want to ask, "Why am I experiencing distress? What's the matter?" Innocent daughter, sometimes you don't even feel like talking. Sometimes your waist hurts. Sometimes it feels as though your body is broken in half, and one part is below and the other is on top. Victory! And there is also pain in your neck. Victory! Victory! Innocent daughter, sometimes you feel like just lying on your cot. Victory!

Woman: Yes, Jī.

Mātājī: Victory! You don't feel like talking and neither do you feel like eating. Innocent daughter, you have given up eating, and you won't even touch food. Innocent daughter, sometimes it feels as though someone has beaten your body. Sometimes there is pain in your head too, sometimes in half of it and sometimes in all of it. Sometimes there's no pain at all. Innocent daughter, because of this you want to ask, "Why is this happening?" Innocent daughter, a mighty enemy is the cause of this. Because you have had a new residence built for yourself. Innocent daughter, you have had a very beautiful residence built. For this very reason, they turn on those who become great. They turn on those who become fortunate. They think, "We'll grind them to dust." For this, take cardamon, holy water . . .

Woman: Who is it?

Mātājī: He's of your own caste. He has quarreled with you also.

Woman: Mātājī, will we be all right?

Mātājī: Innocent daughter, why not? For this take cardamon, holy water, and a five-colored thread. Victory! . . . In the middle, there's a square-faced watch . . .

QUESTION 13

[*A foreign woman in her early forties, wearing Indian clothing, comes forward.*]

Mātājī: Victory! Victory! You want to ask about your career. You want to ask, "Will I be successful in the work I have undertaken or not?" Victory! "Will my wishes be fulfilled or not?" Innocent daughter, why are you worrying?

Last year, too, you profited well. Did you or didn't you? Innocent daughter, what lies ahead is also good.

This watch belongs to the author, who placed it there before the session began. She is a scholar who has come to study Mātājī, her devotees, and her practices, and is consulting Mātājī concerning the success of her research project. She remains silent and simply nods in response to Mātājī's questions. At this point in their acquaintance, she has told Mātājī very little about herself except that she is a university professor and has certainly not mentioned the fact that the previous year was a good one professionally.

Mātājī: Victory! Victory! There's a white handkerchief in the back.

QUESTION 14

Mātājī: Victory! Innocent daughter, you want to ask about your distress. You want to ask, "Why am I experiencing distress?" Victory! You want to ask about your little girl, and you want to ask if what was thought of will work out or not. But her mind is not settled. Victory! Innocent daughter, she is engaged in work, and then that is broken. Innocent daughter, on Thursday, make a donation of something yellow. Innocent daughter, this little girl will be deeply wounded. Victory! Victory!
Woman: Mātā, who is the emeny?
Mātājī: Victory! Victory! Innocent daughter, the enemy is some distance away. For this take cardamon, holy water, and a five-colored thread.
Woman: Mātā, does the enemy have a job, or is he in business?
Mātājī: He has his own business, not a job. Innocent daughter, she'll be all right soon. I protect my devotees who are attached to me. I become their servant and protect them. Victory! Victory! Next question . . . In the back there's a bangle.

QUESTION 15

Mātājī: Victory! Innocent daughter, you want to ask about your health. You want to ask, "Why am I having problems with my health?" Innocent daughter, how much trouble you've borne. Innocent daughter, both of your arms have broken. Victory! Your body has become leaden. You don't even feel like talking. You don't feel like eating. Innocent daughter, your whole body feels numb. It feels heavy. Sometimes it feels as though it is bound in a noose.
Woman: Yes, Jī.
Mātājī: Innocent daughter, you have been taking medicine, too. Even so, there is no difference. Sometimes, peace comes by itself. Other times the pain increases by itself. Therefore, you want to ask, "Is this my fault or someone else's?" Innocent daughter, this is caused by a mighty enemy. For this take

cardamon, holy water, and a five-colored thread. Next question . . .Victory! In front there is a white-stoned ring.

QUESTION 16

Mātājī: Victory! Victory! Innocent daughter, you have pain in your head, and your eyes feel as if blinded. Victory! Innocent daughter, sometimes when you have head pain it feels as if your head is splitting. Victory! Victory! Because, innocent daughter . . . Victory! Afterward your body trembles and you feel exhausted. Innocent daughter, every time you go to a doctor, it is futile. The doctors go on prescribing, and your suffering goes on increasing. It hasn't decreased. Innocent daughter, you have come under the influence of both the Sun and Saturn. For Saturn, I have already given you the remedy. For the Sun, offer a libation with red sandalwood paste mixed in and accompanied by kuśa grass and flowers. Victory! And wear a thread of five colors. Innocent daughter, this is the work of a mighty enemy. To be saved from this . . .

Woman: Is the enemy from nearby or far away?

Mātājī: From very nearby, not from far away. For this take cardamon, holy water, and a five-colored thread.

Woman: Is it a man or a woman?

Mātājī: It's a woman . . . Next question . . .There's a ring lying next to the watch.

QUESTION 17

[*A husband and wife approach together. Mātājī addresses each in turn.*]

Mātājī: Victory! Victory! Victory! Innocent son, you want to ask about your distress. You want to ask, "Why am I experiencing distress? What is the reason?" Victory! How much distress you have borne! Innocent daughter, he has already become like a crazy person. He doesn't even want to sit in the house. He comes into the house and it's as though he were sitting in a jungle. Only people outside the home are his friends. Innocent daughter, Saturn is dwelling in his fourth house. Victory! For Saturn he should look at the reflection of his face in bitter oil and then should light a flame in a Śiva temple. Victory! Victory! Then there will be a difference. For this give cardamon and holy water.

Man: How should I light a flame?

Mātājī: After looking at your face. Victory! Is there another question, one about a document?

QUESTION 18

Helper: Whose is this?

[*A woman steps forward and picks up the rolled-up document on the floor.*]

Mātājī: You want to ask about someone else's work. You want to ask about auspicious work.

Woman: I want to ask about [his] business.

Mātājī: Victory! Victory! You want to ask about auspicious work, and you want to ask if the business will go well or not.

Woman: Yes, Jī.

Mātājī: Victory! It was going along and then went down. What's the matter? Will it improve or not? Innocent daughter, of course it will improve.

Woman: Mātājī, it's just like that. What's the matter?

Mātājī: Victory! Because, innocent daughter, [someone] has bound it all up.

Woman: Who bound it up?

Mātājī: Innocent daughter, the one who built a residence fell into a quarrel. Innocent daughter, the one who bound it up is someone like that. For this matter, an eighty-four-part fire sacrifice and ritual recitation should be done.

Woman: Will it be all right?

Mātājī: There will be good fortune. Next: a checked cloth.

Question 19 is omitted, due to incomplete tape recording.

QUESTION 20

Mātājī: This is a watch on the other side. Victory! Victory! Innocent daughter, your chest hurts, and you also want to ask about some work. Victory! Innocent daughter, your chest hurts, and there's pain in your head, sometimes a little and sometimes quite a lot. Victory! Sometimes it feels as though your head is being cut off. You don't have the heart even to talk.

Woman: Yes, Mātājī.

Mātājī: Victory! Your heart says, "I should leave everything and go off somewhere and sit alone." Therefore, you want to ask whether it is your fault or someone else's doing. Innocent daughter, four years have passed and the fifth has started. Innocent daughter, for this place pure oil in the temple for eight days and then take it, and also wear a seven-colored thread.

Woman: Who has done this, Mātājī?

Mātājī: The one who has done this is a woman from around here.

Woman: Mother, is she one of my in-laws or my own family?

Mātājī: She's an in-law.

Woman: Is she a widow or an auspicious married woman?

Mātājī: Innocent daughter, she is a widow, not an auspicious married woman.

Woman: All right, Mātājī.

Mātājī: For this, take cardamon, holy water, and a seven-colored thread.

Woman: Where should I put the pure oil, Mātājī?

Mātājī: Innocent daughter, in the temple. It should stay for seven days.

Woman: Then should I rub it on my neck, Mātājī?

Mātājī: Victory! Innocent daughter, why not? Victory! Victory! On this side there's a handkerchief.

QUESTION 21

Mātājī: Victory! Victory! You want to ask about some work. Innocent son, now you are begging forgiveness for your own mistake. Innocent son, listen! It was a matter having to do with money. In five months, there will be good fortune.

Man: Mātājī, will there be an answer or not to the letter which was sent outside?

Mātājī: Innocent son, why not?

Man: Mātājī, will the work be accomplished or not?

Mātājī: Innocent son, why not? Victory! Victory! There's another question; this checked cloth.

QUESTION 22

Mātājī: Victory! It's a question about a boy. Innocent daughter, you want to ask about distress. You want to ask, "Why is this distress occurring?" It's a question about a man, and you want to ask, "Will there be good fortune in the work he's doing now?" Victory! On Saturday [the day of Saturn], make up a packet of mustard greens.

Woman: Mātājī, there is obstruction in the work.

Mātājī: Innocent daughter, make up a packet of mustard greens. His work will go on.

Woman: The work is so precarious . . .

Mātājī: Innocent daughter, it will definitely work out. Why are you worrying?

Woman: It must be sorcery.

Mātājī: Innocent daughter, the might of an enemy has brought this on.

Woman: Who is it?

Mātājī: The one who is doing this kind of deed, he is doing this one, too.

Woman: All right.

Mātājī: Next question, a polythene envelope.

QUESTION 23

Mātājī: Victory! Victory! This is a question for someone else.

Man: Yes, it is my son's, about his interview.

Mātājī: Victory! Victory! Innocent son, I am Kanyākumārī, the Virgin Goddess, I can speak for myself. There will be a little obstacle, but he will definitely obtain work. . . . Next question . . . Victory! A watch on this side . . .

QUESTION 24

Mātājī: Innocent daughter, you want to ask about your future, whether your future will be bright or not. Innocent daughter, it will be bright. Victory!

Innocent daughter, your studies are a bit shaky. Innocent daughter, offer a flower at the time of twilight. You will have good fortune. . . . Ahead, there's a checked handkerchief . . .

QUESTION 25

Mātājī: Innocent daughter, you want to ask about your distress. You want to ask, "Why am I experiencing distress; what is the matter?" Victory! For, innocent daughter, the affairs of the household were going on as usual, but all of a sudden, there is this. That's why you want to ask, "When things have been peaceful, why has an obstacle befallen us? Must we continue to bear this difficulty, or will we again have peace?" There is affliction in your home; there is no prosperity.
Woman: Yes, Mātājī.
Mātājī: It comes from one side and goes off in another. One can't tell where it's coming from or how it's snatched away. Therefore, you want to ask, "Is this our own fault or someone else's doing?" Victory! Innocent daughter, this is an enemy's might over your household. Innocent daughter, there is no shortage of money coming into the house, but no one knows how it is all spent.
Woman: Yes, Jī.
Mātājī: Victory! Sometimes it seems as though someone is walking around. Whenever you lay your hand on a cooking pot, it becomes empty. Innocent daughter, the harijan caste's mountain spirit has been cast upon you. That's why there is no brightness in your work.
Woman: Mātājī, who cast it on us?
Mātājī: Innocent daughter, the casters are from nearby. They're not from far away. They're of your own caste.
Woman's husband: Are they from our very house?
Mātājī: They're from your very own caste. They work in a job. Have an eighty-four-part fire sacrifice and recitation done. Take cardamon and holy water.
Woman: Mātājī, will it be all right?
Mātājī: Innocent daughter, why not? . . . In front, there's a "wide bangle" question . . .
Woman's husband: Mātājī, for how many days will we have to do the sacrifice and recitiation?
Mātājī: Daily. For some days you'll have to keep this regimen. Then there will be good fortune. . . . Wide bangle question . . .

QUESTION 26

Man: Mātājī, will the work I am doing turn out well or not?
Mātājī: Victory! Innocent son, why not? Even this month has gone well.
Man: Mātājī, this month has gone very badly.
Mātājī: All right, innocent son, just yesterday something came up.

Man: Mātājī, nothing came up with anybody yesterday.

Mātājī: What do you mean, nothing came up? Didn't something happen with a certain man?

Man: Yes, Jī. There was a little something. Mātājī, what will come to pass with him?

Mātājī: Innocent son, there will be good fortune.

Man: Mātājī, my aunt has received a letter. What will happen to her?

Mātājī: For the time being, nothing.

Man: Mātājī, should we hold out hope or not?

Mātājī: For now, there's nothing.

Man: Oh, misfortune.

Mātājī: Innocent son, there will be good fortune. . . . Next question, handkerchief . . .

QUESTION 27

Mātājī: Victory! You want to ask about your distress. Victory! You also want to ask about work, and you want to ask, "Will the work I am doing turn out well or not?" Innocent son, what a misfortune has happened! You are also having trouble getting a position. Innocent son, victory! No one has done anything or sent anything to you. This is the astrological influence of Rāhu [dragon's head] and Saturn. In the midst of this there has been and will be trickery by friends and quarrels with your kinsmen. Innocent son, make a bundle of mustard greens, a bundle of sesame seeds, and a bundle of wheat. Make these three bundles, and you will have good fortune.

Man: Mātājī, when will there be a result?

Mātājī: Innocent son, there will be a result in March or April. You will get a position. . . . Next question . . . this cloth . . .

QUESTION 28

Mātājī: Victory! Victory! Innocent daughter, you want to ask about your future. And you want to ask why you are having difficulty concerning your future. Innocent daughter, your attention is not fixed on your studies. Victory! If work comes up in the morning, you leave it until evening, and in the morning the same thing happens again. Innocent daughter, the evil eye has been cast on you. Innocent daughter, for this take a three-colored thread, cardamon, and holy water.

Girl: For how many days?

Mātājī: Innocent daughter, for eight days. Victory! It will definitely bear fruit.

QUESTION 29

Mātājī: A "leaf" question.

Helper: Who put this leaf here?

Mātājī: It belongs to a woman wearing a Coca Cola-colored suit. [*A middle-aged peasant woman wearing a brown outfit steps forward.*] It's a question about the household. You want to ask a question about an animal of the household.

Woman: Yes.

Mātājī: Victory! Victory! Innocent daughter, there is the disappointment of "white water." [*This is an infection that prevents a cow from conceiving.*] Therefore, you want to ask, "Will the hope that we have held out be fulfilled or not?" Innocent daughter, the cow's womb is softening. For this, take black neem leaves and holy water and give them to her. The "white water" will go away. . . . On this side, a silver ring . . .

QUESTION 30

Mātājī: Victory! Victory! You want to ask about distress; you want to ask why this distress is occurring.

Woman [*who has already asked a question*]:Yes, Jī.

Mātājī: Innocent daughter, I have already given you a remedy. Do it, and you will have good fortune.

Woman: Mātājī, this is a question for someone else.

Mātājī: Innocent daughter, you want to ask about distress. Victory! There is pain in the stomach, pain in the head, nervousness. The right side of the body is numb.

Woman: Yes, Jī.

Mātājī: Innocent daughter, someone has bound her with coercion. Victory! For this, give cardamon, holy water.

Woman: Mātājī, who has bound her with coercion?

Mātājī: The binder is from another jāt, from another caste.

Woman: Should we give it [the cure] to her now?

Mātājī: Why not? There will be good fortune. Devotees, I am gone!

Mātājī shudders and then relaxes. Her eyes gradually refocus as she takes a few deep breaths, straightens her clothing, and smooths her hair. She smiles at those around her and begins to greet the devotees who have lined up outside. She knows many by name and inquires about their family members. One by one they come into the temple to collect the items she has prescribed. She dispenses the cardamon seeds in small newspaper-wrapped packets and cuts the threads in neck-length sizes. The holy water, which earlier in the day has bathed the stone Goddess image, has collected in a small chamber underneath. Mātājī scoops up some of this water, mixing it into a bucket of tap water. She then taps it with a flower while reciting a mantra under her breath. At Mātājī's direction, the helper uses this water to fill containers that devotees have brought. Mātājī distributes prasād (consecrated offerings) of candies or bananas to everyone. Some of the devotees circumambulate her temple or visit the adjacent temple to Lord Śiva.

Some stay awhile to chat with her, ask advice, or seek a blessing for their children. Others leave monetary offerings. A family that has traveled some distance unpacks their lunch and sits down to eat on the veranda. When everyone has left, Mātājī tidies up her temple, says a prayer to the Goddess, and retires to her own quarters.

Kings and Priests

—6—

The Consecration of the Monastic Compound at Mount Koya by Kūkai

David L. Gardiner

Although Japanese Buddhism is probably best known in popular circles for its rich tradition of Zen teachings and practices, from a historical perspective it is plausible to contend that no form has had more of a pervasive impact on the overall development of Japanese religion than the esoteric or Tantric Buddhist schools known in Japan as mikkyō ("secret teaching"). Mikkyō was first formally represented in the Tendai and Shingon schools founded in the early ninth century, but its roots are discernible in the eighth century and its branches, to continue the metaphor, extend throughout virtually all the subsequent schools that emerged in the Kamakura period (around the thirteenth century), in particular in the Zen, Pure Land, and Nichiren schools, where its presence bore significant and recognizable fruits. Among the variety of ways mikkyō seems to have influenced religious expressions other than those formally identifiable as Tantric are the inclusion of elaborate rites with a profusion of liturgical paraphernalia, the employment of dhāraṇīs or mantras in recitation of prayers, and the utilization of some form of painted maṇḍala diagrams. In addition to these more concrete instances, one might add the basic religious paradigm that mikkyō offered, which encompassed elements such as the perfect identity of practitioner and Buddha (in body, speech, as well as mind) and the generally affirmative view of the ordinary world as being a manifestation of the sacred body of the Buddha.

Kūkai and Mount Koya

Kūkai was the founder of the Shingon school, which has long stood as the most exclusively Tantric form of Buddhist practice in Japan. Shingon means "true word," and is derived from the Chinese translation of the Sanskrit word *mantra*. Although the Tendai and other Buddhist schools incorporated Tantric elements into their study and practice, the Shingon school prides itself on being less eclectic than any other. The two texts translated below chronicle ceremonies associated with Kūkai's founding of the monastery named Kongōbuji (Temple of the Vajra Peak, named after the *Vajraśekhara sūtra*) on Mount Koya. Of the various monasteries at which Kūkai lived and worked, none held as much significance for him as Kongōbuji. The temple complex, together with the surrounding community of Koyasan that occupies the top of Mount Koya, has remained as an important center for Japanese religion for nearly 1,200 years. Koyasan is located two hours south by train from Osaka in the hills of Wakayama prefecture. It continues today to draw around one million tourists a year, many of whom perform a pilgrimage to Kūkai's tomb, where many believe the master (some call him a saint) still sits in meditation awaiting the future Buddha, or to the gravesite of a relative—for the mountaintop houses probably the largest, and surely the grandest, cemetery in all Japan. Mount Koya is one of Japan's greatest holy spots and, because it has served for many centuries as a thriving religious center, it stands as a repository of a fabulous cultural and artistic heritage.

The first text below touches briefly on Kūkai's relation to the mountain. It notes that after he had returned from studying esoteric Buddhism in the Tang capital of China for two years, he sought far and wide for a suitable location to build a monastery devoted to its practice. In a letter he wrote in 816 C.E. requesting the Japanese emperor to bestow the land to him, he indicated that he came to know the area when he had passed through it during his younger peripatetic days as a mountain ascetic practitioner. Although it is accurate to say that he founded the monastic compound of Kongōbuji, it would be misleading (though in accordance with popular legend) to assert that Kūkai "discovered" Mount Koya as a holy spot. The mountains of Yoshino just to the east had for generations been favorite grounds for practitioners of various spiritual disciplines, and it is clear that Mount Koya had seen the footsteps of many a seeker. Kūkai indicates in his writings that he may have employed some geomantic methods for discerning that it was a suitable location for a monastery. Yet it is also evident that the simple facts that it is a large basin of approximately four square miles at the top of a three-thousand-foot peak, with good running water and sufficient distance from the urban life of either Nara or Kyoto (a few days' travel away), were all points in its favor.

The two texts translated below chronicle rites that mark the establishment of the grounds as a monastery. The texts themselves are not dated, but other reliable documents that can be dated, and that are likely to have been produced shortly before and after these rites, indicate that the rites must have taken place in 818 or 819. In his 816 letter requesting the emperor to permit him to use the mountain for a monastery, Kūkai indicated that there were not enough religious centers situated in quiet mountains in Japan. He cited the scripture *Dainichi-kyō* (*Mahāvairocana-sūtra*) as recommending isolated mountain spots as ideal for the practice of meditation. A text dated one month after Kūkai's request purportedly documents the emperor's permission to build a center, but the authenticity of this letter has been called into question on several points. Nevertheless, various correspondences reveal that Kūkai dispatched some of his disciples to the mountain in 818 to begin to construction there and that he intended to follow them shortly afterward. Letters he sent to acquaintances in Kyoto and elsewhere reveal that he resided on the mountain for about eight months from the winter of 818 until the summer of 819, and it is likely that the present texts were composed during this period. This was twelve years after he had returned from his studies in China.

When Kūkai returned in 806 from Tang China, where he had studied as a Japanese government-sponsored "foreign student," he was not well known in court circles. It took several years for him to develop contacts with important senior monks (such as the Tendai founder Saichō), influential court officials, and eventually the Emperor Saga, whose interest in things that were vogue in Chinese literary and cultural circles is legendary. Before establishing his center on Mount Koya, he did manage the affairs of a few temples near the capital, such as the Jingōji on Mount Takao. Jingōji served Kūkai well, as it was an older temple with strong connections to established court families. While residing there he performed two very significant initiation ceremonies into Shingon Tantric practice, which scores of well-known monks and lay aristocrats attended. This allowed him both to gain some repute as a new specialist in an attractive tradition, and to gather some able disciples. But it seems that for many years Kūkai desired to build a place far from the busy life of the capital that would be dedicated solely to the training of students in Shingon practice. In fact, a letter survives in which he tells a friend of a vow that he had made en route back from China to do just that. It appears that when his ship had encountered a severe ocean storm, he had promised the gods that if he were allowed to arrive safely in Japan he would generate great benefits in the world by establishing a center devoted to the practice of the Tantric Buddhism he had learned in China. Other letters also indicate that his building of the complex at the top of Mount Koya was indeed an expression of his commitment to realize this vow.

The construction of the Kongōbuji monastery, however, did not proceed quickly. Its distance from the capital, coupled with Kūkai's many responsibilities there, permitted neither the procurement of supplies nor the management of labor to run smoothly. By the time of Kūkai's death in 835, it is not likely that more than a few buildings had been completed: a stūpa, a worship hall, and a residence for monks. From 823, Kūkai became engaged in supervising the completion of the Tōji temple in the capital. The construction of this important temple at the southern entrance to Kyoto had languished for several years, and the invitation to Kūkai to revitalize the project was both a clear indication of his growing reputation and a stepping stone to other obligations in the capital. His correspondence reveals that, as his duties in Kyoto expanded due to his newly found prominence, he felt frustrated at becoming increasingly distanced from his dream to build a center on Mount Koya. In 832, he led Kongōbuji's first large ceremony of offering to the Buddha, known as the mandōe or ceremony of ten thousand lamps, a ritual that had a long tradition in major Japanese Buddhist temples of Nara. Soon afterward he pleaded with the court to be released from his responsibilities in the capital—he had recently been appointed in Kyoto to the high-ranking position of a chief supervisor of monks—in order that he might return to his retreat at Mount Koya. One of his reasons for requesting retirement was his ailing health, and indeed it was not long after his return there in 834 that he passed away, on the mountain, in the third month of 835, at the age of sixty-two. The supervision of the construction was left to his disciple Shinzen, who made much progress during the next twenty years.

The Consecration Rite

The particular ritual for which these texts stand as our introduction is known in Japanese as kekkai, meaning "to bind a realm." The Japanese term is derived from the Chinese translation of the Sanskrit *sīmā-bandha*. Buddhist texts on vināya, or monastic rituals and regulations, apparently used the term in non- or pre-Tantric contexts to refer to the prescribed rules serving to formally separate the monastic community from lay communities in terms of such categories as spatial demarcation and restrictions regarding clothing and food. In Japanese history, kekkai has generally denoted the divisions between monastic and lay territory. There are signposts known as kekkai stones that stand at the entrance to some temple buildings (especially ones set aside for assiduous contemplative practice), which frequently contain the engraved admonition that women, alcohol, and garlic are not permitted beyond the sign. The term may also refer to the railing (commonly wooden) within a temple building that separates the altar, on which Buddha images usually stand, from the surrounding space for worshipers. The kekkai thus demarcates sacred and profane space, and might be considered in the Japanese context to circumscribe an area in which the healing/saving power of deity is seen to be concentrated.

These two texts were most likely recited as prayers before or during the consecration rites. Furthermore, much in the way that the Shintō tradition recites norito (formal prayers to a diety) under similar circumstances, the texts are addressed to deities in the form of announcements of what will transpire. The core of this announcement, however, is the actual invitation of the deities to enter the realm under consideration, thereby sacralizing and protecting it. The kekkai rite described by Kūkai for the founding of Kongōbuji declares the bounded realm to be an area with a radius of seven ri, or approximately two to three miles. Although some scholars have noted that this distance seems to fit quite naturally with certain geographical features of the area surrounding Mount Koya, it is also a distance that has some precedence in Buddhist literature. Chinese translations of the biography of Śākyamuni Buddha give an account of how the nāga (a serpentine deity) king Mucilinda made a gigantic umbrella-like covering that protected the Buddha, which extended for a radius of seven ri (about two miles). There also exist Chinese Tantric texts that describe rites aimed at protecting an area designated by the same distance. Some kekkai rites performed in Japan prior to Kūkai's day were known as "binding the realm of the nation" (*kokudō kekkai*), and seem to have had a protective purpose, albeit less explicitly related to Tantric texts and deities than was Kūkai's kekkai. Most Japanese encyclopedias note the rites Kūkai performed for Kongōbuji in their entries for kekkai. The Shingon tradition recognizes three types, or scales, of kekkai. The largest is the "binding the realm of the nation," and some scholars say that the rites in the texts below fall into this category because of the vast area they designate (this interpretation implies that "nation" might simply indicate "land"). The two other kekkai rites are for a temple building and for an altar within such a building.

In Indian Buddhist Tantric ritual, the term *sīmā-bandha* sometimes referred to "binding" the area of a horizontal maṇḍala platform, which was often constructed on a raised earthen surface. Pillars known as kīlas were inserted into the circumference of the platform and a multicolored thread was tied around their tips to create a ring around the platform. There were also rites known as sīmā-bandha that purified a given area by expelling evil forces from the ground level, the air above the ground, and even from the area beneath the ground. Kūkai's texts follow a similar pattern because their central aim seems to be the elimination of obstructive spirits from the area and the invitation of helpful ones to stay. It is worthy of note that the native Japanese Shintō tradition also uses the word "binding" (*musubi*) to refer to the demarcation of sacred space.

Related Texts and Deities

Apart from their overall purpose, and the fact that the second ceremony took seven days and involved a number of deities named by him, we have little concrete knowledge about the actual rites performed by Kūkai. The primary deity of the second text is Kuṇḍali, who is called a "knowledge king" (*vidyārāja* in Sanskrit, *myōō* in Japanese); Kūkai indicates that he will rely on a "Kuṇḍali rite" for this consecration. There are a variety of Chinese texts containing rites that center on this deity, including one written by Amoghavajra, the great Tantric adept of the Tang dynasty who instructed Kūkai's master Huiguo. Kuṇḍali is said to manifest a fierce or wrathful appearance and is known as a destroyer of obstacles. In the Buddhist Tantric symbol system, he is often connected with Vajragarbha Bodhisattva as well as Ratnasambhava Buddha, and is associated with the southern direction.

A number of other deities are mentioned in the second text, including Śākyamuni Buddha, Avalokiteśvara, and the Medicine Buddha from the Buddhist tradition; the non-Buddhist Brahmā and Indra; other unnamed heavenly beings (*ten* in Japanese, a common rendering of the Sanskrit *deva*), and a variety of Japanese spirits, most notably the souls of the imperial line and the ancestors of members of the court. The rite targets in particular the enemies of the Buddha-dharma known as the vināyakas, who are depicted as potential obstructors to the spread of Kūkai's Shingon practice, in opposition to the aforenamed deities, who are called upon as protectors. The vināyakas are commonly portrayed in the Buddhist literature as opponents of the Dharma. Twice Kūkai repeats the phrase that the vināyaka, who destroy the true Dharma, and other maleficent spirits should get out of his newly established grounds to the distance of seven ri.

The Maṇḍala

Because both texts refer to the Shingon Buddhist maṇḍala, the concept needs some elaboration. The first text begins with a proclamation to the "oceanlike assembly" of the two great maṇḍalas, which are the Diamond and Womb Realms. These maṇḍalas are often represented in colorful painted form with intricate geometrical designs that incorporate myriad deities. In short, the maṇḍalas are visual representations of two simultaneous, overlapping aspects of the enlightened mind variously described either as emptiness and form, wisdom and compassion, or subject and object. Essential to a proper understanding of these maṇḍalas is the recognition that they are symbols for actual realities—pictorial embodiments of dimensions of the experience of a buddha. They represent a dimension of awakening *from* which a practitioner is guided, from the buddha's side so to speak—and *toward* which s/he developes through spiritual aspiration and specific methods. In essence, the Shingon practitioner is taught to believe that the maṇḍala represents an as yet unmanifested dimension of his/her own experience: an original buddhahood residing within. Thus the painted form, together with the visualizations, prayers, and ritual gestures of the contemplative regime, serve as a catalyst to this potential manifestation, which could be described as an inner transformation. The maṇḍala can thus be understood both as a means and an end of religious practice. Kūkai's use of the term maṇḍala focuses on its role as a description of the sacrality or sacredness of the world of enlightened experience, a sacrality that manifests when the true purity of one's mind is realized. At the same time, one can say that the sacrality of a geographical realm is also a potency that already resides within the land, which is made manifest in conjunction with an individual's own spiritual realization. Speaking of the maṇḍala in both of these senses—as both catalyst and aim—Kūkai writes in the first text of his "transmission" of the esoteric Buddhist teachings (which are also called a maṇḍala) to India and then ultimately to Japan, that "Mahāvairocana Buddha, the great compassionate one, enjoying for himself the taste of the equality that is enlightenment, was saddened by the plight of the beings in the six realms of rebirth. And so it was that the thunder of his wisdom that is one with reality trembled throughout the Dharma realm, and the secret maṇḍala was thereby transmitted to our world."

When later in the text he mentions how he "safely returned [from China] with the two maṇḍalas of the Diamond and the Womb realms," it is to the actual paintings on cloth that he refers. A little later he again mentions them by saying that he intends to "establish both the great maṇḍalas" on Mount Koya. But here it seems that he is indicating not so much the paintings, nor even their transmogrification into the statues inside stūpas that did take place on the mountain, but rather more significantly the actual engagement in the practice of the realization of these sacred realms of experience within the practitioner. It was this practice at the heart of the Shingon tradition that Kūkai wished to establish at Mount Koya. And so it was natural for him to regard a location that was dedicated to such noble aims as a sacred space.

But the concept of the sacred space of the maṇḍala can extend beyond that of just the immediate religious precinct of Mount Koya. It is equally likely that Kūkai believed that by "establishing the two maṇḍalas" at Kongōbuji he was creating a sacred center for all of Japan, thereby consecrating the entire land by his act. The area around Mount Koya was already in Kūkai's time a popular site for practitioners of asceticism, but its transformation into a major center of esoteric Buddhist practice from the early ninth century onward represented the emergence of a remarkably visible "power spot" in Japan. Earlier sacred mountains of Buddhist history easily come to mind: China's Tian-tai and Wu-tai mountains, as well as the holy Gṛdhrakūṭa in India where the Buddha himself is said to have preached. In the case of Wu-tai shan, where the Tantric master Bu-kong (Amoghavajra) established a center for a national cult of the bodhisattva of wisdom Mañjuśrī, we may see something like a model for Kūkai's vision for Mount Koya, which became one of Japan's most sacred mountains. An irony in this case might be that, instead of a heavenly bodhisattva such as Mañjuśrī serving as the focus as in the case of Wu-tai shan, at Koya, beside some interest in a cult devoted to the future Buddha Maitreya in which Kūkai himself displayed some zeal, the main object of worship assuring the locale's sacrality became the holy relic of Kūkai's own body, which many faithful still believe remains in meditative equipoise today.

The second text focuses on the "Assembly of the Dharma Altar," where Kūkai states that for one week he would, in order to consecrate the realm, offer worship to the buddhas of all directions (throughout the reaches of the universe) and to other deities. The title of this text indicates that it was written for the kekkai of the "altar place" (*danjō*), an expression that connotes the platform on which various deity statues are placed as a three-dimensional maṇḍala. In this case the meaning of maṇḍala is more concrete. Nevertheless, it is noteworthy that the sense here of an altar as a horizontal platform for the maṇḍala, which was the original style in early Tantric Buddhism in India, may resonate better with the broader spiritual sense of maṇḍala, in both a visual and a somatic (because three-dimensional) sense, than does the vertically hanging painted form. It is also noteworthy that in spite of the second text's apparent focus on consecrating an altar, the area said to be "bound" by the rite consists nevertheless of a radius of seven ri.

Conclusions

The esoteric Buddhist rites to which these texts refer, related as they are to the consecration of religious space, may in some sense be considered magical or at least apotropaic, a term that indicates the warding off of evil forces by ritual means. But equally characteristic of these and similar esoteric Buddhist rites is the invocation of beneficial forces to protect the realm. It is commonplace to acknowledge the extent to which the emergence of Buddhist Tantra introduced entirely new rites into the repertoire of Buddhist monastic specialists. Nonetheless, we know that the historical Buddha affirmed the existence of spiritual beings, whether of the heavenly or ghostly realms. Biographies also report that part of his daily routine included the teaching of deities that came for instruction in the Dharma. We also know that he acknowledged the effectiveness of particular incantations (*parittas*) for protection against harmful animals. But we do not possess any accounts of his performing rites like the ones Kūkai documents here, whose aim is to invoke and expel spiritual forces from the saṅgha residence. However, without going back to the lifetime of the Buddha, a period for which we have little historical evidence, it is possible to confirm that certain beliefs inherent in Kūkai's rites, in particular those regarding the efficacy that monastic rituals may have over the spirit realms, can be traced to an early stage in Indian Buddhism. We know, for example, that monks (even the more scholastically trained, learned ones) often performed and sponsored rites to benefit the spirits of their ancestors. Recent research reveals that, contrary to a common scholarly misconception that the practice of ancestor veneration entered Buddhism only after the religion had been transported to China, and equally contrary to the normative textual descriptions of monastic regulations, Indian Buddhist monks engaged in rituals that aimed to "manipulate" spiritual beings and ancestors. Thus, regardless of whatever Buddhist monks may have written about what they ought to have been doing, we can verify that they did perform rituals for the benefit of spirits.

Kūkai also wrote many texts contained in the *Shōryōshū* (a collection of his miscellaneous writings from which the present texts are taken) that commemorate rites performed on behalf of persons recently deceased. However, the rites discussed in the present texts include references not only to ancestral spirits—in this case of the imperial family and members of the court—but to a variety of "heavenly" beings (many of Indian origin), as well as to autochthonous spirits of Japan. In fact, in all of Kūkai's writings that document rituals, those translated below appear to be the only two in which he mentions such spirits. There must have been some great significance to the fact that it was only in the consecration of the monastic compound at Mount Koya that he chose to call upon such spirits for aid. One explanation for this may be found in the striking parallels between these rites performed by Kūkai and similar rites for the consecration of an area that are central to the native Shintō traditions that he surely knew well. This significance is clearly mirrored today in the presence on Mount Koya, at the heart of the compound near the central Great Stūpa, of a large shrine dedicated to the local deity known as Kōya Myōjin, where rites continue to be performed on a daily basis. It is justifiable to conclude that the symbolic and cosmic acts of consecration and invocation are to be renewed on a continual basis, albeit perhaps on a smaller scale.

The two documents translated below are preserved in a collection of Kūkai's writings known as the *Shōryōshū* (sometimes read *Seireishū*). In most printed editions, they correspond to the texts numbered 99 and 100. The *Shōryōshū* is a collection of over one hundred poems, letters, documents commemorating rituals (as in the present case), and other miscellaneous materials. Although the *Shōryōshū* does not contain any of Kūkai's major doctrinal works, many of its texts portray esoteric Buddhist theories as refracted through the lens of actual practice, thereby revealing how Shingon Buddhism took shape in its initial stages, during his lifetime. The *Shōryōshū* is thus an important historical resource for understanding the concrete means by which Kūkai propagated Shingon Buddhism. The translations here are based on texts 99 and 100 of Katsumata Shunkyo's *Kōbōdaishi Chosaku Zenshū*, vol. 3 (Tokyo: Sankibo Busshorin, 1968), pp. 392–96. The earlier Chinese source from which much of the language in Kūkai's second text derives is located in *Taishō* vol. 18, text no. 901, p. 813c. Kūkai's later ritual writings bear a great similarity to various texts found in this same *Taishō* vol. 18.

Further Reading

The best introduction to Kūkai's life and thought, which includes translations of some important doctrinal works, remains Yoshito Hakeda, *Kūkai: Major Works* (New York: Columbia University Press, 1972). A good source for more details on theory and practice in Shingon Buddhism is Taiko Yamasaki, *Shingon: Japanese Esoteric Buddhism* (Boston: Shambhala, 1988). My dissertation covers in depth several factors involved in Kūkai's introduction of Shingon into Japan: "Kūkai and the Beginnings of Shingon Buddhism in Japan" (Stanford University, 1995). On the significance of the maṇḍala concept, both as philosophy for the sake of individual practice and as incorporated into the design of the Kongōbuji monastic compound, see my "Maṇḍala, Maṇḍala on the Wall: Variations of Usage in the Shingon School," *Journal of the International Association of Buddhist Studies* 19.2 (1996): 245–79. Finally, a partial translation of each of the present texts, as part of a discussion of the influence of esoteric Buddhist concepts of space on Japanese religion, is presented in Allan G. Grapard, "Flying Mountains and Walkers of Emptiness: Toward a Definition of Sacred Space in Japanese Religions," *History of Religions* 21.3 (February 1982): 195–221.

Text of Declaration for the First Consecration at the Founding of Mount Koya

The śramana (monk) Henjō Kongō (Universally Illuminating Vajra) respectfully declares to the buddhas of the ten directions, to the oceanlike assembly of the Two Great Maṇḍalas, to the five kinds of devas and the heavenly and earthly divinities of this land, as well as to the various spirits of earth, water, fire, wind, and sky of this mountain:

That which possesses both form and consciousness is necessarily endowed with Buddha nature. Buddha nature and Dharma nature pervade the entire Dharma realm and are inseparable: this body and that body are of one essence and so are equal. One who has awakened to this truth always roams freely in the realm of the five wisdoms of Mahāvairocana Buddha, whereas those lost and unaware are constantly sinking in the mud of the three realms of desire, form, and formlessness that comprise saṃsāra. Mahāvairocana Buddha, the great compassionate one, enjoying for himself the taste of the equality that is enlightenment, was saddened by the plight of the beings in the six realms of rebirth. And so it was that the thunder of his wisdom that is one with reality trembled throughout the Dharma realm and the secret maṇḍala was thereby transmitted to our world. It was passed on to Vajrasattva, to Nāgārjuna and down to the present without a break in continuity. Vajrabodhi and Amoghavajra came east, bearing their staffs from India to China, and transmitted the esoteric teaching in order to liberate all beings. And yet, here across the broad ocean in Japan, worthy vessels of this teaching had yet to appear and so the teaching remained hidden in the secret palace of Mahāvairocana without being transmitted to our land.

Fortunately, due to the power of the grace of the Buddha and the forces that mature beings for spiritual work, I was able to travel to Tang China in 804, whence I safely returned with the two maṇḍalas of the Diamond and the Womb realms and over one hundred scrolls of Vajrayāna scriptures. Still, people in Japan were not ready and the time was not right. Month after month passed in rapid succession and it is now more than twelve years since I returned. At last, since our devout sovereign has taken it upon himself to help promote this teaching, we are in need simply of a place to practice. I have searched far and wide and am convinced that Mount Koya is a most suitable location. The sovereign, deciding to spread this teaching, has granted the mountain for this purpose. The location was deemed proper after careful divination in all directions. Thus will a monastic complex be constructed on this land bestowed by the sovereign.

And so, in order to repay above the kindness of the buddhas by spreading the esoteric teaching, and to augment below the resplendence of the five kinds of deities by liberating sentient beings, in sole reliance upon the secret teaching of the Vajrayāna, I wish to establish both the great maṇḍalas of the Womb and Diamond realms. With reverence I beseech all the buddhas to rejoice in, and all the devas to protect, my efforts here and ask that all virtuous spirits vow to help realize my wishes.

To the east, west, south, and north, and in the four intermediate directions, as well as above and below, within a circumference of seven ri: all maleficent spirits and deities within this area, each and every one, get out of my sacred ground. All beneficent deities and spirits in this area, those who can bestow advantage, may reside as you please.

Further, I request that from all directions, may the five kinds of devas, the deities of the five elements of earth, water, fire, wind, and sky, together with the revered spirits of the emperors and empresses of the court since its inception, and all the divinities of heaven and earth: may all these serve as sponsors of this place of religious practice. I most humbly beseech that all spiritual presences offer their protection day and night to help to realize this wish.

Respectfully declared.

Text of Declaration for the Consecration of an Altar at Mount Koya

I respectfully declare to all the buddhas, Prajñā, vajra-devas, and all the visible and invisible spirits still bound in the paths of karma: I hereby declare that this is my land. I will now set up, for seven days and seven nights, a great assembly on the Dharma altar. There I will worship all the buddhas, world-honored ones, in the ten directions of the Dharma realm; Prajñā-pāramitā; the many bodhisattvas with their followers, and I will firmly establish the teaching that is hard to comprehend and which is the repository of all esoteric dharmas. By thus availing myself of the superior power of these teachings, I will perform rites to protect myself and these sacred precincts.

In the east, west, south, and north of this compound, in the four intermediate directions and above and below, all the vināyakas who destroy the true Dharma, maleficent spirits and deities, every single one here: get out of the area of my sacred precincts, to the distance of seven ri. If there be beneficent deities and spirits who protect the true Dharma, who will bring advantage to my Buddha Dharma, you may remain in this compound as you please.

Before an image of the Tathāgata in this compound, with one mind in harmony with the Dharma, many monks will maintain the practice of the Buddha dharma, repay our gratitude to the four benefactors (of parents, kings, sentient beings, and the Three Jewels), and bring vast benefits to all beings. In reliance upon the rites of Kuṇḍali bodhisattva, for seven days and seven nights we will perform the ceremonies for establishing the sacred boundary, undergo repentance and engage in worship.

Within this monastic compound, to the east, west, south, and north, in the four intermediate directions and above and below, all the vināyakas who destroy the true Dharma, maleficent spirits and deities, every single one here: get out of the area of my sacred precincts, to the distance of seven ri. If there be beneficent deities and spirits who protect the true Dharma, who will bring advantage to my Buddha Dharma, you may remain in this compound as you please.

With the sincerest of hearts I invoke the palace of the Three Jewels, our most revered teacher Śākyamuni Buddha, the greatly dignified and powerful divine heart mantras, the excellent protector and liberator Avalokiteśvara, Vajra Kuṇḍali bodhisattva and the two Medicine King bodhisattvas who deliver from suffering, along with their holy assemblies, Vajra-garbha-rāja bodhisattva and his holy assembly, Brahmā, Indra, the four Deva kings, the Nāgas—all the deities and holy beings who protect the Dharma—I implore you all to enter this place of religious practice to assure the success of these rites. Please accept my request with pity.

—7—

Praises of the Drunken Peacocks

Richard H. Davis

Near the head of the Mahuar River in Madhya Pradesh, in the small backwater village of Rannod, sit the ruins of an ancient Hindu monastery built sometime in the tenth century C.E. On a wall of the veranda, carved on a stone tablet, a lengthy inscription praises the community of Śaiva monks who built and inhabited this monastic retreat in medieval times. The poet speaks of the Śaiva lineage called the "Drunken Peacocks" (*Mattamayūra*) as a stalk, "free of knots, its strong branches spreading widely." The poetic figure is historically apt, because other inscriptions from the same period found in many different parts of the subcontinent speak of more ascetics and teachers linked to the same lineage. The Drunken Peacocks appear to have been a broadly dispersed, celebrated, and influential group of religious specialists in early medieval India of the tenth and eleventh centuries.

Here I translate selections from three inscriptions praising the Drunken Peacock lineage. The first is from Rannod, ancient Aranipadra, about five miles from Kadwaha, which archeologists believe to be the ancient Mattamayūra, the "Town of Drunken Peacocks." Filled with the remains of some fifteen medieval Hindu temples, the hamlet of Kadwaha was probably the capital of a minor dynasty of Cālukya rulers in the tenth century, and became the prime seat of the community of Śaiva sages who derived their name from the town. The other two come from monasteries located about 200 miles to the east, in the villages of Chandrehe and Gurgi, along the Sona River in eastern Madhya Pradesh. In the tenth and eleventh centuries, this area was controlled by the Kalacuris, a powerful dynasty of rulers based in Tripuri, near present-day Jabalpur. As the inscriptions tell us, Kalacuri kings persuaded eminent teachers of the Drunken Peacock lineage to resettle in the Kalacuri dominion, where the monks were treated royally. A poet named Devadatta composed the Rannod epigraphical poem. The inscription at Chandrehe was composed by one Dhāmsaṭa, a Kalacuri court poet, Damodara wrote it out, and Nīlakaṇṭha engraved it into the temple porch stone on Friday, February 10, in the year 973. The praiseworthy poet Madhu wrote the Gurgi poem a few years later.

Courtly poets like Devadatta, Dhāmsaṭa, and Madhu speak in the intricate and highly laudatory rhetoric typical of medieval Indian inscriptional verse. Most often the poets direct their tributes toward kings, but in the examples here they single out religious specialists for special praise. Hyperbolic as the inscriptions may be, they nevertheless allow us to retrace some of the activities and travels of these Śaiva monks and to reconstruct a kind of collective portrait of this remarkable lineage. The poets describe the mythical origins of the lineage and its transmission from teacher to pupil, in disciplic succession over many generations. They praise the ascetic practices and virtuous conduct of the Drunken Peacocks, and their knowledge of Śaiva teachings. Most important for the court poets, these monks also come to interact with kings and queens. Drunken Peacock preceptors teach and perform rites like Śaiva initiation for Hindu rulers, and in return receive the royal patronage that enables them to construct temples and substantial stone monastic centers. Of course, it is also thanks to their intimate relations with royalty that we have these contemporary accounts of the Drunken Peacocks, for court poets celebrated only those religious specialists the court deemed worthy of royal favor.

The preceptors of the Drunken Peacock lineage adhered to the medieval Hindu school of Śaivism known as Śaiva Siddhānta, the "completed" form of Śaivism. By the tenth century it had become conventional to speak of four main categories of Śaivas: Pāśupatas, Kāpālikas, Kālāmukhas, and Siddhāntins. Of these, the Pāśupatas appear to be the oldest distinct school. Followers of Śiva as Paśupati, the "Lord of All Creatures," the Pāśupatas most often followed a renunciatory regimen of yogic practices along with certain special vows such as bathing in ashes, and conduct that was often intentionally provocative to orthodox sensibilities. More unconventional still, the Kāpālikas named themselves after the skull each carried as begging bowl, much like the one attached to Śiva's hand after his slaying of the god Brahmā. Kāpālikas tended to frequent cremation grounds, and used meat, wine, and other noramlly polluting substances in their propitiations. The Kālāmukhas, "black-faced" Śaivas, constituted a branch of Pāśupatas prevalent mainly in southern India. Of the four schools, Śaiva Siddhānta was the most respectable according to standards of ordinary Indian society. Followers of the Siddhānta based their practices and their theology on a group of texts called the Āgamas, revelations of Śiva himself (see Davis 1991). Like their fellow Śaivas, they practiced yogic austerities, and they were closely affiliated with Śiva temples, which became prominent in the religious life of early medieval India. As the inscriptions of the Drunken Peacocks indicate, these Siddhāntins were respectable enough to compete successfully with other long-established groups of religious specialists such as Vedic brahmans for royal support. The monks of the Drunken Peacock lineage gained their name from the monastic center Mattamayūra, apparently, and not by emulating the kind of wild behavior we might expect of inebriated peacocks.

All things must have a beginning, and an eminent medieval Hindu lineage of sages required a suitably ancient and holy source. In the Rannod inscription,

Devadatta provides a brief origin myth. Once in the Pine Forest, a famous Himalayan hermitage, the orthodox god Brahmā approached Śiva with all due devotion at the completion of a sacrifice. Śiva was so pleased by this sign of respect that he initiated Brahmā. This act of divine favor, claims the poet, engendered the line of Śaiva ascetics later to be known as Drunken Peacocks, as a fruit might contain a seed that grows into a far-reaching tree. The inscription goes on to trace a number of teachers of the lineage, culminating with the sage Purandara, who initiated King Avantivarman of Mattamayūra. Thus Haridatta traces the lineage's trajectory from forest retreat to royal capital, from the mythical interactions of gods to the worldly domain of kings and priests.

All the Drunken Peacock inscriptions describe interactions between sages and rulers. The Rannod inscription narrates what can be taken as a paradigm for proper and respectful reciprocal relations between ascetic preceptor and king. King Avantivarman hears about Śaiva initiation and immediately travels to visit Purandara at his ascetic retreat. The king shows his profound respect to the sage and finally persuades him to travel to his own domain. When the sage has been resettled, the king asks to receive Śaiva initiation (*dīkṣā*), the most significant and efficacious ceremony in the Āgama system of ritual. Purandara performs the rites, and the king subsequently becomes successful in all his endeavors. As a gift for his guru, the king offers Purandara the "essence" of his kingdom, and Purandara utilizes some of these royal resources to construct a great monastery in the capital city, Mattamayūra. Subsequently he builds a second monastery, identified as a "retreat for ascetics," some distance from the capital at Rannod, on whose veranda this account was inscribed. The remains at Mattamayūra and Rannod are among the very earliest Hindu monasteries archeologists have identified.

Although most inscriptions portray relations between sages and royalty in an equally ideal light, an inscription found in the Mattamayūra (modern Kadwaha) monastery (too fragmented to be included among the translations here) allows us to see some sensitive points in these interactions (see Mirashi and Shastri 1968). An emperor named Harirāja visits the monastery to receive an audience (darśana, literally, a viewing) with the pontiff, probably Sadāśiva, second in disciplic succession after Purandara. However, Sadāśiva first makes diplomatic enquiries into his identity: "Who is this king, who seems so full of life?" Only after an officer in the royal retinue has assured the sage of the king's pure descent within the Pratihara clan—the Pratiharas being the most powerful dynasty of northern India in the tenth century—does the sage agree to confer Śaiva initiation upon Harirāja. The king then tries to give Sadāśiva some of the royal elephants, apparently, as a preceptor's gift. Understandably Sadāśiva considers this inappropriate, and forces the king to make repeated offers before he finally acknowledges that "villages would satisfy me." The annual revenue from agricultural villages, of course, could support a community of monks in a way that no elephant, no matter how distinguished, possibly could.

More intriguing, the Kadwaha inscription also seems to describe a magical vendetta carried out by Dharmaśiva, Purandara's successor, against an intrusive local ruler. King Gobhaṭa comes to Dharmaśiva's hermitage and apparently causes the death of one of the monks. Giving way to rage, Dharmaśiva arms himself with magical weapons and emulates the god Śiva in his destructive capacity. For Śaivas, Śiva is simultaneously the agent of creation and destruction, the one who brings new worlds into being and who also annihilates them when their time has run out. Here, the poet tells us, Dharmaśiva defeats his enemy completely, as Śiva destroys the world at the end of the eon. Unlike Śiva, Dharmaśiva apparently dies in his effort, for the next verse compares him to the sun sinking behind the western mountain as his successor, like the moon, rises to dispel the ensuing darkness. The Kadwaha inscription is too dilapidated for us to reconstruct this event fully, but we are left with a fascinating fragmentary glimpse of a seemingly weaponless ascetic gaining revenge on a king who had failed to observe proper decorum toward religious seekers.

The inscriptions from Gurgi and Chandrehe trace one branch of the far-spreading Drunken Peacock lineage. As Dhāmsaṭa tells us in the Chandrehe eulogy, one of Purandara's successors at Mattamayūra was Prabhāśiva, who became famous far and wide as "crown jewel" among Śaivas. So esteemed was he that the Kalacuri ruler Yuvarājadeva declared him "master of all ascetics" and managed to bring him some two hundred miles to his own kingdom, where at great expense he constructed a monastery to accommodate the sage and his students. Yuvarājadeva's wife Nohalā had much to do with this invitation, for she was apparently granddaughter of the king Avantivarman initiated by Purandara, and she appears in other inscriptions as a great patroness of Śaiva institutions. Prabhāśiva and his followers constructed more monasteries and temples, making the Drunken Peacock lineage a powerful religious presence throughout the Kalacuri kingdom.

The Kalacuri branch was not the only limb growing from the Drunken Peacock stalk. During the early medieval period, religious figures affiliated with this monastic order appear in inscriptions found in Gujarat, Rajasthan, Maharashtra, Orissa, Andhra Pradesh, and Tamilnad, as well. The Drunken Peacocks were evidently at the center of a mobile pan-Indian network of Śaiva Siddhānta teachers and ascetics.

Although it is difficult to discern the sages described in these inscriptions as distinct individuals, one can see in the laudatory poems a collective portrait of the Drunken Peacocks as a distinctive community of religious specialists, differing from other religious figures who receive royal favor. During the early medieval period independent Hindu kings, members of the royal courts and other wealthy elites patronized worthy religious specialists by giving them land, gold, and livestock, and by setting up religious institutions like temples and monasteries for them. They did so, in the typical phrase, to acquire merit for themselves and others, or as the poet Madhu puts it, "to gain the great fame that comes from serving the good." But there were many who claimed the mantle of the good. Kalacuri inscriptions, for example, honor orthodox Vedic brahmans, courtly brahman ministers, and Pāśupata yogins as well as the Śaiva Siddhānta sages of the Drunken Peacock lineage. All are described as virtuous, but their virtues differ.

The sages of the Drunken Peacock lineage are, first of all, ascetics. They are renouncers who have left their homes and families. We do not hear of their caste, clan, or parents, as we do in inscriptions praising orthodox Vedic brahmans. Drunken Peacocks trace their genealogy from guru to disciple, in spiritual succession, rather than from father to son. As renouncers, they practice sexual continence, and the poets often remind us that the sages have extinguished all sexual desire through their austerities. They also fast or otherwise restrict their diets. Even as a young child the precocious ascetic Prabodhaśiva eats only fruits, roots, seeds, and greens. In addition to these bodily abstentions, the Drunken Peacocks practice yoga and meditation. In meditation they especially focus their minds upon the god Śiva. They seek to "perceive" Śiva or visualize him in meditation, rather than seeking to gain a state of objectless contemplation, as in classical yogic meditation. These ascetic practices are collectively known as tapas, a key term in these inscriptions that I have generally left untranslated. The poets envision tapas as a source of brilliant, fiery energy (often called *tejas*) that emanates outward from the ascetic. Like those other energy sources, fire and the sun, tapas produces both heat and light: it burns up impurities and sins and it dispels the darkness of ignorance and delusion.

Although the Drunken Peacock sages are renouncers, they are not as rigorous in their ascetic regimen as Pāśupata ascetics like Bhāvabrahman, who appears in another Kalacuri inscription (Mirashi 1955: 186–95). Whereas Drunken Peacocks sleep securely in their monastic retreats and receive regular stipends from their land holdings, Bhāvabrahman wears only a loincloth, makes his bed on a heap of ashes, eats only scanty alms, and is "addicted" to his practice of yoga. His yoga is the classical eight-limbed yoga outlined in Patañjali's *Yogasūtras*. The Drunken Peacocks seem less attached to the full scope of Patañjali's prescriptions, and more flexible in adapting specific yogic techniques to their own needs. Bhāvabrahman's Pāśupata austerity may place him farther from the hand of royal favor than the Śaiva Siddhānta sages of the Drunken Peacock lineage, for when he builds a Śiva temple near the Kalacuri capital, he does not rely on gifts from the king, but rather obtains the necessary resources by begging.

Second, the Drunken Peacock sages are knowledgeable teachers. They understand the great doctrine of Śaiva Siddhānta, which they have acquired through meditation on Śiva and through study of the Āgamas. The poets often compare the sages' knowledge and their beautiful elucidation to such sources of illumination as the sun and the moon, in their capacity to overcome darkness and ignorance. Like Tolstoy's proverbial hedgehog, the Drunken Peacocks know only one thing, but they know it very well. The poets seldom praise the Śaiva sages for their mastery of other traditional Indian disciplines of knowledge like grammar, or for knowing other genres of religious texts such as the Vedas. Compare this focus with the foxlike comprehensiveness attributed to Someśvara, an orthodox brahman who served as minister at the Kalacuri court: "He never felt doubt when it came to the Vedas. His knowledge of grammar was complete, he surpassed all reason in his logic, and he was not bad in his understanding of the

Tantric path either. He was first in Vedānta, and adroit when it came to remembering poetry" (Mirashi 1955: 305–9). Someśvara also knew about painting, music, the evaluation and care of elephants and horses, and the science of gemology. The Drunken Peacocks would respond to the challenge of such autodidacts by asserting the sufficiency of the one doctrine they did know. As Devadatta says of Purandara, "Even today scholars expert in worldly ways have still not refuted his teachings."

The inscriptional poets praise the Drunken Peacock sages for their good and pious conduct. Here the sages follow ideals of conduct largely accepted by ordinary Indian society, as well. They are selfless, benevolent, and pure. The personal purity of the sages seems to emanate outward from their persons and act autonomously on the world. When Prabhāśiva walks from Mattamayūra to the Kalacuri kingdom, his footsteps "purify the earth" along the way. Notwithstanding their name, the Drunken Peacocks do not engage here in deliberately provocative or challenging behavior, as Pāśupatas or Kāpālikas might.

The Āgamas divide their teachings into four main rubrics: yoga, theology, proper conduct, and ritual action. In Āgama texts the section on ritual is often the most extensive and detailed, reflecting the great emphasis Śaiva Siddhānta placed on the efficacy of ritual activity. In the Drunken Peacock inscriptions we hear surprisingly little about rituals performed by the sages—with one exception. The sages repeatedly perform the rite of initiation (*dīkṣā*) for kings. The Āgamas consider initiation to be the most potent of all ritual acts. There are two (or more) levels of initiation, suitable to aspirants at different stages of attainment. The first is "common initiation," which awakens the initiate to the knowledge and presence of Śiva and brings one into the Śaiva community. The Āgamas convey esoteric knowledge; only those who have undergone this common initiation may learn their teachings. More advanced seekers may subsequently undergo "liberating initiation" (*nirvāṇadīkṣā*), a much more ambitious ceremony that is said to burn up all one's fetters, as a blazing fire consumes a heap of cotton. According to Śaiva Siddhānta, only those who have been initiated in this way may attain the highest degree of final emancipation from all worldly impurities. The initiation that kings receive in these inscriptions is common initiation. Anything more would be inappropriate for rulers who continue to exercise sovereignty in the everyday world. This initiation is powerful enough, however, to bring them success in all their endeavors. The Śaiva sages who perform the royal initiations, on the other hand, have necessarily undertaken liberating initiation, as well as a supplementary "preceptor's consecration," which together confer on them the capacities to act as preceptor and priest for others.

For their great religious attainments, the sages of the Drunken Peacock lineage receive great fame (*kīrti*). The poets seem particularly fascinated by the charisma of these religious specialists, and describe it with many hyperbolic tropes. The reputation of the Drunken Peacocks shines forth to reach all people in the world. Note here again the use of light imagery, to evoke the glittering, glowing, emanating quality of celebrity. It is also reflected figuratively in their feet, glowing in the beams of light that radiate from the gems set in the crowns on the heads of kings who bow before them. Here the poets turn a common Indian act of etiquette, where a powerful political figure bows to show respect for a religious teacher, into an elaborate image of the universal fame of the Drunken Peacocks. According to the Chandrehe inscription, even the residents of heaven get into the act of celebrating Praśāntaśiva's glory.

Fame and glory bring us back to the king and court, for it is the fame resulting from their spiritual practices that first brings these sages to the attention of political authorities and court poets. The collective narrative of the Drunken Peacock lineage begins far from such royal centers, in the forests and caves where Śaiva ascetics initially practice austerities and meditate on the god Śiva. Once they come to royal notice, however, their lives may well change. Kings bow, propitiate, flatter, and ultimately persuade them to resettle in or near the royal capital. New associations with the elite allow the sages to receive substantial resources in the form of preceptors' gifts and royal land grants. They construct temples and monasteries, and increasingly take on administrative roles as priests and preceptors in these new religious complexes. The institutionalization of the Drunken Peacocks offers great opportunities for the promulgation of Śaiva Siddhānta. It enables the sages to transmit the teachings of the Āgamas to a wider audience, to maintain disciplic succession by training new monks, to worship Śiva in temples on a much grander scale, and to be available to the royal family for special spiritual counseling.

For some of the Drunken Peacocks, however, such responsibilities must have interfered with the simpler, purer ascetic practices with which the lineage began. We hear of preceptors like Praśāntaśiva who build special retreats for adepts (*siddhas*) and ascetics far from the madding crowd, where he could meditate peacefully on Śiva and converse with his more austere Śaiva cousins, the Pāśupatas. I end these selections with the poet Madhu's celebration of Praśāntaśiva's happy retirement in his spiritual retreat, while his disciples carry on the public works in the Kalacuri capital.

The story of the Drunken Peacocks, then, reflects an ambivalence toward worldly conventions and court life, a theme that runs through much Indian religious literature. The Drunken Peacocks are renouncers, but respectable ones. They move from the periphery to the royal center, but are then tempted to return to the more peaceful margins. They interact successfully with royalty, and use the patronage that comes their way to construct considerable religious institutions, but in the final reckoning a sage like Praśāntaśiva appears happier conversing with Pāśupata yogis than with courtiers and kings.

Were the sages of the Drunken Peacock lineage Tantric? When the Kalacuri minister and scholar Someśvara refers to his understanding of the "Tantric path," was he referring to the Śaiva Siddhānta teachings of his religious competitors? Much depends, of course, on how broadly or narrowly one defines the term "Tantra." It is clear that, among the four Śaiva schools of early medieval times, the Pāśupatas and the Kāpālikas were the most direct precursors (in style, if not necessarily in theology) to later Śaiva tāntrikas such as the Nāth Yogīs and the Siddhas. By this measure, Śaiva Siddhānta and the Drunken Peacocks appear on the conventional side. On the other hand, these sages distinguished themselves from Vedic brahmans and orthodox religious categories. They relied on the Āgamas revealed by the god Śiva, not the Vedas, as their primary textual authority. Through ascetic practices they sought to harness for themselves special supernormal energies or powers. They used initiation as a central act in their ritual system, and initiation acted as a necessary condition for receiving the esoteric teachings of the Āgamas. Finally, the system outlined by Śaiva Siddhānta employed many of the ritual actions that formed the basis for later Tantric practice—mantras, mudrās, the imposition of powers onto the body (*nyāsa*), meditative visualization, and the like. However we define Tantra, though, the collective portrait offered by these and other inscriptions of a far-flung community of sages and teachers who initiated kings in Śaivism and constructed monasteries to house their many disciples may give us a revealing sense of the diversity among the nonorthodox religious specialists wandering and teaching throughout India in early medieval times.

The inscriptions translated here were published in *Epigraphia Indica* 1 (1892): 351–61; and *Corpus Inscriptionum Indicarum* 4 (1955), edited by V. V. Mirashi, pp. 198–204 and 224–33. The fragmentary Kadwaha inscription was edited by Vasudev Vishnu Mirashi and Ajay Mitra Shastri in *Epigraphia Indica* 37 (1968): 117–24.

Further Reading

Other Kalacuri inscriptions referred to in this introduction may also be found in volume 4 of *Corpus Inscriptionum Indicarum*, edited by V. V. Mirashi. For historical reconstructions of the Drunken Peacock lineage and the Kalacuri dynasty, see Mirashi's erudite introduction ibid., pp. xvii–cviii; cxlv–clxiv. My book *Ritual in an Oscillating Universe: Worshiping Śiva in Medieval India* (Princeton: Princeton University Press, 1991) describes Śaiva Siddhānta theology and ritual based on the Āgamas.

Inscription at Rannod (Aranipadra)
Composed by Devadatta (ca. Tenth Century)

6. Once upon a time in the lovely Pine Forest
Brahmā performed a sacrifice following every rule.
Then he approached with devotion the One

Who can be perceived only through firm devotion
And He who knows every rule, Śiva granted him grace.

7. The holy fruit of that rite was the seed of great happiness
For from it arose a perfect new line of sages,
A tree whose strong limbs spread far and wide,
A flawless raft for us to cross the passions within.

8. In that line was born the sage who lived in Kadamba Cave
Like the Moon come to earth, rising daily, a form honored by all.
From him came that Indra among sages,
The pontiff of the Conch-shell Monastery.

9. By defeating desire, Terambipāla was equal to the Highest Lord Śiva.
Next came the head of Amardaka Tīrtha, a sage of great austerity and learning.

10. After him the guru Purandara, as weighty as the Guru Śiva,
Became head sage in the learned line.
Even today scholars expert in worldly ways have still not refuted his teachings.

11. That worthy sage glowed with unthinkable luster, bright as the sun,
Scattering his elevated words like rays beaming out from the eastern mountain.
When good King Avantivarman heard his lovely teachings on the subject of initiation
He immediately arranged to have that sage brought here.

12. King Avantivarman went to see the ascetic in Upendrapura, honored him profoundly,
Somehow or other brought him to his own territory and again he worshiped him.

13. The wise king requested and received complete Śaiva initiation. As gift to the preceptor
He offered the essence of his own realm and so achieved success in his own lifetime.

14. With a portion of his bounty the sage built a celebrated monastery, equal to Mount Meru,
Fit for those true gems, the good sages of the royal town known for Drunken Peacocks.

15. Once again that Indra among sages, matchless in virtue, built a splendid monastery,
A retreat for ascetics, known as Aranipadra, and consecrated it.

Inscription at Chandrehe
Composed by Dhāmsaṭa, 973 C.E.

1. In his cloud of twisted tangled hair
Black with hissing snakes and thundering
with the waters of the never-dying Ganges,
Flashes lightning from his forehead-eye.
Like moonbeams raining from his crown
his necklace of skulls gleams like a wreath of campaka flowers.
That Śiva rules!

2. White as a parade of swans it spreads across the face
of one dressed in elephant hide.
Then, for an instant shadowed by the blue of his neck,
it suddenly regains its glow,
The luster of the moon emerging from a cloud.
May Śiva's smile bring you good fortune!

3. The great snake's hood bows down as the bowl of Earth spins,
turned by nimble feet dancing a quick step.
The elephants of the quarters flee.
The Cosmic Eggshell whirls without end, twirled by his long arms
to the dense beat of the ḍamaru drum.
May Śiva's wild dance bring you delight!

4. And may the holy line of Drunken Peacocks purify the three worlds,
as does the Ganges!
In that line was born Purandara, ascetic and teacher of kings.
His pupil was Cūḍāśiva, bright
as the flame of a lamp burning on the fuel of tapas
to dispel the black pitch of impurity,
He stood on the path of liberation.

5. After that lord of the Madhumati came Prabhāśiva. He piled up great
tapas
Until he was crown-jewel among all Śaivas. Many rulers honored him.
King Yuvarājadeva declared him Master of All Ascetics.
He purified the very earth with his feet.

6. Then came his pupil Praśāntaśiva, a veritable Moon.
Pure, he showed his true form in a battle to dispel the dark.
He made good Śaivas blossom as the Moon does the lotus.
The radiance of his fame brightened the whole face of the sky.

7. He lived on fruits, roots, and bulbs.
Wherever his feet left tracks he purified the earth.

This friend of sages built the Ashram of Peace, known well by the people,
Where the Sona River meets the foot of Bee Mountain, covered in *priyāla* thickets.

8. In Indra's court celestial singers and dancers rejoice.
Nandi the bull drops his instrument to please his shaggy master.
The charioteer of the sun playfully shakes his hair, drops the reins,
And sings praises from on high.
So was the ascetic's eternal glory celebrated in the gardens of heaven.

9. Then followed Prabodhaśiva, best in the class of all his pupils
As Paraśurāma was best among Śiva's.
Defeating every rival, he projected his glory in every direction.
Giving money to the virtuous, he made Earth his debtor.

10. Like the god Kumāra he kept his hand busy
feeding the high flames of sacrificial fire
as Kumāra feeds his peacock,
He always avoided the company of women as did the young Kumāra,
The force of his power was proclaimed by a proud king
as Kumāra showed his dart to the high Krauñca Mountain,
He was devoted to Śiva, enemy of Kāma, as Kumāra is his beloved son,
And he accomplished all his divine duties just as Kumāra did.

11. He went through all the Āgamas. He saw God in ritual and meditation.
He ate only fruit, radish, seeds, greens, and lotus root.
Imitating his teacher, he did tapas on the river banks.
Even as a child he amazed the world.

12. He resembles the rising sun:
Kings light his feet with their crowns, as the sun's first rays glisten on mountain peaks.
He destroys ignorance, as the sun breaks up the darkness.
Starting from dawn everyone praises him, as they do the sun.
What more can I say?
Now he has risen to full glory, his brilliance spreads across the three worlds!

13. Digging up a great multitude of heavy stones, splitting them up, spreading them out,
He struck a path through the mountains, over streams and rivers,
Through woods and thickets, as Rāma did across the ocean.
A wondrous deed, this great work among the great
spreads wonder through the world.

14. The ashram at night: Breezes cooled
 With waterdrops from the Sona, the sky echoing
 With lions' roars, clouds of black bees hovering on mountain peaks,
 And from the glow of luminous herbs people become fearful of lightning.

15. Here troops of monkeys kiss the lion cubs
 A fawn drinks from a mother lion's breast
 Rivals set aside their hatred, for
 In the groves of ascetics every mind is pacified.

16. Near the temple of his teacher, Prabodhaśiva built a monastery
 High and wide as a white cloud, as is his own glory.
 And near the mountain that peaceful man dug a tank,
 Clear as a river, and a well with lots of water.

17. With time the well Praśāntaśiva made here
 Had collapsed and filled with fallen wood.
 But devoted to his teacher Prabodhaśiva fixed it up again,
 With a charming pattern of heavy stones, and dug it deep.

18. Mehuka was an initiate, famed on earth as a leader of good people.
 He had a son, Jeṭuka. From him, in Amarikā's womb, came the poet Dhāmsaṭa
 Who composed this poem of praise, bound with big letters.

19. Wandering through twists in Śiva's matted hair, waters stumbling over rock cliffs
 In the Himalayas, leaping in a wave to Earth, cleansed, thanks to Bhagiratha—
 As long as the Ganges, river of gods, flows to the ocean, master over all rivers,
 So long may Praśāntaśiva's fame remain firm on earth!

20. Renowned and intelligent Damodara, son of Lakṣmīdhara, brother of Vāsudeva
 Wrote out this poem of praise in elegant letters.
 By order of Superintendent Suraka, Nīlakaṇṭha inscribed it
 On the fifth day of the bright half of Phalguna, in the [Kalacuri] year 724.

Inscription at Gurgi

Composed by Madhu (Late Tenth Century)

1. Dreadful with the echoing shrieks of birds covering the earth
 Terrified, thinking it the end of the world, as
 the strong arms of demon Rāvaṅa, lord of Laṅka,

Shake and pile up crystal rows of Himalayan peaks—
May the Lord who lives on the mountain peak
Who by himself created this earth
  and wears the moon as his crest
Increase our joy!

2. "Nandin, who is this that has entered Śiva's home?"
"I think she must be the Goddess."
"Wrong, for I am not she and she is not me.
  Tell me, Śiva, who is that in your tangled hair?"
"Silly woman! It's the enemy of the gods, taking your beautiful form!
  Look, I've thrown him down before me."
"With what weapon?" Defeated by Pārvatī's sharp reply, silent—
May Śiva protect us!

3. The best of teachers of impeccable conduct,
Peacocks dance and shriek in drunken joy when
  out of season clouds appear
  arising from billows of thick smoke from constant sacrificial offerings,
Circles of dazzling light
  from the big glowing gems in the palace windows
  mock the world of heaven—
In all the world the Madhumati River is the home of the Siddhānta sages.

4. There in former times godlike ascetics, the turnings of their minds stilled by vows,
Came down and taught their pupils the great flawless doctrine of Śiva.
And even today their fame glows like the moon, whitening the earth,
Celebrated by all, delighting the excellent scholars as the moon pleases the breeze.

5. In this great line of Śaiva sages arose the most esteemed Cūḍāśiva.
With his blazing splendor he burnt up sin as a forest fire burns dry grass.
His fame, most radiant, which came from gaining perfection in knowledge
And meditation on Śiva's two feet, wandered through
  the palace of the three worlds.

6. His pupil was the wise sage Prabhāśiva, worthy of praise
  in all the three worlds,
Whose footstool glowed with the beams from the jewels in the crowns
  on the bowed heads of every king.

7. King Mugdhatuṅga's son Yuvarājadeva, who knows good conduct,
Brought him here on account of an innate trust
And made him take a monastery built with endless wealth,
In order to gain the great fame that comes from serving the good.

8. His pupil was the esteemed sage Praśāntaśiva
Where all desirable virtues willingly made their sole abode.
He became known throughout the world for his flawless tapas
And the power of his nourishing knowledge.

9. Enticed by the tapas he had collected so long
Goddess Fortune desired to join her body with him,
who always turned his face from pleasure to seek the Highest.
But when she received his command to serve others,
She dwelled faithfully in the homes of good people dear to him,
Like a devout wife who follows the vow of absolute truth.

10. Supported by the stake of his beneficence, sprinkled with the water
Of his gleaming knowledge, protected all round by the power of his spreading tapas,
The tree of plenty made up of his fame grew in time until
It forcibly filled the whole hollow of Brahmā's egg, this universe.

11. North of the temple glittering like Kailāsa's peak built by Yuvarājadeva
He too built a temple for Śiva. People thought it a rival
For the tip of Mount Sumeru, and all three worlds called it a marvel—
A stairway of his own fame leading up to heaven.

12. In the shrines connected to the main temple
That learned man of far-flung fame placed Pārvatī,
Śiva and Pārvatī together, and six-faced Skanda.
At the gates he posted Gaṇeśa and Sarasvatī.

13. And after he had satisfied seekers of wealth with gifts of burnished gold
He built a place for the Siddhas, away from the temple on the Sona River bank.
Yogis enter there and—inner commotions curbed in discipline, peaceful,
Undeterred in meditation, clear in mind—
they go straight to the land of the liberated.

14. For the complete rest of those whose minds are intent
On staying at a holy place the sage built a retreat for ascetics
on the banks of the holy river Ganges.

Those who live in Varanasi, who love to worship Śiva, after they visit it
Consider the ocean of worldly existence, though weighty, to be as
slight as the water in a cow's hoofprint.

15. The generous master of yoga sat still in solitude, tasting inner joy,
His firm mind fixed meditating on the Firm One, Śiva, at the center
of his heart,
And passed the days with those virtuous self-deniers
Wise in the Pāśupata philosophy of the Self.

16. Meanwhile, his pupils by their own lights lit things up as brightly
as all the rays of the sun—
Daily enlightening those who had fallen into the deep darkness,
Their fame ripening as they served others with the gift of vision,
the splendor of their commands carried by kings on their heads—
They moved about honored by the best sages and the people.

—8—

Precepts for an Emperor

Allan G. Grapard

The document translated here represents the views of Kūkai (774–835) on ritual and power, and gives insights into his articulation of the relationship between esoteric Buddhism and the imperial cultic system of Japan at the beginning of the Heian period (794–1185). This document was written for an important occasion: Emperor Heizei (774–824), who had withdrawn from public life in 809, asked Kūkai to confer upon him Shingon precepts, and to grant him an initiatory unction (*kanjō*) normally reserved to practitioners of esoteric Buddhism. Kūkai did so in 822. This was the first, but not the last time, that an emperor requested initiatory rites. As a matter of fact, such rituals became, during the medieval period, a regular part of enthronement rites.

In order to understand the conditions that guided the relations between power and ritual during the Heian period and thereafter, it is necessary to emphasize two issues. First is the way in which Japanese Buddhist ecclesiasts of the two major lineages of Tendai and Shingon esotericism cultivated good relations with the leaders of the Fujiwara house and the imperial family. From their inception and for much of their history, both Tendai and Shingon were geared to the elite, without whose political and economic support they might have faltered and disappeared. The relationship that was to evolve between these Buddhisms and the leading houses of Heian Japan was one of reciprocity: the aristocracy needed legitimacy, as well as relief from what it thought were certain obscure causes of disease and otherwordly causes of internecine and exterior unrest; on the other hand, Buddhist schools needed economic and other forms of support for their institutions and to uphold their own claims to legitimacy. Saichō (767–822) had been successful in restoring a modicum of communication between Buddhist institutions and the imperial state after the debacle that had led to the abandonment of the Nara (Heijōkyō) capital and the creation of the Kyoto (Heiankyō) capital in 794. Kūkai was instrumental in making esoteric Buddhism the main intellectual and ritual operative of the elite. One important step in that direction was his establishment of esoteric initiation and the taking of precepts as the late-life counterpart of autochthonous rites of enthronement. Kūkai established esoteric Buddhism at court by positing himself as the ritual guarantor of imperial legitimacy, by making esotericism the practice of aristocrats during the last years of their life, and by assuming responsibility for funerary rites.

The second issue is the place of ritual in Heian culture. Ritual was obviously more than rule-governed activity serving to bond sacerdotal and policy-making functions, institutions, and people. Even though sacerdotal authority and policy-making power were supposed to be merged in the imperial person, it seems that there was generally, at the social level, a perceived opposition between purity and power; and that ritual may have served either to annihilate or minimize the polluting aspects of the use of power and violence, especially in the context of territorial expansion and maintenance. This motif seems to undergird some of the passages in the texts presented below. Of greater importance, however, is the fact that Heian culture was marked by the development of a ritual economy of power, by which the legitimacy of the rulers was grounded in ritual codes and laws (elaborated in 859 in the *Jōgan-gishiki*, and further developed in 967 in the *Engishiki*), which were applicable to (Shintō) shrines in the entire country under imperial rule, and which stipulated what rituals should be performed where and when, and at what price—a price to be exacted from local governments and the general labor force. In the case of Buddhist temples, Shingon and Tendai both developed large-scale rituals to be performed on the levels of the state, aristocratic houses, and individuals. Heian Japan thus evolved into a highly ritualized state, in which both shrines and temples played a sometimes complementary, sometimes competitive, role. In other words, ritual was considered a powerful activity in both Shintō shrines and Buddhist temples, as well as in policy-making circles. The overall institutional framework within which these rituals were performed was named *kenmitsu taisei* (exoteric-esoteric regime) by the late Japanese historian Kuroda Toshio; its goal would have been the establishment of the Heian period's leading ideology of mutual support between Buddhist temples and Shintō shrines on the one hand, and, on the other, the imperial power structure (*ōbō-buppō*) through the maintenance of institutions and rituals for the protection of the imperial and aristocratic houses ruling the country (*chingo-kokka*). This arrangement manifested itself materially through grants of landholdings to shrines and temples, which the Buddhist temples and shrines associated with them used to establish themselves as major economic and political powers. In this set of arrangements and institutions, esoteric Buddhist rituals became dominant, and left such a deep mark on Japanese culture during and long after the Heian period that to ignore them would lead to gross distortions in our understanding of that culture as a whole. Needless to say, the type of rationalization provided by Kūkai in the text below was responsible, in part, for the success of this feature of Japanese cultic and political history.

By Kūkai's time, Buddhism had already become a tool of imperial ideology in China and Korea, and it would not have been accepted by Japan's Heian court if it did not provide, on the one hand, a comprehensive system for analyzing the human condition and, on the other, a beneficial political arrangement between the emerging imperial state and Buddhist institutions. For reasons yet to be determined, Kūkai felt a need to place Buddhist rather than Shintō shrines at the service of interests of the imperial house and its surrounding aristocratic houses. He also wished to convince his contemporaries that esotericism was a comprehensive world of symbols and an effective ritual system. There is no question that the overwhelming concern of the early ninth-century courtiers was to establish the supremacy of the imperial house, as seen in the establishment of Chinese law, the definition and codification of autochthonous ritual, and general support for, but control of, Buddhism. Kūkai's thought and activities fit this concern in the sense that he saw Buddhism as supportive of the imperial system in two ways. First, he posited the emperor as a manifestation on earth of the cakravartin, the universal monarch discussed in a number of Buddhist scriptures, apocryphal and otherwise. Second, he arranged for Buddhist rituals of protection of the imperial lineage to be performed in the imperial palace, and encouraged individual aristocrats to have various Buddhist rituals performed for a vast array of reasons and situations.

One of the ways Kūkai established Shingon esotericism in ninth-century Japan was through an emphasis on lineage. This satisfied a number of parties: the state with its intrinsic interest in state-sponsored historical records and genealogies, and several Buddhist schools' interest in grounding the legitimacy of new statements in (mainly fictitious) genealogies. The emphasis on lineage thus worked to locate new schools in the overall understanding of varied and often contradictory Buddhist doctrines and practices, and formally to establish normative access to new knowledge and ritual, as well as to legitimate secret transmissions from master to disciple. Kūkai wrote several documents on his lineage, and mentions it and his place therein in the document translated below; by initiating a retired emperor, Kūkai co-opted him, so to speak, and thereby attempted to assert the supremacy of esoteric Buddhist ritual. Secrecy and lineage became integral parts of the transmission of knowledge and practice in relation to power, and this system remained in place, both in and out of Buddhist esoteric circles, for better or worse, for nearly one thousand years.

One of Kūkai's central concerns is visible in his lifelong efforts to position Shingon at the apex of the various Buddhisms in existence in his time, both for the elite and other members of the society in which he lived. Nowhere is this more evident than in his most important and lengthiest work (still untranslated), the *Ten Stages of the Mind* (*Jūjūshinron*), in which he applies the doctrine of expedient devices or skillful means (*upāya* in Sanskrit, *hōben* in Japanese) to suggest that Shingon esotericism was at once the matrix and culmination of all Buddhist schools, as well as of Confucianism and Taoism. In this and other works, including the document translated below, Kūkai ranks eight schools of thought and practice in terms of two major analytical concerns: the depth and complexity of their philosophical achievements, and their appropriateness to radically different types of human psychological and intellectual tendencies and abilities. It may be argued that this double analytical concern dominates all of Kūkai's works; it is the central feature of his earliest work comparing Confucianism, Taoism, and Buddhism, as well as of his latest works.

In the document discussed here, this analytical concern manifests itself as a discussion of the relative merits and applicabilities of the "eight schools of Buddhism," which in Japan were more or less institutionalized by 822. These are the Ritsu, Kusha, Jōjitsu, Hossō, Sanron, Tendai, Kegon, and Shingon schools. Ritsu (*vinaya* in Sanskrit) refers to the disciplinary rules transmitted to Japan by the Chinese monk Ganjin (Jianzhen, 688–763); Kusha (*abhidharmakośa-śāstra* in Sanskrit), refers to the abhidharma set of philosophical, cosmological, and cosmographic considerations set forth in the document of the same name; Jōjitsu (*satyasiddhi* in Sanskrit), refers to a commentary that went largely ignored in Japan. Hossō refers to the so-called "idealistic" school of Yogācāra Buddhism that originated with Asaṅga and Maitreya in India; in Japan, this school was based in the Kōfukuji temple, the private institution of the Fujiwara aristocratic house. Sanron refers to the three treatises said to have been authored by Nāgārjuna, the central figure of the philosophy of emptiness that in fact forms the core of the various schools of Mahāyāna Buddhism. Tendai is the Chinese school based on the *Lotus Sūtra* and its Chinese commentaries, imported by Saichō (767–822). Tendai was so influenced by Shingon, however, that one came to speak of two esotericisms, the Shingon-based Tōmitsu, and the Tendai-based Taimitsu; these two sets of esoteric thought and practice were closely related. Finally, Shingon ("spell," *mantra* in Sanskrit) is the name given to the school established by Kūkai in the early ninth century.

Although he made it clear that he saw fundamental value in each of the schools, and different sets of people for whom these schools' teachings and practices would be appropriate, Kūkai insisted that Shingon was both superior to and inclusive of all of them. Kūkai was not, of course, the originator of this type of ranking and competitive assessment of Buddhist schools; known in China as *pan-jiao* ("doctrinal critique"), this practice had its origins in India. It subsequently evolved in China, within complex social and political circumstances, in order to demonstrate which school of Buddhism the emperor was to sponsor as the main guarantor of his legitimacy. Kūkai simply imported and refined the technique, using it to further his desire to convince his audience of the validity of his argument, that is, that Shingon was to be the principal philosophical and ritual arm of the imperial state. Although it is clear that esotericism prevailed, Shingon alone did not. Important questions with regard to this comment cannot be answered without further examination of the subtle and important differences between Taimitsu and Tōmitsu esotericisms, and of their sponsorship by competing political factions. Japanese scholarship is, in this respect, seriously lacking, in that it is usually dominated by modern but thoroughly outdated sectarian concerns.

Kūkai was well aware of the traditional distinction between the three parts of the Buddhist canon (the so-called Triple Basket consisting of teachings, disciplinary rules, and commentaries). He insisted, however, on a division into five parts that resulted in the separate treatment of a corpus of treatises on wisdom (*prajñā*) and of esoteric treatises and formulas (*dhāraṇīs*). He thus speaks in the document translated below not of a triple basket but rather of a quintuple system (the "five storehouses" or "containers"), in a move to assert the autonomy and legitimacy of esoteric teachings and practices.

Esoteric Buddhist traditions emphasize the transmission of doctrines through series of secret initiatory unctions (*kanjōs*), but accord greater importance to ritual practices considered to be the main vehicle for attainment of buddhahood in this body, that is, in the present lifetime. The Triple Mystery of body, speech, and mind is a set of technologies of the self ("the great self of no-self," *muga no daiga*), which consists of physical practices of control of the body, practices related to speech (the utterance of mantras and dhāraṇīs, and their corresponding meditations), and highly ritualized meditative practices based on a number of esoteric documents.

These practices are subsumed under the umbrella of the "four types of maṇḍala," graphic representations of the parallel structures of the cosmos (the body of the buddha Mahāvairocana) and of sentient beings. The four types of maṇḍalas are dai mandara, or painted maṇḍalas that represent deities; sammaya mandara, or convention maṇḍalas, in which the various deities are represented by various ritual emblems; hō mandara, in which the deities are represented by their seed syllables (*bījas*) and corresponding sounds; and katsuma mandara, in which the deities are represented separately in various forms and by symbols identifying their varied functions and virtues. Maṇḍala-based ritualization of the body, speech, and mind were thus held to transform common passions into their corresponding wisdoms, leading from the illusory notion that commoners and buddhas are different to the realization that people ensconced in passions are not separate from the Buddha. This highly organized and structured realm of practices that engaged the entirety of being obviously drew imperial and aristocratic support.

The text translated below comprises four separate parts. The first part offers definitions of Shingon's main characteristics: that the Body of Essence of the Buddha does preach; that the doctrine of the Three Mysteries is central; and that Shingon has its own precepts, which the retired emperor is about to take upon himself. This is followed by a description of the lineage of transmission of these teachings, that of the so-called Eight Patriarchs, to legitimate Kūkai's own position. In the second part, Kūkai outlines the differences between exoteric and esoteric Buddhisms, which differences account for the different types of precepts. He then discusses the eight schools of Buddhism in existence at the time, and stipulates that the precepts to be taken at this point are the samaya ("pledge") precepts particular to Shingon. Kūkai then discusses the various meanings of the Sanskrit term *samaya*, which is variously interpreted as equality, original vow, removal of obstacles, and attainment of awakening. The third part outlines the categories of canonical texts, classified by Kūkai as the "five storehouses": sūtra (scriptures), vinaya (codes of conduct), abhidharma (philosophical treatises), prajñā (wisdom literature), and dhāraṇīs (esoteric formulas, bearers of wisdom). Kūkai then discusses the eight schools of Buddhism current at his time, enumerating the different types of texts that form their basis, thereby characterizing the schools' tendencies and audiences. He uses this discussion to clarify the position of Shingon precepts within the overall framework of Buddhist teachings and practices. Finally, in the fourth part, Kūkai analyzes the Shingon precepts and emphasizes that practitioners of esoteric Buddhism are to develop four types of mental achievement: the confident mind, the great compassionate mind, the critical mind, and the awakened mind. Kūkai then defines the term "precept," discussing two of its features: vinaya (discipline) as control, and śīla (morality) as calm.

The source for this reading is *Heizei tennō kanjōbun* (Text for the Initiatory Unction of Emperor Heizei), dated 822 C.E. I have used the version contained in Katsumata Shunkyo, *Kōbō Daishi Zenshû* (Tokyo: Sankibo, 1970), vol. 2, pp. 117–45.

Further Reading

On the ritual economy of Heian Japan, see Allan Grapard, "Aspects economiques du rituel," *Cipango* 6 (Autumn 1997) (Paris: Publications Langues'O, 1997), pp. 111–50; Grapard, "Religious Practices in the Heian Period," in *The Cambridge History of Japan*, vol. 2 (Cambridge: Cambridge University Press, 1999), pp. 517–75; and Grapard, "The Ritual Economy of Power," in J. Breen and M. Teeuwen, eds., *Ways of the Kami* (London: Curzon Press, 2000). On the difficulty of translating the term *samaya*, see David Snellgrove, *Indo-Tibetan Buddhism* (Boston: Shambala, 1987), vol. 1, pp. 165–66.

Precepts for an Emperor

I.

Lest one be endowed with the legs of the asura, the eight-yojana-deep [seventy-one-mile-deep] oceans shall remain unfathomable; and lest one be endowed with the wings of the phoenix, the wind-blown summits of the nine mountains shall remain forbidden to sight. As the wide and solid earth will be reduced to cinders, so the mighty billows of black clouds will be dispersed by raging gales. Only upon the appearance of a great dragon does the wish-fulfilling gem produce its treasures. Should it be taken improperly, even the miracle drug [concocted by] the Universal Sovereign will turn to poison. What then should be said of the rare possibility of hearing the treasury of the Mysteries of Shingon, since they transcend the three categories of self-substance, self-aspect, and self-function? And what of the difficulty inherent in gaining the Adamantine Buddha precepts that transcend the ten stages leading to bodhisattvahood?

Who but members of the lineage of the Universal Monarch and the great bodhisattvas could unite the five wisdoms in their heart-minds and realize the Triple Mystery in their bodies? Under the insightful gaze of a doctor, a hundred poisons are as good as medicine, just as in the light of the Buddha's wisdom all living beings appear as buddhas. The corporeal nature of all living beings and the realm of essence of all buddhas are originally of a single flavor and are not distinct. However, those living beings who do not awaken [to this truth] are subjected to pain during their long slumber, while the buddhas are fully awakened and reside permanently in a state of bliss.

In disclosing the doctrine of Shingon, the Buddha showed the right way to those who are lost, so that all living beings might immediately awaken to their Buddha mind and swiftly return to the original source. That is why it is said in the *Kongōchōgyō* [*Vajraśekharasūtra, Taishō* 865]:

> The storehouse of dhāraṇīs and mantras contains the ultimate secret teachings of the Tathāgata [a title for the Buddha]; it contains the doctrine of self-awakening, its attendant knowledge, and the practice leading to its demonstration. Furthermore, it is the samādhi ("concentration") gate through which all bodhisattvas must pass in order to receive the incommensurable meanings of the pure precepts of the Buddha; it is the location at which, ascending the platform of the ocean-assembly of all tathāgatas, they will receive the various degrees of initiation and, transcending the triple world, will acquire the teachings of the Buddha. When all causes are collected, they will immediately bring together wisdom and broad virtues and, reaching the "awakening without superior," attain the point of no possible return. Having left all the gods and demons behind, with absolutely every passion, fault, and obstruction dissolved in each moment of thought, they will come to realize the quadruple body of the essence of the Buddha. This is known as the Buddha of Self-Nature."
>
> . . . It is also said in the *Rokuharamitsukyō* [*Taishō* 261], "All the teachings of the Buddha are contained in the five storehouses." Of these five storehouses, the sūtra-piṭaka is tantamount to milk, while the dhāraṇī-piṭaka is tantamount to ghee. Furthermore, it is said in the *Kongōchōgyō*, "The Buddha's metamorphic body achieved awakening in the kingdom of Magadha in the land of Jambu-dvīpa and expounded the teachings of the Three Vehicles to the various bodhisattvas, śrāvakas ["auditors," persons who attain emancipation while listening to the Buddha], pratyeka-buddhas ["lone buddhas,"who attain emancipation as a result of causal factors], and common folk he met. He would now employ teachings conforming to their minds, and then teachings conforming to his own. Those who, according to their capacities and in congruence with the expedient devices, put his teachings into practice—they shall gain the fruit available to men and gods. Or, obtaining the fruit of liberation of the Three Vehicles, they will—either by advancing or retreating—obtain the realization of buddhahood upon com-

> pletion of ascetic practices over three incommensurable periods of time, at the level of "awakening without superior." Born in a royal palace, extinct in the śāla grove, the Buddha bequeathed his body as relics. Those who build stūpas and revere him will gain the wonderful reward available to men and gods, and shall initiate the course whose end is nirvāṇa.

The above segment interprets the sermon of the Buddha in his body of bliss, residing in the heavenly palace of akaniṣṭha, in the fourth ecstasy at the summit of the realm of form. The proof thereof is visible in all bodhisattvas who have completed the ten stages and in all tathāgatas who fill the all-pervasive realm of essence. That Buddha jolts his own heart-mind into awakening; therefore, this [interpretation] is different from the demonstration of the immediate "awakening without superior."

The Buddha of Essential Nature thereupon released, through emanation from his heart-mind, an incommensurable number of bodhisattvas, all having one and the same diamond nature. Encountering that cosmic buddha, they acquired the various degrees of initiation. Expounding the doctrine of the Triple Mystery one by one, these bodhisattvas approached Mahāvairocana and all the tathāgatas, and requested the teaching of empowerment. The venerable Mahāvairocana then declared,

> As members of the Supreme Vehicle, in the future and for an incommensurable number of [time-]worlds, you shall be enabled to achieve both mundane and extra-mundane completions in the course of your lifetime.

Having thus received the Tathāgata's behest, all those bodhisattvas revered the buddha's feet. Circumambulating Mahāvairocana, they then withdrew, each to his original quarters in the cosmos where, becoming five-storied stūpas, these bodhisattvas held forth the banner of the teaching. And thus, whether by vision, by audition, or by penetration of the five circular maṇḍala platforms, they became proficient in extracting the karmic obstructions of sentient beings who wander about in the wheel of transmigration. Seated in the midst of five lunar circles, they moved from one buddha to the next, revered him and received his teaching, and thereby gained the "awakening without superior" and produced the confirmation of "no more rebirth." This is similar to the diamond that cannot be crushed. Such is the Assembly of Mahāvairocana. Thus did they become the symbolic body of Mahāvairocana. Each bodhisattva, each diamond, residing in its own deliverance, residing in its own concentration—and all residing in the power of the vow of great compassion—thus assists all sentient beings, far and near. Either by vision or by audition, all fully confirm their concentration and realize the immediate completion of all virtues and wisdoms.

This Mahāvairocana tathāgata, in his physical body in the realm of essence as well as in his quadruple body of essence in which the five wisdoms are realized, resides together with an assembly of vajrasattvas [thunderbolt-beings] and buddhas as numerous as specks of dust, either within the palace of the realm of essence or in the heart-mind palace of [the bodhisattva] Samantabhadra, and unceasingly expounds the secret storehouse of Shingon, the Unique Diamond Vehicle.

A long time ago, following the extinction of the tathāgata Śākyamuni, there lived a great master named Nāgārjuna; he was initiated by [the Master of Mysteries] Vajrasattva and thus gained access to the teaching of mysteries. His disciple Nāgabodhi received these teachings from Nāgārjuna. Nāgabodhi lived for over nine hundred years and had more than thirty faces. He resided in southern India, where he spread those teachings. His disciple Vajrabodhi transmitted those teachings to China when he arrived there in 720. His superior disciple Amoghavajra went to India between 742 and 746 to study under Vajrabodhi, gained [access to] the *Kongōchōgyō* and the *Dainichikyō* [scriptures] as well as to the five kinds of maṇḍalas [forming the Diamond maṇḍala], and then returned to China. Three emperors were initiated by him: they took the Buddha precepts and entered the practice of the Triple Mystery. Among Amoghavajra's disciples, eight received his dharma seal [confirmation]. One of those was Huiguo of the Qinglong-si [temple], versed in the teachings of the two [maṇḍala] realms and in no way inferior to his master's style. He bestowed the precepts to Emperor Dezong and to an imperial prince, and granted them the initiation. Huiguo was the seventh patriarch, the ācārya [supreme master] of the transmission of the doctrine. As for my humble self, I was fortunate enough to live in a peaceful world and to have developed a thirst for the Buddhist teachings. Living under the august protection of this sacred court and resting upon the compassionate power of the great master, on the thirteenth day of the sixth month of the year 805, I took the Buddha's samaya precepts in the Initiation Hall of the Eastern Hall of the Qinglong-si [temple] in Chang-an, and was granted initiation into the five parts of the maṇḍala. [Subsequently] undertaking a lengthy voyage, I forgot the brevity of existence and, throwing my life, precarious as a bubble, onto the seething waves of the ocean, I brought the two maṇḍalas and more than one hundred scrolls of scriptures of the Diamond Vehicle back to Japan, hoping thereby to repay my debt to the court. Favored by chance again, I was greeted by this imperial court, a manifestation on earth of the buddhas and a court that follows the enlightened policy of a cakravartin. Thus, in the year 806 I was able to present the court with the two maṇḍalas and a number of scriptures. Due to my own lack of a sense of urgency, however, seventeen years have already elapsed since that time. However, Heaven sometimes grants human desires, and due to a favorable convergence of circumstances I now face the dragon-face of the emperor and thus realize my humble wish. Simultaneously feeling exultation and sadness, it is is difficult to remain poised.

When reflecting upon the topic, it is clear that the present emperor has reached such an exalted status as a result of karmic conditions that developed long ago, and because the consequence of those conditions came to fruition in the lifetime preceding the present one. It is because compassion has not exhausted itself and because all living beings are here that he now manifests himself in this domain and exerts himself for the salvation of all. At the present juncture this [retired] emperor has withdrawn from public affairs and has set his mind to wu-wei [non-interference]. In order to protect the stronghold of the Buddhist teachings (*dharma*) he now temporarily displays his capacity for investiture in the Buddhist code (*dharma*) and, out of compassion for all living beings, deigns to listen to a sermon pronounced by an unworthy commoner. Is it not cause for joy that today the four classes of ecclesiasts, as well as the great and small of this world, have come to see the emperor and his son the imperial prince take these Buddha precepts so that they may quickly reach the stage of the buddha?

I thus humbly formulate the following vow. . . .

II.

This heart-mind of ours is greater than the Great Void; the buddha that is inside this self of ours transcends the realm of essence. Even the metaphor of the number of specks of dust in the universe is ill-suited to describe the number of temples; even the metaphor of the brilliance of the sun and moon is inadequate to express the radiance of the cintāmaṇi [wish-fulfilling] gem. There is no need for practice, since the pure awakened one is present within from time immemorial; there is no need for meditation, since the essence (*sattva*) of innate awakening is already naturally obtained.

The godhead endowed with the five wisdoms stands atop our neck, and the four types of maṇḍalas are comprised in our four limbs. The principle of utter suchness and the wisdom of absolute emptiness cannot be separated from one's body, in the same way that if one were to cut its feet off, one could not advance, or if one were to cut its hands off, one could not grasp anything. Ah, wonderful indeed are the maṇḍalas, wonderful indeed this Triple Mystery of ours! But it is precisely there that violent winds surge and stir immense waves on the ocean; it is there that dark clouds evolve and kick stunning dust storms into being. The tigers of empty dreams crowd every corner of the triple world, while the flowers of illusion shed their radiance in the homes of the four classes of beings. Foolish attachments to a self conceived either as a source or as an agent of being push their roots ever deeper into the heart, while the illusions of materialism and being further obscure our consciousness with their thickening foliage. Three types of foolish attachments cast their shadow to hide the light of the great sun, while the illusory thought of a true being as permanent, blissful, pure, and autonomous cloud the moon of awakening. Deeply ensconced in a sleep from which we fail to awaken, we dwell in the raging fires of the triple world. As a consequence, the twelve causal factors never cease to spur the wheel of transmigration, while the five aggregates (*skandhas*) and their ensuing eight types of frustrations never tire of their illusionist tricks. Father and son go on engendering father and son, and body-minds go on reproducing body-minds that appear and disappear. The suffering of birth, the suffering of death, the pain of aging, the pain of disease, the frustation of poverty, the frustration of wealth—these six types of suffering constantly threaten us, while hell awaits us all. When even the gods know no peace, what might be said of the human condition?

It is because the compassionate father of great awakening has clearly appreciated this situation that he dispenses antidotes for the types of disease we suffer from, that he devises method upon method to show how lost we are and to show us the way back to the original source. Just as there are distinctions between weak and strong poisons, so there are distinctions between shallow and deep doctrinal medicines. The vehicles, be they double or triple, are offered according to situation, just as the rafts of exoteric and esoteric doctrines are offered according to merit. But they are offered. Such is the reason for which the types of precepts vary structurally, in accordance with types of doctrine. As Nāgārjuna stated, "There are five types of precepts: men-and-god precepts, śrāvaka precepts, pratyeka-buddha precepts, bodhisattva precepts, and samaya precepts."

The precepts taken today are those of this final fifth category. The [conventional] ten good precepts are similar in the five classes outlined above; they merely vary in depth, according to the breadth of the issues. Furthermore, just as there are four and ten types of distinctions in the śrāvaka and bodhisattva precepts, there are distinctions in the samaya precepts [taken today]. However, their meaning varies even though their name remains the same. Thus, although the four types of precepts offered in the śrāvaka and bodhisattva categories are here as usual, they have a different meaning in the present case, to which we will return. [However,] let it be clear that it is not only the precepts but also the corresponding wisdoms that change accordingly.

If one is speaking of vehicles, there are five. If one is speaking of schools, eight offer different directions. These are: Ritsu, Kusha, Jōjitsu, Hossō, Sanron, Tendai, Kegon, and Shingon. The Ritsu school prevents harm from the seven factors that issue from body and speech: its four introspections lead toward the ultimate goal in which the body is reduced to ashes and knowledge extinguished. The Kusha school discusses the concept of the true existence of the three temporal worlds, whereas the Jōjitsu school teaches the emptiness of all phenomena (*dharmas*). Their aim is to realize arhatship, the goal of the Lesser Vehicle. The three preceding schools form the Lesser Vehicle. The Hossō school teaches the concepts of the eight forms of consciousness and the triple nature, proposes in a wonderful fashion the principle of consciousness-only without objects of perception, and broadly develops a universal doctrine of causation. It establishes a vertical hierarchy of fifty-two degrees, and expounds the view of three incommensurable units of time. The Hossō [teachings] thus put an end to those who are foolish enough to dispense with the law of cause and effect, and to those ignorant people who are led astray by the objects of perception outside the mind: they are a balm that soothes all living beings that are bursting with arrogance, and are [collectively] known as the doctrine of the samādhi of great compassion of [the bodhisattva] Maitreya. The Sanron school excels at teaching the principle of the eight negations, and in a wonderful fashion lays all false opinions and views to rest. It affords insight into what it calls the unique truth of nonproduction, whence it develops the concept of middle path of absolute and relative truths. This doctrine may be compared to a violent fire that consumes the three poisons and the four demons, or to a raging wind that disperses the clouds of false reasoning. It ranks as a superior medicine capable of sweeping away all attachments of body and mind, and of loosing all inner and outer obstacles. It is also known as the practice of the Mother of the Buddha of Wisdom, or of the samādhi [concentration] of [the bodhisattva] Maitreya. The Tendai school offers the teachings of the Unique Vehicle and of the Triple Introspection, brings forth the concepts of four teachings and of undivided suchness, and reaches its wonderful culmination in the concepts of a single thought-moment, triple truth, and mediate idealism. It is grounded in the foundations of the *Lotus Sūtra* and of the Treatise of Middle Introspection, and is centered on Mount Tiantai [in China, and Mount Hiei in Japan]. It is known as the practice of Avalokiteśvara, the bodhisattva of great compassion. The Kegon school is wonderfully apt at expounding nonobstruction in the Realm of Essence, and discusses at length the concept of harmonization of fact and principle. It thus annihilates the disease in which phenomena (*dharmas*) are conceived of as having an unchanging nature, and prescribes the medicine of nondistinction between mind and Buddha. Should one attempt to define its practice, it might be called the practice of the samādhi in the realm of essence of [the bodhisattva] Samantabhadra. The various teachings of the schools outlined above are as so many decrees from the Law (*dharma*) King, issuing from his governmental offices. They expand in depth and breadth, and display great limpidity and radiant effulgence; they are miraculous remedies applied in accordance with the occasion by Śākyamuni, the emperor of the Buddhist law (*dharma*) and king of medicine.

The code (*dharma*) that is about to be sworn to at the present moment is the Secret Maṇḍala performed by the tathāgata Mahāvairocana, who resides in the mind palace of the adamantine realm of essence, and who manifests himself as the five tathāgatas, who represent as many wisdoms in their quadruple body-form, together with their many inner cohorts. The tathāgata Mahāvairocana's attributes are virtues as numerous as the grains of sand in the desert, of which none whatsoever is lacking. That is why he also receives the name of maṇḍala, which has the following meanings: incomparable flavor, unsurpassable savor, and perfect circularity. Those who are to enter this vehicle must first abide by these precepts. These are named samaya, and the teaching is called mantra [Shingon]. The term *samaya* is Sanskrit; in its Chinese rendition it means original vow, equality, acquisition.

The term equality refers to the triple equality, since it indicates the equality of the triple mystery of body, speech, and mind. It is also known as the Three

Parts, which refer to the Buddha, the Lotus, and Diamond. All buddhas of these Three Parts possess the four types of maṇḍala and the quadruple body of essence. All these divine entities are equal to one other and there is no distinction of increase or decrease, of superiority or inferiority between them. That is why one uses the term equality. These divine entities exist in an incommensurable number; and this incommensurable number of buddhas all exist within a single being. This doctrine holds that one must fully contemplate all these buddhas within [oneself], and then go on to contemplate the buddhas within other living beings. It is in order to contemplate the buddhas within himself that the Buddha exerts himself in the contemplation of the Triple Mystery, and it is for the sake of other living beings that he practices according to that vow.

The term "original vow" indicates the lack of distinction that the Buddha maintains between himself and all other living beings. It is for this reason that he formulated this great vow, and that he practices compassion accordingly. This vow consists of the Four Incommensurables and the Four Acquisitions. It is of benefit to all living beings and saves all forms of life. This makes him the father of all living beings, something to keep in mind.

The term "acquisition" means entrance into the self and entrance of the self. The buddhas of oneself, numerous as specks of dust, easily enter the self of others; while the buddhas of another self, numerous as specks of dust, easily penetrate one's own mind's buddhas, and thus in complete reciprocity carry out the functions of acquirable and acquired, of potential and realization. If one meditates on this principle, one acquires the universal mind.

Furthermore, one may propose an interpretation based on linguistic grounds. The term *sa-ma-ya* refers to the Three Treasures, namely, to the Three Parts. The term *sa* refers to the various doctrinal truths. Truth is something that can be gained only through meditation in the practice of the samādhi of great compassion of [the bodhisattva] Avalokiteśvara. The term *ma* refers to that which the self cannot gain, namely, emptiness. Emptiness is another name for the tathāgata who does not promote false reasoning—[that is, the bodhisattva] Maitreya—and it is known as the practice of great wisdom. The term *ya* means vehicle, but refers to a vehicle that cannot be boarded. The vajrasattva of primordial being is without beginning or end, and knows neither production nor destruction; its nature is constant and equal to the void. Since it neither comes nor goes, who could board it? Its course has already been run. This is why it is termed "unboardable vehicle." The three virtues delineated above form the attributes of the tathāgata Mahāvairocana. Mahāvairocana's physical attributes are all subsumed under these three syllables, and it is in order to reveal this that the term *sa-ma-ya* is used. Should one grasp this concept and chant these three syllables, one will acquire absolutely all of the tathāgata Mahāvairocana's virtues and wisdoms. Expand on these concepts. I have been unable to offer them in a compact form. Of all the doctrines of the Greater Vehicle, this doctrine is the most venerable and the most noble. That is why it is stated in the *Rokuharamitsugyō* and in the *Shugokokkyō*: . . . [these two quotations are missing in the original].

III.

However imperceptible the dragon's breath may be, it can instantly stir the clouds of the entire universe into motion; and small though the eye may be, it can at once perceive immense depths and horizons. And what can one say of the asura's legs, able to fathom the depths of the ocean; or of the wings of the phoenix, able to carry it to immense heights? But these are still unconsequential metaphors: when it comes to evaluating the bodhisattvas' production of the mind of awakening, or the mental preparation of the vajrasattva whose heart-mind comprises the entire realm of essence and who treats all living beings as if they were the object of his fourfold duty, what can one say? They extract suffering from all living beings and replace it with pleasure. The extraction of suffering cannot be effected without correct practice, and it is impossible to grant pleasure without correct teaching (*dharma*). The terms "correct practice" and "correct teaching" cover practices and doctrines that are manifold by virtue of the multiplicity of occasions [for which they are appropriate]. The means to deal with situations and occasions vary accordingly. There are five major means to grasp the end and return to the origin. As is stated in the *Daijōrishū-rokuharamitsugyō*, immeasurable are the treasures of doctrine the tathāgatas have at their disposal:

> Five broad distinctions can be made. First comes the sūtra-piṭaka; second, the vinaya-piṭaka; third, the abhidharma-piṭaka; fourth, the prajñā-piṭaka; and fifth, the dhāraṇī-piṭaka. The sūtra-piṭaka is intended for those who enjoy ecstatic introspection in the forests. The vinaya-piṭaka is for those who enjoy living in cities and monasteries, who are interested in proper form, who wish to harmonize themselves and hold on to the correct teaching. The abhidharma-piṭaka is for those who do not enjoy the above two and prefer to polish the aspect of nature, or for those who enjoy the examination of deep principles. The prajñā-piṭaka is either for those who, not enjoying any of the above, distance themselves from attachments and false reasoning, and who, swiftly reaching a state of nondiscrimination, enjoy abiding in calmness; or it is for those who, not enjoying any of the above, quickly cut off all passions and enjoy exiting from the round of transmigration and who thereby attest to the body of essence. Finally, the dhāraṇī-piṭaka has been devised by the Buddha for those who break the quadruple injunction for monks; the octuple injunction for nuns; for those who perpetrate the five major sins; for those who ridicule the *Vaipulya sūtra* corpus, and for icchantikas ["willful ones" who never attain awakening] and other similar beings. The five storehouses [of doctrine] as described above are classified along the

> five stages of production of ghee: the sūtras are like milk, . . . and the dhāraṇīs are like ghee. Ghee is the most wonderful and delicate of all flavors and is able to cure disease in the same way as the dhāraṇīs. Dhāraṇīs enable one to destroy all obstructions to the cutting off all passions, to the swift realization of happiness and wisdom, and the witnessing of the immediate realization of the body of essence.

Thus five categories are established to classify the teachings expounded by the Buddha. As for those teachings that are expounded by bodhisattvas and men, there are eight schools: first, Ritsu; second, Kusha; third, Jōjitsu; fourth, Hossō; fifth, Sanron; sixth, Tendai; seventh, Kegon; and eighth, Shingon. The first three make up the Lesser Vehicle; the next four constitute the Greater Vehicle. The last one is called the Diamond Vehicle of Mysteries. . . . Thus the first seven schools constitute exoteric Buddhism. It is possible to suggest that their contents range from shallow to deep; nevertheless, these are teachings of various manifestations of the Buddha, medicines granted according to situations. Thus the great king of medicine dispenses his cures according to the type of disease and in virtue of the type of recipient. That is why the precepts vary in accordance with these categories of teachings. And this is why Nāgārjuna stated, "There are five types of precepts: men and gods precepts, śrāvaka precepts, pratyeka-buddha precepts, bodhisattva precepts, and samaya precepts." The precepts to be taken presently are the samaya precepts.

IV.

The twelve hundred herbal cures and the seventy-two kinds of medicinal preparations have been devised out of compassion for the ills of the body, just as the wonderful teachings (*dharmas*) in twelve parts and eighty-four thousand stanzas were expounded to relieve kindly the ills of the mind. Since the ills of the body are many, there is no panacea; and since the affections of the mind are manifold, the teachings found in scriptures are not universal. Thus the World-honoured One dispenses various drugs to cure equally varied kinds of afflictions. The five virtues of Confucianism and the five prohibitions form the basic medicine geared to the indigent child; the six practices and four introspections are best for that indigent one. The 250 precepts, the four introspections and the eight powerful concentrations, the twelve causal factors and the twelve practical vows (*dhūtas*) allow one to take evasive action from the human self and to affirm concentration (*sanmai*)—to keep the Dharma to oneself, and thereby attain nirvāṇa. These are soothing teachings for the śrāvakas, and a remedy for the pratyeka buddhas. Beyond these, the causation of compassion, the introspection of consciousness to fight illusions, the practice of the six perfections, and the application of the four means of conversion enable one to accumulate such deeds for three incommensurable periods of time and thereby gain the fruit of the four wisdoms: such are the medicines of the Great Vehicle.

Yet beyond gaining emancipation through rejection of the no-self, gaining insight into the unborn and awakening to the essence of mind—activities such as these enable one to wield the eight negations and cut through the eight errors, whereas rejecting the five attachments empowers one to expunge the five great prejudices. The four types of language thus lead beyond language and enable one to penetrate the realm of noninterference, while the nine types of perception are laid to rest: these are wonderful techniques that enable one to awaken to the unborn character of the mind. Or, contemplating one's own heart-mind in the middle of a lotus blossom, one reaches the point of unity between wisdom and the object of the senses. The three truths are harmonized and thereby shed light on the six types of immediacy; these are like acupuncture and cauterization, and lead to the unique heart of the way of truth. What then is to be said of the relationship between the realm of essence and Indra's net? One who contemplates one's heart-mind's buddhas, and realizes that gold and the lion are not separate and that waves and wetness are one, thereby delineates the intricate patterns of the doctrine of the six aspects and ten mysteries. One then perceives the distinctions between the five teachings and the four vehicles, realizes at once the correct awakening, and confirms the buddha fruit at the end of three lifetimes. That is, namely, the buddha fruit of the heart-mind of ultimate no-self-nature. All these wonderful doctrines cure the various affections of the mind in an undescribable manner. Such is the nectar expounded by the manifestations of the Buddha for the sake of others.

The samaya Buddha precepts to be granted presently are those of the Shingon maṇḍala teachings expounded by the body of essence of self-nature of Mahāvairocana. Should there be any good man or woman, monk or nun, or men or women of pure trust who should wish to board this vehicle and practice accordingly, they should first produce four types of mind. The first is the confident mind, second the great compassionate mind, third the critical mind, and fourth the awakened mind.

First, the confident mind is produced so that one may be empowered to maintain strong resolve without faltering. There are ten meanings to the term "confidence": purity, so as to purify and render the mind clear and bright; resolve, in order to fortify the nature of the mind; joy, in order to cut short all frustrations; lack of disdain, so that negligence might be abandoned; equanimity, in order to hold the same attitude in all situations; respect, in order that the venerable ones not be the object of spite; acquiescence, in order that one not react aggressively to words or actions; praise, in order that all actions be the object thereof; indestructibility, in order that the mind may remain set; and love, in order that the great compassionate mind may appear.

This great compassionate mind is also called the mind of the vow to practice. The so-called external ways and Two Vehicles do not give rise to it; however, bodhisattvas do produce it in such manner that when they look at all beings without exception in the realm of essence, they think that they are in fact looking upon themselves. The mindset of a good person puts others before oneself, and puts oneself after all others. Elsewhere, when looking at the three periods of time, all a compassionate mind sees are the four debts of gratitude, whose objects have fallen prey to the three evil destinations and thereby endlessly suffer. However, a good person regards all and anyone as his father, or regards himself as their disciple. Who therefore is in need of salvation but oneself? That is why one must produce the great compassionate mind. Great compassion is good at dispensing cures, whereas great wisdom is good at removing pain. . . . Though there are ten thousand distinctions in doctrines and medicines, their basis is formed by the eight vehicles described above.

As already stated, depth of treatment and speed of recovery vary with the types of afflictions and situations; it is in order to be able to decide which among many teachings is correct that one must develop the third mind, the critical mind. This is also called the mind of deep wisdom. How does one reach a judgment? It is like a superior man who, wishing to return to the home of his heart-mind through the practice of the Dharma, first requires a choice as to what kind of vehicle he will use. Should he desire to come to a decision concerning the superiority of certain modes of transportation, he should not rely upon the knowledge of the common man, of the Two Vehicles, or even of the bodhisattvas of the ten stages. He should rely solely upon the teachings of the Tathāgata.

The Tathāgata has clearly expounded those differences. One should therefore rely on his predictions and knowledge in order to reach a judgment. Commoners are engaged in producing a karma based on the ten defilements; they are enmired in the three poisons and the five types of desires and, what is more, ignore that they will be subjected to the sufferings of hell. This is why a Shingon man of knowledge does not become attached to pleasures. As far as the doctrine of the human vehicle for commoners is concerned—although it may be said that it instills belief in the law of cause and effect, and that it entices one to practice the five constancies and the five precepts—it must be emphasized that that is still a totally human cause and does not grant the joy of rebirth in heaven. Thus, one should not be attached to [its] pleasures. The vehicle of external ways, which allows rebirth in heaven, grants the pleasures of the twenty heavens that span the space between the residence of the four heavenly guardians at the bottom and the realm of nonthought at the top. Nonetheless, it still leads to the hells, and is unable to release one from transmigration. Thus, one should not be attached to [its] pleasures. The next vehicle enables one to exit the triple world; nonetheless, it is really of an inferior order. Is it not, in fact, unsatisfactory for those auditors (*śrāvakas*) who must pass either three lifetimes [if intelligent] or sixty kalpas [if foolish: a kalpa is an extremely long period of time], or seven or eight lifetimes just to take vows; or [for the pratyekabuddhas] four lifetimes [if intelligent] or eight kalpas [if foolish] of practice? Thus, one should not seek [its] pleasures. The two doctrines of the Great Vehicle require that one forget about life and grant his wife and children to others, and that one enter the ten thousand practices of the six perfections for a duration of three great incommensurable periods of time. The unbelievably great cosmic stone is high and wide and difficult to encompass, and the heart-mind is frail and therefore eager to retreat and unable to advance easily. Knowing that as a rule for every ten steps forward one takes nine steps backward, how can one persist? The "way similar to reality" wipes away the mind's filth and enables one to penetrates the realm of purity, and by harmonizing the realms of perception and wisdom it allows one to attest to suchness; nonetheless, it is still representative of the pleasure of knowing that one is on the path to truth and purity, and it therefore does not permit entry to the diamond storehouse. Thus, one also avoids this sort of path. It may be said that the mind of ultimate no-self-nature harmonizes with the realm of essence and attests to the body in the three periods of time, and that it is comparable to Indra's net and allows gain of the great unique body of essence; nonetheless, it is still the cause of realization of buddhahood as incipient buddha. It is not possible to complete the realization in the five aspects or the fourfold maṇḍala. One should not take this path either, because it seems to suggest that nonrealization is realization, and that nonarrival is arrival.

In this manner, basing oneself upon the teachings of the Tathāgata and forming the supreme wisdom, one is able to choose the best of all vehicles, and thereby give rise to the mind of awakening. Should one board any of the preceding vehicles and tread these paths, however, one will not be able to realize the pure mind of awakening. That is why the bodhisattvas of Shingon transcend these various stages of the mind and give rise to the mind of awakening, and practice such awakening. It is because they know the distinctions between the vehicles that they produce the critical mind of profound wisdom.

As far as the term "mind of awakening" is concerned, there are two major distinctions. First is that which is potential, and second is that which is fictive. In the case of the potential mind, imagine someone who wishes to do either good or harm: first, he must have such an intention, and then he must perform an act. Those who are in quest of the mind of awakening are not unlike persons in this situation. Or take the case of a madman. . . . Thus it is clear that [madmen] are like drunken people who find themselves in the prison of the triple world, and that, overcome by sleep, they lay themselves down in the bushes of the six destinations. How could they possibly board the vehicle of supernatural powers and swiftly return to the decorated seat of original awakening?

The fictive mind of awakening is the body of the inexhaustibly beautiful Diamond realm. The quadruple body and the fourfold maṇḍala of Mahāvairocana are coexistent with all living beings, with which they forever share absolute equality. However, people fail to realize this [truth] because the five obstacles obstruct the way, or because the three delusions block their view like a dense fog. If one meditates on the radiance of the sun and of the moon, chants the mantras, is empowered by the triple mystery, and is versed in the wonderful technique of the mystic hand gestures *(mudrā),* then the rays of the universal sun will shine forth, and all obstacles of ignorance will instantly dissolve in the ocean of mind. Ignorance will instantly become knowledge, and poison will become cure. The divinities of the seven parts of the diamond and of the three parts of the womb maṇḍalas will appear together in their circular perfection, and buddhas and bodhisattvas as numerous as the specks of dust in the desert or as drops of water in the ocean will spontaneously surge forth. To establish residence in this meditation is called the samādhi of mysteries.

The various tathāgatas take these three—the compassionate mind, the critical mind, and the samādhi mind—and make them their precepts, which they never abandon, even for a single moment. Why should these be called precepts? There are two kinds of precepts. The first one is vinaya, which translates as "control." The second is śīla, which translates as "purity" and "calm." When the Buddha sees living beings, he sees himself or the four objects of gratitude. That is why he refrains from killing. When he contemplates living beings, he sees his own body; that is why he does not steal their property. When he sees living beings, he sees the objects of gratitude; that is why he does not think ill or insult. . . . Since a buddha practices the compassionate mind, he naturally stays away from the ten evil deeds. To stay away from the ten evil deeds is, namely, the [semantic value of] precept as control. And since he stays away from the evil mind, his mind is pure and calm; that is the precept of śīla. It is also called the precept of benefiting animate beings.

Finally, when one looks at the preceding nine stages of the mind with profound wisdom, it appears that they have no self-nature. It is like the winter freeze that flows away with the thaw of spring, or like a piece of flint that disappears as it produces fire. All phenomena (*dharmas*) are born of causes, and therefore have no self-nature. That is why, ultimately, the resident of the first stage, though he be one-sided in his evil mind, can become a resident of the second stage if he comes into contact with the teachings of a good friend. . . . It is because all these stages have no self-nature that one can go from one to the next. Should one use wisdom to look at everything, then one naturally avoids evil, practices only absolute good, and benefits all living beings. These precepts are complete and perfect. It is the same for the samādhi of mysteries: [armed] with these precepts, those who board this [Adamantine] Vehicle can control their own body-mind and convert other living beings. Such are the Buddha precepts of samaya of mysteries.

Devotees and Deities

—9—

Raising Snakes in Bengal: The Use of Tantric Imagery in Śākta Poetry Contests

Rachel Fell McDermott

What is Tantra in Bengal? The Sanskrit Tantras important to the region since the fifteenth century list several central elements: selection of the proper teacher; initiation; mantra repetition; fire worship; construction of mystic diagrams (*yantras*); image worship; the honoring of young girls as embodiments of the Goddess; cremation-ground rituals performed to gain mastery over death; and the notorious "five M" ritual, in which wine, fish, meat, a type of intoxicating grain, and sexual intercourse (these are the makāras, all of whose Sanskrit and Bengali names begin with M) are used in controlled ritual circumstances—either literally (the hero's way), through comestible alternatives (the bestial way), or by enjoying mental substitutes (the divine way). Meditative techniques are also crucial to Tantra. The most famous of these is kuṇḍalinī yoga, or the practice of raising the serpent power through the seven lotus-shaped spiritual centers in the body (*cakras*) to the top of the head, where she unites with her consort Śiva. Each of these cakras—mūlādhāra (at the base of the spine), svādhiṣṭhāna (at the genitals), maṇipura (at the navel), anāhata (at the heart), viśuddha (in the throat), ājñā (between the eyebrows), and sahasrāra (at the top of the head)—has a different number of petals, with letters of the alphabet engraved on them, and is assigned a resident god, goddess, animal, element, one-syllabled mantra, and sound to be enjoyed as one passes through it. These lotuses are strung on a subtle channel called the suṣumṇā, "the path of knowledge" or "the path to liberation." Flanking it are two more channels, the iḍā to the left, symbolized by the moon, and the piṅgalā to the right, which represents the sun, whose influence is said to be poisonous, causing attachment to the senses. Especially significant are the beginning, middle, and end points of the journey: the mūlādhāra, where the serpentine kuṇḍalinī lies coiled three and a half times around the Śiva liṅga, waiting to be awakened and induced to enter the door to the suṣumṇā; the anāhata, where the Goddess is installed and visualized in the heart; and the sahasrāra, where Śiva and Śakti, often as male and female swans, make love, dripping nectar for the tasting. It is here that the soul achieves liberation and attains the blissful status of Lord Śiva. Often Tantric practitioners will meditate on special seats erected over the buried skulls of five "unclean" beings (jackal, snake, dog, bull, and śūdra). A final category of Tantric arts relates to the tāntrika's superhuman skills: he can cure with charms and protective mantras; prognosticate via astrology; and even attain mastery over nature through special powers. Because of these sometimes eccentric rituals, and the philosophical principle that worldly enjoyment can be a means to spiritual realization, Bengalis have often viewed Tantra as the upside-down path of the mad.

Although each of these topics is praised in the Sanskrit Tantras, they are not emphasized uniformly by Bengali tāntrikas. This chapter investigates what Tantra has meant to a tradition of Bengali Śākta poets who utilized its themes for their own purposes. What has been maintained, what ignored, and why?

The tradition of "Śyāmā Saṅgīt," or songs composed to the black goddess Kālī, began in the middle of the eighteenth century with a gifted poet and devotee of the Goddess, Rāmprasād Sen (ca. 1718–1775). In more than three hundred poems of praise, petition, complaint, self-exhortation, and meditative contemplation, he set the standard for the genre, and his literary followers—over two hundred as of the present day—have continued his lead in style and content. Two of his most famous heirs, Kamalākānta Bhaṭṭācārya (ca. 1769–1820) and Mahendranāth (Premik) Bhaṭṭācārya (1843–1908), mirrored his achievement not only in their composition of Śākta poetry but also in their religious lives; like Rāmprasād, they too are famed as Tantric adepts. All three have also inspired a hagiographic tradition, Rāmprasād since the 1850s, Kamalākānta since the 1880s, and Premik since the 1920s. Contemporary poets continue to add luster to the tradition, with new poetry collections and recordings appearing every year. One especially fine example is a man whose pen name is Dīnrām. Although the introductions to his published work contain almost no information about him, his literary output demonstrates that even if he is not a practicing Śākta, he has mastered the imagery superbly.

I take these four poets as representative of the Śyāmā Saṅgīt tradition; together they span two and a half centuries and include three men who are household names in Bengali Goddess-worshiping contexts. Although the Tantric images, valences, and messages of their poetry are of primary interest here, one must not forget the hagiographic lore that has grown up, particularly around Rāmprasād and Kamalākānta—and that "interprets" for us the Tantra of the poets' compositions. Such stories, when placed beside the poems they are meant to "explain," demonstrate the disjunction between poetry and commentary.

A caution: Tantric themes, though important to the Śākta poetric genre as a whole, never touch more than fifteen percent of any poet's total output. This is true even of Rāmprasād and Kamalākānta, the two figures whose Tantric proclivities are most famed. Far more common are Kālī-centered poems of adoration, supplication, and self-abnegation. Indeed, many poets omit Tantric themes altogether from their compositions. But the fact that contemporary poets like Dīnrām, a retired government employee, still incorporate Tantra into their work is evidence of its continued importance—even if it is ignored or feared by most.

Is the Snake Charmer's Son a Fool? Tantra's Redeeming Features

The most obvious Tantric influences on the Śakta poets are the dhyānas, or iconographic descriptions of the various forms of Kālī, to be visualized in or just below the heart cakra. The Sanskrit Tantras enjoin the adept to construct a jeweled alter in a temple of jewels underneath a wish-filling tree, on an island in a sea of nectar, and to establish the deity there for meditation. As so depicted, Kālī kills demons on the battlefield and then stands triumphantly on the chest of Śiva, also referred to in the poetry as the Great Lord (Mahādeva), the slayer or bewitcher of Lust (Madana or Kāma), and the enemy of the demon Tripura (Tripurāri). She is beautiful—a bejeweled sixteen-year-old—and her vision grants liberation (poem 1). This emphasis upon the installation of Kālī in the heart, or mind's eye, is consistent with the biographers' characterizations of the poets: Rāmprasād, Kamalākānta, and Premik were said to be proficient in meditation, which they performed on their five-headed Tantric meditation seats.

Sometimes the Goddess is not a static icon but an active partner with Śiva in erotic love making (poem 2). Watching this is so intoxicating that it befuddles the senses and opens the final door for the rising kuṇḍalinī (poem 3). The poet's demeanor changes, too; he becomes mad, like Kālī's crazy Bengali devotees Rāmakṛṣṇa and Bāmākṣyāpā (poem 4)—and like the Goddess herself, who is pronounced a crackpot for mating in the poet's head (poem 3) and blighting the creation with her injustice. You must have been on drugs, complains Dīnrām, who vows to be compassionate to the victims of her caprice, while nevertheless refusing to leave her (poem 4).

What about real sexual union? And the five Ms? In spite of the scope given to Śiva and Śakti in the sahasrāra, Bengali Śākta poetry makes almost no reference to the fifth M. This is true of all poets, from Rāmprasād to the contemporaries of Dīnrām. Indeed, by their stock denigration of the "six enemies" (lust, anger, greed, delusion, pride, and envy) and the "three strands" (goodness, activity, and ignorance), the poets display their mistrust of earthly passions. With the exception of a poem by Rāmprasād on cremation-ground rituals (poem 5), there are no poems in the entire Śākta corpus on external rites—whether exoteric deity worship or esoteric rituals involving the five Ms. On the contrary, a common theme in the poetic literature is the uselessness of physical rites, which cannot aid in the task of raising the kuṇḍalinī to the city (a common image for the sahasrāra) where there is no darkness, sleep, or unconsciousness. Expecting to find happiness from the world is like marrying a widow (poem 6). However, one can use the world to liberate oneself from it. Like the water poured into the ear to induce it to drain, or like the grandson Knowledge who kills the grandparents Worldly Attachment into whose family he was born (poem 6), Tantric philosophy encourages a careful recourse to earthly enjoyments. Hence the importance of the teacher, Śrīnāth, or the Lord.

Although the poetry of Rāmprasād, Kamalākānta, and Premik is thus strikingly lacking in references to ritual practice of any sort, the legacy of the biographic tradition is less clear. All three men were known as Tantric practitioners, and one can still visit the sites of their five-headed seats. However, all three were also householders. Although Kamalākānta is depicted as a man who learned the five M practice at Tarapith, a famous Tantric temple in Bengal, his biographers are quick to point out that he only engaged in the ritual with his wife, and never ejaculated. Premik deliberately gave up his overt Tantric practices—even ceasing to use his five-headed seat—when he began to have children, and counseled his followers to live a spiritual life within the acceptable confines of worldly expectations. Hence the poets' lack of interest in ritualized sex accords with the orientation of the Bengali tradition as a whole, which has a stake in representing its tāntrikas as practicing the "divine" or internalized path. From such a perspective, watching Śiva and Śakti in union is the equivalent of engaging in the fifth M oneself.

If ritual is not the main focus of the Śākta poets, let us turn to what is: the intricacies of kuṇḍalinī yoga. A few poems describe the entire upward journey, but most focus on a single lotus. One example we have already discussed: the heart lotus, where one enshrines one's chosen deity and worships her according to prescribed iconographic descriptions. Another is the ājñā lotus, where the three subtle channels, iḍā, piṅgalā, and suṣumṇā, come together in a plait between the eyebrows. This confluence, called the *tribeṇi* in Bengali, is said in the poems to be a spiritual Kāśī (Varanasi); "bathing" in its waters brings the highest spiritual cleansing and pleasure.

All four of our Tantric poets write about the merits of immersion at this confluence. One representative sample by Rāmprasād is an extended metaphor about pilgrimage, except that the destination is not a physical site. The horse of the mind pulls the six-wheeled chariot of the body (a reference to the first six lotuses of kuṇḍalinī yoga), with the soul for a charioteer and the two- syllabled Goddess, Kā-lī, as a passenger. Coursing past the five senses and their objects, impelled by the five vital breaths, the soul reaches Tribeni Ghat, where he refreshes himself (poem 7).

This type of poem has an odd history in the biographic literature. In Rāmprasād's corpus it acts as a proof-text for a story in which the poet plans a trip to Kāśī, but gets only as far as Tribeni—a town in northern Bengal—when the Goddess tells him that she is pleased with his efforts and requires him to go no further, since all pilgrimage places lie at her feet. The biographers have externalized the theme of the poem and devotionalized the moral, never hinting at the embedded poem's Tantric implications. The strain between poetry and biography is still more pronounced in Kamalākānta's case. He too writes poems on bathing at Tribeni, and his biography contains an almost exact copy of Rāmprasād's pilgrimage story. But the poems are not used as proof-texts. It is tempting to conclude that the narrative cloak created by Rāmprasād's biographers to obscure the meaning of the Tantric poems took on such a life of its own that later interpreters missed the connection between story and poetry. Premik's biography contains no reference at all to pilgrimage, internal or external, though he too composed poems on the subject of the Tribeni bath. As poets become less famed and the knowledge of Tantra less widespread, stories necessary to "translate" Tantric allusions for a devotional audience decrease in frequency.

The lotus that receives the most attention is the sahasrāra, where the kuṇḍalinī meets her mate. The bliss experienced here by the aspirant is encapsulated by two unusual images: inebriation and moonlight. In translating both through a narrative venue, the biographic literature is once again at odds with the poetry it is aiming to illuminate.

All four poets compose songs on divine drunkenness. In a kuṇḍalinī yoga context, the nectar or honey in question drips from the citriṇī, a narrow channel within the suṣumṇā, the entrance to the final ascent for the kuṇḍalinī at the sahasrāra. Generated by the blissful sport of Śiva and Śakti in union, it is the drink for which the aspirant thirsts (poems 8 and 9). Real drunkards are not tāntrikas, but those intoxicated by the sense objects, and the truly spiritual can tell the difference. Rāmprasād hints, however, that his erratic behavior may be more than just a spiritual trope; in defending his right to be "unrespectable," since the Goddess cares for the insane, he may also be justifying the use of wine in a religious context (poem 8).

Indeed, it is possible that these poems contain veiled clues to the first M. Rāmprasād and Kamalākānta not only devote songs to the subject of inebriation but also inspire their biographers to frame stories to justify their unconventional behavior. Both are accused of wine drinking by respected men—sometimes depicted as Vaiṣṇavas. Rāmprasād defends himself by singing about divine nectar. Although the poem does not make explicit mention of the juice dripping from the sahasrāra, it is clear from other poems in the corpus that this is his intention. No commentator or biographer ever warns the reader that this is what is being referred to, and prefers instead to let the poem be read as a devotional reference to the nectar of Kālī's name. Kamalākānta too is defamed as a drunkard, but instead of singing a song in his defense, he takes the jug of wine he has been caught with and turns it into milk. Although there are songs in his repertoire that demonstrate his familiarity with the "wine" dripping down from the thousand-petaled lotus in the head, none is ever attached to this story. The masks created for Rāmprasād's Tantric poems have once again, with Kamalākānta's life story, gained their independence. No biographer tells the reader that the poets may be defending the actual use of wine in a Tantric ritual, or that they are definitely promoting the idea of drinking divine ambrosia in the sahasrāra.

A third example of the disjunction between poetry and legend also concerns the sahasrāra: the rising of the full moon. In kuṇḍalinī yoga, the difference between the darkness of ignorance, as experienced in the mūlādhāra, and the light of consciousness, as realized in the sahasrāra, is explained by comparing the new moon, where all is dark, to the full moon, where light brightens everything. Thus when the poets exclaim that they have arrived in a city where the moon always shines, dripping nectar; where there is neither night nor sleep; and where opposites cease, they are referring to the topmost cakra (poem 10). Rāmprasād and Kamalākānta's biographers either did not know this or tried to conceal it in a common story. Both poets are challenged by irreverent contemporaries as to what day of the lunar cycle it is. When they reply, "the full moon," they are ridiculed for their ignorance; it is, they are told sneeringly, the new moon. No matter. That night both perform a miracle of self-justification and cause the full moon to rise, out of season. Poets like Premik and Dīnrām who are familiar with this Tantric moon imagery continue to use it in their compositions, though Premik's biographers feel no need to explain it away by recourse to his planetary prowess.

The Śākta poets also use kuṇḍalinī yoga imagery to exhort spiritual awakening through homey metaphors. The poet is a snake charmer learning his duties (poem 11). His body is a boat, where the kuṇḍalinī is the mast (poem 12), or a house where the sleepy mistress lies around with her man (poem 13). Alternatively, the kuṇḍalinī is homologized to elements of popular festivals. For instance, Dol, the Vaiṣṇava fair in which Kṛṣṇa and Rādhā are rocked back and forth on a swing and showered with red powder by their devotees, is used to describe the motion of Kālī seated on the platform of the heart lotus, held by the ropes of the three subtle channels (poem 14).

In sum, Bengali Śākta poets are selective in their appropriation of Tantric themes. Meditation is central; human teachers, external rituals, the five Ms, yogic powers—almost none of these make their way into the poetry genre. It is the biographers who are far more intent on the poets' supernatural powers: their abilities to command rivers, change the properties of liquids, and control planets. The fact that the events in these stories bear such a striking resemblance to kuṇḍalinī yoga imagery leads one to conclude that the poems came first, and were transformed by the contexts into which they were placed. Did the biographers do this purposely or not? We may never learn. One indication, however, that the earliest writers may have known what they were doing is a comment by Īśvarcandra Gupta, Rāmprasād's first biographer in 1853. After quoting one of Rāmprasād's most explicit poems about the raising of the kuṇḍalinī, Gupta says: "A sincere tāntrika, with a deep feeling for spiritual matters, will appreciate these immortal songs; no one else will be able to do so. This subject is extremely difficult. There are only one or two great souls left who can grasp the significance and concealed meanings of certain of Rāmprasād's poems, in order to explain them; nowadays almost all such people have disappeared" (*Īśvar Gupter Racanābalī* 2:23).

Whatever the intention of our poets and their interpreters, three things are certain today. First, poets writing in the genre continue to draw upon Tantric metaphors and language. Second, the average person continues not to understand such poetry, and even if the modern biographers do, they tend not to explicate it. Śākta anthologies routinely omit poems on kuṇḍalinī yoga, and recording studio employees freely admit that Śyāma Saṅgīt does not sell as well as Vaiṣṇava songs—both because the imagery is so abstruse and because the vision of Kālī or the kuṇḍalinī copulating with Śiva does not fit with the majority view of the Goddess as Mother, or Mā. Third, although one does not know whether the evidence preserved in the Śākta songs represents the whole of the poets' Tantric activities—one suspects not—one can understand the reticence an adept might feel in revealing everything in his poetry. Besides, although the literal use of ritual substances like wine, meat, and sex might awe the outsider, Bengali or Western, the tradition itself devalues it. Meditation takes precedence because Bengali Tantra places the "divine path," the path of mental worship, highest in the spiritual hierarchy. Sanskrit Tantras describe a range of Tantric injunctions. Bengali poets leave records that—although in an upside-down language—do not ultimately compromise their respectability.

The poetry translated below is taken from four anthologies, referenced in abbreviated forms: Kamalākānta Bhaṭṭācārya, *Śyāmā Saṅgīt*, collected by Nabincandra Bandyopadhyay and Bripradas Tarkabagish Bhattacarya (Calcutta: Barddhaman Maharajadhiraj Mahtabcand Bahadur, 1857), hereafter *ŚS*; Mahendranāth Bhaṭṭācārya, *Āndul Kālīkīrtan o Bāul Gītābalī*, 7th ed. (Calcutta: Prabodh Printers, 1987), hereafter *ĀKBG*; Satyanarayan Bhattacarya, *Rāmprasād: Jībanī o Racanāsamagra* (Calcutta: Granthamela, 1975), hereafter *RJR*; and Dīnrām and Kṛṣṇa Bhaṭṭācārya, *Sādhan Gīti o Svaralipi* (Calcutta: Sahityam, 1985), hereafter *SGS*.

Further Reading

At various points in the essay above I have mentioned "the early biographers" of Rāmprasād, Kamalākānta, and Premik. For Rāmprasād, the three most important are Īśvarcandra Gupta; see *Īśvar Gupter Racanābalī*, edited by Santikumar Dasgupta and Haribandhu Mukthi, 2 vols. (Calcutta: Dattacaudhurī & Sons, 1974); Dayalcandra Ghosh, *Prasād Prasaṅga*, 2nd ed. (Calcutta: East India Press, 1876); and Atulcandra Mukhopadhyay, *Rāmprasād* (Calcutta: Debendranath Bhattacarya, 1923). For Kamalākānta, see *Kamalākānta Padābalī*, edited by Srikanta Mallik (Calcutta: Aghornath Barat, 1885); Barddhaman Maharajadhiraj Bijaycand Bahadur, *Kamalākānta* (Burdwan: Rajbati, 1913); and Atulcandra Mukhopadhyay, *Sādhak Kamalākānta* (Dhaka: Ripon Library, 1925). Premik's biography is given in the introduction to his poetry booklet (see the sources, above). Almost nothing is known about Dīnrām. All of these, and more, are discussed in my *Singing to the Goddess: Poems to Kālī and Umā from Bengal* (New York: Oxford University Press, 2000).

Other English translations of Śyāmā Saṅgīt include: *Bengali Religious Lyrics, Śākta*, translated by Edward Thompson and Arthur Spencer (Calcutta: Oxford University Press, 1923); *The Cult of Shakti: Ramaprosad's Devotional Songs*, translated by Jadunath Sinha (Calcutta: Sinha Publishing House, 1966); and *Grace and Mercy in Her Wild Hair: Poems to the Mother Goddess*, translated by Leonard Nathan and Clinton Seely (Boulder: Great Eastern, 1982). For introductions to Tantra and secondary literature on the poetry tradition in Bengal, consult Asitkumar Bandyopadhyay, *Bāṅglā Sāhityer Itibṛtta*, 4 vols. (Calcutta: Modern Book Agency, 1955); S. C. Banerji, *Tantra in Bengal: A Study in its Origin, Development, and Influence*, 2nd rev. ed. (New Delhi: Manohar, 1992); Narendra Nath Bhattacharyya, *History of the Tantric Religion: A Historical, Ritualistic, and Philosophical Study* (New Delhi: Manohar, 1982); Mircea Eliade, *Yoga: Immortality and Freedom*, translated by Willard Trask (Princeton: Princeton University Press, 1969); Teun Goudriaan and Sanjukta Gupta, *Hindu Tantric and Śākta Literature* (Wiesbaden: Otto Harrassowitz, 1981); Malcolm McLean, *Devoted to the Goddess: The Life and Work of Ramprasad* (Albany: State University of New York Press, 1998); and Sir John Woodroffe, *The Serpent Power, being the Ṣaṭ-Cakra-Nirūpaṇa and Pādukā-Pañcaka*, 2nd ed. (Madras: Ganesh, 1989).

1. Rāmprasād Sen, *Śyāmā bāmā guṇadhāmā*

That black woman
full of virtue
stands playfully on Kāma's Killer.
What is She
  goddess, demon, elephant, serpent, woman?
The pearl hanging from Her nose
  like a *cakora* bird
  in the lap of the full moon
swings back and forth
  back and forth.
She smiles gently.
Now what's She doing?
Catching elephants on a battlefield
  with Her hands?
She's only a naked thin sixteen-year-old!

Her face is prettier than a blue lotus;
Her sweet smile flashes lightning.
As yet undeveloped,
Her budding breasts are bashful, and a slivered moon
illumines Her forehead.
How seductive! How beautiful! My heart throbs.
The sweetheart is young and well-behaved, with graceful movements
  and a gorgeous figure.

Demon throngs thrust themselves into the furious waves of battle.
Who is this, crushing my sorrows, breaking my pride?

She Who Destroys Everything.

Servant Rāmprasād says:
Remover of deep dense darkness,
the black, long-haired Goddess always dwells in my heart-lotus.
Victorious in this life and the next, I spit on Time.
My words are extreme
but for me
death is stilled.
I have entered God.

RJR no. 300

2. Kamalākānta Bhaṭṭācārya, *Bhālo preme bhulecho he*

So, forgetful Mahādeva,
You have fallen in love!
You got Her footprints
and now there's no separating You;
staring, staring,
You worship Her.
Her heavy locks of hair
darker than a mass of clouds,
fall disheveled over Her body.
Incomparably glamorous!
Who knows the greatness of either of You—
You, sky-clad sixteen-year-old,
and You, naked Tripurāri?

There is no end
to the bliss of Madana's Bewitcher.
Lying lazily under the woman's hold,
He thirsts for the taste of love play.
Saying endearing things
He makes love to the beautiful one
in the lotus heart of Kamalākānta.

SS no. 131

3. Mahendranāth Bhaṭṭācārya, *Baṛa dhum legeche hṛdi kamale*

There's a huge hullabaloo in my lotus heart;
my crazy mind is getting me in trouble again.

It's a carnival for crazies—
two madcaps copulating!

Again and again
the Bliss-Filled Goddess collapses
in ecstasy
on the Lord Ever-Blissful.
I stare at this, speechless;
even the senses and six enemies are silent.
Taking advantage of this confusion,
the door of knowledge opens.

Crazy Premik says,
everyone tells me I'm muddle-headed,
but can the son of confirmed crackpots
be normal?

Listen Mā Tārā, Remover of the World's Sins,
I'm going to cherish this moment;
and when at the end
I'm submerged in the water
take Your son onto Your lap.

ĀKBG no. 6

4. Dīnrām, *Kī sukhe tor paṛbo pāye*

Do You think I'd be happy
to fall at the feet
  of a mad bitch Mother?
You eat raw meat.
I'm so scared of You
my clothes fall off.
Rāmakṛṣṇa and Bāmākṣyāpā
went mad in Your embrace.
Who can be healthy and sane
when he loves You?

Your creation is so bizarre
You must have been on drugs.
I see Her swinging Her sword at a corpse
  hitting a man when he's down
and my eyes burn.
People line up in this world
to suffer and die.
That's why Dīnrām moves among them
sharing their sorrow.

SGS no. 29

5. Rāmprasād Sen, *Jagadambār koṭāl*

The World-Mother's police chief
goes strolling
  in the dead of night.
"Victory to Kālī! Victory to Kālī!" he shouts
  clapping his hands
and "bab bam!"
  striking his cheeks.

Ghosts, goblins, and corpses roused by spirits
  also roam about.
In an empty house at the crossroads
they hope to unnerve the devotee.

A half-moon on his forehead
a big trident in his hand
clumps of matted hairs falling to his feet,
the police chief is arrogant
  like Death.
First he resembles a snake
then a tiger
then a huge bear!

This may alarm the devotee:
ghosts will kill me!
I can't sit a second more!
He's turning toward me
  with blood-red eyes!

But can a true practitioner
fall into danger? the police chief is pleased:
"Well done! Well done! Kālī
of the Grisly Face
has empowered your mantra.
  You've conquered
  now and forever!"

Poet Rāmprasād the slave
floats in a sea of bliss.
What can trouble a practitioner?
Are frightful scenes a threat?
He stays sitting on the hero's seat
with Kālī's feet
for a shield.

RJR no. 134

6. Rāmprasād Sen, *Ār baṇijye ki bāsanā*

Tell me:
do you still want to trade, oh Mind?
Be content; do your austerities.
Then She'll owe you
  that Goddess Filled with *Brahman*
and you can collect your reward.

There's always air around a fan,
but only when you move it
do you feel the wind.
Oh Mind, that Goddess Filled with *Brahman* sleeps in your body;
stir Her up; wake Her.

If water gets in your ear, someone who knows the trick can drain it:
Oh Mind, he adds more water, and then it all comes out—
  or so the worldly say.

You house a great jewel,
but labor foolishly
in search of glass.
Oh Mind, the Lord gave you knowledge; hold onto it!
Open Time's door.
Then will be born
a strange being:
a grandson who kills old grandpa's wife.
Oh mind, birth and death rituals, prayers, worship—
they're all just trouble.

Prasād says,
not recognizing yourself, oh Mind,
is like dabbing vermillion
on a widow's forehead!
My God! What impeccable judgment!

RJR no. 37

7. Rāmprasād Sen, *Kālī Kālī bala rasanā re*

Tongue, call out
"Kālī! Kālī!"
Mind, my Śyāmā Mā
sits in a six-wheeled chariot with three reins
fastened to the mūlādhāra.

Endowed with five powers, Her charioteer
drives Her from country to country.
Her horse
charging ahead with the chariot
can cover ten krośas in a single day—
though when the chariot breaks down
he can't even move his head.

Going on pilgrimage is a false journey, Mind;
don't be over-eager.
Bathe at Tribeni; cool yourself
in your inmost chamber.

When your body's finished, decomposing,
Prasād will be cast away.
So, Mind, seize the moment;
time's running out:
call the Two-syllabled One
as best you can.

RJR no. 97

8. Rāmprasād Sen, *Man, bhulo nā kathār chale*

Mind, don't be duped by others' sneers.
They call you drunkard? Let them.
It's not wine I love
but nectar. Today my mind the drunk
is drunk, but drunks say
I'm drunk on drink.

Day and night sit at the feet of Śiva's queen.
If you don't
   and swallow the wine of the deadly senses
you'll fall under the influence;
your head will spin.
The cosmic egg itself
   filled with yantras and pierced with mantras
floats in that ambrosial water.
She saves us all
   Tāntrikas and non-Tāntrikas
so don't leave your path because of what others say.

Some believe the three strands birth all:
   Goodness gives us righteousness
   Ignorance feelings

  and Activity deeds.
They're deluded, Mind.

If you get drunk the conventional way
you'll fall out of beat, and the Out of Beat Goddess of Death
  will take you on Her lap.
Rāmprasād says, if
at your final hour
you've abandoned this path
you'll be shut out.

RJR no. 233

9. Dīnrām, *Prāṇjaṭhare agni jvale,*

From the time of the womb
a fire burns;
  Come, Mind, let's sit at Kālī's feast.
I am hungry for nectar,
  always in search of it.
The flame of my appetite burns;
look at all those delicacies of love
daubed with sandalwood paste
and arranged in layers
on the platter of devotion!

To the right of my tongue stands one woman,
  another to my left;
through austerities involving these two channels
the kuṇḍalinī awakes.
In the lap of darkness, on the empty path
  amongst the lotuses in the body
Dīnrām, the bee
delights in drinking that honey.

SGS no. 10

10. Mahendranāth Bhaṭṭācārya, *Ār kena man e saṃsāre yāi*

Mind,
why should we go any more
to the world?
Instead let's proceed to that town
where day and night,
blissful,

the full moon shines bright
   no waxing or waning
   no opposites reigning
no hunger or thirst and no eating or drink —
everyone plays with delight.

Nectar oozes from an ambrosial moon
but poison streams out from the sun.
With no *cakora* bird
   to follow your whim
   and drink to the brim
the moon steals its nectar away. Mind,
he who swallows this poison's exactly
   like you—
going to and fro
forgetting his learning
in the grip of a venomous
   burning.

Says Premik:
It's a fortunate person
who lives in that town.
For those who believe
in a personal God, The Unformed
   to Form
   makes a turning.

ĀKBG no. 181

11. Rāmprasād Sen, *Man re tor buddhi e ki?*

My Mind,
what sort of intelligence is thus?
You never learned to catch a serpent,
and now you wander
in search of tricks!
A hunter's son kills birds,
A fisher's son catches fish.
O Mind, if the snake charmer's son is a fool
will the snake spare him?
Playing with snakes is your caste duty;
don't despise those mantras
Mind, when your father asks you to catch a snake,
you'll hang your head in shame.
You got a treasure

but lost it through negligence.
What fool would reach for anything else?

Prasād says,
I won't lose it;
while there's still time,
I'll learn.

RJR no. 240

12. Kamalākānta Bhaṭṭācārya, *Tanutari bhāsilo āmār*

The boat of my body is floating on the ocean of existence.
My Mind, my good helmsman,
row carefully. See that you
don't drown me at sea.
Our oarsmen are the five senses and their objects—
but they're paddling the boat in the wrong direction.
  Please try to control them.
Steer the rudder in Kālī's name,
hoist the kuṇḍalinī sail,
and let's set off in a favorable wind.
Thwart the six
  lust and his band
with the great mantra
lest they harass us on our way.

Take Kamalākānta. Let's sing a boat song
in Kālī's name, and be happy.
For we're heading to the city
of ceaseless bliss.

ŚS no. 12

13. Rāmprasād Sen, "*Ghar sāmlā biṣam leṭhā*

Managing the house is a big problem.
The master of the house
is completely undisciplined;
he does whatever he pleases.
To him everything seems gross.

This house is attacked at its nine dread gates;
because of them I
constantly flail about.

The housewife always sleeps; day and night
She never rises. It's not just tiredness,
either. That female conspires
with Her man.

Prasād says,
if you don't shake that snake
who will wake Her up?
But once you wake Her
She'll start biting—
causing total panic.

RJR no. 128

14. Rāmprasād Sen, *Hṛt-kamalmañce dole karālabadanī Śyāmā*

The Black Goddess
with the rodent's teeth
swings on the lotus platform of my heart.
Mental winds swing Her day and night.
Eternal *brahman*, Black Śyāmā,
She's tied to the beautiful suṣumṇā rope
strung between iḍā and piṅgalā.

How She gleams
  Her body coated
  with blood-red dyes.
Lust, delusion, and the rest
take one look—and bolt.

He who sees the Mother swing
gets the Mother's lap.
So declares Rāmprasād
boom booming these words
like a drum.

RJR no. 320

—10—

The Wedding of Śiva and the Goddess in the *Kulālikāmnāya*

Teun Goudriaan

In our endeavor to understand the Hindu scriptural tradition in its astounding variety, we have to set up a number of distinctions as guidelines for our analysis. But such distinctions should not be understood as so many watertight compartments, because these hardly ever exist in Hindu religiosity. Two instances of such analytical preliminaries are the distinction between "ideology" and "practice" in the Tantric traditions, and that between "Tantric" and "Puranic" religiosities or literary traditions. The translated Sanskrit text presented below, *Kulālikāmnāya* 3.1–39 (this is the main version of the *Kubjikāmata Tantra* [*KMT*]), provides a good illustration of their relative validity. It contains a version, admittedly unique, of one of the best-known myths of the Epic-Puranic religious tradition; and it firmly connects mythological timelessness with the psychosomatic realization of spiritual truth and power which is the goal of Devī's rebirths

We translate *Devī* by "the Goddess"; the title Devī is very frequent in the Tantras as a name and a means of address. At first sight, the heading "Devī's rebirths" seems paradoxical, because the gods cannot die, and especially Devī, being the tangible manifestation of eternal Power, cannot be held to undergo death or rebirth. But in mythology this theological truth is not always respected. On the contrary, there are several mythological (and ritual) references to death and regeneration of divine beings (see, among others, Marglin and Mishra 1991). Without a doubt, the most important tradition about the succession of Devī's earthly existences is the mythological cluster around her death as Satī and successive rebirth as Pārvatī. The religious historian might be tempted to explain the paradox as follows: Devī's different existences are systematizations of different, even contradictory revelations about manifestations of Power within the realm of time. But the same could be maintained about Śiva or his manifestations, which are nevertheless only seldom said to undergo rebirth. It would seem therefore that "rebirth" is a typical prerogative of the feminine manifestation of the godhead—at least in the mythological sphere, where it probably reflects the observation of the recurrence of death and rebirth in the natural world. This state of affairs implies that the union of God and Goddess, absolutely necessary for the continuance and renewal of the world process, is periodically repeated—or rather, reenacted, actualized.

Satī and Pārvatī

The Puranic authorities generally agree that in her last but one temporal existence, Devī appeared as Satī, "the Faithful [wife]." She was born as one of the many daughters of a primeval father named Dakṣa. All these women, like Satī, bear allegorical names such as Śraddhā (Confidence) or Khyāti (Fame). We momentarily follow the authority of the *Viṣṇu Purāṇa* (1.7), where we are told, quite significantly, that Satī did not belong to the oldest group of thirteen who were married off to the god Dharma; nor to a second group of eight who were destined to become the wives of Brahmā's sons. In fact, the name of Satī (and, by the way, those of Svāhā and Svadhā) was undoubtedly appended to those of the original group at a later time. The mythic compilers may have felt that the ideal of the "faithful wife" was too important to be left out of this collection of allegories. Be that as it may, Satī was joined in wedlock to Rudra-Śiva. When her father on a certain occasion organized a magnificent sacrificial ceremony but forgot to invite her husband, she could not brook the insult. In a terrible rage she killed herself by means of a yogic procedure, as related in Kālidāsa's famous court epic, the *Kumārasambhava* (1.21). The *Kulālikāmnāya* author does not refer to this prelude; however, because of its extreme popularity, he cannot have been unacquainted with it.

The Purāṇas tell us how Śiva, inconsolable over the death of his wife, began to lead the life of a naked ascetic. In the meantime, Devī decided upon a new incarnation as the daughter of the divine mountain Himavant (the Himalaya) and the fairy Menā or Menakā (*Liṅga Purāṇa* 1.101.24ff.). Of special interest in connection with the fragment translated below is the version recorded in the Pārvatīkhaṇḍa of the *Śiva Purāṇa* (2.3.1–20).

Although the Goddess as Daughter of the Mountain is generally known as Pārvatī, she is occasionally given other names. Kālidāsa (*Kumārasambhava* 1.26) informs us that Pārvatī was the patronym by which she was known to her relatives, but that her mother Menā introduced another name, Umā, when she tried to dissuade her daughter from asceticism: through a strained etymology, Umā is explained to mean *u mā*, "Oh, don't (do it)." According to the *Liṅga Purāṇa* (1.101.24f.) however, the name Umā was already known to Brahmā before Pārvatī's birth. In the literature, Umā Haimavatī is mentioned much earlier, in an early Upaniṣad (*Kena Upaniṣad* 3.12). According to the *Rāmāyaṇa* (1.35.17), Umā was the usual name of Himavant's daughter. But these sources are silent about another famous name of Devī, that of Kālī or Kālikā. In the *Śiva Purāṇa*, this name appears in the present myth in a dual context. First, the Goddess is invoked as Kālikā by Menā, her future mother, who implores her to take birth as her daughter. Second, when this has been granted and the daughter has been born, she is given the name Kālī, along with other designations, by her father Himavant. Also here, the variant Kālikā (Blackie) occurs. The same name is prominent in the *Kulālikāmnāya*, especially in its first chapter, which deals with her premarital encounters with Śiva. Kramrisch (1981) records a remarkable explanation for the girl's dark complexion from the *Matsya Purāṇa*, which is generally recognized as a relatively early Purāṇa: Brahmā purportedly ordered his eldest daughter Rātri (Night) to enter the body of the pregnant Menā and provide the embryo with a black color. However that may be, it is clear enough that it would be wrong to associate the name Kālī solely with the well-known fearsome apparition who, bedecked with skulls and other gruesome ornaments, dances upon Śiva's corpse.

How Śiva Becomes Her Husband

When their splendid daughter approaches marriageable age, her parents consult the sage Nārada about the girl's future (here we continue to follow the *Śiva Purāṇa* version). The sage notices an inauspicious line in her hand and concludes that her future husband will be a naked yogin of shabby dress and devoid of family relations. The parents are shocked at first, but Kālikā is happy, because from this description she recognizes her eternal husband Śiva. She is more determined than ever to win him back. This purpose coincides with the gods' project of causing Śiva to procreate a son. Only such a son, they know, will be able to destroy a most dangerous demon who is about to conquer the threefold world. The demon's name is usually given as Tāraka. The *Śiva Purāṇa* (2.3.10) also records the origin of another enemy of the gods, Bhauma, "Son of the Earth"—a reference to his birth from a drop of sweat that fell from Śiva upon the ground. In his battle against the gods, Tāraka is assisted by his general Krauñca (*Śiva Purāṇa* 2.3.16.14). In the version found in the *Kulālikāmnāya* (3.3), Krauñca himself is the world-conquering demon; typical of this Tantra's different outlook is the fact that Krauñca is here said to have been born from the Goddess' (and not from Śiva's) perspiration. This must have happened when she roamed the earth as a virgin in order to install sacred centres of Tantric worship (as described in chapter 2 of the text, see also below).

In the meantime (we return to the standard *Śiva Purāṇa* version) Śiva, still overcome with grief and disgusted with the outside world, chooses to continue his asceticism in the region of the Himalayas. Himavant goes out to welcome him courteously; Śiva accepts his greeting but expresses his desire not to be disturbed in future. Nevertheless, Himavant (having noted Śiva's poor condition) soon returns with his daughter, whom he presents (with her full assent) as a housemaid. Śiva opens his eyes for a moment but closes them again immediately when he sees her dazzling beauty. Slightly irritated, he requests Himavant to leave his daughter at home on future occasions. But this is unacceptable to Kālī, who addresses Śiva with philosophical argumentation, proving that he as the cosmic Self cannot do without her as Śakti, eternal Power (*Śiva Purāṇa* 2.3.13.1–22). Śiva cannot refute her demonstration and has to acquiesce in her daily service. All this is told with a Puranic prolixity that tends to obscure the dynamism of the story. The Tantric version, as we shall see, is quite different.

The course of events now moves more rapidly. The gods, realizing that the time is ripe, send Kāma (Love), assisted by his friend Vasanta (Spring) and his wife Rati (Passion)—in verse 19 of the *Kubjikāmata Tantra* version, a second wife, named Prīti (Charity) is mentioned—to Śiva with the command to shoot him with his flowery arrows. He manages to release but a single arrow: Śiva feels its impact and because he happens to have Pārvatī in full view, he is seriously assailed by erotic passions. But he regains his self-control, and with a fiery glare from his third eye opened ever so slightly, reduces Kāma to ashes (this god too can die!). The episode is one of the most widely known of Hindu mythology.

The concerted attack on Śiva's chastity having failed, Kālī, in tears, returns home. But she soon finds herself again, and decides upon a course of the most terrible asceticism, the likes of which has never been experienced on earth (*Śiva Purāṇa* 2.3.22.61ff.). All the world's creatures begin to feel its impact. Even cats and mice live in temporary friendship. The gods, alarmed and once again fearing destruction, approach Śiva under Viṣṇu's leadership to request humbly that he marry Pārvatī. After some hesitation, the god, moved by their devotion, agrees. The world is again saved, and everyone joyfully takes part in the marriage ceremony, in which the most important gods act as officiants. As a matter of course, the rites are conducted according to the Vedic prescriptions. Viṣṇu (and not the bride's father, Himavant) takes it upon himself to give away the bride (*Liṅga Purāṇa* 1.103.45f.), and Brahmā acts as the invoking priest (*hotar*). Contrary to what one might perhaps expect in a Tantra, the *Kulālikāmnāya* (3.25f.) has preserved these time-honored ritual details. In verse 25, Śiva even complains (with a show of self-pity) that he cannot marry because the requisite participants are missing from the ceremony; but the gods provide a solution to this problem.

At the end of this rapid survey, we cannot but note the paradox offered by the myth in its different stages: is Śiva won over by Kāma's feat of archery, by Pārvatī's asceticism, or by the gods' devotion? In the *Kulālikāmnāya* version, the problem is less prominent, although present between the lines. Here (*KMT* 3.18), it appears that Kāma is burnt only after Śiva is already in Pārvatī's arms, when he, however love-stricken he may be, catches sight of his attacker from a corner of his eye (a masterly detail). But the god's passion is strong and the marriage seems unavoidable. On Devī's asceticism, the text remains almost silent, except for two brief allusions (*KMT* 3.12 and 24). But then, the gods' devotion is again described (*KMT* 3.21ff.) as the decisive factor by which the god's self-centered hesitancy is finally put aside.

The *Kulālikāmnāya* and Kubjikā

In the *Kulālikāmnāya*, the myth of the marriage of Śiva and Pārvatī is retold and adapted as a divine context for its description of meditation and yoga. In this way, the text firmly proves its attachment to the classical Hindu religious tradition. At the same time, it recognizes Śiva as the Lord of Kula (*KMT* 3.31), that is, of the "family" or "community" of those who follow the esoteric path and whose aim is final release through realization of the identity of their own self, the guru, Śiva, and Śakti. But its most remarkable feature is its introduction of an original conception of the Goddess characterized as Kubjikā (the Hunchbacked).

This cult of Kubjikā (also called Kujā, in *KMT* 3.22; or Kubjī, in *KMT* 3.31) must be an old subtradition from within the Kula, one that seems to have been limited to certain communities of Siddhas and yogins in northern India. Due to historical and climatological circumstances, the manuscripts of its Tantras and ritual guides have been recovered almost exclusively from Nepal. In this still imperfectly known literary heritage, we find several explanations of the Goddess's surprising deformity. The most probable view is that "hunchbacked" is an oblique reference to the coiled form (elsewhere compared to a sleeping serpent) in which she remains hidden in the lowest power center of the human body (the mūlādhāra; in the *Kubjikāmata Tantra*, perhaps the second center, the svādhiṣṭhāna). It may also be a reference to her crooked, serpentine upward course within the body of the meditating yogin. An attractive mythological explanation is offered in a secondary text of the school, the unedited *Kularatnoddyota* (1.75–76): the Goddess is so named because she huddled herself together out of shame when Śiva declared his love to her. This "down-faced" position might very well refer to the "sleeping" position of the kuṇḍalinī serpent mentioned above. Curiously enough, the Goddess after her wedding is still suffering of her deformity and professes to be ignorant of its origin (*KMT* 3.32). To the best of our knowledge, the Puranic traditions (with the exception of a late and secondary passage in the *Agni Purāṇa*) know nothing of this theme.

In any case, the *Kubjikāmata Tantra* makes clear that the premarital phase in the relationship of Śiva-Bhairava and the Goddess Kubjikā has not been without obstacles. On the contrary, a serious altercation between the predestined lovers has taken place, as described in the text's first two chapters. The bone of contention seems to have been the possession of the authorization to teach (*ājñā*) and the right to transmit teachings. The Goddess has even gone so far as to show herself in a fear-inspiring form (*KMT* 2.4f.), which later becomes one of her worshiped manifestations. While still a virgin—and therefore independent and awesome—she had taken a trip around the world (in practice, India) to establish sacred places devoted to her worship and populated by her manifestations. In the view of this Tantra, it is only after this task has been fulfilled that she is ready for her marriage with the god.

When the newlyweds are happily sitting together on Mount Kailāsa, the time is ripe for Devī to question Śiva on those matters that are of crucial importance to the earthly practitioners of the Tantric path—in short, the further contents of the *Kulālikāmnāya*. In this way, our text conforms to the general pattern of Tantric contextual anchoring. It must of course be realized that Devī poses her questions merely out of compassion for these devotees, being herself the source and final goal of all teaching. By her pretended ignorance, she even leaves herself open to her husband's ironical remarks (such as in *KMT* 3.33).

The first subject explained is the selection and excellence of the right guru (*KMT* 3.38f.). Thereafter, the text proceeds with the exposition of mantras and mudrās (gestures) in chapters four through six, followed by a discussion of Kubjikā's root mantra: the thirty-two-syllabled samayāvidyā (vidyā being the type of mantra directed to, and identified with, goddesses). In chapters 11–22, the bulk of the *Kubjikāmata Tantra*, Kubjikā's aniconic manifestations (mainly phonic and geometrical), as well as the yogic and meditative methods to realize these, are described. The final three chapters contain additional matter of importance to the Siddha's or yogin's way of life.

In this way, all the practical teachings of Tantric ritual and yoga are embedded in the context of the creative union of Śiva and Śakti or Devī. But this erotic frame does not refer to the sexual ritualism that the West has often considered, quite unappropriately, to be the main feature of Tantra. There are no clear allusions to such rituals in the *Kulālikāmnāya*.

A remark on the literary character of the *Kubjikāmata Tantra*: most of the text is in the śloka meter. This is also the case in the translated fragment, except for stanzas 17, 18, and 31 (which are in varieties of triṣṭubh meter); and 19 (in āryā meter). The *Kubjikāmata Tantra*'s manner of presentation is often unsystematic, incomplete, and at times even mystifying. The fragment translated below is no exception. The descriptions of events, and especially the dialogues and other fragments of direct speech, are allusive and evocative rather than factual. It is therefore possible that the translation contains a few misunderstandings of a speaker's intentions (for example, in verses 9 and 10). Moreover, the manuscripts show up a great number of variants.

The present translation of the *Kulālikāmnāya* 3.1–39 is based upon the text published in Goudriaan and Schoterman (1988). While translating, I have tried to remain faithful to the idiosyncracies of the Sanskrit, undoubtedly at the cost of the fluency of the English.

Further Reading

The only available edition of the *Kubjikāmata Tantra* is *The Kubjikāmatatantra, Kulālikāmnāya Version: Critical Edition,* by Teun Goudriaan and Jan A. Schoterman (Leiden: E. J. Brill, 1988). This edition has a preliminary character because many details of this difficult text are as yet imperfectly understood. A survey of the Tantra's contents may be found in pages 110–30 of the introduction.

A general study of the Kubjikā cult and its Tantric literature (which was written, as far as we know, entirely in Sanskrit) does not yet exist. The reader may turn to Jan A. Schoterman's pioneering study, *The Ṣaṭsāhasrasaṃhitā, Chapters 1–5* (Leiden: E. J. Brill, 1982), pp. 3–16; or to Dory Heilijgers-Seelen's carefully worded introduction to her *The System of Five Cakras in Kubjikāmatatantra 14–16* (Groningen: Egbert Forsten, 1994), pp. 1–12. The chapter entitled "The Pañcacakra" in the same book (pp. 16–38), although difficult, is worth the trouble as an introduction to the school's intricate microcosmic symbolism. Mark Dyczkowski's *The Canon of the Śaivāgama and the Kubjikā Tantras of the Western Kaula Tradition* (Albany: State University of New York Press, 1988), is of only partial relevance. A still useful general treatment of Hindu Tantric doctines and practices is Sanjukta Gupta, Dirk Jan Hoens, and Teun Goudriaan, *Hindu Tantrism* (Leiden: Brill, 1979). For the Puranic accounts of Śiva's and Devī's wedding and their earlier relations, see Stella Kramrisch, *The Presence of Śiva* (Princeton: Princeton University Press, 1981), pp. 301–83 ("The family of Śiva"), especially pp. 340–83 ("The Lineage of Parvata, the Mountain"); the rich material is, however, poorly organized. A selective reading of Wendy Doniger O'Flaherty's *Śiva, the Erotic Ascetic* (New York: Oxford University Press, 1973, 1981) provides an idea of Śiva's difficult character. A compendium of Puranic literature in general is Ludo Rocher, *The Purāṇas* (Wiesbaden: Harrassowitz, 1986). Orthodox Hindu marriage ritual is treated, rather technically, by Raj Bali Pandey, *Hindu Saṃskāras*, 2nd ed. (Delhi: Motilal Banarsidass, 1969), p. 153–233. An attractive (although somewhat remote) article on the death and regeneration theme is Frédérique Apffel Marglin and Purna Chandra Mishra, "Death and Regeneration: Brahmin and non-Brahmin narratives," in Diana L. Eck and Françoise Mallison, eds., *Devotion Divine: Bhakti Traditions from the Regions of India* (Groningen: Egbert Forsten, and Paris: Ecole Française d'Extrême-Orient, 1991), pp. 209–30. The article is also useful as an indication of the relationship between mythology and ritual, as well as of the social background of different types of oral and written textual transmission.

The Wedding of Śiva and the Mountain's Daughter

The Venerable Goddess said:

1. Relate to Me, O Bhairava: how was the marriage realized
   of You with Me; what was its cause,
   and what its object held in view?
   The Venerable Bhairava said:

2. You, O fair Lady, [having roamed
   the earth, enjoying maidenhood],
   had reached again Your father's home;

but as to Me: I was approached
with respect by the throng of gods
whose aim was to have Krauñca killed.

3. And how that demon had been born,
that I will tell You faithfully:
from You, while traveling with haste,
a drop of sweat fell down on earth.

4. From that, a demon was born
whose name was Krauñca; glorifying in strength.
By him, the host of gods in seven worlds

5. was put to flight: he was so mighty.
They, then, retired to Brahmā's place.
But Brahmā, at their head, went on
to seek refuge at Viṣṇu's side.

6. He then conferred with Viṣṇu thus:
"What can we do, being put to flight
by Krauñca, that powerful antigod;
please, Lord, point out [to us] a way

7. by which to crush him, Lord of the Bird!
Because of this, I sought Your presence."
But Hari spoke in answer thus:
"No being is able to take his life

8. if not Śiva's and Devī's son.
And why? He [Krauñca,] too sprang from that source."
Considering this, the Grandfather Divine,
[Brahmā,] spoke thus: "[Śiva,] that mighty Lord—

9. Where does He live now [as an ascetic], far away
from the Goddess's presence?" And he produced
a laugh: "Does a protector act like this?"
These were Grandfather's very words.

10. [And he continued, warning them:]
"Is He not full of power? his fire
might rise; scorched by that burning wrath
nobody who came with a request can live.

11. You, dwellers in heaven, will be lost,
laid low because of some presumptuous act!"
Thus they were brought to realize
by Viṣṇu['s message,] intimated by Brahmā.

12. But then, they spoke again and said:
"A means should be devised right now!
The Daughter of Mount Himavant
sits there alone in concentration.

13. The Lord's feet are her sole delight;
the Lord Himself is not so far away."
After these words, the famous pair
of youths, called Spring and blameless Love,

14. were summoned by the gods, and charged
to charm the minds of God and Goddess both;
and thus they did, after preparing flowers
and sprouts, in short: all [Nature's gifts].

15. Resounding with sweet melodies of cuckoos,
teeming with swarms of bees restlessly humming;
[Brahmā] duly observed Spring thus appearing,
and, with a voice steadied by his contentment,

16. at that great moment he proclaimed this [message]:
"the god of Love now hits the Fearsome One!"

17. And He, staring with eyes filled to the brim
by bliss, as He surrendered to his passion;
fixing a steady gaze upon that maiden
[and grasping her body,] He put her on his thigh;
while She [also] was full of longing, as her hands
were clasped around his neck. But even so,
in tight embrace, He cast a glance aside, and saw.

18. His mind aroused to shame, clouded by wrath
—that cosmic fire, destructive of the threefold world—
He wrapped [Love's] body in a flame. That god fell down,
dispatched within a moment by the Lover's lethal gaze.

19. When Love was burnt, the source of their delight,
his spouses, Charity and Passion, were reduced
to wailing long and loud, and hard to bear!
He saw them crying and [spoke]: "Forever gone
is now your common spouse, henceforth
the Bodiless; you both, please weep no more !"

20. The three-eyed God thus meted out
the punishment to Kāma. Punishment or grace,
Bhairava's wish becomes a fact.

21. But then, when things had reached this stage,
the throngs of gods together came;
the sages, demigods, and perfect beings
also arrived; Brahmā and Viṣṇu were presiding.

22. These two, Hari and Brahmā, praised aloud
with divine songs and lauds, the Lord of Kujā;
having thus satisfied Him, they spoke these words:
"Oh God, we have a pressing need forward to bring:

23. We lost [the blessing presence] of Your feet;
we gods, Oh God, have fallen on evil days:
pressed down are we by that impetuous being
of violent nature, Krauñca; Oh supreme Lord!

24. Protector, be benevolent to us, and by compassion—
we mean to say, grant us security . . .
Be kind, Protector, take the Goddess as Your wife,
her state is pitiful, She mortifies herself."

The Fearful One spoke:

25. "Where is She now, whose daughter is She,
who is her mother, who her [father and] father's father;
who will give her to Me, to whom
should I apply the wooing for her hand,
what can I do, a lonesome being without relations ?"

26. But Brahmā answered Him: "I am the one
to whom You can apply; I shall [on Your behalf]
ask for her hand; the sacrificer is [her father]
the Himavant; [Viṣṇu] the Ruler is the acting priest."

27. After these words, the Elder god
ordered Vasiṣṭha, being the chief
of sages: "quickly organize
the marriage celebration rites!"

28. The [sages] took their leave; they bore the order
faithfully on their heads. A festive scene
of wedding was prepared in costly style:

29. most glamorous, with excellent forebodings,
joyful and merry. From that time, every wish
of these [participants] was realized completely.

30. Now that the Fearsome's passion was aroused,
the Cosmic Womb became the ever fertile source;

with the creation of a threefold world in view
the God was then engaged in sexuality.

31. While He was lost in all too greedy passion
by fanciful varieties of love play,
intent upon the ritual production
of what the Kula knows as "fluid of immortality,"
that Lord of Kula, much attached to Kubjā,
was humbly questioned by his Lady, as follows:

32. "By the love You made to Me, My body melted down;
but, Fearful Lord, my burden is heavy:
this hunchbacked form of Mine."

The Fearsome One spoke:

33. "Goddess, expert in love play,
fulfiller of many desires:
today, You satisfied Me.
Dear Lady, ask whatever You like,
ask, even what may be hard to get."

Verses 34–37 are omitted.

The Venerable Kubjikā spoke:

38. "Be so kind as to explain to me, what is proper behavior; a Guru, how [should he be, because] the realization of all [spiritual] aims is dependent upon him alone.

39. "[Such realization] comes to pass by his mantras and ritual instruction, by his yoga; [in short,] his traditional authority. Dear Lord, please relate this all in a relaxed manner, but [if possible] within one session."

—11—

An Advertised Secret: The Goddess Taleju and the King of Kathmandu

Bronwen Bledsoe

The text presented here is an inscription from Nepal, a praise-poem named *Sarvāparādhastotra*, which King Pratāp Malla had hammered into the golden doors of the temple of the Tantric goddess Taleju in the middle of the seventeenth century. A public and literary text, the *Sarvāparādhastotra* offers a concise—if difficult—instance of Tantra's deployment in one historically specific social world.

Mise-en-scène

In late medieval Nepal, the temple of the goddess Taleju commanded the skyline of the city-kingdom of Kathmandu, while her principal servants—rulers of a dynasty named Malla—commanded the world of the Newar people. No structure in the realm could be build higher than the goddess's imposing temple in the royal palace at the heart of the maṇḍala-patterned city-kingdom. The Tantric goddess Taleju was literally and conceptually the most exalted being of the realm. No one could miss the fact of the goddess's existence or her power, yet access to her sanctuary was jealously restricted. Full initiation into the method of her worship amounted to consecration into kingship itself in the late Malla period (ca. 1600–1768 C.E.).

And just who might this goddess named Taleju be? There is still no definitive answer to this question, at least none openly spoken. The name may be derived from the Newari *tale*, meaning high or upper, and the honoric suffix *ju*; thus, "the deity of the high temple." Or, it may be a transformation of Tulajā, patron deity of the great Maratha king Śivājī (1630?–1680). In this poem the king addresses her as Kālī, a fierce Śaiva goddess with both exoteric and esoteric forms aplenty; he also calls her Kālikā, "little Kālī." Both the latter name and certain details of the poem suggest the authority of the *Kālikā Purāṇa* of Assam. Elsewhere King

Pratāp addresses the goddess as Caṇḍikā, Ambikā, Umā, Durgā, and Bhavānī. No doubt we are to understand that she is any and all of the Śaiva goddess's many forms. Informed scholarly speculation opines that her true esoteric identity is Siddhilakṣmī, high deity of the Northern Transmission of Kaula Tantra, but Taleju is not called by that name in public. Just who she is for practical purposes emerges from her supremacy in the kingdom, and her mastery over the king.

Pratāp Malla (reigned 1641–1674) was perhaps the most flamboyant king ever to rule in Nepal. Local chronicles and oral tradition remember him as a great tāntrika, a pupil of several famous gurus, and a protagonist of Tantric duels and deeds of daring. Pratāp was a great self-publicist, particularly fond of elaborate Sanskrit inscriptions, where he where he invariably signed himself "kavīndra", or poet-king. Pratāp's favorite topic of conversation was the divine company he kept, and his favorite conversation partner was the goddess he addresses in this poem.

Politics and Tantra

Kings had powers, responsibilities, problems, and potentialities that set them apart from other mortals. With our modern presupposition of a clear division between the domains of religion and politics, it might be thought that the proper concern of kings would be the exercise of power in statecraft, in the sense of administration and warfare. The historical record is, however, scanty on such mundane matters. What texts of all types do choose to speak of is the continuing quest of mortals to integrate their lived world with the worlds of the divine. Nowhere was this quest of more consequence for society as a whole than in the case of kings, for their extant words and works all indicate an overriding concern with what might be called "cosmopolitical order." By this term I mean a social and/or political order whose constituency was not confined to mortals but was actively extended at every turn to include divine as well as human beings in a single conceptual and practical frame.

Constructing an inclusive cosmopolitical order around a Tantric deity involved one major problem. Tantric knowledge and practices are by definition secret, whereas political life must be public. How could Tantra be deployed for public purposes without compromising its essential secrecy?

In general, the Mallas negotiated this problem by recourse to what Robert Levy has called "advertised secrets." This useful oxymoron breaks down as advertising, calling attention to the existence and importance of private deities, plus secrecy, maintaining resolute silence on particularities of content. Taleju's conspicuous yet inaccessible temple is a prime example of the advertised secret rendered in architectural terms. Royalty were not the only agents of the period to make use of the advertised secret: Newar Buddhists and some brahman lineages had also taken one or another variety of Tantric knowledge as the highest and most efficacious form of truth. Their deities too were announced and concealed in special architectural structures; their initiations too authorized roles of privilege in society.

Kings had the responsibility to maintain continuities between sociopolitical order on earth and an encompassing universe of divine powers. That is, they were concerned with the lives of the gods, and with the lives of mortals defined as servants of the gods. In the Kathmandu Valley, temples by the hundreds and thousands were the principal sites for the articulation of cosmopolitical order, for service to deities new and old generated complex networks of obligation and privilege among mortals of all classes. Inscriptions on these temples constituted a public and permanent discourse on relations of cosmic and mortal power. It is probably true that only a small proportion of the king's subjects could read the letters placed on display in inscriptions, and even fewer would have been able to penetrate the stylized Sanskrit verse. But we should not doubt that most people would have had a substantial understanding of what was being said. The king was the foremost servant of the goddess; thus he was foremost among mortals; therefore he should be served by all other mortals. This was the logic in force.

The poet-king Pratāp did not put the matter so bluntly. Inscriptions were traditionally a medium for display of Sanskrit literary virtuosity, and more than any Nepali king, Pratāp turned the subtleties and sophistication of Sanskrit poetic convention to the articulation of power. His problem with respect to the Tantric goddess was to speak of her without compromising the esoteric heart of the relationship. His solution, I suggest, was to preserve the intimacy of the king/goddess dyad by overlaying its esoteric heart with a reformulation centered on exoteric devotion. Within the frame of exoteric devotion, Pratāp constructed his own kingly persona by juxtaposing the special forms of knowledge of which he was master with a posture of extravagant humility. Among these special forms of knowledge was his understanding of the goddess's role in the realm as a whole: she commanded not only him, but his city-kingdom, and ultimately the universe. As an open and public production, the inscription is amenable to an exoteric surface reading. But the poem's very construction—through display and concealment, contrast and camouflage—invites penetration beyond its façade.

Explicit Arguments and Counterevidence

The overt message of Pratāp's *Sarvāparādhastotra*, or "Hymn for the Forgiveness of All Faults," is resolutely exoteric. It is quite possible to read past its esoteric component with barely a pause. In mood, the poem is confessional rather than perfection-seeking; goddess and practitioner relate as mother and child, without hint of erotic charge. Its literary category is stotra, "praise," "eulogy," or "hymn." Its genre in the conventional division of Indic religious modes is that of bhakti, "devotion" or "participation." What the poet craves is an intimacy with the goddess that is profound but in no way secret. The poem's overall thrust and overriding tone are encoded in an insistent refrain, "O Mother, let my faults be forgiven! Kālikā, Treasure of Victory, be gracious."

The poem's explicit argument centers on the king's abject failure to accomplish what he should have accomplished, namely, service to the deity—service in the form of worship and knowledge, or at least exquisite eulogy. The obstacles to her service, his lapses, and his inadequacies are inventoried and examined one after another. The impossibility of achieving her grace through individual effort is argued in the first half of the poem, which presents obstacles and inadequacies by category. It opens with four strong verses on the impediments entailed in the various stages of life: infancy, childhood, youth, and old age each constrains mind and body in some way to prevent her worship. Then the king speaks of the failures of paths (*mārgas*) and performative practices (*vidhis*). Orthodoxies include revealed and "remembered" brahmanical wisdom, esoteric knowledge and practice, simple acts of devotion performed by bodily and mental faculties—according to the poem, the king has succeeded in none of these.

One important result of the inventory of failures is to focus attention on Pratāp Malla. It is the figure of the poet-king, not of the goddess, that is carefully constructed throughout the stotra. The critical point in the poem's construction of the king is the status of the faults or failings (*aparādha*) around which it revolves. The word *aparādha* could be taken more strongly: "offense" or "outrage" is not going too far. In large measure, the force of the poem derives from the tension between the king's self-deprecation and the mass of internal and external evidence to the contrary.

Few of the poet's statements concerning his failings can be taken at face value. Some are indeed rooted in human inevitabilities, as with the age-determined constraints on mind and body. Most demand active interpretation. One clear example is the king's apology (at verse 16) that the goddess's worship had not been performed at her temple at festival time, through his "wrong-headed negligence." This is extremely unlikely, for the Festival of the Nine Nights (*navarātri*) was and remains a great state occasion, hardly subject to lapse. Elsewhere (verses 11–12) Pratāp exhorts his body's limbs and senses—ears, tongue, nose, thoughts, spirit—to partake of her, and then laments that he did not do so. Again, one must wonder if it were possible for him not to have performed these acts. What Pratāp must mean is that he has in fact done all of these things, and yet something eludes him. Other portions of the poem, such as the difficult quasi-esoteric verses (6–10), are hard to understand at all without supplying this sense of oblique dissatisfaction. (My translation does so.) "Failings" or "faults" here serve to prove discriminating excellence, in a way that boasting could not.

The text itself offers evidence contradicting the poet's self-deprecation. The king calls himself feeble-minded, yet he gives voice to keen sensibilities, and in poised and polished Sanskrit verse. Speaking to the goddess, he calls himself a child, yet his signature epithets outside the poem proper address mortals in proud and magisterial tone:

> Thus ends the *Sarvāparādhastotra* composed by him who excels in all fields of expertise, including war, book-learning, and music, the ruler of great rulers, the lord of Nepal, the great scholar, the lord of the circle of all kings, the supreme king of kings, the most worshipful poet-king, Jaya Pratāpa Malla.

With regard to the goddess, the king is all humility; with regard to men, he is all majesty. As he serves, so should he be served.

The king's expertise as a master of knowledge and as a master of men comes into active play in the latter portion of the poem, where the stock refrain gives way to specific inflections, and the deity's merits are moved to the fore. Particularly significant is Pratāp's account of the way the goddess pervades the polity and integrates the world of mortals. Specific mārgas are still said to be inadequate: the competing doctrines of Vaiṣṇavas, Śaivas, and Buddhists—among others—all miss the mark set forth as paramount; that is, they fail to truly serve her. Yet, argues the poem, she is integral to each approach: the brahmanical Gayatrī mantra is the goddess personified; the Vaiṣṇava goddess Lakṣmī and the Buddhist Vajravārāhī are none other than she; she is even the abstract principle niyati ("necessity") of the non-theist Mīmāṃsā school of classical philosophy. Pratāp knows that "She is the One whom all mārgas serve." (We should note that the followers of these other mārgas may themselves have known nothing of the sort.) She is the one who pervades the city-kingdom and renders it auspicious, a śāṅkarī nāgarī. The same phrase implies that she belongs to both the cosmic order of Śiva and its citizenry on earth. Pratāp's knowledge of unity in diversity is ultimately political, for it manages both to affirm and subordinate the contending views of ultimate truth that flourished in his realm.

And what of the poem's overt message concerning methods of approach to the divinity? None of his many efforts has succeeded in bringing the king to the state he desires, which is total intimacy with the goddess. The poem of devotion appears to be his last hope. Can we therefore take it that bhakti-style submission was truly Pratāp's preferred mode of relation to the goddess? More broadly, is this really evidence that in late medieval Nepal, Tantra was thought to be a less efficacious approach than emotional bhakti?

Bhakti and Tantra

Precisely what the *Sarvāparādhastotra* has to say on Tantric topics is unfortunately not altogether clear. Published transcriptions of the poem present variously problematic readings, and direct access to the lettering on the golden doors is not readily obtained. The three verses (6–8) that pertain directly to Tantra may have been somewhat obscure in their own time, for the poet's intent seems to have been simultaneously to display and to camouflage an initiate's special knowledge. In modern times, the problem of construing technical terminology in an exoteric framework is yet more difficult. From the number of points at which the poem touches upon esoteric topics, it is clear, however, that among the paths of approach to divinity alternative to that of bhakti or self-surrender, it is in Tantra that success might have been expected.

The poem's final verses offer an important closing reflection on the goddess's grace. Because tāntrikas of all six Kaula schools of transmission (*ṣaḍāmnāya*) achieve success (*siddhi*) at her pleasure, so does Pratāp hope that she will be pleased with his poem of praise, and thus forgive every conceivable sin. The juxtaposition of esoteric and devotional approaches makes the important suggestion that poetry is the sādhanā (perfection-oriented practice) of the king—the king as devotee, that is.

The discussion in this paper has followed discursive convention in treating bhakti as an approach to divinity distinct from other Indic forms of religious practice. The bhakti mode is usually glossed as devotionalism, emotional in nature, with humility and self-surrender as key stances. As such, bhakti is distinguished from Tantra's esotericism on the one hand, and the ritualism of professional liturgies on the other. More technically, the term *bhakti*—a derivative of the verbal root *bhaj*, "share" or "participate"—refers to the project of mortal participation in the very being of the deity concerned. In this sense bhakti may be an important component of both Tantra and professional liturgies. The *Sarvāparādhastotra* is, however, centered on emotion and devotion.

Two other important contrasts between bhakti and Tantra are pertinent to the question of what texts such as the *Sarvāparādhastotra* meant in late medieval Nepal. The first is bhakti's amenability to aestheticization in self-consciously literary endeavors: Tantric texts typically have a different thrust and texture entirely. Similarly, the sorts of intimacy that Tantra and bhakti respectively seek to establish between worshiper and deity pertain to entirely different domains. Devotional bhakti is appropriate to exterior and public contexts; esoteric Tantra is predicated on privacy and concealment.

My suggestion is that in the *Sarvāparādhastotra*—and throughout his inscriptional career—Pratāp Malla used bhakti as the public face of Tantra. The fact of his relationship with the Tantric goddess was no secret; in important senses, it was the pivot of late Malla kingship. But articulating that relationship in the verbal medium and in the public realm required Tantra's paraphrase or overlay, and the bhakti brand of intimacy was eminently suitable for purposes of display. Bhakti added an exoteric and aesthetic dimension to the relationship without compromising its secret core.

This introduction to the *Sarvāparādhastotra* has tried to relate Pratāp's inscription to the lived social world of its particular time and place. All the evidence indicates that the problem which most engaged agents of the period was that of constructing the world of mortals for maximum interface with the worlds of divinity. The problem for the late Malla kings was to deploy power ultimately referable to Tantra for real-world political purposes. Pratāp's poem makes it clear that the knowledge that bound devotee to deity constituted the conceptual center of the cosmo-political order realized in his realm. Far from being a free-floating text, the inscription's situation as a physical object in the real lived world is also highly significant. Emblazoned on the golden doors of Taleju's high temple in the heart of the city, the inscription—like the temple itself—advertised the secret at the pivotal point of the city-kingdom's life.

If what is at stake here were only Pratāp Malla's poems, or only the history of late medieval Nepal, consideration of inscriptional texts would be tangential to the greater study of Tantra. But the larger point is that Tantra in practice—real historical practice—must always negotiate some interface with the public gaze, for even in maintaining secrecy its practitioners shape the social world.

Transcriptions of the *Sarvāparādhastotra* have been published several times. Transcriptions show significant variations, corresponding in part to the three times Pratāp had the poem inscribed at different sites, none of which is open to foreign researchers. My translation follows the unpublished reading graciously supplied by the learned Gurusekhara Rajopadhyaya Sarma of Kathmandu. The textual integrity of the inscription is best retained in the edition published by Yogi Naraharinatha et al. in *Saṃskṛta-sandeśa* 1 (Kathmandu, 1953): 26–30. Naraharinatha transcribes the stone inscription Pratāpa Malla had erected at the shrine of the goddess Guhyeśvarī in N.S. 780, or 1659/1660 C.E. More readily available is the reading supplied by Gautamavajra Vajracarya in his *Hanūmānḍhokā Rājadarabāra* (Kathmandu: Nepala ra Esiyali Adhyayana Sasthana, Tribhuvana-Visvavidyalaya, 1978), pp. 225–27. This transcription is of the poem embossed on the doors of Taleju's temple, in or near N.S. 792, or 1671/1672 C.E. At pages 208–9 of the same work, Vajracarya presents an earlier version of Pratāp's poem, carved into the now-crumbling stone bath of an inner courtyard of the Kathmandu palace between N.S. 772 and 773, or 1651–1653 C.E. Most problematic is the reading of Taleju's doors by D. R. Regmi, in his *Medieval Nepal*, vol. 4. (Patna: the author, 1966), pp. 97–101. Regmi does not supply a date, but inserts the inscription in sequence at N.S. 775.

Further Reading

The phrase "advertised secrets" was coined by Robert Levy, whose *Mesocosm: Hinduism and the Organization of a Traditional Newar City in Nepal* (Berkeley and Los Angeles: University of California Press, 1990) contains meticulously compiled ethnographic data on one Newar city. On the goddess Taleju, see Bert van den Hoek and Balgopal Shrestha, "Guardians of the Royal Goddess: Kumār and Daitya as Protectors of Taleju Bhavānī of Kathmandu," *Contributions to Nepalese Studies* 19.2 (1992): 193–222. An important account of the Tantric practitioner's—very different—interface with the lived social world is presented in Alexis Sanderson's "Purity and Power among the Brahmins of Kashmir," in *The Category of the Person: Anthropology, Philosophy, History*, edited by Michael Carrithers et al. (Cambridge: Cambridge University Press, 1985). On the Śaiva deities and knowledges to which this paper has alluded, see Sanderson's "Śaivism and the Tantric Traditions," in *The World's Religions*, edited by Stuart Sutherland et al. (London: Routledge, 1986). Mary Shepherd Slusser's *Nepal Mandala: A Cultural Study of the Kathmandu Valley*, 2 vols. (Princeton: Princeton University Press, 1982) is an indispensible compendium of information on the history, deities, architecture, and folklore of the area.

Many of Pratāp Malla's other inscriptions are well edited in *Abhilekha-Saṃgraha* 3 (Kathmandu: Samsodhana Mandala, 1961). Two Purāṇas that had particular currency in the late medieval period are helpful for understanding the poem's arguments concerning the goddess. On Kālikā and her "oneness" with Śiva see the *Kālikā Puāṇa*, usefully translated in three volumes by B. N. Shastri (Delhi: Nag

Publishers, 1991–1992); verse 9's specification of the male gods as her vehicles is set forth in chapter 58, verses 59–71 of this work. On the goddess's supremacy over and subsumption of a range of deities normally held as distinct, see the *Devībhāgavata Purāṇa*; readily available is the edition *The Srimad Devi Bhagawatam*, translated by Hari Prasanna Chatterji, Sacred Books of the Hindus, vol. 26 (New Delhi: Oriental Books, 1977 [1921–1923]).

Sarvāparādhastotra by Pratāpa Malla

Homage to the thrice-illustrious Kālikā.

1. The sort of anguish felt by the child, whose body is tortured by the garland of flaming digestive fires producing waves of piss and shit, reborn from his mother's cavernous womb as a result of past evil's excess,

Can someone like me, or one still more simple-minded, describe it?

O Mother, let my faults be forgiven! Kālikā, Treasure of Victory, be gracious.

2. In childhood's painful state—incapable of knowledge, in a body wet with its own filth—one cries constantly because it is impossible to say what hurts, and because one is greedy to drink milk,

In this state, which is totally dependent on others, there is not even recollection of the mother who makes suffering cease.

O Mother, let my faults be forgiven! Kālikā, Treasure of Victory, be gracious.

3. Wealth and youth feed egoism, and that mind-set respects no one. I adored sexual games with women, and became so enchanted with this foul adoration that not for a moment did I adore you, the Primal One, the most deserving of those who deserve to be honored.

O Mother, let my faults be forgiven! Kālikā, Treasure of Victory, be gracious.

4. In the decrepitude of old age—which consists of diseases starting with coughing, wheezing, and being bent over, when walking and breathing are like punishment, and the heart finds pleasure only in eating—one's thoughts are empty of her who is Made of Pure Thought,

When I am sinking into Death's snare, befouled by my own filth, and worries grow ever greater,

O Mother, let my faults be forgiven! Kālikā, Treasure of Victory, be gracious.

5. I was unawakened in yoga, I was inattentive to the commands of the Veda and indifferent to the orthodox smārta path, I lacked the power to apply myself to Sāṃkhya metaphysics and the like, I had no ears to hear talk of governance and conduct.

My thoughts lack focus even when turned to praise and reflection on you, who are Speech Embodied.

O Mother, let my faults be forgiven! Kālikā, Treasure of Victory, be gracious.

6. Located like the Supreme Śiva at the Brāhma-lotus atop the head, you were never worshiped through mental acts, nor were you worshiped by means of external rituals, such as those performed in the yantrarāja by me, even though my thoughts were pure,
Though every act was faithfully performed, fire-oblations and the rest, still none really reached you.

O Mother, let my faults be forgiven! Kālikā, Treasure of Victory, be gracious.

7. In my material body composed of the five gross elements, and of Brahmā and other deities, I did not honor you—who are eternal in the form of mantra and the Inner Sound, who are the Queen of Breath, who are Made of Pure Thought—
I did not honor you by means of the unparalleled sacrifice of evils cut like animals with the sword of knowledge, because the blaze of desire and anger is brighter than the sun and moon.

O Mother, let my faults be forgiven! Kālikā, Treasure of Victory, be gracious.

8. She is that which moves in the element-free subtle body, and in the mind, and in the essence of the self as known through insight; she is transcendent, an extraordinary thing composed of bliss, whose own self consists of ultimate truth,
And yet she is hidden from me. I have not even for a moment managed full consciousness of her subliminal presence.

O Mother, let my faults be forgiven! Kālikā, Treasure of Victory, be gracious.

9. Dhātā [Brahmā] in the form of a lotus, Hari [Viṣṇu] in the shape of a lion, Śambhu [Śiva] as a ghost—these gods who are portions of yourself serve as your illustrious vehicles at particular times,
But I am just a mortal who does not know single- and multi-forms at the time of sacrifice.

O Mother, let my faults be forgiven! Kālikā, Treasure of Victory, be gracious.

10. You merely fixed your gaze on the best of yogins and that Great Lord—scorcher of Madana, bearer of the trident, holder of the bow—became the Lord of the Simple, for his heart was stolen away,
So how shall I, of the dull and wandering thoughts, offer elegant verses of praise to you?

O Mother, let my faults be forgiven! Kālikā, Treasure of Victory, be gracious.

11. Ears! Listen ceaselessly to the stream of goodly descriptions of her.

Tongue! Sing out, I say. Thoughts, meditate on her feet! You pair of eyes, behold her body. Spirit! Merge yourself here. Nose! Smell the flowers offered to the daughter of the Best of Mountains.

But I did not do this.

O Mother, let my faults be forgiven! Kālikā, Treasure of Victory, be gracious.

12. Feet! Go forth to circumambulate daily. Hands, do pūjā! Head, bow yourself in reverence. Heart, do continuous japa. Spirit, go to the state of absorption in her!

But I, who am deeply corrupt, did not perform your worship by sharing in Bhavānī thus.

O Mother, let my faults be forgiven! Kālikā, Treasure of Victory, be gracious.

13. Let her be served—by those who have realized that wisdom, wealth, land, all forms of grandeur, immortality, and the like are but trifles made of fear, mixed with a little happiness, and thus doomed to be consumed by Time,

With body, speech, and mind let her be served—by those who have realized that she and Śaṅkara are One, for she is made of Endless Bliss, she is the Woman of the Beautiful City, she is the blessed Śaṅkarī of our City.

14. Neither in fate, nor in the opinions of the Kāpālikas and their like, nor in the collected Vedic teachings, nor in the doctrines of the Vaiṣṇavas, the Saugatas, the Śaivas, the Sauras, nor of those who put Gaṇeśa first, nor in the path of devotion to the guru, nor in the service prescribed by the Kaulikas who teach the rules for your observances, with perpetual, occasional, and other rites,

In none of these is your worship accomplished.

Mistress of the afflicted! Protect me who takes refuge at your feet.

15. You are the Gāyatrī of the Vaidikas, Daughter of the Ocean (Lakṣmī) of the Vaiṣṇavas, Maheśī of the Māheśvaras, according to the categories of doctrine on earth, Vajravārāhī of the Saugata yogins and, further, Necessity of the Mīmāṃsakas.

Mother, let my faults be forgiven! Treasure of Victory, the One whom followers of all *mārgas* serve.

16. Kālī! Even at a power-seat pleasing as this, even when festival time came around, the pūjā of your two feet was not openly rendered, due to my wrongheaded negligence. Thus you have been slighted, but don't be angry with foolish me, who has come to take refuge in you.

Lady, mother, giver of auspiciousness! when a bad son is born, let not the mother turn bad too.

17. Mother! the world's Kaulikas partake of you with Six Transmissions of teachings, and the Success of their six types of practice rests at their fingertips easily, through your grace.

But how might I sing your praises? Even this poem is no true praise. Mother of Speech, be content with what has been uttered by the illustrious King Pratāpa.

18. That which I have done or caused to be done—in morning, noon, evening, or night; through thought, speech, or deed; with feet, hands, or eyes; through smelling, hearing, or touch; by myself, through another person, or at the word of the guru; by virtue of fate or by force—

Every single fault of mine, overlook it! O sea of compassion, O Devī Kālī!

Thus ends the *Sarvāparādhastotra* composed by him who excels in all fields of expertise, including war, book-learning, and music, the ruler of great rulers, the lord of Nepal, the great scholar, the lord of the circle of all kings, the supreme king of kings, the most worshipful poet-king, Jaya Pratāpa Malla.

—12—

Tantric Rites in Āṇṭāḷ's Poetry

D. Dennis Hudson

"Shoot me into Kṛṣṇa,"

Āṇṭāḷ told desire,

and performed the rites that made it happen.

The poet known as Āṇṭāḷ, who called herself Godā, lived in the early ninth century, in the deep south of the Indian subcontinent. She performed Tantric rites of the Bhāgavatas and described them in her poems, excerpts of which follow. Bhāgavata theology and the stories of her life will introduce them.

Bhāgavata Theology

"Bhāgavata" is the ancient name for the devotees of Vāsudeva Kṛṣṇa who believe him to be the human manifestation of the *brahman* they name Nārāyaṇa. Today they are more commonly known under the less precise name of Vaiṣṇava. *Brahman*, a neuter noun, signifies the infinite power of beginningless being and becoming. Nārāyaṇa, a masculine noun, defines the *brahman* as "the abode (*āyana*) of humans (*naras*)." The name Nārāyaṇa means that the *brahman* in whom we live and move and have our being, in essence, is personal in a manner impossible to comprehend. Nārāyaṇa is the Supreme Person (*parama-puruṣa*) of the *Ṛg Veda* and is the Supreme Self (*parama-ātman*) of the Upaniṣads. Nārāyaṇa, essentially formless, is the source of all consciousness and being whose innate power of creativity (*māyā*) produces all forms.

The form Nārāyaṇa first imagines through māyā is Vasudeva-with-Lakṣmī in a realm called Vaikuṇṭha composed of a supremely pure mode of matter (*śuddha-*

sattva) beyond our reckoning. The non-dual Vaikuṇṭha is changeless, transcendent to sun, moon, and fire, and any who reach it do not return to space and time. Vasudeva-with-Lakṣmī (Tirumāl) is the primordial "Father-Mother," the highest mode of Nārāyaṇa that beings can worship. Through māyā, Vasudeva-with-Lakṣmī makes formations (*vyūhas*) of himself to produce the cosmos and us, and differing forms (*mūrtis*) to act for us and to be served by us. Notable among these are three goddesses (*devīs*) called Śrī (kingship), Bhūmi (the material realm), and Caṇḍikā-Durgā (victorious conquest); three gods (*devas*) called Viṣṇu (pervading sustenance), Śiva (destruction), and Brahmā (emanation); and two humans called Balarāma and Kṛṣṇa. All the while, however, the formless Nārāyaṇa at whose "center" Vasudeva resides with Lakṣmī remains imperishable, omnipresent, and unthinkable.

The name Vasudeva repeats the meaning of Nārāyaṇa, but more intimately. It means "God (*deva*) in whom all things dwell (*vasu*) and who dwells (*vasu*) in all things." Lakṣmī denotes his auspicious and properous sovereignty. With her, Vasudeva is known as the Bhagavān, "Possessor of Glorious Excellences" by which he-with-she acts to conceive the universe at the uterine "center." As the Bhagavān in the form of Kṛṣṇa said to his friend Arjuna, "My womb (*yoni*) is the transcendent *brahman*, and I plant the embryo (*garbha*) in it; the arising of all living beings comes from that, O son of Bharata. In all wombs, O son of Kuntī, whatever comes into being with a form, the transcendent *brahman* is the womb, and I am the father who gives the seed" (*Bhagavad Gītā* [*BG*] 14.3–4). Just as the fetus resides within the womb of a pregnant woman, the universe resides inside God as if God were a pregnant king.

Perception of Vasudeva in Vaikuṇṭha is the purest wisdom possible in Bhāgavata thought and the content of omniscient knowledge (*jñāna*). In the end, however, this is Vasudeva's gift, normally given to those of undefiled consciousness, which means that in the Kali Yuga few will receive it, for in our time, passion and ignorance overwhelm everyone. Only by omniscient knowledge can anyone know who he or she truly is and act accordingly; without it, a soul (*puruṣa*) will live forever inside the wheel of time (*saṃsāra-cakra*) at Nārāyaṇa's "center," propelled by a profound anxiety (*bhayam*) that will cause it to cling to ephemeral objects for a security they can never give. Anxiety generates desire (*kāma*), which, when frustrated, produces anger (*krodha*), causing greed (*lobha*) to emerge. Desire, anger, and greed are doorways to painful purgation and ceaseless wandering (*BG* 16.21–24).

Nevertheless, Bhāgavatas believe there is hope, for by means of māyā, Vasudeva appeared as Kṛṣṇa very near the end of the previous age, the Dvāpara Yuga. He was born in the city of Mathura on the Yamuna River in northern India through the warrior aristocrat named Vasudeva and his wife Devakī, who at the time were imprisoned. Miraculously, Kṛṣṇa escaped the prison to join his elder brother Balarāma in the household of Nanda, the chieftain of the cowherd village of Gokula. Nanda and his wife Yaśodā mistakenly thought Kṛṣṇa would inherit the position of cowherd chieftain; he was therefore known as Gopāla ("Protector of Cows"), Govinda ("Lord of Cows"), and Govardhana ("Increaser of Cows").

Kṛṣṇa and Balarāma were human modes of the Bhagavān, but not equally so. Balarāma, the elder, embodied omniscient knowledge (*jñāna*) and its indefatigable power (*bala*); like the purity of insight, his skin was white. Kṛṣṇa, the younger, however, embodied the complete Vasudeva; like our deluded Kali Yuga perception of God, his skin was dark as sapphire.

Kṛṣṇa as son of Devakī appears briefly in the ancient and esoteric *Chāndogya Upaniṣad* of the *Sāma Veda*, but the *Mahābhārata* and the *Bhāgavata Purāṇa* (hereafter *BP*) develop that identity at great length. The epic *Mahābhārata*, for example, contains as its theological center the secret teaching that Kṛṣṇa gave Arjuna after he had abandoned his cowherd disguise: this is the famous *Bhagavad Gītā*, "Song of the Possessor of Glorious Excellences." There he revealed his identity and the mysteries of our existence (*BG* 7). Along with Buddhists, Jainas, and Śaivas in the early centuries B.C.E., Bhāgavatas spread throughout the Indian subcontinent, telling the story of Kṛṣṇa and Balarāma and establishing their worship. For those who thought of Kṛṣṇa only as a great hero and lover, his first name "Vāsudeva" was a patronym; but for those who believed him to be Nārāyaṇa, it referred to his true identity as God. By the ninth century C.E., the Kṛṣṇa story and cult had been in southern India for at least a millennium, and Āṇṭāḷ, thoroughly immersed in both, was intensely in love with the Dark Cowherd.

Āṇṭāḷ in History

In her poetry, Āṇṭāḷ calls herself Kōtai ("Garland"), which in Sanskrit is Godā ("She gives cows"). She lived in Villi's New Town, which she calls Putuvai ("New Town") and is known today as Srivilliputtur; it lies about forty miles southwest of the Pāṇḍya capital, Madurai, the "southern Mathura." New Town's newly constructed temple, facing east, housed a long stucco icon of Vasudeva reclining on a huge snake in his form as Madhusūdana, "Slayer of Delusion." That icon depicted the theme of māyā at the beginning of the universe, which Godā and her father Viṣṇucitta creatively developed through their skill in ritual visualization (*dhyāna*).

The Madhusūdana story begins after the previous universe has disappeared into the waters of darkness within Vasudeva's womb. Vasudeva has "eaten" the universe, has kept it unmanifest in his "uterine center," and now at the end of "night," it has emerged in the form of his first-born son, Brahmā (*BP* 8.17–19). Once awakened, Brahmā's nature of purified Passion will enable him to reorganize himself into the universe, following the guide of Veda or sacred knowledge. The reclining icon in New Town's temple represented the last part of that primordial night known as "Brahmā's Hour" (*brahmamuhūrta*).

According to the story, this time when Brahmā awoke in the lotus-womb, two asura demons named Madhu and Kaiṭabha (Delusion and Passion) had stolen the

Veda. To assist Brahmā, Vasudeva became Purity (*sattva*) in the form of a person with the head of a horse (Hayagrīva)—a visual allusion to the mantras of Veda. Horse-head then descended into the waters of darkness, tricked Deluded Passion into leaving the Veda unattended, seized it, and carried it up to Brahmā. While the asuras were searching in the dark waters for their deceiver, Purity removed his horse-head form and took on the form of a white-skinned man lying on a snake and sleeping—a visual allusion to the mantras of Tantra. Yet Purity was not really asleep, for he had allowed māyā to envelop him in the "Sleep of Unified Consciousness" (*yoganidrā*), a state of complete awareness that only appears to be sleep. When the asuras embodying Deluded Passion found him, they mocked his white body and snake bed, and attacked. Immediately, Yoganidrā released Purity, who then arose, battled the asuras, and slew them on the thigh of his own white body. Brahmā was now free to express his undefiled passionate nature by transforming himself into the universe for a new daytime. Thereafter, that form of Purity was known as Madhusūdana, "Slayer of Delusion."

That cultic background explains why Godā made Yoganidrā, "Sleep of Unified Consciousness," central to her rites. After Brahmā had emanated space and time, Yoganidrā appeared within it as Goddess Caṇḍikā-Durgā, famous for slaying asuras with her spear, as told in the "The Glorification of the Goddess" (*Devī Māhātmyam*). She embodied the Bhagavān's brilliant conquering power (*tejas*). Yet Godā did not address Yoganidrā as Caṇḍikā-Durgā, but as Pin̲n̲ai, or as Nappin̲n̲ai, "the lovely Pin̲n̲ai," a figure in Tamil Bhāgavata tradition who was Kṛṣṇa's beautiful "cousin-to-be-married." Having entranced Kṛṣṇa with her alluring beauty, Pin̲n̲ai lived with him as wife in his cowherd parent's house. Still, Caṇḍikā-Durgā is part of Pin̲n̲ai's identity. In Sanskrit poems, Pin̲n̲ai is known as Nīḻadevī, the "Dark Goddess," but Tamil poems call her Āymakaḷ, a name whose double meaning is revealing. Āymakaḷ can mean "Cowherd (*āy*) Goddess (*makaḷ*)," who is the cowherdess Pin̲n̲ai; at the same time it can mean "Goddess (*makaḷ*) who Strikes (*āy*)," who is Caṇḍikā-Durgā. Pin̲n̲ai plays a crucial role in both of Godā's poetic works, and we shall return to her shortly.

The historical account of Godā is slim, known primarily from her poems and those of her father, Viṣṇucitta. They belonged to a brahman caste called Veyar that specialized in music and served in temples. In New Town, Viṣṇucitta was known as "Lord of Priests" (*Bhaṭṭapirān̲*), adept in the art of visualization and a devoted servant of Kṛṣṇa. He apparently provided garlands of fresh lotus for the daily rites in New Town's temple, and he interpreted his own name, Viṣṇucitta, to mean "Whose mind is a temple housing Gopāla" (*Tirumoḻi* 5.4.11). In one poem, he identified himself with the Pañcarātra Āgama, the mixed Vedic and Tantric liturgy of the Bhāgavatas, for he said that his family lineage was branded with the Wheel and Conch that the four-handed Vāsudeva Kṛṣṇa holds in his back right and left hands, respectively (*Tiruppallāṇṭu* 6–7). That branding is a Pāñcarātra rite of purification.

The origins of the Pañcarātra Āgama remain obscure, but evidence points to its presence by the third century B.C.E. in both the northern and southern portions of the Indian subcontinent. Bhāgavatas who followed that Āgama believed that to supplement the rites of the Veda, which in theory are restricted to males of certain classes, Vasudeva in his various formations (*vyūhas*) revealed the ritual knowledge now contained in the texts (Saṁhitās) of the Pañcarātra Āgama. He addressed that knowledge specifically to people living in the Kali Yuga, including females as well as males, low castes as well as high castes, the innately "defiled" as well as the innately "clean." Followers of the Pañcarātra Āgama believed that it possessed powerful mantric rites to "clean up" the impure, notably the "Man-Lion Consecration" (*narasiṁha-dīkṣā*) taught in the *Sātvata Saṁhitā*, perhaps the oldest literary form of that tradition now available. Once cleansed, initiates could then receive consecrations that gave them access to mantras, icons, maṇḍalas, and temples in their worship, all of which were believed to be based on the Veda.

In contemporary India, the Śrī Vaiṣṇava tradition (*sampradāya*), which descends from the famous eleventh- to twelfth-century ācārya Rāmānuja, follows the Pañcarātra Āgama. Its initial consecration includes a purifying sequence of rites during which the initiate is branded by the ācārya on his or her shoulders in imitation of Vāsudeva Kṛṣṇa. Once marked, that devotee is Vāsudeva's purified possession, a "slave" who in bodily form now represents the "master" to the world. Such devotees, called prapannas or refugees, are then qualified to receive further consecrations if they wish. Each consecration requires commitment to specific disciplines of daily life and ritual practice (*sādhana*) to attain a specific religious goal, for example worldly longevity and prosperity, or emancipation from time and space altogether, or both.

According to Godā, her father was a religious virtuoso, "the king of those in New Town who do not swerve from the enjoyment (*bhoga*) of God." He followed a ritual practice or sādhana focused on temple worship. As part of his offerings, it appears, he sang and mimed the poems he had composed while absorbed mentally in the inner visions (*dhyāna*) they portrayed. Godā said that his behavior stimulated others: "our Lord reclining on the cobra bed is wealthy and great, so what can we mere humans do to reach him? But in Villi's New Town, Viṣṇucitta makes his deity come in a powerful way and then we see him" (*Nācciyār Tirumoḻi* 10.10). The numerous Tamil poems her father composed to the cowherd Kṛṣṇa, collected as the *Tirumoḻi* ("Auspicious Speech"), earned him the title, "Great Saint Immersed in the Consciousness of God" (*Periyāḻvār*).

Viṣṇucitta projected onto the reclining Madhusūdana another story about the deluge of Brahmā's "nighttime," this one concerning the seer and great scholar of *Ṛg Veda* known as Mārkaṇḍeya (*Tirumoḻi* 1.1.6 and 2.2.6). The story appears in *Mahābhārata* 3.186–87 and a "corrected" version appears in the *Bhāgavata Purāṇa* 12.9.20–34. One day, it says, while Mārkaṇḍeya engaged in visualization at his ashram, God gave him an experience of māyā. Mārkaṇḍeya suddenly found himself totally alone in the dark waters of the cosmic deluge, floundering, it seemed, for years. Then he saw a shining baby boy lying on the leaf of a banyan tree, sucking his foot. When he approached the leaf, the dazzling infant inhaled the seer into his mouth. Suddenly inside the baby, Mārkaṇḍeya now saw the entire universe and his own ashram. The baby, of course, was Vāsudeva, who had "eaten" the universe and would, as a mature male, emit it again through his own lotus-womb as his son, Brahmā. Suddenly, the baby exhaled Mārkaṇḍeya, and he found himself back in the dark waters. He realized he had met the *brahman* of Veda in a manner beyond his own understanding of the *Ṛg Veda* and took refuge in him. Suddenly again, Mārkaṇḍeya found himself back in his ashram, meditating.

Kṛṣṇa's cowherd mother Yaśodā had similar experiences. One day while she was nursing him, Kṛṣṇa yawned, and Yaśodā saw all things, moving and non-moving, inside his mouth (*BP* 10.34–37). Another time, Yaśodā was told that her little boy Kṛṣṇa had eaten earth. She grabbed him, but Kṛṣṇa denied it. He offered to open his mouth to prove it, and when he did, she saw the universe inside. But through *māyā*, Kṛṣṇa allowed her to forget (*BP* 10.32–45).

Viṣṇucitta's visualization of the reclining Madhusūdana as the baby of the deluge who was also the baby Kṛṣṇa changed the icon's identity permanently. Today he is known in Sanskrit as "He who reclines on the banyan leaf" (Vaṭapatraśayi), and in Tamil as "He who has the banyan leaf for his great palace" (Vaṭaperuṅkoyiluṭaiyāṉ). Following in her father's liturgical footsteps, Godā then added another story of even greater cultic impact.

Āṇṭāḷ in Hagiography

The hagiography of Godā explains her vision of the reclining icon. It is longer than the historical story, more widely known, and is the basis of her annual marriage to Kṛṣṇa in Srivilliputtur. Written down in the twelfth to thirteenth centuries, it depicts Godā as so passionately and single-mindedly attached to Kṛṣṇa that she first compelled him to wake up from Piṉṉai's bed, and then she compelled him to marry her. That is why she received the title Āṇṭāḷ, "She who rules Kṛṣṇa." Their union was so literal, the story says, that after Viṣṇucitta betrothed her to Kṛṣṇa, he processed her in a palanquin northward to the island temple of Śrī Rangam in the Kaveri River. There she walked into the temple's sanctum, climbed up on the altar, and disappeared into its long and reclining stucco icon, known appropriately as "The Handsome Bridegroom."

To explain how that could happen, the story says that Āṇṭāḷ was an avatar of Goddess Earth (Maṇmakaḷ or Bhūmidevī). At the beginning of the Kali Yuga, Goddess Earth appeared as a newborn under a basil plant in the garden of the New Town temple. Goddess Earth, who is māyā as the material universe, is noted for her patient separation from Vasudeva, in contrast, for example, to māyā as the prosperous kingship (Śrīdevī), who is always with him. In order to experience union with him even while remaining separate, however, Goddess Earth took a human form; it was a gracious act, for right at the beginning of the Kali Yuga she exemplified the goal of uniting with God in perception while remaining separate from him in body. Viṣṇucitta found the baby, raised her as his daugher, but when she grew into sexual maturity, her extraordinay passion for Kṛṣṇa revealed her true identity.

Āṇṭāḷ, the story says, was highly skilled in the practice of visualization. Kṛṣṇa was no longer alive on earth, but out of her longing for him, she perceived Villi's New Town to be his cowherd village, and the Madhusūdana Temple to be the house of his cowherd parents, and its sanctum to be his bedroom where he slept with Piṉṉai. So adept was she, raised a brahman girl, that she lived like a cowherd girl and even smelled of sour milk. Out of that transformed consciousness, the story says, she composed her poems for the benefit of the Kali Yuga, the *Tiruppāvai* and the *Nācciyār Tirumoḻi*. Not surprisingly, the rites we find in those poems do not avoid desire or burn it up, as ascetic renunciants might try to do; rather, they stimulate desire, harness it, and use it to focus the five senses—with the mind as sixth—on Kṛṣṇa.

The *Tiruppāvai* and Communal Rites

In Tamil, *Tiruppāvai* (hereafter *TP*) means "Auspicious *Pāvai*," and in Āṇṭāḷ's poem the term *pāvai* has three referents: Yoganidrā as Goddess Caṇḍikā-Durgā; the rites performed for the Goddess during the month of Mārgali by unmarried girls; and the vow (*nonpu* or *vrata*) those girls made to perform those rites for the thirty cold mornings of the Mārgali month. That month, known in Sanskrit as Mārgaśīrṣa, ends at the winter solstice day; Kṛṣṇa had identified himself with it in the *Bhagavad Gītā* 10.35. The committed girls would arise in the cold before the dawn of each Mārgali day, gather a drum and other ritual implements from the headman's house, go together to the river, bathe, and then fashion an image of the Goddess from sand. As a group they would then worship her for practical benefits in the year beginning with the winter solstice. For the sake of the land and its people, they asked the Goddess for regular rainfall; for their own sake, they asked for a good husband.

Although the hagiography provides a rich theological interpretation of Āṇṭāḷ's poems, the history of Godā, thin as it is, provides insight into her profound genius. Godā based the thirty stanzas of *Tiruppāvai* on a Mārgaśīrṣa temple ceremony prescribed for Bhāgavatas by the Pañcarātra Āgama. Onto that ceremony she visually projected the rites of the Goddess's bathing vow; she then visualized the actors of that vow, herself included, as cowherdesses living in Kṛṣṇa's village of Gokula, far to the north, in the previous age. Out of that complex perceptual patterning she spoke a poem believed by Śrī Vaiṣṇavas to contain the essence of the Upaniṣads. It was so important to their famously learned teaching priest (*ācārya*) of the eleventh to twelfth century, Rāmānuja, that he was known as the "Pontiff Devoted to the *Tiruppāvai*" (*Tiruppāvai-jīyar*). Having spoken out of a desiring consciousness focused on Kṛṣṇa, her words now embody that consciousness as mantras do the *brahman*; any adept singer of them will become immersed in the consciousness that produced them.

In early ninth-century New Town, we may reasonably conjecture, observant Bhāgavatas arose during the last hour of each Mārgali night, gathered at the temple's sanctum, and sang songs as they waited for the priest to open the doors. They then addressed the newly awakened Madhusūdana directly and offered him songs in Sanskrit and Tamil, the special foods he enjoys, and their own loving service. For thirty days they fed him, but fasted until the last day, when in his iconic presence they gathered to eat the sweet milk-rice, rich with the ghee in which he delights.

Of those thirty days, the full moon was the most important, and the *Tiruppāvai* describes it. Godā envisions male and female Bhāgavatas rising in the predawn hour as cowherdesses gathering to worship the Goddess in the Yamuna River. Those same Bhāgavatas standing at the door of the temple's sanctum she sees as cowherdesses at the door of Kṛṣṇa's bedroom. She hears the songs they sing as cowherdesses calling out to Pinnai to open the door so that they might ask Kṛṣṇa for the drum essential to their Goddess rites—for as the headman's son, he is its keeper. When the priest finally opens the sanctum doors to reveal the awakened Madhusūdana, she sees him as Pinnai opening the bedroom door to join the cowherdesses, who now admit to Kṛṣṇa that they had really come for *him*—the drum was merely a pretext. All they want is the desire to serve him as they would serve a husband, but for "seven times seven rebirths," which means forever in the wheel of time. In her last stanza, Godā says he fulfilled their request.

Later commentators noted that the cowherdesses in the *Tiruppāvai* do not go off alone for solitary union with Kṛṣṇa, but remain together; they unite with him collectively, as if bathing together in the cool waters of his stunningly beautiful presence. Here erotic imagery depicts communal experience as it does in the famous "Dance of Delight" (*rāsa-līlā*) described in *Bhāgavata Purāṇa* 10.29–33. Dancing in a circle in the Vṛndāvana forest, Kṛṣṇa appeared to each cowherdess as if he were with her alone, and yet they were all there together, united in their focus on him. Shared love of the Supreme Male is the basis of human community, Bhāgavatas believe, for all souls in relation to God are like dependent females: their own fulfillment comes from giving God pleasure in the way servants give to a master, or polygamous wives give to a shared husband.

The *Nācciyār Tirumoli* and Solitary Rites

Equal in fame to the communal "Dance of Delight" is Kṛṣṇa's special love for a single cowherdess (*BP* 10.30). Later northern tradition knows her as Rādhā; earlier Tamil tradition knows her as Pinnai. Apparently, communal "bathing in Kṛṣṇa" on the full moon day of Mārgali was not enough for Godā, who wanted to be alone with him as a unique lover like Pinnai. Godā could not have literal sexual union with Kṛṣṇa, of course, because he was no longer alive as a man. He was bodily present now in icons of wood, stucco, stone, or metal; or in the teaching priest (*ācārya*) on ritual occasions; or in her own visualizations.

Being adept in visualization, Godā sought solitary union with Kṛṣṇa through it. She sought the enstatic consciousness called samādhi. Her method was to envision herself as Pinnai, Kṛṣṇa's cousin-to-be-married as she grew in Gokula from a child of about five to full sexual maturity at the age of twelve when Kṛṣṇa was sixteen. Out of those visions she produced the fourteen poems called the *Nācciyār Tirumoḻi* (*NT*), "The Venerable Beloved's (*nacciyar*) Auspicious (*tiru*) Speech (*moḻi*)."

Of the fourteen poems of the *Nācciyār Tirumoḻi*, eleven consist of ten stanzas and three of eleven. In the first poem, translated below, Godā describes the rites of her ritual discipline (*sādhana*). She had begun the sādhana on the winter solstice day, the first day of the month called Tai, immediately after the Mārgali rites of the *Tiruppāvai*. She continued it through the following month called Māsi. Now, she tells us, she is on the first day of the following month called Paṅguṉi, when the vernal equinox falls, and is looking forward to its full moon. Her sādhana thus extends from the winter solstice to the vernal equinox, the period of slowly increasing heat in southern India that matches the increasing heat of her passion, felt especially in her swelling breasts, which "will go into no other mouth than Govinda's" (*NT* 12.4) In the poem she begins her sādhana's climactic sequence of daily visualizations, producing a poem out of the experience of each day except for the last; the samādhi she attained on the full moon day apparently left her speechless.

In the first poem, Godā describes her rites as centered on a maṇḍala, a cosmic mapping, that she had ritually drawn on the ground outside the temple sanctum during the month of Tai. In the meantime, she had laid a fire and had performed appropriate rites for the season, including, it appears, commemoration of Śiva's burning of the God of Desire (Kāmadeva), which made him bodiless. Any doubts about Kāma's reality thereafter, however, she banished, and used his name inscribed on a wall to represent his bodiless presence. By addressing Kāmadeva outside of herself, she addressed the passion inside her that propelled her toward Kṛṣṇa, who in these rites stood as an icon over three hundred miles to the north, on the mountain called Veṅkaṭam. Her rites took her in processions on New Town's streets (verse 6), involved priestly chanters and the leadership of her ācārya (verse 7), and her own fasting (verse 8). Her ācārya appears in verse 7 as Viṣṇu in the form of a Dwarf, a small man who embodied the owner of everything, including the initiate (*BP* 8.15–23); that is, the status of the ācārya infused with mantras during consecration (*dīkṣā*) rites conducted at a maṇḍala. In the rite, he touches her body to divinize it, and she envisions this to be Kṛṣṇa's loving touch.

Godā's ritual focus on Kāmadeva as "Churner of the Mind" (Manmatha) reveals her Pāñcarātra liturgical context. Kāmadeva derives from the Preeminently Mighty Formation (*Pradyumna-vyūha*) of the Bhagavān. In Kṛṣṇa's later life as ruler of Dvaraka, this formation appears as his son and heir-apparent, Pradyumna, who looked just like his father. Pradyumna was born to Rukmiṇī, but he had a younger half-brother named Sāmba, born to Jāmbavatī. Sāmba embodied Skandadeva, God of War. Pradyumna and Sāmba were Desire and Anger as Kṛṣṇa's sons, which means they were expressions of Vāsudeva Kṛṣṇa himself. That is why Godā addresses both in the poem: desire for, and anger at, Kṛṣṇa are modes of his "Preeminently Mighty" Pradyumna presence.

Godā's remaining thirteen poems describe her visualized journey to samādhi. In the second poem, she introduces herself as the child Pin̲n̲ai building sand castles that the older Kṛṣṇa—"Nārāyaṇa praised with a thousand names who was a man"—playfully kicks down (*NT* 2.1). Each poem captures a scene in Pin̲n̲ai's life as she swells, like the Paṅgun̲i moon, to full sexual maturity and intense desire. In poem 3, her sexual maturation has begun: While she is bathing with other cowherdesses in a pond, Kṛṣṇa steals their clothes and teases them erotically. "We won't do *that*," she says, "it's not right—You're a boy and you know these things, don't be in such a hurry" (*NT* 3.2). Following the conventions of ancient Tamil poetry, in poem 5, her breasts have swollen with pleasure and give her grief, and she has already met her lover in secret; he penetrated her, stole her "bangle," but did not show his face. In desparation she addresses a *kuyil* bird in passages translated below. He has to marry her to save her honor, yet as time goes by, he does not come, and so, in poem 13, she breaks into a rage: "If I see Govardhana, I'll grab my fruitless breast by the root, rip it out, and throw it on his chest, and then I'll be free of my burning" (*NT* 13.8). But she retreats quickly: "If only he would take me to his superbly auspicious chest, then, if one day he looked me in the face and told me in truth to leave, still it would be wonderful" (*NT* 13.9).

Godā also weaves into her poems a pilgrimage route that she must have made at least once by palanquin, oxcart, and foot. She begins her envisioned pilgrimage at the temple in New Town, where the icon is sculpted reclining. Then she visually moves northward to icons sculpted in various postures—sitting, reclining, or standing—housed in the temple in Madurai, in the mountain temple of Alagakoyil, and in temples along the Kaveri River. For example, at the closed doors of the reclining icon in Kumbhakonam, she says to her visualized companions:

> I was initiated into the vision of the Black God
>   Kṛṣṇa,
> And in my pure state,
> Don't stand there talking of his beauty
>   as if pouring acid in a wound,
> Take the gold cloth from the room of the Bhagavān
>   who doesn't know women's sorrow
> And throw it over me
>   to end my withering.
>
> *NT* 13.1

She completed her envisioned pilgrimage route in the Pallava capital of Kāñcipuram, the last major stop before the Veṅkaṭam mountain about sixty miles to the north. The pilgrims she would have met returning from the forest shrine appear in her last poem as Pin̲n̲ai's friends. As the selected stanzas translated below illustrate, they tell her they saw Kṛṣṇa walking in the Vṛndāvana forest toward which she is headed. The final stanza, moreover, makes it clear that she would attain her goal, for it refers to a well-known story of Gajendra, the king of elephants, caught by a "grasper" in the lake of ordinary sensual pleasure. After struggling for a thousand years and near exhaustion, Gajendra remembered Vāsudeva, mentally took refuge in him, and asked him to free him—not from "grasping" sensual desire, however, but from ignorance. Instantly, Viṣṇu appeared, slayed the "grasper," and took the stout-legged "Indra of Elephants" to Vaikuṇṭha, never to return (*BP* 8.2–4).

Despite the journey she embedded within her visualizations, Godā remained at the maṇḍala in New Town during the rites underlying her fourteen poems; she traveled only in her consecrated and impassioned mind. She attained, we are told, what all pilgrims seek, the end of ignorance and the emergence of omnisicent knowledge (*jñāna*), whose content is Vāsudeva Kṛṣṇa.

For the Tamil texts of Āṇṭāḷ's poems, I have used P. Annangaracaryar Swami's edition of *Tiruppāvai* (Kanchipuram: P. B. Anangaracaryar, 1962) and *Nācciyār Tirumoḻi*, 5th ed. (Madras: P. B. Annangaracaryar, 1966). For Sanskrit texts and English translations, I consulted Swami Tapasyananda, tr., *Śrīmad Bhāgavatam: The Holy Book of God*, 4 vols. (Madras: Ramakrishna Math, 1982); R. C. Zaehner, tr., *The Bhagavad-Gita: With a Commentary Based on the Original Sources* (London: Oxford University Press, 1969); J. A. B. van Buitenen, tr., *The Mahābhārata*, 3 vols. (Chicago: University of Chicago Press, 1973, 1975, 1978) (English only); and Thomas B. Coburn, *Encountering the Goddess: A Translation of the Devī-Māhātmya and a Study of Its Interpretation* (Albany: State University of New York Press, 1991).

Further Reading

Vidya Dehejia provides a complete translation of Āṇṭāḷ's poems, with insightful commentary, in *Āṇṭāḷ and Her Path of Love: Poems of a Woman Saint of South India* (Albany: State University of New York Press, 1990). Translations of Viṣṇucitta's poems are available in Lynn Marie Ate, "Periyāḻvār's Tirumoḻi—A Bāla Kṛṣṇa Text from the Devotional Period in Tamil Literature," Ph.D. dissertation, University of Wisconsin-Madison, 1978. For more detailed discussions of Āṇṭāḷ and Piṉṉai, see Dennis Hudson, "Bathing in Kṛṣṇa: A Study in Vaiṣṇava Hindu Theology," *Harvard Theological Review* 73.3–4 (1980): 539–66; "Piṉṉai, Kṛṣṇa's Cowherd Wife," in *The Divine Consort*, edited by John Stratton Hawley and Donna Wulff (Berkeley: Graduate Theological Union, 1982), pp. 238–61; Hudson, "Āṇṭāḷ Alvar: A Developing Hagiography," *Journal of Vaiṣṇava Studies* 1.2 (1993): 27–61; and Hudson, "Āṇṭāḷ's Desire,"*Journal of Vaiṣṇava Studies* 4.1 (1995–96): 37–76.

For studies of the Bhāgavata religion among the Tamils, see also Dennis Hudson, "Vāsudeva Kṛṣṇa in Theology and Architecture: A Background to Śrīvaiṣṇavism," *Journal of Vaiṣṇava Studies* 2.1 (1993): 139–170; Hudson, "Vraja among the Tamils: A Study of Bhāgavatas in Early South India," *Journal of Vaiṣṇava Studies*

3.1 (1994): 113–40; and Hudson, "The Śrīmad Bhāgavata Purāṇa in Stone: The Text as an Eighth-Century Temple and Its Implications," *Journal of Vaiṣṇava Studies* 3.3 (1995): 137–82. The texts of the Pañcarātra Āgama are summarized and discussed by H. Daniel Smith in *A Descriptive Bibliography of the Printed Texts of the Pañcarātra Āgama*, 2 vols., Gaekwad's Oriental Series, nos. 158, 168 (Baroda: Oriental Institute, 1975, 1980). Sanjukta Gupta discusses Pāñcarātra thought in "The Pāñcarātra Attitude to Mantra," in *Mantra*, edited by Harvey Alper (Albany: State University of New York Press, 1989), pp. 224–48; and in "Yoga and *Antaryāga* in Pāñcarātra," in *Ritual and Speculation in Early Tantrism: Studies in Honor of André Padoux*, edited by Teun Goudriaan (Albany: State University of New York Press, 1992), pp. 175–208.

Vasudha Narayanan provides the Śrī Vaiṣṇava theological and liturgical contexts for these and other Āḻvār poems in *The Way and the Goal: Expressions of Devotion in the Early Śrī Vaiṣṇava Tradition* (Washington, D.C.: Institute for Vaiṣṇava Studies; and Cambridge: Center for the Study of World Religions, Harvard University, 1987); Narayanan and John B. Carman, *The Tamil Veda: Piḷḷāṉ's Interpretation of the Tiruvaymoḻi* (Chicago: University of Chicago Press, 1989); and Narayanan and Carman, *The Vernacular Veda: Revelation, Recitation, and Ritual* (Columbia: University of South Carolina Press, 1994).

Excerpts from the *Tiruppāvai*

1. Mārgali month and the full moon,
   what a grand day!
   If you're going to bathe, let's go
   You well-adorned wealthy girls
   of the herders' town flowing with riches!
   The son of Nanda the cowherd,
   man of sharp spear and ruthless deeds,
   The young lion of Yaśodā,
   her eyes full of beauty,
   He with the body dark like a cloud
   with red eyes,
   a face like the sun and moon,
   Nārāyaṇa himself,
   Will give us the drum,
   And people of this land will praise us,
   So plunge in, everyone, O my Goddess.

2. O you who live on earth,
   Listen to the deeds we do for our Goddess:
   We exalt the Transcender's foot,
   who sleeps lightly on the Sea of Milk,
   We don't eat ghee, we don't eat milk,

Before daybreak we bathe,
But we don't paint our eyes,
We don't braid flowers in our hair,
We don't do what isn't to be done,
Nor do we spread evil words around,
But we do give gifts and alms to the limit,
And we ponder the path to life,
Rejoicing, everyone, O my Goddess.

3. The Exalted One grew tall to measure out this world,
And if we extol his name and bathe,
  saying it's for our Goddess,
All the land will be free from harm,
For with rains three times each month,
  carp will leap in fine paddy growing tall,
  spotted bees will slumber in blue waterlilies,
  milkers without qualm will enter, sit,
  seize swollen teats, and tug
  as bounteous great cows overflow their pots,
Unceasing wealth will abound
For everyone, O my Goddess.

4. Ocean-deep Lord of Rain, hold back nothing,
Plunge into the ocean, lift up its water,
Roar and soar high with a body dark like the Deluger,
Flash like the Wheel he holds,
  he with a lotus navel
  and shoulders of power and beauty,
Thunder like his Conch curling to the right,
And without delay
  like a rain of arrows shot by his Bow,
Pour down on earth for its thriving
So we may bathe in Mārgali rejoicing,
Everyone, O my Goddess.

5. Coming in purity to the Owner of Māyā,
  hero of everlasting Mathura in the north,
  chief of the Yamuna pure and deep,
  jewel lamp blazing in the cowherd caste,
  child with a rope tied round his belly
    bringing radiance to his mother's womb,
We scatter bright flowers and worship,
We exalt him with our words,
Ponder him with our minds,
And, they say, our past faults,

and even those yet to come,
Will become like cotton in a fire,
Everyone, O my Goddess.

18. He is a bull elephant in rut,
His mighty shoulders never flee,
He is Nanda the protector of cows,
And you are his daughter-in-law,
O lovely Pinnai,
Won't you with coiled and perfumed hair
Open the gate, please,
for cocks are crowing all around us,
and look, on the *mādhavī* bower,
flocks of *kuyil* cry out over and over;
So that we may sing the names of your husband,
As you hold the ball in your fingers,
Won't you come
with graceful bangles tinkling
And with with your red lotus hand
Open the door,
Rejoicing everyone, O my Goddess.

19. A standing lamp burns,
While stretched out on a smooth bed
of the five finest qualities
over a frame with tusks for legs,
You rest, holding on your full-blown chest
The breasts of lovely Pinnai,
clusters of flowers blooming
in her coiled hair,
Speak to us, please;
And you there with those long shadowed eyes,
Won't you let your husband awake from sleep
even for a moment?
Look, can't you stand to be apart
even for a second?
That's not your nature, not your way,
Please open up,
Rejoicing everyone, O my Goddess.

20. You led the thirty-three Immortals
and dispelled their fear,
Such strength is yours,
please wake up;
You are faithful, you are brave,

You are the Uncorrupted who gives
  sorrow to your foes,
  please wake up;
And lovely Pinnai, best of women,
  breasts soft, small like pots,
  mouth red, waist slender,
    O Śrī,
  please wake up,
Give us a fan,
  a mirror,
  your husband,
So we may bathe this very moment,
Open up, please, rejoicing everyone,
O my Goddess.

27. O Govinda, you always slay the enemy,
  for such is your sovereignty,
And in praising you we shall take the drum,
Receive your largesse,
And with gifts the land extols—
  bracelets and armlets,
  rings and baubles for the ears,
  anklets and many other jewels—
We shall adorn ourselves, dress in cloth,
We shall be served milk-rice covered in ghee
  flowing down our elbows,
And sitting together with you we shall be cooled,
Everyone, O my Goddess.

29. In the small hours of morning we come and serve you,
Praising your golden lotus foot and no other,
Listen please to the meaning of this,
  for you too were born in the caste
  that grazes cattle for a living,
  so don't go on not taking our intimate service,
Because, keeper of cows,
Today isn't for taking the drum—
Every day for seven times seven rebirths
We will relate only to you,
We will slave only for you,
So please dispel any other desire we may have,
Everyone, O my Goddess.

30. The finely dressed girls with moon-bright faces
Approached and revered Keśava,

who was Mādhava
churner of the sea of ships,
And there received that drum,
as told in a garland of classic Tamil by Godā,
the daughter of the best of priests at lovely Putuvai
whose garland is fresh and cooling lotus,
While here whoever recites these stanzas
all thirty
without error,
Will receive holy grace from wealthy Tirumāl
with four vast mountainous shoulders,
red eyes,
a brilliant face,
And will dwell in delight everywhere,
Everyone, O my Goddess.

EXCERPTS FROM THE *NĀCCIYĀR TIRUMOḺI*

POEM ONE

1. The whole month of Tai
I purified the ground
and laid a graceful maṇḍala,
And from the first day of Māsi
I decorated the streets
with fine sand and made them beautiful,
O God without a body,
And wondering, "Will I ever live?"
I worshiped you and your younger brother—
You can appoint me to the Lord of Veṅkaṭam
Whose hand holds the incomparable Wheel that spits hot fire,
can't you?

2. I decorated the streets with fine white sand,
I immersed myself in a pond before the sky grew light,
I fed thornless branches into a fire,
Enduring those things for you, O God of Desire—
You can take a flower full of honey for an arrow,
Write on it the unique name,
"He the Color of the Ocean,"
And shoot me into the singular target,
"He Split the Mouth of the Bird,"
can't you?

3. Taking flowers of intoxicating sweet fragrance
And the blossoms of coral trees
I worshiped your feet three times a day,
And when my heart burned and said, "He is not real,"
I refused to say it and did not slander you at all—
You can take a cluster of blooming flowers for an arrow,
Write the unique name "Govinda" on it,
And shoot me into the singular lamp,
"The Mysterious and Wise Herder,
Resident of Veṅkaṭam,"
can't you?

4. I wrote your ancient name on a wall,
Showed you auspicious flags with shark emblems
And horses and ladies waving yak-tail fans
And sugarcane war bows
And gave them to you,
Didn't you notice, O God of Desire?—
Since I was young my full breasts have craved constantly
and have swelled up,
But I have resolved they are only for the Lord of Dvaraka
And have been worshiping you,
For you can make that happen quickly,
can't you?

5. My full and swelling breasts meant for the Supreme Being
Whose body bears the Wheel and the Conch
Are like the food set aside by brahmans
in the fire sacrifice
for the gods dwelling in heaven—
So if you say they are meant for a man,
That would be like a fox that wanders in a forest
who enters, licks, smells,
and picks over the food,
And I won't go on living,
don't you see, Manmatha?

6. Every day I appear on the street with handsome men
And young men and learned men
And skillful reciters of hymns,
Observing the days of Paṅkuṉi perfectly,
O God of Desire—
So you should be gracious and make him
who is the color of a black cloud
and the color of the purple *kāyā* flower
and the color of the sky-blue *karuvilai*

Look at me directly with his auspicious eyes
In his splendid face the color of a lotus,
don't you see?

7. I cook green paddy with sugarcane
And I cook *aval* from fresh rice with brown sugar,
And I worship you with the *mantras* of Brahmins with good voice,
O Manmatha—
So you will give me the greatest glory in this world,
The experience of the Thrice-strider
who long ago measured out the land,
Touching me with his auspicious hands
on my lustrous belly and soft full breasts,
won't you?

8. With my body tarnished,
My hair disheveled,
My lips colorless,
And eating only once,
O splendid and able God of Desire,
Don't you notice the vow I endure?—
Don't you see my lord,
Only one thing is left to say:
Be gracious in a way that crowns my womanhood
And grant me this boon,
"She will seize the feet of Keśava the Beloved."

9. Worshiping three times a day,
Venerating your feet,
Tossing pure flowers in worship,
I sing your praise,
Yet flawlessly I serve him alone,
He whose color is the sea that surrounds the earth—
And if I don't receive true life,
I shall run wild
and weep
and wail
and cry out "Mother!"
And that will disgrace you entirely,
don't you see,
Just as if you had yoked an ox to the plow
and worked it
but never gave it food.

10. By venerating the two feet of Lord Kāma
whose bow is sugarcane
and whose arrows are flowers,

And by saying,
  "The one there who ripped off the tusk
  of the incomparable roaring elephant
  and split the mouth of the bird,
  he the color of blue gem,
  set me aside for him,"
Godā, daughter of Viṣṇucitta,
  king of those who live in New Town
  where storied houses spring up in abundance like mountains,
Composed this garland of Tamil with desiring love,
And those adept in reciting it will,
  without a doubt,
Reach the feet of the King
  of those dwelling in Viṣṇu's realm.

POEM FIVE (EXCERPTS)

1. Just because I take pleasure in the Lord of Spring,
  that man the color of black gem
  wearing a jewel crown,
Is it right that I lost my bangle? . . .

2. That spotless one holding a sparkling Wheel
  in his left hand
Didn't show his body to me,
But penetrated me
And hurt me
And all day as my life pours out,
He dances about, watching. . . .

3. I haven't see that hero coming anywhere. . . .

4. O *kuyil*, my bones melt,
The lids of my splendid spearlike eyes
  won't close,
And many days now I've been tossing about
  in the sea of sorrow
  without the boat Vaikuṇṭha,
But you, too, know the ache
  a lover's separation gives,
Don't you? . . .

5. Longing to see the golden feet
  of him who lives in Villi's New Town,
My eyes fight like fish
And I can't sleep. . . .

6. The Lord of Senses
    whom gods everywhere worship and praise
Pains me,
And the beauty of my white pearl teeth
    and my red lips
    and my breasts
Has vanished. . . .

7. Longing to make love to him
    who sleeps on the billowing Ocean of Milk
My breasts swell with pleasure
And boil my spirit over
To grieve me. . . .

8. But that man
    whose powerful broad hand
    bends his bow
Is a gentleman and decent,
And we have an agreement between us
That only he and I know. . . .

9. O *kuyil*, I've been caught in a snare
    the color of a young parrot
Called Śrīdhara, Bearer-of-Kingship. . . .
If you want to live in this grove,
You'd better tell him
    who holds the Conch and Wheel
To come,
And you'd better make him
Bring my golden bangle
    And give it back. . . .

10. He measured the world that day
    and I desire him,
But in his slavery
    he treats me cruelly,
    I didn't know the way I would suffer
    when the southern breeze
    and the moon
    cut me through,
If you want to go on living in this grove,
    O *kuyil*,
Don't hurt me—
Go tell Nārāyaṇa to come today
Or I'll chase you right out of here. . . .

POEM FOURTEEN (EXCERPTS)

2. Govardhana the young bull
Left me to suffer
While he plunders Gokula,
eating everything,
reeking of sour milk,
Did you see him?
Yes we saw him, indeed,
There in Vṛndāvana playing with others,
his garland of wild flowers
flashing like lightning in clouds.

3. The beloved Lord born as Desire,
The bridegroom who creates Desire
and tells all kinds of lies,
Did you see him coming here?
Yes we saw him indeed,
There in Vṛndāvana under Garuḍa's wings
Vinatā's son stretching out
to protect him
from the spreading heat above.

8. The gracious and auspicious Tirumāl
holds a white Conch
wears a golden Cloth
has a Wheel
Have you seen him?
Yes we saw him playing in Vṛndāvana
Standing with bunches of fragrant flowers
Coiling around his broad shoulders
like a swarm of drunken bees.

9. "Create the universe," said the Lord
who is Purity itself,
And in play gave Brahmā and the others
The cool and large flower of his navel
to make into a home,
Have you seen him?
Yes we saw him there in Vṛndāvana
Where he entered the wilderness
to hunt down Dhenuka,
the elephant
and the bird,
And slew them instantly.

10. In Vṛndāvana here on earth,
Viṣṇucitta's Godā saw the Supreme Being
who was gracious to the elephant
of stout legs,
And whoever believes her words
to be medicine,
Living with them constantly in mind,
Will exist forever at the feet of God
whose legs, too, are stout,
Never to leave.

Traditions in Transition and Conflict

—13—

The Jain Monk Jinapati Sūri Gets the Better of a Nāth Yogī

Paul Dundas

Perhaps more than any other Indian religious tradition, Jainism has placed a high value on maintaining barriers of physical and moral restraint and self-discipline in order to advance on the path to liberation. The entire regimen of the religion's adherents, at least as ideally conceived, has been oriented toward the ascetic quieting of the mind, body, and speech. The aim is to reduce and ultimately eliminate the flow of karmic matter, which brings about both the soul's embodiment, whether in human or lesser form, and loss of its perfect qualities of bliss, energy, and knowledge, with consequent entanglement in the time-bound world of rebirth. Tantric practices have tended to flourish in India whenever a religious establishment that claims a monopoly on purity of behavior has erected boundaries against what it perceives to be the encroaching dangers of society and nature. The response that is generated would see true religiosity in radically experiential terms, linked to the deliberate breaching or ignoring of these boundaries. From this perspective, Jainism would appear to provide a classic scenario for the eventual emergence of a reorientation of its soteriological path that would fall within the general sphere of Tantra. Even to those well informed about the dynamics of South Asian soteriological traditions, however, it might seem strange to think of medieval Jain monks as Tantric adepts.

Here we should be clear about what is meant by "Tantra" in the Jain context. Although some Jain teachers from the early medieval period onward did advocate judging the external world in terms of the one true reality, the innermost soul, and consequently downgraded workaday experience by reference to it, there cannot be found within Jainism any serious claim that conventional social and moral values should be turned upside-down by engaging in antinomian sexual and ritual practices. Extreme forms of behavior indicating an attempted direct engagement with some variety of unconditioned or unmediated reality seem to have been advocated only within those South Asian traditions that had nondualism as an ideological basis. The Jains, pluralist realists throughout their intellectual history, have consistently rejected nondualism and its philosophical affine, monism, whether of a Hindu or Buddhist provenance, as equivalent to idealism.

However, the possibility of using sanctified language of a general Tantric idiom in the attempt to gain worldly goals has never caused the Jains any difficulty, and in common with the Hindus and Buddhists they cultivated an elaborate science of mantra and yantra (*mantraśāstra*) that enabled them, often with the aid of tutelary deities, to participate within a performative world of magic and esoteric ritual. Mantras and magic spells are, in fact, credited with great antiquity in Jainism, having supposedly constituted the whole of the tenth section of the massive Pūrva ("prior") scriptures that finally disappeared very early in the common era, if indeed they ever existed at all. Legends also accrued around a number of mantrasiddhas, or "mantra masters," named Revatī, Rohiṇī, Nāgārjuna, Khapuṭācārya and Yaśobhadra who are given traditional datings that would locate them as living from about the second century B.C.E. to the tenth century C.E. However, these individuals, who are regarded as Jain exemplars in the practice of magic, have little reality beyond legend; Nāgārjuna, for one, also appears in a large number of guises in Buddhist tradition. The early medieval literature prescribing correct monastic behavior is clearly uneasy with the performance of magic ritual by Jain monks, which suggests that this may have been a common practice. Unfortunately, the trajectory of early Jain mantric practices cannot be precisely delineated much beyond this. Nonetheless, it can be said that probably through a combination of the influence of the requirements of a burgeoning life-cycle and temple ceremonial and increasing exposure to prestigious Śaiva styles of mantric usage, by around the eleventh century the Jains had evolved their own particular brand of *mantraśāstra* and attendant ritual. Monastic participation within this mantric culture was no longer frowned upon. Indeed, the ability to manipulate magic spells successfully and thus overcome human or divine opponents came to be seen as one of the major ways by which a monk could bring glory to the Jain religion.

Jain use of mantras has, broadly speaking, been centred on alloforms or variants, often of some length, of the *Pañcanamaskāra*, "The Five Homages," a benedictory formula of salutation to the omniscient saints, liberated beings, teachers, preceptors, and monks, which was composed in the vernacular Prakrit language and in its complete form perhaps dates from around the beginning of the common era, although in Jain tradition it is reckoned to be eternal. From early medieval times to the present day, Jain scholars have analyzed this mantra and speculated on the nature of its power and its correlation with the constituent parts of the human body. However, an important mantra that came to preoccupy medieval Jains greatly (and that will be encountered in the passage translated below) has only tangential connections with "The Five Homages," at least in external form. This is the sūrimantra, a mantra from whose power the very continuity of Jainism was regarded as deriving.

Strictly speaking, the sūrimantra is the formula (once again couched in Prakrit, not Sanskrit, as is normal in other Indian mantric cultures) transmitted privately by a senior Jain teacher, or sūri, of one of the Śvetāmbara ("White-Robed") image-worshiping sects to a pupil during the ceremony in which the latter is promoted to that same rank. Many elaborate cloth paintings, called paṭas, exist with sūrimantras inscribed on them within elaborate yantra-like designs that were presented to newly appointed sūris to commemorate their promotion. One of the regular obligations of a sūri is to recite this mantra and meditate upon it every night for the well-being of the members of his sect, both ascetics and lay followers. Meditation upon the sūrimantra by the leader of a sectarian group was in the late medieval period also a vital element in the location of an appropriately qualified successor.

Although the hagiographies of the post-eleventh-century Śvetāmbara sectarian leaders take care to hedge the sūrimantra around with secrecy, the medieval ritual handbooks, or kalpas, show no reticence about recording the mantra's wording and the ritual by which the powers located in it could be realized. Indeed, so many different transmissions have been preserved that it is impossible to talk of one central version of the sūrimantra, whatever claims to exclusivity the competing sectarian traditions might have made. The kalpas describe how the mantra was originally transmitted by Ṛṣabha, the first of the twenty-four saving teachers, or tīrthaṅkaras, of this world age—and gradually became differentiated and diminished from its original length of three hundred verses, as the physical and moral stature of humanity slowly but inexorably declined over vast periods of time, until it was finally reduced at the very end of this world age to a mere two and half verses in length.

The earliest evidence for the sūrimantra simply links it to the ritual for teacher consecration and image installation. By the eleventh century, however, it had also become a crucial element of legitimation for the leaders of the various Śvetāmbara Jain sects (*gacchas*) that emerged at that time. By means of the sūrimantra, a sūri could demonstrate his authority within his sect by mastering through meditation and ritual the various magic powers embodied in the mantra, such as curing disease and overcoming enemies, and thus ultimately transform himself into the latter-day equivalent of Gautama, the miracle-working favourite disciple of the twenty-fourth tīrthaṅkara, Mahāvīra. Although the result gained from the sūrimantra ritual is not specifically stated to be enlightenment and subsequent freedom from rebirth, it can nonetheless be said that here Jain Tantra, normally oriented toward material and worldly goals, becomes more soteriological than at any other point.

A typical example of the sūrimantra is divided into various sections, as many as five, called prasthānas or pīṭhas, each of which has a presiding deity. The first section, standard in all transmissions of the sūrimantra, contains expressions of homage (similar in form to those found in the *Pañcanamaskāra* formula referred to above) to a variety of Jain advanced spiritual types and also a formally expressed expectation of success in the ritual linked to the mantra. The next two sections generally invoke the various labdhis, or magic powers, possessed by Mahāvīra's disciple Gautama and offer praise to the great warrior-ascetic Bāhubali, the son of the tīrthaṅkara Ṛṣabha, whose attainment of enlightenment without scriptural knowledge seems to have provided an attractive model for those monks who saw themselves as following the Jain path in debased times during which serious learning was at a premium.

The fourth and fifth sections usually contain strings of mantric language, Prakrit combined with esoteric words such as *meru*, framed by the power syllable *Oṃ* and the ancient Vedic invocation *svāhā*. These sections are more overtly oriented toward spiritual attainments and the transformation of the sūri into the equivalent of Gautama. According to some monastic commentators, the fifth and most advanced section of the sūrimantra, called mantrarāja, "king of mantras" (a designation that is often used by synecdoche to refer to the whole mantra) encompasses and is equivalent to the preceding four sections. Contemplation of the mantra by the sūri was ideally to take place within a maṇḍala-like diagram modeled on the balustraded assembly hall where gods, humans, and animals gather to hear each tīrthaṅkara preach. The restrained and ascetic activities of fasting and confession were necessary components of the accompanying ritual, thus marking it out as specifically Jain. Making offerings in consecrated fires, indicative of a more general Tantric idiom, is also advocated in the ritual handbooks.

One of the Śvetāmbara Jain subsects that placed particular emphasis on the sūrimantra was the Kharatara Gaccha, which took its name from the epithet "Sharpwitted" (*kharatara*) bestowed in 1024 C.E. by a king on one of its early teachers after a victory in public debate. The passage translated below focuses upon three of the sūris of this sect, Jinadatta Sūri (1075–1154), perhaps the greatest leader of the Kharatara Gaccha, his successor Jinacandra Sūri (1140–1166), known as Maṇidhārin, "Jewel Bearer," because he had a precious stone in his forehead (an attribute not fully explained by the chroniclers but possibly connected with the narratives about the legendary mantrasiddha Yaśobhadra, who was similarly endowed), and his successor Jinapati Sūri (1153–1220). The chroniclers of the Kharatara Gaccha are particularly concerned to portray these monks as protectors and enrichers of their followers through their magical powers and, in particular, as vying for supremacy with the yoginīs who controlled some of the major cities of western India.

The cult of the yoginīs, the sixty-four semidivine sorceresses and shape-changers, although of indeterminate origin (sixth century C.E.?), had become extremely popular in north India by around the tenth or eleventh centuries. Benevolent protectresses and agents of inner transformation when propitiated by their Śaiva votaries but malevolent and vengeful if crossed, these sorceresses were particularly associated by the Jains with Delhi, called in the Kharatara Gaccha sources Yoginīpura, "City of the Yoginīs," a dangerous place of the black arts. They are also portrayed as having strongholds in the cities of Ajmer, Ujjain, and Broach. The yoginīs represent for the Jains a malign form of Tantric magic, as does the mysterious Nāth yogī who appears later in the passage below as a stock representative of a Śaiva sect with which the Jains contested for local patronage in western India for centuries and also at times achieved a kind of accomodation.

The early chronicler of the Kharatara Gaccha, Jinapāla, who probably wrote around the middle of the thirteenth century, refers only in passing to the perils of Delhi and Jinadatta's conversion of the yoginīs at Ujjain, and he says nothing of Jinacandra's having had a jewel in his forehead. A cycle of traditional stories quickly emerged, however, as the Kharatara Gaccha expanded its sense of identity and history; it described how Jinadatta compelled the yoginīs of Delhi to bestow boons upon the sect and how the young Jinapati Sūri won back his master Jinacandra's jewel through the power of the sūrimantra. Here we gain a glimpse of Tantra as it was perceived to operate "on the ground" in medieval India, functioning not as an esoteric and learned soteriology but as a magic weapon in the struggle for sectarian dominance. A consistent theme in these narratives is the ability through spells to paralyze an opponent. This is one of the "six acts" (*ṣaṭkarmāṇi*), a form of black magic common to most Tantric traditions, with the other five being calming disease and inimical spirits, bringing others under one's control, sowing dissension among one's enemies, causing psychological turmoil in an individual so that he abandons his normal life, and killing. Jain monks saw no moral difficulty in engaging in such magic.

The following extract is taken from the third of three anonymous Sanskrit chronicles or paṭṭāvalīs, "Lists of the Holders of the Paṭṭa," which describes the main events in the lives of the leaders of the Kharatara Gaccha up to 1617. The term *paṭṭa* signifies the seal tied on the forehead of a traditional Indian monarch at the time of his consecration and indicates the royal imagery with which the Jains surrounded their great teachers. The style of this particular paṭṭāvalī is clipped and unembellished (although without the strong vernacularization that characterizes much Jain Sanskrit literature of this period), and I have occasionally smoothed it out. In the interests of providing a self-contained narrative, I have also omitted the paṭṭāvalī's descriptions of the miracles performed by Jinadatta in the period prior to his death. Although according to Jain usage the title of sūri is incorporated into a teacher's name (for example Jinapatisūri), I have throughout kept it separate.

An equivalent narrative recorded by an earlier anonymous Prakrit chronicle entitled the *Vṛddhācāryaprabandhāvali*, "Series of Biographies of the Old Teachers," provides some explanations that amplify the version below. Thus we are told that on his deathbed Jinadatta had forbidden his successors to travel to any of the cities that fell within the influence of the yoginīs. Jinacandra's otherwise odd and ultimately fatal visit to Delhi is explained as the result of an earnest request by the Jain community there. In addition, this same chronicle attributes the vindictive behavior of the Nāth yogī to his anger at the unwillingness of the Jain laity to give him alms. It is noteworthy that, according to the second of the paṭṭāvalīs edited by Muni Jinavijaya, Jinapati magically summons his dead teacher Jinacandra to help him against the yogī.

The passage translated below, the third of three anonymous chronicles, is taken from the *Kharataragacchapaṭṭāvalīsaṃgraha*, edited by, Muni Jinavijaya (Calcutta: Puran Chand Nahar, 1932), pp. 49–52.

Further Reading

Paul Dundas, "Becoming Gautama: Mantra and History in Śvetāmbara Jainism," in John E. Cort, ed., *Jain Communities and Cultures in Indian History* (Albany: State University of New York Press, 1998), pp. 31–52, provides a contextualization of the sūrimantra, along with an analysis of one particular transmission of it. The bibliography of this article should also be consulted for primary sources on Jain mantraśāstra and the Kharatara Gaccha, including the *Vṛddhācāryaprabandhāvali*. Phyllis Granoff provides a study of the hagiographies of the two greatest Kharatara Gaccha exponents of Tantra in "Jinadattasūri and Jinaprabhasūri: Two Studies from the Śvetāmbara Jain Tradition," in *Speaking of Monks: Religious Biography in India and China*, edited by Phyllis Granoff and Koichi Shinohara (Oakville, Ontario: Mosaic Press, 1992), pp. 1–96. Lawrence A. Babb, *Absent Lord: Ascetics and Kings in a Jain Ritual Culture* (Berkeley and Los Angeles: University of California Press, 1996), chapter 3, places the episode I have translated in the ritual and devotional context of current-day Śvetāmbara Jainism in Rajasthan.

For the yoginī cult in medieval India, see Vidya Dehejia, *Yoginī Cult and Temples: A Tantric Tradition* (New Delhi: National Museum, 1986); R. Nagaswamy, "The Sixty-Four Yoginīs and Bhūta Worship as Mentioned by Śaṅkara in His Commentary on the Bhagavad Gītā," *Berliner Indologische Studien* 9–10 (1996): 237–46; and David Gordon White, "Transformations in the Art of Love: Kāmakalā Practices in Hindu Tantric and Kaula Traditions," *History of Religions* 38:2 (November 1998): 172–98. A description of the role of the yoginīs in contemporary Himalayan Hinduism can be found in Hélène Desirens, "Les Yoginī de la haute vallée de Kulu (Himachal Pradesh)," *Bulletin d'Etudes Indiennes* 9 (1991): pp. 61–73.

The Nāth yogī may be described slightly anachronistically by the chronicle translated below, whose vantage point is around the second half of the seventeenth century. For the chronology and origins (probably late twelfth- to early thirteenth- century) of the Nāth sampradāya and for the relationship of this sect with the Jains in western India, see David Gordon White, *The Alchemical Body: Siddha Traditions in Medieval India* (Chicago: University of Chicago Press, 1996), pp. 90–101 and 117–19.

Kharataragacchapaṭṭāvalīsaṃgraha, Third Paṭṭāvalī

Once Jinadatta Sūri went to Delhi where the sixty-four yoginīs had their ritual sites. He did not pay homage to them, and so in anger the yoginīs thought, "Let us bewitch him." Then a friendly deity, who traveled between the various worlds, visited Jinadatta and warned him, "There are yoginīs living here who will try to bewitch you. Be careful." During the night Jinadatta summoned a layman called Mahaṇasī and said to him, "Get sixty-four fresh mats ready and bring them here. There is an important task to be performed." The layman brought the mats that night, and Jinadatta recited mantras over them. In the morning, when the time came to expound the scriptures, he told another layman, "Today sixty-four laywomen will come in a crowd. They will stand in the south, the inauspicious region of death, wearing white clothes. You must give them the mats to sit on." While Jinadatta was preaching, the women came as he had said, and the layman gave them the mats, as result of which they all remained rooted to the spot, for they were in reality the yoginīs who had been paralyzed by the power of Jinadatta's mantras. At the end of his sermon, Jinadatta said to them, "Be off now, but come again tomorrow morning."

The yoginīs were deeply embarrassed, realizing that Jinadatta was a repository of great mantric power, and they asked that their offense be pardoned before they left. Jinadatta said, "Give me something in return." So they gave him seven boons, namely, that Kharatara monks would generally not be fools; Kharatara nuns would not follow the normal worldly behavior of women; Kharatara monks and nuns would not die from snakebite; statements made by followers of the Kharatara Gaccha would be efficacious; there would be no danger to the leaders of the Kharatara Gaccha from lightning; witches (*śākinīs*) would not enchant members of the sect; and all Kharatara laymen beyond Delhi would be rich and learned. The yoginīs asked for a pledge in return, namely, that if any of the monks who succeeded Jinadatta as leader of the Kharatara sect should come to Delhi, Ajmer, Bhṛgukaccha, or Ujjain, the abodes of the yoginīs, then he should simply take food and then go, without staying the night. If, however, he were to stay the night for some reason, then he should not take food. With this stipulation, the yoginīs went back to where they had come from.

Jinadatta Sūri died at the age of eighty-four at Ajmer, where the lay community erected a funerary monument to commemorate him. Jinacandra Sūri, who had become a monk at the age of nine, had been personally installed by Jinadatta as his successor at Vikramapura in 1149. He had a jewel in his head. One day a powerful Nāth yogī saw him and realized that the sūri had only five years to live. At a later time Jinacandra went to Delhi. The yoginīs there said, "He has ignored the command we gave to Jinadatta. Let us bewitch him." So they came at night, but through the power of the Jain flag on the monastic lodging house their witchcraft did not work. They then turned themselves into mice and carried off the flag. Waking up, Jinacandra turned himself into a cat and chased after them. However, they managed to bewitch him. In the morning the teacher entered the death-fast and said to the layman Kocara, "There is a jewel in my head. At the time of my cremation, put a bowl of milk near the funeral pyre and the jewel will fall into it. Worship it at home and you will gain unfailing wealth." But when Jinacandra died, Kacora forgot what he had told him to do. The Nāth yogī, however, prepared a bowl of milk when the cremation was taking place, got hold of the jewel, and went off with it. Kacora saw this and argued with him, but the yogī would not give him the jewel.

Jinapati Sūri was appointed Jinacandra Sūri's successor at the age of fourteen by Ācārya Jayadeva in 1167 at the village of Bavveraka, where a great festival was held by two laymen to celebrate the event. He had attained this rank not long after becoming a monk as a boy. Jinapati then went off with five hundred monks to the town of Hāṃsī in the vicinity of Hiṃsār to the north of Delhi, where the laypeople had gotten an image of the tīrthaṅkara Pārśva made and had built a new temple to house it. At the time of the installation of the image, the Nāth yogī who had taken the magic jewel also came there. He knew that Jinacandra had possessed magic power and wanted to see whether his pupil Jinapati had it as well. To this end, he employed a spell to immobilize the image that was near the temple so that it would not move from its position. The yogī then challenged the Jains, saying, "I have immobilized the image. Let your leader raise it up."

At this, the senior monks became deeply despondent, for none of them had any magic power, and as a result the installation of the image could not take place. The laywomen, egged on by a nun, mockingly sang, "The new moon doesn't shed strong moonlight, so what can this young teacher of ours know?" Hearing this, Jinapati thought that his life was not worth living. But then he looked at his sūrimantra yantra, with the "king of mantras" portion, three and a half words in length, inscribed in the middle. He put it aside and recited the mantra, at which Padmāvatī, the tutelary goddess associated with the tīrthaṅkara Pārśva, appeared to help him.

In the morning, while the senior monks and preceptors were expounding the scriptures, Jinapati went to the temple and played with the children who surrounded him. The yogī once again announced that he had immobilized the image. But then Jinapati threw magically consecrated powder on his head and so immobilized the yogī in turn. The entire Jain community assembled and the installation ceremony was carried out to the accompaniment of praise of the power of its teacher, even though he was so young. The yogī said, "Let me go. Have pity." Jinapati replied, "Hand over the jewel from my teacher's head that you took in Delhi." The yogī did so and said, "My dear sir! Take this source of magic. However, a spell of the sort I have employed with it only succeeds if betel nut is used." Jinapati replied, "We Jains are not allowed to chew betel nut, because it is the equivalent of flesh. I do not care whether the spell is successful or not." Then the yogī spat betel nut from his mouth and said, "Worker of magic spells! Go back to the underworld where you came from. There is nobody else in this world who can possess you." And the jewel, the source of magic, went straight to the underworld.

—14—

Longchenpa and the Possession of the Ḍākinīs

David Germano and Janet Gyatso

Lay communities of itinerant yogins and yoginīs have been a vital dimension of Tibetan Buddhist culture from at least the ninth century onward. These communities were almost always irreducibly Tantric in character, in their ritual and contemplative practices, their textual traditions, and the very structure of their communal life. Although much of our information about early Tantric Buddhist communities in India and Tibet is fragmentary and heavily mythologized, detailed biographical and historical narratives that emerged in in later centuries in Tibet give a fuller portrayal of the nature of these communities, and afford us a glimpse of actual male-female relationships. We have chosen to translate a depiction of the fourteenth-century Tibetan saint Longchenpa's (Klong chen pa, 1308–1363) ritual empowerment of a group of Tibetan yogins and yoginīs into esoteric Tantric practices. The action portrayed here occurred in the spring of 1339. The work is signed by Longchenpa himself in the colophon and is specifically referred to as his composition in his own catalogue to *The Seminal Quintessence of the Ḍākinīs*, which is the larger cycle of his texts in which it is found. It refers to him throughout in the third person, however, usually calling him "the lama"; it is possible that the text was actually recorded by a disciple on the basis of Longchenpa's oral autobiographical account, or that Longchenpa actually wrote it in the third person, a practice not unknown in this period of Tibetan autobiographical writing; or, finally, that the text was recorded by a disciple some time after the events reported in it. Whatever the case, it seems fair to conclude that the basic sequence of events reported, at least in their bare outer appearance, in fact occurred, and that the interpretations offered were current in the early community of Longchenpa's followers. This exceptional narrative offers much to ponder with regard to the social dynamics of an esoteric Tantric community, to claims that were made regarding the production of sacred Tantric scriptures, and to the transic practices in which members of the community engaged, and which yielded extraordinary performances that were then interpreted within the context of an elaborate system of Tantric beliefs.

The broader Tibetan Tantric Buddhist movements within in which Longchenpa and his disciples participated are at least three in number. One consists of what was by then the standard set of Indian and Tibetan scriptures and practices surrounding the Tantric practice of deity yoga: the procedures in which people visualized themselves as Tantric deity/buddha figures and participated in what was thought to be those figures' experience. Another is the Seminal Heart or Nyingthik (*snying thig*) form of the Great Perfection (*rdzogs-chen*) movement, which is a Tibetan syncretic Tantric tradition consisting of Chan-like practices of formless meditation combined with exercises that cultivated spontaneous visions of buddhas. The third salient tradition that informs the account translated below is called Treasure (*gter ma*). A few comments concerning this uniquely Tibetan Tantric tradition of scriptural revelation will aid in understanding the distinctive conceptions about personal identity, time, and sacred scripture that lie at the heart of the activities in which Longchenpa engages in the narrative to follow.

The Tibetan "Treasure discoverers" (*gter ston*) were part of a movement in Tibet that had its origins in the tenth to eleventh century in Tibet, alongside other movements centered on the figure of the *lotsawa*, or translator. The discoverers were often exceptional yogins and teachers who revealed special texts and other objects that, they maintained, had mainly been concealed in the eighth- and ninth-century imperial period of Tibetan history for the express purpose of being revealed at the "right time" in the future. Furthermore, a distinction was made between "Earth Treasures" (*sa gter*) and "Mind Treasures" (*dgongs gter*), the former being actual material manuscripts recovered from the earth and the latter being visionary revelations with no physical substrate. Regardless of the modality, however, Treasures usually consist of collections of works, most of which contain instructions for special forms of Tantric practice. As discussed below, Longchenpa, in addition to being a renowned academic scholar, was also intimately involved in the revelation of Treasure. He inherited the two main streams of Treasure scriptures of the Seminal Heart—among the most important products of early Treasure revelations, which derived from the eighth-century Indic saints Vimalamitra and Padmasambhava, respectively—and went on to produce new revelations that extended both and integrated them into a single stream. In essence, the events that Longchenpa describes here trace out the process of how he first came into possession of new Padmasambhava revelations entitled *The Seminal Heart of the Ḍākinīs*, and then gradually came to reveal—in a very distinctive manner—his own exegetical revelations, entitled *The Seminal Quintessence of the Ḍākinīs*. This process most notably involved a series of encounters with women who were understood to be possessed by certain Indic and Tibetan deities and humans, all of whom play critical roles in authorizing Longchenpa's involvement with these past and future revelations of the ḍākinīs.

Treasure discoverers typically display doubts about whether they are the person who has been prophesied to reveal the Treasures that they have found, and Longchenpa is no exception. He repeatedly checks the identity of his spiritual informants to determine if they are indeed the rightful "protectors" of the Treasure. Most centrally, he asks questions about his own identity and prophesied destiny. One of the main reasons why Treasure revealers like Longchenpa talk about their self-doubt is precisely to demonstrate their care and caution in assuming the exalted role of scripture revealer. Many sectors of Tibetan Tantric society had grave concerns about the validity of the Treasure tradition as a whole, to say nothing of the authenticity of any particular individual's claim to have found such ancient materials. Even in Tibetan society, in which most persons firmly believed in reincarnation, many were skeptical of the claim that someone could recall a special teaching that they had been entrusted—by a master such as Vimalamitra, or more often, the "Precious Guru" Padmasambhava (circa 800 C.E.)—to bring to light five hundred years hence, in a future lifetime. Padmasambhava is the Indian Tantric master who introduced Tantric Buddhism to Tibet, and who is the source credited with of most of the Treasure texts in Tibet. Critics went so far as to doubt that figures such as Padmasambhava and Vimalamitra would have ever designated and then concealed special materials for future revelation in the first place. It is important to remember that such critics of the Treasure tradition were in many ways acting to protect the claims to legitimacy of their own Tantric corpora. The Treasures were probably often formulated precisely as an alternative to the more mainstream Tibetan Tantric materials that were transmitted in the large monastic institutions of central Tibet. In many ways, then, we can understand that the situation in Tibetan Tantric religion in which Longchenpa was participating was a conflict between Tantric corpora—between the mainstream canonical Tantric texts and their commentaries and ritual cycles and those introduced through the more unconventional modes of the Treasure tradition.

The Visionary Autobiography

It is because of the Treasures' controversial claims of origins that their discoverers often wrote detailed accounts, like the one by Longchenpa translated here, of their individual odysseys to revelation. Often written as glorified diaries with precisely recorded dates, the detailed events reported in such autobiographical works served to "engender confidence" in the authenticity of the revelatory process, and to convince their readers that the protagonists were in fact not the charlatans that everyone, even the Treasure proponents themselves, believed many so-called Treasure discoverers to be. Among the principal events that such autobiographical accounts report—and again, we see many examples in the present account—are the visions of the original concealers of the Treasure, including Padmasambhava, his Tibetan consort Yeshe Tsogyel (Ye shes mtsho rgyal), and other masters. Many of Longchenpa's encounters with local deities such as Remati and Vajra Turquoise Lamp (rDo rje g.yu sgron ma) also attest to the authenticity of the discoverer and the Treasure he is purporting to introduce, for such deities are said to have been appointed to protect the Treasure during the period of its interment, and to assist the appointed discoverer in locating it at the proper moment. It is in this context that we are to understand the many passages in which such deities speak directly to Longchenpa and give him information concerning the history of *The Seminal Heart of the Ḍākinīs* as well as his own relationship to that history in the past, present, and future.

Another type of experience that is typically reported in Treasure "autobiographies" such as this is the attainment of special Tantric meditative states. This connected with one of the other principal Tantric founts of Longchenpa's experience, the Great Perfection tradition. States of Great Perfection insight might be reported in any work of the "secret autobiography" genre; but the relevance of these experiences to the Treasure narrative lies in the fact that Treasure discovery is in fact closely related to those states themselves. Experiences akin to "the rainbow colored visions of radiant light" frequently referred to here are often singled out as having been salient in that past moment in which the discoverer-to-be originally had the Treasure implanted in this deep level of consciousness. That initial concealment was made in a highly encoded form, which would have been both covert and durable enough to remain in deep memory over many lifetimes until the time for revelation was at hand. In order, then, to bring out the Treasure in its fully unfolded form in that future moment, the discoverer needs to gain access to that deep state of consciousness again; hence, his ability to realize such states of consciousness serves to demonstrate that he is a person capable of revealing a Treasure.

The reader should also bear in mind the extent to which the Treasure tradition is dependent upon the more general Tibetan belief that humans can be emanations, or even reincarnations (tulkus; *sprul sku*), of past Buddhist masters. In general, the buddhas' and bodhisattvas' mastery of the Buddhist principle of emptiness is thought to allow them self-consciously to manifest "emanations" (*sprul pa*) to different parts of the cosmos, in the service of the Buddha's teachings. In the Tibetan Buddhist world, there is a more specialized belief that historical figures who were religious masters could also reincarnate deliberately in the right place and time to accomplish particular compassionate goals. These ideas underlie the Tibetan institution of the tulkus, a word that literally means "the emanated body of a buddha," but which in practice refers to the person who is discovered through the distinctive practice of seeking out the young reincarnation of a recently deceased saint, in order that that child be "reinstalled" in the religious community that the old master had left behind. Alternately—and this is the case in the selection translated here—adults can claim such a mantle for themselves later in life. Thus we witness Longchenpa reincarnationally recreate himself before our eyes, or at least before the eyes of the ḍākinī.

It is usually said that other "secondary conditions," beyond the discoverer's mastery of the succession of his or her lives and memory of the one in which the Treasure was first received, also contribute to the discovery of Treasure scriptures. The discoverer will often be granted certain props, such as a fragment of a text buried in the ground, or even a fascicle of writing handed to him in a dream.

Once such materials are in hand, the discoverer is often unable to understand them or decode them from their encrypted form. Advanced Tantric teachings and practice are said to be necessary for one to be fully qualified to codify the main Treasure scriptures, compose the necessary commentary texts, transmit the codified scriptures in a ritual Tantric empowerment, and finally teach their content in detail. At an even more esoteric level, discoverers are often said to engage in a form of sexual consort yoga as a means of accessing the necessary states of mind for Treasure revelation and decoding. Although such practices are not referred to explicitly in this text, it is quite possible that Longchenpa engaged in them during the period he is reporting. In this context we should also understand the active role of yoginīs, who are possessed by female deities. These members of the larger Tantric retreat community in which Longchenpa wrote and taught during the years reported here seemed especially gifted for channeling the spirits of the Treasure protectors and communicating their intimate messages, in esoteric form, to the discoverer. In the account we read here, Longchenpa shows a certain disdain for the revelation of Treasures out of the ground, and instead eventually identifies his own authorial voice with the voice of his ḍākinī-mediated Treasure inspiration. In other words, his extension of *The Seminal Heart of the Ḍākinīs*, rather than being a revelatory core of other-voiced texts fleshed out by his own compositions, reflects an inseparable unity of personal intention and transcendent inspiration, a subject to which we shall return.

The Seminal Heart of the Ḍākinīs

Beyond the general role of the feminine in Treasure revelation, *The Seminal Heart of the Ḍākinīs*, the tradition that Longhcenpa is engaged with here, has much to do with the particular feminine roles. This is patent in the work's title: *ḍākinī* is an Indic term, translated by the Tibetan term Kandroma (*mkha' 'gro ma*), which means "one who goes in space." It signifies a female spirit who can either be a transcendent buddha or a vengeful demoness; in addition, the word can also signify an historical female saint in Tibet. Seminal Heart is the name for a syncretic Tantric tradition that came to be the most normative variant of the Great Perfection. What *The Seminal Heart of the Ḍākinīs* Treasure did, in fact, was to bring a greater focus, in its meditative practices, on the distinctively Tantric practice of sexual yoga as integrated with the Seminal Heart. The latter include the belief in dynamically active buddhas within the ordinary body which, when cultivated, flow spontaneously out through the eyes and into the surrounding visual field. As the rainbow-colored light gradually shapes itself of its own accord into maṇḍalas, the practice culminates in visions of pure lands.

The Seminal Heart literature prior to Longchenpa consisted of three major collections, all of which emerged, between the eleventh and fourteenth centuries and through the revelatory processes of the Treasure movement, as Tibetan-language literature. They are *The Seventeen Tantras*, *The Seminal Heart of Vimalamitra*, and the very *The Seminal Heart of the Ḍākinīs* that is of principal concern in the material translated below. *The Seventeen Tantras* are largely Tibetan syntheses, and function as the primary texts upon which the other two collections are based. *The Seminal Heart of Vimalamitra* is a three-volume collection that also contains a few Tantras, but consists mostly of ritual, contemplative, and philosophical texts attributed to Vimalamitra and other Indian teachers. Vimalamitra and his disciples are said to have buried both *The Seventeen Tantras* and *The Seminal Heart of Vimalamitra* as Treasure, where they remained until the late tenth or early eleventh century, at which time their excavation began, a process that culminated in the mid-twelfth century. It appears, however, that these texts were in fact largely composed by their Tibetan discoverers themselves.

In any event, the Seminal Heart tradition had little to do with Padmasambhava until the early fourteenth century, when against the backdrop of the increasing predominance of a larger revelatory cult organized around Padmasambhava, an obscure Tibetan by the name of Tsultrim Dorje (Tshul khrims rdo rje, 1291–1315/1317) produced a two-volume collection known as *The Seminal Heart of the Ḍākinīs*. Although clearly indebted to its predecessors, its narrative frames claimed that the collection had been authored by Padmasambhava in eighth-century Tibet and concealed as Treasure by Padmasambhava's Tibetan consort Yeshe Tsogyel. The important role of the Tibetan queen Yeshe Tsogyel in the burial of Treasure is one of the reasons for which female consorts, not to mention female epiphanies, play such an important role in the revelatory processes of the Treasure discoverers. In particular, emanations of this supreme Tantric female consort are believed to be essential in helping the discoverer decode the Treasure, since it was Yeshe Tsogyel herself who encoded the Treasure in special "ḍākinī sign-language" at the moment of the Treasure's burial. Yeshe Tsogyel receives special attention in *The Seminal Heart of the Ḍākinīs* Treasure, inasmuch as it is she who originally requested Padmasambhava to grant the many texts and teachings contained in this Treasure.

Another female figure in *The Seminal Heart of the Ḍākinīs* is of paramount significance for Longchenpa. This is the eighth-century Tibetan princess Lhacam Pemasel (Lha lcam pad ma gsal) who, according to the story, died suddenly at the tender age of eight in Samye Chimphu (bSam yas mchims phu), in the presence of both her father, the Tibetan Emperor Trisong Detsen (Khri srong lde'u btsan, 742-c. 798) and Padmasamabhava. Padmasambhava explains to the grieving emperor the karmic reasons for this sudden death—namely, her transgressions of past lives—but then discloses that he has decided that the princess will reveal his own Seminal Heart teachings in a future life. He proceeds to bring her back to life in order to give her an initial transmission of those teachings: this is *The Seminal Heart of the Ḍākinīs*. Padmasambhava annoints her as Pema Ledreltsel (Pad ma las 'brel rtsal), "The one with the Dynamism of a Karmic Connection to Padma," That is, Padmasambhava.

These events are central to the the fourteenth-century narratives of Tsultrim Dorje, who claimed to be the prophesied reincarnation of the princess and thereby the inheritor of the mantle of Pema Ledreltsel. However, following his stunning revelations of 1313, when he was in his early twenties, Tshultrim Dorje himself abruptly died under mysterious circumstances, in which an ill-fated sexual liason with a woman and an inability to keep his Treasure revelations secret while he mastered his own contemplative practice of their teachings were rumored to have played a part. He left behind no institutional basis for the perpetuation of his revelations, the first new Seminal Heart cycle in over a century. However, Longchenpa, following his reception of the older traditions of *The Seminal Heart of Vimalamitra* in his early thirties, came into possession of this major Seminal Heart work. How he came into possession of this cycle, the concomitant possession of his female disciples by the ḍākinīs who redacted, concealed, and guarded the cycle, and Longchenpa's own eventual visionary extension of the tradition lie at the heart of our story.

Overview of the Translation

The passages excerpted here mark Longchenpa's emergence as a teacher, transmitter, and revealer of the Seminal Heart. When Longchenpa was in his late twenties, Kumārāja, his principal lama, gave him an array of teachings that highlighted *The Seventeen Tantras* and *The Seminal Heart of Vimalamitra*. Longchenpa followed these transmissions with a three-year period of retreat. At the opening of our translated passage we find him emerging as a teacher of the Seminal Heart in his own right, as he takes on a circle of disciples of his own. Not surprisingly, he chooses the famous Chimphu Valley to inaugurate this new identity. Chimphu is a retreat center in the mountains above Samye, the first Buddhist monastery in Tibet, which also bears strong associations with Padmasambhava, who is believed to have been instrumental in its construction. Samye was also the site of important events relating to *The Seminal Heart of the Ḍākinīs*, including the death and ressurection of Princess Pemasel. Here Longchenpa began ritually to initiate a nonmonastic group of eight yogins and yoginīs into the tradition of *The Seminal Heart of the Ḍākinīs*, after which he gave them detailed contemplative instructions on the tradition's esoteric meditative system.

Against the backdrop of these rituals, transmissions, and celebrations, Longchenpa and his disciples enter a spiritually excited state, which gives rise to a stream of visions and states of possession in the group. The visions are often seen by everyone present, but the possessions are performed exclusively by the women. We can also note that the overwhelming majority of the visionary apparitions and possessing spirits that enter into this exceptional milieu are female, whether they be Buddhist goddesses, Dharma protectresses, or historical Tibetan women. The possessions are characterized as the "descent" (*babs*) of the spirit into the yoginī, after which the latter begins to "perform" (*'khrab*) in the identity and voice of the former.

The first such spirit appears abruptly during an empowerment ritual. She identifies herself as the Dharma protectress Ekajaṭī, a famous wrathful female figure particularly associated with the Seminal Heart tradition. Dharma protectresses are generally depicted as indigenous spirits wrathfully subjugated by Padmasambhava or other masters, both to prevent them from hindering Buddhist activities and to bind them into the ongoing service and defense of Buddhism. They therefore have a hybrid nature that retains traces of their origins in the violent and unpredictable nature of certain older, non-Buddhist spirits, now reinterpreted in Buddhist ethical terms. Indeed, such protectresses are often viewed as emanations of buddhas or bodhisattvas, with their ferocity subliminated into a kind of playful creativity, as we see here repeatedly. Ekajaṭī chides Longchenpa on the quality of his performance of the ritual, imparting nuanced revisions of the master's teachings and actions. The other disciples present are skeptical and taken aback by the yoginī's daring actions before their respected guru, but he reassures them that she is indeed possessed by an authentic and enlightened spirit, and also that he himself has the knowledge and charisma to keep the performance under control. The episode marks an important breakthrough for the small community, as its members begin to recognize the special insights and information that these possessed women are able to offer their teacher. These positive results reinforce the value of what might otherwise have been viewed as dangerous—or inauthentic—trance states.

The next possession episode provides even more crucial information. A yoginī is taken over by Vajra Sow (rDo rje phag mo, in Tibetan, Vajravārāhī in Sanskrit), one of the most famous Buddhist Tantric buddhas and Longchenpa's own personal deity. Vajra Sow tells him about the other Tibetan spirits bound into the service of Longchenpa's teachings who have come to visit him as well, and also reassures him about the current state of health of his teacher Kumārāja. She then settles into an extended dialogue with him concerning his true identity. She begins by revealing that Longchenpa's teacher, Kumārāja, is one of the prophesied centennial emanations of Vimalamitra in Tibet, which implies that Longchenpa had received *The Seminal Heart of Vimalamitra* from Vimalamitra himself, in reincarnate form, just a few years earlier. Still more dramatically, she goes on to disclose that Longchenpa is none other than the contemporary reincarnation of Tsultrim Dorje, who was in turn the reincarnation of Princess Lhacam Pemasel, who had originally received, from Padmasambhava, the very Seminal Heart teachings Longchenpa now is transmitting. She thus identifies him as the principal heir and, in fact, the original revealer of *The Seminal Heart of the Ḍākinīs*, the second great stream of the Seminal Heart. As a consequence, she gives him the prophesied names Drime Özer (Dri med 'od zer) and, by extension, Pema Ledreltsel (Pad ma las 'brel rtsal). The former, literally "Stainless Light Rays," comes to be one of Lonchenpa's most important authorial names invoked in colophons, while the latter, literally "The One with the Dynamism of a Karmic Connection to Padma(sambhava)," is employed throughout Longchenpa's own subsequent commentary, entitled *The Seminal Quintessence of the Ḍākinīs*.

Vajra Sow then discusses his present lifespan and his future lifetimes and Treasure revelations, and gives critical instructions on when, where, and by what means the revelations would transpire. This passage thus works to accomplish a momentous feat, namely, the recreation of Longchenpa into a authorized revealer and teacher of the esoteric *Seminal Heart of the Ḍākinī*, who in a future life would attain buddhahood in the sacred land of Oḍḍiyāna to the west of Tibet. It should be recalled that all of this self-transformation takes place in the very valley where, in a distant past life, the subject in question had already been resurrected and blessed as a ḍākinī him/herself by Padmasabmhava.

These grand claims, however, are undermined by two seeming contradictions, which actually are noted by Longchenpa himself: Tshultrim Dorje's death date (1315/1317) seems to have come after Longchenpa's birth date (1308), and the prophecies in the Treasure cycle itself indicate that Tsultrim Dorje's next rebirth will be in Bhutan, whereas Longchenpa was born in southern Tibet. As the passage proceeds, we see the ḍākinī ingeniously solving these problems. Her strategy turns on a skillful interpretation of a seemingly irrelevant detail in the prophecy, namely, that Tsultrim Dorje would, prior to rebirth, spend a "brief sojourn in a pure land." This would seem to indicate that the few years' gap separating the saint's death and rebirth would have been passed in a buddha's pure land outside of the ordinary world system. The ḍākinī, however, interprets the statement as referring to Longchenpa's own life, in which he is immersed in visions of Buddhist pure lands through his contemplative practice of the Seminal Heart. This renders the prophesied Bhutanese rebirth as one yet to come. As for the incongruous death date of Tsultrim Dorje, she exploits the obscurity of his life to push his death date back by eight or ten years to 1307, just in time to coincide with the conception of Longchenpa. This passage ends with Longchenpa in a state of inspiration, singing a Tantric song about the interior reality of the five Tantric buddhas.

The next major episode of possession involves a distinctively Tibetan Dharma Protectress by the name of Vajra Turquoise Lamp (rDo rje g.yu sgron) who, again, descends into a female disciple of Longchenpa. She first invites him to her domain, which refers to the retreat place of White Skull Snow Mountain (Gangs ri thod dkar) to which he would eventually repair and compose most of his major works. The two then discuss various doctrinal and meditational points, reiterating the nonconceptual, immediate, and even "nonmeditational" nature of the kind of enlightened realization most valued in the Seminal Heart tradition. They also review a range of pedagogical problems that relate to the transmission of certain esoteric Tantric empowerments. She further reminds Longchenpa of a former vision he had had of her, revealing that in reality she is Vajra Sow who has only temporarily taken the form of Vajra Turquoise Lamp; in this way, this local Tibetan deity becomes identified with the famed Indic Buddhist goddess.

In the course of their conversation, Longchenpa critically displays anxieties about his own qualifications and about the necessity of teaching the Seminal Heart at all: the teaching had already been transmitted by one of the most famous tulkus of the time, the third Karmapa Rangjung Dorje (Rang byung rdo rje, 1284–

1339), as well as by a well-known Treasure finder Rinchen Lingpa (Rin chen gling pa, 1295–1373). The deity again bolsters Longchenpa's sense of confidence. She immediately dismisses his doubts, making a clever pun based on the dual sense of *lung* as both "handle" of a vessel and "verbal transmission" in which a teaching is ritually read out loud to disciples prior to its study. She thus implies that Longchenpa's two perceived rivals are simply mouthing the words of the texts without real comprehension—they are mere "handles" of a reality that only Longchenpa fully "owns." Thus does the yoginī, speaking in the voice of the ḍākinī, play a crucial role in reinforcing Longchenpa's sense of legitimacy and self-worth for the throne of Seminal Heart transmission.

Soon after this self-empowering exchange, Longchenpa commissions his most trusted disciple, Özer Gocha ('Od zer go cha), to retrieve the actual manuscript of *The Seminal Heart of the Ḍākinīs* Treasure. Upon his return with the text, we have another extensive possession episode that endures for several days, this time by none other than Yeshe Tsogyel, the queen of Treasure concealment and the principal ḍākinī of the Treasure tradition. As on the previous possession, the yoginī-as-ḍākinī intervenes in some of the ritual proceedings, at one point even granting teachings and empowerments to the teacher, and engages in mysterious symbolic actions and performances that are meant to impart an esoteric message to her audience. She also reiterates the essential importance of nonattachment and openness, pronouncing *phaṭ*, a mantric utterance designed to cut off obsessive thinking whenever such small-mindedness occurs. Again, the more cautious disciples are not sure how to take these strange and supremely self-confident female performances, but the lama Longchenpa assures the doubting disciples of the performances' worth.

The inspired yoginī proves her prescient powers in the next episode when she is able to give a nuanced assessment of a deep meditative experience that Longchenpa has just had. She approves heartily of his perception—classic for this school of Tantra—that beholds the apparitions of saṃsāra and the visions of nirvāṇa simultaneously. Nonetheless, she is critical of a previous moment in his experience when he had momentarily swooned. With its insistence on the necessity of engaging with all appearance, the Great Perfection tradition repeatedly resists the temptation to retreat into a near-unconscious cocoon of formless meditation. Rather, the meditator is advised to perfect the skill of "emanation" in order to work most effectively in *saṃsāra* and aid sentient beings.

This esoteric guidance is followed by further ritual interventions and attempts to bolster Longchenpa's self-confidence. There are a number of explicit references to the ḍākinī authorizing and announcing his enthronement or investiture as the regal inheritor of Padmasambhava's legacy. She offers him the texts of *The Seminal Heart of the Ḍākinīs* (evidently the copy that Özer Gocha has just procured), along with its transmission, though presumably in a somewhat condensed manner. In addition, she is portrayed as guiding his hand, with help of Vajra Turquoise Lamp, as he composes some explanatory notes associated with the Treasure, which would appear to be an allusion to the seminal inspiration which at the end of the text yields his own masterly extension of the Treasure entitled *The Seminal Quintessence of the Ḍākinīs*.

In the next episode of possession, we witness the kind of repartee that often ensues between the sometimes unruly protector deities and the Tantric lama. Remati is another female guardian deity who descends, yet again, into an unspecified yoginī disciple, this time with a retinue of other female deities. She begins by rebuking Longchenpa for his supposed lapses in devotion to her. However, he eventually responds with a defiant dismissal of any need to be fully dependent upon her. It appears that he is beginning to assimilate the messages of encouragement he has been receiving, and is no longer willing to value every channeled message sent to him, especially those sent by less than fully trustworthy local protector deities. Particularly interesting in this light is his explicit criticism of the unqualified valorization of Treasures—particularly the material Treasures pulled out "of the cracks of rock mountains"—and his claim to transcend any concern for their revelation by himself, since he has "revealed the gateway to the Treasure of radiant light within myself." This is a critical moment in which we witness not only his own growing self-confidence in the face of these imposing ḍākinīs who descend suddenly into his world (and depart just as abruptly) but also his assertion of his own authorial voice and its intrinsic value amidst the dramatic landscape of Treasure revelation and the channeling of sacred voices of the past.

The final episode translated here shows the Tantric community engaged in the celebratory rituals that are appropriate to the conclusion of a profoundly meaningful retreat period. With the playfully magical assistance of Longchenpa, they produce the customary pints of beer out of their meager resources and proceed to become inebriated. In the midst of the festivities, Turqoise Lamp returns to invite Longchenpa to her residence on White Skull Snow Mountain, and he has to hold off the jealous intervention of Remati, who also reappears to take issue with his impending move to that mountain retreat. Her dangerous nature is revealed when she admits to taking a toll on the livestock of the northern Tibetan pasturelands as her deserved tithe, but this unpredictable spirit nonetheless remains part of the protective organization of Longchenpa's Treasure pantheon.

The community begins to part company, many fulfilling Longchenpa's wishes by promising to go into meditative retreat. The narrative also refers to certain violations and disturbances caused by at least one member of the lama's circle from eastern Tibet, but provides no detail on their nature. Longchenpa proceeds to White Skull Snow Mountain located in the headlands of Shukseb, on the col of which he builds his small hermitage, named Oḍḍiyāna Fortress (U rgyan rdzong). This is to become his most favored hermitage, and he retreats there continually over the final two and half decades of his life to write many of his greatest masterpieces. Shortly after establishing the hermitage, at the urging of the devoted Özer Gocha, Longchenpa composes his own textual extension of *The Seminal Heart of the Ḍākinīs*, which brings to fruition the fragmentary inspirations and multiple allusions to his own impending Treasure revelation that one finds woven through his dialogues with ḍākinīs at Chimphu. The seminal insights of

Chimphu thus become the three volumes of *The Seminal Quintessence of the Ḍākinīs* at White Skull Snow Mountain.

Although the text's composition takes place amid a continuing flow of visions and omens stemming from the ḍākinīs, and represents the culmination of the ḍākinīs' and Padmasambhava's inspirations conveyed in the numinous headlands of Chimphu, Longchenpa's account leaves no doubt that it is his own composition. Indeed, colophon after colophon of *The Seminal Quintessence of the Ḍākinīs* uses the language of Treasure revelation, but ultimately clearly ascribe its composition to Longchenpa himself, albeit in his reincarnational identity as Pema Ledreltsel, "the one with the dynamic karmic connection to Padmasamabhava." Unlike his previous life's revelations, which involved earth Treasures attributed repeatedly in framing narrative and colophon to the literal authorial agency of Padmasmabhava and Yeshe Tsogyel, Longchenpa in his present life discloses the same bravado and self-assertion he had increasingly exhibited in the headlands of Chimphu, in a literary form. He is the Treasure revealer and the author, thereby incarnating a moment in which revelation and inspiration, reincarnation and incarnation, Treasures and compositions coincide on shifting registers. Never before, and perhaps never again, was the Tibetan Treasure tradition of channeled authorial voices so exquisitely invoked and deconstructed, simultaneously, in the same voice and the same texts. This multivalent identity, on authorial grounds, of the possessed and the possessor constitutes the textual landscape on which Longchenpa perhaps most adequately responds to the enigmatic possessions of the ḍākinīs, the result being a text of intertwined voices, human and ḍākinī, past and present, Tibetan and Indian, which mirrors the intertwining of ḍākinī and yoginī at Chimphu.

The translation below is an abridgment of *The Luminous Web of Precious Visions* (*mThong snang rin po che 'od kyi drva ba*) by Padma Ledreltsel (Longchenpa). The text is located in *sNying thig ya bzhi* [A-'dzom Chos-sgar edition] (Delhi: Sherab Gyaltsen Lama, 1975–1979), vol. 9 [*Mkha' 'gro yang thig*, Part III], pp. 203–66. The passages translated here are on pp. 209–11, 215–25, 237–48, 250–52, 256–60, and 265–66.

Further Reading

For further details on Longchenpa's life, as well as other important figures in the Treasure tradition, see Dudjom Rimpoche, *The Nyingma School of Tibetan Buddhism: Its Fundamentals and History*, translated by Gyurme Dorje and Matthew Kapstein (Boston: Wisdom Publications, 1991), vol. 1. Tulku Thondup's *Buddha Mind* (Ithaca, N.Y.: Snow Lion Publications, 1989) provides an excellent anthology of Longchenpa's doctrinal writings. His *Hidden Teachings of Tibet: An Explanation of the Terma Tradition of the Nyingma School of Buddhism* (London: Wisdom Publications, 1986) is an in-depth study of the phenomenon of revelation itself in Treasure tradition. Janet Gyatso's *Apparitions of the Self: The Secret Autobiographies of a Tibetan Visionary* (Princeton: Princeton University Press, 1998) provides analysis of the significance of the Treasure cult, especially within the context of autobiographical writing in Tibet. David Germano's *Prophetic Histories of Buddhas, Ḍākinīs and Saints in Tibet* (Princeton: Princeton University Press, forthcoming) offers a detailed study of the events surrounding the revelation of both *The Seminal Heart of the Ḍākinīs* and *The Seminal Quintessence of the Ḍākinīs*, and their broader social and philosophical significance.

All but one of the literary collections referred to in the introduction are found in *The Seminal Heart in Four Parts* (*sNying thig ya bzhi*) by miscellaneous authors in eleven volumes (New Delhi: Trulku Tsewang, Jamyang and L. Tashi, 1971). *The Seminal Heart of the Ḍākinīs* (*mKha' 'gro snying thig*) by Padmasambhava constitutes volumes 2–3; *The Seminal Quintessence of the Ḍākinīs* (*mKha' 'gro yang thig*) by Longchenpa constitutes volumes 4–6; and *The Seminal Heart of Vimalamitra* (*Bi ma snying thig*) by Vimalamitra and other early Great Perfection Masters, volumes 7–9. Finally, *The Seventeen Tantras* (*rGyud bcu bdun*) has been published in a three-volume edition based on the Adzom Drukpa blocks (New Delhi: Sanje Dorje, 1973).

The Luminous Web of Precious Visions

At the age of twenty-seven, [Longchenpa] encountered the glorious lord of religion Kumārāja, from whom he obtained the empowerments, guidances, and instructions for the esoteric Seminal Heart of the Great Perfection. The next year [Kumārāja] gave him the seal of entrustment for the higher empowerments, along with their Tantras, scriptures, and esoteric precepts. [Longchenpa] then practiced contemplation for three years. At the age of thirty-one he decided to leave at the conclusion [of the retreat]. At that time a traveler to Nyiphu Shukseb (sNyi phu shug gseb) came to see him, and he was supplicated by many disciples with the right fortune. Hence he gave them guidance on the Seminal Heart of the Great Perfection. At that time the yogin Özer Gocha offered the lama a totally intact manuscript of *The Seminal Heart of the Ḍākinīs*, which he had obtained after great hardships from Loro (*Lo ro*). [Longchenpa] dreamt at the same time that the goddess Vitality Accomplishing Mistress (*Srog sgrub ma*) hand-delivered the manuscript [to him].

Then at the age of thirty-two in the following year, in the middle spring month of the year of the earth female hare [1339], [Longchenpa] began giving instruction in the esoteric Seminal Heart of the Great Perfection to eight male yogins and female yoginīs with the right fortune in the forest of Rimocen (Ri mo can) at Chimphu valley. Upon the descent of blessings during his performance of the nonelaborate empowerment, the glorious and great Mantra Protectress [Ekajaṭī] descended into one of the yoginīs, and she began to perform. When everyone else became full of doubt, the lama said, "Because a ḍākinī has actually descended here [in her], get over your worries! I am a yogin who has realized the single flavor of appearances and mind, and thus no obstacles will ensue!"

The yoginī prostrated to the lama, and having gazed at the offering cakes, she inquired, "Why haven't you included the peacock [feather?]" He replied, "I have conjured it mentally!" She in turn said, "What use is doing it mentally in the symbolic doctrine? [that is, one needs the actual object to function as a symbol in these teachings]. [Also] this [basin] isn't necessary." She then put aside the basin from the platform atop the vases, and placed there three vases linked together. Then when the lama performed the ritual in full detail, she joined her palms together, said "excellent!" and kept nodding her head [in approval]. But when [Longchenpa] left off the final letter *s* in pronouncing the word *rigs*, she said, "No, no! You should say *rigs*!" When he was reciting the [mantra] letters—*Oṃ* and so forth—she said, "Imitate me!" and proceeded to sing the mantras in a sweet melody in Ḍākinī language, connecting them without mixing them up.

During the eight words in the context of the main phase [of the ritual], she made restitution for the omission of no-meditation, singing it as a song: "When the intellect is free from meditation, joy! When meditation is free from the intellect, how happy!" Saying that the offerings were of poor quality, and moreover that nothing would ensue by means of them, she again sang a sweet melody as an offering. When a large bowlful of ambrosia was presented to the lama at the time of the ritual communion (*gaṇacakra*), she said, "This is the sacrament of the ḍākinīs, and thus must be relied upon no matter what!" She thus invited him to consume all of it without remainder.

At this time the yogin Rinchen Ötro (Rin chen 'od 'phro) also saw the blue-black Glorious Savior (dPal mgon po) with his complete set of ornaments. Then special blessings of the ḍākinīs occured right up until daybreak. Thereupon, until [Longchenpa began] the guidance [in the morning], the yogins and yoginīs sang and danced in a state of intense exhilaration. Their experiences blazed with cognitive experiences of bliss, clarity, and nonconceptuality, all day and night. They entered a special visionary state that was neither asleep nor awake.

[*The intervening passages describe further visions of various ḍākinīs and other figures who appear on the twenty-fourth and twenty-fifth of the lunar month.*]

After a while [still on the twenty-fifth], one yoginī also saw gathering cloud banks of ḍākinīs showering all over the land and space. Therefore [we] dedicated the cakes of the feast offering to them. Then after a while, that yoginī was shaking her long tresses and had the experience of Vajra Sow with a dark blue-colored body filling up the sky and then dissolving into [her]. Then she began to perform [as the goddess].

She said: "Its coming, its coming." [We] asked: "What is coming?" She replied "Tomorrow morning obstacles are coming; if not then there will be many high guests." [We] asked, "Who has come?" She replied: "The seven medicinal goddess (*sman mo*) sisters have come. They are white, youthful in complexion, wearing multicolored silk garments adorned with various gold, turquoise, and jeweled ornaments, and are surrounded by immeasurable medical goddesses as retinue. There are still more to come. Ode Gungyel ('O de gung rgyal) has come surrounded by many retainers similar in appearance—a black man with a black horse, black cloak, black spear, and with his long hair forming a turban wrapped around his head. There are still more to come. Nyenchen Thanglha (gNyan chen thang lha)—a white man with white horse, and surrounded by many similar retainers is here. Offer them torma!" [We] offered them torma.

Then the yoginī said, "I have come here newly—why don't you offer me a torma?" [The lama] asked, "Who are you?" She replied, "I am the lama's personal deity, Vajra Sow." At that time [the lama] asked everyone, "What do you see her as?" The yogin Özer Thaye explained that he saw a dark blue woman larger than the others, adorned with bone, and adorned by nets of jewels and bones.

Then the lama asked her, "Why have you come here? Is [my] holy lama [Kumārāja] healthy?" The yoginī replied, "Since tonight is a wild night, I have come to spy on these karmically worthy disciples. Your lama is in excellent health." [Longchenpa] then asked, "Well, if that's the case, since this year is a dangerous point in his life, should we be worried?" She responded, "What obstacles could there be to an emanation of the Buddha? It merely depends on his perception of the needs of disciples. Don't you understand that [in him] Vimalamitra has come to Tibet?" He then asked, "Then how long will he live?" She replied, "He will live until the next year of the sheep. After that it is uncertain, since [his life span] depends upon his disciples."

[Longchenpa] then asked, "Well, if that's the case, are you now urging me [to act] for the welfare of others as the lama himself urged me to do [previously]?" She replied, "Yes, precisely!" He then inquired, "Should I stay in solitude to accomplish the body of light, or bring benefit to sentient beings through acting for the welfare of others? How much longer have I to live?" She replied, "Though you could accomplish the body of light, you must benefit sentient beings—much welfare to others will ensue. You will be able to live for thirty more years beyond the present." At that point, the yogin Özer Gocha said, "Please stay for a long life!" The lama responded, "This ḍākinī has no obessive fixations—it may be that [my life span] can be calculated in terms of days, months, and years, but I have no idea what that would be."

Again, the lama questioned her, "How many Word Protectors (*bka' srung*) do I have?" She replied, "Many! You have all of those of your lama, and in particular Goddess Vajra Turquoise Lamp." He then inquired, "Where will I benefit other beings?" She answered, "That will be in the southwest. To expand on that, it will be in the areas of Dra (Grwa), Drachi (Grwa phyi), and Trengpo ('Phreng po)." He asked, "Well, is it definite that I will benefit others?" She replied, "From this point onward much [benefit] will ensue. In your next life, [you will bring] even vaster benefit than that to beings." [Longchenpa] asked, "Where will my future life [transpire]?" She replied, "[Your activities] will be very vast in the Lhodrak (Lho brag) region, and in the border areas between Mön, Tibet, and India." He asked, "Will that be Mön Bumthang?" She replied, "Precisely! The Guru is named Drimay Özer." He then asked, "Is that [the rebirth of Tshultrim Dorje] explained in *The Seminal Heart of the Ḍākinīs*?" She replied, "Yes, precisely! You're not mistaken at all!"

He asked, "Well, if that's the case, am I now allowed to give the empowerments and guidance just as explained from *The Seminal Heart of the Ḍākinīs*?" She replied, "Since [these teachings] are yours, certainly!" He asked, "Won't people come to see me as a charletan?" She replied, "What's the point in those people's gossip? The fortunate ones will gather [around you] out of faith, while those without the fortune wouldn't show up even if no one at all slandered you. They would slander even the Buddha himself."

I asked, "Well then, where should I disclose these sacred precepts of the Seminal Heart? Should I disclose them at the site of the Goddess Vajra Turquoise Lamp?" She replied, "Since this is a place where ḍākinīs naturally gather, you should disclose them up here." I asked, "Will I extract the Treasure at Bumthang in this life?" She replied, "If you have three or four disciples with exceedingly immaculate commitments, you will extract it." I asked, "Do I have such disciples now?" She replied, "No. A Tantric practitioner named Karsang who is slender and exceedingly beautiful will come. At that time you will extract it."

I asked, "And the Treasure letters?" She replied, "At that time a prophet will manifest—you needn't ask." I asked, "And the rock moutains where the Treasure is located?" She replied, "There are rock moutains on the eastern side near the end of the valley where the central river in Bumthang flows to the southwest. At their edge, at the border of the neck [of the mountains] running up to its head [top], projecting outward like a sitar standing upright, there is some swamp water coming hither. Atop that is [an outcropping] resembling a leaf of a rhododendron flower. If you tie a rope to it and go twelve fathoms [upward], you'll find a square rock in the manner of a vessel. It has a triangular crevice in its lower center, which is where [the Treasure] is."

[Longchenpa] asked, "When will I meet the Great Master [Padmasambhava]?" She replied, "In the uplands of three valleys, in the lowlands of three mountains, is a small rock formation facing southwest. Beneath the right corner of the third rock mountain, you will meet him and he will give prophecies." [He] asked, "When will I meet Vimalamitra?" She replied, "You have already met him [i.e., Kumārāja]. [He] asked, "Does my realization reach the ultimate meaning of the Seminal Heart?" She replied, "It is the ultimate."

[He] asked, "What about other Treasures?" She replied, "In the northwest border from here is an exceedingly high rock mountain—from its side resembling spears' tips pointing upward in disarray, you will extract [Treasures]. But don't go there [now]." [He] asked, "Well, if that's the case, should or should I not take out the Treasures of Tramo Rock Mountain in the east at present?" She replied, "You have already taken them out [that is, *The Seminal Heart of the Ḍākinīs*, extracted in his previous incarnation]." The yogini Özer Gocha asked, "Where is Pagang Rinchen Dorje (sPa sgang pa rin chen rdo rje, another name of Tshultrim Dorje)?" Saying "Pagang Rinchen," she was unclear for a while. [He again] asked, "Master Rindor?" (sLob dpon rin rdor, a contraction of Rinchen Dorje), and she replied: "Yes, yes. He is that one, he is sitting right here." And she pointed her finger [at Longchenpa].

The lama asked her: "It is said that after that birth he was to be reborn in Bumthang. So how could that [rebirth] be me [since I was born instead in southern Tibet]?" She replied, "[The prophecies say] that following that incarnation, he will be reborn in Bumthang after a brief sojourn in an Enjoyment Body pure land, rather than being reborn directly there [in Bumthang]. Now you [represent] that sojourn in an Enjoyment Body pure land." [He] responded, "Why do [you say] I now [represent] the sojourn in an Enjoyment Body pure land?" She answered, "When Master Rindor took out the Treasures, if he had kept them secret for several years and practiced, he would have refined his skill [during that life] during a sojourn in a luminous Enjoyment Body land for his own welfare, while benefit to others would have ensued through the Seminal Heart teachings. Since in fact he didn't keep them secret, he wasn't able to live out his full life span. Thus now in this birth your meditation and practice of the rainbow-colored visions of radiant light should be understood as that period of 'a brief sojourn in an Enjoyment Body pure land.' Others don't understand how to interpret the intention of that statement, but in fact your life right now is the intent of that prophecy."

[Longchenpa] then asked, "At what point will I achieve [liberation] without any remaining residue?" She replied, "If you meditate in solitude you will achieve it in this current [life], whereas if you act for the welfare of others you will be liberated within the [postdeath] intermediate state. Your emanation will take rebirth in Bumthang, display many magical powers, and act for the welfare of others. Then that emanation—surrounded by the five types of ḍākinīs—will also depart to the land of Oḍḍiyāna, to the northwest of the Vajra Seat (*rDo rje gdan* in Tibetan; *vajrāsana* in Sanskrit) in Magadha, where he will act as if becoming awakened into buddhahood."

[He] asked, "Where did the Master Rindor die and how many years have gone by?" She replied, "He died in Kek, since which thirty-two years have passed [that is, 1307]." [He] asked: "Which Seminal Heart tradition will be most beneficial for me to teach—*The Seminal Heart of Vimalamitra* or *The Seminal Heart of the Ḍākinīs*? And how long will each last?" She replied, "Both will be beneficial, but the *Vimalamitra* will be more vast. The *Vimalamitra* will last one hundred years, and the *Ḍākinī Seminal Heart* will last five hundred years, beginning from this year."

At that time, she made prophecies concerning the lifespan and beneficial actions of the [gathered] yogins and yoginīs as well. After a while, the yogin Özer Thaye ('Od zer mtha' yas) had a vision of a white woman with multicolored silk clothes, a silk turban, and adorned with gold and turquoises. He saw her dissolve into the lama, who then stood up and said, "I will sing a previously unknown vajra song." [Longchenpa] then sang the following:

> I prostrate to and praise the Blissful One [Buddha] All Good consort pair,
> Spontaneity which is primordially empty and originally pure!

1. As the condition of reality which is Mind as such beyond all elaboration,
   The very essence of the purity of ignorance right where it stands,
   [Buddha] Vairocana exists internally, not externally—
   I supplicate the buddha affinity of the Blissful Ones:
   Inspire me with blessings to self-recognize as self-manifestations
   The abiding reality of the unborn beyond all mental objects!

2. As the mirror of the unceasing ground for the shining of awareness's dynamism,
   The very essence of anger's liberation right where it stands,
   [Buddha] Akṣobhya exists internally, not externally—
   I supplicate the vajra affinity of the Blissful Ones:
   Inspire me with blessings to self-recognize as self-manifestations
   The abiding reality of mentation in its empty radiance devoid of grasping!

3. As the sameness devoid of acceptance and rejection as well as affirmation and negation,
   The very essence of the purity of pride right where it stands,
   [Buddha] Ratnasambhava exists internally, not externally—
   I supplicate the jewel affinity of the Blissful Ones:
   Inspire me with blessings to self-recognize as self-manifestations
   The sameness of abiding reality evenly pervading everything!

4. As the complete realization of [all] subsiding in the expanse of bliss and emptiness,
   The very essence of the purity of desire right where it stands,
   [Buddha] Amitābha exists internally, not externally—
   I supplicate the lotus affinity of the Blissful Ones:
   Inspire me with blessings to self-recognize as self-manifestations
   The abiding reality of dualistic apprehension subsiding in bliss and emptiness.

5. As the efficacious action of awareness's penetrating emergence and self-liberation,
   The very essence of the purity of jealousy right where it stands,

[Buddha] Amoghasiddhi exists internally, not externally—
I supplicate the action affinity of the Blissful Ones:
Inspire me with blessings to self-recognize as self-manifestations
The abiding reality of whatever manifests in its unceasing dynamic flow.

When ḍākinīs deliver prophecies tonight
On the tenth day of the waning half of the lunar month
[A day in which the ḍākinīs' influence is believed to be very strong],
This is a sign of the internal conjunction of auspicious factors
A sign of pure commitments among the faithful,
A sign of the nonbiased emergence of welfare for the living,
And a sign of traversing the ocean of cyclic existence!

Joy! Happiness! A pure field,
This world realm in its external environment of radiant light,
Is like arriving at the site of the Highest Heaven (*'Og min*, in Tibetan; *Akaniṣṭha*, in Sanskrit)
With everything having the identity of gods and goddesses:
I feel self-awareness transcends misery,
I feel acceptance and rejection as well as affirmation and negation are destroyed,
I feel delivered from the treacherous path of hopes and fears,
And I feel primordially free from the three fictive states of existence.

Conceptuality in its projections and contractions subsides within the five lights,
And the visions of five lights subside into the primordial.
Appearances and mind having the identity of the groundless Reality Body,
Even this life is blissful, the next life will be blissful,
And through self-recognition, bliss will also be in the intermediate state—
Now I go from bliss to bliss.

I offer this song as worship, O Three Jewels!
Rejoice, O host of Ḍākinīs!

[Longchenpa[performed a dance, and then, after a while, up in the sky opening, a red woman with jeweled ornaments manifested three times. Several saw her and greeted her, after which she dissolved into the lama. When a white woman also came in similar fashion and dissolved [into him], the entire landscape and space was seen to be filled with ḍākinīs. . . .

[Omitted sections describe the ensuing rituals and visions from the twenty-fifth through the twenty-ninth of the lunar month, including many more ḍākinīs as well as Padma-

sambhava himself. This culminates in a yoginī's vision of Padmasambhava and many ḍākinīs dissolving into Longchenpa, at which point he again sings a lengthy vajra *song.*]

. . . The next day [the thirtieth] the yogins and yoginīs in general saw immeasurably many ḍākinīs all over the sky. At twilight, the yogin Özer Thaye saw a woman with braided hair filling the sky, who said, "Present an offering cake to me!" Then, after a while, everyone heard "kiki soso" ("hail," used in addressing deities), roaring sounds, the sound of cymbals, thudding sounds, and so forth, from all directions. After a while, [we] presented feast-offering cakes, upon which the guests, who had previously manifested during the daytime on the twenty-eighth, arrived.

Rinchen Ötro thus saw a dark blue woman dissolve into the crown of a yoginī, who then began to perform. The yoginī [herself] saw the trio of the Master Padmasambhava, Vimalamitra, and Yeshe Tsogyel arrive. At this time, the seven white Turquoise Lamp goddess sisters arrived, wavering and modest. Prostrating to the lama, each dissolved into the yoginī, who then said, "I am Vajra Turquoise Lamp, and I request you come to my place!" The lama responded, "I want to stay forever in your place." She replied, "I would be happy if you stayed [there] forever, but you won't even be able to stay beyond the first winter month." He then asked, "What do you want with me?" She replied, "Guru [Padmasambhava] bound me to an oath of allegiance, and hence I have come to look after his Treasure precepts." He inquired further, "[But] the precepts are yonder, and their revealer has passed away. So what are you doing here?" She responded, "Though the precepts are yonder, their meaning is here. Since your good fortune didn't pass away even after you passed away [in your former incarnation], I have come."

[Longchenpa asked], "How many Word Protectors do [these Treasures] have?" She replied, "They have many. In particular, there is glorious Vajra Sow, Black Vitality Accomplishing Mistress, Dark Red Harm Giver (gNod sbyin dmar), and Vajra Turquoise Lamp. In addition, there are the Nine Divine Generation Siblings (*lha rabs mched dgu*), the Twelve Teaching Guardian goddesses (*bstan ma bcu gnyis*), and the Dang deities (*ldang lha*)." [Longchenpa] followed by asking, "How many people should be introduced to the guidance? How many guidances are there to give?" She replied, "There are eleven [guidances; she then specifies a total of twelve]. Since the first three are fraught with danger, you should sequentially introduce three, four, and then five individuals to them. The remaining nine [guidances] should be done for groups of seven [disciples]. Since in general [these Treasures] are fraught with danger, they could pose obstacles to your lifespan. If you give guidance on them only a little, I would be happier." [Longchenpa] asked, "Do you have my Treasure scrolls?" She replied, "They'll come slowly—we'll make sure to remind you!"

Then, after a while, she asked, "Do you remember my granting you a spiritual attainment on your head?" The lama responded, "When I was practicing meditation at Cokla (lCog la), at daybreak one day a ḍākinī with golden mail came. She put a diadem on my head, thereby engendering a wonderful experiential realization in me. Was that you?" She answered, "Yes!" He asked, "Are you Turquoise Lamp"? She replied, "No, no! I am Vajra Sow! Don't you recognize me?"

[Longchenpa] asked, "When the seminal nuclei (*thig le* in Tibetan; *bindu* in Sanskrit) are explained as primary in this [system], the third empowerment is conferred to one with a sexual partner—how is this?" She replied, "That is intended for engaging those given to desire. It is conferred only mentally for those without desire." He further inquired, "In the context of the introduction [ritual], what is 'settling concepts into the unborn,' and 'settling mentality beyond into the incalculable' all about?" She answered, "What can antidotes do to conceptuality? Introduce them to the intention of the extremely expansive matrix, which is primordially free!"

Longchenpa asked, "Well, then, there are many explaining these Seminal Heart [teachings]—what is the point of myself explaining them as well?" She replied, "It is said that there are such figures as the Karmapa and Rinchen Lingpa giving verbal transmissions (*lung*), but I don't like their explanations. Even a clay pot has a handle (*lung*); how could that be sufficient? Because each [pot] also has an owner, these [teachings] need one [as well]!" Longchenpa further inquired, "How are the Treasures of Rinchen Lingpa?" She replied, "Of course they exist, but they aren't pure or authentic." He then asked, "How is it that I have actualized you without meditating upon you?" She answered, "Am I simply a deity who musţ be meditated upon, a mantra to be recited, an object of offerings? Don't you understand that I am always present for all yogins and yoginīs with intact commitments and realization? I have been in seamless union with you in all your rebirths."

Then [Longchenpa] inquired, "What does the location of Princess [Pemasel]'s wealth that is concealed in Chimphu look like?" She replied, "It is in a flat area in a rock mountain that resembles an offering of divine foods. But the time has not come for it yet." He then asked, "How long will it be until that Treasure of Vimalamitra is extracted?" She answered, "Fifteen years from now, it will be extracted by a white Tantric adept, who will translate them and spread them. In it will be the four profound volumes, which will come into your hands."

Then on the first of the next month, he sent the yogin Özer Gocha to get the text [of *The Seminal Heart of the Ḍākinīs*]. When he was on the road back, the tip of a rainbow touched and encircled the text. In particular, all the male and female yogins saw it linked to Rimocen by a five-colored rainbow on the night that he arrived at Chukpo ('Phyug po) rock mountain. In a dream of Geshe Lorin (dGe bshes blo rin), a woman told him, "Though he is considering departing to the border area, I must not allow it." On the ninth [Özer Gocha] escorted the texts [back]. That evening when [Longchenpa] was enjoying the communal feast offerings after performing ritual confessions as part of fulfillment rituals, a ḍākinī descended. Saying, "The lama and disciples have congregated for instruction," she performed many dances.

Then on the tenth, many yogins and yoginīs saw an even vaster gathering of ḍākinīs than before. During the day of the eleventh, when the earlier guidance finished and the yogins and yoginīs who were senior students were dispersing, Yeshey Tsogyel descended into one yoginī. She gave voice to a lot of ḍākinī sounds. When a grand fire ceremony was done at twilight, she gave a little siddhi [substance] one by one to some people, and then told them, "Don't talk at all [and stay] to one side." [She] opened all the vessels and prepared auspicious connections for the siddhi to descend, and [she] sequentially directed all the siddhi substances to the lama. He said, "Great benefit to living beings and sublime prosperity will ensue [from this]." The siddhi substances were then carried to the lama's quarters, and dawn broke. When the sun rose, and a yogin and yoginī went outside to demarcate borders for a strict retreat, she [again] gave voice to various ḍākinī sounds and danced.

Then on the twilight of the twelfth, she was contemplating opening the gateway for these teachings, and performed all the ḍākinī-empowerment symbols with a skull cup, mirror, and vase. At that time, she taught the instructions on the manifestation of all appearances and beings as luminous visions by means of an introduction to the space of the female consort (*yum mkha'*). That night the introduction to the fourth [empowerment] was born in the Lama's heart for the first time. At that time, he asked, "What are these—the stars in the sky and so forth?" She replied, "They are lamas who think they are gods, and so forth." One person thought to himself that she was lying, but that [despite this] whatever she did was permitted [by Longchenpa]. She acted in the same way for all five senses [which were being evoked in this ritual introduction]—in the context of sound, she strung a bell on her staff and beat it on the ground, questioning insistently, "What do you hear it as? What is being said?" Some voiced their doubts [about her] as before. [However], at that time the lama himself obtained the introduction to [the realization that] all phenomena are impossible to pinpoint as such; they appear in the manner that they are imputed.

During this, the yoginī was able to read [everyone's] mind, and when they became attached to mental states of faith and so forth, she said, *Phaṭ* to the demon of exultation! *Phaṭ* to the demon of arrogance! *Phaṭ* to the demon of dualistic grasping!" and raised a great commotion. Everyone thus became frightened and panicky. The Lama [however] understood all phenomena as serving to refine his skill in being divested of presumptions and objectification, and knew it as the mirror of realization. That night [he transmitted] the ritual introduction into the way of gazing for the empowerment to primordial gnosis and so forth. Similarly, she danced the next day and gave voice to a lot of ḍākinī sounds. At daybreak the next day, as the lama was sleeping, his mind spaced out into radiant light: upward was the vision of original purity, in between were clusters of Enjoyment Bodies, downward the modes of manifestation of the six types of living beings; and he heard a variety of sounds and languages. He was aware of all of this with his mind, yet it appeared devoid of any coarse [substantiality]. The continuity of his ordinary memory and thought had become broken in the preceding moment, and he spaced out as if fainting in a state of intense red vision with a blue tinge. Then his awareness projected out into the coarser manifestations of spontaneity, and he spaced out within the upper original purity, the intermediate Enjoyment Bodies, and the lower Emanational Bodies. After a while, the yoginī came, and said, "That previous [experience] was an introduction to remaining without ignorance [as everything] dissolves into internal radiance within primeval original purity. The so-called 'fainting' was a fainting within the state of reality, and hence you must raise [yourself out of it.] The subsequent [experience] was an introduction to the external radiance of emission of Emanational Bodies along with the manner of gradually straying." Then many rainbow colors previously absent manifested all over the sky in forms resembling the individual Word Protectors. When he asked what they were, she replied, "It is those [Word Protectors themselves]." When the sun rose, she gave an introduction to many different symbols and their meanings.

At noon, as the lama was sitting on the throne, [Yeshe] Tsogyel put three layers of garments [on him], and said, "Everyone offer donations and prostrate! Today [you] sons must be diligent!" When each [of the disciples] prostrated and made offerings, she made prayers for immeasurable auspiciousness, and the sky was filled with rainbow colors. At that point she said, "This type of sky appears when a lama who is a spiritual guide who will accomplish vast benefit for others is appointed to his religious seat of authority." When she gave the lama some siddhi [substance], he asked, "What is this?" She replied by saying such things as, "It is an ocean of glorious wealth! It is the spontaneous accomplishment of others' welfare!" He asked, "How many if they are counted?" to which she responded by saying, "innumerable hundreds of thousands." Because of these answers, [Longchenpa] said, "Sublime benefit will come to living beings!" In the afternoon, holding [it] to the five clusters of guests [miniature images of the five buddhas?], she hung a diadem of blue and red silk on the lama's head as a crown, and performed an investiture of him with many auspicious verses. At twilight he made auspicious connections for the emergence of sublime benefit for others. There was an intense commotion of ḍākinīs after the introduction, and so he asked, "Would such [manifestations] accompany the opening up of any other dharma Treasure?"

Just as the sun was about to arise during the subsequent introduction, he saw in the sky above the facing mountain to the west a lion throne with a soft seat of the finest silk, adorned with a backing curtain of delicate lattice designs, decorated with a variety of jewels, and topped by a peacock canopy. The yoginī said, "This is the throne of the great knowledge-holder Master [Padmasambhava]. It is a sign that you should sit on it. Look at it further!" And when he looked, he saw in all directions a great vision of the nature of the five [-colored] lights adorned by seminal nuclei. "It is an apparition of the field of buddha bodies and primordial gnosis," he said.

Then when the lama was sitting on the throne at noon, [she] offered to him the volumes of *The Seminal Heart of the Ḍākinīs*, a scroll painting of the peaceful and wrathful [buddhas], a Vajrasattva mirror, a [long-] life vase, and a skullcup [filled] with ambrosia. She also had each of the others offer a gift [to Longchenpa]. Having then prostrated and invoked [prayers] of auspiciousness, she implored [him], "I request that you act for the welfare of others." So he performed a permission [ceremony]. That afternoon, the lama said, "I need to compile a guidance course," and opened up the text. One yoginī saw the Guru [Padmasambhava] come in the fashion [described in] his mind-evocation [ritual] and dissolve into the lama, while [Yeshe] Tsogyel [appeared] on his right and Turquoise Lamp on his left, dictating the words of the guidance. At that time, he separated out the texts of two guidance courses, and composed them as notes.

In this way, Yeshe Tsogyel descended in actuality for six days, from the first to the thirteenth, and she gave to the holy lama [Longchenpa] Drime Özer Pema Ledreltsel (Pad ma las 'brel rtsal) the complete threefold introduction to the symbols, meaning, and analogies of *The Seminal Heart of the Ḍākinīs*, along with the seal of entrustment. She then departed to Oḍḍiyāna. . . .

[*Over the next sixteen days there are further visions of Padmasambhava and other figures. Various women appear who assist in some of the ritual performances, and there are signs of meditative success among several of Longchenpa's disciples.*]

At midnight on the twenty-ninth, Namdru Remati descended and said, "Why haven't you given me an offering cake? I've endured hardship for a long time!" Everyone was panic stricken, and [Longchenpa] asked, "Who are you?" She replied, "I am in all phenomena! I am present right up to the top of your head!" He asked again, and she said, "I am Namdru Remati. Since I have been guarding your Treasure, [I] am going to give it to you." He inquired, "What do you have?" and she responded, "I have some clothes along with the Master [Padmasambhava's] religious robe and skull cup. I have come [here] with the intention of conferring these upon you. I showed you a miracle before, but you didn't recognize me. The other day you gave everyone else an excellent communal feast of offering cakes, but there was nothing for me. I was thus ashamed, and felt like stealing everything!" As she said this, she seemed to become quite reduced in presence. He asked, "How many are you?" and she replied, "We are five [in number]." He further inquired, "What are your body color and hand-held accoutrements?" She replied, "I, Namdru Remati, am black and ride on a four-footed mule. My right [hand] holds a sword and my left [hand] holds a bag of disease. Red Mistress of the Desire Realm ('Dod khams dbang phyug) rides a three-legged mule, green Vajra Creature-Headed Goddess (rDo rje phra men ma) rides a bear while waving her hand, yellow Vajra Mistress (rDo rje dbang phyug) [rides] a three-legged mule, and white Vajra Action Lamp (rDo rje las sgron ma) [rides] a three-legged mule—all of them hold skulls and ritual daggers as hand-held accoutrements. I am the Mistress of the Desire Realm holding a saber and bag of disease."

Then for three days she performed many miracles relating to Treasures and caused an intense commotion. Then she descended again on the night [that Longchenpa was transmitting] [teachings on] breakthrough, and displayed miracles. At that point, the lama said,

> Having revealed the gateway to the Treasure of radiant light within myself,
> I have no need for Treasures in the cracks of rock mountains.
> If I have Treasures, that's fine; if I don't that's fine, too.
> If I have the right fortune, it's fine; fine, if not.
> There is no point in bartering your boasts of guarding Treasure
> With me, a yogin who has exhausted phenomena, exhausted intellect.

They each responded, and conversed back and forth a few times. Then the time came, and [he] accepted [the duty to] extract [the Treasure], so [that they] were pleased. . . .

[The text proceeds to describe Longchenpa's transmission of further empowerments relating to the Great Perfection visionary techniques, which causes some of these abstract visions to be seen by all in the sky. The figure of Yeshe Tsogyel is sighted again, and predictions are made about Longchenpa's successors.]

Then after a while, when the sun was setting, the lama said, "Since the empowerments and guidances of *The Seminal Heart of the Ḍākinīs* have all been completed [and it is time for the communal feast], be careful tonight!" When he said that, [someone replied], "There is no beer." [The lama said], "The other day the ḍākinīs gave us *siddhis*. Let's call them tonight and see if they come. Pour water in the malt dregs jug and collect [the beer that is thereby produced]. I will bless it." By thus straining out the beer, they obtained one jugful and asked, "Isn't this enough?" He replied, "Since this won't even suffice for what is needed tonight, collect [more]!" They strained more, yet all of it came out as fresh as a first straining of beer from malt. When all the yogins and yoginīs were intoxicated, [Longchenpa] said in a playful manner, "This represents my activity of emanating and transforming material things!"

Then Turquoise Lamp requested, "I entreat you to come to my place [that is, White Skull Snow Mountain]." [Longchenpa] pleased her by assenting, saying, "Let me go first," and she departed. Then the Mantra Protectress descended, and when leaving, said, "Something that you will find upsetting is approaching." Namdruma came down after a while, and said "I request that you not depart." The lama refused her, saying "I explain such profound teachings to all of you nonhuman spirits but you don't understand. Being pleased or displeased are [both] a miraculous show of mind. You can come to wherever

I am." He then performed the conferral of an empowerment for meditative contemplation. She said, "That was amazing; I am bound to [your] heart-mind."

He asked her, "Where did you go since the other day?" "I went to the pasture lands to collect a first-fruit tithe offering," she said. In fact, at that time there had occurred considerable disease among the cattle.

Then all the yogins and yoginīs offered a maṇḍala of their own clothes, ornaments, and jewels, and made vows to practice [the teachings he had transmitted]. The lama rejoiced, saying "Many will emerge who will strive to be generous and to practice in these teachings of mine." He then taught very profound instructions on entering into the sheath of radiant light. At that time he said, "Since my instructions are very rare in this world, you will be able to accomplish rapidly a body of light."

Then on the thirteenth, when performing the higher empowerment, a previous disciple from eastern Tibet (Khams) upset [Longchenpa] with inappropriate behavior. [Longchenpa] said "Some disciples in these teachings will have impaired religious commitments." He thus performed ritual confessions as part of fulfillment rituals, and departed [for Shukseb]. [Turquoise Lamp's] previous statement that someone would come to upset him just as he was leaving referred to that [situation].

Then, on the road by which he was coming, he performed a communal feast offering at Chukpo ('Phyug po) rock, and there were many rainbow-colored lights and portents of the ḍākinīs. Then, on the road along which he was going it was sunny without clouds, and he suffered from the heat. He prayed and at once clouds gathered and a wind, not too strong, arose and he also had a vision of Turquoise Lamp welcoming him. When doing a communal feast at Chilmo (mChil mo), again there were many omens of the ḍākinīs. Then, when he was invited to Shukseb, a ḍākinī descended into one yoginī and for six days she gave voice to ḍākinī sounds, and said, "I beseech the lama to come to Oḍḍiyāna." During this period, rainbows continuously appeared every day.

Then he built a hermitage on White Skull Snow Mountain [above Shukseb] which he named Oḍḍiyāna Fortress, and stayed there. He gave empowerments, guidances, and instructions, and again ḍākinīs spontaneously descended. There were many omens and the sky was filled with rainbows. Periodically his residence was linked to five-colored rainbows in the sky, which everyone witnessed.

Then the one with the deepest spiritual attainments from the empowerment crowd, the yogin Özer Gocha, requested that he compose a text on the empowerment, guidance, introduction, and so forth for the instructions of *The Seminal Heart of the Ḍākinīs* that had been previously [transmitted], and sponsored a communal feast offering with tormas [for that purpose]. [Longchenpa then] stayed in retreat from the eighth of the first autumn month, and from the tenth began the [composition] of the text. The sky was filled with rainbows and expressions of the ḍākinīs. In his dream, many crowds of supplicating men and women were prostrating [to] and circumambulating [him]. They beseeched him, "We are bound to your heart-mind! Please look after us compassionately!" At night there was the sound of ḍākinīs in all directions. Also many unprecedented miraculous displays manifested to the great meditators in the area. The first [autumn] month was like that, and up until the second autumn month the lama spent his time supplicating ḍākinīs and composing the text day and night. Throughout this period, there occurred immeasurably many auspicious connections that would benefit others, dreams, and visionary experiences. Every day, rainbow-colored light swirled above his residence on the col of White Skull Snow Mountain, and many amazing visions of light occurred. Then, on the first of the third autumn month, he performed a celebration for the full completion [of the text entitled *The Seminal Quintessence of the Ḍākinīs*]. All the yogins made prayers of auspiciousness, at which point the sky was filled with rainbows, and inconceivably many auspicious signs occurred. . . .

[The text then concludes with lengthy celebratory verses].

The Luminous Web of Precious Visions is set forth here by Yogī Pema Ledreltsel—the one illuminated by the light rays of the sun, who is the glorious Oḍḍiyāna Master [Padmasambhava]—through summarizing a portion of the chronicle of the manifest emergence of the profound Treasures. It is completed.

—15—

The Anonymous *Āgama Prakāśa*: Preface to a Nineteenth-Century Gujarati Polemic

Robin Rinehart and Tony K. Stewart

In 1874, a substantial Gujarati book was published in the city of Ahmedabad by an anonymous author, with a lengthy English title: *Exposition of the Nigamas or that portion of Hindoo Shastras which the dukshinas or Right Hand sect follows as their books of revelation. i.e. Vedas, Sootra, Smritis, Pooranas &c. For the use of reformers in India by the author of the "Nibandha Sangraha."* The author prefaced the text, which included extensive Sanskrit passages from more than seventy different texts, like this:

> We dedicate the following pages to the thinking Public, who have curiosity to know the ancient mode of worship proclaimed by the revelation called Nigamas. The ancient practices of a nation are often buried in oblivion, but those of India are well preserved in its sacred literature. It is necessary that Reformers, in order to be successful, ought to possess a knowledge of the ancient literature, which the people have, through habit, ignorance and Priest-craft learned to venerate. The secrecy which is attached to the sacred literature of the Brahmans, principally arises from the ignorance of the language in which it is written and by its being to a great extent, out of vogue. The primeval sacrificial system, which is the basis of the ancient Vedic Religion is cruel, uncouth, as well as opposed to the ideas of the present age. It would not have been satisfactory to describe it without referring to authorities on each point asserted and discussed. The book therefore is filled with authentic extracts from Vedic literature, which is considered as revelation from the Most High. It has been hitherto a special privilege of the Brahmans to recite it by rote and offer sacrifices in a manner handed down from generation to generation, without understanding their purport or condition of civilization in which they were ordained. Various miraculous powers are attributed to the mantras and sacrifices and various stories, inculcating the holiness of the Brahmans and power of their ritual are industriously circulated, in order to create awe and respect among the ignorant masses. It becomes therefore necessary

> to unveil this ritual as far as the limits of a small book will admit and to place within the reach of the Reformers such portions of the ancient mode of worship as required notice. This it is hoped may stimulate a further research, in those regions of antiquity, which appear to be utterly neglected in India by those, whom they concern most. The Religion of a nation greatly affects its destinies and progress. Adherence to the ancient prejudices combined with the thickly prevailing ignorance and a powerful priest-craft has produced baneful effects, such as early-marriages, miserable and forced widowhood, prevention of travelling to foreign countries, slavery of female sex, waste of money on useless objects, eleemosynary habits of one-tenth of the population, internal dissentions, want of fellow-feeling and patriotism and above all false worship of God. When reformers try to remove these effects, where do they stumble? At the religious difficulty.

The text purports to explain those features of the Hindu tradition that are deemed admirable by the author, then explained by one pandit and further elucidated by a second, but for the special purpose of encouraging emerging notions of "progress" into "modernity." Apart from the diction, which appears a trifle stilted to our contemporary sensibilities, there is nothing remarkable about such a publication; it is typical of many such productions in the nineteenth century. But later in that same year, a companion volume appeared by the same still nameless author, which in its contrast with the first reveals not only the extent of this reforming agenda but a remarkable taxonomic organization of the various dimensions of Hindu practice and theory that anticipate the creation of the category of Tantrism, which, as André Padoux has argued in the *Encyclopedia of Religion*, was a newly recognized independent category of religious experience constructed in the nineteenth century.

The title of our anonymous author's companion volume and its preface, which opens with the same telltale phrase, are worth quoting in full and with original punctuation (pp. 1–2):

> *Exposition of the Agamas or that Portion of Hindoo Shastras, which Vamees or Left Hand Sect Follow as Their Books of Revelation, i.e. Tantras, Vamalas, Rujusias, &c. for the Use of Reformers in India*, by the Author of the "Nigama Prakash"

> We dedicate the following pages to the thinking Public, whose education and natural public spirit have excited in them a curiosity for knowing the doctrines & dogmas contained in that portion of the Hindoo Shastras which enjoy the title of "Agamas" and which for a long time have remained a secret store, though they continue to attract veneration from ignorance, habit or the pretentions of the professors of what is called "Mantra Shastra." It is evident that they can not be properly appreciated, unless they are in some degree unveiled and thrown open to the Reformers, who wish to introduce changes, in order to establish a pure form of religion. The object of these pages, is to hold up to light the most filthy, infernal and obscene superstitions and pretended miraculous power of Mantra Shastris, who abound, in every town in India, especially in native states, where they find a large-patronage. It would have

> been useless simply to describe their practices without referring to their authorities. The book, therefore, is filled up with extracts from Sanscrit-books, which enjoy the notoriety of having been composed by Shiva, the great object of worship throughout India. It would be easy to imagine what should be the degeneration and debasement of a nation which not only gives currency to such literature as the Tantras, but venerates them as revelation from the Most High. It is hoped that this publication will induce all those, who are concerned in the welfare of this great nation to unite in one common effort to put down the diabolical tenets inculcated by the "Vami" and "Kowl" sects. The secrecy with which they are practiced & propagated, is a real obstacle, which must, to a great extent, baffle the exertions of Reformers but it must be recollected that perseverance overcomes all difficulties. It will be a grand triumph to free Hindoos from the snares of these knaves, who pass by the polite names of Mantra Shastris and Upasakas but who deserve to be denounced as enemies to all that is decent, virtuous, and moral.

What follows this remarkable preface is an introduction that names dozens of groups who are seemingly indiscriminately lumped together into this category of "Vami" or left-hand practitioner, followed by an anthology of some two hundred pages of Sanskrit and Gujarati.

These twin texts are follow-up companions to an initial volume entitled *Nibandha Samgraha*, which unfortunately has not surfaced in any repository we can locate. Based on the title and vague references in the following texts, we infer that it reflects an initial commitment to a defense of the rational injunctions of religion, in which the *Nigama Prakāśa*, with its generally Vaiṣṇava orientation, represents the salvageable dimension of Hindu practice, and the *Āgama Prakāśa*, with its Śaiva, Śākta, Nātha, and general tāntrika orientation, that which is despicable. Whether they were conceived originally as a set or logically grew from the initial argument is impossible to say, although the latter is most probable because of the exclusively backward reference; that is, the title page of the *Āgama Prakāśa* refers only to the author of the *Nigama Prakāśa*, which in turn only refers to the (for us) anonymous *Nibandha Prakāśa*. But we do have a probable author in the figure of one Gopal Rao Hari Devmukh, whose name appeared on the title page of a translation of the *Āgama Prakāśa* in a handwritten manuscript. There are very few additional clues to the authorship or dates, save the following.

Based on a single explicit intertextual reference in the *Āgama Prakāśa* to a datable text, the Sanskrit *Śikṣāpatrī* (*Shikshapatri*) of Swaminarayan published in 1826, it seems reasonable to conclude that the texts were compiled in the mid-nineteenth century, not long before their publication, but they may well have been circulated before printing, as inferred from the simultaneous publication dates. Swaminarayan's *Śikṣāpatrī* features a pro-Vaiṣṇava, anti-advaita and anti-tāntrika polemic (for example, it implies that the philosopher Śaṅkara was a tāntrika), but is equally critical of *brahman* priests, particularly those who prescribe expensive rituals, which are precisely the two overriding themes of the twin volumes by our (tentatively identified) anonymous author. Those texts deemed reliable by the *Śikṣāpatrī* are the very ones so deemed in the *Nigama Prakāśa*, and vice versa for the *Āgama Prakāśa*, suggesting that the author of our text is a follower of this important new tradition. This Swaminarayan connection is significant, because the group was seen as a reforming agent of Gujarati society, both by locals and by British administrators and clergy. Followers of Swaminarayan were opposed to animal sacrifice, forbidden to consume liquor or meat, sing vulgar songs, engage in practices for the appeasement of ghosts or evil spirits, and were strictly forbidden to participate in sexual rituals. The Swaminarayan religion was progressive in that the group was open to all castes, even though caste hierarchies were still observed, and the group came out strongly against the practice of satī (widow burning) and female infanticide, while promoting widow remarriage and allowing women to take formal vows of renunciation. The urge to reform, however, is not simply the outgrowth of the colonial project but has deep roots in the Hindu traditions.

Since the emergence of the devotional cults of the early centuries of the first millennium, the orthoprax vaidika and smārta rituals have come under criticism from those who have argued that the meaning and point of the rituals was no longer known, and therefore that the rituals were performed out of ignorance, inviting karmic and other forms of disaster for all who participated. With the resurgence of vernacular devotionalism in the premodern, precolonial, era, the critique extended to include sincerity of religious feeling, that is, devotion (*bhakti*). In the nineteenth century, the Western conception of religious hypocrisy, coupled with a sweeping indictment of all that could not be defended rationally or scientifically, brought these ongoing critiques together in works such as the *Āgama Prakāśa*.

The criticism was two-pronged: the first was aimed at those *brahman* ritualists who, in the arrogance of their ignorance, were accused of perpetuating a meaningless ritual system that took advantage of the ordinary Hindu to no positive end, producing a parasitic (and therefore useless, but not debased) class of priests. The second target was the group of practitioners (not limited to priests) who, seeing only gain and pleasure for themselves, debauched the rituals to include sexual indulgences and other unseemly activities transgressive of ordinary social sanction, such as drinking liquor and eating meat—the so-called "left-handed" practitioners of Tantra. What was criticized first was the arcane and the secret, for both groups depended on the inability of their participants to fathom the mysteries of their liturgies. This accounts for some, at least, of the groupings of individuals castigated by the author of the *Āgama Prakāśa*: Nāthas and Śāktas were connected to propounders of Vedic lore (*śāstris*), household priests (*paṇḍitas*), and hired performers for specialized, often magical, rituals (*māntrikas*). The texts are similarly grouped, with Tantras and Rahasyas finding a place beside the Vedic Brāhmaṇas, Upaniṣads, and Sūtras.

Clearly, the *Āgama Prakāśa*'s critique of Indian religion has strong links to the past, but it also reflects the climate of British colonial rule, which gave its impulse a greater social claim and a much wider audience, aided not only by the introduction of the printing press (a vernacular press was established in Ahmedabad in 1845) and improved systems of travel and communication but also by the adoption of institutional models from Western organizations such as the Young Men's Christian Association, which was active throughout India. The new institution of the vernacular newspaper and the inexpensively printed pamphlet and book (such as the *Āgama Prakāśa*) provided powerful input to the increasingly vocal public arena, which was marked by organized lectures and debates among traveling religious leaders. New popular Indian religious leaders (many of whom who were educated in schools run by Christian missionaries) incorporated many of the colonial social issues directly into their platforms; because the public debate was shaped in forums often conforming to Western sensibilities, the terms of that discourse were not entirely in the control of locals. These religious figures occasionally adopted stances as a show of solidarity with their British rulers, but in other instances they advocated reform to show that any necessary changes in Hindu practice could be implemented from within the tradition itself, with no need for outside assistance—a position that reflected independence, pride, and an emergent nationalism.

Our text seems on the surface to be sympathetic to British rule, for the author is keen to show that the tāntrika practices he finds so despicable are most prevalent in the princely states ruled by Indian kings, and not those areas under direct British rule. Such sympathy was typical of the mid- to late nineteenth centuries, before an organized movement for independence from the British got underway. But it should be noted that elsewhere he labels Bengal, which at the time of composition was the capital of British India, to be the hotbed of debauched practices, the stronghold of mantra-śāstra, which he labels "Bengali vidyā" (arcane knowledge of Bengal). His zeal for religious reform is coupled with a strong nationalist proposal—a unified nation working together to cleanse the religion of its excesses—but his sentiment often spills over into a ready regionalism tied both to language and locale. In the opening pages of his introduction, he claims to know of no more than two, or at most, four hundred men who practice these left-handed rituals in his own locale of Ahmedabad. Yet when one travels so far as Banaras, the figure jumps to the thousands, and when one ventures to the edges of India, to Draviḍa in the south (especially Kerala), to Kashmir in the north, and most of all to Bengal in the east—that is, away from the heartland of Hindu India defined by Ahmedabad as its center—the practitioners are numbered in the millions. The tendency to exoticize those who are "not like us," that is, the projection of an "other," is a common feature of this indictment.

Although these characterizations may seem somewhat unsophisticated in light of our most recent reconstructions of India's religious heritage, they were part of a larger nineteenth-century effort to map and catalog the full terrain of Indian religious cultures. Importantly, this effort included the "scientific" control of populations through the enumerations of the census, which tracked religious affiliations (and in cases of an ambiguous response, assigned one). It became the task of many religious writers to ground their critiques in enumerative, if not statistical, analysis. The surprising pluralism that emerged from such analyses was quick to be characterized in starkly delineated terms, because the categories that these rulers and reformers erected were exclusive in ways that reflected, at the very lowest level, the census taker's inability to check two boxes at once. As such, it revealed a predilection for exclusive "group membership" as the defining feature of identity (an individual could not have two identities at once), whereas it appears that individuals who participated in these traditions did not always follow this exclusionary approach. As religious identities became politicized in the latter stages of the nineteenth century, thought and rational assent were given unprecedented priority over action in categorizing "proper" religion in India, and membership in a clearly defined "group" was a prerequisite for being counted. With a litmus test of a self-articulated "purity," the response of many reform groups, including the Swaminarayan, was to accept specific texts and practices as representative of a "true" Hinduism while declaring others debased or degenerate forms of religion, and in many cases not even Hindu at all. The author of our text adopted a similar strategy as he brought to light not only the "filthy, infernal, and obscene superstitions" of the tāntrika tradition, but also the Vedic texts previously kept secret as "a special privilege of the *brāhmaṇas*."

Although it is common nowadays to think of the texts and practices of Tantra as shrouded in secrecy because of their connection with transgressive activities, our text reminds us that the recitation and rituals associated with the Vedas were an equally mysterious arena for those who were not *brahman* males trained in Vedic tradition. Indeed the stated aim of many of the translated versions of Sanskrit texts printed in the nineteenth century (including our text) was to make them available to those who otherwise had no access to them. Reformers argued that many Hindus were ignorant of their own religious tradition, and that the best path to religious reform was for them to study the proper texts and subsequently bring their practices into conformity with the texts, and thereby to rationalize those practices. Essential to this argument was a reading of Indian history that posited an initial golden age of religious purity and consistency (typically the age of the Vedas) followed by a period in which religious knowledge fell into the hands of a small group of *brahmans* who either inadvertently or through greed and corruption gradually forgot the true meaning of the Vedas, causing the tradition to enter a lengthy period of degeneration. Our author, along with others who subscribed to this model of India's religious history, saw the decline of an "original" Hindu tradition as responsible for the spread of Buddhism throughout India, which in turn led the god Śiva to institute the sensual practices of Tantra as a radical antidote to the ascetic, world-negating tendencies of Buddhism. The conflict engendered by trying to exalt the ancient while indicting it forced the author of the *Āgama Prakāśa* to restate his position, according to context. Thus he believed it essential that the secrets of the Vedas and other texts deemed acceptable be revealed so that people could bring their practices into conformity with them, even as he sought to reveal the secrets of Tantra in order that that their practice be eradicated. Where those secrets were mixed (*miśra*) with Vedic secrets, problems abounded. We should note that this purported "secrecy" is as much a rhetorical device as a reflection of reality, for our author himself had been able to learn of this "secret" in extenso (although his translator seems a bit unsure from time to time, so we might infer the that the details were not widely known in spite of the general recognition), and he asserts that at least one-fourth of the people in every city of India practiced it (sometimes even publicly), making it a very well-known secret indeed. Importantly, and contrary to many of our contemporary characterizations of Tantra, our author routinely highlights secrecy over sexual indulgence as the dominant trope of these practices.

The argument for the eradication of tāntrika practices, by Indian and British reformers alike, singled out those aspects of it which they found the most troubling to a modern society on moral grounds. The consumption of liquor and meat, and participation in sexual rituals, were often paired with ignorance and a laxity of discipline as the source of the problem. This strategy was clearly evidenced in the introduction to the *Āgama Prakāśa*, as the author acknowledged a wide variety of texts and practices from different regions of India but lumped them together as a "sect" known as the Vāmamārga ("left-hand path"), Tantramārga, or Kaulamārga, whose adherents were united in their practice of "despicable" and "immoral" rituals, whether they had any historical connection or not Our text is thus part of a larger nineteenth-century trend toward conceiving of a new entity called "Tantrism" as a specific modality of Indian religious experience, where previously these groups would have remained categorically distinct.

The printed edition of this text, which is probably not its original publication, can be found under the full title *Exposition of the Agamas or that Portion of Hindoo Shastras, which Vamees or Left Hand Sect Follow as Their Books of Revelation, i.e. Tantras, Vamalas, Rujusias, &c. for the Use of Reformers in India*, by the Author of the "Nigama Prakash"; the Gujarati title is simply *Āgama Prakāśa eṭale Tāntrika Dharmano Khulāso*. Both title pages indicate the publisher to be Sumsher Bahadoor in Ahmedabad, with the imprint dates of 1874 C.E. and Saṃvat 1930. The translation of the preface comes from a ninety-six-page manuscript purchased in an antiquarian book stall in London by Stewart in 1997. The bound and undated anonymous translation—done in a hand that suggests English schoolboy education—the first part of what would have covered at least four volumes, was copied on rag bond with the watermark "M and J Lay 1817," with the putative original author named on the verso of the endpaper that serves as a title page.

We have transcribed the anonymous English translation of the preface to the *Āgama Prakāśa*, checking every line against the printed text, preserving its somewhat awkward phrasing, but editing inconsistencies in transliteration, and supplementing with glosses those phrases the translator chose not to translate, either out of frustration with the long lists or out of a healthy respect for those places where the original author's understanding far exceeded his own. The translator's glosses appear in parentheses and our glosses appear in brackets. Hyphenation of technical terms generally follows the translator's original, which, along with his choice of vocabulary, suggests a heavy reliance on Monier-Williams's 1899 *Sanskrit-English Dictionary*. We have retained the translator's preference for capitalizing proper names or titles. Our transcription preserves the paragraph breaks of the original Gujarati text, which, as readers will surely note, is somewhat haphazardly organized, and shifts from gross generalizations appropriate to an inexperienced reader to the advanced technical descriptions of ritual and practice. A second editor's hand can be detected in our translation manuscript, and those suggested changes have been routinely incorporated without comment, since it appears that the translation was at one time intended for publication, although it appears that never occurred.

Further Reading

For good introductions to the religious movements of the nineteenth century, see Kenneth W. Jones, *Socio-religious Reform Movements in British India* (Cambridge: Cambridge University Press, 1989) and Raymond Brady Williams, *A New Face of Hinduism: The Swaminarayan Religion* (Cambridge: Cambridge University Press, 1984). For the scholastic constructions of India, see Ronald B. Inden, *Imagining India* (Oxford: Basil Blackwell, 1990), and for religious identity as political identity, see Kenneth W. Jones, "Religious Identity and the Indian Census," in *The Census in British India: New Perspectives*, edited by N. Gerald Barrier (Delhi: Manohar, 1981), pp. 73–101; and Barnard S. Cohn, "The Census, Social Structure and Objectification in South Asia," in *An Anthropologist among the Historians and Other Essays* (Delhi: Oxford University Press, 1990), pp. 224–54. For comparison as a basis of category formation in religion, see Jonathan Z. Smith, "Adde Parvum Parvo Magnus Acervus Erit," *History of Religions* 11.1 (August 1971): 67–90; and for a critique of the concept of group inclusion as the primary marker of identity, see Tony K. Stewart, "Alternate Structures of Authority: Satya Pīr on the Frontiers of Bengal," in David Gilmartin and Bruce B. Lawrence, eds., *Beyond Muslim and Hindu: Rethinking Religious Identity in Islamicate South Asia, 1200–1800* (Gainesville: University of Florida, in press).

Explanation of Āgamas (or Tantras or Vāmamārga) Translated from the *Āgama-Prakāśa* of Gopal Rao Hari Devmukh

PREFACE

Āgama-śāstra is called the *Mantra-śāstra*; and it is also known as the *Vāma-mārga*, the *Tantra-mārga* and the *Kaula-mārga*. This sect advocates the three doctrines, viz., action or sacrificial rites, worship, and knowledge; there are books written on the subject and Śiva is regarded as their author; there are also other books to the same effect and they are composed by the Nātha-sectarians and they inculcate the ceremonies called *nyāsa* [imputation of mantras to different body parts in order to sanctify], *mudrā* [gestures], *japa* [chanting], and *pūjā* [worship] as well as the worship of the different gods, and goddesses, Bhairava, etc. These people repeat the *pañcāṅga* [five modes of devotion] which includes [prayers such as the] *sahasra-nāma*, *stavarāja*, *kavaca*, *hṛdaya*, and *pañjara*. There is also another ceremony called the *Puraścaraṇa* which is observed in connection with the various *gāyatrīs* [verses] and mantras [utterances]. One has to be initiated, before he is admitted into this sect and that ceremony is called the *pūrṇābhiṣeka* and the *paṭṭābhiṣeka*. It is said that the sound "*soham*" is made 21,600 times while inhaling and exhaling and this process is [named] *japājapa* and *ajapājapa*. There are many treatises on the subject of the Śākta worship; in some places the Vedic hymns are also used [but] the actions are quite different from the Vedic. The different actions are the worship of *damanaka* (jackal), the sacrifice of *dūtī* (female go-between), the worship of a virgin, of a female ascetic, and of hair, the placing of a vessel and the making of a thread. The books are called the Tantra and Rahasya; some are known as the Yāmala and Āmnāya, while others are named the Kalpa. All these books, if collected, will be equal in number to the Vedas, the Śāstras and the Purāṇas. Some ceremonies are mentioned to gain the desired objects and to reduce, to sicken, kill or ruin an adversary (*jāraṇa*, *māraṇa*, and *chāṭṭan*). Intoxicating drinks, flesh, fish, and women are necessarily required in all these ceremonies. Flesh and fish are consecrated and placed in a plate and afterwards the devotees partake of the food. It is mentioned in the Tantra books that the spiritous liquors ceased to be drunk, as Brahmā, Kṛṣṇa and Śukra cursed them all, but that there is no sin in drinking them after removing the curse by some peculiar ceremony. There are some technical terms in the Tantra which contain *bīja* [seed] *mantras* of one word only. The ways of such men as are versed in this *Mantra-śāstra* are quite different; they have their own distinct years, months, days, astronomical divisions of time, worship, *śrāddha* [ceremony for deceased relatives], *guru-tarpaṇa* [libations to gods and ancestors], precepts and general ceremonies. The books on the subject are also different in various countries. The *Gauḍa-pāṭha* [the reading proper to Bengal] and the *Gurjara-pāṭha* [reading proper to Gujarat] are different from one another on account of the different countries in which they are accepted. The principal treatise on the subject is the *Caṇḍī-pāṭha* which is included in the *Mārkaṇḍeya Purāṇa* as well as in the *Kātyāyanī-tantra*. Taking this book to be an authority, the devotees perform the sacrifices, *mārjana* [rite of purification], *tarpaṇa* [libations to gods and ancestors], *japa*, etc. by reciting [praise of the goddess in the forms of] *haracaṇḍī*, *śatacaṇḍī* and *sahasracaṇḍī*. The ten *Mahāvidyas* [personifications of the śaktis or powers of Śiva] are regarded as the principal goddesses in the Tantras. There are many books which give description of sacrificial receptacles or pits and pavilions called the *huṇḍa* [latrine?] and *maṇḍapa* respectively; and all this system is attributed to Mahādeva [Śiva]. Some people recognize three distinct features of these ceremonies, viz. *Vaidikī* [Vedic], *Tantrikī*, [Tantric] and *Miśra* [combined]; *Miśra* is that in which *Tantrikī* and

Vaidikī are used together. It is difficult to separate from the Tantras the part promiscuously accepted by the *Brāhmaṇas* [brahmans] in their religious rites. Various Tantras and *Mantras* are found in the *Dakṣiṇa* [southern]-*mārga*. From this, it appears that the *Brāhmaṇas* did not differ from the *Tantra-mārga*. Had there been any difference of opinion, they would not have taken anything from the Tantras; but, that is not the case: the *Tantra-mārga* that is to say, *Kaula-mārga* is prevalent in many parts of India. The *Brahmacārīs*, *Sannyāsis*, *Paramahaṃsa Paṇḍitas* and many other people belong to this sect in every city and town, but their ways of life are kept very secret and hence it is that they are not brought to light. It is after a long search that we have come to know something about them. About two or four hundred men are connected with the *Śākta-mārga* in Ahmadabad and in the same way there are many in Nadiyad, Baroda, Broach, Surat, Puna, Satara and Karbir; thousands of *Brāhmaṇas* follow the *Śākta-mārga* in Benares, while in Bengal, and the Dravidian countries millions are found; wherever there is a temple of the Devī, there this system is in vogue and liquor and meats are offered to the various goddesses, viz, Bechrājī, Ambājī, Kalaka, Hīnglāj, Tuljāpura, Vindhyavāsinī, Kāmākṣī, Mātāpura, and Kālī of Calcutta. The Vaiṣṇavas despised all liquors and meats and they therefore do not go to such places, but the Gosāvīs, Atītas and the Nātha sectarians do go there. It is clearly mentioned in the *Śikṣāpatrī* of the Svāminarāyaṇa that no one should salute a god to whom liquors and meats are offered; the followers of this sect do not make a bow to such a god but many of them have faith (in those gods) in order to serve their purpose. In native states, the *Mantra-śāstras* are employed to perform some mystical ceremonies. There is not a single native state which does not engage such men and spend lakhs of rupees on these peculiar ceremonies.

The object of this book is to show what *Āgama-śāstra* is, what particular gods are worshipped, and what the names of the books and the technicalities are; the names of the authors of the various books, the *mudras*, the mystical powers of accomplishment and *bīja*, etc., are mentioned in this book. The Vedic and the Tāntrika ceremonies are these days mixed together to a very large extent but in the original books of the Vedas there is not such a mixture; no traces of the Tāntrika ceremonies are found in the Brāhmaṇa and the Sūtra works but they were introduced into the *Karma-mārga* by the later *Prayoga-kāras*. If we examine the present system of the Brāhmanical *sandhyā* [daily rites], we find that the *nyāsa*, *mudrā*, *āsana* [posture] and *arghyapradāna* [ritual presentation of water] etc., are taken from the Tantras, the *Prāṇāyāmas* [breathing exercises] from the Yogaśāstrā, *japa* and *upasthāna* [worship] from the Vedas and the repetition of the names and praises (*nāma-smaraṇa*) from the Purāṇas. It is difficult to separate and classify all this. In the same way, there are other *Tāntrik* ceremonies, viz, *kuṇḍa, maṇḍapa vidhi, laghunyāsa, and mahāṣoḍhānyāsa*.

It is said that the pioneers of this system were the nine *Nāthas* and eighty-four *Siddhas*. It appears from the thousands of books on the subject that this work was carried on long ago and that the Brāhmaṇas were not opposed to it, because many people believe that a follower of this sect pleases god and gratifies all his desires by the virtue of the mantras. It can be inferred from the *Śaṅkaravijaya* [a biography of the Advaita Vedānta philosopher Śaṅkara] that Śaṅkarācarya was also a Śākta, for the worship of *cakra* [meditative wheel; bodily center of energy; chiromantic circle; zodiac?] is highly praised in that book, and because the *cakra* is found in the Shin-geri and Dvarka [monasteries] established by him; this sytem therefore existed before Śaṅkarācārya. The opinion of some people is that, when Buddha appeared, all men became ascetics by his precepts; so much so that they would not marry, fight or cultivate the land; there being no government, all worldly affairs ceased; some people left everything aside and observed fasting days and thought that they would attain to salvation by dying in that state. At that time, Śiva instituted the *Kaula-mārga* to set the people to worldly affairs, and allowed them to use liquors and meats freely, and determined that the woman was the only supreme deity. It is said in the *Bhāgavata Purāṇa* [4.2.2]: "Let the foolish and impure men who wear long hair, apply ashes and carry bones, be admitted in the Śiva-*dīkṣā* (religious rites, initiation etc. of Śiva) in which intoxicating drinks is held sacred or divine." The two chapters of the *Padma Purāṇa* are devoted to the origin of *pākhaṇḍa* or heretical doctrines and it is said by Śiva therein that the Kaula system was made to pollute people. Perhaps, these statements are made by the Vaiṣṇavas themselves, but it appears that this system followed Buddhism and that it was carried on for a very long time, because, how can one account otherwise for thousands of books which treat of the said system?

Afterwards, [the philosopher] Kumārilabhaṭṭa insisted on the Vedic rites inculcated by the Pūrva-mīmāṃsā and after including some ceremonies in which many animals were killed, and which were intended for the attainment of the desired objects, he settled that salvation can only be obtained by performing religious ceremonies. This system lasted for some time as well and afterwards, there appeared Śaṅkaracārya who revised the Uttara Mīmāṃsā and declared that the *ātmā* [individual spirit] was *brahma*[*n*] and that salvation or absolution could not be obtained by performing *karman* or religious rites but by knowledge. According to him knowledge is superior; heaven is the fruit of observing religious rites [*karman*] but one cannot have salvation thereby. The system of the Vedānta bears in many respects a very close resemblance to that of the *Kaula*. (The *Kaula* is called Rājyayoga.) The *yoga* system of Patañjali is called Haṭhayoga while the Vedānta is known as Jñānayoga, while the system which is advocated in the *Gītā* is termed Karma-yoga. The difference amongst the four systems is that one gets salvation, according to the Rājyayoga, by enjoyment, while the Haṭhayoga declares that he should desire to obtain final beatitude by performing religious austerities, viz, *samādhi* (mortifying the body, etc.); the Jñānayoga recommends asceticism and the Karmayoga suggests that absolution can be had by performing ritual actions (*karman*) advocated by the *varṇāśrama* [classical system of caste, life stages, and goals]. There is a story in the *Padma Purāṇa*, which affirms that Śiva will manifest himself in order to propagate heretical doctrines (*pākhaṇḍa*). Now some people ascribe this statement to the *Vāmamārga*, while the Vaiṣṇavas say that it is applicable to Śaṅkaracārya because the latter was a great heretic in calling the personal soul (*ātmā* or *jīvātmā*) *brahma*[*n*]. This is the opinion of the Vaiṣṇavas belonging to the Mādhva-saṃpradāya [followers of Dvaita Vedānta teachings of Madhva]. The Vaiṣṇavas of all denominations believe that *ātmā* (personal "soul") is not *brahma*[*n*] but that it is an object created by *brahma* who is its master and whose service is its duty. All doctrines opposed to this are called heretical. According to the *Kaulika-mārga*, the *ātmā* is *Brahma-rūpa* [in the body or form of *brahma*]—and all those who do not belong to that sytem are termed *Paśu* and *Kaṇṭaka* (beasts and thorns). It also asserts that all prescribed rules and prohibitions should not be followed and that one should act independently without any restraint. The system of religion of the *sannyāsi* Paramahaṃsa as well as of the Aghoris is identical with that of the followers of the *Vāma-mārga*. In these times, many Aghoris are not found but formerly there were many; they used to live in forests and partake of urine and excrement. Near Siddhapur, there is a village called Avaghaḍasthalī where dwelt the head of the Aghoris; he used to catch scorpions, small lizards and other animals and then place them in a pot and, when they were naturally decayed, he would drink their extracted juice from the skull of a dead man and after throwing their bones away, bring other animals. Some people eat the flesh of corpses while they are being burnt and others take out the dead body of a woman from the grave and make *āsana* [i.e., mount it] in the burial ground in order to accomplish their mystical powers. A guard is always kept in a graveyard that none may tamper with dead bodies; there is a saying current among the people that a *mantraśāstrī* or one versed in mystical science has power to snatch away the bodies of the Ḍheḍa or the Bhanghi clan from the *śmaśāna* [cremation ground].

Many immoral and horrible practices which are contrary to the Dharmaśāstra (the science of law or morality etc.) are advocated by the *Mantra-śāstra*. As a rule the followers of this system worship various incarnations of the form of Śiva and Śakti, and thinking that the power of the Vedic hymns has ceased but that of the *Tāntrika* is still in force, they observe this form of worship and believe that Viṣṇu is in the form of Śakti. There are many stories in the Purāṇas giving the origin of the worship of Śiva and Śakti in the form of the male and female generative organs (*liṅgam yonī* [respectively]). This worship of the generative organs is taken from the Tantras, because they not only mention it clearly but also the *Pañcamakāra* [five Ms] containing *kuṇḍa* [menstrual blood] and *golāmāta* [semen], etc.; as it seems to be a *Tāntrika* custom, the Vaiṣṇavas do not worship Śiva nor do they take the *Tīrtha-prasāda* (of Śiva); they only salute the image of Śiva. The religious ceremonies (*karma-kāṇḍa*) observed in the *Vāma-mārga* are quite different. The followers of this sect perform very secretly the non-Vedic ceremonies, viz, the *pratasmaraṇa* (morning prayer), *snānaviddhi* (ceremony of bathing), *tripuṇḍra-dhāraṇa* (making marks with red or white powder on the forehead etc.), *bhū-śuddhi* (purification of the earth), *bhūta-śuddhī* (purification of animals), *prāṇāyāma* (restraining the breath), *sandhyā* (morning and evening prayers), *japa*, (muttering certain syllables of phrases), *puraścaraṇa* [preparatory rite], *karāṅganāsa* [nyāsa of the elephant's trunk?], *antaramātrikā* [internal mystical diagrams], *bahirmātrikā* [external mystical diagrams], *citrānyāsa* [placement of symbolic diagrams on body], *nāthādividyā* [supreme knowledge of the Nāthas], *mūlāvidyā* [knowledge of the root or base], *nityādividyā* [knowledge of the eternal], *tattvanyāsa* [imputation of metaphysical truths?], *dvāra-pūjā* [worship of the opening], *tarpaṇa* [libations], *daśa-vidyānyāsa* [imputation of the ten goddesses], *pātra-nirṇaya* [removal of the vessel], *nityā-pūjā* [daily worship], *sūryārghya* [offering to the sun], *tīrtha-saṃskāra* [pilgrimage rites], *gurvādi-pūjana* [worship of the *guru*, etc.], *dīkṣhā* [initiation], *prāyaścitta* [rituals of atonement], *nimba-puṣpa-pūjā* [worship of the sexual organ of a young virgin], *damanaka-pūjā*, *vasanta-pūjā* [spring-worship of Śītalā(?)], *śrī-cakra-pūjā* [worship of the mystical śrīcakra diagram of masculine and feminine united], *dīkṣā-kāla* [the black consecration], *dikṣābheda* [consecration of non-differentiation], *sarvatobhadra* [square diagram], *puṇyāha-vacana* [proclamation of auspiciousness], *nāndī-śrāddha* [offerings to ancestors], *kūrma-cakra* [diagram in shape of a tortoise], *nava yoni* [sexual organ of a prepubescent girl], *kaula-śrāddha* [rite for the Kaulas], *mantra-śodhana* [purification through mantras], *mantroddhāra* [selection of mantras], *nātha-pārāyaṇa* [knowledge of the Nātha system], *tattva-pārāyaṇa* [study of metaphysics], *nāma-pārāyaṇa* [study of the names], *pañcanyāsa* [five nyāsas noted above], *mahāśoḍhā-nyāsa* [nyāsa of great purification], *mahā-nyāsa* [great nyāsa], *sammohana-nyāsa* [nyāsa of bewitching], *saubhagya-vardhana-nyāsa* [nyāsa of increasing good fortune], *antyeṣṭhi* [funeral sacrifice], &c.

There is a place of Bhairavanātha, in Kākariā at Ahmedabad and the ceremonies peculiar to the *Vāma-mārga* are observed there; such places are found in every city. The ceremonial consists in making some gestures with the hands called *mudrās*. There are many *mudrās*, viz, *maccha-mudrā* (gesture in the form of a fish), *kūrma-mudrā* (a gesture in the form of a tortoise), *kuśa* (sacred grass), *tārkṣa* (bird or Garuḍa), *dhenu* (a cow), *vidrāvaṇi* (literally act of defeating), *vaṣakarī* (subduing), *khecarī* (moving in heavens), *bāṇa* (an arrow), *pāśa* (a snare), *musala* (a pestle, a club &c), *śankha* (a conch-shell), *kaustubha* (a jewel found from the ocean [jewel worn by Kṛṣṇa]), *śrīvatsa* (a particular mark or curl on the breast of Viṣṇu or Kṛṣṇa.) &c. [These are all marks of the worship of Kṛṣṇa.] The Śāktas have a different mark (*tilaka*) on the forehead and a line of red powder is produced between the eyes; when two Śāktas meet they make presents of liquors, meats, and fish, but, as they do such things very privately, no one knows who a *Śākta* is. Many *Śāstrīs*, Pandits, *Vidiyās* (those who learn the Vedas by heart), householders, *Sannyāsis*, *Paramahaṃsas*, and other people belong to this system of *Vāma-mārga*. Some say that they can convert wine into milk and show it to others in the form of milk and fish as bananas by the virtue of their mystical powers. They have pretensions or claims to magic to a very great extent. It is said that the king Gopīcanda abandoned his kingdom and his queens through listening to the precepts of Macchendranātha (Matsyendra-nātha) and that in the same way Gorakṣanātha (Gorakhanāth) made dead men alive.

The followers of the *Vāma-mārga* do not salute any other gods except Devī (goddess) and Śiva. They say that gods and men perish if they bow down to them (gods), that the *vaitāla* [vampires], *bhūtas* (evil spirits), *yakṣas, yakṣaṇīs* [male and female class of tree-dwelling spirits], Datta, Hanumān and all other gods are ready at their service, and that they can kill and make any one sick or mad. The credulous and ignorant people take all this for truth. At Benares, there was a certain Śākta, named Bhāskarācārya who is author of many books. Once upon a time, he was not invited to a dinner party by some gentlemen and the consequence was that all the food cooked for other persons was changed into a dirty substance or excrement; but the tradition says that, when Nārāyaṇa Dīkṣita Patanakara saluted Bhāskarācārya and took him to his house, all the dirt assumed the form of the original food. The same man (Bhāskarācārya) carried bottles of liquors on the back of an elephant and gave a spirituous bath to the Kāśī-Viśveśvara ([Śiva liṅgam] of Benares) together with a grand procession. Even in these days, some *Brāhmaṇas* sprinkle the water extracted from the *bhāṅga* [hashish] on the image of Śiva; the king Śivājī of Deccan had a preceptor named Gaṇeśadeva who got a temple built in a sacred place called Makulī; his system is now followed in Satārā, while that of Bhāskarācārya is prevalent in Benares. According to the Śāktas, no worship of any sort can be observed without liquors, meats, eggs and women. As the *pañcagavya* [five products of the cow], which consists of five things, viz, cow dung, urine, milk, ghee and curds, is taken according to the Vedic rites to perform a penance for the bodily purification, in the same way, liquors are drunk and used for *mārgana* [rites of request]. The religious ceremonies called the *dīkṣā, śrāddhā, pūjā, antyeṣṭi* &c cannot be performed without intoxicating drinks. The liquors, meats and fish are called *Tīrtha* (sacred waters [fords]), *śuddhi* (purification) and *kadalī* (a deer &c) respectively. It is mentioned in the *Tantra-śāstra* that liquors are considered extremely pure and that Devī (goddess) is pleased beyond measure, if any one would partake of them. Some portion of the Sanskrit text is attached to this book, which when read will clearly show the import of the subject. It will not be worthwhile to give meaning of all the Sanskrit passages, as a specimen, a few of them are translated in the first part.

This book is intended for those men who wish to make a religious reform (dharmanī sudhāraṇā), and they should think of its merits and demerits.

Some *Brāhmaṇas* are *upāsakas* (worshippers [conductors of worship]) from times immemorial; they observe the worship (*upāsanā*) in their family from generation to generation; some kings become the pupils of the *Brāhmaṇas* versed in the mystical science and believe that they will be greatly benefitted thereby. Gaṇeśa-śastrī of Nasik was the religious chief (*danādhyakṣa*) of Gaikwar Malhāvara and was publicly recognised as an *upāsaka* (worshipper). Some prime-ministers of the Baroda State also belonged to this sect, and, as a rule, the native states have many such men. Śivājivās[?] Mahārāja had a mason, named Ladabā-bhagata from Deccan, as well as four or five *Brāhmaṇas* who were Drāviḍas [from the south]; they showed some mystical tricks to the Mahārāja and he gave them a *jāgīr* or property worth a lakh of rupees and paid money to build a temple. As many men are patronised by the kings, this system is carried on without any detention. Every city has one-fourth part of its population as Śāktas—and the ceremonies are performed very secretly in the middle of the night; if a king be a supporter, they are also observed publicly. It is very curious to see that, in case a *Brāhmaṇa* is accused of drinking spirituous liquors, the men who drink always are considered pure or virtuous and they themselves insist on giving *prayaścitta* [rites of atonement] to that man accused. It is said:—The world is deceived in the broad day light by those cheats who pretend to be omniscient, initiated (*dīkṣitā*), *agnidāva* (having a great conflagration by fire), knowers of Brahma[n] (God) and observers of religious austerities, and who while away the nights of the full moon at the houses of harlots, in enjoying pleasures characterised by profound love and fragrant mouthful of liquors.

When a country is characterised by dark, gloomy, thick, blind, and terrible ignorance, heresy is considered a religion and a true religion is regarded as heresy (*pākhaṇḍa*), while the credulous people are deceived by their cunning preceptors. Formerly, there was the Vedic religion in this Gujarāt, and it was followed by the *Śrāvaka, Vāma-mārga,* Śiva, and Vaiṣṇava religions successively. It is said in the *Mahimān stotra* to this effect: "The Vedic, the Sāmkhya, the Yoga, the Paśupati (Śaiva) and the Vaiṣṇava systems (came out after the other)."

All of these religions are now lost in oblivion and no one knows what his religion is. The native princes and their subjects are sinking into ignorance; there are no schools and teachers to impart religious instruction, and, as all religious books are written in the Sanskrit language, no one knows their import; thus truth (artha) is confounded with untruth (anartha) and the wicked and deceitful men serve their selfish motives.

Some modern *Vedias* (those who learn the Vedas by heart) and Joṣīs (astrologers) say that they are *upāsakas* (worshippers) and that the Devī (goddess) is pleased with them; the kings do not take medicine from them unless they (*Vedias*) say so. When such statements are made, the princes think that the Devī is kind to those men and that they will be cured of the disease; these (credulous) fellows are initiated by the *Śāstrīs, Paṇḍitas*, and *Māntrikas* (versed in the mystical science) who are regarded as their preceptors (*gurus*); they believe that they will be greatly benefitted by tying talismans prepared by those mystical men with coals (*aṅgāra, yantrā, tavija*).

The *Mantra-Śāstra* is also called the *Bengāli Vidyā* (the learning of Bengal), because the Gauḍa *Brāhmaṇas* of Bengal used to come to Gujarāta and Deccan and circulate there the mystical books (*mantra-śāstra-grantha*), a large number of which are even now found in Bengal and Kerala; they have not yet come to this side. In Gujarāta, temples dedicated to Kālikā (*kālikā-sthāpana*) are found in Ḍabhoi, Pāvāgaḍha, Ahamadabad, and Pāṭaṇa. The Bengali *Brāhmaṇas* visited this country in the times of the Hindu kings and made some pupils; they circulated some books and introduced Kālikā. The killing of various animals is sanctioned by the books on the *Mantra-śāstra*, but no mention is made anywhere about killing cows, though it is mentioned in many places in the Vedas; from this it appears that the prohibition of killing cows was made in the Kaliyuga or the iron age and that the *Mantra-śāstra* came into existence afterwards. The devotees or advocates of the last mentioned system require necessarily a secluded place and *śakti* (literally power) that is to say a woman in all the ceremonies (*anuṣṭhāna*). The five *makāras* (beginning with *madya*, *māṃsa*, *mīna, mudra*, and *maithuna*) [liquor, meat, fish, grain, and sexual intercourse] are also called *prathama* (first), *dvitīyā* (second), *tritīyā* (third), *caturthī* (fourth), and *pañcamī* (fifth) respectively. In case all objects be not secured, the ceremony is observed by taking the single *prathama* (*madya* = liquor); if two or three things be had, they are only used in performing the rites. The *pañcamī* (fifth, viz, *maithuna* = cohabitation) is considered as *amṛta* (nectar or immortal[ity]) and it is produced from *śakti* (power = woman); and hence it is that cohabitation with the woman is termed *yajña* (sacrifice) or the *dūtīyāga*.

Śiva is regarded as the founder (*ācārya*) of this sytem. Now the question arises why Śiva should produce or advocate heresy (*pākhaṇḍa*), as all the books treating of the *Tantra-mārga* are said to be authorised by Śiva. There is a logical maxim [in Sanskrit] that even a fool does not move without having a special object or aim in view. The meaning of the statement is even an idiot does not do anything without some reason; what should be then the cause of such a heresy (*pākhaṇḍa*); how did people believe in it and should we call him a god or man who propagated a heretical system (*pākhaṇḍa*)?

The *Vāma-mārga* is diametrically opposed to all religious or law books (Dharma- śāstra), morals and good customs. Not only do they not observe caste-distinctions but they also disregard the marriage ceremonies. The men and women perform the ceremony called the *ghaṭa-kañcukī*. *Ghaṭa-kañcukī* is a peculiar and immoral rite according to which the bodices of different women are placed in a pot and the men present at the ceremony are allowed one by one to take out each bodice from it. Each then cohabits with the woman to whom that particular bodice belongs. Any man takes any woman he happens to find; the followers worship a naked woman and consider that they attain to greater merit by getting a female of the Bhangiṇa caste or one in her monthly course. They worship her, eat the remainders of her food, and come into contact with her; they do not observe any distinction between what should be eaten and what should not be eaten. It is mentioned in the books of the *Vāma-mārga* that one is highly benefitted by acting thus and taking this statement into consideration, people join this sect (*dharma*). From this it appears that there is no telling how mean one may become in the hope of deriving some benefit; though he may be mistaken in his ideas as to right or wrong, still, as soon as he sees some advantage, he does not shrink from committing the most horrible deeds. All such men are naturally mean and wicked. There are indeed many instances in history showing that a single man killed thousands of men, burnt their city, committed dacoity, and put millions of people into an ocean of misery for his own insignificant good. There have been instances, also, of great men who made millions of people happy. Many efforts are necessary for the nourishment and growth of man; no one would nourish the child of some other person, even if thousands of rupees be offered but as God has given instinct to the parents who nourish their children, this difficult task is attended with success and thousands of men attain to maturity; their overgrowth becomes so very rapid that some of them cannot be supported, because many men waste money in giving dinners and in marriage ceremonies and nourish their children to no purpose. Good men are sorely wanting, but, if all parents make their children virtuous, strong and useful, the world will abound in good men. In these days, many useless people wander about for their livelihood and are not afraid of acting in any way they like. The principle of education must be such as would make men more useful and religious and must be accessible to all men. As there was no education at all in this country many heretical systems (*pākhaṇḍas*) took rise and people became wicked; their greatest exploit is to quarrel and annoy one another. There is nothing like material confidence. In a great kingdom like that of Baroda, the clerks, state-officials &c would envy and destroy one another. Two men do not trust each other; that is their hearts or thoughts are not in accord; in the same way the enmity inherent in the caste-system has increased to such an extent that any reform is impossible. The natives of this country are inferior even to the lower animals or beasts, because they serve their selfish motives by ruining others; the enmity and wickedness which they possess are not found even in beasts. When all this is considered, it appears that the reasoning power vanished and futile learning (*avidyā*) and ignorance were on their increase. One should dispel foolishness (*avidyā-ajñāna*) and propagate good and true religion.

The *tithis* or days of a month are called *tattva* (essence) in the *Devī-mārga* while the days of a week are called *nātha* (lord); there are thirty-six days in a month and they are thus pronounced: "*pha-māse, kha-yuge, pa-parivarte*" (In the month *Pha*, in the cycle *Kha*, in the year *Pa*). There are five *pārāyaṇas*, viz, *nityanātha* (eternal lord), *caturaṅga* (four limbs), *haṃsa* (a swan), *cakra* (a wheel), *deva* (god), and their fruit is mentioned as follows [in Sanskrit from] *Saubhāgya-ratna-tantra*: "The *Nitya-pārāyaṇa* gives all accomplishments and the *Haṃsa-pārāyaṇa* affords the highest object" (*paramārtha*).

The prefixes and suffixes called *bījas* are applied to some *mantras*. The *mantra* which is recited to gratify the desires is pronounced repeatedly, and this repetition is called the *samputi-pāṭha*. In the same way, when a *Brāhmaṇa* recites generally the *caṇḍī* (*caṇḍī-pāṭha*) [glorification of the goddess Caṇḍī], he receives two annas (3 pence) and if he were to repeat the *samputi-pāṭha* with all its ramifications, which is recited four times, he would charge eight annas (one shilling) for every recitation. In the same way if he were to recite it nine times, it would be called *nava-caṇḍī* and if hundred times, *śata-caṇḍī*. All these actions are mentioned in the Tantras and though some *Brāhmaṇas* censure the *Tantra-mārga*, still they observe the *tāntrika* ceremonies. It is originally arranged that, if prayers are to be said to God or some other deity, they must be offered from the mouth of a *Brāhmaṇa*; if a man of some other denomination were to say such prayers, God or any other deity would not listen to them. Prayers offered by a man of another caste do not become fruitful, therefore, if men of any caste have to say prayers they must have them done through a *Brāhmaṇa* who accords the merit or prayer to the sacrificer (*yajamāna*). If a child be born to some one in the *mūla* asterism, the *mūla* is appeased (*mūla śānti*), that is to say a *Brāhmaṇa* is sent for and thus requested: "You say that this child was born in the *mūla*-asterism; sit and suggest some means to avoid this danger." This ceremony is called "*Varuṇī*." After the *Brāhmaṇa* is thus requested, he makes *āvāhana* [invocation] of a particular deity mentioned in the book which is intended for appeasing gods, or in other words, he invites the god and appeases him by offering prayers (*pūjā*), *japa*, sacrifice, &c; the sacrificer thinks that his difficulty is avoided thereby. In case the sacrificer were not to observe this, the *Brāhmaṇa* would tell the women of the house, "As the child is born in the *mūla*-asterism, there is a great danger to the master (of the house) and if you do not make *śānti* (the act of appeasing)—just for the sake of money (*paisā*), you may do anything you like. If you want to spend a small sum (in performing the ceremony), you can invite four *Brāhmaṇas* and spend five rupees whereby everything will be propitious and you as well as your child will be happy." Having heard these words of the *Brāhmaṇa*, the wife, if unexperienced, annoys her husband and puts him to expense. In the same way, the *Śuklas* (the priests of the *Brāhmaṇas*) order many *śānti*s to be made in the marriage ceremonies, and looking at the horoscopes of the bride and the bridegroom says that the marriage should be brought about after appeasing Maṅgala (Mars) because that planet is inauspicious. Thus the priest has his claim on all things. If it does not rain or cholera and fever be ravaging, the *śānti* should be made and the disease disappears while the rain falls; such statements are made in books but all this must be done through a *Brāhmaṇa* and at the end of all ceremonies the *Brāhmaṇas* should be fed, otherwise the rites observed are of no avail. If a complaint be made to a god (*devatā*) it must be mentioned to a *Brāhmaṇa* who will convey it to that particular deity who gives such a reply as would satisfy the *Brāhmaṇa*, therefore it is considered better to feed more *Brāhmaṇas* and give more *dakṣiṇā* (alms in the shape of money). No one should give less than what he can afford to pay. It is said: "One should not be cunning in money matters."

No religion has such methods (*sādhanā*) as that of the *Brāhmaṇas*. There are answers found in the Śāstras to whatever you may ask. If one drops a lamp from his hand there is a *śānti* for it and it is called the *dīpa-patana-śānti* (the act of appeasing for dropping a lamp). If you invite a *Brāhmaṇa* at the time of death, he would afford final beatitude (to the dead man) for two pices (penny) which sum is regarded as a lakh of rupees spent (for the purpose). They show a way to the poor as well as to the rich men in proportion to their abilities; there is no difficulty or refusal to a question of any kind. There is no reply only to one who enters into discussion or uses reasoning. There is no liberty in the Śāstras to ask what this is and what its cause is. If any one questions that, he is called an atheist or scorner (*miṇḍaka*) of the Śāstras. There is everything in the Śāstras, if you listen without a discussion. If a goat is to be sacrificed, it (the ceremony) is found in the *caṇḍī-pāṭha*; while if a pumpkin is to be cut, if a *japa* is to be made or a *mārjana* [purification] is to be performed, there is a sanction found in the *Śāstra*. You get whatever you require. Whence can such a *kāma-dhenu* (a cow fulfilling all desires) be had? One should only give his consent to hearing what is said. This is the state of the Hindu-Śāstras, and particularly in the Āgamas, this principle is carried on to a very great extent.

The ceremonies of the followers of the *Vāma-mārga* are ten times greater than those of the adherents of the Vedas. In the *Vāma-mārga*, the *pūjā* (worship) is called *yāga* [yajña](sacrifice), the Kālī-*yāga* is named as *anuṣṭhāna* in which a sacrifice is made by repeating a thousand names of Kālī. In all the ceremonies (*anuṣṭhāna*), there is a great deal of *nyāsa*, *mudrā*, and *japa*. In some ceremonies, red peppers and *bhīlāna* [?] are sacrificed. They make a doll of the man by the name of whom the ceremony is undertaken and after piercing a knife in the body of the doll and destroying its eyes, sacrifice it piece by piece and recite mantras; this ceremony is called *māraṇa* [killing] or *abhicāra-karman* (act of killing). The *Śyena-yāga* mentioned in the Tantras is intended for killing enemies but there are thousands of such ceremonies in the books of Āgamas and the credulous men consider them valid, while the heretical *Mantra-śāstrīs* take an undue advantage. Thus there is a great deal of mischief in this subject. If you go to a city like Baroda and examine the state of the thing, there you will see much of it.

—16—

Conversation between Guru Hasan Kabīruddīn and Jogī Kāniphā: Tantra Revisited by the Isma'ili Preachers

Dominique-Sila Khan

Isma'ilism, a form of Shi'a Islam, entered the Indian subcontinent toward the end of the eighth century C.E. In 1094 it underwent a major split, from which there emerged two main branches. The Nizārī sect, originally known as the "new mission," was first based in Iran, but soon spread to Syria and Central Asia, as well as into the subcontinent, perhaps as early as the twelfth century. As Daftary and Corbin have shown, Isma'ilism can be broadly defined as a well-organized revolutionary type of movement, undergirded by a complex esoteric philosophy. Persecuted by the Sunni rulers of Delhi, who cast themselves as the representatives of an "orthodox" or "normative" Islam, the Indian Isma'ilis, viewed as heretics, generally resorted to the Shi'a custom of precautionary concealment of one's true faith *(taqiyya)*. At the same time, they adopted a strategy that involved accepting most of the beliefs and practices of the people they sought to convert while gradually transforming the same to fit the requirements of their own doctines. This method, however, should not be viewed solely as a tactic for conversion but rather as an essential part of Isma'ili philosophy: not merely a later evolute of Islam, their faith was also a "culmination of Hinduism." Rather than rejecting the established beliefs and practices of local populations, the Nizārī missionaries absorbed and adapted them in order to create what Maclean has righly called "an innovative synthesis," in which Muslim and Hindu elements were harmoniously combined.

In fact, the syncretic form of Isma'ilism that developed on the subcontinent closely resembles many other religious movements of the medieval period, and as such, was referred to as Satpanth (literally the "true path" or "true sect")—a name retained until recent times. This historical phase of acculturation came to a gradual end toward the close of the nineteenth century. The first changes occurred with the arrival of the Aga Khan (the living Imam of the Isma'ilis) on the subcontinent in the 1840s. As increasing numbers of Isma'ilis, convinced that they were no longer subject to persecution, came out of concealment and began searching for a new identity, the whole movement was gradually re-Islamicized—a process that has continued down to the present day. Nonetheless, the "syncretic" phase—some six to seven centuries in duration—has left a lasting mark on the Nizārī sect, in the form of readily accessible rituals and texts. This "innovative synthesis" was clearly the fruit of extensive exchanges and interactions with the many indigenous (Jain and Hindu) belief systems that were prevalent in the medieval period. Because of the practice of taqiyya, as well as of a typical conversion strategy, Nizārī missionaries on the subcontinent never revealed themselves for whom they were: as Nanji has stressed, they presented themselves, according to the context in which they were preaching, as Sufi dervishes, or as Hindu jogīs (yogī in Hindi, from the Sanskrit *yogin*, "practitioner of yoga").

On the Hindu side, the Nizārī preachers drew from a variety of sources, both Vaiṣṇava and Śaiva. They developed their own doctrine of Viṣṇu's descents (*avatāras*), equating Kalki, the tenth of these, with their Imam who, apart from being a religious leader, was considered to be a manifestation of Divine Light. Of greater impact, however, were Śaiva ideas and practices, most particularly those involving Tantric forms of yoga. It is obvious, from numerous references found in the Nizārī textual sources, that the followers of Gorakhnāth and other of the Nāth masters (also referred to as jogīs) deeply influenced the literature and rituals of subcontinental Isma'ilis.

The Nizārī literature is revealing in this regard. So, for example, the Āgākhānī Khojās who now form the majority of Nizārī Isma'ilis in India and Pakistan, have preserved a rich and wide-ranging corpus of sacred texts generally referred to as *ginān*s (the word *ginān* means "knowledge" or "wisdom," and is derived from the Sanskrit *jñāna*). Composed in a blend of north Indian vernacular languages, most of these were intended to be sung (and many still are sung) in jamāt khānas, their sacred assembly and prayer halls. Gināns may be replete with terminology proper to Tantric yoga, and at times entire gināns will be devoted to haṭha yoga and the Nāth tradition. These include an Isma'ili version of the story of the illustrious royal renouncer Gopīcand and his sister (a work signed by Pīr Shams, a famous thirteenth- or fourteenth-century missionary and saint); a series of poems explicitly referred to as Jogvāṇīs ("discourses on yoga," attributed to Imām Shāh, a fifteenth-century figure); and the text that will be presented here, a meeting between Jogī Kāniphā and Imām Shāh's father, Hasan Kabīruddīn.

At this point, we need to say a few words about the rituals of the subcontinental Nizārī Isma'ilis, insofar as they have been influenced by Tantric practices. As Shackle and Moir have noted, the organization of religious life in the Satpanth (the acculturated form of subcontinental Nizārī Isma'ilism) differs from the familiar patterns found in "orthodox" Sunni Islam. Traditionally, Nizārīs neither went to mosque nor recited the five daily prayers, but rather maintained and continue to maintain their own jamāt khānas, open exclusively to members of the community, the "assembly of the faithful" (*jamāt*), where they recite the morning, evening, and nighttime prayers, and sing ginans. Their most characteristic ritual is the ghaṭ-paṭ ceremony (*ghaṭ* means "pot," and *paṭ* refers to the low wooden table on which this vessel is placed), which centers on the distribution of sacred water from the pot, which is either mixed with clay from Karbala (a Shi'a holy site) or blessed by the imām. As Ivanow has rightly stated, this rite may be viewed as a symbol of conversion and participation in the religious life of the community. Typically, the holy water of which all the followers partake—in a kind of communion—is referred to in the sacred literature as ami (from the Sanskrit *amṛta*, the "ambrosia" or "nectar of immortality"); the same term is used in Hinduism for the sacred fluid in which the feet of a divine image or one's guru have been bathed.

A number of scholars consider this ritual to have been inspired by Tantric or Śākta cults, especially those "of the left-hand" (*vāmmārg; vāmamārga* in Sanskrit), which may well have been prevalent among such major convert groups as the Lohanas (a trading caste of the Sindh region) and untouchables. By accepting certain of their practices, and recasting them into a new mold to meet the requirements of Nizārī Isma'ili ideals, the process of conversion was presumably made smoother. Let us briefly mention the elements of the Satpanthī ritual which recall the Vāmmārgī ceremonies.

secrecy: those who had not been initiated into the Satpanth were not allowed to attend their ceremonies
joint participation of men, women and children
caste mixing: all communities, including untouchables, commune in the assembly halls
communal drinking of consecrated water which, as Ivanow has observed, is intended to replace the semen partaken of in Śākta or left-handed Tantric rituals
the pot itself in which the water is kept is traditionally worshiped by Hindus as the Goddess, of whom it is a symbol

Here, it is worth noting that, perhaps due to the secrecy that surrounded the Nizārī rituals, Indian Isma'ilis, viewed as heretics by the Sunni rulers (including the fourteenth-century Sultan Alaūddīn Khiljī), were accused of indulging in "free licence and incest"—an accusation more accurately leveled against Vāmmārgī practitioners.

In conclusion, it may be said that, in conformity with the spirit of Isma'ilism, the ritual complex of the Satpanthīs ought not to be regarded solely as a "revision" of Tantra, but also as its "consummation," in the same way that the Nizārī sect as a whole, in its Indian form, may be viewed as the culmination of earlier Hindu systems. This is further corroborated by the fact that the spiritual message of the Satpanth and its religious literature were considered to be a secret "fifth Veda," called the *Athar Ved* (literally, the "immobile, stable Veda," not be confused with the fourth Veda, the *Atharva Veda*). Here as well, we may detect a reference to Tantric revelation, which is also viewed as a fifth Veda that, unlike the four original Vedas, is accessible to women as well as men from every caste.

The text translated here deals with the imaginary encounter between two prestigious religious figures: a Nāth jogī who is an exponent of Tantric yoga, and a Nizārī missionary. In spite of its obvious anachronisms and other implausible elements, this dialogue—in which the representatives of two different spiritual paths exchange their views—undoubtedly reflects an historical situation in which interactions took place between Nāth jogīs and Isma'ili pīrs (even if this ginān in its written form is the creation of a much later period, the eighteenth or nineteenth century). It is worth noting that some of its parts are still sung in the sacred assemblies of the Khojās, as Zawahir Moir, who remembers entire portions of it, has informed me.

The choice of Kāniphā Nāth as the central figure of the text, in the role of the jogī, is certainly not a concidence here. On the one hand, he is one of the foremost masters of the Kānphaṭā ("split-eared") jogīs and is listed as one of the renowned Nine Nāths. In addition, as Briggs has noted, there is a tradition that traces the origins of the Vāmmārg to this disciple of Jālandhar Nāth, who was himself one of the original Nāths. Even today Kāniphā is revered as the head guru of the Kalbelyā jogīs of northwest India, a community of snake charmers who have preserved various traditions and customs connected with Tantric yoga.

The story opens with Kāniphā being cursed by his guru, Jālandhar Nāth. With the curse, however, the jogī predicts that his disciple's salvation will eventually come through a saint named Guru Hasan Kabīruddīn who was, as we know, a famous Isma'ili missionary. According to Isma'ili tradition, Hasan Kabīruddīn concealed his identity in the course of his missionary activities, appearing either in the guise of a Sufi pīr (a Muslim "saint"—he continues to be revered by the Sunni Suhrawardi order of Sufis as Hasan Daryā); or, as Upanga has noted, as a vegetarian Hindu sādhu dressed in white or saffron robes.

Jālandhar Nāth adds that his disciple will recognize his new master when Kāniphā's miraculous chariot, now suspended in mid-air, suddenly falls from the sky. This happens on the day that the jogī reaches the city of Uch (at that time the center of the Nizārī mission on the subcontinent). Although Hasan Kabīruddīn is but a child, he has attained true wisdom. The dialogue begins when, surprisingly enough in a Nāth context, Kāniphā's new guru reveals to him the "true" secret of Viṣṇu's ten avatāras. (Here, as in other cases, it is obvious that the prestigious Vaiṣṇava model is being used to counterbalance the Śaiva and Śākta idioms of the Kānphaṭā jogīs). This new revelation, however, concerns the "true" (according to the Nizārī doctrine) identity of the tenth incarnation of Viṣṇu. This is Kalki, whom he equates with Imām Ali (the Prophet's son-in-law) and, as such, with every living Imam considered to be his cyclic reincarnation. Guru Hasan Kabīruddīn claims that 'Ali, the manifestation of Divine Light, is the original founder of the Satya Dharm, the "religion of truth," an equivalent of the term Satpanth. Oddly enough, this appears in the manuscript form of the ginān as Śaiv Dharm, the "Śaiva religion"; once more, this may be viewed as an allusion to the fact that the Nizārī spiritual message does not contradict or negate the faith of the Śaiva Nāths but ought rather to be viewed as a kind of "super-Śaivism," a new revelation that supercedes the earlier one.

Although he is impressed at first by his new guru's knowledge, Kāniphā still considers himself to be the wiser of the two, and seeks to please the pīr by asserting that he will be rewarded for his wisdom and will obtain miraculous powers (*riddhi-siddhi*), liberation (*mukti*), and immortality (*acal pad*). To his surprise, the child-guru retorts that all these achievements (typical of Tantric yoga) are devoid of value. There then follows a discussion of the four yugas (cosmic ages); the nature of the world and of God; and the role played by Hasan Kabīruddīn's predecessor, the great pīr Sadruddīn, who is credited with most of the syncretic features of the Satpanth. Recognizing the differences between this new teaching and his former beliefs, Kāniphā wishes to know to which sect (*panth*, literally "path" or "way") Hasan Kabīruddīn belongs. Everyone, answers the guru, belongs to a sect (or follows a path), but it is he who will reveal the "true path" (Satpanth). He begins with a stinging criticism of all the outward signs by which the Kānphaṭā jogī distinguishes himself: "What kind of jogī are you," asks Kabīruddīn, "if you shave your head but do not shave your mind?" The true jogī should don "mental" earrings (*mudrās*), smear the "ashes of truth" on his body, and so on. Emphasis is thus given to "inner religion," which actually coincides with the essential Isma'ili doctrine of the superiority of the esoteric truth (*batin*) over the externals of religion (*zahir*). The dialogue continues in question-and-answer form, the answers being much longer than questions, and often takes the form of short devotional songs (like the gināns sung in Ismaili assemblies).

The passage translated here corresponds to the second and final portion of the text and represents sightly less than half of its total length. Differing in its content and tone from the first portion, it treats of what might be termed "inner yoga"; that is, everything a yogin should be and do, according to Satpanthī philosophy. Curiously enough, direct references to Islamic or typically Nizārī terminology are scarce; however, a few bear mentioning: Allah and the Prophet; paradise depicted as Amrāpurī, the "City of Immortality"; Islām Shāh, the living Imam who was a contemporary of Hasan Kabīruddīn; the "true believer" (*momin*, a term that refers to a Muslim in general and, in the Isma'ili context, to a member of the Nizārī community); and the community of the faithful (*gat*).

In contradistinction, the passage is replete with words belonging to the sphere of Hinduism and of Tantric yoga. These include: intellect (*cit*); consciousness (*caitan*); the elixir (*rasa*, literally "essence," "flavor," or "meaning"), the three principal channels of the yogic body (idā, pingalā and suṣumṇā) and the moon (*canda*, identified with the idā channel), the stage in which the *yogin* experiences the "inner sound" (*surat-nirat*), the mystical sound (*nad*), supernatural powers (*riddhi-siddhi*), and so forth. The soul is called *hansa* (literally, "migratory bird"), and the Spiritual Master the *Hansa Purus*, literally, the "Man of the soul or breath." The body is also described as *navsar* (literally "nine-head"), and inhabited by "five ministers," probable allusions to the yogic image of the nine bodily orifices and the five senses.

The lesson that is transmitted by the Isma'ili pīr to his Nāth disciple does not, therefore, deny the value of such purely haṭha yogic techniques as postures (*āsanas*), breath control (*prāṇāyāma*), and meditation (*dhyān*). However, it simultaneously emphasizes the necessity of true knowledge and of following a guru who alone can show the true path. "Search with your breath, and place your hope in the Invisible Master (*Alakh Purus*, literally, the "Cosmic man who defies description") is a message comprehensible to Nāth and Nizārī alike. The Isma'ili Guru is also represented by alchemical symbols, which are an essential part of Tantric yogic imagery: " If you find the Guru you will be transmuted"; and "The true Guru is like mercury, the sādhu is like copper: if the two are rubbed together one obtains gold." As will be seen throughout, characteristically Tantric "intentional language" (*sandhā bhāṣā*) is also used extensively, for example to describe the state experienced by the accomplished yogin: "sound (*nad*) is resounding without a mouth . . . without feet you come and go."

The final portion of the text, immediately preceding the brief conclusion (in which it is related that Kāniphā is released from his guru's curse and granted liberation) is actually a devotional song, a short ginān that, in the Nizārī tradition, is also attributed to an earlier missionary, Pīr Shams, and which appears in Kassam's selected translations of the gināns. It seemingly sums up the entire message of the Satpanthī preachers, asserting what a "true jogī" or fakir (holy man, literally "poor man") should be. Therefore, in accordance with the imaginary vision of the poets who composed this text, one could say that Kāniphā does not, by becoming a member of the Isma'ili community, cease to be a yogin, because the Satpanth is a kind of "super-yoga" that encompasses and complements the traditional values of Tantra.

The *Conversation between Guru Hasan Kabīruddīn and Jogī Kāniphā* exists in both manuscript and printed form. The manuscripts are written in the sacred (and once secret) alphabet of the Nizārī Khojās known as Khojki, whereas the printed texts use both the Khojki and the Gujarati scripts. No critical texts have yet been established, and the publications that are available are more or less revised copies of a collection of gināns brought together by an Isma'ili named Lalji Devraj at the beginning of the twentieth century; these constituted the official canon at that time. Here we have used a version published in Bombay in 1921; no other publication data are available. I am deeply indebted to Zawahir Moir, who not only provided me with the text in Gujarati script but also helped me to understand its meaning and establish the translation.

Further Reading

For the sake of comparison and as an overall survey of the Nāth sect, see George Weston Briggs, *Gorakhnāth and the Kānphaṭā Yogīs* (reprint Delhi: Motilal Banarsidass, 1990). For a comprehensive study of Isma'ilism see Farhad Daftary, *The Isma'ilis, Their History and Doctrines* (Cambridge: Cambridge University Press, and Delhi: Munshiram Manoharlal, 1990). The esoteric Isma'ili philosophy is best presented in Henri Corbin, *Histoire de la philosophie islamique* (Paris: Gallimard, 1986). Other useful works dealing with Nizārī Isma'ilism are: R. E. Enthoven,

The Tribes and Castes of Bombay, 3 vols. (reprint Delhi: Asian Educational Services, 1989); John Norman Hollister, *The Shi'a of India* (reprint Delhi: Oriental Book Corporation, 1979); D. N. Maclean, *Religion and Society in Arab Sind* (Leiden: Brill, 1989); and Azim Nanji, *The Nizārī Ismaili Tradition in the Indo-Pakistan Subcontinent* (New York: Caravan Books, 1978). The earliest source (in Gujarati) is Sachedina Nanjiani, *Khojā vṛttānt* (Ahmedabad: Samasher Bahadur Press, 1892). A brief hagiography of Pīr Hasan Kabīruddīn is found in A. A. Upanga, "Pīr Hasan Kabīruddīn" in *The Great Ismaili Heroes* (Karachi: Religious Night School, 1973), pp. 91–93. On acculturation and interactions with Hinduism, see Françoise Mallison, "Hinduism as Seen by the Nizārī Isma'ili missionaries of Western India" in Gunther Dietz Sontheimer and Hermann Kulke, eds., *Hinduism Reconsidered* (Delhi: Manohar, 1989), pp. 93–113; and Dominique-Sila Khan, "Deux rites tantriques dans une communauté d'intouchables au Rajasthan" in *Revue de l'Histoire des Religions* 210.1 (1994): 443–62; and Khan, *Conversions and Shifting Identites: Ramdev Pīr and the Ismailis in Rajasthan* (Delhi: Manohar, 1997). Translated gināns are found in Vladimir Ivanow, "Satpanth," in the Ismaili Society Series (series A, no. 2) *Collectanea*, vol. 1 (Leiden: E. J. Brill, 1948); Tazim R. Kassam, *Songs of Wisdom and Circles of Dance: An Anthology of Hymns by the Satpanth Ismaili Muslim Saint Pīr Shams* (Albany: State University of New York Press, 1995); and Christopher Shackle and Zawahir Moir, *Ismaili Hymns from South Asia: An Introduction to the Ginans* (London: School of Oriental and African Studies, 1992).

Conversation between Guru Hasan Kabīruddīn and Jogī Kāniphā

PART ONE

Kāniphā says: O respected Guru, I wish to ask you some questions: answer, if you please!

The guru says: Do ask, O Kāniphā!

1. The jogī says: What has come to me I do not give up; neither will I go and take it. My Master says, "Be with me," O Pīr!

2. The guru says: Give up what has come and go and take the truth, says my true Guru. Eat only after having carefully considered, O Jogī!

3. The jogī says: Impurity says, "I am the queen of the world." Impurity is removed by water, and the impurity of water by wind—but who will remove the impurity of the soul, O Pīr?

4. The guru says: The body is like a pot, the mind is like musk, and knowledge is the light of the soul. The man in whose heart Allah and the Prophet dwell—why should he be affected by impurity, O Jogī?

5. The jogī says: Who is the learned brahman (*pandit*)? What is the flesh

(*pind*)? Whose children are you [the Nizārīs]? With whom should one eat? How may one reach the City of Immortality [paradise], O Pīr?

6. The guru says: the mind is called the pandit; the body our *pind*; we are the children of the venerable Islām Shāh; in the assembly of the pious, meditation should be your food: in this way you shall reach the City of Immortality, O Jogī.

7. The jogī says: What is your sacred thread? What is your loincloth? What is your word? What is your sacred book, O Pīr?

8. The guru says: The absence of grief is our sacred thread; the suppression of grief is our loincloth; permanence is our word; the body is our sacred book, O Jogī!

9. The jogī says: What is the city? What is the place? Who are the ministers? Who is the king? Who is the vizier? Tell me this, O Pīr!

10. The guru says: The city is the body; navsar ["nine-head"] is the place, and there are five ministers within. The soul (*hansa*) is the king, the breath (*pavan*) is the vizier: know [the secret of] this city, O Jogī!

11. The jogī says : Who is asleep? Who is awake? Who identifies the ten directions? Who recognizes the Guru? Who brings one to the [true] path, O Pīr?

12. The guru says: The soul is awake; the flesh is asleep; cosmic illusion (*māyā*) identifies the ten directions and knowledge recognizes the Guru. It is therefore knowledge that brings one to the [true] path, O Jogī!

13. The jogī says: Which are the pilgrimage centers of the four cosmic ages, and which are the pilgrimage sites of the true believers? Which is the pilgrimage site of the running river, and which is that of the six philosophical schools, O Pīr?

14. The guru says: The pilgrimage sites of the four cosmic ages are nonexistent; the pilgrimage sites of the true believer are [composed of] knowledge; the pilgrimage site of the running river is within [you]; the Satpanth is the true pilgrimage, [replacing] the six philosophical schools, O Jogī!

15. The jogī says: How many years will the clouds give rain? Who will obtain salvation, heaven, or the inner world?

16. The guru says: The clouds will give rain for thirty-six years; both heaven and the inner world will be saved. Therefore, take heed in your mind, O sādhu: there is no other salvation—it is ahead, it is far away where there is no teaching, no sound, no ego, no primeval chaos. So says Pīr Hasan Kabīruddīn, O Jogī!

O Jogī, take heed in your mind! Here is the path to salvation—listen!

PART TWO

1. O renouncer, if you conquer the mind you can fulfill your desires, and if you conquer the mind you will experience great bliss. If you conquer the heart you will experience happiness; in this way [the fruit of] the yoga is ripened.

2. O renouncer, if you conquer lust and anger then the truth will become sacred. If you conquer the intellect the moon will become pure—it becomes totally pure, O sādhu!

3. O renouncer, they ask for the elixir, and they wish to taste the nectar of immortality, and they seek the lord of knowledge. The king of heaven has made the body a throne, yet they go on searching for the Supreme Master [outside of themselves]!

4. O renouncer, the body is full of lust and desire is a goddess. But it is consciousness that is the abode of the Supreme Master. Anger and selfishness are the kings of the armies, and meditations on the inner sound are his ministers, O renouncer!

5. Above everything it is the Name that leads you to your inner depth. Action (*karma*) is the true throne of the Master. When both yoga and practice are conjoined, O Lord, then any action you perform is done well.

6. O renouncer, slay your desires, keep your mind concentrated, and do your own cooking [work for your own transformation]. Control the postures, do not fall asleep—and all will take place as the Lord ordains, O renouncer!

7. O renouncer, if you find your Guru he will tell you the meaning, and the doubts of your mind will be removed. Without water the lotus flower does not bloom: only the fool would laugh at this, O renouncer!

8. O renouncer, if you find your [true] Guru, you will be transmuted! O sādhu, without a guru you cannot find the path. Within the circle of knowledge shining lamps appear: therefore without a guru [whose knowledge provides light to his disciple], this will remain out of reach, O renouncer!

9. O renouncer, the night is dark! Your companions are your enemies, and you are dwelling in another man's house! How will you find the path without a guide? Make haste and consider this, O renouncer!

10. O renouncer, the true Guru is like mercury, the sādhu is like copper: if the two are rubbed together one obtains gold. Just as you see yourself mirrored in water, so your vision is made pure, O renouncer!

11. O renouncer, purity is the door to the true Guru's dwelling and compassion is the Supreme Master's fragrance. The heart is like a pot—search with your breath, and place your trust in the Invisible Master!

12. O renouncer, it is easy to slip in the narrow passage of the heart! There even a needle cannot find its way, so ride the chariot of your breath and be like a king on a throne. Control it, letting it enter in and exit regularly.

13. O renouncer, blossoms are blooming and there is no tree; sound (*nad*) is resounding without a mouth! Without speech the praises of the Lord are sung; without feet you come and go, O renouncer!

14. O renouncer, make your mind your seat, strap in your consciousness, and enjoy the giddy ride! Idā, pingalā and suṣumṇā are your slaves—they are the servants of the true Guru, O renouncer!

15. Search your body to find its silken thread and do what the Guru says. Like the mother-of-pearl that anxiously waits for the rain [that produces the pearl], so the soul swells with eagerness to meet the Lord, O renouncer!

16. O renouncer, when the Spiritual Master appears before you the body is purified. Meditate without the body, O you whose limbs are smeared [with ashes], then [you will not be a god] but will reach a divine state.

17. O renouncer, both sound and the absence of sound are the manifestations of the Guru. Intellect and truth are your companions. The Guru's renewed miracles will be yours to experience. [Learning to practice true] knowledge and meditation is like [riding] an elephant.

18. O renouncer, those who wake to enjoy the divine elixir will ripen, while those who remain asleep will lose it. They will therefore lose the path, O Gusain! It is only fools who wish to sleep, O renouncer!

19. O renouncer, it is in the inner self that the miraculous powers dwell and it is there that the eternal play goes on. In the inner self the Lord has planted a garden and therein the gardener dwells.

20. O renouncer, in the inner self is the earth with its nine continents; within it is Mount Kailāsa; and within it are the seven seas. Without a guru the cup [of the nectar of immortality] is lost!

21. O renouncer, the Lord has said, "Look into your inner self!" Only then will you gain the sacred vision of the Master. Pīr Hasan Kabīruddīn says, "Listen, O people of the jamāt, you will then have no more rebirths!

O Jogīs, you must live in this way—listen!

DOHA [COUPLET]

> Famished and exiled, the heart is sad—on your seat be firm!
> Those who vanquish the fear of the grave deserve the name of fakir!
>
> O Jogī, this is the [true] way of begging alms—listen:

PART THREE

1. O renouncer, make the world you mendicant's bag and satisfaction your begging bowl; may your reflection be your staff! Place the two earrings of forgiveness and compassion in your ears, and let knowledge be your food. O renouncer! He is the true jogī in this world: he whose mind is one, he is the true jogī!

2. O renouncer, knowledge is my guru, [true] renunciation is of the senses. May the conjunctions [of opposites?] be your ashes! He who accepts the true religion and meditates on the truth, he is the true jogī! O renouncer, he is the true jogī!

3. O renouncer, stop both the moon and the sun [the left and right channels], choosing concentration as your staff. Then the suṣumṇā [the central channel] will begin to reverberate: few indeed are those who know this secret!

4. O renouncer, wash your sins away in the triple confluence; play the unstruck sound! Hasan Kabīruddīn says: "Die while your are living, and you shall not be reborn. O renouncer, he [who does so] is the true jogī in this world!"

Having listened to this ginān of spiritual teaching, Kāniphā prayed and spoke:

Kāniphā says: O Guru, thanks to you I have found the path to liberation and through the grace of the blessed Guru Jālandhar I have had darśan [vision] of you! You have imparted to me the knowledge of liberation! I offer you obeisance!

Thus, in various ways, the path to liberation was revealed to him by Guru Hasan Kabīruddīn—and he enjoyed it.

Tantric Paths

—17—

Emptiness and Dust: Zen Dharma Transmission Rituals

William Bodiford

Although the Shingon lineage of Kūkai (774—835) and the Tendai lineage of Saichō (767—822) can be most readily identified as the Tantric mainstream within Japanese Buddhism, we must not overlook the pervasive influence of Tantric rituals, Tantric deities, and Tantric symbolism on Japanese religious traditions in general. Even today fire invocations (*homa* in Sanskrit, *goma* in Japanese), for example, are ubiquitous not just in Shingon and Tendai, but also in Hossō, Nichiren, and Zen lineages, as well as in Shintō (Japan's so-called "native" religion), mountain asceticism (*shugendō*), and many New Age religions, such as Agonshū. In medieval times, before the eighteenth-century renaissance of Buddhist scholarship gave birth to a heightened sense of sectarian identity among these lineages, Tantric imagery was even more common than it is now. For this reason, scholars of Japanese culture often refer to medieval Japanese religions as *kenmitsu* (combined exoteric and esoteric Tantric) Buddhism.

Prime examples of Tantric tendencies within medieval Zen can be found in the once common practice of secret initiations into the esoteric lore of Zen, and in the documents (*kirikami*) on which the contents of such initiations were recorded. These initiations were reserved for the most advanced disciples, those who would inherit the dharma lineage of their master and thereby become Zen masters in their own right. Conducted in absolute secrecy over a period of several weeks or months, the initiations would reveal to the disciple both special ritual techniques, which the master and disciple would rehearse, as well as the symbolic associations from which the ritual techniques derived their religious power. Over the course of the initiations, the disciple would record on separate single sheets of paper (the original meaning of the term *kirikami*) key terms, signs, and gestures for each ritual. Some of the rituals taught in this way were exactly the same as the ones transmitted in Shingon or Tendai lineages. The most interesting initiation documents for students of Zen, however, are the ones that focus on Zen itself.

Two such documents are translated below. While reading these translations, it is important to remember that these documents have become available to the general public only because modern-day Zen masters no longer maintain the tradition of esoteric initiations that such documents represent. They have also abandoned, therefore, the traditions of hands-on knowledge and oral explanation necessary to understand fully the content of these texts. For this reason, much of the symbolism remains obscure.

The first document, entitled "Emptiness and Dust Ritual" (*Kūjinsho*) concerns the ritual of dharma transmission in which the disciple merges his mind and his body with that of his teacher. Its title implies the merging of the universal, timeless truth of emptiness (*śunyatā*), or buddhahood, with limited, historical phenomena (the dust of ordinary existence). It explains the mythological origins of the Zen lineage in just such a ritual union and how this same form of union must be reenacted in present-day dharma transmission ceremonies. The mythological origin of Zen, of course, lies in the oft-told story of how one day on Vulture Peak (Gṛdhrakūṭa) Śākyamuni, the historical Buddha, preached a sermon not with words but by holding up a flower. Mahā Kāśyapa was the only one of Śākyamuni's many disciples who grasped the true significance of this wordless teaching, which he expressed by a slight smile. Śākyamuni thereupon selected Mahā Kāśyapa to inherit his dharma robe and his dharma lineage as the second Zen ancestor. Although this story might seem to suggest that the secret, wordless, mind-to-mind transmission of the true dharma occurred at the moment when Śākyamuni's flower met Mahā Kāśyapa's smile, in reality, according to our document, the formal conveyance of the dharma did not occur until a secret ceremony later that night.

The *Emptiness and Dust Ritual* document explains how the spiritual union of Śākyamuni and his disciple was symbolized by a wide variety of ritual forms that the contemporary Zen master and his disciple must reenact: flames leap from one torch to the next (symbolized in the document by a two-headed flaming chicken); teacher and disciple reflect one another by covering their faces with mirrors; they mix their blood together, and they use their mixed blood as ink to write their names together; the teacher anoints the disciple, who then anoints the teacher. After each ritual element the teacher and disciple must recite together: "Future generations must never terminate the lineage of the buddha-to-buddha transmission."

The most powerful tangible symbol created during this ritual is a genealogical table known as "blood lineage" chart (*kechimyaku*). Beginning with Śākyamuni, the table lists the names of each generation (both real and imagined) of Zen ancestors down to the present. This list of names constitutes a "blood lineage" (*kechimyaku*) in several senses of the word. First, as mentioned above, the master and disciple physically mix their blood together to produce ink for writing the chart. The spiritual connection between each individual person named provides the life blood that sustains the religious experience of Zen awakening, and the written list of names forms a text that can be used as a magical talisman to confirm the faith of the present generation in the reality of that awakening. In popular religious lore, a properly written blood lineage chart can exorcise ghosts and free the dead from the torments of hell. The intangible, wordless essence of the Buddha wisdom is symbolized by Vajra Jewel Precepts (*kongō hō kai*) that are transmitted along with the blood lineage chart. For this reason, the *Emptiness and Dust Ritual* document identifies dharma transmission ritual as a special kind of precept ordination ceremony.

The second document, entitled *The Unsurpassed Ultimate Blood Line of the Bodhisattva Precepts in the Orthodox Transmission of the Buddhas and Ancestors* (*Busso shōden bosatsukai kechimyaku saigoku mujō no koto*), makes explicit the soteriological implications of the first document. It begins by asserting that the blood lineage is the fundamental body of all buddhas and all living beings. The circle surrounding the names of Śākyamuni Buddha and Mahā Kāśyapa at the head of the lineage chart signifies the true blood lineage, which is none other than the bright "moon disk" of wisdom that "constitutes the fundamental mind of living beings." It goes on to explain that the disciple attains sudden awakening at the moment when he receives the ordination with the Vajra Jewel Precepts. In this awakened state, all dualities, including all distinctions between good and evil, collapse. Every aspect of the precept ordination is charged with soteriological significance. The teacher's bowing to the disciple enacts the descent of the universal (*honji*) into the particular (*suijaku*), whereas the disciple's bowing to the teacher represents the ascent of the particular into the universal. The union of both ascent and descent is achieved as both teacher and disciple leave the initiation site together. A five-colored string is tied around the blood lineage chart because living beings fundamentally are the Five Wisdom Buddhas of the Womb Maṇḍala. The string is tied with nine knots because living beings possess nine types of consciousness, and so forth.

The physical layouts of the original documents are also noteworthy. The *Emptiness and Dust Ritual* document is long and thin, with a circle at the top of the document, followed by text, followed by a list of names, and concluding with more text. The circle at the top of the document contains the names of Śākyamuni Buddha and his disciple Mahā Kāśyapa. The circle itself is labeled as depicting a small mirror of the type that the teacher and disciple will wear on their heads during the dharma transmission ritual. The list of names in the middle of the document consists of all the Indian, Chinese, and Japanese patriarchs in the Zen genealogy. The dictionary forms of the names of the first ten Japanese Zen masters listed are as follows: Dōgen (1200–1253), Ejō (1198–1280), Gikai (1219–1309), Keizan Jōkin (1264–1325), Gasan Jōseki (1276–1366), Tsūgen Jakurei (1322–1391), Tenshin Jishō (d. 1413), Kidō Chōō (d. 1410), Sessō Ichijun (1377–1455), and Tennō Soin (d. 1467). A red line, written in the blood of the master and disciple, runs from the top circle down the right margin of the text through the list of names and then back up the left margin back to the circle. The *Emptiness and Dust Ritual* document also contains a brief glossary of the esoteric meaning of each word in the phrase "I entrust (*fuzoku*) so-and-so with the Lineage of the Wisdom Eye that Perceives the True Dharma (*shōbōgenzō*), the Marvelous Mind of Nirvāṇa (*shōbō genzō nehan myōshin*)." Both documents conclude with fictitious stories that tell how the original copies of the documents were brought to Japan from China by Dōgen, the founder of the Sōtō lineage of Japanese Zen. Finally, both documents are signed and dated by Kyūgai Donryō, about whom nothing is known other than the fact that he once served as the abbot of Yōkōji Zen monastery.

The *Kūjinsho kirikami,* copied in 1637 by Kyūgai Donryō is a Yōkōji (Ishikawa prefecture) initiation document. It was photographed September 5, 1980 by Kaneda Hiroshi. (Kaneda serial nos. 2–5). The transcription is in Ishikawa Rikizan, "Chūsei Sōtōshū kirikami no bunrui shiron, 12: shitsunai (shihō, sanmotsu, kechimyaku) kankei o chūshin to shite," *Komazawa daigaku Bukkyō gakubu ronshū* 19 (1988): 165–167.

Busso shōden bosatsukai kechimyaku saigoku mujō no koto, copied in 1622 by Kyūgai Donryō, seal by Meian Tōsai, is also a Yōkōji (Ishikawa prefecture) initiation document. It was photographed September 5, 1980 by Kaneda Hiroshi (Kaneda serial nos. 101–2). The transcription is in Ishikawa Rikizan, "Chūsei Sōtōshū kirikami no bunrui shiron, 14: shitsunai (shihō, sanmotsu, kechimyaku) kankei o chūshin to shite," *Komazawa daigaku Bukkyō gakubu ronshū* 20 (1989): 129.

Further Reading

Regarding the roles of secret initiations and precept ordinations in the development of Zen Buddhism in Japan, see William M. Bodiford, *Sōtō Zen in Medieval Japan* (Honolulu: University of Hawaii Press, 1993), as well as two of his forthcoming articles: "Bodhidharma's Precepts in Japan," and "Documents of Insight: Initiation Documents (*kirikami*) in Japanese Zen." The ways that Zen monastic rituals serve to construct religious authority from dharma lineages is illustrated in Robert H. Sharf, "The Idolization of Enlightenment: On the Mummification of Ch'an Masters in Medieval China," *History of Religions* 32 (1992): 1–31. Although a serviceable overview of the full range of Japanese Tantric Buddhism does not exist, readers will find in Taiko Yamasaki, *Shingon: Japanese Esoteric Buddhism* (Boston: Shambhala, 1988) an excellent account of how one contemporary Shingon practitioner views his own tradition. Stanley Weinstein, "The Beginnings of Esoteric Buddhism in Japan: The Neglected Tendai Tradition," *Journal of Asian Studies* 34 (1974): 177–91, points out how Shingon historical scholarship tends to slight the contributions of Saichō. Nonsectarian accounts of specific Tantric rituals can be found in Michel Strickmann, "Homa in East Asia," in *Agni: The Vedic Ritual of the Fire Altar*, edited by Frits Staal (Berkeley and Los Angeles: University of California Press, 1983), vol. 2, pp. 418–55, and in two articles by James Sanford: "The Abominable Tachikawa Skull Ritual," *Monumenta Nipponica* 46 (1991): 1–20, and "Breath of Life: The Esoteric Nenbutsu," in *Esoteric Bud-*

dhism in Japan, edited by Ian Astley-Kristensen (Copenhagen and Aarhus: Seminar for Buddhist Studies, 1994), pp. 65–98. The same volume (pp. 37–64) also contains Ian Reader's account of the Agonshū, "Appropriated Images: Esoteric Themes in a Japanese New Religion." Finally, parallels between the Shingon teachings of Kūkai and the Zen teachings of Dōgen are discussed by David E. Shaner, *The Body-Mind Experience in Japanese Buddhism* (Albany: State University of New York Press, 1985).

Emptiness and Dust Ritual

[Written inside a circle:] A bright mirror, 4.2 inches in diameter. The great master Śākyamuni Buddha—Mahā Kāśyapa—. . . . [A line extends down the right margin of the text to the remainder of the lineage chart found below.]

First year of Shōan [1299], senior water year of the horse, fourth moon, fifteenth day; lecture concerning Śākyamuni holding up the flower:

Śākyamuni raised the flower before a huge audience of eighty thousand, including five hundred senior disciples. Although the entire audience turned their heads and looked at the same sight, they did not fathom Śākyamuni's heart. Only Mahā Kāśyapa smiled. Śākyamuni said: "I have the Lineage of the Wisdom Eye that Perceives the True Dharma, the Marvelous Mind of Nirvāṇa (*nehan myōshin*). I entrust it with Mahā Kāśyapa. Later tonight I will perform the Buddha-to-Buddha Dharma Transmission Ceremony."

In the middle of the night Mahā Kāśyapa silently sneaked past the gaze of the audience of eighty thousand, including five hundred senior disciples, and entered Śākyamuni's cave at the base of the Uḍumbara Tree next to the mountain stream on Vulture Peak. The cave was four bays wide. Śākyamuni sat facing west on the golden-lion throne situated on the east side of the room. Mahā Kāśyapa sat on the west side, facing east. Because of the darkness outside it was difficult to discern their shared location. Just then a flaming chicken flew into the room. A flaming chicken is a type of bird with two heads and red and white spots in nine places. Flames blaze from between its two heads. In that room it appeared just like the flame of a lamp. Thus, it signifies the location where dharma fires of wisdom erupt.

Śākyamuni turned toward heaven and kowtowed three times. Mahā Kāśyapa placed his seating mat over Śākyamuni's mat and kowtowed three times. Then they performed the ceremony of the past buddhas and present buddhas. Facing two mirrors toward each other, they performed the kāṣāya robe ritual, covering their heads with the mirrors. Śākyamuni took the upper mirror and Mahā Kāśyapa took the lower mirror. Their reflections shifted. Śākyamuni's mirror reflected the image of Mahā Kāśyapa, while Mahā Kāśyapa's mirror reflected the image of Śākyamuni. This is the mutual embodiment of buddhas. Having completed the above, next they performed the kāṣāya robe ritual, raising their heads. Śākyamuni rubbed Mahā Kāśyapa's forehead and said: "Just as these two mirrors function together, so too is the Lineage of the Wisdom Eye that Perceives the True Dharma bequeathed. Throughout the infinite future this lineage must never be allowed to terminate." These are the words that are chanted buddha to buddha.

Then the image in one of the mirrors shifted to reflect the name of Śākyamuni. Likewise, Mahā Kāśyapa's name appeared reflected in the other mirror. They performed the rite of mixing blood from their tongues to form ink and, using a wooden stylus, linked the two names together. The dharma transmission ceremony of past buddha to present buddha is performed thus. Do not allow it to become lost to buddhas of future generations. Buddhas and bodhisattvas have halos of light or purple clouds around their heads because they perform this ceremony.

In the same manner as when the Buddha spent twenty years in Heaven of the Thirty-three Deities (*trāyastriṁśa*) preaching the Mahā Māyā Scripture to his mother, the huge audience of eighty thousand addressed the Buddha and asked: "According to the scriptures, this is the dharma of equality. But what about the blind people of the triple world? How can they be saved? Please by your compassion provide them with a means of salvation." In response, the Buddha preached the Ten Vajra Precepts.

The appearing in the mirror, the placing it on one's head, the appearing of Śākyamuni's name, the linking together names of past buddhas and present buddhas, the ink from the blood of the tongue, the sprinkling of sanctified water on one another's heads, the transmitting the flame of the flaming chicken with its spots in nine places, the lighting of the torch: these constitute the dharma transmission ceremony of all buddhas. They are the life root of the buddhas.

The Wayfaring Site [*bodhi-maṇḍa*, or site of awakening] of Śākyamuni and Mahā Kāśyapa became a stūpa. It is the appearance of the Transmission Returning Stūpa. The bodhisattvas, auditors (*śrāvakas*), and solitary buddhas (*pratyekabuddhas*) gathered around it like clouds. The king of Magadha and his sixty thousand attendants came to that assembly of equality. The earth and heavens shook with six kinds of earthquakes. The demon of the Sixth Heaven tried to disrupt the Buddha by throwing rocks to smash the stūpa. But at that moment many additional stūpas began to appear. They were too numerous to count. As soon as rocks were thrown by the demon they appeared as letters and fell from the sky. The many stūpas appeared and the letters became attached to their back gates. Within ten years they spread throughout central India. As Master Tendai said, from there to this Vimalakīrti-like abbot's quarters [that is, the room in a Zen monastery where the initiation is conducted], thus has the dharma been transmitted. This buddha-to-buddha lineage must never be allowed to terminate.

Later generations must never doubt this *Emptiness and Dust Ritual*. Deviation from this format is the heresy of naturalism (*tennen gedō*, that is, denial of karmic connections). This document was originally written in an Indic script.

After a long time the Indic letters became corrupted. During later generations this document required special study of Sanskrit and the proper procedure began to disappear. During the time of Ejō, the second ancestor of Eiheiji, this version was drafted. The original text is inscribed on Chinese paper and is stored inside the heart of the sacred image of Dōgen, the founder of Eiheiji. It is never revealed.

("True Dharma" is the ancient mirror. "Lineage of the Wisdom Eye" is the blood from the tongue. "Nirvāṇa," which is complete Parinirvāṇa, is liberation from the cycle of birth and death. The "Marvelous Mind" is the flaming chicken, which is the shining flame of the torches. "Entrust" is shared use.)

[Lineage continued from above:] . . . —Ānanda—Śaṇavāśa—Upagupta—Dhṛtaka—Miccaka—Vasumitra—Buddhanandi—Buddhamitra—Pārśva—Puṇyayaśas—Aśvakhoṣa—Kapimala—Nāgārjuna—Kāṇadeva—Rāhulata—Saṅghānandi—Gayaśāta—Kumāralabdha—Sāyanta—Vasubandhu—Manorhita—Haklenayaśas—Siṁha—Basiasita—Puṇyamitra—Prajnātāra—Bodhidharma—Second Ancestor Huiko—Third Ancestor Sengcan—Fourth Ancestor Daoxin—Fifth Ancestor Hongren—Sixth Ancestor Huineng—Qingyuan Xingsi—Shitou Xiqian—Yaoshan Weiyan—Yunyan Tansheng—Tongshan Liangjie—Yunju Daoying—Tongan Daopi—Daoan Guanzhi—Liangshan Yuanguan—Taiyang Jingyuan—Tousi Yijing—Furong Daokai—Danxia Sichun—Changlu Qingliao—Tiandong Zongjue—Xuedou Zhijian—Tiandong Rujing—Eihei Dōgen—Eihei Ejō—Daijō Gikai—Tōkoku Jōkin—Sōji Jōseki—Yōtaku Jakurei—Jigen Tenshin—Kidō Chōō—Sessō Ichijun—Tensō Soin—Kōkoku Genshin—Ekkei Rin'eki—Chikuo Reishu—Dairin Meifu—Sekigan Eikaku—Tennō Ryōin—Daikō Zen'yū—Tsūsan-rin—Buddhas and ancestors properly penetrate—*buddha bodhi*—. . . . [This line extends up the left margin of the text back through the circle to Śākyamuni.]

Rub the disciple's forehead and say: "This ceremony shall be taught orally in verse. But it must be performed according to the *Emptiness and Dust Ritual*. If the *Emptiness and Dust Ritual* document is not transmitted, it is a heretical lineage."

—First year of the Great Song-dynasty Baoqing Period [1225]; ninth moon, eighteenth day: Rujing, the former abbot of Jingde Zen monastery on Mount Tiantong bequeathed the above document to Dōgen in accordance with proper ceremony. The attendant Zuyue offered incense. The guest prefect Zongrui and the attendant Guangping performed obeisance. This Song-dynasty style precept ceremony was propagated during the Baoqing Period.

—Fifth year of the Japanese Shōō Period [1292], eighth moon, thirteenth day: the above document was carefully copied from the original stored in the Myōkōdō Memorial Hall at Eiheiji monastery.

—Fourteenth year of the Japanese Kan'ei Period [1637], junior fire year of the ox, eighth moon, auspicious day by Kyūgai Donryō.

The Unsurpassed Ultimate Blood Lineage of the Bodhisattva Precepts in the Orthodox Transmission of the Buddhas and Ancestors

What is the blood lineage? The blood lineages of all previous buddhas and ancestors as well as the blood lineages of all deluded, ignorant living beings fundamentally are not two. They constitute the undifferentiated true body of a single flavor. Because the buddhas and ancestors have awakened, they constitute original awakening like the moon shining bright in a cloudless sky. Because ordinary people are deluded, they experience darkness as if the moonlight is obscured by clouds. When ordinary people of deluded minds receive the bodhisattva precepts all filth and obstructions are eliminated, completely allowing this spiritual luminosity to appear for the first time. For this reason the Brahmā Net Scripture states: "Living beings who receive ordination with the precepts enter into the ranks of the buddhas, attaining the same great awakening. Truly they are the Buddha's children." Based on this principle, the person receiving the precepts sits in the Dharma Throne in the Wayfaring Site, and the teacher bestowing the precepts bows to him. This ritual signifies the attainment of the Way, as the fundamental Buddha [the teacher] descends and the manifest trace [the disciple] ascends. Then the disciple bows to the teacher. This ritual signifies the attainment of the Way, as the fundamental ascends and the manifest trace descends. The preceptor bestows and the disciple receives. The teacher hands over the blood lineage chart and the disciple humbly grasps hold. This ritual signifies the attainment of the Way, as the fundamental and the manifest trace together descend. Once the lineage has been bestowed, teacher and disciple leave the Wayfaring Site together. This ritual signifies the attainment of the Way, as the fundamental and the manifest trace together ascend.

The round circle drawn at the head of the blood lineage chart signifies the bright moon disk that constitutes the fundamental mind of living beings. It is called the "blood lineage." Therefore, the blood line that links together the upper and lower names signifies the undifferentiated body of teacher and disciple. A five-colored string is used to tie these two together, because living beings are inherently endowed with the marvelous virtues of the Five Wisdom Buddhas of the Womb Maṇḍala. Ascending without knowledge of this principle, they become stained with the mud of the five defilements (*kleśas*). Because the seed of the Five Wisdom Buddhas is thereby concealed, in ascending they defy the five planets, in descending they defy the five mountains, in between they defy the five constant ethical norms. Day and night, dawn and dusk, they accumulate the karmic conditions of their evil actions. Therefore they defy the spiritual standards of the three jewels of Buddha, Dharma, and Saṅgha and of the local gods. Nonetheless, by cultivating the courageous vigor of spiritual practice one purifies his six sense organs, and at the moment one receives the Vajra Jewel Precepts of the buddhas and ancestors he suddenly eliminates the five defilements and realizes the fundamentally awakened body of the Five Wisdom Buddhas. Although each of the five colors has a different name, they are neither different nor distinct from the awakened body. This is why a five-colored string is used to tie these together.

Blood-lineage charts are rolled up and bound with nine knots. This indicates that the eighty-four thousand dhāraṇīs [spells] and the eighty-four thousand defiled practices, the good and the evil, ultimately are not two. True and false are one and the same. All return to the perfect dharma body of the nine types of consciousness. The nine knots express this.

The Chinese graph for the word "union" (*gō*) is used to state the doctrine of all nine types of consciousness being perfectly endowed. When the ways of host and guest achieve union, all insignificant matters, petty humans, and non-sentient things end up in the coal pit. This one Chinese character is composed of three graphic elements: "man," "one," and "mouth." This means that man uses his mouth to eat things to sustain his life. Union with this blood lineage thus sustains the life of the buddhas and ancestors. Buddhas use their one mouth to preach the unsurpassed dharma wheel to save all beings of great and small, real and provisional spiritual capacities. Zen uses the one mouth to pluck out the stakes hammered in by monks. In such ways, is there any affair of day or night, secular or sacred, that is not accomplished with the mouth? Other extensive ways of examining the graph "union" also exist and should be handed down.

This tradition was first transmitted when Dōgen, our country's first ancestor, traveled to Song-dynasty China in accordance with the instructions of Eisai, the founder of Kenninji monastery, and entered into the innermost chambers of Master Tiandong Rujing, thereby completing his studies. Wanting to return to our country, Dōgen humbly requested leave. Master Rujing replied: "Don't be so hasty. There exists this document called *The Unsurpassed Ultimate Affair of the Buddhas and Ancestors*. It is rare. I have not yet permitted you to learn it. At this time you must keep this a deeply held secret. After you receive it, take it back to Japan and use it to benefit all beings." Dōgen obeyed his teacher's command and remained for another month. After he finished receiving it, he returned to this land to save all deluded beings, the good and the evil, the elite and the base.

What is the great affair of the buddhas and ancestors like? You must guard this well. Guard it well. You must keep it secret.

—Copied on a good day, second moon, eighth year of Genwa Period [1622] by Kyūgai Donryō.

—18—

The Necklace of Immortality: A Seventeenth-Century Vaiṣṇava Sahajiyā Text

Glen A. Hayes

The Vaiṣṇava Sahajiyās were Hindu tāntrikas who lived in northeastern India, especially in the region of greater Bengal (Bengal, Bihar, Orissa, Assam), from approximately the sixteenth through the nineteenth centuries. Many things about the medieval Vaiṣṇava Sahajiyās remain unclear to modern scholars, including their origins, social standing, major personalities, esoteric practices, authorship of texts, and their continued existence into current times. Although much about their beliefs and practices is elusive—we have, for example, no existing written commentaries to help us in understanding key words and phrases, and apparently no living connections to the medieval teachers—what we do know suggests a truly distinctive approach to Tantric expression and experience. This chapter explains why the medieval Vaiṣṇava Sahajiyās are unique, and selected passages from an important text, *The Necklace of Immortality (Amṛtaratnāvalī)* of Mukundadāsa (ca. 1650 C.E.) will illustrate this distinctiveness.

The goal for Sahajiyās was to achieve the ultimate state of *sahaja*, a Sanskrit and Bengali term that literally means "together (*saha*) born (*ja*)," and by extension of the semantic domain, "innate," "easy," "spontaneous," or "primordial." In the translations that follow, I use "primordium" or "primordial." Basically, sahaja is the original state of cosmic unity and bliss; a state that transcends the realm of saṃsāra (phenomenal reality), in which all created beings exist, subject to pain and endless rebirth. Sahajiyā ritual practices (*sādhanas*) were developed to guide both men and women to the realization of this state of liberation. These groups of Tantric practitioners are generally called "Vaiṣṇava" Sahajiyās, as their worship focused on one of Viṣṇu's most important manifestations: the playful and erotic cowherding god Kṛṣṇa, the "Dark Lord." To Sahajiyās, Kṛṣṇa was not regarded simply as a supreme being. Like most tāntrikas, the Sahajiyās connected human and divine natures, so the Dark Lord was reinterpreted as the inner divine aspect of a man, and Kṛṣṇa's mythical consort, Rādhā, was reinterpreted as the inner divine aspect of a women. Furthermore, some Sahajiyā beliefs and practices, including concepts of religious love and the use of devotional songs, were adapted from the famous medieval devotional (*bhakti*) tradition known as Bengali (Gauḍīya) Vaiṣṇavism, which grew up around the famous Bengali religious leader Kṛṣṇa Caitanya (ca. 1486–1533 C.E.). It is largely due to their historical (and controversial) connections to Bengali Vaiṣṇavas that the label of "Vaiṣṇava" Sahajiyās has been used by scholars like Manindramohan Bose, Shashibhushan Dasgupta, Edward C. Dimock, and Paritos Dasa. In Sahajiyā texts themselves, the religion is typically referred to as the Primordial Way (*sahaja-dharma*).

There was much more to the Vaiṣṇava Sahajiyās than their reinterpretations of Bengali Vaiṣṇavism and the Caitanya movement. Sahajiyā gurus adapted a wide range of beliefs and practices into complex ritual systems and elaborate views of the universe, and composed hundreds of texts of varying length in Bengali (with occasional Sanskrit passages), many of which have survived to this day. A few manuscripts have been edited and published, but most remain unstudied in archives in West Bengal and elsewhere. Discernible in these texts are hints of Sanskrit aesthetics and dramaturgy, classical and medieval Hindu devotionalism, Sāṃkhya philosophy, Āyurvedic medicine, Siddha Tantra and alchemy, haṭha yoga, and perhaps even Sufi Islam and Tantric Buddhism.

The Vaiṣṇava Sahajiyās are distinctive partly because most of their texts were composed in the Bengali vernacular; Sanskrit passages, when they do occur, are typically only quotes from earlier works, mantras, or opening invocations, whereas most other Hindu Tantric traditions rely extensively on Sanskrit. This choice of language reflects the regionalism and local flavor of Sahajiyā beliefs and practices. In Bengal, Sanskrit never attained the prominence that it did elsewhere in India, and although some Sahajiyā gurus may have been versed in Sanskrit, the evidence suggests that they preferred to convey their teachings in Bengali. In *The Necklace* (v. 13), Mukunda-dāsa goes further, rejecting the Vedas and Vedic rituals, the ancient foundations of Sanskrit authority and religious life. The most popular works of Bengali Vaiṣṇavism, especially the *Caitanya-caritāmṛta* of Kṛṣṇadāsa Kavirāja (ca. 1575 C.E.), were composed mainly in Bengali—(although some important treatises were composed in Sanskrit). In *The Necklace* (v. 4), Mukunda-dāsa even claims that Kṛṣṇadāsa was his own guru, so this choice of the local vernacular may have been a matter of tradition, also deemed appropriate for the majority of Bengali devotees.

Before we discuss the more obvious Tantric and yogic dimensions of the Sahajiyās, we need to emphasize the ways in which Sahajiyā gurus adapted Bengali Vaiṣṇavism—much to the chagrin and outrage of the rather orthodox followers of Caitanya then (and even now). Orthodox Bengali Vaiṣṇavas developed much of their belief system from classical Sanskrit devotional texts such as the *Bhāgavata Purāṇa* and medieval poems like Jayadeva's *Gītagovinda*. Their basic view is that Kṛṣṇa is the supreme god and creator of the cosmos, and that his creative powers (*śakti*) extend to the vast reaches of the universe. Human souls (*jīvas*), created by Kṛṣṇa, long to return to a loving and blissful relationship with him. Fortunately,

Kṛṣṇa wants to experience the love and devotion (*bhakti*) of the souls, and so he has used his cosmic powers of magic (*māyā*) and playfulness (*līlā*) to fashion an eternal heavenly abode (*dhāman*) that is identical to the idyllic setting of the *Bhāgavata Purāṇa*: the pastoral village of Vṛndāvana, in the forested region of Vraja. These gorgeous heavenly realms are also called Goloka ("Cowland") and Gokula ("Cowhouse"). Here, Kṛṣṇa grows up as a handsome youth, enticing the lovely young milkmaids (*gopīs*) to leave their husbands for furtive lovemaking in the groves and gardens of Vraja. Many Bengali Vaiṣṇavas quickly allegorize these figures: the milkmaids represent the human soul, and their desires to frolic with Kṛṣṇa in the woods is understood to be the quest of the soul to rejoin the creator. Since Kṛṣṇa has thoughtfully reproduced this mystical scene in all of its details in a blissful heaven, it is possible for devout Vaiṣṇavas to travel there if they take on the role of one of the characters in that heavenly abode. Much of Bengali Vaiṣṇavism is dedicated not only to singing and dancing praises to the Dark Lord, but also to developing an inner spiritual identity as one of the Vraja residents. As David L. Haberman has shown, this process of "acting as a way of salvation" allows one to adopt the identity and "spiritual body" of fellow villagers of Kṛṣṇa, especially one of the impassioned milkmaids. Those who choose to "become" female attendants to Kṛṣṇa's beloved consort Rādhā (herself a married woman) experience the most intense love, as they visualize the divine couple's erotic sports in the inner heavenly worlds. But for Bengali Vaiṣṇavas, this means that their souls are returning to an eternal relationship with god. And although in the mythic drama and in heaven Kṛṣṇa seems to be involved in adulterous affairs, they are not really adulterous, since this is really god just playing with his creation. Human beings, on the other hand, following Hindu caste rules and good family values, should never be adulterous. Human beings are not divine, only Kṛṣṇa is; their souls were made by god, but they themselves can never become god. This dualistic theological relationship was aptly phrased by the later Bengali poet Ramprasad Sen when he argued that "I don't want to become sugar, I want to taste sugar"—with the "sugar" standing for the divine, and the taster as the human soul.

The Vaiṣṇava Sahajiyās had their own interpretations of the erotic drama of Kṛṣṇa, the milkmaids, and Rādhā. For Tantric Sahajiyās, as noted above, Kṛṣṇa is not regarded as a supreme god, a creator who dwells in a distant heaven, and Rādhā is not merely his chosen consort or emanation of blissful energy. In contrast to Ramprasad, Sahajiyās have wished to transform "tasting sugar" into "becoming sugar." They therefore have adapted the sophisticated theological dualism of Bengali Vaiṣṇavas (which is not a pure dualism) into their own monistic system, in which humans reunite with their inner divine natures. According to Sahajiyās, every man has within himself his "true form" (*svarūpa*) as Kṛṣṇa, the divine masculine principle, and every woman has within herself her divine feminine principle as Rādhā. And rather than trying to visualize and then participate in the lovemaking of a god and his consort in heaven, Sahajiyās call upon all men and women to make love themselves in order to unify their essences and get to heaven. In doing so, Sahajiyās are using the physical world and their human bodies as platforms and tools for their experiments with the sacred. Both of these Sahajiyā claims—that men and women are really Kṛṣṇa and Rādhā, and that adulterous relationships and ritual sexual intercourse can be salvific—have caused some scandal or at least discomfort in Bengali Vaiṣṇava communities. Regarded by the orthodox Vaiṣṇavas as loathsome heretics, and transgressive to the extreme, Sahajiyā practitioners, who may have seemed on the surface to be regular devotees of Kṛṣṇa, have often felt compelled to perform their ritual practices without the knowledge of their neighbors or risk certain public condemnation. In various sources from the sixteenth century to the present day, outraged Bengalis and shocked European colonial administrators have written of what they regarded as the depraved sexual practices of various Tantric groups, including the Sahajiyās.

Although the influence of Bengali Vaiṣṇavism on the Sahajiyās is clear enough, the Tantric influences are harder to trace; many Vaiṣṇava Sahajiyā texts claim that their own gurus were noted Bengali Vaiṣṇavas like Kṛṣṇadāsa Kavirāja, Nityānanda, and even Caitanya himself. And although one text claims that a legendary writer on dance and drama, Bhārata, was the founding Sahajiyā guru, virtually all Vaiṣṇava Sahajiyās see themselves as intimately connected to Bengali Vaiṣṇavas. Although Sahajiyā texts were clearly influenced by earlier Tantric yogic traditions, most existing manuscripts seem to have been composed after the time of Caitanya. How can this be? Part of the problem has to do with the claims of Caitanya and his followers in Bengal that the renowned leader was himself the "incarnation" (*avatāra*) of both Kṛṣṇa and Rādhā in one body. The belief is very Tantric in nature: the idea that both male and female cosmic principles are latent within the microcosm of the human body. But it is also a plausible reading of Bengali Vaiṣṇava theological views concerning the ultimate relationship between the divine Kṛṣṇa and his creative female powers. Much like the Śaiva and Śākta tāntrikas, who saw the existence of both the god Śiva and the goddess Śakti within the human body, Sahajiyās utilized the Caitanya model to argue for a similar indwelling of both Kṛṣṇa and Rādhā. And since the Caitanya movement was growing in popularity at the time, it was perhaps inevitable that Sahajiyā gurus would adapt what they saw as a congenial tradition—giving it, however, their own "Tantric" reinterpretation. By adopting the Caitanya traditions, however, Sahajiyās also appropriated something that most other Hindu tāntrikas did not: the fundamental roles of human passion (*rāga*), divine love (*prema*) and devotion (*bhakti*) in practice.

In *The Necklace*, Mukunda-dāsa presents the outlines of a basic Sahajiyā worldview and ritual system, although he does so in a language that is highly technical, difficult to translate, and challenging to understand. To begin, the words are often grammatically uninflected, lacking the usual markers for noun case, number, and verb tense. This means that the relationships between adjectives, nouns, and verbs are often unclear. I have tried to render the most inclusive reading of each passage, but many passages could be read in alternative ways. This is fairly typical of Tantric language in general; due to its grammatical indeterminacy, however, the form of the Bengali language adapted by the Sahajiyās creates additional hurdles to scholarly interpretation. In choosing passages for this volume, I have tried to use material that presented a basic picture of Sahajiyā beliefs and practices. For translations and studies of other Vaiṣṇava Sahajiyā texts, readers may consult the recommendations for further reading.

Of the complete text of *The Necklace of Immortality*, only four verses are in Sanskrit: the opening invocation and three quotations from earlier Vaiṣṇava works. Following these invocations (vv. 1–5) to Kṛṣṇa, Caitanya, famous Bengali Vaiṣṇavas, and his own guru Kṛṣṇadāsa Kavirāja, Mukunda-dāsa sketches out some of the basic beliefs and practices of his system. In simplest terms, the process of realizing sahaja requires the yogic mastery of one's emotions, mental states, physical body, and sexual energies in order to create a type of subtle inner yogic body or "divine body" (*rūpa*, *deva-deha*)—that provides a vehicle for the soul (*jīva*) to travel to the blissful realms of sahaja. The basic system revolves around the complex and important term *rasa*, which literally means "juice," as from fruit or sugarcane, but which has several levels of meaning for Sahajiyās. Although rasa is a term already found in Sanskrit aesthetics and Bengali Vaiṣṇavism, it can also be used to describe an elevated state of religious rapture, in which one experiences the purified emotion of love for the divine. Drawing on more obscure Tantric and alchemical influences, Mukunda-dāsa plays with the additional significant meaning of rasa as "male semen" and "mercury," and it is this meaning—of an essential fluid—that predominates in the text. I have translated it as "Divine Essence," but the multiple referents should be kept in mind. By performing ritual sexual intercourse (*sambhoga*) with a female partner (*rati*), the male Sahajiyā is understood to yogically "reverse" his rasa-semen and propel it, along with the sexual fluids of his partner, along his urethra into a mystical yogic channel, the Crooked River (*bāṅkānadī*), that flows upward and inward into the inner body and worlds. Only by sexual ritual can the vital fluids of men and women be transformed into *vastu*, a technical term meaning "truth, essence, thing," or "object," but which I translate as "Cosmic Substance," the most fundamental constituent unit of the universe. It is this Cosmic Substance, created only through Sahajiyā rituals, which forms the subtle inner body, in much the same way as the physical body is made of flesh and blood. As indicated in verses 7–12, this realization of rasa as Divine Essence, and its transformation into the Cosmic Substance of the Inner Body (*rūpa*) is needed to reach the ultimate state of sahaja. One can only learn about this from those who have already experienced rasa, advanced practitioners called *rasikas*, which I translate as "Experienced Ones."

This powerful and liberating process of ritual sexual intercourse is controversial; it is a tool that is not universal and a modality of religious ritual that takes years to cultivate. As with all tāntrikas, one must first receive initiation and a mantra from a guru (vv. 14–15). Additional and subsequent instructions are received from a second person, the śikṣā ("teaching") guru, who according to another Sahajiyā guru, Ākiñcana-dāsa, should be a woman. There are three stages of Sahajiyā practice (v. 18): beginner (*pravarta*), accomplished (*sādhaka*), and perfected (*siddha*). Beginners should start their practices using the standard ritual devotions (*vaidhi-bhakti*) of Bengali Vaiṣṇavas (vv. 20–23), including singing hymns, chanting, dancing to Kṛṣṇa, and developing an alternative spiritual body and identity as one of Kṛṣṇa's followers. At this level, Sahajiyā practices resemble those of orthodox Vaiṣṇavism. Such devotional actions result in the experience of a mystic emotional state called a *bhāva* ("mood, condition"), which I have translated as "Divine Existence."

After using these techniques from Bengali Vaiṣṇavas, clearly discussed by Edward C. Dimock, Jr., and David L. Haberman, the more obviously Tantric dimensions of Sahajiyā practice begin. During the second and third stages of practice, the rituals involving coitus and erotic activities are gradually introduced—after all, the Sahajiyā couple are acting out the divine loveplay of Kṛṣṇa and Rādhā. Like rasa, the term *rati*, which I translate as "Female Partner," also comes from Sanskrit and Vaiṣṇava traditions and has a distinctive Sahajiyā meaning, as well. It does mean an actual female ritual partner, and in Vaiṣṇavism generally refers to a woman loved by Kṛṣṇa. However, consistent with the fluid-based cosmology of Sahajiyās and other tāntrikas, it can also mean female sexual fluids, which are "reversed" along with male semen in order to create the inner body. The Female Partner must also be visualized (vv. 33–39) as having an "Inner Damsel Body" (*rūpa-mañjarī*), which is an elegant blend of Caitanyaite and Tantric visualization techniques. As adapted from the erotic adventures of Kṛṣṇa, the ideal female partner should not be one's own (*svakīyā*) spouse, but rather one "belonging to another" (*parakīyā*). Such a dangerous liaison, risky in itself, only serves to heighten the passions of forbidden love, as the relationship could end if known to others. Underlying this process, however, is the need to transform worldly passions (*rāga*) and lust (*kāma*) into pure divine love (*prema*). These basic positions are complicated by amplifying the roles of emotions and by including various erotic games (*vilāsa*) as part of the sexual ritual. These features help to distinguish the Sahajiyās from most other practitioners of Tantra.

The Sahajiyā model of the inner or subtle body is also quite different from most Śaiva and Śākta Tantric systems. In addition to incorporating ideas from the mythology of Kṛṣṇa with its beautiful gardens, forests, and villages, the basic structure of the subtle body in *The Necklace* consists of the Crooked River and four inner lotus ponds (*sarovaras*)—rather than the more typical six or seven *cakras*, *suṣumṇā-nāḍī*, and fiery *kuṇḍalinī-śakti* of other Tantric traditions. This emphasis on rivers and ponds clearly reflects the watery deltaic geography and topography of Bengal, and it also expresses the Sahajiyā emphasis upon physicality, substances, and fluids. In contrast to other South Asian traditions, such as the philosophy of Vedānta, which regarded the natural world and the human body as illusory obstacles to liberation, the Sahajiyās saw the world and body as very "real" and useful for salvation—a basic Tantric understanding. This allowed them to transform the human body, its parts, and processes, using them to give "birth" to the inner subtle body, thereby reaching the blissful realms of the primordial state of sahaja.

There are several realms and states of consciousness associated with sahaja, all of which are said to be places of bliss (*ānanda*). *The Necklace* has often vivid descriptions of such places (vv. 43, 45–47, 54–57, 96–99), visualizing them as particular villages and gardens alongside a mystical river. The Crooked River is of great importance, since it connects the four inner ponds. For the Sahajiyās, this subtle physiology functions in much the same way as the cakras and suṣumṇā-nāḍī of other Tantric systems; but the river and ponds convey the reversed sexual fluids, not the fiery kuṇḍalinī. These four ponds (vv. 97–98) may be thought of as a set of holding tanks within the male body, and each one represents a different level of purity, consciousness, and bliss. The lowest, the Pond of Lust (*kāma-sarovara*), is said (v. 96) to be reached through the "ninth door" of the human body, probably a reference to the urethra, where the Crooked River begins. Next is the Pond of Arrogance (*māna-sarovara*), where lingering feelings of egotism and selfish desire must be purified—again, through continuation of the sexual and other rituals. The third reservoir is the Pond of Divine Love (*prema-sarovara*), where the pure and selfless affection between the two partners is developed. Reflecting influences from Tantric alchemy, each of the ponds also serves as a type of alchemical vessel, into which the base sexual fluids are drawn through sexual intercourse. It is out of these yogically transformed sexual fluids that the immortal elixir of Cosmic Substance is fashioned. The uppermost vessel is the Pond of Immortality (*akṣaya-sarovara*), which has such features as a thousand-petaled lotus and is the abode of the cosmic mountain Sumeru (similar to the highest cakra in other Śaiva and Śākta systems). The fourth pond is thus closest to sahaja, the realms of bliss, and the realization of the androgynous state of the Primordial Inner Being (*sahaja-mānuṣa*)—the complete union of male/female and Kṛṣṇa/Rādhā.

Many details of these yogic processes and visualized realms are difficult for us to understand, as the text was composed with the intent of concealing such cosmic secrets and powers from outsiders. Some verses seem impossible to understand at all. But we can still glimpse some salient aspects of practice. For example, it seems that the word rasa itself is used as a mantra during sexual intercourse (vv. 55–56), and uttering ra-sa helps the practitioners to reach sahaja. But difficulties and dangers lurk along the way: if one can bypass the pitfalls of passion and lust, described as the flower arrows of the love god or as a deadly serpent (vv. 104–7), then one may discover the myriad yogic channels of the inner body (v. 110) and use coitus and eroticism to escape ordinary worldly decay (v. 115), that is, to overcome mortality, the goal of many yogic sādhanas.

Each of the four ponds is described in varying detail in the complete text, with multicolored and multipetaled lotuses, bathing and entry steps, surrounding villages, and mystical qualities. Each is beautiful and adorned with precious gems (vv. 162–63), a typical Tantric reference not only to their great value but also to the fact that each pond is fashioned out of Cosmic Substance—a commodity that is most difficult to obtain. Some of this imagery is derived from Bengali Vaiṣṇava visualization techniques involving the ponds and other locations where Rādhā and Kṛṣṇa met for their secret loveplay. But the Sahajiyā depictions of the ponds are also based upon the gurus' experiences of these ponds as important realms of the subtle body. As such, the ponds are vital reservoirs for the yogically manipulated sexual fluids, and reflect a standard Tantric motif of the reversal (*ulṭā*) of the cosmic process. For the Sahajiyās, this process requires a journey along the Crooked River as it flows "upward against the current" (v. 180) to sahaja. Found in these inner realms are a variety of different beings and special places, such as the Self-perfected Inner Being (*svataḥ-siddha-mānuṣa),* the Primordial Inner Being (*sahaja-mānuṣa*), the Place of the Hidden Moon (*guptacandrapur*), and the Primordial Citadel (*sahajapur*). Attaining these places also entails mastery of breath control, which leads to mystical visions of different colors and objects (vv. 184–90). Like other tāntrikas, Sahajiyās must visualize inner forms of the Female Partner, known as the eight Heroines (*nāyikās*), enthroned in the delicate lotuses of the ponds (vv. 242–44). Although few details of the Heroines or the Female Partner are given (in one passage she is described as a lovely sixteen-year-old maiden), the process of coitus is likened to the "churning" (*mathana*) of the partner (vv. 256–58). Although this image possibly refers to the vigorous mixing of the sexual fluids, it also recalls the mythical effort of the gods to extract nectar from the cosmic ocean, the making of butter, and the preparation of alchemical elixirs.

The concluding passages of the text emphasize the centrality of the Female Partner in the attainment of sahaja (vv. 309–10), review basic dimensions of the cosmos (vv. 311, 317–19), and extol the importance of *The Necklace* itself (vv. 329–30); the text ends with "Blessed Mukunda-dāsa presents *The Necklace of Immortality*." Some scholars, such as Paritos Dasa, have argued that this text and several others were originally composed in Sanskrit by one Siddha Mukunda-deva, and that various disciples such as Mukunda-dāsa prepared the Bengali translations that have come down to us. Until more evidence is found, this argument must remain unproven, leaving us further mystified by the Vaiṣṇava Sahajiyās of medieval Bengal.

So what do we learn from a text like *The Necklace of Immortality*? To begin, it suggests that human beings have experienced their bodies and sexuality in many different ways, and that some have used these experiences as the basis for expressing vivid, sensual, religious worlds. The Sahajiyās used all of their sense capacities—sight, sound, taste, touch, and scent—to bring together the spiritual and the material. But this is true of many other Tantric traditions. The Vaiṣṇava Sahajiyās are distinctive in the ways in which they combined the physicality of the body, sexual energies, emotions, passions, and senses in order to express their elaborate models of reality. In simplest terms, gurus like Mukunda-dāsa attempted to blend the best of the complex worlds of Tantric yoga and bhakti devotionalism, offering both men and women a powerful means of liberation from the apparent limitations of the ordinary world and their bodies. Such a bold use of sexuality definitely has the power to offend. Yet such a dangerous rejection of social norms, found throughout Tantra, is deemed necessary for salvation.

Beyond the controversies surrounding sexual practices, the text also raises profound questions about perceptions of gender and power. Most Sahajiyā texts seem to have been written by men, from a male perspective, and privilege the male body by locating the ponds within the man (v. 169). If anything, ritual coitus is a form of what some scholars have called "inverse intercourse," in which the man takes the fluids from the woman and draws them into his body. The subtle body is "born" within the male body, unlike the physical body, which is born in a womb. It should be pointed out that although these are clearly male-centered features, they are not therefore anti-female, since the Sahajiyā system is dependent upon the harmonious interaction of both male and female cosmic principles. Without the Female Partner and her fluids, the male can never reach sahaja; without the man and his essences, she is also denied final liberation. In the end, both must experience the ultimate state of sahaja, or it does not happen. Sahaja itself is transcendent, beyond the duality of male and female, but unobtainable without their interaction. The *Vivarta-vilāsa* ("Erotic Games of Transformation") by Ākiñcana-dāsa (ca. 1700 C.E.) states that the *śikṣā* or teaching guru, who provides instruction on the advanced ritual practices, is identified with Rādhā and should thus be a woman. This reflects the Sahajiyā view that all woman are teachers, and that men must learn from them. And though much of Bengali society at the time was dominated by men, Bengal was still the center of the worship of such great goddesses as Durgā, Kālī, and Śakti. We see this regional emphasis on the divine feminine reflected in Sahajiyā texts like *The Necklace,* as well: in the importance given to the Female Partner and the Damsel, to Rādhā and the milkmaids, the visualized Heroines, and the female gurus. Much about the medieval Vaiṣṇava Sahajiyās will remain a mystery to outsiders, as gurus like Mukunda-dāsa seem reluctant to loosen their grasp on the jewels in *The Necklace of Immortality*.

The Necklace of Immortality exists in two manuscript editions found in the archives of the University of Calcutta, and a printed version edited by the Bengali scholar Paritos Dasa. The manuscript version used for these translations is Bengali ms. no. 6451 in the collection of the University of Calcutta. Another version exists as ms. no. 595 in the same collection. I would like to thank the University of Calcutta, especially Asitkumar Bandyopadhyay, P. K. Dasa, Tushar Mahapatra, S. C. Banerjee, and the Department of Bengali, for providing me with access to these and other Sahajiyā manuscripts. Ms. no. 6451 consists of 330 verses (to which I have assigned line numbers) and was written using several different poetical meters. The meter used in all of the translated verses is called *payāra*, consisting of two rhymed lines of fourteen syllables each. A printed edition of *The Necklace of Immortality* (*Amṛtaratnāvalī*) may be found (in Bengali) in Paritos Dasa, *Caitanyottara prathama cāriṭi sahajiyā puṅthi* ["Four Primary Post-Caitanya Sahajiyā Manuscripts"] (Calcutta: Bharati Book Stall, 1972).

Further Reading

For translations of selections from other medieval Vaiṣṇava Sahajiyā texts, including several short poems, another text attributed to Mukunda, and the *Vivarta-*

vilāsa of Ākiñcana-dāsa, see Glen A. Hayes, "The Vaiṣṇava Sahajiyā Traditions of Medieval Bengal," in Donald S. Lopez, Jr., ed., *Religions of India in Practice* (Princeton: Princeton University Press, 1995), pp. 333–51. The relationship between the Sahajiyās and Bengali Vaiṣṇavas is treated in Edward C. Dimock, Jr., *The Place of the Hidden Moon: Erotic Mysticism in the Vaiṣṇava-sahajiyā Cult of Bengal* (Chicago: University of Chicago Press, 1966; Phoenix Press, 1989). Dimock examines many Sahajiyā texts, and includes a complete translation of a ritual text concerning the Heroines. The details of Bengali Vaiṣṇava visualization and devotional practices are presented in David L. Haberman, *Acting as a Way of Salvation: A Study of Rāgānugā Bhakti Sādhana* (New York: Oxford University Press, 1988), and more recently in his *Journey through the Twelve Forests* (New York: Oxford University Press, 1994). Earlier useful works on the Vaiṣṇava Sahajiyās now available in reprinted editions are: Manindra Mohan Bose (Basu), *The Post Caitanya Sahajiā Cult of Bengal* (Delhi: Gian Publishing House, 1986) and Shashibhushan Dasgupta, *Obscure Religious Cults*, 3d ed. (Calcutta: Firma KLM, 1976). Bose tends to focus on the connections between the Sahajiyās and Bengali Vaiṣṇavism, whereas Dasgupta argues for influences from earlier Tantric Buddhism. Dasgupta also examines other contemporary Bengali Tantric traditions, including the Bāuls and Nāths. For an excellent study and translations of Bāul materials, which have definite links to the Sahajiyās, see Carol Salomon, "Bāul Songs," in Lopez, *Religions of India in Practice*, pp. 187–208.

The Necklace of Immortality (*Amṛtaratnāvalī*) of Mukunda-dāsa

OPENING INVOCATIONS

1. Glory to the eternally blissful Kṛṣṇa, resplendent in his heaven of Gokula.
   To Him Mukunda dedicates this book called *The Necklace of Immortality*.

2. Salutations to the blessed Kṛṣṇa Caitanya, an ocean of Divine Essence.
   Salutations to his disciple Nityānanda, salutations to the other humble friends.

3. Salutations to his disciples Rūpa, Sanātana, and Raghunātha Bhaṭṭa,
   and to Jīva, Gopāla Bhaṭṭa, and Raghunātha Dāsa.

4. Salutations to my own Master, the blessed Kṛṣṇadāsa Kavirāja.
   Through the power of your compassion, all has been revealed.

5. I offer greetings to the companions of Caitanya.
   I am energized by their profound compassion.

BASIC CONCEPTS OF PRACTICE AND COMMUNITY

7. Listen closely, for I am going to speak about the principles of Divine Essence (*rasa*).
Only with the help of Experienced Ones (*rasikas*) can you taste this Divine Essence.

8. Devotees who are Experienced Ones will attain their Inner Body.
Their minds are constantly overwhelmed by the experience of Divine Essence.

9. With their minds flooded by experiences of Divine Essence, they float along.
Yet such Divine Essence can be generated only with the guidance
of Experienced Ones.

10. You must discover the Cosmic Substance (*vastu*)
hidden within the Divine Essence.
This Primordial Cosmic Substance and Divine Essence are like gems.

11. Transformed into this gemlike Cosmic Substance, the Divine Essence assumes the shape of the Inner Body (*rūpa*).
The Inner Body is given birth through the rituals involving Divine Essence.

12. Then, with the help of Experienced Ones, you will meet a woman who knows the Inner Body.
To realize your inner self you must frolic with a woman who knows Divine Essence.

13. Divine Love for Kṛṣṇa is always pure, it is never stained.
Get rid of the Vedas and never perform any Vedic rituals!

14. The first step on the path is to seek refuge at the place of the mantra-guru.
Ordinary physical birth is from a womb, but this only results in old age and hell!

15. When you are accepted by the guru you will be sheltered by the power of the mantra.
Keep the instructions of the guru close to your heart!

16. With great care, the guru who has initiated you with the mantra
will guide your practices.
You must continue to follow those instructions for as long as you practice!

17. One of those commands is that you associate with a special
community of practitioners.

Through following such instructions, you will reach the state of consciousness of the Divine Existence.

18. The three stages of practice are called: beginner (*pravarta*), accomplished (*sādhaka*), and perfected (*siddha*).
These are the three conditions: Divine Existence (*bhāva*), Divine Essence (*rasa*),
and Divine Love (*prema*).

19. When you are initiated and receive your mantra, the guru will protect you.
While in the beginner's stage, your practices involve the use
of your physical body.

20. The kinds of practices appropriate for the physical body consist of the sixty-four types of ritual devotions developed by Gauḍīya Vaiṣṇavas.
Such ritual devotions have been written about and explained elsewhere.

22. You must master these different ritual devotions as a beginner.
The initial awareness of Divine Existence will continue for so long as
no Female Partner (*rati*) is actually present.

23. The sixty-four types of ritual devotion for the physical body
are intended for the beginner.
Devotions that are influenced by worldly karma should be avoided by the Adept.

25. One joins the spiritual lineage of the guru at the precise moment
one receives a mantra.
After this initiation, however, you must continue your practices under
the guidance of a teaching guru.

26. Through such sustained practices, the adept will develop the finest physical body.
Even older men and women can benefit from the consciousness
of Divine Existence.

TRANSFORMATIONS OF THE BODY

27. A Divine Body (*devadeha*) must be born within the physical body.
So how may men and women come to know that they possess a Divine Body?

28. With effort, you will discover the Divine Body within the physical body.

One may produce the Cosmic Substance of the Divine Body
by following the teachings.

29. By performing ritual practices with a woman, the Divine Body will be discovered within the physical body.
A woman who has realized her divine inner nature should serve as
the passionate Female Partner.

30. When both the male and female principles are brought together within the physical body,
then one is ready to perform the advanced practices
leading to consciousness of Divine Essence and Divine Love.

31. Without following these steps, you will never acquire the Cosmic Substance.
How then will you know about the transcendent Cosmic Substance?

32. That transcendent Cosmic Substance seems to be very remote.
The person who is able to obtain it is a hero in the ways of passion.

33. The form of that blessed Inner Body must be without impurity, as must the Female Partner.
One can't reach the Vraja heaven without traveling the way of passion.

34. The blessed Inner Damsel Body (*śrīrūpamañjarī*) leads the adept to the Vraja heaven.
With her body of eternity, she helps the adept to master the passions.

35. Without her, you'll never taste the passion-filled Cosmic Substances
of the Vraja heaven.
For adepts seeking Vraja, she is the very essence of the way of passion.

37. The Female Partner who is imbued with Divine Love shimmers with erotic energies, and is herself a well of Divine Essence.
Having a splendid body like Rādhā, she is the well of both Divine Essence and Cosmic Substance.

38. The Female Partner who is imbued with Divine Love is the vessel
of shimmering Divine Essence.
The Inner Body was born in that ocean of Divine Essence.

39. In the Vraja heaven, the adept acquires an eternal Inner Body.
That is why it is called the blessed Inner Damsel Body.

40. Through Divine Essence, the Inner Body is born, becoming a vessel of Divine Love.
And through that inner body one becomes conscious of the true nature of passion.

COSMIC REALMS OF BLISS

43. Along the far shores of the Virajā River is a place called the Homeland.
There is a village there called the Primordial Place, a realm of eternal bliss.

45. In that region there is a Tree of Emptiness, and lotuses
of one hundred and one thousand petals.
The Homeland spreads out around that tree and the waters of a pond.

46. To its north is a village called the Place of Bliss.
The abode of the god of love, it has a lovely grove
where the Experienced Ones taste Divine Essence.

47. Forever blissful, forever overwhelmed, forever desirous,
The Primordial Being (*sahajamānuṣa*) makes its home there.

54. In that realm there is a lake called Moon Pond.
It is located near the left side of the inner ocean.

55. The Pond of Lust (*kāma-sarovara*) is to be generated out of that Moon Lake.
Through uttering the syllable *sa* [of the mantra *ra-sa*: Divine Essence] a vast empty space is revealed within the human body.

56. In the making of the other syllable, *ra*, the Female Partner
becomes the secret vessel of semen.
In the Place of the Hidden Moon, the male and female principles
are joined together.

57. That Place of the Hidden Moon is apprehended
by joining the two principles together.
Behold how all the regions of the vast cosmos emerge in that special place.

96. The Pond of Lust is reached through the ninth door of the human body.
This is a subject that has been revealed by all the holy books.

97. There are four ponds within the body: the Pond of Lust, the Pond of Arrogance, the Pond of Divine Love, and the Pond of Immortality.

98. The four ponds exist within the human heart.
Only if you have a physical body can you reach the other shores of reality.

99. The Pond of Lust is the most sought-after thing of all.
Without fail, you must be diligent in your ritual practices.

RITUAL SEXUAL INTERCOURSE AND EROTICISM

104. The five flower-arrows of the god of love are the enchanters of Kṛṣṇa.
But a deadly serpent of death and time lurks within the human body.

105. That deadly serpent can strike day or night.
Even a mind in total control of the body cannot prevent the serpent from striking.

106. But, a mind in control of the physical self is really the cause of Phenomenal Reality.
Such a soul is of the lowest kind, unable to prevent lust.

107. That is why such conditions hinder the worship of Kṛṣṇa.
The soul's thirst for a Female Partner can drive one mad.

108. When engaged in these kinds of practices, you must be very, very careful.
You should visualize an inner mental form of the Female Partner.

109. Performance of religious rituals with a devout woman belongs to the second stage of the practitioner.
The god of erotic love helps to transform the Female Partner
into her inner visualized form.

110. Within the physical body there are nine major yogic channels
and 320 million finer channels.
Who is the person who knows which one goes where?

115. The ultimate ritual is ritual sexual intercourse and eroticism with a Female Partner.
If you perform such practices with a Female Partner,
you will escape worldly decay.

INNER WORLDS AND A CROOKED RIVER

154. This path of practices is difficult to travel; it seems to be near, but then remote.
From a distance it seems close, from close up it seems distant.

155. You must be able to come to know the principles of your own body.
Whoever does not learn about the body suffers the consequences.

156. The ponds and all of Phenomenal Reality exist within the body.
Who can truly worship without knowing the principles of the body?

158. Without the instruction of the guru, you cannot know the guru's principles.

Distracted day and night by so many things, just eating and defecating.

162. Those ponds should be visualized as having a pleasing shape.
I will tell you about them, please listen carefully!

163. Those ponds are adorned with precious jewels.
Those eternal abodes are encrusted with gems.

168. You must perform your practices with the physical body of your Female Partner.
Through such practices, you will attain your own Cosmic Substance.

169. The ponds are within the man, but the woman becomes conscious of them.
A Female Partner suitable for such practices should be
a desirable and joyful woman.

170. During sexual intercourse, the ponds and lotuses shimmer with erotic energies.
The Pond of Divine Love, where Divine Love blossoms, is eternal.

179. The Village of Eternal Bliss is located along the far shores of the Crooked River.
The Crooked River flows in a northerly direction.

180. Its undulations are pleasing and well formed.
Its waters flow upward against the current.

181. To its west is the village called the Primordial Place.
That eternal abode is the place of the Self-Perfected Inner Being.

182. The community of Experienced Ones dwells in the Place of Eternal Bliss.
The Experienced Ones are youthful; the Experienced Ones are numerous.

183. The people of the Primordial Place perform the rituals of the Primordium.
The Primordial Being is the vessel of all Divine Essence.

MYSTICAL LIGHTS AND BREATH CONTROL

184. Following the sunrise, nothing remains in that Land.
Please hear, all Experienced Ones, about the truths of that place.

185. Please hear, all devotees, the story of the Land of Eternal Bliss.
In that place, neither the moon nor the sun rise; the wind moves not at all.

186. There is blue light, white light, and yellow light.
The three lights glow like the rising sun.

187. The vessel of nectar is carried along by the rippled waters of the Crooked River.
The nostrils force air into that vessel of nectar.

188. The nose quickly exhales the air that has been inhaled.
The rising sun doesn't glow, yet there are different kinds of light.

189. The rising sun is absorbed by the brilliance of the lights.
These matters have been covered by other books.

190. Just as the breath is quickly exhaled through the nose,
so too I narrate this book, *The Necklace of Immortality*.

HEROINES OF DIVINE LOVE

242. The eight Heroines appear in the eight petals of a lotus.
They float in blue lotuses, yellow lotuses, and white lotuses.

243. Thus the Heroines are visualized in the eight petals.
The eight Heroines who appear in the eight lotus petals are
the Inner Bodies of the Female Partners.

244. If by this you are able to understand the principles concerning
the realization of the body,
then, with great devotion, you will know the nine major yogic
channels and the 320 million finer channels within the body.

256. Divine Love came into being through the churning of the Female Partner during intercourse.
Thus there comes into being a place
called the Pond of Divine Love (*prema-sarovara*).

257. Kṛṣṇa's home is in that pond, which contains drops of Divine Love.
A Female Partner who embodies Divine Essence is a woman suitable for Kṛṣṇa.

258. Continually churning the Female Partner produces the essence
of the Female Partner.
Deeply entranced day and night, a state of wonder develops.

THE FEMALE PARTNER AND THE COSMIC REGIONS

309. The Female Partner and Divine Essence will lead you to the heavens of Goloka and Vṛndāvana.
By understanding these principles, you will master your own lusts.

310. You should carefully realize the Female Partner in the Pond of Lust.
Through such practices with a Female Partner, you will attain
the Primordial Cosmic Substance.

311. The Land of the Hidden Moon is the essence of everything.
There is no Cosmic Substance beyond this Cosmic Substance.

317. There are seven heavens, seven hells, and eight protectors of the directions.
There are the nine major yogic channels, 320 million finer channels,
the cosmic mountain Sumeru, and the jungle.

318. The Crooked River spirals around them in the four directions,
as the eight Heroines wrap themselves around the trees like creeping vines.

319. There is a village called the Place of Eternal Bliss.
You must certainly make your home in that land.

328. An ocean of Divine Essence, this book is a like a great god among the gods.
This is not paradoxical for the followers of the blessed Inner Body.

329. That Inner Body is made of eternal Cosmic Substance and is
the essence of practice.
This book, *The Necklace of Immortality*, is the vessel of Divine Essence.

330. The nectar of the celestial river Mandākinī is delightful ambrosia.
Blessed Mukunda-dāsa presents *The Necklace of Immortality*.

—19—

The Tibetan Practice of the Mantra Path According to Lce-sgom-pa

Yael Bentor

The text translated here is an exposition of the Buddhist Tantric path written in Tibet in about the twelfth or thirteenth century. It was chosen for the present volume because of its relatively concise and straightforward style of explaining Tibetan Tantra. The uncertainty concerning the author's exact identity, dates, and sectarian affiliation need not concern us here. According to the testimony of the text itself, its author relies (specifically in the section on the completion process) on the authority of Nāropa. The work from which our selection is taken, *The Outline of the Jewel Mound of Instructions* (*Man-ngag-rin-chen-spungs-pa'i-dkar-chag*) is devoted to the entire Buddhist path. The five opening chapters are concerned with general Mahāyāna topics, including the Bodhisattva path, the Perfection of Wisdom, emptiness, the two truths, and the true nature of things. Our excerpt is the first part of the sixth chapter entitled "The Teaching of the Practice of the Mantra Path." The name of the author is given in the work variously as Lce-sgom-rdzong-pa, Gces-sgom Mkha'-skyong-brag-pa, and other names. For the sake of brevity we will simply call him Lce-sgom-pa (pronounced Cegompa). This introduction will be devoted to clarifying Lce-sgom-pa's presentation of the Mantra path as a guide to the translation. It will closely follow the logical progression of the text itself. Some may prefer to read the translation first and the introduction second.

The author begins his essay by placing the Tantra/Mantra path within the general context of the path to enlightenment. The Buddhist Great Vehicle (Mahāyāna) is said to comprise two paths, the path of the Sūtra and the path of the Tantra, also called the Perfection of Wisdom and the Mantra path, respectively. According to our text, the path of the Sūtra was taught by the Buddha for people who are only slightly afflicted by desire and who are able to renounce the world. This seems rather tongue-in-cheek, since it is obvious that most people are greatly afflicted by desire and are not able to renounce the world. It is precisely for this great majority that the Mantra path was taught.

Lce-sgom-pa distinguishes three methods for overcoming suffering in saṃsāra, which results from the emotions afflicting all unenlightened beings. These three methods reflect the three paths within the Great Vehicle delineated by him—the Sūtra, Tantra/Mantra, and Great Seal. The Sūtra path of the Perfection of Wisdom is the classical method of the Great Vehicle based, for the most part, on the bodhisattva ideal and the notion of emptiness. The Tantra path is further divided into two—the common Tantric method, which Lce-sgom-pa calls the path of purifying the mind in stages, and the path of the Great Seal (*mahāmudrā*), which he defines, in contrast, as an instantaneous practice. This Great Seal is, according to him, the pinnacle of all Mantra path practices, yet at the same time superior to it. In the path of the Sūtra, the afflicting emotions are regarded as adversaries to be conquered with some countermeasure. The afflicting emotion of desire may be overcome through nonattraction, aversion though loving kindness, and ignorance through correct understanding of Buddhist views. The Tantra path, on the other hand, employs a homeopathic approach—a remedy of a type similar to the affliction is applied. This method is stated in a famous verse from the *Hevajra Tantra* (2.2.52): "By passion beings are bound and by that very passion they are released." Other examples are a thorn stuck in one's finger, which may be removed by another thorn, or an Indian washerman who removes the dirt from a cloth by dirt itself (used in India as cleanser). These examples are easier to understand than the one given in our text. Lce-sgom-pa emphasizes that the remedies of corresponding type employed in the Tantra path are not the actual afflicting emotions. Ordinary desire is cured not by ordinary desire but by sublime desire—desire that has been transformed. Hence, in the Mantra path as well, the ordinary afflicting emotions are in fact renounced.

How are one's afflicting emotions transformed? This occurs as part of the practice (discussed below) in which meditators transform themselves into enlightened beings, and their world into the celestial mansion of the maṇḍala in which they abide. With such a transformation, their enjoyment of objects of desire is said to be like that of enlightened beings who are making offerings to enlightened beings. In this case, both offerer and recipient are said to experience perfect enjoyment untainted by any trace of affliction, such as attachment, miserliness, or jealousy. They realize that all offerings that appear as forms, sounds, tastes, and so on, are in actuality nondual enlightened wisdom and emptiness. As such, they function as objects of the senses that no longer induce ordinary clinging, but rather immaculate bliss. In other words, offerings made on the path to enlightenment serve to transform ordinary attitudes with respect to offerings into a blissful mind that realizes their true nature. One example of this occurs in the generation process, wherein practitioners who have been transformed into enlightened beings express their gratitude to these enlightened beings. Since the practitioners are no longer distinguished from the enlightened beings, they generate from themselves another maṇḍala of enlightened beings that is like a reflection in a mirror. This replica splits off from themselves in the same way that one butter lamp lights another, without the first losing any of its light. In making the offerings to the enlightened beings emanated from themselves, practitioners worship these enlightened beings, express their gratitude to them, and accumulate merit on the level of conventional truth. At the same time, at the level of the highest truth, they meditate on the true nature of the recipients of these offerings as illusion empty of inherent existence. After making their offerings, the recipients of the offerings merge back into the offerers indistinguishably, like water into water. On the basis of this visualization, the practitioners meditate on all offerings, offerers, and objects of offering as empty illusion. They realize that all appearances arise as the role-playing of enlightened wisdom. The empty and unobstructed nature of everything enables them to dissolve one enlightened being into another. Such is precisely the true nature of things dissolving in the true nature of things. Therefore our text explains, in words similar to those employed by Milarepa, "One enjoys in the manner of enlightened beings making offerings to enlightened beings, of the playfulness of enlightened wisdom in enlightened wisdom, and of the dissolution of the nature of things into the nature of things. Thereby, the ordinary afflicting emotions that afflict one's stream of being are cleared away."

What is the method for overcoming afflicting emotions according to the Great Seal? Here the meditators do not neutralize them with counteractive antidotes, nor do they apply remedies of a similar type, but rather realize that they are the result of their own conceptualization. The workings of the mind cause objects of desire to appear in the way they appear, and bring about the afflicting emotions that grasp at them. The example our text provides for the existence of afflicting emotions is the appearance of water in the desert that arises from optical illusion. Once the beholders comprehend the phenomenon of a mirage, they understand the true nature of water in the middle of a desert, and their former mistaken perception, which holds to the existence of this water, ceases. Because no antidote is applied in this case, the afflicting emotions are said to be released or liberated by themselves.

This classification of the Great Vehicle into three paths that differ in their cure for the afflicting emotions is not meant so much to illustrate historical developments within Buddhism as to serve as a didactic means for presenting the different approaches and clarifying their unique features. The classification of the three paths as gradual stages, ranging from the inferior to the superior, allows the presentation of newer developments—such as the paths of Tantra and the Great Seal—as both belonging to the Great Vehicle and surpassing it. This presentation is modeled after the older method of the Great Vehicle itself, which presents Buddhism in general as consisting of three paths, with the Great Vehicle included within it in the highest position. In order to emphasize this parallelism, Lce-sgom-pa first introduces the three vehicles for the path in Buddhism in general—those of the Hearers (*śrāvakas*), the Solitary Buddhas (*pratyekabuddhas*), and the Bodhisattvas—while adding that only the last of these is capable of leading to buddhahood itself. The two others were taught for people with lesser capacities, as skillful means for gradually leading them into the Great Vehicle of the Bodhisattvas. Similarly, the paths of Mantra and the Great Seal are part of the Great Vehicle, yet are reserved for practitioners with the highest capacities.

Before practitioners may embark on the Tantric practices that lead to liberation, they must receive initiation from their gurus. This initiation is called ripening initiation, since it activates the disciples' capacities to engage in the practice. In receiving initiation, the disciples gain the first inner experience of the meditation, such as seeing themselves as enlightened beings. When both guru and disciple are worthy, the disciple shares in the meditation of his or her guru. They also share in the meditation of the entire lineage of teachers, who have achieved direct experience in that meditation. Our text lists two essential roles of the initiation: cleansing the disciples' impurities and endowing them with efficacy. The first is said to purify the disciples' entire being—expressed in terms of their body, speech, and mind—by removing obstacles that prevent access to the practice, such as habitual tendencies. Each of the inner experiences in the initiation is represented by an external symbolic ritual action. The purification is symbolized by the vase initiation, in which gurus or their helpers pour consecrated water from a decorated vase into the disciples' hands. At that time the disciples visualize, in the space above themselves, a maṇḍala of enlightened beings, with the female enlightened beings holding up decorated vases filled with nectar, which they pour on the disciples' heads. They are to feel that the nectar completely fills their bodies and purifies them of all their defilements.

The second role of initiation is to endow the disciple with the ability to perform the practice. The literal meaning of the Tibetan word for initiation is "empowerment." It empowers disciples with the spiritual powers of the entire lineage of gurus, rendering them appropriate recipients for the practice. Here the disciples should visualize that the nectar filling their bodies transmits the powers of all their gurus. The initiation consists of four parts, each empowering the disciples with the capacity to engage in a successive practice on the path. First, the vase initiation transforms disciples into vessels suitable for the generation process in which they transform themselves into enlightened beings. Second, the secret initiation renders the disciples suitable vessels for engaging in the practice of the subtle body, composed of cakras, channels (*nāḍīs*), and winds (*prāṇas*). This practice is based on the practitioner's own body, in contrast with the following initiation, which relies on another person's body. This is the initiation of enlightened wisdom (*jñāna*) with a consort (*prajñā*) that consists of sexual yoga and turns the disciple into a suitable vessel for engaging in meditation on bliss together with a consort. The fourth initiation, which is nonconceptual, empowers the disciple to practice the meditation of the Great Seal.

According to the tradition of the new schools as followed by our text, the Tantric system is divided into four cycles. In the lowest of these, that of Action (Kriyā) Tantra, only the first initiation, the vase initiation, is conferred, whereas in the fourth one, that of Highest Yoga (Anuttarayoga) Tantra, all four initiations are conferred. In the second Tantric cycle, that of Performance (Caryā) Tantra, and in the cycles beyond it, the five initiations of knowledge are conferred. These five initiations transform one's five afflicting emotions and five aggregates into the five enlightened wisdoms and the five buddhas (*tathāgatas*) of the maṇḍala. The water initiation puts out the fire of hatred, actualizes the mirrorlike enlightened wisdom, and transforms the aggregate of form into Vairocana. The crown initiation destroys the mountain of pride, actualizes the enlightened wisdom of equanimity, and transforms the aggregate of feeling into Ratnasambhava. The vajra initiation overcomes the poison of desire, actualizes the enlightened wisdom of particularized understanding, and transforms the aggregate of perception into Amitābha. The bell initiation releases the chains of jealousy, actualizes the enlightened wisdom of accomplishments, and transforms the aggregate of conditionings into Amoghasiddhi. The name initiation dispels the darkness of ignorance, actualizes the enlightened wisdom of the nature of reality, and transforms the aggregate of consciousness into Akṣobhya.

In the third Tantric cycle, that of Yoga Tantra, the initiation that authorizes the disciples to become teachers or gurus is also conferred. The complete set of initiations conferred in the cycles of Highest Yoga Tantra enables its recipients to engage in the two main practices that will be explained below, the generation process and the completion process. The initiations are of varying degrees of complexity. According to Lce-sgom-pa, these depend on the preferences and economic means of the disciple. In the most elaborate initiation, multicolored precious stones, or at least colored grain or powder, are used to draw the maṇḍala. In the Kālacakra initiation, conferred nowadays by the fourteenth Dalai Lama in the West, it is such a colored-powder maṇḍala that is used. Some maṇḍalas have even found permanent homes in European and Northern American museums. This permanence goes against the intent of the traditional ritual, at the end of which the colored-powder maṇḍala is destroyed and scattered into a body of water. Although an initiation based on a colored-sand maṇḍala creates a profound impression in disciples, a true disciple does not require any ritual or implement.

The effect of the initiation is explained in terms of the disciples' basis, path, and fruit. The basis is the disciples' ground state before receiving initiation. The initiation purifies the basic condition of the disciples' body, speech, and mind. In terms of the path, the four initiations endow disciples with the ability to engage in the four practices on the path to enlightenment (the generation process, the practice of the subtle body, the meditation on bliss that relies on a consort, and the Great Seal). The fruit of these practices is an awakened or enlightened being, a buddha endowed with the four bodies (or embodiments)—the emanation body (*nirmāṇakāya*), the embodiment of enjoyment (*saṃbhogakāya*), the *dharma* embodiment (*dharmakāya*) and the embodiment of the essential nature (*svābhāvikakāya*).

Having explicated the initiations, Lce-sgom-pa explains the practices on the path, beginning with the generation process. The generation process is so called because, by means of visualization, practitioners generate themselves as chosen enlightened beings at the center of a maṇḍala. Our text emphasizes that regardless of the visualization technique, this meditation is a progressive and gradual process, in contrast to the instantaneous practice of the Great Seal. The first purpose of this practice, as listed by Lce-sgom-pa, is the purification of ordinary conceptual thoughts. Since classical Buddhism, conceptual modes of thinking have been counted among the core roots of saṃsāra. Things do not exist in the way they appear to the ordinary mental apparatus. By means of the generation process, ordinary perception of the world and its contents—all its inhabitants—dissolves away and is replaced with the maṇḍala and the enlightened beings inhabiting it. Through such practice, one conceptualization is replaced with another—though the later conceptualization is somewhat more "true," since it is in this form that actual reality appears to enlightened beings. However, the shift from one conceptualization to another demonstrates both the relative nature of each and the workings of the human mind in creating such conceptualizations. The nature of mental construction is more apparent with regard to the maṇḍala than with regard to the external world, and this serves to illuminate the dreamlike nature of ordinary reality, as well. Eventually both conceptualizations will dissolve.

The generation process aids not only in recognizing conceptualization as conceptualization but also in utilizing the power of practitioners' minds to transform and recreate their reality. The control achieved over the visualization of themselves as enlightened beings at the center of a maṇḍala can also be employed for manipulating the ordinary reality that has been replaced by this visualization. Once the nature of the workings of the mind is realized, one can, by knowing their true nature, create whatever appearances one wishes. Hence, one can "truly" transform the ordinary world into that of the divine maṇḍala, while comprehending the true nature of this new reality.

The second purpose of the generation process, according to our text, is the actual engagement in the meditations of tranquil abiding (*śamatha*) and penetrative insight (*vipaśyanā*). These two meditations are the paradigmatic meditations of classical Buddhism that the Tantra, being both unable and unwilling to discard, appropriates. The Tantra path maintains that its practice not only fulfills both of these meditations but also supersedes them. Tranquil abiding can be attained through one-pointed concentration on the visualized enlightened being, while penetrative insight can be accomplished by understanding the true nature of this enlightened being as a dreamlike illusion, empty of intrinsic existence. This is in addition to the other attainments of the generation practice.

The third purpose of the generation process, according to the general Tibetan tradition, is to prepare a basis for the completion process. It seems that the generation process has at times been taken to be an autonomous meditative transformation able to achieve the goal of attaining buddhahood in and of itself. In combining the different Tantric practices into a systematic path, however, the generation process is usually allotted a position subordinate to that of the completion process.

The fourth purpose is to attain the form body (*rūpakāya*) of the Buddha. The three or four bodies or embodiments of the Buddha are divided into the form bodies and the dharma embodiment. Whereas the completion process is said to accomplish the latter, the generation process with its visualization of oneself in the form of a chosen enlightened being is considered to effect the realization of the form body.

In addition to the completion process performed in the cycle of Highest Yoga

Tantra alone, there is yet another practice by the same name that is performed at the conclusion of the generation process in the various Tantric cycles. Lce-sgom-pa points out that these two completion processes should not be confused, and lists three types of completion processes that belong to the generation process. The first is sealing with the four seals (the seal of union, the seal of dharma, the seal of action, and the great seal), which effects the realization of the meditator as an enlightened being whose true essence is nondual emptiness and appearance. The second completion process within the generation process is meditation on the enlightened being as illusion. Here, meditation on the form of the enlightened wisdom with all its intricate details, as well as the practitioner's identification with this form, is infused with a meditation on its illusory empty nature. The purpose of the generation process is not to replace practitioners' fixations on their ordinary existence and their ordinary world with yet another fixation on themselves as enlightened beings in a wonderful celestial maṇḍala. Therefore, the generation process is not complete without this meditation on those enlightened beings as intangible—a rainbow in the sky, having the nature of light empty of intrinsic nature, yet another conceptualization of the mind.

This is also the purpose of the third completion process within the generation process, in which the visualization of oneself as an enlightened being at the center of a maṇḍala is gathered back at the end of the meditative session and dissolved into emptiness. Everything that has been created out of the expanse of emptiness dissolves back into this primordial state. This dissolution serves to demonstrate the true nature of the visualization—an empty illusion—and to prevent attachment to the reality created through the generation itself. In Highest Yoga Tantra, the emphasis is often shifted from these three forms of completion to the completion process per se.

The essence of this completion process is enlightened wisdom characterized by three qualities—bliss, clarity, and nonconceptuality. The discussion is again arranged in terms of the basis, path, and fruit of the completion process. The true mode of being of the *bodily* aspect at the disciple's basis (prior to embarking on the path) is the subtle body that consists of channels, energies, and the pure elements of the white and red drops. Whereas the coarse white and red drops received from the father and mother respectively—drops that together produce one's physical body—lead to rebirth in saṃsāra, the pure white and red drops lead into the spiritual birth of the mind of enlightenment. The true mode of being of the *mental* aspect at the basis is a great bliss that is primordially empty, devoid of essence, and lacking in any mental construct. By realizing the true mode of being of their bodies, practitioners come to know the crucial points of the meditation; and by realizing the true mode of being of their minds, they come to know the crucial nature of the meaning that they should meditate upon. With the realization of these two true modes of being, they proceed to the path of the completion process, which consists of the three practices into which they are initiated through the three higher initiations. The first of these is the practice in reliance on one's own body that, according to our text, consists of the six yogas of Nāropa; the second is the practice in reliance on the body of a consort; and the third is the Great Seal. The fruits of this path are the four yogas of the Great Seal (one-pointedness, lacking mental constructions, the singularity of plurality, and the stream of innate nature without meditation).

When it is instantaneous, the Great Seal is not a practice. A practice is a gradual process with a beginning, middle, and end, composed of meditation, object of meditation, and so on. In the nondual nonconceptual Great Seal, there is neither meditation, nor object of meditation, nor meditator. These distinctions are the source of the problem, since as long as one engages in conceptual thinking, one cannot reach beyond it. Hence, the four yogas of the Great Seal are the natural, spontaneous fruit of the prior practice on the path, and they may be seen as four aspects of a single meditation. Still, in accordance with the faculties of the practitioner, the four yogas may arise simultaneously, gradually, or by leaping to a higher level, as Lce-sgom-pa points out.

Four purposes are listed for the completion process. The first is relinquishing any attachment to the visualized enlightened being and realizing that its nature is suchness, just like that of any other phenomenon—a purpose quite similar to those of the completion processes that belong to the generation process. The second purpose is achieving a direct experience of great bliss that is indistinguishable from enlightened wisdom, through practices relying on one's own body and the body of another. The third is the purification of cognitive obstruction, the counterpart to the purification of emotional obscurations said to be achieved through the generation process. The fourth is attaining the dharma embodiment that complements the attainment of the form body realized in the generation process.

Next in the topics of discussion are practices undertaken outside the formal meditation session, between meditation sessions or in postmeditation. Postmeditation is of utmost importance for the practitioner's meditative experience, and Lce-sgom-pa devotes much space to it. Sitting in meditation withdrawn from everything is not an end in itself. The purpose of meditation is to effect and transform one's entire being. Hence, Lce-sgom-pa explains that after arising from their formal meditation, practitioners should preserve their meditative experiences and combine them with their daily activities. Those who have not attained meaningful meditative experiences in their formal meditation should in the meantime engage in religious practice between meditative sessions.

Like the formal sessions themselves, these practices differ among the various vehicles. Having renounced all sensual pleasures, Hearers and Solitary Buddhas engage in bodily ascetic practices. Lce-sgom-pa refers ironically to the bodily hardship and the difficulty of these practices, implying that these practitioners may not achieve much beyond the hardship itself. Bodhisattvas also abandon objects of desire, while practicing the ten perfections for the sake of leading others to enlightenment. On this point, our text maintains that Tantric practitioners do not renounce the objects of the senses, but understand their true nature. In contrast to the practices of the actual meditative session—which he mentions only in passing, assuming the reader (or hearer) to be already familiar with them—Lce-sgom-pa describes the practices outside the meditation session in some detail. These depend on the practitioners' meditative experiences. Beginners in meditation engage mainly in practices performed between meditative sessions. Since the great majority of the followers of the Tantric path are beginners, these are very popular practices, in both senses of the word. They are considered to be conducive to actual meditative experience, since they contribute to the accumulation of merit and wisdom and to the removal of any impediments to the meditation that may follow. Among the practices that our text lists are recitations of mantras, such as the *Oṃ maṇi padme hūṃ* that springs constantly from the lips of so many Tibetans. The yoga of food means that the daily meals taken between meditative sessions are considered as offerings to the enlightened being one is practicing to become. Tormas, generally, are food offerings made to one's enlightened beings and protectors. A maṇḍal is a symbolic offering of the entire universe, the greatest offering one could imagine. It exhibits both the importance of these offerings to the offerers and their nonattachment to the material world. The seven-limbed practice, in its Tantric version, includes prostration, offering, confession of sins, rejoicing in the joy of others, seeking refuge in the Three Jewels, generating the Bodhisattva's mind for enlightenment, and dedicating one's merit to all. The water offering is made to hungry ghosts tormented by hunger and thirst, whose insatiable craving is iconographically represented by their huge bellies and tiny mouths. Many Tibetans make daily offerings of water to quench their thirst. Tsha-tshas are small images or stūpas stamped in clay or water for the accumulation of merit. Often they also contain ashes of one's parent or lama. Circumambulations of holy places, temples, monasteries, and so forth also serve for the accumulation of merit. Rounding out the list of these popular practices are the recitation and copying of Buddhist scriptures, studying and understanding them, as well as teaching them to others.

The next stage, following that of the beginners, occurs when a slight inner experience arises in meditative equipoise. This experience should be applied to postmeditation activities. For example, when during their formal meditative session practitioners engage in the generation process, they meditate on the illusory empty nature of themselves as enlightened beings. In postmeditation they should apply this realization to everything that appears to their senses. In a similar way, they combine their inner realization during the completion process with their ordinary activities in the external world. Not only are they to apply their meditative experiences to daily life but their everyday experience should also serve to sustain their formal meditation. In their postmeditation, the practitioners should first understand that all phenomena appear to them in the way they appear as a result of their own mental processes; and then realize that these mental processes too are empty of inherent existence. Since everything is empty and unobstructed, one thing can simply dissolve into another, which is tantamount to the dissolution of the nature of things into the nature of things as Lce-sgom-pa describes.

The third stage of this postmeditational practice occurs when the slight inner experience evolves into a slight stability in the experience. In order to enhance that stability, a special practice called "taming the engagement of awareness" is performed. Once again, depending on the distinctive characteristics of the practitioners, this practice may be performed "with mental elaborations," "without mental elaborations," and "completely without mental elaborations." According to our text, the first is intended for practitioners who are rich and young but lack in true understanding, the second for those of medium possessions, age, and wisdom; and the last for those who are impoverished and old but possess great wisdom.

The first group tames the engagement of their awareness by actually acting out the maṇḍala. Together with yogins and yoginīs in a number equal to that of the male and female enlightened beings of their chosen maṇḍala, they withdraw to a solitary place. There they prepare a maṇḍala, and while occupying the abodes of the enlightened beings in it, they practice the generation and completion processes with all the ritual details. The offerings play an instrumental role in the transformation of the practitioners into enlightened beings. In making ritual offerings, they practice in the manner of enlightened beings making offerings to enlightened beings until they actualize this mode of offering.

In contrast to this training, those who tame the engagement of their awareness "completely without mental elaborations" perform the practice known as "the activity of a bhusuku." *Bhusuku* is a Sanskrit acronym for "eating, sleeping, and defecating." Apart from these three life-sustaining actions, these practitioners do nothing but meditate on emptiness. It is by playing on the meaning of the Tibetan word for "taming the engagement" (*brtul-zhugs*) that Lce-sgom-pa explains this practice, which consists of taming (*brtul*) the ordinary mental processes that involve conceptual thinking, and infusing (*zhugs*) all external and internal events into the maṇḍala of enlightened beings. Here, Lce-sgom-pa applies one of the classic Buddhist meditative sequences as the guideline for this Tantric meditation. The practitioners should first see themselves and their world as the celestial maṇḍala and the enlightened beings dwelling in it, while maintaining the conventional temporary nature of that maṇḍala. Second, they realize how that maṇḍala and its inhabitants came into being through the working of their ordinary minds. Third, they realize that in actual fact the true mind does not objectify or perceive external objects (*mi dmigs-pa*), since the true nature of everything is emptiness. Nonperception of objects brings about a new type of perception, a direct realization of the true nature of things. The four steps in this meditation endow the four kinds of offerings—outer, inner, secret, and suchness—with a new meaning.

These three practices for taming the engagement of the awareness—with, without, and completely without mental elaborations—enhance the practitioners' stability of meditative experience, and lead them to the fourth stage of the postmeditative practice, in which a very stable experience is reached. At this stage the practitioners explore the degree to which their meditative experience has been secured by undertaking the so-called "practice of the crazy yogin." This is a serious test for their equanimity and impartiality. For example, their experience of having a nice meal should not be the least bit different from eating excrement; drinking beer from drinking urine, and so forth. They should experience a total equanimity not only toward undertaking these diametrically opposed activities but also with regard to abstaining from them. This is a state of complete freedom from duality. It is no longer a practice of postmeditation, since there is no longer any such distinction to be made.

Lce-sgom-pa warns against the misuse of these highest practices—of taming the engagement of the awareness and the practice of the crazy yogin—by ignorant persons who do not understand their true purpose. He emphasizes that it is only for persons endowed with spiritual qualities that these practices can be factors conducive to enlightenment. Moreover, the subject of the second part of this chapter, the keeping of the practitioner's vows and commitments on the path, which is not translated here, also stresses the moral foundations of this practice. Lce-sgom-pa concludes the present section by reiterating the Tantra/Mantra method of employing the "enemy" for overcoming that "enemy." Whereas in the view of the Sūtras the enjoyment of the senses is the cause of bondage in saṃsāra, the Tantra maintains that this very enjoyment is the key to liberation from saṃsāra. The Tantra, however, makes practitioners' reliance on the enjoyment of the senses conditional on their thorough understanding of the true nature of sense objects. Recognizing the essential characteristics of the objects of desire and their effect on the mind is the foundation of the Great Seal, and the subject of the seventh chapter of Lce-sgom-pa's *Outline of the Jewel Mound of Instructions*.

The work from which our selection is taken, *The Outline of the Jewel Mound of Instructions* (*Man-ngag-rin-chen-spungs-pa'i-dkar-chag*), is based on two sources. One version was printed by The Pleasure of Elegant Sayings Printing Press at Sarnath, 1971, and the other, a copy of which was kindly sent to me by Per Sørensen, is found in the National Library in Bhutan, Inv. no. 282. Passages shown in {curly brackets} in the text indicate notes added by the hand of an unknown copyist. Only those notes that do not interfere with the the flow of the text are included here. This research was supported by The Israel Science Foundation, founded by The Israel Academy of Sciences and Humanities.

Further Reading

For a general discussion of the Buddhist Tantra path, see the last chapter of the fourteenth Dalai Lama's, *The World of Tibetan Buddhism*, translated by Geshe Thupten Jinpa (Boston: Wisdom Publications, 1995). Other such discussions are found in Geshe Kelsang Gyatso, *Tantric Grounds and Paths* (London: Tharpa Publications, 1994) and Daniel Cozort, *Highest Yoga Tantra* (Ithaca, N.Y.: Snow Lion, 1996). On the initiation ritual according to the Kālacakra system see the fourteenth Dalai Lama's, *The Kalachakra Tantra: Rite of Initiation*, translated, edited, and introduced by Jeffrey Hopkins (London: Wisdom Publications, 1985). For a good treatment of Tibetan meditative rituals in general and the generation process in particular, see Stephan Beyer, *The Cult of Tārā: Magic and Ritual in Tibet* (Berkeley and Los Angeles: University of California Press, 1973). For a translation of a Tibetan explanation for both generation and completion, see Jamgön Kongtrul, *Creation and Completion: Essential Points of Tantric Meditation,* translated by Sarah Harding (Boston: Wisdom Publications, 1996). For a translation of another explanatory work on the generation process, together with a lengthy introduction, see Herbert V. Guenther, *The Creative Vision* (Novato, Cal.: Lotsawa, 1987.) Unfortunately this is not easy reading. For a discussion of the generation process according to the Kālacakra system, see Roger Jackson, "The Kalachakra Generation-Stage Sadhana," in *The Wheel of Time: The Kalachakra in Context*, edited by Beth Simon (Madison, Wisc.: Deer Park Books, 1985), pp. 119–38. On the six yogas of Nāropa, see Herbert V. Guenther, *The Life and Teaching of Nāropa* (London: Oxford University Press, 1963), and Glenn H. Mullin, *Readings on the Six Yogas of Naropa* (Ithaca, N.Y.: Snow Lion, 1997). On Lce-sgom-pa, see Per K. Sørensen, "The Ascetic Lce-sgom Shes-rab Rdo-rje Alias Lce-sgom Zhig-po: Prolific, Allusive, but Elusive," *Journal of the Nepal Research Centre* 11 (forthcoming).

"The Practice of the Mantra Path" by Lce-sgom-pa

While bowing down with reverence through my three avenues of being [my body, speech, and mind] to the lama, *yi-dam* [tutelary deities], and ḍākinīs, I have written concisely on the theory and practice of the Mantra, the path of the swift messenger of excellent skillful means.

Thinking about the inconceivable number of types of sentient beings to be trained, the completely perfect Buddha taught, on the whole, an inconceivable diversity of vehicles for the path. But, in fact those vehicles for nirvāṇa are three. Furthermore, the path that brings attainment of the highest buddhahood is nothing but the Great Vehicle (Mahāyāna). The others, the two vehicles of Hearers and Solitary Buddhas, were taught as skillful means for gradually inducting into the Great Vehicle people of lesser mental capacities. The *Sūtra of Great Liberation That Expands in All Directions* teaches:

> O sons of noble families, for example, just as one person has three names—when he is young he is called a child, when he is over twenty years old, he is called a man, and after passing the age of eighty he is called an old person—just so are the three vehicles of mine. To the Hearers whose minds are limited I taught the small vehicle, to the Solitary Buddhas whose minds are moderately expanded I taught the medium vehicle, and to the Bodhisattvas who have entered the great path, I taught the great vehicle. O son of noble family, even though there are diverse doors for understanding, eventually, they are united into one juncture. This juncture is the One Vehicle (Ekayāna), which when separated through skillful means is considered to be three. The vehicles of the Hearers and of Solitary Buddhas are included

as well in the Great Vehicle. The Great Vehicle alone is the vehicle for buddhahood. Therefore, even though there are three vehicles, these are the One Vehicle.

Also the *Song of the Names of Mañjuśrī* (*Mañjuśrīnāmasaṅgīti*) states:

Realizing the advantages for beings of the methods and ways of the different vehicles, he [Mañjuśrī] has gone forth from the three vehicles and abides in the fruit of the one vehicle.

The Great Vehicle, taking into account the two different types of people who are receptacles for the practice, but who have not yet reached the path of Seeing, taught two dissimilar systems for the path. In taking into account those people who are only slightly afflicted by the desire for sense objects, who have the ability to renounce, and who aspire to attain awakening, the path of the Perfection of Wisdom of the Great Vehicle was taught. In taking into account those who are greatly afflicted by the desire for sense objects, who are unable to renounce, and who aspire to awakening, the Mantra path was taught. Also within the Mantra itself two paths were taught: 1. the path of purifying the mind in stages by the outer and inner generation process and by the completion process, and 2. the path of the Great Seal that is the instantaneous practice of the essential meaning.

The method of overcoming the afflicting emotions in the Perfection of Wisdom of the Great Vehicle is as follows: Having placed the afflicting emotions and the objects of desire in the position of an enemy, one overcomes them by means of an antidote of the opposing type, an antidote that contradicts them. By meditating on nonattraction as an antidote to desire, on loving kindness as an antidote to aversion, and on codependent origination as an antidote to ignorance, and so forth, one overcomes them. In the Mantra system of the Great Vehicle, one overcomes the afflicting emotions of passion through antidotes of a corresponding type. One meditates on sublime desire as an antidote to ordinary desire. Having transformed the entire vessel-world and its content-inhabitants into a celestial mansion-maṇḍala with pure enlightened beings, one enjoys in the manner of enlightened being making offerings to enlightened being, of the playfulness of enlightened wisdom in enlightened wisdom, and of the dissolution of the nature of things into the nature of things. Thereby, the ordinary afflicting emotions that afflict one's stream of being are cleared away—in the same way, for example, as one would soothe a burn by fumigating it in the same fire that caused it—in order that the pain of the burn quickly subside. The method of overcoming the afflicting emotions in the instantaneous Great Seal is to recognize their essential characteristics, and thereby abandon them. By realizing the inherent nature or the essential characteristics of the conceptualization of the objects of desire and of the afflicting emotions as the nonarising true nature of reality, the holding of things as real is reversed. By virtue of this reversal, craving and aversion are naturally liberated. For example, one might mistakenly take a mirage to be a body of water, but by carefully investigating, seeing that there is no water there, the clinging to the holding of the mirage as water is naturally liberated. Hence even Tantra does not teach that the actual afflicting emotions are taken on the path. Although there is some variation in their methods of abandoning the afflicting emotions, in terms of abandonment itself there is no difference between the three paths.

Now, generally speaking the majority of the gods and people of the Desire Realm, greatly afflicted by desire for objects of the senses, are unable to renounce, but still aspire to awakening. For them the Buddha taught the method of training on the path through the special means of the Tantra belonging to the Great Vehicle (Mahāyāna). There are two general subjects here: 1. the path of the initiations that bring maturation and 2. the path of the skillful means that bring liberation.

THE PATH OF THE RIPENING INITIATION

1. The essential nature of the initiation is cleansing the impurities of the stream of being of the disciple and endowing them with efficacy. 2. The etymology: It is called "ripening" because it causes the unripe basis to ripen, and it is called "initiation" because having been made into a receptacle suitable for meditation on a particular path, one is initiated, empowered for meditation on that particular path. 3. The divisions of the initiation: In terms of their essential meanings there are four divisions. The first is the vase initiation, the second the secret initiation, the third the enlightened wisdom initiation with a consort (*prajñā*), and the fourth the precious word initiation. There are two divisions to the vase initiation, the initiation of the disciple and the initiation of the teacher (*vajrācārya*). In both the secret initiation and the consort initiation there are two divisions: the initiation of the path of passion [formation] and the initiation of the path of liberation [dissolution]. There are no divisions in the fourth initiation. It is the "leaping over" or the culmination of all four initiations. There are three divisions in terms of the degree of elaboration: {Those who are wealthy and who like mental elaboration} are conferred elaborate initiation by means of a maṇḍala of powdered precious substances, grain, or colored powder. {Those with medium wealth and understanding} are given a medium initiation by means of a body maṇḍala, or a *maṇḍal* of a bouquet of flowers. Those who posses little wealth and do not like mental elaboration are conferred the four initiations in an abbreviated form by means of the body, speech, and mind of the lama, or an emblem, or some small article of initiation.

4. The internal grades of the initiation are four in number: The cycle of the Action Tantra (Kriyā Tantra) teaches that the initiation is conferred with the water of the vase using only a *maṇḍal*. Its initiand becomes a vessel suitable for meditation on the enlightened being by merely bestowing permission for the mantra. The cycle of Performance Tantra (Caryā Tantra) teaches that

through the five initiations of knowledge and the initiation of vajra practice, six initiations in all, the initiand becomes a suitable vessel. The Yoga Tantra explains that through the complete initiation, beginning with the five initiations of knowledge and followed by the initiation of the disciple and the initiation of the teacher, the initiand becomes a suitable vessel. The Highest Yoga Tantra (Anuttara Yoga Tantra) explains that through the complete vase initiation as well as the three supreme initiations the initiand becomes a vessel suitable for meditation on the entire path of the generation process and completion process.

5. This being so, there are three benefits or purposes for conferring the four initiations: The first benefit or purpose is purifying the basis from aspects of impurity. First, the vase initiation mainly purifies the impurity of the bad habitual tendencies of the body. Second, the secret initiation mainly purifies the impurities of speech. Third, the initiation of enlightened wisdom with a consort mainly purifies the impurities of the mind. Fourth, the precious word initiation purifies every impurity of the body, speech, and mind—all three. The second benefit or purpose is making the initiand a vessel suitable for meditation on the four paths. The vase initiation makes the initiand a vessel suitable for meditation on the generation process of oneself as an enlightened being. The secret initiation makes the initiand a vessel suitable for meditation in which one's own body possesses skillful means, such as the "channels and winds" [the subtle body]. The initiation of enlightened wisdom with a consort makes the initiand a vessel suitable for meditation on the bliss that relies on the consort, the body of another. The fourth initiation makes the initiand a vessel suitable for meditation on the instantaneous Great Seal. The third purpose of conferring the four initiations is to bring the initiand into the fortunate state of attaining the four embodiments of the fruit. The giving of the vase initiation brings the initiand into the fortunate state of attaining the emanation body of the fruit. Similarly, the secret initiation brings the initiand into the fortunate state of attaining the embodiment of enjoyment. The initiation of enlightened wisdom with a consort leads to the Dharma embodiment, and the fourth initiation to the embodiment of the essential nature. In short, initiation brings the initiand into the fortunate state of attaining all the good qualities and accomplishments, both mundane and supermundane.

According to the system of Lama Nāropa, there are three general topics on the path of the skillful means that bring liberation: the yoga of the path; the conducive practices; and the companion vows. The yoga of the path is divided into two practices, the generation process and the completion process.

In the generation process there are five topics.

1. The essential nature: One should generate that which is to be generated—whatever enlightened being one chooses with the appropriate components of the skillful method.

2. There are two kinds of divisions: The divisions appropriate to different texts are two: the generation process for attaining the common accomplish-

ments according to manuals of ritual collections, and the generation process for attaining the supreme accomplishment. For these divisions one needs to consider each individual text. The divisions according to the degree of elaboration are three: extensive meditation on the wheel of the maṇḍala; middle meditation; and concise meditation on the main ornament of the male heroic being or of the female heroic being.

3. The etymology: Because this is a process of visualizing the generation of the supporting celestial mansion [the maṇḍala] and the supported enlightened beings [residing in it], it is called "generation process."

4. The methods of meditation are of two types: Those who pursue the profound and are not fond of the elaborate generate the complete visualization in an instant. Then in clarifying the visualization in stages, they meditate. And those who pursue the extensive and are fond of the elaborate, meditate in stages on the proceedings of the practice. Clarifying the visualization in stages for as long as they are not weary, they meditate. The method of meditation for each of these should be known from the practice manual of each meditation.

5. There are four purposes: The purpose of purifying ordinary conceptual thoughts; the purpose of the actual arising of the concentration of tranquil abiding and the spontaneous arising of penetrative insight; the purpose of preparing a basis for the completion process; and the purpose of attaining the perfect form-body of the fruit.

In the generation process [in the cycles] up to Yoga Tantra—apart from merely sealing with the four seals, meditating on the body of the enlightened beings as illusion, gathering back in stages the enlightened being and its celestial mansion at the end of the meditative session, and meditating on emptiness—there is no completion process with its distinctive methods. Above and beyond the generation process, Highest Yoga Tantra also teaches the completion process.

In the completion process there are also five topics.

1. The essential nature of the completion process is the actual generation of the enlightened wisdom of bliss, clarity, and nonconceptual thought in the body and mind by setting the mind on certain supports.

2. There are three divisions according to the system of Lama Nāropa. a. The "natural state of the basic entity": First, the natural state of the basic entity of the body is the natural condition of the bodily channels, the winds and the pure elements of bodhicitta [thought of enlightenment]. By knowing all these conditions exactly, one knows the crucial points of the meditation. Second, the natural state of the basic entity of the mind: The actual natural condition of the mind as such is great bliss, primordially empty, devoid of inherent essence, lacking mental elaborations. By realizing well this natural condition, one knows the essential nature of the meaning on which to meditate. By realizing these two aspects of the natural state of the basic entity in this way, one knows the meaning on which to meditate, and the crucial points of the meditation. b. The

"natural state of the path": Knowing the basic entity in this way leads to the teachings on the natural state of the path. There are three practices here depending on the stream of being of the practitioner: the practice of one's own body as possessing the means; the practice with a consort (the body of another); and the practice of nondual Great Seal. The practice that relies on one's own body as the means is known as the "six dharmas" in the system of Lama Nāropa. c. The "natural state of the fruit": Practicing these leads to the "process of arising of the natural state of the fruit" within one's stream of being. This is "arising in the mode of the four kinds of the yoga of experiencing the true condition": the yoga of one-pointedness, the yoga free of mental elaborations, the yoga of the multitude as one taste, and the yoga of the stream of the innate nature without meditation. These too arise gradually, instantaneously, or in leaping over, depending on the special faculties of the person who is the receptacle for the practice. For the meaning of these you should examine the *Great Guidance of the Path*.

3. The etymology: Because one perfectly completes enlightened wisdom it is called "completion process."

4. You should know the practice of meditative techniques from the transmission.

5. There are four purposes for the completion process: a. The purpose of abandoning clinging to the enlightened being of the generation process, while realizing this enlightened being as the true nature of things; b. The purpose of directly realizing the natural innate enlightened wisdom and great bliss; this purpose is fulfilled by relying on the special method whereby the meditative experience that dissolves and increases the pure elements takes the practitioners through the rebirth process by means of bliss, clarity, and nonconceptuality. In relying on the special method, the meditative experience that dissolves and increases the pure elements takes the practitioners through the rebirth processes by means of bliss, clarity, and nonconceptuality, whereupon they realize directly the natural coemergent enlightened wisdom and great bliss. c. The purpose of purifying all the cognitive obscurations. d. The purpose of coming to attain the dharma embodiment of the final fruit.

Now, the teachings on the conducive practices.

1. The essential nature of these practices: Having been absorbed in a concentration within meditative equipoise, one practices preserving the experiences of meditative equipoise in the postmeditation phase by combining it with various daily activities.

2. The practice is divided into two parts: a. First is the "practice-without-passion," which is subdivided into two parts. The lesser practice is the practice of the Hearers and the Solitary Buddhas: after abandoning completely all the objects of the senses, they undertake practices that cause bodily hardship and weariness, such as the twelve ascetic practices. The extensive practice is the practice of the Bodhisattva: after abandoning the objects of the senses, they

practice the ten perfections for the sake of others. b. The "practice-with-passion" is the practice of the Mantra. By means of thoroughly knowing the true nature of all appearances, they train in the path while relying on the five objects of the senses. The *Guhyasamāja* says: "The enlightened wisdom with passion always relies on objects of the senses with desire." In classifying that practice of the Mantra there are four stages: beginners' practice; the practice of those in whom slight experience has arisen; the practice of attaining a slight stability in the experience; and the practice of attaining a great stability in experience.

3. The methods of the practice:

a. Beginners' practice: Beginners chiefly engage in practice between meditative sessions—in the recitation of mantras, food yoga, tormas, maṇḍals, the seven-limbed practice, water offerings, tsha-tshas, circumambulations, recitation of sūtras, listening and explaining the teaching, realizing the view of the teaching, writing the letters of the scriptures, and so forth, with great devotion. They perform the complete practice, including the preparation, main part, and conclusion. By mainly performing these practices, beginners perfect the accumulations and purify the obscurations, thereby developing the factors conducive to the arising of experience in the mind. These are called the practices of Samantabhadra.

b. The practice at the time of the arising of a slight inner experience, as a result of that beginner's practice: The practitioners unify the slight inner experience that arises in their meditative equipoise with their postmeditation, and combine it with everything that appears to their sense faculties. Further, just as in the meditative equipoise of the generation process they meditate on the maṇḍala of the enlightened beings of their yi-dam, so too in postmeditation, they should meditate on and see all appearances as the illusory maṇḍala of the enlightened beings. They also should combine the experience as it is generated in the meditative equipoise of the completion process with everything that appears to themselves in postmeditation, and unify them. In short, when the practitioners arise from their meditative equipoise and engage in the manifold external world, enjoying forms, sounds, scents, tastes, and objects of touch, they then know all these to be of the inherent nature of the enlightened beings. Further, {since they know them as} their own {mind}, and they know the true nature of their mind as emptiness, they practice in the manner {of enlightened beings making offerings to enlightened beings, in the playfulness of enlightened wisdom in enlightened wisdom} and in the dissolution of the nature of things into the nature of things. Hence, everything that appears to their faculties in the postmeditation phase assists them on their path. This is called the secret practice as well as the practice of realization. They should rely on these ritual actions between the meditative sessions described above—actions that are beneficial to their meditative experience and do not harm it, and avoid any harm to their meditative experience.

c. Performing in this manner brings about the practice at the time of attaining a slight stability in the experience. For the sake of enhancing that experience, they should practice taming the engagement of their awareness. For this there are three practices.

i. The practice with mental elaborations: Those persons who are receptacles for the practice that possess great riches, are young in age, and small in wisdom perform in the following manner. In a very secluded place that is in harmony with their mind, they arrange perfect requisites for the feast offering. In an upper chamber they arrange a maṇḍala, receptacles and offerings decorated with various ornaments, and prepare there a seat for the yogins and yoginīs. They gather consorts, endowed with the essential characteristics, in a number equal to that of the female enlightened beings of the maṇḍala. Then the yogins and yoginīs enter into the abodes of the heroes and heroines in the maṇḍala. They meditate as in the generation and completion processes, beginning with the meditation on the protection wheel. Next, the yogins and yoginīs make offerings, first outer offerings {such as flowers and incense}, then inner offerings {for the five senses}, then secret offerings, and finally, they make offerings of songs and dances again and again. At that time, they entirely abandon ordinary craving in every respect. They make offerings in the manner of enlightened beings making offerings to enlightened beings, the playfulness of enlightened wisdom in enlightened wisdom, and of the dissolution of the nature of things into the nature of things. In this way, they practice uninterruptedly for six months or more. This is the practice with mental elaborations.

ii. Second, the practice without mental elaborations: Persons who are receptacles for the practice with medium riches, age, and wisdom perform everything as above except that they perform the entire practice in a medium way together with one, two, or three consorts, who are endowed with the essential characteristics.

iii. Third, the practice completely without mental elaborations: Persons who are receptacles for the practice with few riches, old age, and great wisdom perform in the following manner. In an isolated place, such as a site for the disposal of the dead, having renounced the actual consort, they engage in meditative equipoise on the natural innate enlightened wisdom. They perform the activity of a bhusuku. Here *bhu* stands for *bhuñj*—the activity of eating; *su* for *sutana* [*svapana*]—sleeping; and *ku* for *kutisara* [*kūṭīsara*]—defecating. In such a manner they are not active: abandoning all but these three involuntary activities, they preserve only the yoga of emptiness. Now, you may ask why these are called "taming the engagement of awareness." Thoroughly comprehending the outer, inner, secret, and suchness, they discipline their ordinary conceptual thoughts by means of their awareness. Thereby all the outer and inner phenomena are infused into the assemblage of enlightened beings of the maṇḍala as mere conventional illusion. They then further realize that all these enlightened beings are emanations of their own minds. In the highest truth, they do not perceive them even as mind itself: rather, they penetrate the equanimity of emptiness. Hence this is called the practice of taming the engagement of awareness.

d. Practicing in this way brings about attainment of great stability in experience and realization: At this stage, through the practice of taming the engagement of awareness great stability and some ability in the three doors are attained. For the sake of examining whether these experiences and realizations are stable or unstable, one should perform the "practice of the crazy yogin." There is pure food that should be eaten and food that should not be eaten {such as excrement}, drinks to be drunk {such as beer} and drinks not to be drunk {such as urine}, places to be gone to {such as the king's palace}, places not to be gone to {such as the house of a butcher}, those to have intercourse with {such as a consort with the essential characteristics} and those not to have intercourse with {such as mother and sister}. When they practice all these things that are to be done and not to be done, they practice with impartiality; and when they give them up, they give them up with impartiality. They practice such a practice at the appropriate time regardless of hope and fear even with regard to whatever is dharma and not dharma, without affirming or negating, and without accepting or rejecting anything. Hence, when they simply abide unceasingly in the actuality of the realization of the equanimity of saṃsāra and nirvāṇa, free of dualistic grasping, without meditation and postmeditation, that is called "practicing the great meditative equipoise." It was taught that the culmination of that experience gives rise to the path of seeing.

4. The etymology of practice: because the practitioner ought to perform it, it is called "practice."

5. Abandoning the faults of objections: Clearing doubts about contradictions within the scriptures. Now the scriptures of the Perfection of Wisdom teach for the most part that enjoying the five objects of the senses is the cause of bondage to saṃsāra. Yet many Tantras of the Great Yoga of the Mantra teach that enjoying anything one likes among the five objects of the senses is the cause for liberation. If you ask, "would not this contradiction cause doubt?" the answer is that these two scriptures are intended for different persons. Who are they? In taking into account those people who are receptacles for the practice, who are ignorant, who do not understand the inherent nature of the five objects of the senses: on that basis, relying on objects of the senses was taught as a cause of bondage. And in taking into account those people who are receptacles for the practice, who have the wisdom of completely understanding the inherent nature of the five objects of the senses: on that basis, relying on anything they like among the five objects of the senses was taught as a cause for liberation. The *Guhyasamāja* teaches: "In relying on desire toward all desirous enjoyments, the yogin would quickly attain buddhahood." The *Jewel Peak Sūtra* (*Ārya Ratnakūṭa*) teaches: "Kāśyapa, it is like this. Just as, for example, a poison enclosed by mantra and medicinal herbs cannot perform the action of killing, O Kāśyapa, so too afflicting emotions enclosed by wisdom and skillful means cannot perform the action of wrongdoing." The same source also states: "Endowed with great means, afflicting emotions become a factor of enlightenment."

6. The benefit of training in the Mantra path: By enjoying anything they like while understanding the inherent nature of the five objects of the senses as the cause, they would attain the untainted bliss of the fruit. The *Guhyasamāja* says: "Though they adhere to intense vows of asceticism, they will not achieve, but when they adhere to all enjoyments of desire, they will quickly achieve." The *Cakrasaṃvara* says: "Therefore by means of bliss you will attain blissfulness, all-awakening." Therefore all the previous buddhas and bodhisattvas also attained the fruit by adhering to the Mantra practice. The *Guhyasamāja* teaches: "Buddhas and bodhisattvas and those who practice the highest Mantra practice attain the unwavering [eighth bodhisattva level], the highest quality, by relying on all desires." If those Mantra practices are not performed in accordance with the timing of the practice, if the beginner performs the taming of engagement of awareness or the "practice of the crazy yogin," that will later become a cause for a lower rebirth. Therefore it is very important to perform in accordance with the timing of the practice. In this way these four practices are conducive to quick awakening. For example, when you urge a good horse on with the conducive factor of a whip, it runs faster. Just so, you should obliterate your ordinary body, speech, and mind with the conducive factor of practicing the experience and realization in meditative equipoise. Thereby you quickly bring about the attainment of the level of buddhahood. Therefore this is called the conducive practice.

—20—

The Ocean of the Heart: Selections from the *Kulārṇava Tantra*

Douglas Renfrew Brooks

Few Sanskrit texts within Śaiva and Śākta Hindu Tantra provide as clear and concise a vision of basic tenets, beliefs, and values as the "Ocean of the Kula" or *Kulārṇava Tantra*. Traditionally regarded as the fifth section of the *Ūrdhvāmnāya Tantra*, a work that has never been recovered, the *Kulārṇava Tantra* as we know it today consists of some 2,060 verses divided among seventeen chapters called ullāsas or "waves." Usually dated between about 1000 and 1400 C.E., the text is as much a repository of traditional materials defining the movement or school called the Kula or Kaulism as it is a singular, original document.

Although there are dozens of verses, sometimes entire chapters, that require technical and deeply esoteric knowledge to grasp even the first layers of meaning, the *Kulārṇava* has much to say in broader terms about what it means to live one's life immersed in the practice of Hindu Tantric yoga as a worshiper of Śiva and Śakti. The *Kulārṇava* does not contain all the materials of this broad Tantric tradition, or even more of them than other texts within Śaivism and Śāktism, but it offers a primer and a base to which various elaborations of lineage understanding and practice are later added. In this way, the *Kulārṇava* seeks to create far-reaching principles of generalization even as it defines and distinguishes a "narrow" vision of the Kula path.

Certainly the *Kulārṇava Tantra* creates its own particular vision of the Kula as a distinctive school or "clan"–as the word *kula* suggests–of esoteric initiation and practice. The *Kulārṇava* appears to view itself as the quintessential Kula text, the single authoritative source that defines both particular and universal aspects of the path. And yet the *Kulārṇava* has been regarded as an authoritative resource and compendium of essential teachings by tāntrikas who subscribe neither to its doctrinal definitions nor to its prescriptions. In this way, the word *kula* refers to the highest or the most secret teachings of the "heart," a meaning of the term that suggests yet another set of broad metaphorical connotations. I have throughout my translation used the English word "heart" as the term that suggests the widest possible meaning of *kula*. This translation is based, in no small part, upon a passage from the *Parātriṃśikavivaraṇa* of Abhinavagupta, which states that there exists a set of meanings that link kula to a reality that is the very core, the center, the heart of the Tantric deity Bhairava himself. That passage reads as follows: "For truly the kula, because it is identical with the essential self of the Supreme, grants that perfection. Kula is called the circle of rays of the splendor of the supreme Lord Bhairava, made up of the fullness of his own light."

Thus, when the *Kulārṇava* discusses such seminal topics as initiation, ritual practice, discipleship, and the nature of divinity, we gain insights and perspectives that apply across many different sectarian lineage traditions. Specific or general points made within the text are subject to further interpretation within the contexts of particular lineages. There is to my knowledge no lineage, historical or current, that defines itself according to the specific data found in the *Kulārṇava Tantra*, despite the text's own narrower self-definition.

The single common link among Kula lineages is their association with the term *kula* as a means of designating their brand of spirituality. Certain philosopher-theologians, such as the famous Abhinavagupta, further differentiate the "Kaula" or "Kaulika" from the tāntrika. But this is not a distinction of importance to the *Kulārṇava,* and not the sort of distinction that applies to later interpreters who identify themselves as Kaulas or who cite the *Kulārṇava Tantra*. It is the wish of all different sorts of Kaulas to define their own versions of the Kula path. The *Kulārṇava* is no different in this sense: it creates its own kula and yet that is not all it imagines itself to be nor what it becomes to later interpreters.

In addition to meanings that imply association by initiation, this Tantra suggests that kula means "the essence of reality one takes to heart," and this is the meaning that clearly captures its larger intent. In this sense, the heart of the *Kulārṇava* is its secretive body of teachings and practices meant for an initiated spiritual elite. To enter the kula, to practice the kula, to learn or achieve the goals of the kula is to engage the secrets of the heart and to penetrate the heart of the divine. To overemphasize the sociocultural aspect of Kula Tantra—as a school or movement of secret initiations and practices meant for a spiritual elite—can lead us to overlook its most fundamental claim: that there is a path leading to the heart of the divine and an experience of the divine that leads one's heart to the source of happiness in the world and liberation from death and rebirth. Although this spiritual goal may not itself distinguish the *Kula* path, it is no less the *Kulārṇava Tantra*'s most important claim.

The selection presented here intends to capture the *Kulārṇava Tantra*'s broadest theological and practical teachings. I have selected verses that any Kaula might cite for the sake of defining the Kula path in the broadest sense. To these verses one would then add any number of more specific sectarian ideas and interpretations and, in this way, capture the flavor of a given Śaiva/Śākta Kula Tantric lineage. *Kulārṇava* verses are quoted by tāntrikas both to support general principles and in the context of very specific arguments and ideas. This is, in fact, one of the text's most appealing characteristics: it can and has been used for nearly every purpose to which one might quote a "scripture." I have not limited the selection to the verses that "all" Śaiva and Śākta tāntrikas might somehow hypothetically agree represent common ideology, but rather have chosen those that provide enough commonly mentioned material to permit a basis for comparison with other texts, lineage practices, and claims of authority. I have avoided a selection that reflects the apparent preference of the *Kulārṇava* itself to define a very particular and authoritative Kula tradition and practice of its own design.

All Hindu Tantras present themselves as very specific and usually highly detailed secret teachings. Śaiva and Śākta Tantras most often appear in the format of revelations of Lord Śiva to his beloved Śakti in answer to her particular queries. In this guise, the Tantras emphasize that what is to be held in general is expressed most precisely by the very particular points of view prescribed in the text. So, for example, by way of demonstrating how Kula practice requires initiation into mantras, the *Kulārṇava* goes into exquisite detail regarding different mantras and the implementation of those mantra practices it regards as defining the path. At stake here is more than the revelation of specific teachings or distinctive Kaula forms of knowledge; at stake is the way a tāntrika learns to generalize, to see the whole from the parts, to become visionary by focusing on a particular subject. In this way, the tāntrika learns generalization not by learning things in general but by extrapolating the general from the particular. The *Kulārṇava* has a penchant for levels of generalization that lead one through the particular.

Historically we find Kaula practitioners, sometimes speaking for lineages, who regard selections of the Tantra's very specific teachings as their own and who vehemently disavow or passively disregard other specifics. At the same time, these individuals may cling to equally selective aspects of the Tantra's broader vision, picking and choosing as their own the themes, issues, attitudes, and practices that the text commends. However, the *Kulārṇava Tantra* is neither definitive nor exhaustive in its presentation of basic Śaiva/Śākta Tantric materials, no matter how authoritative it appears to be for so many traditionalists of different lineage traditions.

What is presented here is, like the full extant text, a feast of the general and the particular, the common and the controversial, the accessible and the esoteric. It would seem that the text presumes selective readings, expansions, emendations, and elisions even as it lays out its specific views and broad sweeping generalizations. Certainly the tāntrikas who today engage the *Kulārṇava* as an authoritative resource are as often reluctant to consider its specifics as they are welcoming of its generalities; however they regard the text as a whole, they select what they wish to emphasize or concentrate upon, and simply leave the rest.

The Tradition of the Kula: Teachings and Practices

The *Kulārṇava Tantra*'s interest in practical methods of self-realization stem from its basic cosmology. The universe is nothing other than the singular, undivided consciousness of God, Śiva, who by his own free will chooses to delimit his nature to experience the joy and ecstasy of his own otherness—his divine complement and consort, Śakti. Śiva is both the material and the efficient cause of creation; nothing exists which is not Śiva. Śakti is his own experience of his original illuminative Self as true reflection or vimarṣa. Śiva chooses to experience his otherness as Śakti for sheer delight, joy, and by the play of his own consciousness. He remains unfettered and unconditioned by the conditions he chooses.

Human beings, however, caught in the web of karma and deluded by the exercise of their own free will, experience themselves as limited, conditioned, and therefore disconnected from the ecstasy of divine consciousness. To put it simply, what God does in limiting himself so that he may enjoy the experience of plurality and diversity, unenlightened human beings experience as their own separateness from the One who becomes the Many.

The universe is God's body and creation is the process by which God assumes two bodies, as Śiva embraces Śakti. The *Kulārṇava* makes clear that human beings must regard their own assumption of embodiment not as a curse of karma but as an opportunity to experience the divine's own forms of embrace. This embrace is the perfect relationship: Śiva in union with Śakti, the guru protecting the loving disciple, the Kula adept committed entirely to the spiritual discipline by which the truth of the Self as God within, and guru as the divine outer form, is fully revealed.

This Tantra maintains that one needs to look to one's own experience as the fundamental test by which the divine relationship and its joys are confirmed. Although texts may instruct and reveal this truth, it is only the example of the guru and the guru's own transmission of this experience that will enable the committed disciple to transform his or her own life into a life of joy and liberation. Thus, the Tantra commends the twin goals of human existence, bhukti, worldly enjoyment, and mukti, ultimate liberation, as its promise to those who keep its secrets and take up its disciplines. The Kula path, it goes on to say, is the sole path that can promise both of these aims in this very lifetime; it is therefore superior to all others. One becomes capable of true enjoyment only to the degree that one is advancing toward liberation; similarly, the liberated are the only ones who experience life's true enjoyment.

To enact this vision of reality, the *Kulārṇava Tantra* places strict requirements on both the aspirant and the Kula guru. The means to achievement are also spelled out in detail. At the heart of the Kula path is initiation into the subtle form of divinity itself: the mantra. *Kulārṇava* teaches specific mantras–several of which are included in this selection and all of which are commended as forms of the supreme consciousness. Its most basic teaching, however, is that these secret mantras form the highest path to divine realization. More than mere means, mantras placed in their proper meditative and ritual contexts are none other than Śakti, whose divine consciousness awakens as the realization of one's own Self in identity with guru and God.

In addition to the mantra, this Tantra endorses the empowerment created by ritually employing the five M words (*makāras*), so called because each begins with *ma* in Sanskrit—wine, fish, meat, fermented grain, and sexual intercourse. The makāras, which induce states proximate to divine ecstasy, reveal divine consciousness as a form of experience that transcends the boundaries of ordinary convention. The heroic adept, in contrast to the mere animalistic person, achieves union with his Śakti by experiencing fully their embodied relationship as a recognition of the one Self in each other. Just as the divine couple are inseparable, so too the true Kula adept experiences all forms of this perfect relationship. With these experiences come the constancy of a state that appears in whatever form or manner of life the perfected yogin adopts. Such uninterrupted states of perfect awareness do not, however, exempt the Kula adept from his vows of secrecy or the need to sustain a practice that reflects outwardly his inward recognition. It is, in the end, the grace of the guru—who from initiation forward has led the Kula disciple to the point where his freedom is as absolute as his discipline is uncompromised—that liberation is realized.

Entering the Ocean of the Heart

The selected verses for translation follow generally the evolution of the Kula teachings as this Tantra presents them in the order of chapters. Certain themes are reiterated in nearly every chapter, and key points are made over and over again. As one studies more deeply the *Kulārṇava Tantra*'s teachings, one experiences more fully the radical nature of this path. The Kula is radical in the sense of its unremitting demands on the adept to make extraordinary efforts and to use extraordinary means to achieve its goals. The goals it sets forth are, in its own view, the most worthwhile, real, and fulfilling one could imagine; one makes every form of consciousness another aspect of the divine's own consciousness of itself. To enter the kula, to penetrate the heart of the divine, is the divine's explicit wish to be united in the ecstasy of its own creative, sustaining, and dissolving experience—at once a unity and a union with its own otherness.

The *Kulārṇava Tantra* was edited with an introduction by Arthur Avalon (Sir John Woodroffe) (reprint Delhi: Motilal Banarsidass, 1965). The verses translated below are based on that edition.

Further Reading

For a discussion of the Kula path as the path of the heart see Paul Muller-Ortega, *The Triadic Heart of Śiva, Kaula Tantricism of Abhinavagupta in the Non-Dual Shaivism of Kashmir* (Albany: State University of New York Press, 1989). For more on the history of Kaula lineages, see Mark S. G. Dyczkowski, *The Canon of the Śaivāgama and the Kubjikā Tantras of the Western Kaula Tradition* (Albany: State University of New York Press, 1988).

SELECTIONS FROM THE *KULĀRṆAVA TANTRA*

THE NATURE OF THE ABSOLUTE AND EMBODIMENT'S CONFUSION

1.7 Śiva, O Goddess, is by his own nature the supreme absolute, without aspects; He is omniscient, the agent of all, lord of all, without any taint and without a second.

1.8 He is his very own light, beginningless and endless, without change, the supreme of the supreme, without qualities, being, consciousness, and bliss. Sentient beings are but a portion of that Śiva: they have come about from their own beginningless ignorance, just as sparks indicate the fire from which they arise.

1.19 One should protect oneself who is the Self of all; the Self is the vessel of the all. For the sake of protection one should make every effort [toward Self-realization], for there is otherwise no true vision of reality.

1.24 For one who does not make every effort for suggestive cures of hell-like bodily diseases here in this body, and so has gone to a place without medicines, what could a person do when such diseases are in place?

1.35 He does not see what he sees, nor even hear what he hears, nor does he know what he recites, and so he is deluded by your māyā.

THE TRUE SPIRITUAL DISCIPLINE: THE SOURCES OF TRUTH AND ERROR

1.42 One should do today what is for tomorrow and what is meant for the latter part of the day in the earlier part of the day. Death does not wait around to see what has been done or has not been done.

1.96 Not knowing that the truth is situated within one's Self, the deluded is confused by looking for it in treatises. One whose judgment is so poor is like the shepherd who sees his goat in a well when it is actually already within the flock.

1.107 The one true knowledge that gives liberation comes from what the guru teaches; all else is imitative, bearing confusion and error. The supreme is the one reality that embodies.

1.109 However, the nondual truth has been spoken by Śiva, freed from rituals and tormenting efforts. Obtained directly from the guru's mouth, it is not otherwise obtained, even by studying tens of thousands of scriptures.

1.115 So long as there is false attachment to the body and so long as there is sense of "mine-ness"; so long as there is no compassion from the guru, how then can there be truth?

THE KULA TEACHING: THE HEART'S SECRET TEACHING

2.6 You must keep this teaching secret; it is not to be given to just anyone but given only to a disciple and to one truly devoted. Otherwise one will surely fall into disaster.

2.7 The Veda is superior. Higher than the Veda is the path that worships Viṣṇu; the worship of Śiva is superior to worship of Viṣṇu; and the Right path is superior to Śiva worship. The Left path is superior to the Right; the Doctrinal path of Śaivism superior to the Left. The Heart path is superior to the Doctrinal, and there is nothing higher than the Heart.

2.9 The most secret of the secret, O Goddess; the most essential of the essential; the best of the best. The Heart path, which comes directly from Śiva, O Goddess, is transmitted from ear to ear.

2.23 In other paths, if one is a yogin, then one cannot be an enjoyer of life. Nor can an enjoyer of life be a yogin. The Heart path has the nature of being for both enjoyment of life and yoga and so, beloved, it is greater than all others.

2.33 The knowledge of the Heart shines in one whose consciousness is pure, peaceful, whose actions serve the guru, who is extremely devoted, and who can keep a secret.

2.50 Even if one performs no other rituals or actions, leaving aside what is commanded according to one's social estate and stage of life, the one who dwells within the Heart is a vessel of enjoyment and liberation, O Goddess of the Heart.

2.68 One yoked to the compassion of the guru, for whom a fallen state has been shaken off by initiation, who finds delight in the worship following the Heart—such a person, O Goddess, comes from the Heart [he is a Kaula], and not another.

2.80 The followers of the Heart, knowers of the essence, do not consider other religion, just as bees who serve themselves the blossom of the coral tree don't seek to obtain other flowers.

THE PATH OF THE MANTRA, THE HIGHEST PATH IS THE HEART PATH

3.49 The supreme mantra that bestows the grace of the Auspicious One (Śrī) is the foundation of the highest path (*urdhvāmnāya*). He who knows this as our supreme form is himself Śiva.

3.50 This mantra is performed, O beloved, with each exhalation [which makes the sound *ham*] and inhalation [which makes the sound *sa*] of breath, repeated by all breathing beings, from Śiva all the way down to the worms.

3.56 Just as the fig tree exists in its subtle form in its incipient seed, so too the three worlds that make up the universe exist within this supreme mantra that bestows supreme grace.

3.63 He who attains loving devotion to the auspicious guru who is my own form is said to achieve the supreme, knowing the supreme mantra that bestows the grace of the auspicious one.

3.82 He who knows the mantra that bestows the grace of the auspicious one knows all mantras, including those belonging to Śiva, Viṣṇu, the Goddess, the sun, Gaṇapati, and the moon.

The esoteric etymology of the mantra, that is, why it is called *prasāda-para* ("grace-giving supreme") is given next, focusing on the two elements of the mantra's name, the prefix *pra-* and the word *para*. Next follow the instructions for "laying down" or nyāsa of the divinities in the form of mantra-names, invoking and placing them within the subtle body. The mudrās or gestures that should accompany the nyāsa process are next mentioned. In this way, the mantra in all its subtle divine forms is identified and invoked onto the subtle body of the Kula practitioner. The details of nyāsa involve the recitation of mantras, gestures of placement on the physical body, and mental identifications. The process of inter-identification brings the ritual of the Kula Dharma into its distinct focus: specific mantras, specific actions and intentions, and specific goals are enunciated. These ritual details need not detain us; more importantly, the text implies their distinctiveness and superiority.

4.12 Performing this inter-identification, O Goddess, wherever a human being goes he shall experience preeminence, benefits, esteem, and human dignity, beloved one.

4.127 Why say too much, O Goddess? This inter-identification is beloved to me. It should not be spoken about to one who is not like a son, nor should it be explained to one who is not a true disciple.

Next follow the ritual prescriptions for the vessels and offerings, including the five M-word substances—māṃsa (flesh), matsya (fish), madya (wine), mudrā (fermented grain), and maithuna (sexual intercourse). These and other offerings are called the kula-dravyas, or heart oblations. They are strictly regulated and their qualifications and benefits detailed. Considered privileged and dangerous, these ritual actions are a distinctive (but not unique) aspect of the Kula path.

THE FIVE M-WORD OBLATIONS ON THE RITUAL PATH OF THE HEART

5.71 Those who offer with loving devotion to us both flesh and drink, they create a blissful experience and, being beloved by us, are the followers of the Heart.

5.72 Our supreme mark—characterized as being, consciousness, and bliss—manifests effulgently when there occurs the true enjoyment of the Kula oblations [the five M-word offerings], and not otherwise.

5.75 For example, just as a dwelling enveloped in darkness becomes lit by a lamp, so the Self covered in Illusion is seen by drinking the oblation [of wine].

5.77 Wine truly is the Terrifying Divinity (Bhairava) and wine is even called Power (Śakti). Ah yes! The enjoyer of wine can delude even the immortals!

5.78 A man who, having drunk a potent wine, is not adversely affected and has become supremely one-pointed in meditation on us, he is liberated and he is the true Follower of the Heart.

5.79 Drink is Power, Śakti; and flesh is Auspicious, Śiva: the Enjoyer becomes the Terrifying One, Bhairava himself. The bliss that arises from this union of the two is called liberation.

5.88 One who serves oneself for the sake of pleasure with wine and the rest is fallen. Having dispensed with one's own lassitudes one should indulge only for the sake of pleasing the gods.

5.89 It is said that indulging in intoxicants such as fish, flesh, and drink, and so on, other than at the time of ritual sacrifice, is prohibited and errant, my beloved.

5.90 Just as the brahman is enjoined to drink intoxicating soma on the occasion of Vedic sacrifice, so drinking wine and the like at prescribed times gives enjoyment and liberation [on the path of the Heart].

5.91 Only when one knows the meaning of the Heart treatises directly from the auspicious guru should one take upon oneself the practice of the five imprinting ritual acts [that is, the five M words], for otherwise one becomes fallen.

5.105 He who practices the five imprinting ritual acts without the proper imprimatur, O Goddess of the Heart, becomes contemptible even though he may experience the Absolute.

5.111 The divine Śakti of animalistic persons is unawakened and that of the follower of the Heart is awakened. One who offers service to that awakened power truly serves Śakti herself.

5.112 One who experiences the bliss of union in sexual relationship as being between the Supreme Power (Parāśakti) and the Self—such a person knows the meaning of sexual relations; others are inferior, indulging only to pursue women.

5.113 Knowing, O entrance of the Heart (*kula-nāyikā*), the true condition of the five imprinting ritual acts in all these ways directly from the mouth of the guru, O Goddess, one truly serves and is liberated.

6.6 Pure in Self and deeply joyous within, bereft of anger and greed, having turned away from the avowed ways of animalistic persons, one should offer sacrificial ritual with a sweet disposition, my beloved.

6.7–8 When by my grace a person has, after a long time, become firm in his feelings of devotion, he should perform the rituals, offering the libations together with the offerings as it has been taught by the Auspicious Terrifying Lord (Śrī Bhairava) and according to the instructions of the guru—for otherwise he will fall.

6.9 One should perform the worship of the auspicious wheel (Śrī Cakra) with the discipline of mantras, O Goddess of Light. Being then in your company I accept that [worship] myself.

6.10 With the experience, "I am the Terrifying Lord," and so possessed of qualities such as omniscience, the lordly yogin should become a performer of the Heart worship.

WORSHIP AND DEITY PRESENCE WITHIN A YANTRA

6.85 A yantra or diagrammatical form is said to consist [actually] of mantras; the deity has the form of mantras as well. The Goddess worshiped in the yantra, O Goddess, is pleased spontaneously.

6.87 As the body is for an embodied soul like oil for a lamp, my beloved, so likewise the yantra is the place of all divinities.

6.88 Therefore, drawing the yantra and meditating on Śiva in the proper manner, and gaining knowledge directly from the guru, one should worship all according to the prescribed rules, my beloved.

Chapters 7 and 8 detail the worship of various deities including Śiva as Baṭuka and the accompanying forms of the Goddess. Included are many of the specific mantras, the yantra prescriptions, and procedures of worship, as well as the benefits and prohibitions of such worship.

AS ARE THE GODS, SO ARE THE WORSHIPERS OF THE HEART

8.106 Just as We the Divine Couple are inseparable; just as the goddess Lakṣmī [is inseparable] from Lord Nārāyaṇa, or the goddess Sarasvatī from Lord Brahmā, so is the Courageous Practitioner with his Śakti consort.

9.3 Meditation is said to be of two sorts, divided accordingly as gross and subtle. The gross sort is said to include a particular form, while the subtle centers on the formless.

9.9 When there is no longer any reflective consciousness and one is as calm as the still sea—the innate form itself being empty—such meditation is called samādhi or Equanimity Consciousness.

9.10 The purely self-illuminating truth is nothing like a cognitive process; one can become that self-illuminating truth instantaneously.

9.22 For one immersed in the state of the singular Self, whatever is done is worship, whatever is recited is a mantra, whatever one sees is a meditation.

9.23 When one has experienced the Supreme Self (Paramātman), the sensation of identifying with bodily consciousness ceases; wherever such a heart goes, there consciousness is in equanimity.

9.24 When the knot of the heart is severed, so all doubts are cut away; and karmas, actions, and intentions—past, present, and future—are destroyed when one sees the Supreme Self from within.

9.41 The body is the abode of God, O Goddess; the embodied self is God, Ever-abiding Śiva (Sadāśiva). Abandon ignorance as if it was old flowers offered in worship and perform worship with the contemplation "I am He," *so'ham*.

9.42 The embodied self is Śiva; Śiva is the embodied self; that embodied self is *only* Śiva. The experience of bondage to one's animal nature is how one thinks of the embodied self; liberated from this animal nature identity one has the experience of the Ever-abiding Śiva.

9.52 Drinking wine, eating flesh, carrying out the practices of one's own initiatory teaching, contemplating the unitive experience of both "I" and "That," so the Heart yogin dwells in true happiness.

9.55 Valuing what is devalued in the world and devaluing what the world values, this the Terrifying Lord who is the supreme Self has pointed out is the path of the Heart.

9.59 There are no commands; there are no prohibitions. There is neither merit nor fall; no heaven and truly no hell for the followers of the Heart, O Goddess of the Heart.

9.62 What is poorly characterized becomes well characterized; otherness becomes one's own heart and what is contrary to righteousness becomes righteous for the followers of the Heart, O Goddess of the Heart.

9.65 Living anywhere, taking on any disguise, and [living] unrecognized by everyone, in whatever social position he may be, he remains a Heart yogin, O Goddess of the Heart.

9.66 Yogins in various guises act for the sake of humanity; they wander the earth, their true nature unrecognized by others.

9.67 They do not reveal their true experience immediately, O Goddess of the

Heart, living in the midst of the world as if they were intoxicated, mute, or just idiots.

9.73 The yogin goes about his own life while the world looks upon him laughing, reproaching, and with contempt, keeping its distance from him.

9.74 The yogin wanders about the ordinary world in different guises, acting on some occasions like a dignified person, sometimes like a vagrant, sometimes like demon or a ghoul!

9.75 The yogin enjoys the pleasures of life only for the sake of serving the world, [and] not out of his own desire. Offering grace to all people, he traverses the earth out of compassion.

9.77 Just as the wind touches everything and space extends everywhere, just as all who bathe in rivers become pure, so the yogin is always pure.

9.81 Wherever the elephant walks becomes a path, and similarly wherever the Heart yogin goes becomes a path, O Goddess of the Heart.

9.88 Whosoever knows the truth of the Heart and is well-versed in the treatises on the Heart should perform the worship of the Heart; he is truly the Heart follower [and] not another, my beloved.

9.90 By initiation (*dīkṣā*) one is a Heart follower who knows the triadic truth [as supreme, ordinary, and both], who surrenders to the auspicious feet of the divine, who possesses the meaning of the root mantras, and who offers loving devotion to God and guru.

9.94 I do not dwell on Mount Kailāsa nor on Meru or Mandara: wherever reside the Heart knowers, I reside there, O my divine contemplation!

9.131 Just as a tree gives up its flowers regardless of [whether it has] once obtained its fruit, so the yogin obtaining the truth gives up attachment to actions and rituals.

Given this statement concerning the state of absolute freedom in which the yogin abides with respect to worldly life and religious requirements, Chapter 10 next describes at length the different occasions for ritual worship and different ritual benefits, violations, and prohibitions. Also mentioned are specific deities, mantras, and manners of worship that the Heart follower may enjoy as part of his privileged spiritual practice.

ULTIMATE IDENTITY AND IDENTIFICATION

13.64 Just as words such as "pot," "vessel," and "jar" all mean the same object [*artha*: goal, meaning, thing], so too are god and mantra and guru said to be the same object.

13.65 Just as divinity is, so is the mantra; just as there is mantra, so there is the guru.

13.66 The fruits of worship are the same for god, mantra, and guru. For the sake of establishing myself in the form of Śiva, I seize upon worship, O Goddess of the Mountain (Pārvatī); for the sake of taking on the form of the guru I break the stranglehold of fear.

SECRECY, INTIMACY, AND PRIVACY ON THE HEART PATH

10.44 One should not enunciate the guru's name except at the time of ritual recitation, my beloved, calling him instead over the course of spiritual life by such titles as Auspicious Lord, Deity, and Svāmī, and the like.

10.45 One should not tell anyone other than one's own disciple the mantras praising the guru's sandals, the imprinting gestures, the root mantra, and one's own grace-giving sandal mantra.

10.46 Lineage, scripture, levels of teaching, the practice of mantras, and such must all be obtained directly from the guru in order to bear fruit—and not otherwise.

14.3 Without initiation, there can be no liberation: This has been said in the sacred Śiva teachings. And there can be no initiation without the preceptor of a lineage.

14.7 Therefore one should make every effort to seek always the guru of unbroken lineage who is in origin the immediate Supreme Śiva.

14.14 The experiential knowledge of the mantra cannot establish itself in the unworthy. So there should be an examination of the disciple; otherwise [initiation, worship, and knowledge] bear no fruits.

14.30 Those persons who at the outset have no true loving devotion, who then in the midst of their spiritual practice gain loving devotion, and at the end experience the expansion of loving devotion, they assimilate the inner practice of yoga.

14.34 Initiation, you will recall O Goddess, is threefold: It is given by touch, by deliberate sight, and by mere mental intention without acts, ritual, efforts, or any other such things, great Goddess!

14.38 The disciple becomes worthy of grace by stepping into the current of the divine Śakti's initiatory power; where Śakti does not descend, no accomplishment can be claimed.

14.78 Initiation is said to be twofold, divided accordingly as outward and inner. Initiation into actions such as ritual is the outer; the inner one creates the experience of pervasive penetration into one's being.

14.86 That initiation by which those who indulge themselves in their animalistic nature become Śivas, opening the eyes to the Self, O Goddess: that is liberation from the noose of being a mere animal.

14.97 O Goddess, for one who is without initiation there is no fulfillment nor true path. So by every effort one should seek initiation from a guru.

LIBERATION IS THE EXPERIENCE OF THE HEART

15.19 There are innumerable hundreds of thousands of mantras and they unsettle the heart of one's own divine consciousness. The one mantra obtained by the grace of the guru will provide every goal and accomplishment.

15.34 Placing oneself in postures such as the lotus, the cross-legged, or warrior pose, one should perform repetition of the mantra and offer worship. Otherwise [initiation, grace, and effort] will bear no fruit.

15.113 One should perform the recitation of the mantra by fixing oneself on it, with life breath coursing through it, setting it within one's consciousness, and making the deep connections that form the meaning of its syllables.

THE NATURE OF THE DIVINE AS MANTRA IMPARTS THE SUPREME GRACE

16.40ab Male divinities' mantras are called mantras while those of female divinities are called vidyās, my beloved.

16.116 One who knows the mantra of supreme grace is liberated whether he dwells in a place of true pilgrimage, or a place without means to ford across the world, or even in the midst of the ocean of worldliness—there is no doubt about it.

17.102 This treatise called the Ocean of the Heart exists within the heart of divine yoginīs. I have illumined it today; and with true effort it should be kept secret.

—21—

Tantric Buddhism and Chinese Thought in East Asia

Fabio Rambelli

The text translated below from the Chinese, entitled *Ritual of the Secret Dhāraṇīs of the Three Siddhis for the Destruction of Hell, the Transformation of Karmic Hindrances, and the Liberation from the Three Conditioned Worlds* (hereafter, *Ritual*), is a short but comprehensive summary of the doctrines and meditative practices of East Asian esoteric Buddhism. The ideas and practices presented in this text circulated in various forms in China between the late Tang and the early Song periods (ninth and tenth centuries), and became very influential in Japan from the twelfth century onward. The earliest known surviving versions were edited in Japan in the early nineteenth century.

The origin of the *Ritual* is obscure: no official Chinese catalogues of Buddhist texts of the Tang period mentions it, and its title does not appear in any Japanese records until the late ninth century. Direct citations from the text appear only in much later works, composed in Japan between the eleventh and the twelfth centuries, particularly those by the Shingon monk Kakuban (1095–1143) and the Zen monk Yōsai (1141–1215). Under its title the *Ritual* includes the note "translated at the imperial behest by Śubhakarasiṁha Tripitaka from Central India," but this attribution is dubious. Śubhakarasiṁha (Shanwuwei, in Chinese: 637–735), traditionally considered to be the founder of the Tantric Buddhist tradition in China, did translate several Tantric works, among them the *Mahavairocana Sūtra*, but it seems unlikely that he was involved in the production of this text. One of the main reasons for which the traditional attribution to Śubhakarasiṁha has been questioned is the content of the *Ritual*. It contains an advanced combination of Indian Tantric teachings and practices and Chinese doctrines and rituals, mainly drawn from medicine (especially from such texts as the *Huang-di nei jing su wen*) and Daoism. Not only is the *Ritual* obviously not a translation from the Sanskrit but the first Tantric patriarch in China could not possibly have been responsible for such an advanced form of religious and cultural syncretism.

Scholars have therefore moved the *Ritual*'s probable date of composition to the late Tang period (first half of the ninth century). The reference to Śubhakarasiṁha, however, is not completely arbitrary. The *Ritual* is in fact heavily influenced by the susiddhi ("perfect siddhi" or perfect spiritual attainment) textual lineage centered on the *Susiddhikara Sūtra*, translated into Chinese by the Tantric patriarch. This textual tradition was popular in China during the late Tang period and became very influential in Japan, especially in the Tendai school of esoteric Buddhism. Recently, it has been suggested that this text may actually have been composed in Japan.

Apart from Chinese medical and Daoist elements, the body of the *Ritual* consists of citations from Tantric texts. Its patchwork-like nature makes this text particularly interesting as a summary of late Tang Tantric doctrines and practices, which later became the template of Japanese esoteric Buddhism and also influenced such aspects of cultural life in medieval Japan as music, linguistics, poetry. The confluence of Tantric Buddhism and Daoism in the *Ritual*, with its systematic correlation of Indian doctrines and practices with doctrines and practices from the Chinese tradition, offers historians of religion an example of cultural interaction. This text also shows the dynamism of the Tantric tradition which, despite its marginal origins, nevertheless became one of the central cultural formations in several regions of the East Asian world.

The main protagonists of the *Ritual* are the five buddhas located on the lotus flower at the center of the Womb maṇḍala and, in various combinations, also in the Vajra maṇḍala (see below). Each represents or embodies some characteristics of the soteriological processes at play in Tantric Buddhism, especially the steps leading to enlightenment and the five types of wisdom acquired through it. Mahāvairocana, the cosmic buddha of East Asian Tantric Buddhism, is the most important among them. Situated at the center of the maṇḍala (see below), he represents both the principle of enlightenment and the whole range of powers associated with it. All around him are the so-called four buddhas. Below him, to the east, is Akṣobhya, to the south is Ratnasaṃbhava, to the west is Amitābha, and to the north is Amoghasiddhi. These buddhas are usually referred to in the text with the honorific title of "tathāgata," meaning "the one who came to this world form the realm of truth" or "the one who came to this world in the same way as the buddhas of the past." The five buddhas serve as the reference point for a number of five-elements cosmic series that structure the Tantric universe and guide the practitioners in their meditations.

As we will see, the practices described in the text enable the practitioners to identify themselves with Mahāvairocana, the paradigmatic buddha of esoteric Buddhism. The text makes several references to the doctrines concerning the nature and characteristics of the buddha. For example, "Buddha body" refers to the buddha's superhuman body, characterized by thirty-two major signs and eighty-eight lesser marks (even though the text also calls a Buddha body the body of the practitioner who has successfully completed the cycle of meditations it describes); "Buddha land" is the paradisiacal pure land ruled by a perfected buddha who preaches the Law and leads beings to salvation; and the "Buddha assembly" is a synonym for maṇḍala.

A maṇḍala is a Tantric representation of the Dharmadhātu, the enlightened universe. In this image, the most representative buddhas, bodhisattvas, and other beings are ordered according to a geometrical pattern. Although a maṇḍala is usually painted, three-dimensional maṇḍalas also exist. East Asian esoteric Buddhism acknowledges two paradigmatic forms of maṇḍala, respectively the Womb maṇḍala and the Vajra maṇḍala. The Womb maṇḍala uses the imagery of womb and fetus to represent both the compassionate soteriological activity of the Buddha that permeates the entire universe and the principle of universal salvation. In contrast, the Vajra maṇḍala represents the absolute wisdom attained by the practitioner with enlightenment, symbolized by the vajra ("diamond" or "thunderbolt"). Both maṇḍalas are divided into "sections" centered on a specific buddha or bodhisattva who represents various aspects of the enlightened cosmos. In this text, as in most esoteric Buddhist materials in East Asia, the term *vajra* is often used without direct reference to the Vajra maṇḍala and its related doctrines, but simply as a marker of Tantric discourse to signify something noble, superior, particularly powerful, and efficacious for salvation. In these cases, vajra is translated in the text below as "adamantine."

As mentioned before, the five buddhas are located on the eight-petaled lotus at the center of the Womb maṇḍala. The lotus is a very important metaphor in Buddhism; the fact that the lotus has its roots in the mud of putrid ponds but develops into a beautiful and pure white flower was primarily used to represent the process of enlightenment. The lotus was later associated with the human heart (*hṛdaya*)—the bodily location of the mind (*citta*) and the physical site at which enlightenment takes place. Indian and Chinese physicians noted a morphological resemblance of the lotus to the heart. As the *Ritual* says, "the shape of the heart of ordinary people is like a closed lotus. . . . In visualization one should open one's heart to form a white lotus with eight petals." Enlightenment results from opening one's heart by means of meditative practices, to reveal within it the shape of the eight-petaled lotus found at the center of the maṇḍala. As a support for meditation, the practitioner uses a white disk representing both the moon as a metaphor for the eight-petaled lotus (which is painted in an almost circular way) and the heart of the practitioner himself, as well as the pure enlightened mind achieved through such practice. Thus, through visualization the ascetic modifies his body/mind to embody enlightenment. In this practice, soteriology merges with physiology: indeed, bodily metaphors of the heart became an important part of the doctrines of bodhicitta, literally "the mind (*citta*) of enlightenment (*bodhi*)." This key concept refers first of all to the "thought of enlightenment," that is, the desire to be saved and to engage in Buddhist practice. This is the very beginning of the individual process of salvation, and therefore it is a very important moment. In East Asia, however, bodhicitta is often interpreted literally as "the mind of enlightenment." In this context, one can arouse the desire of enlightenment because all sentient beings have an innate principle of enlightenment. In other words, we are "always already" enlightened, but we just don't know it. Practice thus becomes a process toward the self-awareness of one's innate buddhahood. Tantric Buddhism added a further important layer of meaning: in a coherent nondualistic fashion it stressed that if everyone is innately enlightened, then the initial desire for enlightenment (*bodhicitta*) is already the final goal of practice. This move enabled Tantric Buddhism to emphasize the possibility of attaining salvation in the present life—or, as the well-known Japanese definition has it, to "become buddha in this very body."

The eight-petaled lotus at the center of maṇḍala, where the five buddhas and their retinue are located, is often described in Tantric literature (and in this text) as the Dharmadhātu Palace, the cosmic palace where the buddha Mahāvairocana, surrounded by the other buddhas, bodhisattvas, and all kinds of beings, meditates and preaches. Dharmadhātu, literally "Dharma element," refers to the absolute reality experienced in enlightenment (the realm of absolute truth, translated in Chinese as "the realm of Dharma"). Dharma refers primarily to the Buddhist teachings, but also to the underlying cosmic principles (the absolute Truth) that the Buddha explained; it also refers, when translated as a noncapitalized and often plural term (*dharmas*), to the constituent elements of reality ("things" or "entities" in general, ranging from material objects to thoughts, mental factors, immaterial relations, and spiritual entities such as nirvāṇa). Because of the complex meaning of the term *dharma,* and because all beings in the universe possess, as we have already noted, the Buddha nature (the innate principle of buddhahood), the term "realm of Dharma" came to be used in Chinese and Japanese texts to refer to the totality of the cosmos as sharing an underlying common principle and/or material substance. This was one of the major innovations of East Asian Buddhism, probably mediated from Chinese cosmological and philosophical doctrines. Once the universe was envisioned as sharing an underlying substance and principles, it became possible to speak of Mahāvairocana's "Dharmadhātu body," constituted by the six elements of reality (earth, water, fire, wind, space, and consciousness). Thus, the entire universe came to be understood as the body of the primary Tantric Buddha, and ascetics could then seek to reproduce such a cosmic body within themselves through the performance of Tantric practices such as those described in the *Ritual*.

In this sense, Dharmadhātu-body is a synonym of another complex term, "Dharmakāya." Literally "the body of absolute truth," it originally referred to what was left behind in this world by the historical Buddha (Gautama Śākyamuni) after his extinction: teachings, later preserved as written texts, relics, and traces of various kinds. This notion of a "body of truth" later appears in the doctrines on the nature and status of the Buddha body, as paradoxically referring to the transcendental, unconditioned aspects of the Buddha. Mahāyāna Buddhism developed the doctrine of three bodies of the Buddha, according to which Buddha exists and manifests himself according to three different modalities: Dharmakāya, Saṃbhogakāya, and Nirmāṇakāya. The latter two bodies have forms. The Saṃbhogakāya (Enjoyment body) is the Buddha body that the ascetic sees as a reward for his countless practices; it transcends the perceptive and mental faculties of common, deluded people and can be perceived only by bodhisattvas. The Nirmāṇakāya (Manifestation body) is the physical body in which the Buddha appears in this world to beings of lesser faculties such as gods, humans, and animals. It is but a shadow of the splendor of Saṃbhogakāya, but it is the only way to lead ignorant beings to salvation. The Dharmakāya is absolute, unconditioned, and formless. It cannot be perceived or known, but is postulated as the substratum of all activities of the buddhas. Tantric Buddhism further distinguishes between the Dharmakāya of Principle and Dharmakāya of Wisdom, a distinction that reflects the cosmological and soteriological implications of absolute truth (the principle) and knowledge (wisdom).

An important contribution of East Asian Tantric Buddhism to the doctrine of the Buddha bodies, brought about especially by certain Shingon lineages in Japan, is a change in the status of the Dharmakāya from a formless and signless entity to an immanent cosmic repository of all possible forms and signs. According to this vision, the entire universe (the Dharmadhātu) as the "body" of Mahāvairocana (Dharmadhātu-body or Dharmakāya) is an immense semiotic machine, a sort of pansemiotic cosmos, continuously and eternally engaged in preaching the Law to all beings and, ultimately, to itself for the sheer pleasure of listening to it. The *Ritual* was one of the key texts for such a development. Thus, Buddhism changed from a doctrine of renunciation into a performance affecting all senses and involving the entire universe. The status of salvation was modified by this change, as is shown by the *Ritual*, in which complex meditative and ritual practices leading to salvation have the status of multimedia performances, as it were, involving sounds, visions, lighting effects, the aroma of incense, and architectural setting.

The *Ritual* is essentially a set of instructions regarding three short mantras and related formulae; as such, the text is characterized by the intermingling of the language of commentary and the language of ritual. It outlines the conceptual background and describes the ritual procedures that may enable one to afford the ultimate soteriological goal of esoteric Buddhism, namely to identify oneself with the buddha Mahāvairocana. The structure of the *Ritual* is as follows: first, the Tantric-Daoist cosmology of the human body is presented, with all the complex correlations governing it and the practices necessary to maintain balance. Then, the three siddhis (spiritual attainments) and the respective mantras are introduced. The text then describes the production of the "living-body relic"—the meditative destruction of the ascetic's ordinary body and the creation of a stūpa-like cosmic body. As the text puts it, "From the letter *A* comes out the syllable *ra*, which burns one's body and reduces it to ashes. From the ashes the syllable *va* is generated. . . . From it . . . the mantra of the five elements [of the cosmic stūpa] is produced. This mantra takes its place on the five parts of the body. . . . This is the pure bodhicitta." The visualizations proceed to ensure the embodiment of both Womb and Vajra maṇḍalas. The *Ritual* finally concludes with a vast cosmic vision of absolute nondualism. In a way, the text reproduces the meditative process and its results.

The practices here described consist mainly in visualizing the universe as a five-element stūpa, also called *caitya* in the text. The stūpa in India is a funerary monument, sometime of large dimensions, that enshrines relics of the Buddha. It symbolizes the formless body of the Buddha and the essential structure of the cosmos. East Asian stūpas are usually wooden towers, known in English as pagodas, which enshrine relics or other sacred objects. The stūpa described in this text, however, is a vertical object in the form of a pagoda composed of five elements (from bottom to top: square, triangle, circle, crescent, and sphere), used as a meditation support. The type of stūpa described in the text is still used in Japanese cemeteries as a small memorial monument. Through the meditations presented in the *Ritual*, the ascetic will reconfigure his body as a stūpa, the mystical body of Mahāvairocana, and thereby become a buddha himself.

Such a goal is achieved through complex visualizations, based on multiple interrelations of several subtle substances (breath, light, sound, writing, and so on), in which the hidden structure of the entire universe is recreated and embodied by the ascetic through meditation on his body. The universe of the *Ritual* is organized on interconnected series of five elements that form closed causal chains. For example, the text correlates the five buddhas, the five stages of the enlightenment process, and the five wisdoms thereby attained, with the cosmic elements (earth, water, fire, wind, and space), the five directions, the five seasons (the four usual seasons plus an intercalary period), the five aggregates (the *skandhas*, the psycho-physical constituents of reality), the five viscera, the five souls, the five phases (*wuxing* in Chinese: the five natural elements according to the Chinese cosmology, namely, earth, fire, water, wood, and metal), and so forth. The body is the privileged site for the experience of such a cosmic structure. Once mastered and embodied through initiation, knowledge, and ritual action, cosmology opens the way to liberation. Such a recursive cosmology is directly reflected in soteriology, as we will see below.

There are essentially two sets of meditations on the body. Whereas one set focuses on the internal structure as envisioned by Chinese medicine (the five viscera), the other set consists in the visualization of three external areas of the body, which are the sites of the "three siddhis" mentioned in the title of the text. Siddhi, meaning "achievement, completion," refers here to different kinds of spiritual attainment and enlightenment. The three siddhis are: the "intruding siddhi," centered in the abdomen; the "protruding siddhi," centered in the heart; and the "perfect siddhi," centered in the top of the head (*uṣṇīṣa*), the location of supreme wisdom. Each of these is related to a specific mantra, a formula used as a meditation support in which are condensed the spiritual powers of the deity it represents. These mantras are, respectively, *a ra pa ca na*; *a vi ra hūṃ khaṃ*; and *a vaṃ raṃ haṃ khaṃ*. By focusing intensely on a mantra's written forms, sounds, and meanings, the practitioner is able to embody and control the mantra's deity.

The sites of the three siddhis in the body correspond to the locations of the three "cinnabar fields" (*dantian*) in Daoism. According to Daoist medical soteriology, control of these three centers of pure energy enables the practitioner to achieve liberation from the coarse body and become an "Immortal" (*xianren*). The impact of Daoist soteriology and, more generally speaking, of Chinese cosmic anthropology, is evident in the *Ritual*, in which the correlations uniting human body and external reality are discussed in detail. By becoming aware of the profound relation between the individual and the universe, the initiate is able to control the cosmic forces and, as a consequence, to embody the cosmos—which, as we have seen, is actually a stūpa, a reliquary body. It should be noted that the soteriological transformation of the practitioner's body into a Buddha body is described in the text as an effect of an "empowerment" (*adhiṣṭhāna* in Sanskrit, *jiachi* in Chinese, *kaji* in Japanese) that results from the ascetic's interaction with the Buddha.

Besides describing the procedures for salvation, the text also mentions the benefits gained through ritual manipulation of the three mantras that constitute its nucleus: wealth, health, and longevity for the practitioner; peace and strong political authority for the country. These are typical Tantric benefits: support of state and imperial power; worldly benefits; and individual salvation in the present life. Protection, in particular, is ensured by the activity of Dharma-protectors, supernatural figures whom the ascetic is able to control through the correct performance of ritual.

Descriptions of visualizations, in which several semiotic substances are manipulated in complex ways in order to effect a transformation of the practitioner's body and universe, occupy the major part of the text. However, these meditations are not an end in themselves. The text is not only concerned with individual spiritual experience but also presents a complex picture of the relationships linking religious knowledge and practices to other fields of social and cultural life, in particular cosmology, epistemology, semiotics, soteriology, and politics and state ideology. We now discuss briefly each of these fields as they are treated in the texts.

The *Ritual* combines Tantric Buddhist ideas and practices with a vocabulary and a repertoire of images, metaphors, and procedures borrowed from Daoism and Chinese culture in general in order to provide a more concrete, bodily description of the processes that lead one to become a buddha. It is interesting to note that the Buddha is characterized in these texts as a sort of Daoist immortal, endowed with a perfect body that is a condensation of the entire universe. In particular, the *Ritual* presents breathing techniques of Daoist origin aimed at harmonizing the various forms of breath-energy (*qi*) inside the body. In addition, visualization of bodily organs and mental apparatus and their relations transforms the body (or rather, the body-mind complex) into a replica of the cosmos.

According to both Indian Tantra and traditional Chinese medicine, the human body is a microcosm. The *Ritual* privileges the Chinese vision of the body as the locus for enlightenment. The central apparatus of the body, the five viscera (liver, lungs, heart, kidneys, and spleen), is directly related to the five phases (wood, metal, fire, water, earth) in the external world. The five viscera also control five souls or spiritual functions of the human organism, namely, the celestial soul (*hun*, in Chinese), the terrestrial soul (*po*), the superior soul (*shen*), the will (*shi*), and the ideas (*yi*), which are produced by different configurations of the *qi* (cosmic breath/energy). Another important network of organs in the body, mentioned only in passing in the text, is constituted by the six receptacles (*liufu*, in Chinese). Whereas the five viscera are basically repositories of breath/energy, the six receptacles function as centers of consumption.

Based as it is on the manipulation of images, signs, and ritual objects, the bodily and mental soteriological process described in the text is primarily semiotic, culminating in the production of a perfect body, a "living-body relic" which, as we have seen, is a condensation of the entire universe. It is possible that the teachings in the *Ritual* and other cognate texts were connected with East Asian practices of self-mummification, by which ascetics sought to achieve a Buddha body in the present lifetime. These ascetics, called sokushinbutsu ("buddhas in their present body") in Japanese, aimed to turn their body into the ultimate stūpa-like, whole-body relic.

The meditative technology described in the text implies a particular kind of semiotics, in which there is no distinction between the practitioner, the signs and symbolic objects he employs, their meanings, and the external reality (the deities of the maṇḍala and, ultimately, the entire Dharmadhātu) to which they refer. The characteristic circularity of esoteric Buddhist practices is particularly apparent in the text: the tool of meditation (the moon-disk maṇḍala) is equivalent to the part of the body it affects (the heart/mind), to the mental functions on which it operates (the apparatus of consciousness), and finally to the results achieved (the three siddhis and the three bodies of the Buddha). On the other hand, it is coextensive as a maṇḍala with the entire universe (Dharmadhātu), the mind, and the substance of semiotic activity (the Sanskrit letter A). As a result of such circularity, salvation is continuously produced and certainly realized. The *Ritual* is a good indication that the soteriology of Tantric Buddhism in East Asia is based on semiotic practices, in which symbols are manipulated in meditation and ritual action. The text attributes enormous importance to language, especially the absolute language of mantras, and to the development of particular macrosemiotic formations composed of a variety of semiotic substances and objects organized in a quinary series, in which each component is an alloform of all the others. The previously mentioned stūpa (or caitya) is one of these macrosigns. Another macrosign, related to the previous one, but based on a nine-element system, is the maṇḍala complex of "moon-heart-lotus" that constitutes a rich support for the practices described in the text.

It is precisely the mastering of these macrosemiotic formations that enables one to attain the goals of practice, be they salvation or this-worldly benefits. In other words, attainment requires initiation; and initiation, as an act generating symbolic capital, is directly related to power strategies. This is what is meant by this text when it warns against careless transmission; easy availability would reduce its symbolic potential. The text is also explicit about its political position: it ensures both individual salvation and the protection of the state. In other words, it presents itself as a tool for state government against rebellious or revolutionary movements. It is not surprising, then, that this text and its variants became one of the ideological pillars of institutional Buddhism in medieval Japan, which described imperial institutions as inseparable from the Buddhist establishment, and which effected a general "mandalization" of state territories, as well as of numerous intellectual and productive practices, thereby turning Japan into a veritable geopolitical maṇḍala. Some of the presuppositions of such a cultural and ideological policy are to be found in the *Ritual* translated below.

The *Ritual*, as it appears in the Taishō Canon (vol. 18, no. 905) and in the Manji Zokuzōkyō (no. 102), is a reprint of older versions published in Japan in the early nineteenth century and based on earlier manuscripts preserved in different temples and copied by several people. Those early manuscripts appear to have been very corrupt. Even though the copyists tried to amend the texts, several mistakes, repetitions, and obscure expressions still appear in the modern published versions. In addition to relying on the aforementioned editions, my translation is based on the partially annotated version of Kanbayashi Ryujo in *Kokuyaku issaikyō: Mikkyōbu* (Tokyo: Daito shuppansha, 1931), vol. 3, pp. 95–111 (which contains a few additional errors). I have made some emendations, for which I am fully responsible. Significant variants, original terms, as well as my explanatory comments have been added in square brackets. Except where indicated, all terms found in italics are Sanskrit.

Further Reading

On esoteric Buddhism in East Asia, see Yamasaki Taiko, *Shingon: Japanese Esoteric Buddhism* (Boston and London: Shambhala, 1988), and Michel Strickmann, *Mantras et mandarins. Le bouddhisme tantrique en Chine* (Paris: Gallimard, 1996). On the semiotics of esoteric Buddhism, see Fabio Rambelli, "Re-inscribing Maṇḍala," *Studies in Central and East Asian Religions* 4 (1991): 1–24; and Rambelli, "Mastering the Invisible," *Japanese Religions* (forthcoming). On the issue of self-mummified buddhas in East Asia, see Bernard Faure, *The Rhetoric of Immediacy* (Princeton: Princeton University Press, 1991), especially pp. 148–78. For an introduction to Taoist ideas and practices concerning the body, see Kristofer Schipper, *The Taoist Body* (Berkeley and Los Angeles: University of California Press, 1982); and Isabelle Robinet, *Méditation taoïste* (Paris: Dervy Livres, 1979). On Chinese medicine, see Paul U. Unschuld, *Medicine in China* (Berkeley and Los Angeles: University of California Press, 1985). The *Huang-di su wen nei jing*, on which many notions of the *Ritual* are based, is translated in Ilza Veith, ed., *The Yellow Emperor's Classic of Internal Medicine* (Berkeley and Los Angeles: University of California Press, 1972). For a history of the *Ritual*, see Jinhua Chen, "The Construction of Early Tendai Esoteric Buddhism," *Journal of the International Association of Buddhist Studies* 21.1 (1998):21–76.

Ritual of the Secret Dhāraṇīs of the Three Siddhis for the Destruction of Hell, the Transformation of Karmic Hindrances, and the Liberation from the Three Conditioned Worlds

Translated at the Imperial Behest by Śubhakarasiṁha Tripitaka from Central India

In the practice of yoga there are a thousand ways, but only a small part of them will be mentioned here. When [Mahāvairocana] opens his mouth and moves his tongue, the Dharmadhātu Palace shakes. All the tathāgatas in the Realm of the Lotus Receptacle emerge from samādhi, hell is destroyed, karmic hindrances are transformed positively, and beings are freed from the threefold conditioned world. One should know that if the Sanskrit letters are properly inscribed on the crown of the king, the ten thousand countries will be pacified. If mantras are written on the banners of the envoys from the central government, the four directions will be peaceful and provincial governors will be under control. Also, if Sanskrit letters are written on drums and shell trumpets [used to give orders in battle], the severe sound of authority will be heard from afar. Evil spirits will be purified, order will reign over a thousand leagues, crops will be abundant, and the people will not suffer calamities and diseases; the deities [will be benevolent], and the weather will be regular. If written upon war drums after empowerment, through visualization and chanting, the armies of the enemies will spontaneously surrender without casualties. Such drums can be called Adamantine drums.

The pure eyes of Vairocana Buddha,
open, are like lotus flowers.
I bow deeply to the master of gods and humans of the three worlds,
the savior with the great bodhicitta.
The sublime Teachings of Mantric Empowerment [that is, esoteric Buddhism]
consist in flowing into the gate of letter A, the unborn.
The [light of the] signless universal knowledge emitted by the curl between the Buddha's eyebrows
permeates and illuminates everywhere, like the sun and the moon;
The karmic activities of body, speech, and mind become the three mysteries
and the three mysteries become the Dharma of the Nirmāṇakāya.
The five natural elements and the five wisdoms become the five parts [five-syllable mantra],
and the five parts completely contain the entire Dharmadhātu.
[The four buddhas] Akṣobhya, the savior of the world Ratnasaṃbhava,
Amitābha, the king Amoghasiddhi,
form the auspicious circle of the siddhi,
transmit this sublime Dharma and convert all living beings;

Trailokyavijaya, the compassionate one with infinite powers,
Vajrasattva, the venerable Acalanātha,
without breaking their vow, at the right time,
when the practice of yoga is finished, return to the Diamond Realm.

The Buddha says:

The letter A corresponds to [Akṣobhya's] Vajra Section and controls the liver. The letter A is Mahāvairocana Tathāgata as Dharmakāya of principle, the originally pure, ultimate, and ungraspable emptiness [one version adds: the great bodhicitta innate in all sentient beings]. It is the seed of the adamantine element earth, the mantra of the Vajra section. In terms of names-and-forms [*nāma-rūpa*], the earth is the forms. Among the five psychophysical aggregates it is forms, that is the body, that controls earth. Its seed is impure. In other words, the five viscera are material dharmas, and since they arise out of the aggregate of forms, in terms of names-and-forms, the earth corresponds to the forms. The liver controls the celestial soul [*hun* in Chinese]. The breath/energy [*qi*] of the *hun* soul becomes the east and wood. Wood is the color of the sky. Wood controls the spring, and its color is green/blue. Green-blue breath is generated by wood, and wood is generated by water. The liver is generated by green-blue breath and by the kidneys; its shape is like a lotus leaf in vertical position. At the center is located the heart. The flesh heart is in the left part of the chest. The liver protrudes outside and becomes the eyes; it also controls the muscles. The muscles stretch out and become the nails. Now, because the five syllables control the five viscera and the six receptacles, inside and outside intermingle, as will be explained. If an excessive amount of sour flavor enters the liver, the liver benefits but the spleen suffers. Should there be no *hun* soul in the liver, one would lose sensibility and the lungs would damage the liver, thus causing an illness. Just as metal overcomes wood, if the lungs are strong the liver is weak. One should be careful with the lungs. If green-blue breath absorbs white breath, the diseases of the liver heal, because green-blue breath predominates.

The syllable *vaṃ* corresponds to [Amithāba's] Lotus Section and controls the lungs. The syllable *vaṃ* is the eleventh transformation of the letter *va;* the syllable *vi* is the third transformation. Its meaning is a development of the meaning of the letter A. In other words, *vaṃ* is the seed of the ring of the element water, the sea of wisdom of Mahāvairocana Tathāgata. The Dharmakāya of Wisdom, as well as the Saṃbhogakāya, have unconditioned supernatural powers. *Vaṃ* is the mantra of the Lotus section. The lungs control the terrestrial soul [*po* in Chinese]. The shape of the *po* is like a flower. It controls the nose and corresponds to the west and to metal. Metal controls autumn, and its color is white. The color white is generated from wind, and wind is generated from the yang breath of earth. Among the five aggregates, it is discerning that controls wind. Discerning is generated from consciousness; consciousness is generated from past intentions; past intentions are generated from ignorance; ignorance is generated from false views; false views in turn are generated from other false views. This is the cycle of twelve causal factors. The lungs are generated from white breath and the spleen. If an excessive amount of spicy flavor enters the lungs, the lungs will benefit but the liver will suffer. Should there be no *po* soul in the lungs, one would become insanely frightened; the heart would damage the lungs, thus causing illness. Just as fire overcomes metal, if the heart is strong the lungs are weak. One should be careful with the heart. If white breath absorbs red breath, the diseases of the lungs heal. White breath is another name for the lungs.

The syllable *raṃ* corresponds to [Ratnasaṃbhava's] Treasure section and controls the heart. The syllable *raṃ* sows the seed of the fire element in Mahāvairocana Tathāgata's pure mind. Fire, being the abode of the buddhas of all times, burns ignorance, defilements, and delusory attachments accumulated by sentient beings over a beginningless period of time, and generates the seeds of bodhicitta. The meaning of the syllable *raṃ* is a development of the meaning of the letter A. In other words, since it represents the Tathāgata as Nirmāṇakāya, *raṃ* truly is the fire maṇḍala [or mantra, that is, the maṇḍala/mantra of Acalanātha's samādhi] of the Dharmakāya of Wisdoṃ. The heart controls the superior soul [*shen* in Chinese], and its shape is like a bird. South is fire, and fire controls the summer. Its color is red. Red is generated from fire; fire is generated from wood. Among the five aggregates it is perception that controls fire; perception is produced by ideation. Moreover, the heart is generated from red breath and the liver. The heart protrudes outside and becomes the tongue; the heart further controls the blood; the blood stretches outside and becomes milk. It also controls the ear, and turns into the nostrils, the septum of the nose, the jaws, and the chin. If an excessive amount of bitter flavor enters the heart, the heart will benefit but the lungs will suffer. Should there be no *shen* soul in the heart, one would lose the sense of time; the kidneys would damage the heart, thus causing an illness. Just as water overcomes fire, if the kidneys are strong the heart is weak. One should be careful with the kidneys. If red breath absorbs black breath, the diseases of the heart heal. Red breath is the syllable *raṃ*.

The syllable *haṃ* corresponds to [Amoghasiddhi's] Karma section and controls the kidneys. The syllable *hūṃ* is another transformation of the syllable *ha*. *Haṃ* means that Mahāvairocana Tathāgata always abides on the seed of the element wind and longevity. Since the three gates of liberation refer to the fact that time is ungraspable, *haṃ* is the maṇḍala/mantra of the great power of the Dharmakāya. Wind is controlled by the aggregate of discerning. The five viscera are: liver, the lungs, heart, spleen, and the kidneys. The stomach is one of the six receptacles; it is the belly, that is, the one among the six receptacles corresponding to the spleen; it is the sea located within the five viscera and the six receptacles. All water enters the stomach, which distributes it to the five viscera and the other receptacles. The five flavors circulate inside the body, and since the best among them enter the stomach first, the kidneys in particular receive them from the stomach. The kidneys are located below the waist and the navel; the one to the left is the kidney proper; the one to the right is called

Gate of Life. They lie upon the abdomen [that is, on the stomach]; when they stretch out they become sperm. The kidneys control the will [*shi* in Chinese], and correspond to the north and water. Water controls winter, and its color is black. Among the five aggregates it is intention that controls water. Intention is generated from perception, and perception is generated from discerning. The kidneys are generated from black breath and the lungs, and control the ear. The kidneys protrude outside and become the bones which control the marrow. The marrow stretches out and becomes the ear holes. The bones in turn stretch out and become the teeth. If an excessive amount of salty flavor enters the kidneys, the kidneys will benefit but the heart will suffer. Should there be no *shi* soul in the kidneys, one will be sad and cry; the spleen will damage the kidneys, thus causing illness. Just as earth overcomes water, if the spleen is strong, the kidneys are weak. One should be careful with the spleen. If black breath absorbs yellow breath, the diseases of the kidneys heal. Black breath is the syllable *haṃ*.

The syllable *khaṃ* corresponds to [Mahāvairocana's] Void section and controls the spleen. The syllable *khaṃ* is the invisible *uṣṇīṣa* [that is, the top of the head, one of the marks of the Buddha representing enlightenment] of Mahāvairocana Tathāgata which, as the site of the wisdom of Great Emptiness experienced by the five buddhas, is both principle and wisdom of extinction (nirvāṇa) and Thusness (*tathatā*). The syllable *khaṃ* is thus the supreme maṇḍala/mantra, the sacred place where the buddhas of the ten directions and of all times attain enlightenment. The spleen controls the ideas [*yi* in Chinese], and becomes the center and earth. Earth controls the summer and its color is yellow. Yellow is generated from earth; earth is generated from fire. As explained before, the aggregate of forms controls earth [therefore, consciousness controls space]. Earth also becomes the orb corresponding to wood [that is, the liver]. The green-blue color of wood corresponds to the sky. The spleen is generated from the yellow breath and the heart; it controls the mouth and becomes the *yi* soul. If an excessive amount of sweet flavor enters the spleen, the spleen will benefit but the kidneys will suffer. Should there be no *yi* soul in the spleen, one would lose the sense of orientation; the liver would damage the spleen, thus causing illness. Just as wood overcomes earth, if the liver is strong the spleen is weak. One should be careful with the liver. If yellow breath absorbs green-blue breath, the diseases of the spleen heal. Yellow breath is the syllable *khaṃ*.

The five viscera are like a lotus turned upside down. What inside the body are the five viscera outside become the five phases. The former protrude outside and become objects. These are the forms. Whereas "forms" refer to the four natural elements and the five senses, "names" refer to the four immaterial aggregates such as discerning, volition, and so on. The sun and the moon, the five planets, the twelve constellations, and the twenty-eight lunar mansions form the human body.

The mountains, the sea, and the earth come from the letter A. The rivers and all the water streams come from the syllable *vaṃ*. Gold, jade, precious gems, the sun, the moon and the stars, and the light of fire, and jewels come from the syllable *raṃ*. The five cereals, the five fruits, and the blossoming flowers are produced by the syllable *haṃ*. Beautiful people perfumed with wonderful fragrances, heavenly longevity, a pretty face, a beautiful aspect, fortune, and wealth display their glory out of the syllable *khaṃ*.

The letter A is the east and the tathāgata Akṣobhya, the syllable *vaṃ* is the west and the tathāgata Amitābha, the syllable *raṃ* is the south and the tathāgata Ratnasaṃbhava, the syllable *haṃ* is the north and the tathāgata Amoghasiddhi, the syllable *khaṃ* is the zenith ["center" according to one version] and the tathāgata Mahāvairocana. The meaning of the letter A is extremely profound; it concerns the substance of emptiness and quiescence and cannot be argued upon philosophically. The mother of the myriad dharmas, the king of the great initiation—this is the letter A.

Since the teachings related to the letter A are difficult to believe in, this text should not be shown, especially to the precept-masters of the Lesser Vehicle. The Sanskrit text of the five-syllable mantra comes from the four hundred thousand words [of the main Tantric scriptures?]; this mantra alone is the supreme Merit Field [*puṇyakṣetra*] containing the essence of the *Mahāvairocana Sūtra* and the *Diamond Head Sūtra*. The virtues acquired by those who chant this mantra are incommensurable, unimaginable, and unexplainable.

Contemplation of the fundamental principle through memorization and chanting of the five-syllable mantra of the *Diamond Head Sūtra* will bring people fortune. Their bones will be strong and their bodies healthy; forever free from calamities and diseases, they will cultivate longevity.

The doctrines concerning this mantra in five syllables are the uṣṇīṣa [that is, the highest form] of the five wisdoms, the essence of the five buddhas, the mother of the wisdom of Śākyamuni [the historical Buddha] and the buddhas of the ten directions and of all times, the caring parents of all sentient beings, the treasury of the entire Dharmadhātu. Since it fights against all demons and always wins, [this mantra] is like armor, halberd, bow, arrow, and staff. For this reason, buddhas and bodhisattvas of all times are immersed in and emerge from these five syllables, which are the seeds of the sprouts of the buddhas of all times.

The throne for this meditation is yellow; it is the circle of the adamantine Dharma [esoteric Buddhism], also called the adamantine throne.

1. *A* [the text here has the picture of a square] is the adamantine earth. The letter A is used in the earth throne- and adamantine throne-meditations.
2. *Vaṃ* [picture of a circle] is the adamantine water. The syllable *vaṃ* is used in the water- and lotus-meditations.
3. *Raṃ* [picture of a triangle] is the adamantine fire. The syllable *raṃ* is used in the sun meditation.
4. *Haṃ* [picture of a crescent] is the adamantine wind. The syllable *haṃ* is used in the moon meditation.

5. *Khaṃ* [picture of a sphere] is the adamantine space. The syllable *khaṃ* is used in the space meditation.

[picture of a five-element stūpa]: this is the visualization that the essence of the Tathāgata is unborn.

The mantra in five syllables is the delicious taste of all the tathāgatas' sweet dew [*amṛta* in Sanskrit] of unbornness, the miraculous medicine of the Buddha nature. If one syllable penetrates the five viscera, no disease will occur. How much more powerful will the practice of visualizations of the sun and the moon be! One will immediately experience the emptiness and the quiescence of the Buddha body.

A vaṃ raṃ haṃ khaṃ: these five syllables are the mantra of the Dharmakāya. As for the amount of merit acquired in chanting them once, or seven times, or twenty-one times, or forty-nine times a day, each chanting is equivalent in virtue to reading one million times excerpts from the whole Buddhist canon. How much greater will be the merit of sitting in quiet meditation and entering samādhi! Thanks to the contemplation of the letter A, the truth is as clear as the sun shining in the sky. Once the Buddha nature has been realized, the virtues acquired are incomparable. The texts of the esoteric canon truly transcend discursive thinking. However, there is the risk that monks with a śrāvaka ["auditor," an original disciple of the Buddha] nature and those who keep the precepts of the Lesser Vehicle will not only arouse doubts and refuse to believe these doctrines, but also increase their sins. This is like the king who, even though he loved his little child so much as to give him all the precious objects in his treasury without regrets, nevertheless refused to give him Ganjiang and Moye [two famous ancient swords], because the child was not able to use them and the king was afraid that he would harm himself. In the same way, the Tathāgata secretly transmits the esoteric teachings only to the great bodhisattvas and does not make them available to the inferior knowledge of the śrāvaka.

Dharmadhātu is the Dharmakāya Tathāgata's true reality. In the human body we distinguish between the upper part, from the armpit to the top of the head; the middle part, from the navel to the armpit; and the lower part, from the feet to the navel. Also in the mantras one should distinguish between three different siddhis [to be acquired].

Lower siddhi: *A ra pa ca na*. It is called the "protruding siddhi." It generates roots and stems and permeates the four directions. To chant it once is like reading excerpts from the whole canon a hundred times (to chant it once is like chanting the 84,012 Vedas; the practitioner will be freed from all troubles and sufferings). When one enters the Tathāgata's state of the indifferentiatedness of all dharmas, all letters are undifferentiated, and one quickly attains the great wisdom. If chanted twice, this mantra eliminates all major sins committed over a hundred million kalpas [eons] of rebirths. [The bodhisattvas] Mañjuśrī and Samantabhadra extend their protection to the four classes of Buddhists [that is, monks, nuns, laymen, and laywomen] surrounding them. The good deities, Dharma-protectors endowed with the fearlessness of compassion, appear in front of the practitioner [to protect him]. If chanted three times, the practitioner will attain samādhi; if chanted four times, the practitioner will be able to remember all the dhāraṇīs, if chanted five times, the practitioner will immediately attain the supreme bodhi.

Middle siddhi: *A vi ra hūṃ khaṃ*. Called the "intruding siddhi," it generates branches and leaves. The intruding siddhi goes from the navel to the heart. Permeating the four directions, its bright light penetrates Buddha's Dharmadhātu, whence its name. To chant [this mantra] once is like reading excerpts from the entire canon a thousand times (this mantra is also called the adamantine formula for the subjugation of the four multitudes of demons and the six destinations and for the attainment of universal wisdom).

Upper siddhi: *A vaṃ raṃ haṃ khaṃ*. This is called the "secret siddhi," the "perfect siddhi," as well as the "susiddhi." Susiddhi permeates the Dharmadhātu. These are the Dharmadhātu's secret words to attain buddhahood and experience the great bodhi; their light permeates everywhere. Only buddhas can trespass this threshold; pratyeka-buddhas and śrāvakas cannot understand it; therefore it is called the "secret siddhi." To chant it once is like reading excerpts from the entire canon one million times.

The protruding siddhi goes from the feet to the waist; the intruding siddhi goes from the navel to the heart; and the secret siddhi goes from the heart to the top of the head; these are the three siddhis. The protruding siddhi is the attainment of the Nirmāṇakāya; the intruding siddhi is the attainment of the Saṃbhogakāya; and the susiddhi is the attainment of the Dharmakāya. These truly are the three eternal bodies, the repository of the true Teachings, the perfect body of the Dharmakāya Mahāvairocana, the true source of the Womb and Vajra maṇḍalas. Therefore I bow my head and pay homage to Mahāvairocana Buddha.

These three five-syllable mantras, that is, [each of] these five syllables, are equivalent to the fifteen adamantine samādhis. One syllable is equivalent to all fifteen syllables, and all fifteen syllables are equivalent to each syllable; each syllable is equivalent to each set of five syllables, and each set of five syllables is equivalent to each syllable. The serial visualization in proper order [from the beginning to the end] or in reverse order [from the end to the beginning] produce the same result, since the beginning and the end are nondual [that is, nondistinct]. The following eight meditative practices contain all dharmas. [The practitioner should see that] each syllable contains all syllables; all syllables contain each syllable; each syllable explains all syllables; all syllables explain one syllable; each syllable makes all syllables; all syllables make each syllable; each syllable destroys all syllables; all syllables destroy the meaning of each syllable. All the preceding constitutes one meditative set that can be visualized in the proper order and in reverse order. One should practice the entire set four times in proper order and four times in reverse order. The benefit for sentient beings in the entire Dharmadhātu is that they will all become buddhas.

The shape of the hṛdaya-heart of ordinary people is like a closed lotus. Its muscles form eight sections. In men it is turned upward, in women it is turned downward. In visualization one should open one's heart to form a white lotus with eight petals. Upon it as a platform one should see the letter *A* in golden color. The letter *A* is like a square yellow altar, and the practitioner sees oneself on it. From the letter *A* comes out the syllable *ra*, which burns one's body and reduces it to ashes. From the ashes the syllable *va* is generated, of a pure white color. From it, *A vaṃ raṃ haṃ khaṃ*, the mantra of the five elements [of the cosmic stūpa], is produced. This mantra takes its place on the five parts of the body, from the waist to the top of the head. This is the pure bodhicitta. These five syllables concur in the creation of the roots of great compassion. The śāla tree of the Buddha grows and fills the entire Dharmadhātu; accordingly, all dharmas are based upon this five-syllable mantra, which is originally unborn and transcends language; its substance is pure, without karmic conditionings, and empty like space. The eight petals of the heart-lotus become a platform, and the area in the practitioner's body going from the navel to the heart becomes the adamantine platform (a pavilion built on the sea). The navel becomes the ocean; beneath is the abode of all deities [of the maṇḍala], which is the coastline. From the ocean of compassion of the buddhas arises the Vajra Wisdom; from the Vajra Wisdom arises the assembly of all buddhas [that is, the maṇḍala]. On this eight-petaled lotus platform which is the heart one should then visualize the letter *A*. This letter emits a massive light that disperses in the four directions from the heart; then the rays converge again to form a sort of garland of light like a floral wreath [used in temple decoration] and pervade all Buddha lands in the universe. This light then encircles the practitioner's body, shrouding it from the top of the head to the feet. One should then visualize the syllable *aṃ* on the top of the head; it turns into the center of the Womb maṇḍala and produces three rays of light. The first ray turns around the throat of the practitioner, reaches to the top of the head, and in the areas brightened by the light, Buddhist deities appear to form the first circle of the Womb maṇḍala. The second ray of light turns around the heart and goes from the navel to the throat; Buddhist deities appear to form the second circle of the Womb maṇḍala. The third ray of light turns around the navel and brightens the area of the body below the navel, where Buddhist deities appear to form the third circle of the Womb maṇḍala. This is the heavenly pavilion of the ordinary world [the residence of the gods between the earth and Brahmā's heaven; or, perhaps, the totality of sacred and profane space]. Forms, colors, and characteristics of the deities vary, but the practitioner has all of them inside his own body, as if he were one of the members of the Buddha assembly [that is, the maṇḍala] himself. His whole body is a mandalic body, that is, the Dharmadhātu body of unlimited salvational powers.

The central part of the aforementioned Womb maṇḍala is the eight-petaled lotus representing Mahāvairocana's heart. This heart-lotus platform is the center of the maṇḍala; the various buddhas are distributed according to their rank on the external lotus. The four directions are the four wisdoms of the Tathāgata, and in the petals situated between them are the four all-embracing [bodhisattva] virtues [giving, affectionate speech, conduct profitable to the others, cooperation with others; but also the four Tantric bodhisattvas who convert beings with hook, rope, chain, and bell]. To the southeast is Samantabhadra, the sublime cause of bodhicitta. To the southwest is Mañjuśrī, great wisdom. To the northeast is Maitreya, great compassion. Great compassion is the second principle. Then to the northwest is Avalokiteśvara, who stands for enlightenment. To realize the goals of one's practices, one should enter the samādhi of this lotus platform. The first letter *A* in the lotus is located in the east and represents the bodhicitta, the beginning of all practices. The yellow color represents the Vajra nature; it is called both the "precious banner" and Akṣobhya Buddha. Next, the syllable *ā* is situated in the south. It stands for the religious practices; its color is red and represents fire. Its meaning is the same as that of Mañjuśrī, namely, the opening of the lotus; it is also called Ratnasaṃbhava Buddha. Next, there is the syllable *aṃ* in the west, standing for the bodhi. The performance of countless practices results in awakening. Its white color represents ultimate wisdom; it also stands for water. Its corresponding buddha is Amitabhā. Next, to the north is the syllable *aṃ*, which stands for enlightenment. Its corresponding buddha is Śākyamuni. The syllable stands for the great nirvāṇa, so called because the practitioner, having expunged the traces, returns to the origin. Since the sun of the Buddha hides beyond the mountains, the color [of this stage] is black. Finally, at the center is the syllable *āṃḥ*, standing for skillful means (*upāya*). One should know that the substance of such Dharmadhātu in the heart is originally and always characterized by quiet extinction (*nirvāṇa*). Accordingly, Mahāvairocana's original body, the substance of the lotus platform, exceeds the eight-petaled lotus, transcends space, surpasses the realm of mind: only the buddhas can understand it. It is thanks to skillful means that [the maṇḍala] can manifest all its images even though it is like the great space; even though its center is empty, it contains all forms. In other words, the maṇḍala, as the universe of empowerment, being the assembly of those endowed with infinite salvational powers, appears everywhere in space. However, this is none other than the single body, the single wisdom, and the single practice of the Tathāgata. Therefore, the eight-petaled lotus is Mahāvairocana Tathāgata's single substance. Therefore, Mahāvairocana at the center of the maṇḍala is the Dharmakāya. Vajrasattva's Seal (*mudrā*) of Vajra Wisdom represents prajñā [that is, the wisdom acquired with enlightenment]. Avalokiteśvara's Seal of the Lotus Holder represents liberation. The mystery of the body is the power of the Dharmakāya, the mystery of speech is the power of prajñā, and the mystery of the mind is the power of liberation. Since one attains liberation as a consequence of prajñā, liberation depends on prajñā. However, both depend on the substance of the Dharmakāya: they are different but inseparable, and if one is missing the other cannot be attained. They are like the three strokes of the letter I [in Siddhaṃ script].

The bodhicitta corresponds to the Vajra section, compassion to the Lotus section, and skillful means correspond to the Nirmāṇakāya. Therefore, the letter *A* represents the stage inside the womb, and its level of attainment is that which precedes enlightenment; the letter *sa* represents the stage outside the womb, and its level of attainment is enlightenment; the letter *va* represents the function [*yong* in Chinese], and all wheels of Dharma depend on it. The two manifestations of arbitrary traces [unclear, perhaps a reference to Saṃbhogakāya and Nirmāṇakāya] save the ten worlds. The Tathāgata's Seal of Wisdom is the true aspect of the heart, that is, supreme wisdom. In other words, bodhicitta is the cause, compassion is the root, and skillful means are the ultimate. The meanings of the series of five elements are the causal factors for the practices leading to wisdom.

If a sentient being knows this text's doctrines, the commoners will make offerings to him in the same way they venerate a caitya [that is, a stūpa]. The caitya is in fact the model of the living body's relics [as described in this text]. Therefore, all devas [gods] and human beings, when praying for good fortune, make offerings to it. If a practitioner believes these doctrines, he is the receptacle of the Dharmakāya's relics. Furthermore, the Sanskrit terms *caitya* and *citta* refer to the same thing [since they share the same root]. Accordingly, what is secretly [that is, technically] called "heart" actually is a stūpa of the Buddha. As in the third circle of the Womb maṇḍala [above], one's heart/mind is the basis. It expands and becomes the center of the Womb maṇḍala, upon which is the color of nirvāṇa. Accordingly, the caitya is very high. Then, it expands gradually from the lotus at the center of the Womb maṇḍala and becomes the universal salvific body of the manifestations of the buddhas, pervading everywhere. Accordingly, the caitya is very wide: its lotus platform is the entire Dharmadhātu, that is, the cosmic relic of the Dharmakāya. If a sentient being understands this Seal of the Bodhicitta he is like Mahāvairocana, and the commoners will make offerings to him in the same way they venerate a caitya.

Therefore, in Mahāvairocana's body-and-land, external world and sentient beings are interpenetrated, essence and signs are identical; Thusness pervades the Dharmadhātu and the body-speech-mind of the Supreme Self [the enlightened one] are undifferentiated, like cosmic space. Space is a sacred place, and the Dharmadhātu is the practitioner's residence. Mahāvairocana Tathāgata, in order to spread this doctrine, manifests two Dharmakāyas. The Buddha as Dharmakāya of Wisdom abides in the true principle and, as the Saṃbhogakāya for his own enjoyment, manifests the central circle of the Womb maṇḍala and makes everyone follow the nondual path. The Buddha as Dharmakāya of Principle abides in the undifferentiated and radiant quiescence; absolute, eternal, and unchanging, he manifests the eight-petaled lotus; as the Saṃbhogakāya working for everyone's salvation, he manifests the three circles of the Womb maṇḍala and makes everyone in the ten worlds attain the Great Emptiness [enlightenment]. The meanings of Principle and Wisdom show dissimilarities in extension, but they are originally one single dharma and therefore have no essential differences. All dharmas return to the letter *A*, and the five syllables are identical with the single Vairocana.

Thanks to Mahāvairocana Buddha,
I have opened the seal of the wisdom of the mind,
I have established the meaning of ritual symbols,
and possess numberless virtues
adorning everything.
Having penetrated the perfection and the powers of the dhāraṇī,
together with those who learn and practice, with whom I have karmic affinities,
I vow to abide in peace in the sea of supreme purity.

Rites and Techniques

—22—

Worship of the Ladies of the Dipper

Charles D. Orzech and James H. Sanford

The Pole Star and the seven stars of the Great or Northern Dipper occupy a prominent place in Chinese imperial and Daoist traditions, and have microcosmic and macrocosmic associations on both the astronomical and the human scales. It was widely believed that the stars and constellations of "heaven" (*tian*) had analogues in the "under-heaven" (*tianxia*) and within the human body, and that events and conditions in one of these systems affected the analogous structures in the other systems. Thus, heaven was the model for earth, and the heavenly bureaucracy the model for the earthly empire. So too, the human body was conceived as a "country" containing palaces and offices, with its gods the functionaries that serve in the "Niwan Palace" (conceived of as "grottos" in the cranium), in the "cinnabar field" (*dantian*) located below the navel, and elsewhere. Certain of these gods were less than beneficent. Indeed, if allowed to leave the body they could ascend to heaven and report misdeeds to the "comptroller of fate" (*siming*), who noted their transgressions in a register. Such entries shortened a person's life. It is notable that one of the texts below details rituals to alter these records and thereby prolong life.

Chinese cosmomagical speculation drew important connections between an emperor's rule and events in the heavens, and the "Palace of the Pole Star" was thought to be the celestial model for the palace of the son of Heaven here on earth. The Dipper asterism was also believed to be the residence of Taiyi, the Great Monad, and the abode of the deified Laozi, who lives there "as a hypostasis of the Daoist cosmic Sage, the anthropomorphic form of the Dao" (Robinet 1997: 50). In resonance with the universe at large, the human body contains its own Great or Northern Dipper. For "located in the very center of the head, the Niwan ('mud-pill,' but also a transliteration of the term *nirvāṇa*) Palace is covered by the seven stars of the Northern Dipper" (Kohn 1993: 209). This inner Dipper is the focus of a wide variety of Daoist meditational practices and is celebrated in innumerable Taoist works. As one Daoist adept put it,

In heaven seven stars; on earth seven treasures
and seven grottos in our heads
seven times the subtle air of yin melts
as a slow fire warms the cauldron, warms the lead.

Attributed to Zhang Boduan, *Daozang qi yao* 128

Because of the centrality and ubiquity of the circumpolar stars in Daoist and imperial ideology, Chinese concern with the religious meaning of the Dipper stars is often thought to be a peculiarly Daoist interest. Yet these motifs of macrocosm and microcosm are often expressed in terms of the Indian cakra system of subtle body organs. The dipper star motif is found in a number of Sino-Japanese venues that range from Daoist alchemical texts (such as the poem translated above) to paintings of the Japanese Shintō-Buddhist deity, Matara-jin. It should not, therefore, be surprising that in the volumes of the Taishō Tripitaka collection of Sino-Japanese Buddhist works devoted to Esoteric or "Tantric" Buddhism (*zhenyan*, "Mantra," or *mijiao*, "Esoteric" teaching, in Chinese; Shingon or *mikkyō*, in Japanese) we find several such works.

Chinese Esoteric Buddhism has a complex prehistory; in brief, between the third century and the beginning of the eighth century, South and Central Asian texts describing maṇḍalas, and studded with mantras and dhāraṇīs (spells), began to pour into China. This piecemeal transmission continued until Śubhakarasiṁha arrived in Changan in 717, followed by Vajrabodhi and his disciple Amoghavajra, who arrived in the Tang capital in 721 to articulate and propagate the comprehensive systems of Buddhist esoterism. Like other South Asian forms of Tantra, Esoteric Buddhism assumed an extensive series of correspondences between the body and the cosmos, between internal yogic physiology (composed of cakras or energy centers strung out along the spinal column and their connecting channels) and the elements (wind, water, fire, and earth), planets, and stars. Progress toward enlightenment proceeded on the external level in ritual, and internally through yogic ascent. Success or siddhi was both a microcosmic mastery of the inner world and a macrocosmic mastery of the cosmos.

A common thread that runs through the Esoteric Buddhism of Śubhakarasiṁha, Vajrabodhi, Amoghavajra, and their disciples in the Late Tang (mid-eighth through mid-ninth centuries) was the interdependence of the achievement of enlightenment and various forms of worldly benefit. Nevertheless, much of these masters' lives were spent in "mundane pursuits" and in constructing rituals mainly of apotropaic and political value. Many of the ritual manuals collected in the Esoteric portion of the Taishō canon (volumes 18–21) are directed toward the ills of the period of the "End of the Dharma" (Chinese *mofa*, Japanese *mappō*). For example, in *The Scripture Expounded at the Bodhimanda Concerning the Single Syllable Uṣṇīṣa*, we find the Buddha instructing Vajrapāṇi concerning a time "after my extinction, during the time of the end of the Dharma." What is then propounded is the *End of the Dharma Siddhi* (Taishō 950: 200c, 205c) to shield the practitioner from a wide variety of impending disasters.

Ritual application fell into two broad categories. There were rituals for the imperial family, high courtiers, and generals, both living and dead; and rituals designed to protect and maintain the state and the cosmic order. Esoteric revamping of earlier Buddhist texts and rituals with these purposes in mind consistently followed the paradigms set out in the *Sarvatathāgatatattvasaṃgraha* (Taishō 865–66; 862), and the treatment of these texts and rituals parallels the treatment of the *Scripture for Humane Kings* (Taishō 245–46). No disembodied Buddhism this: rather, the point was application—fully embodied ritual application with sonic, photic, and somatic dimensions. This was, in short, Tantra, and what dazzled jaded Tang courtiers was its sumptuous ritual, its "smells and bells."

The Tang masters drew upon the vast store of correspondences between the body and the cosmos found in South Asian Tantric systems. Among the most basic homologies are those involving lunar and solar images, night and day, white and red, and the iḍā and piṅgalā channels that pierce the cakras of the yogin's subtle physiology. Extensive correspondences were worked out not only concerning the moon and sun, but also with regard to the planets and stars. The alchemical traditions related planets to colors, jewels, ores, and so forth. This body of lore was developed throughout South Asian yogic traditions. Mainstream Buddhism had relatively little to say on the luminaries in or outside of the body. The *Abhidharmakośa* remarks only that "the stars turn about Meru as though caught in a whirlpool." Despite this laconic sentence, it makes perfect sense to "assume that there is some relationship between the seven circular mountain rings and the seven spheres marked out by the 'planets' of antiquity" (Kloetzli 1983: 46–47). Not unexpectedly, later Kālacakra (Wheel of Time) traditions as summarized by Jamgon Kongtrul Lodro Taye (1995: 156–58), give more details:

> The celestial sphere pervades space between Mount Meru and the mountain of fire. It is a belt of wind, within which the twelve houses and the twenty-eight constellations formed first. [The houses] are situated in a clockwise arrangement. Planets such as the sun and moon arise above them. [Eight] move counterclockwise; the Eclipser [moves] clockwise.

The location of this belt in the body is not specified. The Japanese *Byakuhōkushō* (containing what is purported to be oral transmission of the Tang masters now preserved in Japan) seems to identify it with the mouth and eyes in a fashion that seems to evoke the sacrifice of Puruṣa in *Ṛg Veda* 10.90: "the sun, the moon, and the five planets emerge from the radiance of Mañjuśrī. Emanating beams of light from his mouth in the center of this radiance, he manifests the five planets; from the radiance of his left and right eyes, he manifests the sun and the moon" (Birnbaum 1983: 123 n.128, citing Taishō supplement 6.461a). South Asian sources here parallel Daoist tradition in locating the Dipper in the head and associating it with the sun, moon, and the eyes. As elsewhere in esoteric astral lore, it is Mañjuśrī, the bodhisattva embodiment of wisdom, who is lord of the heavens. The *Mañjuśrī-nāma-saṅgīti-sūtra* speaks of the twenty-eight lodges (the lunar lodges, or groups of stars along the path of the moon; mythically, the abodes of Soma's wives where he rests on his journey) as the diadem of Mañjuśrī (Birnbaum 1983: 102). Given the identification of the throat cakra with the element wind one may tentatively imagine the twenty-eight lunar lodges (*nakṣatras*) as the bodhisattva's "necklace" and as the topmost level of the material world (just below the four transic states or Brahmā heavens) that affects the fate of sentient beings. Here we have, in short, the workings of karma. In his climb to the summit of existence the yogin masters the forces of karma (the planets and nakṣatras) and, by bringing together the solar and lunar forces, transcends the wheel of time.

A major factor in the success of Tantric Buddhism in the eighth and ninth century Tang court was the masters' ability and willingness to adapt their knowledge to the concerns of their new Chinese patrons. Indian astral lore—like that of the Greeks—focused on the ecliptic (the apparent motion of the sun against the background of fixed stars), the heliacal rising and setting of stars (which yields the twelve houses or the zodiacal band of stars confined to the apparent path of the sun in the sky), and the twenty-eight nakṣatras. Chinese astral lore was keyed to the circumpolar stars and meridians drawn from them to the "lunar lodges" (*xiu*). The stars of the Great Dipper were not neglected in South Asian traditions; indeed, they had been identified with the seven *ṛṣis* (sages) since Vedic times. The wives of the ṛṣis were the Kṛtikkās, identified as the Pleiades open star cluster that rises in the east in late autumn, and which itself resembles a small dipper. Perhaps this is the reason why the text locates all of the Dipper stars in the east. The Indian and Chinese traditions shared an interest in the "lunar lodges," and both sought ritually to divine and influence events in the heavens in order to shape events in the mundane world. Thus, the Tang masters introduced new mathematical techniques for the production of accurate calendars (an essential part of the son of Heaven's claim to rule), performed homa (immolation) rituals designed to propitiate the "nine Graspers" (spirits of the planets, which are often associated with disease: *jiu zhi* in Chinese; *navagraha* in Sanskrit), and designed new rites to address the lords of the Great Dipper (an asterism in Ursa Major).

With this in mind, we turn to the Taishō canon, where we may distinguish four categories of texts that concern themselves with astral phenomena. First are those texts in which Mañjuśrī is the lord of astral wisdom. Second is the cycle of texts designed to prevent disasters connected with the Buddha's *uṣṇīṣa* (the protuberance on his head, or "wisdom bump"). Third are those texts primarily concerned with the lords of the Great Dipper. Finally, there is an assortment of texts that, along with their primary purpose, also promise protection from astral misfortunes. A good example of these is the *Scripture for Humane Kings*.

The three brief texts we translate represent a synthesis between Chinese and South Asian astral worship. These are the *Scripture Expounded by the Buddha on Prolonging Life through Worship of the Seven Stars of the Northern Dipper* (*Fo shuo beidou qi xing yan ming jing*), *Ritual Procedures for Invoking the Seven Stars of the Northern Dipper* (*Beidou qi xing niansong yigui*), and the *Secret Essentials for Performing Homa to the Seven Stars of the Northern Dipper* (*Beidou qi xing huma miyao yigui*). Aimed squarely at neutralizing the evil effects of astral divinities and at promoting good fortune and long life, these texts were an integral part of the new Tantric teachings tailored to the concerns of Chinese aristocrats and military men.

The *Scripture Expounded by the Buddha on Prolonging Life through Worship of the Seven Stars of the Northern Dipper* constitutes a short catalog of the apotheosized seven stars of the Dipper. Each of its seven entries consists of the following parts: an illustration of the divinity of the star, the star/divinity's name, the drawing of an appropriate talisman, and a short, formulaic, astrological text.

The seven illustrations are all of individual female figures in ancient court dress, with the exception of the fifth star, which shows its female figure accompanied by a smaller-scale male acolyte. This asterism, zeta Ursa Majoris (the brighter member is also known as Mizar, and the dimmer star as Alcor) is a well-known double star visible to the naked eye from a dark site. Curiously, these gender associations are exactly the opposite of those found in most South Asian sources. There, Vasiṣṭha (zeta Ursa Majoris or Mizar) is accompanied by his chaste wife Arundhatī. However, one verse in the *Ṛg Veda* (1.164.16) says in reference to the Kṛtikkās (the Pleiades), "They tell me that those virtuous women are men; he who has eyes sees this, not he who is blind." Each entry is numbered in these illustrations with a Japanese *kana* symbol, a feature that makes the Japanese provenance of the Taishō text patent (but does not, of course, preclude earlier Chinese provenance, as the text itself proclaims). The talisman shapes, like those of many Daoist talismanic diagrams, are quite similar to Chinese characters; in some cases the likely prototype character seems obvious. Each star name has also been associated with one or more of the "twelve earthly branches," which, in turn, is associated with an astrological animal. We have indicated the associated animal in brackets. Not surprisingly, Mañjuśrī is the recipient of this scripture. Perhaps of greater import is the catalog of woes that the scripture seeks to address, including favorable rebirth, helping relatives out of hell, help in fending off demons and "dead souls" (literally, the yang and yin souls of the dead), illness, agricultural disasters, and difficulty in childbirth.

The *Ritual Procedures for Invoking the Seven Stars of the Northern Dipper* is attributed to the master Vajrabodhi and promises a variety of rewards, including that of lengthening one's life by modifying one's karmic register. One should note that such a register is a decidedly Chinese notion, one that is treated in greater detail in the *Secret Essentials for Performing Homa to the Seven Stars of the Northern Dipper*. Here we find a standard Chinese account of the role of the Comptroller of Fate (*siming*), and of penalties suffered for crimes. The text also notes that the stars of the Dipper are the "essence of the sun, moon, and five stars [the planets], making explicit one of the links between South and East Asian astrological lore. Again, turning to South Asia, we find an intriguing correspondence, since the seven ṛṣis of the Dipper are sometimes regarded as sun, moon, and Agni (fire). But this is a homa text, and it gives details of the construction of the altar, the nature of the offerings, the proper mudrās (gestures) and mantras, and a somewhat cryptic form of divination.

Taken together, these texts illustrate characteristic South Asian Tantric concerns and practices aimed at advancement and protection in the material world, while also demonstrating the adaptation of South Asian Tantric practices into the East Asian milieu.

The *Scripture Expounded by the Buddha on Prolonging Life through Worship of the Seven Stars of the Northern Dipper* (*Fo shuo beidou qi xing yan ming jing*) is found inTaishō 1307: 21.425b-426b); the *Ritual Procedures for Invoking the Seven Stars of the Northern Dipper* (*Beidou qi xing niansong yigui*) is in Taishō 1305: 21.423c-424b; and the *Secret Essentials for Performing Homa to the Seven Stars of the Northern Dipper* (*Beidou qi xing huma miyao yigui*) is in Taishō 1306: 21.424b-425a. All three texts are found in *Taishō shinshū daizō-kyō*, edited and compiled by Takakusu Junjiro and Watanabe Kaigyoku. (Tokyo: Taisho issaikyo kanko-kai, 1924–34). The mantras have been rendered according to the siddhaṃ (a script related to Brahmi) that appears beside the Chinese transliteration in the texts.

The Chinese employ two series of characters, the ten "heavenly stems" and the twelve "earthly branches," to designate a calendrical cycle of sixty years. Each of the twelve branches is associated with an animal and a zodiacal year sign. We have given these associations in brackets where appropriate.

Further Reading

Chinese astronomical and astrological traditions have been amply and sympathetically treated by Joseph Needham and Wang Ling in *Science and Civilization in China*, vol. 3 (Cambridge: Cambridge University Press, 1959). Raoul Birnbaum's *Studies on the Mysteries of Mañjuśrī: A Group of East Asian Maṇḍalas and Their Traditional Symbolism*, Society for the Study of Chinese Religions Monograph no. 2 (Boulder: Society for the Study of Chinese Religions, 1983), and his "Introduction to the Study of T'ang Buddhist Astrology: Research Notes on Primary Sources and Basic Principles," *Bulletin: Society for the Study of Chinese Religions* 8 (Fall 1980): 5–19 are by far the best treatments of this topic in English; his bibliographies are a good starting point for further exploration. Henrik H. Sørensen's study "The Worship of the Great Dipper in Korean Buddhism" appears in *Religions in Traditional Korea: Proceedings of the 1992 AKSE/SBS Symposium* (Copenhagen: Seminar for Buddhist Studies, 1995): 71–105. It contains a translation of a Korean ritual manual that is partially identical to *The Scripture Containing the Buddha's Discourse on Prolonging Life through Worship of the Seven Stars of the Northern Dipper* (T 1307) translated below. For those who can read Japanese, Morita Ryusen's massive *Mikkyō senseihō* (Koyasan: Koyasan daigaku, 1941) is the definitive work. Edward H. Schafer's *Pacing the Void: T'ang Approaches to the Stars* (Berkeley and Los Angeles: University of California Press, 1977) gives the reader the context and feel of Tang-dynasty star lore. On the Dipper and its role in Daoism, see John Lagerwey, *Taoist Ritual in Chinese Society and History* (New York: Macmillan, 1987), and Kristofer Schipper, *The Taoist Body*, translated by Karen

C. Duval (Berkeley and Los Angeles: University of California Press, 1993). Also see Isabelle Robinet, *Taoism: Growth of a Religion*, translated by Phyllis Brooks (Stanford: Stanford University Press, 1997), and Livia Kohn, *The Taoist Experience: An Anthology* (Albany: State University of New York Press, 1993). For Buddhist star lore, see Edward J. Thomas, "Sun, Moon, and Stars (Buddhist)," in *Encyclopedia of Religion and Ethics* (New York: Scribner's, 1922), and more recently Randy Kloetzli, *Buddhist Cosmology: From Single World System to Pure Land: Science and Theology in the Images of Motion and Light* (Delhi: Motilal Banarsidass, 1983); and Jamgon Kongtrul Lodro Taye's *Myriad Worlds: Buddhist Cosmology in Abhidharma, Kalacakra, and Dzog-chen*, translated by Kalu Rinpoche (Ithaca: Snow Lion, 1995). For the Dipper and the ṛṣis in South Asia, see John E. Mitchiner, Traditions of the Seven Ṛṣis (Delhi: Motilal Barnarsidass, 1982). For Esoteric Buddhism in China, see Chou I-liang, "Tantrism in China," *Harvard Journal of Asiatic Studies* 8 (March 1945): 241–332, and Charles D. Orzech, *Politics and Transcendent Wisdom: The Scripture for Humane Kings in the Creation of Chinese Buddhism* (University Park: Pennsylvania State University Press, 1998), chapters 5 and 6. In French, Michel Strickmann has provided what is now the best overall examination of esoteric Buddhism in China: *Mantras et mandarins: Le bouddhisme tantrique en chine* (Paris: Gallimard, 1996). Finally, on homa as practiced in contemporary Shingon see Richard Karl Payne, *The Tantric Ritual of Japan: Feeding the Gods: The Shingon Fire Ritual* (Delhi: Aditya Prakashan, 1991).

The Scripture Containing the Buddha's Discourse on Prolonging Life through Worship of the Seven Stars of the Northern Dipper

A brahman monk brought this scripture and the Tang court received it.

Tanlang [Hungry Wolf]: Persons born under the chronogram *cu* [rat] face this star as they descend into birth. Their wages are husked millet. If in danger they should make offerings to this scripture while wearing their natal star's talisman. Great happiness.

Jumen [Great Gate]: Persons born under the chronograms *chou* [ox] and *hai* [pig] both face this star as they descend into birth. Their wages are millet. If in danger they should make offerings to this scripture while wearing their natal star's talisman. Great happiness.

Lucun (Wage Preserver): Persons born under the chronograms *yin* [tiger] and *xu* [dog] both face this star as they descend into birth. Their wages are nonglutinous rice. If in danger they should make offerings to this scripture while wearing their natal star's talisman. Great happiness.

Wenqu [Literary Song]: Persons born under the chronograms *mao* [hare] and *you* [cock] both face this star as they descend into birth. Their wages are lentils. If in danger they should make offerings to this scripture while wearing their natal star's talisman. Great happiness.

Lianzhen [Pure and Upright]: Persons born under the chronograms *zhen*

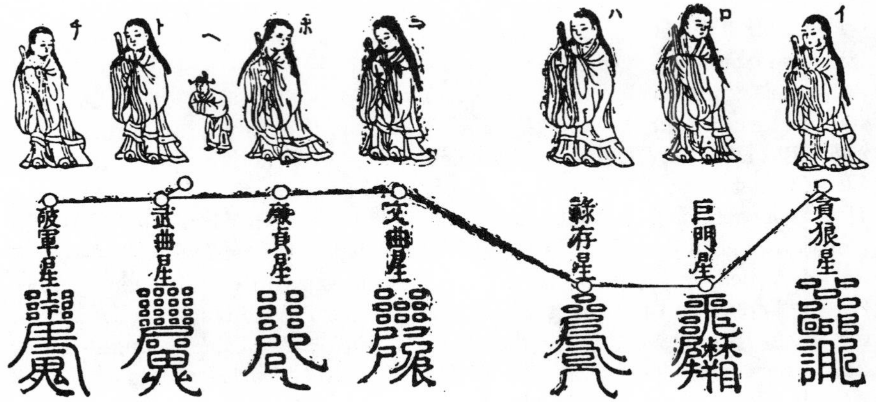

Figure 22.1. The Ladies of the Dipper

[dragon] and *shen* [monkey] both face this star when they descend into birth. Their wages are hemp seed. If in danger they should make offerings to this scripture while wearing their natal star's talisman. Great happiness.

Wuqu [Military Song]: Persons born under the chronograms *si* [snake] and *wei* [sheep] both face this star when they descend into birth. Their wages are soybeans. If in danger they should make offerings to this scripture while wearing their natal star's talisman. Great happiness.

Pojun [Ruiner of Armies]: Persons born under the chronogram *wu* [horse] face this star when they descend into birth. Their wages are lentils. If in danger they should make offerings to this scripture while wearing their natal star's talisman. Great happiness.

Namo Hungry Wolf Star: This is the Buddha-Tathāgata Moves-the-Will-to-Penetrate-Truth of the Most-Surpassing-World of the eastern quarter.

Namo Great Gate Star: This is the Buddha-Tathāgata Sovereign-of-Radiant-Sound of the Sublime-Jewel-World of the eastern quarter.

Namo Wage Preserving Star: This is the Buddha-Tathāgata Golden-Accomplishment of the Fully-Satisfying-World of the eastern quarter.

Namo Literary Song Star: This is the Buddha-Tathāgata Utterly-Surpassing-Felicity of the World-without-Grief of the eastern quarter.

Namo Pure and Upright Star: This is the Buddha-Tathāgata He-of-Broadly-Accomplished-Sagacious-Discrimination of the Pure-Abode-World of the eastern quarter.

Namo Military Song Star: This is the Buddha-Tathāgata He-Who-Wanders-Freely-in-the-Dharma-Ocean of the Dharma-Will-World of the eastern quarter.

Namo Ruiner of Armies Star: This is the Buddha-Tathāgata Medicine-Master-of-Lapis-Lazuli-Radiance of the Lapis-Lazuli-World of the eastern quarter.

If you encounter an inauspicious year or month, pay obescience to this scripture seven times.

At that time the Buddha spoke to Mañjuśrī Bodhisattva, and what he expounded was this scripture. It has awesome spirit and awesome power. It can save all beings from grave offenses and it can eradicate all karmic obstructions.

If there are monks and nuns, officials and administrators, laymen (*upāsakas*), good men and good women, whether wealthy or poor, whether of long or short lifespan, they are all under the sway of the seven stars of the Northern Dipper. If they hear this scripture and receive it, make offerings, and read it repeatedly, and exhort friends and relatives, kith and kin, then in this life they will obtain great fortune and in the next will attain rebirth in a heaven.

If there are good sons and daughters [whose kinsmen] have already died and fallen into hell where they have received all sorts of bitter misery—if they hear this scripture, revere it, and make offerings, then forthwith those who have died will attain release from hell and be reborn in Sukhāvatī [Amitābha's Pure Land].

If there are good sons and daughters who are injured by attacks of imps or troubled by evil demons, or if evil dreams, weird occurrences, or dead souls alarm them—then if they hear this scripture, receive it, and make offerings, forthwith the dead souls will be pacified and they will always be free of fear.

If there are good sons and daughters, and if they serve as personal attendants to an official and—if they encounter this scripture, revere it, and make offerings, forthwith they will [themselves] attain promotion to official [status]. This is great happiness.

If there are good sons and daughters, and if illness racks their bodies and they seek relief, then they should, in a pure room, burn incense and make offerings to this scripture. The illness will abate.

If there are good sons and daughters who desire advancement and through goods-trading travel as brokers, seeking wealth, comfortable living, and prosperity—if they encounter this scripture, revere it, and make offerings, forthwith they will attain the sought-after wealth and comfort they seek, and their transactions will bring them great fortune.

If there are good sons and daughters, and if in raising silkworms [the cocoons] are empty, or if in husbanding the six beasts are discontented, then in a pure room, they should burn incense and make offerings to this scripture. They will attain fields of silkworms according to their wishes, and their six domestic beasts will multiply and [they] will never suffer injury or loss, disaster, or obstruction.

If there are women who are pregnant and in difficulty at the time of parturition, then if they encounter this scripture, revere it, and make offerings to it, forthwith mother and child will be separated and the danger will be eliminated. As a result, the children born to them will attain uprightness and long life as a consequence of their previous good deeds.

If there are good sons and daughters, they should know that the seven stars of the Northern Dipper control human destiny [and that this includes] an entire lifetime's calamities [such as] official notice, disputes, loneliness, or [encounters] with various apparitions. If a person encounters this scripture and reveres it and makes offerings [to it] not a single injury will [befall him]. At that time Mañjuśrī said, "Good sons and daughters, [you should] revere it and faithfully receive it." [Then] they bowed and dispersed.

Ritual Procedures for Invoking the Seven Stars of the Northern Dipper

Translated by the Tripitaka master and South Indian brahmin Vajrabodhi.

At that time on behalf of all the unfortunate beings of the final age [of the Dharma], the Tathāgata expounded the mantra-teaching. At that time the sun, moon, stars, and [lunar] lodges surrounded [the Buddha] and assembled like clouds all around him, and in unison uttered this question, "Would the Tathāgata expound for us the spirit-spell?" At that time the World-honored One uttered the eight-star spell:

> Oṃ sapta-jināya bhajāmi jyaya jambu-dhama svāmi-nakṣatraṃ bhavatu svāhā

This mudrā and mantra come from the Seven Star section of the *Sarvatathāgatatattvasaṃgraha* [note: this section does not exist!].

The Buddha told Hungry Wolf, Ruiner of Armies, and the others, "If there are good sons and daughters who receive and maintain this spirit-spell and preserve it, will you protect them or not?" At that time the Eight Ladies answered the World-Honored One: "If someone chants this spirit-spell every day their evil karma will certainly be completely eradicated and they will accomplish everything they wish. If, moreover, someone is able to chant this spirit-spell 108 times each day, then forthwith he and all his kinsman will obtain our protection. If, moreover, a person is able to chant it five hundred times [each day] then, because of its awesome spiritual power, with a radius of five hundred yojanas none of the māra [demon]-kings, the demon hordes, the obstructers, or the numberless evil ghosts will dare to approach, and we will always protect him. The Eight Ladies of the Northern Dipper, the sun, moon, stars, and lodges, all the divine dragons (*nāgas*) and dryads (*yakṣas*) and those able to create obstructions and difficulties at once will cease their obstruction. If someone wishes to worship them, first arouse an altruistic mind and in a pure place [suitable] for meditation take incense, flowers, drink, and food for offerings. Recite the spirit-spell and make the mudrā. If you make offerings thus, the Eight Ladies and their retinue will manifest and in accord with one's wishes they will serve you, and you will accomplish your limitless desires. If it is kingly status you [desire, you] will have it—[therefore] how much more so the status and glory of lesser worldly positions? If you want long life [they will] scratch out your karmic register and restore your life register. If all the kings of states, the princes, the great officers, those of the rear courts, and so on construct maṇḍalas in their palaces and pay obescience in accordance with the appropriate homa, the Eight Ladies of the Northern Dipper will be delighted. As a result [you will] long abide in a superior position and constantly be happy. The one hundred officers—those superior and those inferior—will be in harmony and not commit acts contrary to the teaching. The people will flourish and the harvests will be abundant. The state will be at peace and without disasters, and weird occurrences will not manifest. Sickness and death will not arise, and all the criminals within the borders will naturally disperse. Therefore keep this method secret from unbelievers and do not transmit it to the ignorant. This is because those who are ignorant have minds that do not discriminate. Being unable to grasp the intent of the teaching they give rise to doubt and criticism. Although ignorant, those born of the Vajra ["Diamond"], sons of the Vajra, and the like constantly chant and maintain the Buddha-Eye-Mother mantra and [this teaching] ought to be transmitted to them. Though ignorant, the Vajra-sons do not doubt or criticize and therefore they attain success with the method. As for those who practice it, even in the joy of the Sukhāvatī they profoundly reorient themselves toward attaining unsurpassed bodhi [enlightenment].

Secret Essentials for Performing Homa to the Seven Stars of the Northern Dipper

Compiled by Master Guanding of the scripture translation bureau of the Great Xingshan monastery.

I will now, on behalf of the multitude of unfortunate beings of this latter age, explicate the sequence of rites for making homa offerings to the seven stars of the Northern Dipper.

In a pure room make a water altar—whether square or round, about a forearm across is adequate. Take thatch incense, sweet pine [valerian] and cense the area. Blend dragon-brain [Borneo camphor?], white sandalwood, and five-flavor [*Schizandra chinensis*?] and daub it [on the altar]. Within the altar around the hearth install drink, food, and fruit. Divide these in seven portions and set them out. Food refers to congee [rice soup], cakes, koumiss [fermented camels' milk], and so on. But as for the choice among the five grains and sapwood, they are to be selected according to a person's natal star.

First make a vow intoning these words: "I earnestly request that the Seven Luminaries, the venerable stars, the daras [the smashers], Hungry Wolf, Great Gate, Wage Preserver, Literary Song, Pure and Upright, Military Song, and Ruiner of Armies, on behalf of the patron so-and-so, [to] free him from danger and lengthen his life so he will see one hundred autumns. I have constructed this maṇḍala and wish that you would condescend to take pity [on him] and approach this place to accept this homa. Protect this patron so-and-so, free him from disasters and lengthen his life in accordance with his heart's desire" (repeat this three times).

Next make the mudrā, clasping your hands before your heart, take your thumbs and press them on the nails of the third finger [such that] the middle and little fingers are like a lotus blossom. Open and close your index fingers slightly.

Next intone the monosyllabic Uṣnīṣa-rāja mantra and the mantra for invoking the seven stars of the Northern Dipper. The Uṣnīṣa-rāja mantra is:

Nama samanta dara dara pacara hūṃ

The mantra for invoking the Northern Dipper is:

Namaḥ samanta darana ehyehi pai hai dai kai rai murdara gharahaṃ svāhā

Pick up the wood, the five grains, the koumiss, oil, etc., and throw it into the hearth to incinerate it. Turn to examine [the patron's] natal star. If its appearance scintillates and changes color and it shines with a yellowish-white light, then you should make a vow to the Tathāgata and in accordance with the previous method do it for seven days and nights. You must not, in such cases, approach this star, as it is concealed and may not be seen. Those referred to as the seven stars of the Northern Dipper are the essences of the sun, moon, and five stars [the planets]. In antiquity these comprised the seven luminaries that shine in [all] eight directions. Above they shine on the celestial spirits, on earth they shine down on men. They control good and evil and apportion calamity and fortune. The host of stars report to them and the ten thousand spirits bow before [them] in reverence. If someone worships and makes offerings to them, that person will have long life and good fortune. He who does not believe and revere them, his fortune will not last long.

The *Book of Wages and Fate* says, "In the world is the spirit who is Comptroller of Fate. On each *keng shen* day (day fifty-seven in the sixty-day calendrical cycle) he turns to the Celestial Emperor to detail the good and evil that people do. If a person [is guilty of] serious offenses then he receives the penalty of destruction. If a person [is guilty of] lighter offenses then he loses twelve years [of his life]. When the twelve-year [sentence] in the reckoning book is announced as having elapsed, forthwith the Comptroller of Fate puts an end to them." Therefore the Tathāgata, on behalf of the multitude of beings in the last generation who are of little fortune and short fate and who die prematurely, has expounded this monosyllabic Uṣnīṣa-rāja [mantra] and proceedures for summoning and offering homa to the seven stars of the Northern Dipper. On behalf of those who make the offerings, these deities will order the appropriate natal star to remove them from the death records and restore them to the life records.

If all the kings of states construct maṇḍalas in their palaces and in accordance with this method offer homa and worship, then [the stars of] the Northern

Dipper will be delighted and therefore will protect you. You will long abide in a superior station and you will continually receive peace and security. Ladies-in-waiting, wives of high officials, concubines of the rear palaces, princes, the multitude of officers, the three dukes, and the one hundred officials will be in concord and will not act contrary to the Dharma. The people will multiply, they will sow and reap bountifully, and the state will be at peace. There will be no calamites, and incongruous events will not manifest themselves. Sickness and death will not arise. Within the borders resentment and opposition and the hordes of bandits will naturally flee and disperse. Therefore keep this method secret!

—23—

The Great Wisdom Mother and the Gcod Tradition

Giacomella Orofino

The tradition of Bdud kyi gcod yul (literally, "the demon as the object that is to be cut off") is a medieval Buddhist practice developed in Tibet in the eleventh century. Becoming widespread soon after the so-called period of the "new translations" of the Indian Buddhist Tantras in Tibetan, it was developed directly in Tibetan rather than imported from India and translated from Sanskrit. It is a syncretic movement that marks the confluence of Indian Tantric Buddhist and pre-Buddhist Tibetan elements that are clearly shamanic in nature, which together gave rise to a religious phenomenon with an identity of its own. It is based on a complex literature that incorporated texts on dance, chanting, ritual music, the nature of mystic hallucinations and visions, geomancy, exorcism, curing plagues, and funeral rites. The basic principle of the practice involves annihilating the ego by severing or "cutting off" demons.

This tradition was little known in the West prior to the last quarter century, when it began to attract scholarly attention. The few Westerners who had previously described the gcod (pronounced chö) practice had provided only a superficial analysis of it, more closely linked to the magicoreligious aspect of its ritual than to its philosophic background and significance. The earliest data concerning the doctrines of this practice had already arrived in the West before the mid-nineteenth century, in the vague and somewhat mystifying descriptions left by the early explorers of Tibet. This was followed in 1929 by the accounts of Alexandra David-Neel, who described the gcod ritual in more detail, defining it as a "macabre banquet" in which the officiant tramples all the passions underfoot, "crucifying" the ego. In 1935 Evans-Wentz published the translation by Kazi Dawa Samdup of *The Laughter of the Ḍākinīs* (*Mkha' 'gro gad rgyangs*), one of the most widespread ritual texts on gcod, from the collection of *Klong chen snying thig* by 'Jigs med Gling pa (1730–1798). The German author compared it to a mystic drama, akin to a mystery play, probably deriving from pre-Buddhist times. In 1953, George N. Roerich translated an entire chapter on the gcod yul system in the *Blue Annals*, his English version of the *Deb gter sngon po*, one of the best-known treatises on the history of Tibet, written between 1476 and 1478 by 'Gos lo tsā ba Gzon nu dpal; and it is here that the Western reader could find for the first time a brief hagiography of the most relevant female figure of this school, Ma gcig Lab sgron (pronounced Ma chig Lab droun). Unfortunately Roerich, in two other chapters of the *Blue Annals*, one on the New Tantras and the Lam 'Bras, (the "Path and Its Fruit" teachings), and another on the lineages of the Zhi byed doctrines, confused Ma gcig Lab sgron with Ma gcig Zha chung ma, a contemporary woman saint. This error, which led other scholars to confuse the two yoginīs, was identified in 1985 by Janet Gyatso in her thorough study of the gcod tradition. Subsequently, since 1990, the Western public has had access to Ma gcig's biography and to the foundations of gcod through the well-documented studies of Karénina Kollmar Paulenz and the more popularized account by Jerome Edou.

In this essay I examine the central philosophy of the gcod school, its origins, and its theoretical premises. This is followed by an analysis of the taxonomy of the concept of "demon" from early Buddhism through Mahāyāna thought to its subsequent development in gcod doctrine. This leads to an examination of the relationship between Vajrayāna Buddhism and the literature of Tantras in Tibet, as well as a description of gcod practitioners, ritual objects, and the structure of the practice. I also discuss the pre-Buddhist and shamanistic elements of death and resurrection, exorcism, and decontamination. Finally, I outline Ma gcig's life as a means of identifying the ways in which the main strands of this tradition were developed in her practice. The translation is an excerpt from a poem attributed by the tradition to Ma gcig Lab sgron, the Great Collection of the Teachings (*Bka' tshoms chen mo*), which was included among the gcod "root texts" by the nineteenth-century Tibetan scholar 'Jam mgon Kong sprul (1813–1899) in his compilation entitled the *Treasury of Profound Instructions* (*Gdams ngag mdzod*). Although a complete Italian translation of this text has been published and a German translation is in preparation, no English edition exists.

The colophon to the *Great Collection of the Teachings* states that the poem is a work by Ma gcig and that it should be considered to be the basis for all the gcod doctrines. This work is renowned by Tibetan tradition as that saint's spiritual testament, and the text that, more than any other, expresses her thought in a clear and essential way. We find in it an analysis of the theory of the "four demons" according to gcod tradition. Starting from the principle that the root of all demons is to be found in one's own mind, Ma gcig examines the mechanisms that form the basis of human suffering, concluding with the consideration that all demons can be incorporated into those of ego-clinging and pride. Her analysis has an apophatic connotation that reminds us of the Prajñāpāramitā (Perfection of Wisdom) literature, and especially of Nāgārjunian thought which holds that supreme reality is neither conceivable nor obtainable through concepts. In this way, her analysis of the mind is transformed into a hymn to the absolute reality, pure in its essential nature and free from religious dogma. It offers us considerable insight into one of the most remarkable traditions of medieval Buddhism.

Theoretical Premises

In the gcod system, liberation from the fetters of existence can only come about through the annihilation of pride. The foremost demon to be severed is attachment to the ego, and all that flows from it: pride, vanity, arrogance, and presumptuousness. This is the fundamental cause of human ignorance and the true obstacle to conquering the suffering of existence and awakening to supreme knowledge. In more general terms, annihilation of the self is the axis around which the whole of Buddhist philosophy has turned from its very inception. In this system, however, cutting off the ego takes on a very specific connotation, as it is based not so much on philosophical speculation as on ritual procedure that, teeming with elements of considerable emotional charge, is deeply rooted in the ancient pre-Buddhist traditions of Tibet. The main rite in gcod is a sacred drama in which the officiant, dancing and chanting to the rhythm of a two-headed drum and the sound of a trumpet made from a human thighbone, invokes all the spirits and gods of the universe and offers them the gift of his body.

It is not easy to establish the phases of the historical development of this tradition. According to Tibetan historical tradition, the gcod system originated in certain Indian Buddhist schools, the foremost being that of the Pacification of Suffering, which was founded by Pha Dam pa Sangs rgyas, a Buddhist master who lived between the end of the eleventh and the beginning of the twelfth centuries. Another important person in the line of transmission was the brahman Āryadeva, who some texts identify as Pha Dam pa's uncle. This master is obviously not the philosopher Āryadeva, the contemporary of Nāgārjuna who played such a major part in the formulation of Mādhyamika thought; nor is he the Tantric Āryadeva, disciple of the Tantric Nāgārjuna who may have lived in the eighth or ninth century. According to tradition, the brahman Āryadeva was the author of a short text called the *Teaching on the Perfection of Wisdom* that is considered to be the theorical basis of the gcod philosophy, which was translated into Tibetan by different authors. A copy of one these versions is also preserved in the Peking Tengyur (*bstan 'gyur*) (vol. 146, pp. 171–72).

Giving up one's body was already a cherished topic of ancient Buddhism, as is evident in certain stories of the Buddha's previous lives (*jātaka*), including those of the tiger and of the hare. In Āryaśūra's rendition of the jātaka of the tiger, the Buddha, before offering his body as food to a starving tigress that was on the verge of eating her own cubs, uttered these words:

> This body of ours is devoid of life, fragile, insubstantial, the source of suffering, unrewarding, always impure. He who is unwilling to offer it for the good of others is foolish! Attachment to our own pleasure and the impossibility of alleviating our suffering render us indifferent to others' suffering. However, why should I remain indifferent to this suffering as long as it exists and as long as it is possible to alleviate it? For if, having the opportunity to alleviate someone's suffering, even if he were the

> greatest malefactor, I were to remain indifferent, then I would feel I had committed a transgression and my mind would burn like dry twigs in a fire. So I will hurl myself down from this cliff and kill my miserable body, so that the tiger will not have to kill her cubs, so that these will not be set upon by their mother.

The theoretical premises of the gcod yul system must be sought, however, in the Buddhist Prajñāpāramitā literature, a corpus composed in India in successive stages from the first century to the end of the first millennium C.E., and which constitutes the foundation of Mahāyāna mysticism. In the Prajñāpāramitā tradition, the Perfection of Wisdom is depicted as a mother goddess, the mother of all the buddhas and bodhisattvas. This element, which comes to be grafted onto such a strongly patriarchal religion as ancient Buddhism, may reflect the cult of the mother goddess that distinguished the matriarchal societies of the Dravidian populations of south India. This literature ascribed great importance to prajñā, wisdom or gnosis. Etymologically, the words *gnōsis* and *prajñā* derive from the same Indo-European stem, and many scholars have pointed out that the Prajñāpāramitā literature shares certain elements with the religious and philosophical traditions that derive from the Hellenistic mysticism that was developing during the same period in the Mediterranean area.

Like the Perfection of Wisdom, all of the various gnostic systems, both Christian and pagan—Hermeticism, Neoplatonism, Neopythagoreanism, and Hebrew wisdom lore—are based on the principle that awakening can only take place through an inner process of knowledge. This knowledge of ultimate reality, in contraposition to ignorance (*avidyā*), can only arise from direct revelation. Moreover, just as in Indian Mahāyāna Buddhism, so too in the gnostic traditions of the Mediterranean and the Near East, Wisdom is a magna mater, likened to ethereal space, pure and immaculate as sunlight, who metes out divine ambrosia.

In the Perfection of Wisdom literature, phenomenal reality is deemed a dream, a mirage, a magical apparition, an illusion. It is only by generating prajñā within oneself that one can rend the veil of ignorance and see the ultimate nature of all existence (*dharmatā*). Thus, the concept arises of two truths—one provisional and conventional, the other absolute and definitive. However, the dualism that might appear to arise from this subdivision has already been surmounted in this phase of Buddhism, since phenomenal reality, being devoid of self-existence, is identical with the absolute truth. This truth, however, is ineffable, beyond the imagination, without form or characteristics, and totally empty.

Alongside emergent speculation on the notion of emptiness (*śūnyatā*), a new ideal starts taking shape within the Greater Vehicle literature; this is the ideal of the bodhisattva, who, like the Buddha, has perceived the supreme truth and yet who renounces nirvāṇa—the complete and definitive extinction of worldly suffering, for the benefit of others—and chooses to continue taking birth in the cycle of saṃsāra in order to help others on their path towards liberation. This new ideal of love for others is most clearly expressed in a work by the eighth-century Indian mystic Śāntideva, the *Bodhicaryāvatāra*, ("The Bodhisattva's Conduct"), a treatise of great spiritual force on compassion and love, which analyzes the inner path of the bodhisattva from the resolution to dedicate oneself to the good of others, to the disciplines (mindfulness, patience, enthusiasm, meditation, etc.) that help to maintain the pledge, up to the attainment of the actual capacity to benefit others. From Śantideva's text (8.129) we read:

All the joy of this world
derives from the wish for anothers' joy;
all the suffering of this world
derives from the wish for one's own joy.

In these words we find already delineated the thought that underlies the gcod system, in which, analogously, attachment to the ego is identified as the factor that determines the suffering and ignorance proper to the human condition. Compassion (*karuṇā*) and awareness of emptiness are thus the fundamental principles that underlie the religious literature of the Perfection of Wisdom, which is the source of the gcod system. It should be noted, moreover, that at times in this tradition the term *gcod* ("to sever") is replaced by *spyod* (pronounced in the same way), which means "practice" or "spiritual exercise," which refers precisely to the virtuous acts and practices of the Bodhisattva path.

The Demons

A significant feature of this system is a demonology of sorts, which comprises an accurate analysis of the various demons (*māra* in Sanskrit; *bdud* in Tibetan) that hinder awakening and hence must be uprooted and removed. The etymological derivation of *māra* (which is also the symbol of the presence of evil in early Buddhism) is the Sanskrit root *mṛ-*, "to die," whence *mṛtyu*, "death." However, whereas mṛtyu indicates the act of death, māra stands for "he who causes death." In Buddhist literature, both Pali and Sanskrit, Māra is the tempter, the offender, who arouses sensual desire, and assails the Buddha to distract him from the spiritual path. He is the demon who holds and binds men in chains, forcing them to perpetuate a life that is under the power of death.

We should take note, however, of the ambivalence of Māra's name. On the one hand, it designates a popular god with his own place within the cosmology of early Buddhism: leader of the Paranirmitavaśavartin gods and lord of the realm of desire; on the other hand, it reflects the etymological meaning of "he who causes death," and Māra is thereby associated with everything that is deceptive, transient, or that brings about spiritual death. These various aspects were subsequently codified in the Greater Vehicle in the formula of the four māras. The *Mahāprajñāpāramitāśāstra* reads: "There are four kinds of māra: Māra of the aggregates (*skandha-māra*), Māra of the mental afflictions (*kleśa-māra)*, Māra of death (*mṛtyu-māra*), and Māra, son of the deities (*devaputra-māra*). The metaphorical function of the four māras in relation to spiritual death is explained in the following way in the *Śrāvakabhūmi* of Asaṅga, the fifth-century Buddhist philosopher of the idealist Cittamatra ('Mind Only') school: Skandha-māra corresponds to the five aggregates that constitute the personality. Kleśa-māra corresponds to the passions that range over the three worlds. Mṛtyu-māra fixes the moment of death of sentient beings. Devaputra-māra is the son of the gods, born in the realm of desire and thus lord over it, who leads those who aspire to transcend the aggregates, passions, and death astray from the practice of virtue." The personage of Māra is also present in the Perfection of Wisdom literature. One of the most ancient texts of this tradition, the *Prajñāpāramitā-ratnaguṇasaṃcayagāthā*, "Stanzas on the Perfection of Wisdom, Heap of Precious Virtue," the original kernel of which probably dates back to the first century B.C.E., reads (27.447–49):

> If as many beings as there are in the fields—countless as the sands of the Ganges—would all, let us assume, become māras;
> And if every single hair on their bodies would again magically create a snare, they could all not hinder the Wise.
> For four reasons does the powerful and wise bodhisattva
> Becomes unassailable by the four māras:
> Because he dwells in the emptiness;
> Because he does not abandon other beings;
> Because he acts as he speaks;
> Because he is sustained by the Sugatas.

In the *Blue Annals*, these verses are indicated as the foundation of the theory and practice of the gcod system. The four principles listed therein: awareness of emptiness, love for one's neighbor, observance of Bodhisattva conduct, and devotion to one's master and spiritual lineage constitute the pivots of the conduct of gcod practitioners. In this system, however, the interpretation of the aspects of Māra is developed still further. The four categories are multiplied, reflecting the multifarious nature of Vajrayāna esotericism, with a division of the symbol of evil under two headings: "outer" and "inner." Later works add further subdivisions: the "secret" and the "particular" māras.

The outer māras correspond to those of Indian Mahāyāna literature, listed above. The analysis of the four demons that we find in Ma gcig's work, on the other hand, refers to the "inner" māras and subdivides them into "tangible," "intangible," "of complacency," and "of pride." The tangible demons (*thogs bcas kyi bdud*, literally, "demons that have obstructions") belong to visible reality and consist of all the phenomena which, through sensory experience, arouse desire and the thirst for possession in people, and enhance the sense of concreteness and of the material reality of phenomena, the worst error according to Buddhist doctrine. The intangible demons (*thogs med kyi bdud*, "demons that do not have obstructions") comprise purely mental events. They arise when the categories of good and evil are separated in the mind and one distinguishes between what one wants and what one rejects. This discrimination is the cause of the continuous alternation between illusion and delusion that generates emotional instability and lack of awareness of ultimate reality. The demons of complacency (*dga' brod kyi bdud*) comprise all those factors that lead to feeling complacent about results obtained regarding philosophical knowledge and powers acquired through the practice of yoga. In reality, these cause obstacles and block spiritual progress. The demons of pride (*snyems byed kyi bdud*) give rise to haughtiness and arrogance. These are the most important of the demons, as they give rise to all the others, because attachment to the ego is deemed the first cause of the death of knowledge.

Cutting off Mental Afflictions

The theme of cutting off mental affliction was already known in earlier Buddhist thought: It occurs in the Hināyāna (Lesser Vehicle) school, as attested in Buddhaghosa's *Visudhimagga*, which states that "relinquishment by means of cutting off takes place in the one who cultivates the supermundane path leading to the destruction of contaminations." According to the *Blue Annals*, the origin of the term *gcod* ("cutting off") is found in the *Abhidharmakośa,* the summa of Sarvāstivādin-Vaibhāṣika thought compiled in the fifth century C.E. by the Indian philosopher Vasubhandu:

> Now, why is this practice defined "the object that is to be cut off" (*gcod yul*)? In Vasubhandu's *Abhidharmakośa* (5.34) it says: "Mental afflictions originate: 1. from habitual attachment (*anuśaya*); 2. from the presence of external objects; and 3. from erroneous mental acts." What have to be cut off are mental afflictions. If these afflictions originate from attachment, from the presence of external objects, and from erroneous mental acts, then as soon as the yogin comes into contact with an external object and traces of past actions (*vāsanās*) arise within him, he must cut off at the root those afflictions [deriving] from objects that are based on erroneous mental acts. This is the reason why this system is called "the object that is to be cut off" (*gcod yul*).

Vajrayāna Buddhism

The Buddhist Tantras, which constitute the final phase of Indian Buddhist literature, constitute a highly complex religious phenomenon, in which Mahāyāna thought coalesced with popular traditions and cults of ancient India to form a mystical and gnostic system that was highly symbolical in character. It was called the Diamond Vehicle or Vajrayāna (from *vajra*, the "diamond" as symbol of the perfect and immutable nature of ultimate reality), and the Mantra Vehicle or Mantrayāna (from mantra, the sacred formulas that were of crucial importance in this system).

The first promulgators of Vajrayāna Buddhism, called Siddhas ("perfect ones"), were yogins, mostly wanderers, living in various regions of India in the medieval period. These ascetics—among them several women—who had absorbed the classical Buddhist theses (the suffering of existence, the transient and fundamentally empty nature of phenomena, and so on), elaborated a system that gave much attention to the practice of yoga. Furthermore, they maintained that the passions which characterize human nature, such as sexual desire, were no longer deemed negative factors to be repressed; instead, the energy they provided constituted the principal means of liberation from the fetters of existence.

The behaviour of the Siddhas contravened the rules and conventions of the Buddhist monastic communities and contemporary society. Like a kind of sacred madness, their quest for ultimate truth and the fundamental identity of all phenomena led them to wander far from towns and to live with outcastes, to eat meat and other impure foods, to drink alcohol, and lie with women—without discriminating. The teachings of the Tantras had a strongly esoteric and initiatory character, and the very words of the sacred texts were incomprehensible without the associated initiation and a master's guidance.

The spiritual heritage of Tantric Buddhism was readily received in Tibet. The Tantras were translated into Tibetan, along with the earlier Buddhist literature, in two successive phases, in the eighth and eleventh centuries. These translations were then arranged and systematized in the Buddhist literary compilations called Kangyur (*bka' 'gyur*), composed of texts that were considered to be the "word" (*bka'*) of the Buddha himself, and Tengyur (*bstan 'gyur*), the commentarial writings. These canons include thousands of works, and are of critical importance to the history of Asian religion, inasmuch as within them are preserved numerous texts, of which the Sanskrit originals no longer exist.

To return to the origins of the gcod tradition, we read further in the *Blue Annals* ('Gos lo tsā va, 870):

> "How can one assert that gcod is similar to the Tantras? Because it conforms to the *Hevajratantra*.
>
> "Good meditation is meditation performed under a lonely tree, in a cemetery, at night, in the places of the Terrible Mothers (*mātṛ*, in Sanskrit; *ma mo* in Tibetan) or in remote places" (*Hevajratantra* VI.6).
>
> Furthermore:
>
> "Having offered his body as a gift, he can start the practice" (*Hevajratantra* VI.19); and:
>
> "Whatever demon appears before him, even if it resembles Indra, he will not be afraid, because he steps forward like a lion" (*Hevajratantra* VI.25).

The three topics indicated in the *Hevajratantra*—the choice of terrifying places, above all cemeteries; the ritual offering of one's body; and overcoming fear—are of such importance in the gcod system as to be considered the fundamental rules for practitioners of this religious system. The gcod pa (gcod practitioners) were yogins who had given up the world and all social conventions to wander from one cemetery to another, carefully selecting for their practice places that were desolate and particularly fearful. Cemeteries in Tibet were grim, uninhabited places, where corpses were devoured by vultures and wild animals. The fear engendered by these places, frequented by ravenous beasts hunting for remains of the cadavers, must have been great, especially at night.

Like the other Tantric yogins, the gcod yogins wore ragged clothing, but were recognizable by certain characteristic ritual gcod objects: a ḍamaru, the two-headed drum played in one hand, thereby enabling the yogin to dance with the other hand free to accompany his chant with the rkang gling (a trumpet made from a human or vulture's thigh bone, whose sound evoked demonic spirits); a ritual bell; the skin of a predatory animal with the claws still intact, a symbol of courage and power; a folding tent, his only shelter against bad weather and symbol of his high aspirations; a trident, which also served to support his tent; a skull (*kapāla*) used as a bowl for his daily meal, a banner made of strips of tiger and leopard skin; a braid of human hair; and a rectangular red hat. This attire was somewhat reminiscent of the garb of the Kāpālikas, the Śaiva sect that took the concepts of Hindu Tantra to extremes, and in which a very important religious role was played by human skulls and bones.

The Structure of the Gcod Practice

The practice of gcod began with a sacred dance in which, to the rhythm of the ḍamaru and the sound of the rkang gling, the yogin visualized himself dancing on his own ego and trampling his dualistic thoughts, fears, desires, and all the fetters of *saṃsāra*. He danced before the buddhas, the Tantric deities, and the ḍākinīs. These latter goddesses, already present as minor figures in the Indian pantheon, acquired great importance in Vajrayāna, where they were considered to be the hypostases of the active energy that arises from wisdom; they were depicted—as attested in the sacred art of Tibet—as female deities who had both a peaceful and attractive, and a terrifying and disquieting mien. In Kaṅha's 800 to 850 C.E. *Yogaratnamāla*, one of the few commentaries of the *Hevajratantra* extant in Sanskrit, we read (2.3.3) that "*ḍākinī* derives from the root *ḍai*, which means to fly in the sky and which corresponds to the power (*siddhi*) of moving anywhere in the sky." As a consequence, the Tibetans translated this word as *mkha' 'gro ma*, "she who flies in space," ascribing a pivotal religious role to these goddesses. In this case, "space" means the essential condition of reality, the pure unconditioned state, the ground of all existence; flight in this dimension indicates the dynamic capacity of transcendent wisdom to turn into action. As we read in the lives of the saints and mystics of Tibet, however, the ḍākinīs can, in addition to belonging to metaphysical reality, also take on the form of flesh-and-blood women, whose tasks it is to aid yogins and to spread and protect the doctrines.

Gcod, elaborated by a woman, presided over by a female deity, with a ritual charged with emotional force, became the ḍākinī practice par excellence. The *Laughter of the Ḍākinīs* states:

I, fearless yogin, practicing
to unite saṃsāra and nirvāṇa,

dancing on the deities and spirits of the ego,
reduce to dust the discursive thought
of transmigration
that generates dualism.

This dance is followed by the evocation of all kinds of gods and spirits, invited to attend the ritual sacrifice of one's body. The gcod pa visualizes the transformation of his consciousness into a ḍākinī, who cuts the head off his physical body and then places the corpse inside the cranium, which stretches to cosmic proportions. The corpse is subsequently transformed in accordance with the wishes of the guests, multiplied infinitely, and offered to them as a gift. Then the offering is divided into various categories: the white offering, in which the yogin visualizes that his body is transformed into ambrosia to be consumed by the higher deities and by the three jewels: the buddhas, devas, and ḍākinīs; the multicoloured offering, in which his body is transformed into all kinds of riches and material goods and offered to the dharmapālas, the protector spirits of the Buddhist law; the red offering, in which the dismembered flesh and blood are multiplied infinitely to appease the demons and fierce spirits; and finally the black offering, in which the officiant visualizes that all the errors and wrongdoings of the world are absorbed into his body, which is then offered as a meal to the demons. These offerings aim to satisfy all spirits, both higher and lower, in order to placate negative impulses and to eliminate definitively the ills of the world.

Having performed the sacrifice, the yogin, who has now transcended hope and fear, is absorbed in absolute reality. This is the most solemn moment of the drama: the gift of the teaching to all the evoked beings and to the entire world. Through this gift, which encapsulates the ultimate meaning of the entire rite, redemption for oneself and others is assured and supreme catharsis realized.

The gcod practitioners are aware of the psychological significance of this macabre banquet. According to the texts, the deities (*lha*) evoked during the ritual are the symbolic images of his desires and wishes while the evil spirits (*'dre*) are nothing but projections of the practitioner's mind, embodiments of his disquiet and fear. Offering one's body and dancing on one's ego represent the means of eliminating discrimination between good and evil, between desire and aversion—the dichotomy that all Buddhist thought deems the root cause of all suffering. In Ma gcig's *Great Collection* we read:

Practicing gcod in terrifying places
is like healing injuries
wreaked by fire
by cauterizing with fire.
This teaching,
which consists in stirring, cutting off,
driving back, and subjugating [the demons]
and which arouses strong sensations, is like
healing through application of fire.

In the gcod system, the horror the yogins seek by evoking demonic spirits in terrifying places is a metaphor for the anguish and fears that characterize human existence. These can only be eliminated by doing away with one's pride and desires, which derive from attachment to oneself. The exacerbation of fear thus becomes the method for definitively conquering fear itself. Ma gcig's text goes on to explain the reason for choosing places that engender fear, and for the visualizations of demonic spirits or other dreadful apparitions. All this is defined as the necessary condition *(pratyaya)* for ripening the cause of liberation inherent in every being:

> As the appearance of the conditions
> is like a weight getting heavier,
> one comes to understand that the secret method
> lies precisely in making the weight heavier.
> Unless all reality is made worse
> one cannot attain liberation
> by means of soothing and pleasing antidotes.
> Wander in grisly places and mountain retreats,
> do not let yourself get distracted
> by doctrines or books:
> no spiritual power can come from them.
> So, just get real experiences
> in horrid, desolate places.

The Pre-Buddhist Elements

The Buddhist elaboration of the theme and practice of gcod is grounded in magicoreligious traditions and popular creeds in which archaic elements are easily perceptible. For example, the gcod initiatory ritual often uses the expression "opening the door of the sky" *(nam mkha' sgo 'byed)*, which denotes ascension to a state of transcendent consciousness. This same expression is also found in the popular religion of Tibet, where it designates ascent into the celestial sphere by means of the magic rainbow light cord *(dmu)*. According to ancient narratives about the epoch of the monarchy, the dmu cord was used by the early kings to descend to earth and then reascend to heaven after their death. To this day, this term refers to the center of a house or tent, above which a hole is made to allow daylight and smoke from the hearth to pass. The dmu cord is the symbol of communication between earth and sky: this word is also found in divinatory rites, in which it connotes the "cord for ascending to the sky," as well as in other popular apotropaic rituals.

Moreover, it should be noted that in terms of the dramatic intensity of the ritual procedure, the gcod practices of dismembering and offering the body to the spirits recall the initiatory dismemberment of the future shaman by demons and the souls of his ancestors, found among Siberian and Central Asian as well as North and South American, African, and Indonesian peoples.

Apart from ritual dismemberment, which partakes of the universal phenomenon of death and resurrection found in many archaic traditions, it is possible to discern other significant elements in the gcod system that evince traces of shamanism, such as the important ritual function of the sound of the thighbone trumpet and the drum as instruments serving to contact "the spirit world." Moreover, it should be noted that the gcod pa, like the shamans in nearby Buryatia, serve a particular role in Tibetan society by virtue of their position as exorcists of the possessed and healers of illnesses—such as plague or other epidemic diseases—that are popularly believed to be caused by demonic spirits. In Tibet there was great fear of epidemics, both of humans and livestock, because they presented a serious threat to the local, and particularly the nomad, economy. On these occasions, the only persons authorized to touch the dead were the gcod pa, who were summoned even from afar to perform the funerary and purificatory rites. According to tradition, the gcod practitioner has transcended all forms of fear, as he has overcome all dualistic considerations created by the ordinary mind concerning good and bad, pure and impure, and so on. In this way he cannot be assailed by demons and fierce spirits, and acquires the power to subjugate them and to heal the diseases they inflict.

Ma gcig Lab sgron between History and Myth

According to her biographers, Ma gcig lab sgron was born in the region of E'i Lab southwest Tibet in the middle of the eleventh century, during a period of great religious and cultural ferment. Born into a Buddhist family, and bearing all the signs that indicate an extraordinary birth, she displayed an early inclination to study the sacred scriptures. From the time she was a child, she had the opportunity of assimilating the basic principles of Buddhist thought, in particular those found in the Perfection of Wisdom texts, of which she was an expert reader. Already at the age of ten she could read four volumes a day, six times faster than other experts, and so she was called Lab sgron, the "Light of the Lab region," because of the knowledge and wisdom she was soon able to display.

Orphaned at the death of her mother, she became a reader in the monastery of Lama A ston. However, the disciple soon surpassed her master and, as he had nothing more to teach her, he sent her to one of the major lamas of the time, the famous gter ston Grwa pa Mngon shes, the discoverer of the Four Tibetan Medical Tantras. For four years Ma gcig remained with this master of the ancient tradition, who taught her the Prajñāpāramitā teachings in depth. Subsequently, she received teachings from Lama Bsod nams Grags pa, who initiated her into the esoteric meanings of the doctrines. The hagiographies of Ma gcig recount that thanks to these teachings she had a deep intuition of the Prajñāpāramitā; she was especially struck by the chapter on demons (*māra*), and through this experience she stabilized her knowledge and was liberated from the dualism of saṃsāra. This episode can be interpreted as the first acknowledgement by her Tibetan biographers of Ma gcig's independence of religious thought, which was then subsumed and organized in the gcod system. Due to her awakening, Ma gcig utterly abandoned worldly conventions, threw away her clothes, donned rags, and went to live with lepers and outcasts.

Subsequently, the yoginī completed her religious training, receiving instruction from several masters of the various Buddhist schools. According to tradition, the most significant spiritual encounter of her life was with Pha Dam pa Sangs rgyas, the Indian Mahāsiddha who introduced the religious tradition known as sdug bsngal zhi byed (The Pacification of Suffering) into Tibet. His teachings were aimed at liberating humans from every form of suffering through the process of the gradual elimination of all attachments and passions. Pha Dam pa is still very popular in Tibet, especially in such areas as the Ding ri Valley in the southwest of the country, not far from the Nepal border, where he plays a significant role in connection with the the local folklore and cult of sacred rocks. He was famous for both his great yogic capacity and his iconoclasm: in fact he destroyed all the depictions of deities that he found, deeming them sources of delusion. He used to exhort his disciples to consider ritual ceremonies and philosophical dissertations as a kind of attachment, and would advise them to leave their monasteries to go practice in the solitude of forests or mountain hermitages. According to one of her biographers, Pha Dam pa immediately entrusted Ma gcig with his spiritual testament, telling her, "Accept what disgusts you. Help those it seems impossible to help. Give up all the things you desire. Go to frightening places such as cemeteries. Always remain vigilant and aware. Find the Buddha within yourself." According to certain accounts, this first encounter took place in Ma gcig's youth, although it was only subsequently, when she was an adult, that the yoginī received the various initiations of sdug bsngal zhi byed and gcod from the siddha. However, recent studies have cast doubts on the centrality and importance ascribed by the Tibetans to Pha Dam pa in the constitution of the gcod system.

All of her biographers tend to highlight the autonomy of Ma gcig's religious inspiration. An episode—recounted in the *Blue Annals* and told in greater detail in one of her biographies (*Rnam bshad,* 35–38)—which occurred during the initiation of the Tantric cycle of Mahāmāyā *(sgyu 'phrul chen mo)* conferred by Skyo ston Bsod nams bla ma, will serve as an example. We examine here the account drawn from the *Rnam bshad*, as it contains an abundance of symbolic details.

The initiation rite had been celebrated during the night, and when at dawn the lama was preparing to commence the most important phase of the ceremony, in which he conferred the Wisdom initiation, Ma gcig had a direct intuition of the teachings and suddenly withdrew from the temple. The yoginī, who had entered a deep contemplative state, rose into the air, dancing the sacred dances of the peaceful goddesses, and teaching in Sanskrit. When she had finished the dance, she alighted on a tree that was near a lake inhabited by a terrible and much feared snake (*nāga*). Ma gcig, who felt no fear of that demonic being, remained in deep meditation for a long time. Both angered and intimidated by the yoginī's presence, the demon called a throng of other demons and spirits who assailed her, seeking to terrify her, but the saint did not let herself be frightened by those monstrous beings and instead offered them her body. The *Rnam bshad* biography recounts that the demons could not harm her because they had not found any form of ego in her to attack. After she had conquered the demons, all the divine manifestations of the *Mahāmāyātantra* and the *Cakrasaṃvara,* all the buddhas of the ten directions, as well as the goddess Āryatārā herself came and conferred on Ma gcig the four Tantric initiations and numerous other spiritual instructions. Then Āryatārā predicted: "Yoginī, you will help all sentient beings and will practice in the 108 cemeteries and terrifying places. Your teachings will shine like the sun high in the sky and your disciples will attain the knowledge from which there is no turning back."

As soon as day broke, the lama and the others participating in the rite went looking for Ma gcig. They found her sitting in the tree, naked and free from all worldly misery. Descending from the branches, she prostrated before the lama, saying: "Those who prostrate sincerely before their master will be purified of all obstacles caused by their past deeds!" The other participants in the initiation then accused her of having interrupted the consecration, but the master said that, whereas they had all only received the initiation of the word *(tshig dbang)*, Ma gcig had been the only one to receive the initiation of the deep meaning (*don dbang*).

An examination of the allegorical elements in this brief episode enable us to comprehend Ma gcig's unique place in the Tibetan tradition. The central theme is that of her spiritual autonomy. Ma gcig is directly inspired by transcendent reality: she withdraws alone from the temple, hovers magically in space, dances the sacred dances, and teaches in the original language of the Tantras. These extraordinary elements mark the authority the Tibetans have ascribed to her. Her awakening is perfectly depicted in the image of the saint on top of the tree, dominating the snake with the power of meditation. To Ma gcig are ascribed the requisites for the founder of a new school. Furthermore, the religious ideal underlying the doctrine of gcod—whose core practice is the meditation on offering one's body—is actualized in the image of Ma gcig offering her body to the demons, by which she exorcizes herself of all possibility of harm. Finally, the initiations directly conferred by the divine manifestations, Āryatārā's auspicious prophecy concerning the yoginī's religious tradition, and the master's confirmation of the authenticity of her spiritual inspiration, all assert the undisputed authority the Tibetans ascribe to Ma gcig as the founder of a religious tradition.

The latter part of her saintly life is marked by her encounter with Thod pa Bhadra (Sanskrit Kapālabhadra), an Indian yogin from Kośala. After having received certain auspicious omens, Ma gcig married him and they had several children. Some biographies relate that Ma gcig was harshly criticized for renouncing her monastic vows and was given the name *'bka log ma* ("the renegade"). The couple visited various pilgrimage sites in Tibet over a long period, but after twelve years Ma gcig decided to give up family life to return to her Buddhist masters and resume a lifestyle entirely devoted to spiritual practice. In Ding ri she met Pha Dam pa again, who gave her further teachings on the Perfection of Wisdom and yoga. Then the yoginī resumed her pilgrimage, and following her master's instructions, she practiced in 108 cemeteries and holy places. She then went to Zangs ri khang dmar, where she went into retreat until her death, at the age of ninety-five.

In the last years of her life, Ma gcig taught numerous disciples, especially her own children, who played a prominent part in the continuation of the gcod tradition in Tibet. The lineages of transmission reported in the various historical treatises are somewhat complex, and the names vary according to the different authors. They are subdivided, along the same classificatory lines as the Tantras, into a male-paternal or method (*upāya*) lineage and a female-maternal or wisdom (*prajñā*) lineage. These genealogical trees of the tradition include a variety of individuals. All of them, however, mention the Indian yogins Āryadeva and Pha Dam pa at the beginning of the lineage, prior to Ma gcig. There is another transmission lineage, called "esoteric" in some hagiographies and "direct" or "very direct" in others, in which the transmission of the gcod doctrines passes unmediated from the goddess Tārā to Ma gcig. This transmission lineage suggests the desire, already visible in her various biographies, to recognize Ma gcig as the originator of an autonomous religious system. In fact, the idea is fairly widespread that it was only with Ma gcig that this tradition began to be defined as gcod.

Also noteworthy is an episode that occurred in the final years of Ma gcig's life, and is recounted in most of her hagiographies and in several texts on the history of the gcod tradition. One day when Ma gcig was already in retreat in Zangs ri, three learned Indian scholars from Varanasi came to visit her. The paṇḍits had heard about the yoginī's teaching and had reservations about a Buddhist tradition that did not come from India. So they asked Ma gcig whether they could challenge her in philosophical debate, as was customary at the time among exponents of the different Buddhist schools. Ma gcig did not hesitate, and started to debate with the scholars in Sanskrit, astonishing them with her wisdom and great doctrinal learning. The paṇḍits were thus forced to concede the yoginī's supremacy and to acknowledge her as the manifestation of the Great Mother, Prajñāpāramitā, in person. From that moment the gcod teaching spread throughout Tibet and, crossing the Himalayan frontiers, spread rapidly in India as well. According to tradition, this was the first Buddhist teaching originating in Tibet to be promulgated in the Indian subcontinent. We cannot ascertain how much truth lies in this belief, which is handed down to this day among Tibetan lamas; however, it betokens the importance ascribed in Tibet to the gcod tradition and its foremost promulgator.

Ma gcig Lab sgron's poem, the *Great Collection of the Teachings (Bka' tshoms chen mo)*, is published in *Gdams ngag mdzod, A Treasury of Instructions and Techniques for Spiritual Realizations*, compiled by 'Jam mgon Kong sprul Blo gros mtha' yas, 12 vols. (Delhi: N. Lungtog and N. Gyaltsan, 1971), vol. 9, pp. 456–66. An Italian translation of the entire text may be found in Giacomella Orofino, *Contributo allo Studio dell'Insegnamento di Ma gcig Lab Sgron* (Supplemento n. 53 agli Annali, vol. 47, fasc. 4) (Naples: Istituto Universitario Orientale, 1987); and in a new revised edition by the same author, in Ma gcig, *Canti Spirituali,* (Milan: Adephi Edizioni, 1995). The Peking edition of the Tengyur (*bstan 'gyur* has been edited by Daisetz T. Suzuki as *The Tibetan Tripitaka: Peking Edition* (Tokyo amd Kyoto: Suzuki Research Institute, 1957).

Further Reading

For an early account of the gcod and zhi byed ritual, see Emil Schlaginweit, *Buddhism in Tibet* (London: Susil Gupta, 1863), pp. 162–63; and Lawrence Austine Waddell, *The Buddhism in Tibet or Lamaism* (London: W. H. Allen, 1895), p. 74. The description of the gcod practice by Alexandra David-Neel may be found in *Mystiques et magiciens du Tibet* (Paris: Plon, 1929), pp. 148–66. The first translation of a gcod ritual was published by Walter Yeeling Evans-Wentz, *Tibetan Yoga and Secret Doctrines, or Seven Books of Wisdom of the Great Path, according to the late Lama Kazi Dawa Samdup's English Rendering* (London: Oxford University Press, 1935), pp. 280–334. George Nicholas Roerich's English translation of the *Deb gter sngon po* (*The Blue Annals)* was published in 1949 (Calcutta: Royal Asiatic Society of Bengal, Monograph Series, vol. 7). The Tibetan text by 'Gos lo tsā va, the *Deb gter sngon po*, was published by Lokesh Chandra (New Delhi: International Academy of Indian Culture, 1976). An interesting description of the gcod practice may also be found in GiuseppeTucci, *The Religions of Tibet*, rev. ed. (London: Routledge & Kegan Paul, 1980), pp. 87–92. On Pha Dampa see *The Tradition of Pha Dam pa Sańs-rgyas*, edited by Barbara Nimri Aziz, 5 vols. (Thimphu: Druk Sherik Parkhang, 1979), and Aziz, "The Work of Pha Dampa Sangs rgyas," in *Tibetan Studies in Honour of Hugh Richardson*, edited by Michael Aris and Aung San Suu Kyi (New Delhi: Vikas, 1980), pp. 21–29. For a closely argued study on the gcod tradition, see Janet Gyatso, "The Development of the Gcod Tradition," in *Soundings in Tibetan Civilization*, edited by Barbara Nimri Aziz and Matthew Kapstein (New Delhi: Manohar, 1985), pp. 320–41. On Ma gcig's biography, see Karénina Kollmar-Paulenz, "Die Biographie der Ma gcig Lab sgron ma-Quellenanalytische Vorarbeiten," *XXIV Deutscher Orientalistentag vom 26 bis 30 September 1988 in Köln,* edited by Werner Diem (Stuttgart: Abdoldjavad Falaturi, 1990), pp. 372–80; and, by the same author, the thorough study, *"Der Schmuck der Befreiung": Die Geschichte der Zhi byed und gCod-Schule des tibetischen Buddhismus* (Asiatische Forschungen, 125) (Wiesbaden: Harrassowitz Verlag, 1993). See also Jérôme Edou, *Machig Labdron and the Foundation of Chöd* (Ithaca, N.Y.: Snow Lion, 1996). On the Prajñāpāramitā literature, see especially the various studies and translations by Edward Conze: *The Prajñāpāramita Literature* (The Hague: Mouton, 1960); *The Perfection of Wisdom in Eight Thousands Lines & Its Verse Summary* (San Francisco: Four Season Foundation, 1983). An English translation of *Hevajratantra* may be found in D. L. Snellgrove, *The Hevajra Tantra: Sanskrit Text, Tibetan Version and Commentary and English Rendering.* 2 vols. (London: Oxford Universitary Press, 1959), and in G. W. Farrow and I. Menon, *The Concealed Essence of the Hevajratantra with the Commentary Yogaratnamālā* (Delhi: Motilal Banarsidass, 1992).

For a discussion of the expression "opening the door of the sky" in ancient Tibetan civilization, see Rolf A. Stein, *Tibetan Civilization* (Stanford: Stanford University Press, 1972). On initiatory dismemberment in shamanism see Mircea Eliade, *Shamanism, Archaic Techniques of Ecstasy* (Princeton: Princeton University Press, 1972). For an interesting study of the Buryat shaman as exorcist and healer of epidemic diseases, see Roberte Hamayon, "Les héros de service," *L'Homme* 18.3–4 (1978): 17–45.

One of the best-known Tibetan hagiographies of Ma gcig is *Phung po gzan skyur gi rnam bshad gcod kyi don gsal byed,* in *Gcod kyi chos skor* (New Delhi: Tibet House, 1978), pp. 9–410 (abbreviated as *Rnam bshad* in the introduction above). This has been partially translated into English in Jérôme Edou, cited above; and in Tsultrin Allione, *Women of Wisdom* (Henley on Thames: Routledge & Kegan Paul, 1984). Other historiographical texts on the gcod tradition are: *Zhi byed dang gcod yul gyi chos 'byung rin po che'i phreng ba thar pa'i rgyan* by Khams smyon 'Jigs bral chos kyi seng ge, in *Gcod kyi chos skor* (New Delhi: Tibet House, 1978), pp. 411–597, translated by Kollmar-Paulenz in, *"Der Schmuck der Befreiung,"* cited above. See also *Ma gcig gi rnam thar mdzad pa bco lnga ma* by Gshongs chen mkhas btsun bstan pa'i rgyal mtshan, in *Thang stong chos mdzod* (Thimpu and Delhi: Kunsang Topgay, 1976), vol. 1, pp. 21–41. A biographical sketch of Ma gcig may also be found in Dpa'bo Gtsug-lag 'phreng ba, *Chos 'byung mkhas pa'i dga' ston,* edited by Lokesh Chandra (New Delhi: International Academy of Indian Culture, 1962), p. 763.

The Great Collection of the Teachings on the Noble Practice of Severing the Demons, Perfection of Wisdom

Praise to that unconditioned state
which transcends objective considerations,
the pure, inexpressible,
unimaginable condition
that goes beyond any thought.

I have written down
this Collection of the Teachings
on severing the demons
thinking that someone, someday
may benefit from it.

The root of all demons is one's own mind.
If one feels attraction and desire
in the perception of any phenomenon,
one is captured by the demons.
When the mind grasps at phenomena
as if they were external objects
one becomes contaminated.

The demons are divided into four categories:
the tangible demons
(whose basis is external objects)
the intangible demons
(whose basis is mental images)
the demons of complacency
(whose basis is the desire for obtainment) and
the demons of pride
(whose basis is dualistic discrimination).

The tangible demons are numerous:
when phenomena appear
before the sense organs,
if one discriminates between
what one desires and what one rejects
the tangible demons arise.
In this way, perceiving phenomena as concrete,
one is chained to the wheel of existence.

As form is empty in its nature,
do not feel attachment to it
but meditate on the emptiness.
If one feels no attachment to form,
one is liberated from the demon of eternalism.
If one does not conceptualize emptiness
one is liberated from the demon of nihilism.

The manifestation of visible phenomena
can not be impeded,
but if they are not considered as concrete
one's vision manifests as light.
In this way one is liberated from sight, sounds,
tastes, odors, touch, and the mind.
The mind itself is the intangible demon.
On the other hand, if it arises through the door of the five senses,
it is defined the tangible demon.
Phenomena that appear to the sense organs
are instantaneously interrupted
in the state of spontaneous liberation

and are transformed in the great
essential dimension of reality.

The way in which the intangible demon manifests:
In that discriminating thought of good and evil
which arises in one's own mind when phenomena appear
is defined the intangible demon.
If one separates oneself from the natural
and spontaneous state of the mind
and clings to the idea of benevolent gods and evil spirits,
because of the oscillation between hope and fear
one's own demon manifests in oneself.

From the clear and immense space
of the essential dimension of reality,
thought and memories arise in all directions
just as ripples and waves arise
on the immutable ocean.
Whoever has this understanding
has no need of contrivances
and naturally remains in his own condition.
One liberates oneself in the space in which
neither benefit nor harm is born.
As wisdom arises spontaneously
from the space of essential reality,
it is not necessary to nurture jealousy,
aversion, or affection.
If one feels no aversion or affection
the spontaneous mind becomes manifest.

The way in which the demons of complacency arise:
The ordinary demons and the superior ones
arise from illusory mind.
If, practicing in horrifying places,
one is not disturbed by the evil spirits
self-satisfaction is born in oneself:
this is the demon of complacency.
When the signs of spiritual power appear—
merits and material wealth—
the demons of distraction arise.
Glory, fame, happiness,
friends, and enemies
are the demons of complacency.
When gods and spirits confer their magical power,
and one is surrounded by sons and faithful friends

getting pleasure and satisfaction,
the demons of complacency arise.

Whichever virtue one achieves
with mind empty of dualism
between subject and object,
do not grasp at it
as if it were concrete.
Act naturally without any attachment
to the nature of virtues,
considering them as the objects of dreams.
Like a beautiful woman
with ornaments who makes herself
even more beautiful,
anything that arises
is as an ornament
of one's own condition.
There is no reason for vanity
but if it arises one is contaminated
by the various categories of illusion.
May this noble conduct
of remaining in one's own natural state
without attachment to phenomena
be kept in secret in the very heart
of those who know!

Because all things are the spontaneous mind,
he who meditates has nothing to meditate.
Let any perception which manifests spontaneously
be left in its natural condition
of union, clarity, and splendor.
Because the meaning is immutable
it is unified,
because one gets real understanding
it is clear,
because one is liberated in one's own condition
it is resplendent.
Thus just as butter freely remains in butter,
this contemplation without meditation
is the supreme meditation.

If one abandons oneself
and seeks externally,
even if one practices for ten million eons,
he will have no obtainment.

Seek nothing, undertake nothing,
remain freely in the nature of essential reality.
Not having any hope is the supreme practice
of cutting off the demons.
Without the limitation of human hopes and fears,
if one cuts the rope of attachment,
where is the Buddha, in reality?

Although they are divided into four categories,
all demons are included in the demons of pride.
Just as the lion on the high snowy peaks has no fear,
if one eliminates ego-clinging,
confidence will develop
and one will not fluctuate
between the gods and the evil spirit of existence.
Even if hundreds of them rise up
the doctrines will shine upon them.
If they can be recognized as one's own projection
one will proceed with great dexterity.
Eliminating the flow of thoughts
and not undertaking any meditation,
it is sufficient to obtain a profound insight of inner wisdom
that bursts out strong and spontaneous
like an epidemic.
This practice of severing the demons
which arises from the profound insight
that there is no root
is the supreme teaching of all!

Emaho! Marvelous!
Eliminating one's own pride and ego-clinging
one pacifies the demons!
Having a profound insight that there is no root
one obtains the real state of complete awakening!
So be at ease in a free condition
and let everything be, in its own natural state.

—24—

Worship of Bell-Ears the Great Hero, a Jain Tantric Deity

John E. Cort

Tantra in Jainism has two distinctive features: it is largely centered around the use of verbal spells or mantra, and Jain Tantric practices are aimed at improving one's condition within the realm of rebirth rather than liberating one from rebirth. Although Jain Tantric rites, such as that given in the second text below, also involve the use of diagrams known as yantras, these play a subsidiary role compared to the mantras, and most yantras have the ritual mantra written on them. Mantras are used directly to effect desired results, and to call on nonliberated deities to effect those results. Jain Tantric rites rarely involve any elaborate form of meditation or visualization; usually the simple repetition of the mantra suffices. Some Tantric rituals invoke the central cultic figures of the tradition, the twenty-four Jinas or tīrthaṅkaras, the enlightened and liberated souls who showed the path to liberation. More often, though, the rituals invoke other figures, such as the wonder-working monk Gautama in the Śvetāmbara ("White-Robed") tradition, various goddesses in both the Śvetāmbara and Digambara ("Sky-Clad") traditions, and male figures such as Ghaṇṭākarṇa Mahāvīra and Nākoḍā Bhairava in the Śvetāmbara tradition.

According to Jain theology, however, none of these beings has the power to grant liberation. The Jinas are inactive icons of the liberated state; the other deities, although active in the world, are themselves unliberated, and so cannot give what they themselves have not attained. As a result, most Jain Tantric rituals are aimed at accomplishing a variety of goals in this world, such as health, wealth, and power. The texts translated below are a veritable catalogue of these worldly goals. Many Jain Tantric texts and rituals categorize these goals within the framework of the "six actions" (*ṣaṭkarmāṇi*) of pan-Indian Tantra. What is not found in Jain Tantra is the development of a full-scale alternative Tantric path to liberation such as is found in some Hindu and Buddhist Tantric schools.

The cult of Ghaṇṭākarṇa Mahāvīra, "Bell-Ears the Great Hero," exemplifies these two distinctive features of Jain Tantra. (This Mahāvīra should not be confused with Vardhamāna Mahāvīra, the twenty-fourth and final tīrthaṅkara of this era). The worship of Bell-Ears is found exclusively among Śvetāmbara Mūrtipūjaka Jains, and in particular is special to one mendicant lineage, the Tapā Gaccha. He is one of the fifty-two vīras or "heroes," a class of powerful male deities who protect faithful Jains and defeat enemies of the Jain community. Bell-Ears is described as a fellow Jain, and so is dangerous only to the opponents of Jainism. The traditional Sanskrit texts of the cult are the seventy-one-verse *Ghaṇṭākarṇa Mantra Stotra*, (a hymn that is also considered to be a mantra), and several Ghaṇṭākarṇa Mantras. The hymn was composed sometime in the latter half of the sixteenth century by an otherwise unknown monk named Vimalacandra, who was a disciple of Sakalacandra, who in turn was a disciple of the great leader of the Tapā Gaccha, Hīravijayasūri (1527–1595).

These mantras were used in a variety of Tantric rituals performed over long periods of time, by which the practitioner gained the allegiance of Bell-Ears and so was able to gain the worldly powers associated with this deity. The nature of these worldly powers, which ranged from cures for diseases and increasing one's material wealth to defeating and even slaying foes of the Jain community, show clearly that Jainism is as much about how to live successfully in the world as it is about ascetic practices to liberate oneself from the world. The inclusion of māraṇa or killing foes in the list of Jain Tantric goals—although many Jain Tantric texts exclude it—also shows that the Jain ethical injunction of ahiṃsā or non-harm does not result in Jains being strict pacifists, as ahiṃsā is more applicable in the sphere of dietary practices than in the sphere of relations among states and religious communities.

For many centuries, the worship of Bell-Ears was a largely private aspect of Jain practice, performed within certain monastic lineages, and possibly by some laymen as well. Vimalacandra (verse 67) claims that this worship dates to the time of the great Haribhadrasūri (c. sixth to eighth century), although there is no other evidence to corroborate this. The nature of the transmission of the cult from teacher to disciple is seen in the third text below, which describes the initiation of Buddhisāgarsūri (1874–1925) into the cult in the late nineteenth century. For several decades, Buddhisāgarsūri 's practice was firmly within this largely esoteric tradition. The texts translated here also indicate ways in which this Jain esoteric tradition shared many practices and concepts with the pan-Indian yogic and Tantric streams of religious expression, while giving them a distinctly Jain flavor.

Buddhisāgarasūri effected an important change in the cult after his direct experience of Bell-Ears, when he established an anthropomorphic image of the deity in a small shrine attached to the Jain temple at Mahudi in northern Gujarat. This is the first known three-dimensional anthropomorphic image of Bell-Ears; previously he had been worshiped only in the forms of abstract and anthropomorphic yantras. Toward the end of his life, Buddhisāgarsūri was responsible for converting the cult into a highly public one. In part, Buddhisāgarsūri 's goal was to create a way for Jains to perform rituals aimed at worldly goals and still be good Jains. According to Jain theology, the Jinas cannot respond in any way to ritual petitions, and so it is considered inappropriate and fruitless to worship the Jinas for worldly ends. Worship of non-Jain deities is fraught with danger, especially as such worship in the early twentieth century frequently involved sacrificing animals. Buddhisāgarsūri arranged for the construction of a much larger temple at Mahudi, and wrote several hymns and rituals for the worship of Bell-Ears, including the one translated as the fourth text below. In line with the transformation of the cult from an esoteric one followed by initiated adepts into a public one followed by hundreds of thousands of Jains, we also see in this text a reformulation of the worship of Bell-Ears along more devotional (*bhakti*) lines than traditional Tantric ones. Such interaction between Tantra and devotion has long been a feature of all South Asian religious traditions.

The shrine of Bell-Ears at Mahudi is now one of the most popular Jain shrines in all India. It is visited by hundreds of thousands of pilgrims every year, who come to offer Bell-Ears his favorite food, a sweet dish known as sukhaḍī, in return for his assistance in their lives. In particular, tens of thousands of people come for the special worship of Bell-Ears on the day before Dīvālī, the autumnal festival of lights that also marks the New Year according to the western Indian calendar. The worship of Bell-Ears is therefore an important aspect of insuring that any possible malevolent influences from the previous year are negated, so that one can start the new year with an auspiciously clean slate. Images of Bell-Ears are also found in a growing number of Jain temples throughout western India.

The Sanskrit *Ghaṇṭākarṇa Mantra Stotra* is found in Acarya Buddhisagarsuri, *Maṅgal Pūjā* (Sanand: Sri Sanand Sagargacch Jnan Khata, 1953; originally published ca. 1922), pp. 33–71; Acarya Buddhisagarsuri, *Śrī Ghaṇṭākarṇ Mahāvīr Dev* (Mahudi: Sri Mahudi Jain Svetambar Karkhana Trust, 1983–1984; originally published 1924), pp. 69–74; Sarabhai Navab and Muni Candrodayvijay, eds., *Ghaṇṭākarṇ-Māṇibhadra-Mantra-Tantra Kalpādi Saṅgrah*, 4th rev. ed. (Ahmedabad: Sarabhai Manilal Navab, 1985), pp. 1–10; and Narottamdas Naginbhai Shah, ed., *Ghaṇṭākarṇ Vīr Jaypatākā* (Bombay: Meghraj Jain Pustak Bhandar, 1972), pp. 33–35. The Gujarati *Ghaṇṭākarṇ Kalp* is here translated from Navab and Candrodayvijay, pp. 12–19; a similar version of the rite in Hindi is found in Chandanmal Nagori, ed., *Ghaṇṭākarṇ Kalp* (Choti Sadri: Candanmal Nagori Jain Pustakalay, 1951). The anthropomorphic yantra of Ghaṇṭākarṇa Mahāvīra (Figure 24.1) is illustration 10 in Navab and Candrodayvijay. The Gujarati narration by Muni Candrodayvijay of Buddhisagarsuri's initiation is from Navab and Candrodayvijay, pp. 33–36. The Gujarati *Worship of Ghaṇṭākarṇ* is from Buddhisagarsuri, *Maṅgal Pūjā*, pp. 18–26; and Buddhisagarsuri, *Śrī Ghaṇṭākarṇ Mahāvīr*, pp. 56–62. I have used different spelling systems to indicate the differing pronunciations in Sanskrit and Gujarati, especially where the latter does not pronounce the final short *-a* of most words.

Further Reading

Background on Jain ritual culture and Tantra is found in the following: John E. Cort, "Medieval Jaina Goddess Traditions," *Numen* 34 (1987): 235–55; Cort, "Tantra in Jainism: The Cult of Ghaṇṭākarṇ Mahāvīr, the Great Hero Bell-Ears," in *Bulletin d'Etudes Indiennes* 15 (1997), 115–33; Cort, *Jains in the World: Religious Values and Ideology in India* (New York: Oxford University Press, 2000); Paul Dundas, *The Jains* (London: Routledge, 1992); Dundas, "Becoming Gautama: Mantra and History in Śvetāmbara Jainism," in John E. Cort, ed., *Open Boundaries: Jain Communities and Cultures in Indian History* (Albany: State University of New York Press, 1998), pp. 31–52. For a modern example of a synthesis of Jain, yogic, and Tantric practice by a former Sthānakvāsī monk who broke with the strict interpretation of Jain monastic rules and came to the United States, where he established a temple and retreat center, see Acharya Sushil Kumar, *Song of the Soul: An Introduction to the Namokar Mantra and the Science of Sound* (Blairstown: Siddhachalam Publishers, 1987). There are a number of books written in Hindi and Gujarati by Jain monks and laymen in which haṭha yoga, elaborate use of mantras and yantras, and other yogic and Tantric elements are presented within a Jain framework.

1. Vimalacandra, the *Ghaṇṭākarṇa Mantra Stotra*

1. *Oṃ hrīṃ śrīṃ klīṃ* Great Hero Bell-Ears Greatly Strong! Destroy anxiety, illness, misfortune, and great dread.

2. The mantra of your name is perfect. It creates all that is holy. Increase the perfection of what I want, my powers, victory, and wealth.

3. May there be great śakti [power] from faith and devotion of you. May vicious, hostile, and very bad people be defeated.

4. Protect me in times of distress. Illuminate my knowledge. Protect me from all misfortune and destroy raging illness.

5. May my actions be successful due to my radiant devotion of you. Protect the kingdom, protect wealth. Protect my body and keep it strong.

6. Protect from great harm, protect from dreadful fires. Protect in the forest, battle, home, village, and the royal court.

7. Protect from hostile kings, protect from lions and hostile serpents. Protect from divine obstructions and unexpected difficulties.

8. Ward off witches, ghosts, vampires, and demons. Destroy, destroy great obstructions born of the nine planets and the like.

9. Save from the four-day fever and plague, quickly save from snake venom. Save from the bites of rabid dogs and jackals.

10. Ward off and take away the stinging poison of scorpions. Always give help in unexpected difficulties.

11. Give direct vision in response to my loving devotion and faith. Give wisdom, give wealth, give sons and grandsons.

12. Give fame, give glory, give character and women. Give all that I desire, give me pleasure and peace.

13. Give me bodily health, defeat my enemies. Quickly calm fever of the joints and plague.

14. Bell-Ears Great Hero, you are the crest-jewel of all heroes! Protect me from beatings, night, day, and always.

15. Ever protect me from untimely death. Lord of gods, protect me from beatings. Make me a hero, Greatly Strong!

16. Bell-Ears Great Hero, give me universal śakti. Protect me in times of distress, protect my fame.

17. Always be near me with your universal śakti. Protect the fourfold Jain congregation everywhere.

18. *Oṃ hrīṃ śrīṃ klīṃ* Great Hero Bell-Ears Greatly Strong! Create my peace, satisfaction, pleasure, and well-being. *Svāhā*!

19. Bell-Ears Great Hero! Create the welfare of the whole congregation. Quickly create pleasure and peace in the country, kingdom, and provinces.

20. Peace, great satisfaction, and pleasure are quickly present wherever you reside in the form of a yantra with the mantra of the letters of your name.

21. Make peace. Quickly ward off plague in the country, kingdom, city, and congregation, in all castes, people, and assemblies, in herds of animals and flocks of birds.

22. Create welfare for ācāryas, upādhyāyas, and sādhus [the three levels of Jain monks], and for brahmans. Quickly create peace for kṣatriyas and śūdras.

23. *Oṃ krauṃ droṃ drīṃ* create welfare, Great Hero Bell-Ears! Destroy boils and other illnesses in the body of your devotee.

24. *Aiṃ jhrauṃ srauṃ hrīṃ* Great Hero Bell-Ears Greatly Strong! Give knowledge, give power, give me purity and wisdom.

25. Embodiment of śakti, remove knots and worries. Show the path to liberation by the gift of pure knowledge.

26. *Aiṃ jhrauṃ srauṃ hrīṃ* Great Hero Bell-Ears Greatly Strong! Increase pure wisdom by destroying ghosts and other obstacles.

27. Destroy all illnesses of [the three humors] wind, bile, and phlegm. Purify my nature. *Oṃ hrīṃ svāhā* may you be praised.

28. Yoginīs, heroes, vampires, ghouls, ghosts, and magicians all flee when I repeat your mantra. Create my pleasure!

29. *Om hrāṃ hrīṃ blāṃ* praise to you Great Hero Bell-Ears! Protect my feet, thighs, hands, and head *svāhā*! Create my welfare.

30. Devotion is firm in my heart, so create all my welfare. Destroy curses from gurus and others. Praise to you! . . .

49. Help everywhere, give desired wealth. Instantly protect welfare, beneficence, and yoga by being present in the yantra.

50. *Oṃ* Bell-Ears Great Hero Great Strength of All the Heroes! Protect the embryo in the womb, protect infants from diseases.

51. Give sons and grandsons, give wealth, strength, and women. Give a long life, give me what I desire.

52. Give understanding, wealth, peace, and goodness. Give the strength and might of Brahmā. Give me lofty status, everywhere do what is dear to me.

53. May I be successful due to your śakti and the śakti of my devotion. *Oṃ hrīṃ śrīṃ klīṃ* Great Hero assist me at once.

54. *Oṃ āṃ krauṃ hrīṃ* Great Hero Bell-Ears Greatly Strong! Instantly give what I desire, give me great strength.

55. Bell-Ears Great Hero, there is no doubt that people gain what they desire through the power of your mantra and yantra.

56. The one who desires a son obtains a son; the one who desires wealth obtains wealth. The student obtains wisdom; the one who desires a wife obtains a wife.

57. From the performance of the mantra of Bell-Ears Great Hero the fruit quickly matches the desire.

58. By sacrifice with five nectars, by sacrifice with bdellium gum resin, the mantra is quickly successful according to the experience and instructions of the guru.

59. He is the hero of the Jain teachings, the great strength of right faith, the increaser of the fourfold congregation, and the doer of good deeds.

60. May Bell-Ears Great Hero be victorious on the earth. He is the presiding deity of righteous Jains.

61. By your mantra and yantra beings will attain the fruit of success in what they desire everywhere in the Kali Age.

62. You illuminate the world in the Kali Age, you protect the congregation. Bell-Ears Great Hero, create pleasure and holiness.

63. Bell-Ears Great Hero, create peace, pleasure, contentment, true happiness, and holiness in response to hearing and reciting your mantra.

64. Bell-Ears Great Hero, may there be holiness in the home of whoever hears and recites due to the glory of your mantra and yantra.

65. Bell-Ears Great Hero, may whoever recites this mantra 108 times daily in purity receive his desired holiness.

66. Those suitable devotees who study this secret mantra receive the guru's blessing, and for them the mantra is successful and holy.

67. In order to spread Jainism the disciple of Haribhadrasūri performed the practice of Bell-Ears Great Hero at his teacher's instruction.

68. Then it was propagated by others of right faith, and it was explained in the *Pratiṣṭhākalpa* by Sakalacandra.

69. Then Vimalacandra made this kalpa [manual] famous. May people be happy from remembering and reciting it.

70. I don't know the invocation, I don't know the dismissal. But by the repetition alone I attained the highest success of your mantra.

71. O best of gods! Forgive whatever is recited without measure, without verbs, without letters, backwards, or without knowledge.

2. *Ghaṇṭākarṇ Kalp*

[Sanskrit invocation:] I bow to Gaṇeśa, the giver of wealth and success, and beloved son of the mountain-born Pārvatī. Now I tell the kalpa of Bell-Ears, which removes enemies and troubles.

The best times for auspicious actions are an auspicious month, the bright fortnight, and the fifth, tenth, and full moon in that fortnight. The auspicious days and conjunctions are Sunday in the Hasta lunar mansion, Sunday in the Mūla lunar mansion, and Sunday in the Puṣya lunar mansion. The best days for killing (*māraṇa*) and causing to flee (*uccāṭana*) are the eighth, fourteenth, and new moon in the dark fortnight. The best conjunctions are Siddhi, Amṛtasiddhi, Ānanda, Śrīvaccha, and Chatra. Before commencing, you should consider the auspicious omens and the power of the lunar position in the horoscope for the performance of the mantra.

The performance should be in a pure building, the walls of which have been attractively washed and rubbed with cow dung, or in a pure forest, in a garden, on the banks of a river, in a temple, or else in your residence. The mantra for purifying the earth is: "*Oṃ hrīṃ śrīṃ* I bow to the earth deity." Recite this mantra seven times while offering incense, lamp, and whole rice.

The mantra for bathing is: "*Oṃ hrīṃ klīṃ* I bow to Ganges water." Recite this mantra seven times while bathing. The mantra for donning clothing is: "*Oṃ hrīṃ klīṃ* I bow to the bliss deity." Recite this mantra while donning pure clothing.

For a pure rite, meditate using the Bell-Ears mantra:

Oṃ Bell-Ears Great Hero, destroyer of all ailments. Protect, protect those in mighty fear of boils, Greatly Strong. Wherever you stand, O god, diseases and gout are destroyed by the written lines of letters [of your yantra]. Instantly from the recitation in the ear there is no fear of kings. Witches, ghosts, vampires, and demons do not arise. There is no untimely death, nor are snakes seen, nor is there fear of fire or thieves, *hrīṃ* Bell-Ears. Homage to you *ṭhaḥ ṭhaḥ ṭhaḥ svāhā*.

Recite this mantra 33,000 times over forty-two days. After that, recite it daily 108 times each at dawn, midday, and dusk. If you accompany the recitation by offering black pepper and mustard seeds into a sacrificial fire, there will be no fear of hostile deities. If you fear enemies, then offer a mixture of curds, milk, ghee, saffron, and bdellium gum resin into the sacrificial fire, and establish an anthropomorphic yantra (Figure 24.1). This will destroy fear of enemies.

THE RITE OF THE ANTHROPOMORPHIC YANTRA

On the stomach of a human figure make twelve sections, and in them write the twelve-syllabled mantra *Oṃ hrīṃ śrīṃ klīṃ sarvaduṣṭa nāśanebhyaḥ* [*Oṃ hrīṃ śrīṃ klīṃ* for the destruction of all malevolence]. On the throat of the figure write *śrī namaḥ* [obeisance to wellbeing], on the right hand *sarva hrīṃ nama* [obeisance to all], on the left hand *śatrunāśane namaḥ* [obeisance to the destruction of foes], on the right foot *rāṃ rīṃ ruṃ namaḥ*, and on the left foot *hvāṃ hvīṃ hūṃ namaḥ*. Write the Bell-Ears Mantra around the border of the figure.

Offer grain, lime paste, a coconut, and raisins into a sacrificial fire. Offer to the yantra vermillion powder, and make a ring from cotton thread spun by a young girl. You will be freed of fear of hostile deities, enemies, and kings, and your fame will increase.

Here is another ritual with this yantra. On the day of Dīvālī, eat a single meal of rice pudding, set up an unextinguished lamp of ghee, light ten-scented incense, and recite the mantra 12,000 times. Lie on the ground as if dead. After the recitations, make an offering into the sacrificial fire of the five nectars [milk, curds, ghee, honey, sugar], and you will see the form of your success in a dream.

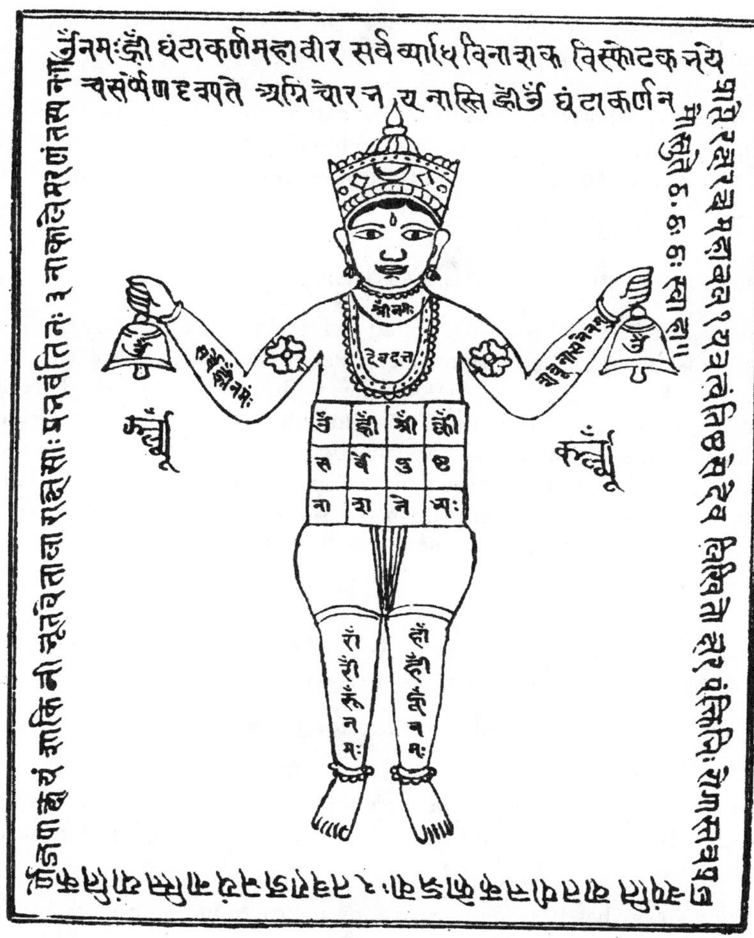

Figure 24.1. The anthropomorphic yantra of Bell-Ears

The text then gives instructions for rituals for specific goals, including obtaining wealth, gaining control over others, killing, causing victims to flee, eliminating ignorance, and preventing miscarriage. Two of these are given here as examples.

THE METHOD FOR OBTAINING WEALTH (LAKṢMĪ)

Recite the Bell-Ears mantra. Make a six-cornered yantra. In its six corners write *Oṃ hlīṃ hvīṃ hūṃ hloṃ namaḥ*. Write the Bell-Ears Mantra around the border. Perform the following rite. To obtain wealth sit facing the west, wearing white cloth, holding a white rosary, seated on a white cloth. With mind, speech, and body in single-pointed attention, recite the mantra 125,000 times in seventy-two days. While reciting eat once per day, and eat something made with wheat. Offer into a sacrificial fire raisins, dried cārolī fruit, almonds, and coconut. Throughout offer incense, lamps, and food to the yantra. It is certain that after six months you will obtain wealth. From maintaining the yantra you will obtain all sorts of pleasure.

THE METHOD FOR SUBJUGATING OTHERS (VAŚĪKARAṆA)

Recite the Bell-Ears mantra while seated facing north, wearing red cloth, holding a red rosary, and seated on a red cloth. Recite the mantra thrice daily (dawn, midday, dusk) for a total of 225,000 times within forty-two days. Establish a four-cornered yantra. Throughout this time offer incense, lamp, and food to it. Offer into a sacrificial fire red sandalwood, pepper, and ghee. While making the offerings, say the name of the deity whom you wish to subjugate. This can be used either to imprison someone or free someone from prison. For this you need to establish a yantra of 132 squares.

Sanskrit colophon:

1. Whoever reads this in a spirit of devotion, and hears the mantra-bells in his ear, will have no obstacles and so be successful in the three worlds.

2. I have made thousands of mistakes: forgive me for all of them, god, be merciful, O Supreme Lord.

3. For what I have not known in the invocation, for what I have not known in the dismissal, and for what I have not known in the worship: forgive them, O Supreme Lord.

4. For whatever has been deficient in my instructions, actions, and mantras: forgive me for all them, O god, be merciful, O Supreme Lord.

3. Buddhisāgar's Initiation and Direct Vision of Ghaṇṭākarṇ

It was Thursday, the eleventh of the bright half of the month of Fāgaṇ, in the year V.S. 1954 [late February 1898 C.E.]. On that day in Vijāpur, Ravisāgar decided to give the siddhamantra [mantra of success] of Bell-Ears, which was in his mendicant lineage, to the young yogin Buddhisāgar, who was his grand-disciple, and who was both most fortunate and firm in his practice. The practice of constantly remembering this siddhamantra had come down in the lineage, and by it those illustrious men had been saved from harassment by animals and undesirable elements. But there had been no direct vision of the hero Bell-Ears, the presiding deity of the mantra, for two or three generations in the lineage. Ravisāgar saw in the young Buddhisāgar the power to generate a direct vision.

As preparation for the initiation into the mantra, Ravisāgar had instructed Buddhisāgar to consume only mung beans, rice, and water for one day, and to maintain complete silence until midnight of the second day. At midnight on the second day, Buddhisāgar sat before Ravisāgar . Ravisāgar twice repeated into his ear the nineteen-syllable mantra that had been passed down in the lineage: *Oṃ hrīṃ aiṃ klīṃ ghaṇṭākarṇa namostu mama kāryāṇi sidhyantu* [*Oṃ hrīṃ aiṃ klīṃ* praise to Bell-Ears may my actions be successful]. Then Ravisāgar used his right hand to rub vāskṣep [sandalwood powder that has been charged by reciting a mantra over it] on the middle of Buddhisāgar's brahmarandra [crown of the head, from which spiritual energy can flow forth], and by pressing his hand gave śaktipāt [establishment of yogic power]. An awareness awoke in Buddhisāgar's entire body, and his six cakras [centers of yogic energy] opened. Then for three days Buddhisāgar followed his teacher's instructions and recited the mantra.

On the first day of the recitation, Buddhisāgar saw wheels of unlimited light, star disks, and minute points in his ājñā cakra [point between the eyebrows]. Then the points gradually opened up and became glowing lamps. The light of the lamps came together in his forehead. In this light for a brief time he saw the dim form of a black figure. On the second day, he became absorbed in an indescribable bliss, and his ājñā cakra glittered with a shining light. All six cakras opened. All his kuṇḍalīs [circles at the six cakras through which the yogic power travels] were awake. His entire body experienced an unprecedented and stimulating sensation. On the third day, he had the same experience. In three days he recited the mantra 27,000 times. Mantra-consciousness was awake throughout his body.

After the three days, Ravisāgar instructed Buddhisāgar to incorporate this supreme mantra in his life, and to give mantra initiation to those among his followers who were suitable to recite it. Then he instructed Buddhisāgar to sit in one place and recite the mantra. Buddhisāgar commenced the recitation, reciting in his mind for eight hours every day. After nine months he had finished 1,800,000 recitations. When he had finished 800,000, mantra-consciousness awoke in him. After 1,000,000, he gained the power over dreams, after 1,400,000 he gained the ability to tell the future, and after 1,800,000 he gained the power to untangle problems and ward off misfortune.

After he had finished the 1,800,000 recitations, Buddhisāgar made a statement of intention, in accordance with the science of mantra, to have a direct vision of his chosen deity. He obtained Ravisāgar 's consent, and decided to to go to Mahudi and there have a sacrifice performed by five laymen who were dispassionate, faithful, and who daily recited the Navkār mantra [mantra to the Jain spiritual hierarchy]. He instructed the five laymen that until the sacrifice was completed they had to maintain complete celibacy, renounce all anger and wrong actions, and every day recite at least five cycles of 108 recitations each of the Navkār mantra. For the sacrifice they had to wear white, red, yellow, blue, and tan clothes. As an introduction to the sacrifice, Ravisāgar recited the Bell-Ears mantra.

On the day before the sacrifice, the sacrificial ground was prepared by worshiping it at 4:00 A.M. in front of four young girls. Each girl held in her hands a coconut, some sukhaḍī, and eleven and one-quarter rupees. The *Ghaṇṭākarṇa Mantra Stotra* [Text 1] was recited three times. As the laymen offered the coconut water on the ground to the ringing of a bell, a peacock suddenly crowed. The sky began to lighten. A cowherd passed with his herd. A man came running with some fragrant flowers and offered them. All of these were taken as auspicious signs.

Before sunset, a three-tiered altar was constructed. It was painted white. In the four cardinal directions *Oṃ* was painted with sandalwood paste, and *hrīṃ* was painted in the four intermediate directions. Eleven and one-quarter rupees in silver coins were placed on it, and vāskṣep sprinkled on them. Sweets were placed on the coins, and this was all covered with a white cloth. Coconuts were placed on the four corners of the cloth.

The fire was lit at the auspicious time of 10:15 in the evening. Buddhisāgar sat facing it. The five laymen took up their positions. They made 18,000 offerings. The first sacrifice was made with bdellium gum resin, the second with ghee, the third with five nectars of milk, curds, ghee, honey, and sugar, and the fourth with sticks of wood. At 11:05 Buddhisāgar started reciting the mantra. At 2:00 A.M. there was an unprecedented light in his ājñā cakra. In the ājñā cakra he saw a divine form with bow and arrow in hand, a smiling face, a powerful body, wearing golden clothes, a diamond-studded crown, and a diamond necklace. Twice he heard the words, "attention, attention, blessing, blessing." Buddhisāgar folded his hands in thanks at the blessing, and performed veneration. At the end he heard in his right ear the words, "The god is present right before you." For a while the deity was visible. Thus it was that Buddhisāgar, the great ascetic, the great king of yogins, the greatly fortunate, greatly knowledgeable, and most worshipful, received that direct vision which is difficult to obtain.

4. Buddhisāgarsūri, The Worship [*pūjā*] of Ghaṇṭākarṇ

INTRODUCTORY VERSES

1. Supreme Lord, Supreme Soul, Mahāvīr, Jina-King, the crown jewel of the gods: Indra, the king of deities, forever does pūjā to you.

2. The twenty-four tīrthaṅkars are the salvific gods. The gods and goddesses lovingly serve them.

3. Protector gods, protector goddesses, and yoginīs sit in meditation, focused on Lordship. The fifty-two heroes serve, destroying the miseries of the faithful.

4. Bell-Ears Great Hero is the crown, the best of all the heroes. Bell-Ears honors us with his presence as an incarnation of devotion to the Lord.

5. This powerful one is the supreme devotee of Supreme Soul [Vardhamāna] Mahāvīr. Bell-Ears is famous for his virtuous assistance.

6. He removes obstacles for those men and women who are devoted to the Excellent Jina God Mahāvīr. He helps those who remember him.

7. Bell-Ears is the devotee of right faith. He serves fellow Jains, and firmly illuminates the soul.

8. With hands lovingly clasped over their hearts, men and women householders do pūjā to their fellow Jain Bell-Ears Great Hero in their faultless right faith.

9. The renouncer Bell-Ears Great Hero glorifies the religion. Religion is increased when one recounts his virtues by reciting the mantra.

10. The hero is attached to religion. He has right faith. He serves. He conquers obstacles by kindling right faith.

11. The excellent pūjā with incense, lamps, flowers, sukhaḍī, gold foil, and other offerings: this pūjā creates well-being.

INCENSE, THE FIRST PŪJĀ

Refrain: Deity Bell-Ears Great Hero, your glory is marvelous.

1. You help those who remember you, and break oppressing obstacles. Your glory is unprecedented. You destroy the illnesses of devotees.

2. The guru says in the Tantra that all worldly works are successful by means of the mantra of Bell-Ears and by the yantra rite done in faith.

3. Give direct vision and pervade the devotee's mind. Give what is needed for religion, and destroy millions of troubles.

4. Śakti is impressed on the heart by repeating your mantra. You establish religion in the world, and so men and women are attached to you.

5. Your glory thunders in the world. The drum beats victory everywhere. Masters firmly remember you. Those opposed to you are shameless.

6. In the forest, in the field, at sea, on the earth, in the sky: you do what is necessary for religion in the house and the royal court.

7. Doing incense pūjā, counting your virtues, and taking correct faith into his heart: Buddhisāgar establishes the god of the teachings in the world.

Mantra: *Oṃ* to Bell-Ears Great Hero, pacifier of illness and obstacles, granter of desires, I sacrifice with incense for peace, satisfaction, and prosperity, *svāhā*.

LAMP, THE SECOND PŪJĀ

Refrain: Bell-Ears Great Hero, firm in strength, spread peace in the world. Your glory is unprecedented, O Hero. Spread peace in the congregation.

1. You beg for food not like a selfish beggar, but rather to observe the vows. Jain devotees don't try to own you, they love you selflessly.

2. I keep the vows selfishly, I hold to religion like a kinsman. I do the lamp pūjā out of love, spreading the intention of nondesire.

3. In my entreaties I'm not asking from you, for I am pleased in my love of the soul. I help kinsmen from pure love. Daily I'm absorbed in the supreme truth.

4. You give shamelessly, O Hero, you help us. You give, but your glory isn't besmirched. Your virtues are grounded in right faith.

5. The righteous people remain with the hero. Help us in religion. Our pūjā is aimed at the lofty ones; keep us lowly ones in your meditation.

6. Your glory spreads throughout the world, yet doesn't block the sun. Remain alert in this dark age, and from affection help your fellow Jains.

7. May those who are fit to be friends remain firm in religion. Buddhisāgar directly experienced the message of Mahāvīr.

Mantra: *Oṃ* to Bell-Ears Great Hero, I sacrifice with a lamp for peace, satisfaction, and prosperity, *svāhā*.

FLOWERS, THE THIRD PŪJĀ

Refrain: Bell-Ears is a good hero within the teachings of the excellent Jina Mahāvīr. He is a god who enjoys the teachings. Destroy the oppression of the devotees, spread Jainism in the world, come and help the congregation, remember and help us.

1. You have a flower garland around your throat. My mind is established in joy. My heart is pure from the love of god who is a fellow Jain.

2. I request worldly things from the god who is a fellow Jain. When religion is exhausted and in trouble, you protect your suffering fellow Jains.

3. The god compassionately spreads happiness through strong divine medicine. You do what is needed for devotees on the path to liberation.

4. In their affection, men and women have good intentions in many lives. Attaining the fruit of their desires, they fall into rebirth; but seeing them, you lift them up.

5. Hero, you are the chief devotee of the Excellent Jina God Mahāvīr. You are deep like the ocean. Remain alert everywhere in the world.

6. Absorbed in the service of the Excellent Jina Mahāvīr's congregation, Buddhisāgar is in devotion, like a fish swimming in the water.

Mantra: *Oṃ* to Bell-Ears Great Hero, I sacrifice with a garland of flowers for peace, satisfaction, and prosperity, *svāhā*.

SUKHAḌĪ, FOOD, THE FOURTH PŪJĀ

Refrain: Bell-Ears Great Hero comes like a river of help. He helps these loving righteous ones, he adorns them.

1. You are firm in your shrine. You give shelter in the name of the Supreme Lord Mahāvīr. Your devotees sing their devotion.

2. They come seeking you in love and faith. Without devotion, they have no claim. They offer the auspicious garland of victory, they wave the flag of fame.

3. Suddenly the earth shakes, suddenly Mount Meru trembles. But such is your greatness that it incinerates all curses.

4. You halt hostile foes, you spread Jainism throughout the world. You spread the recitation of the name of the Lord Blessed Mahāvīr throughout the world.

5. Your devotee offers an auspicious garland in his home to obtain wealth, sons, and other success. You give all he desires, you spread peace of mind.

6. You are the means by which merit arises. It spreads through faith, love, and yoga. You apply yourself to the service of illuminating the teachings.

7. Great Hero appears directly to each devotee. The protector of the teachings is sweet. The message of the Lord appears in Buddhisāgar's heart.

Mantra: *Oṃ* to Bell-Ears Great Hero, protector of the Jina's teachings, I sacrifice with a garland of flowers for peace, satisfaction, and prosperity; increase, increase, do what is known, *svāhā*.

COCONUT, THE FIFTH PŪJĀ

Refrain: O come, come, come, come to me Great Hero. Strongly grace me with the presence of faith and love, create knowledge of religion.

1. Dedicate yourself to Jainism and appear directly to the devotee. A string of lotuses is above you. Don't come to nonbelievers.

2. You adorn the eyes of devotees who are lost in the form of your name. You fulfill the devotion of the saints, you bring absorption in self-awareness.

3. You are fond of the teachings, you illuminate religion, you love the Lord. You perform the great service of the whole congregation and so attain to Supreme Lordship.

4. May the righteous man who wants to do pūjā to you be firm in the wisdom of religion. May Buddhisāgar attain success, increase, and the glory of fame in the world.

FULL-POT SONG

Refrain: Sing loudly, sing of the hero of the teachings. Describe the fivefold pūjā, the shelter for right faith and purity.

1. Do the pūjā of Bell-Ears Great Hero, and attain his virtues from singing. Sing with joy the praises of the god of right faith.

2. Mine is the Sāgar branch of the Tapā Gacch, Nemisāgar is my guru. Before him were Ravisāgar guru and Sukhsāgar guru. Thus may Jainism grow.

3. May the whole congregation of monks and others increase. May they progress in all matters with the aid of his blessings.

4. On Immortal Third, 1978 [April 1922 C.E.] in the town of Vijāpur, Buddhisāgar made offerings for three hours so men and women can attain happiness.

Mantra: *Oṃ* to Bell-Ears Great Hero, remover of all niggling obstacles and illness, granter of desires, I sacrifice with a fruit. *Oṃ arhaṃ* Mahāvīra peace.

OFFERING OF THE LAMP (ĀRATĪ)

Refrain: Sing to Bell-Ears Great Hero, the strong-minded one who deserves world fame.

1–2. Fulfiller of the mind's desires, remover of the devotees' fears. Remover of affliction, disease, and pain, alleviator of illness, affliction, and sorrow, you quickly help those at your feet by giving wealth, success, and auspiciousness. What is desired is obtained by remembering you. The auspicious time of the devotee arrives.

3–4. O Bell-Ears Great Hero, men and women offer the lamp to you. Remover of harsh worries and pain, remover of the mistakes against religion, roar loudly in the world, in the home, on the ocean, in the forest. Help in arguments and disputes so that auspiciousness isn't ruined by the wicked.

5. Bring peace in the country, city, and congregation. Increase the glory of the devotees. Destroy obstacles and fears. May the world live in health and joy.

6. Auspicious garlands shine in every house, stopping harmful influences. May peace and joy shine forth. Come at once to those who remember you.

7. Soul, Mahāvīr and the teachings reign; this the devotees sing to the world. In every moment help Buddhisāgar in the worldly affairs of his soul.

—25—

Secret Yantras and Erotic Display for Hindu Temples

Michael D. Rabe

The *Śilpa Prakāśa* is the only surviving text on Hindu architecture that was written from an explictly Tantric perspective. Its author, Rāmacandra, was an architect who belonged to a community of Kaula brahmans residing in the Mahanadi delta of Orissa. Composed during the reign of an obscure local rāja, the text's date can be approximated by the fact that its prescriptions are best exemplifed by one particular temple. That is the Varāhī temple at Chaurasi, located midway between the great temple towns of Bhuvaneshvar and Puri, and assigned on stylistic grounds to the early eleventh century.

Chief among distinguishing features shared by text and its closest physical exemplar is the prominence given to erotic sculpture. Of course, images of mithuna (couples) had long been components of the north Indian architectural idiom. Their auspicious presence on doorframes was called for by the sixth-century *Bṛhat Saṁhitā* of Varāhamihira, for example, but they were seen centuries earlier even on Buddhist monuments before the Christian era. What distinguishes their tenth- and eleventh-century permutatations is graphic excess. Not only on the Varāhī temple at Chaurasi (which enshrines a striking image of a sow-faced goddess, the Śakti or personified energy of Viṣṇu's boar avatar, Varāha), but on numerous others throughout Orissa and most famously at Khajuraho in the neighboring state of Madhya Pradesh, the depiction of couples embracing so intensified that one may say emphasis shifted from nouns to verbs—from depictions of mithuna to maithuna—to the acts engaged in by couples.

Again, it is the *Śilpa Prakāśa* alone among surviving architectural treatises that offers, from an avowedly Tantric perspective, a rationale for this profusion of erotic art on medieval Indian temples. As divulged in the final two verses of the second passage translated below, erotic sculpture panels (*kāma-bandha*) should be used as "divertissements"—to titillate the general public while hiding from the uninitiated any glimpse of secret diagrams inscribed beneath them, called yantras. However, the employment of sexual imagery should not be construed as endorsement of hedonistic indulgence. In fact, the Tantric understanding of sex begins with full acceptance of the orthodox Hindu presumption that kāma—broadly, the pursuit of pleasure—is one of four legitimate aims in life. Tāntrikas agree with the righteous majority, moreover, that liberation (*mokṣa*) from the vicious cycle of rebirth (*saṃsāra*) is life's ultimate objective—the other two being duty (*dharma*) and prosperity (*artha*). Where they diverge, more in practice than affirmation, from followers of *right*eousness, is in their bold assertion that a left-hand path can also be efficacious. Harnessing the kāma impulse itself, albeit under the most rigorous if not pleasure-subverting ritual conditions, can also be empowering and effective in the pursuit of mokṣa—not to speak of many lesser attainments along the way, including a wide variety of magical powers (*siddhis*) like levitation, astral projection, enticement, and worse.

The deployment of yantras as visual "instruments" with which to demarcate sacred spaces, and to invoke within tightly constructed grids the inhabiting presence of deities, is a commonality shared by nearly all Tantric practitioners, both Hindu and Buddhist private meditators and communal ceremony officiants alike. As such, the *Śilpa Prakāśa* is consistent in that site- or icon-specific yantras are enjoined to underlie virtually every structural component or image type belonging to both the temple's front worship-hall (*mukhaśāla*, the subject of Prakāśa 1, excerpted below) and the sancturary building proper (*vimāna*; see Prakāśa 2, excerpted below). The two passages translated here constitute the major examples from each of the text's two chapters.

First, the Yoginī yantra may be considered a Tantric substitute for the almost ubiquitous Vāstupuruṣa maṇḍala of other Sanskrit treatises on architecture (Figure 25.1). This presumption gains credence from the fact that the *Śilpa Prakāśa* does not even mention the latter, much better known, example of an underlying geometrial grid upon which to build. Mythic acounts of the Vāstupuruṣa maṇḍala vary considerably, but according to the *Matysa Purāṇa* (chapter 226), a demon of global proportions grew from a drop of the great god Śiva's sweat. Ravenously, he proceeded to devour everything until all the gods united and managed to press him face down upon the earth, and to bind him in an eightfold mesh of parallel cords (*aṣṭa-bandha*). There they were obliged to hunker down indefinitely—whence he became known as the Vāstupuruṣa, the "person" upon whom they "reside." By extension, or alternatively, Vāstupuruṣa personifies the building site itself, in essence a local guardian spirit (like the genius loci of ancient Rome) who must be appeased to insure successful construction (of vāstus or habitations) upon it.

As a geometric schema, there are two main variants on the way the god's aṣṭa-bandha is conveived as the Vāstupuruṣa maṇḍala. In both cases the grid is square; the difference arises from whether the intersecting sets of eight parallel lines produce sixty-four or eighty-one subdivisions: either there are eight squares on each side or eight lines between sets of nine (Figure 25.1). Either way, care is taken to insure that there are thirty-two domiciles for as many gods around the perimeter (through a diagonal subdivision of the corner squares in the case of the sixty-four-square grid). With a larger brahmā-sthāna residence at the center for a pre-

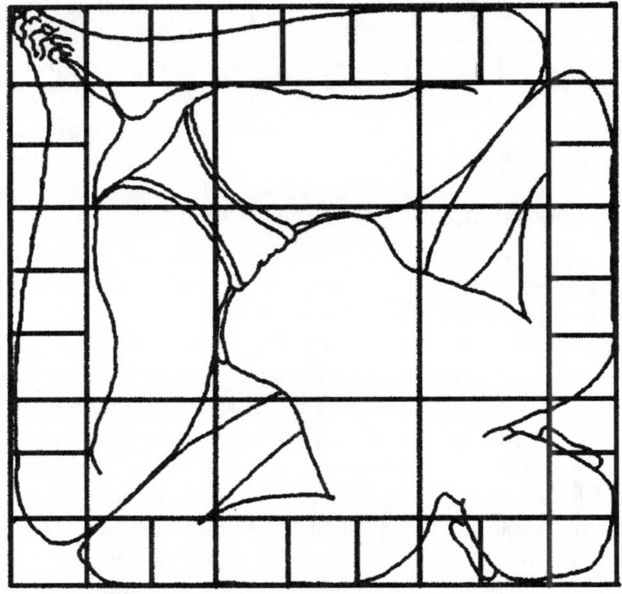

Figure 25.1. Vastupuruṣa maṇḍala with ninefold grid

siding supreme being, one may discern a lingering influence of early references to a Vedic pantheon of thirty-three gods. In actual practice, however, many additional deities are assigned to other interior subsections of the Vāstupuruṣa maṇḍala, and still others are posted to vital points of its exterior perimeter. These and many other finer points are eloquently expounded by Stella Kramrisch in early chapters of *The Hindu Temple*.

One additional aspect of the Vāstupuruṣa maṇḍala as actually deployed at construction sites is reported by S. K. Ramachandra Rao. Although subdued, the site-personifying Vāstupuruṣa is neither dead nor entirely immobilized. Throughout the year his froglike tucked position is conceived as rotating; his head is in the east in September and moves in a clockwise direction (*pradakṣiṇa*) progressively toward due south by December, and so on. The demon is also thought to be dormant most of the time; however, intermittent ninety-minute periods of wakefulness are considered propitious occasions for the commencement of new construction.

Much less is known about the analogous Tantric deployment of the Yoginī yantra. The *Śilpa Prakāśa* passage concentrates on details of its construction and investiture with goddesses. But given the parallels of occasion and audience with the Vāstupuruṣa maṇḍala, its underlying rationale and function in practice can be imagined. Like its better-known correlate, the Yoginī yantra is drawn out on a site or sanctuary floor and then covered over before construction upon it begins.

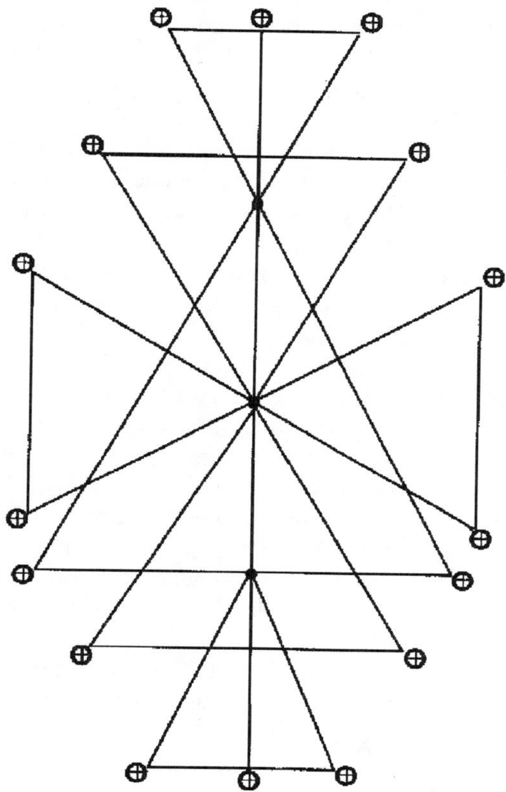

Figure 25.2. A Yoginī yantra

In neither case do the grid lines actually serve to demarcate architectural forms; rather, they serve to position pantheons of empowering and protective deities, with the obvious difference that the Tantric sets are predominantly female. By "audience" I allude to the essential presence of a temple's patron—typically a king—who like the yajamāna (chief sacrificer) of Vedic sacrifices is homologized in his essence with the building (or sacrificial victim) so that attendant benefits may accrue to him.

One fundamental reason why female deities should predominate in Tantric yantras is that worshipers of Śakti, namely Śākta Hindus, consider the energizing goddess to be dominant over her otherwise quiescent male counterpart. The best-known visual expression of this conviction is the iconic Kālī standing on the corpselike body of Śiva. The motif plays upon assonance shared between the male god's name and the Sanskrit word for corpse, *śava*. Tantric deities of both genders frequently come in multiples of eight—or nine, considering that eight subordinates frequently form a protective circle around a supreme central deity. Thus, in one sense at least, the sixteen goddesses (called mātṛikās, "little Mothers") consigned to the periphery of the Yoginī yantra constitute a simple reduplication: a protective circle of sixteen guardians is superior to one with only eight. Even better, by this logic, is the total of sixty-four, reached when an additional four yoginīs are assigned to each vital point of the encirclement. However simplistic this explanation may appear, it is not trivial in actual practice, given the fact that a large number of Sixty-Four Yoginī temples were constructed throughout central India and beyond between the ninth and twelfth centuries. These are accompanied by a truly bewildering number of textual variants on the goddesses' actual names and attributes, with virtually no two lists or sculpture sets identical (see the numerous examples compiled in Vidya Dehejia's book on the subject). But again, such quantitative minutia are not unique to Tantric contexts, as evidenced by the sixty-four- and eighty-one-square variants of the Vāstupuruṣa maṇḍala.

Yet another current of thought joins these primarily architectural traditions. Especially with respect to the sixteen component triangles of the Kāmakalā yantra as detailed in the second passage translated here, the two works by David Gordon White mentioned below bear a close reading. They demonstrate that since Vedic times, sixteen has been considered the number of the moon's waxing and waning digits, and that in the full moon's plenitude—equated with soma, the divine ambrosia—there is hoped-for immortality.

In purely formal terms, the distinguishing feature of Tantric yantras, including the two examples presented here, is their incorporation of triangles. Sometimes, as in the famous Śrī Yantra, overlapping and reverse-directed equilateral triangles are conceived as gendered pairs. The resultant stars thus constitute two-dimensional equivalents of the cylindrical stone liṅgas (phallic images of Śiva) set into discoid yoni-pīṭhas (denoting the Goddess's vulva) in the sancta of Śiva temples. However, in both yantras presented here, where large numbers of triangles come into play, they all signify yonis. An overt statement to this effect is verse 531 of Prakāśa 2, wherein the presiding goddess of the second yantra, Mahā-Kāmakaleśvarī, is described as making a gesture called yoni-mudrā. A rare survival of this mudrā, in an erotic sculpture tableau of the sort recommended for diverting attention from the underlying Kāmakalā yantra, occurs on the Lakṣmaṇa Temple at Khajuraho (Figure 25.3).

Both passages translated here include allusions to the physiological centrality of sexual fluids in Tantric schemata wherein semen, ideally fortified by female secretions (*rajas*) produces a nectar of immortality (*amṛta*) that the adept aspires to redirect through successive cakras of the spinal column upward to the cranial vault. As such, the sexual activity referred to as rajaḥ-pāna (literally, "drinking female discharge") in *Prakāśa* 2.534 may be urethral suction (*vajrolī mudrā*). With respect to the cakras, this same verse describes the divine love making as taking place in the ājña cakra, topmost among the six psychospiritual nodes arrayed

Figure 25.3. Kāmakalā Yantra superimposed over an erotic sculpture on the Lakṣmaṇa Temple, Khajuraho, dated 954 C.E.

along the spinal column in Tantric yoga, commonly visualized as a two-petaled lotus at the level of the eyebrows (or Śiva's third eye). Even without further delving into this subject of great complexity and extremely varied traditions among practioners, it may be seen that homologies are presupposed between the physical space and forms of temple architecture, the divine order of the universe, and a mapping of the individual worshiper's subtle body—or more simply, between the macro- and micro-cosms: as it is in heaven, so may it be on earth.

The *Śilpa Prakāśa* has been published only once, with a full translation, text in Devanagari script, and lengthy introduction by Alice Boner and Sadasiva Rath Sarma: *Śilpa Prakāśa: Medieval Orissan Sanskrit Text on Temple Architecture* (Leiden: E. J. Brill, 1966). The volume was illustrated with photographs of the Varāhī temple at Caurasi, among others, plus reproductions from the one illustrated palm-leaf manuscript of the text, with an eighteenth-century colophon. The published text is based on three such manuscripts, all of a similar age and written in the Oriya script.

Further Reading

The search for texts of this nature was prompted by a more speculative earlier publication by Alice Boner, *Principles of Composition in Hindu Sculpture, Cave Temple Period* (Leiden: E. J. Brill, 1962), wherein she posited the existence of compositional diagrams for a number of well-known rock-cut sculptures at Mamallapuram and Ellora, dating from the seventh and eighth centuries. Subsequently she published two additional studies of manuscripts purported to preserve architectural traditions of Orissa: *New Light on the Sun Temple of Konarka; Four Unpublished Manuscripts Relating to Construction History and Ritual of This Temple*, translated into English and annotated by Alice Boner and Sadasiva Rath Sarma, with Rajendra Prasad Das (Varanasi: Chowkhamba Sanskrit Series Office, 1972); and the *Vāstusūtra Upaniṣad : The Essence of Form in Sacred Art*: Sanskrit text, English translation, and notes by Alice Boner, Sadasiva Rath Sarma, and Bettina Baümer (Delhi: Motilal Banarsidass, 1982).

Two books are recommended for further reading on the use of maṇḍalas in temple construction: the magisterial Stella Kramrisch, *The Hindu Temple,* 2 vols. (1946, reprint: Delhi: Motilal Banarsidass, 1976), and S. K. Ramachandra Rao, *Maṇḍalas in Temple Worship* (Bangalore: Kalpatharu Research Academy, 1988). For a well-illustrated introduction to a variety of Goddess temples belonging to the same period and region as the *Śilpa Prakāśa*, see Vidya Dehejia, *Yoginī Cult and Temples: A Tantric Tradition* (New Delhi: National Musuem, 1986). The leading authority on Orissan temples is Thomas E. Donaldson, *Hindu Temple Art of Orissa*, 3 vols. (Leiden: E. J. Brill, 1985, 1986, 1987); see also his article, "Propitious-Apotropaic Eroticism in the Art of Orissa," *Artibus Asiae* 35 (1975): 75–100, and my on-line publication: Michael Rabe, "Sexual Imagery on the 'Phantasmogorical Castles' at Khajuraho," *International Journal of Tantric Studies* 2.2 (http://www.asiatica.org/publications/ijts). Finally, as mentioned with respect to the underlying Tantric ideology, the reader is advised to consult David Gordon White, *The Alchemical Body: Siddha Traditions in Medieval India* (Chicago: University of Chicago Press, 1996), chapter 2, "The Universe by Numbers"; and White, "Transformations in the Art of Love: Kāmakalā Practices in Hindu Tantric and Kaula Traditions," *History of Religions* 38.2 (November 1998): 172–98.

Śilpa Prakāśa 1.90b- 106

90b. Hear now about the supreme Yoginī Yantra upon which Śākta temples [for goddesses] are to be grounded.

THE YOGINĪ YANTRA

91. According to Tantric texts, the installation of yoginīs is paramount. On the ground align three bindus (points) at an equal distance from each other [along

a north/south axis, plus two outer points at an equivalent distance, as well. The three interior points are equated, respectively, with the metaphysical qualities (*guṇas*) of sattva, rajas, and tamas, that is spirit, energy, and darkness].

92. [Two equilateral] triangles [pointing south] should be made to meet at the upper [sattva] bindu. (Let the sattva bindu mark the apex of the upper triangle whose base aligns with the north perimeter point, and the base of the second triangle whose apex extends a double distance to the tamas bindu). The top triangle denotes sattva and the lower one (with twice the elevation, and centered on the rajas bindu) may be considered the rajas triangle.

93.–94. [Likewise,] the central axis connecting the three points is called the rajas line. From its southern [tamas] bindu, a tamas triangle should be drawn (of equal size to the sattva triangle above), facing the opposite direction and with its apex meeting the central rajas triangle at the tamas bindu. [A variant recension of this passages adds the following gloss as verses 92b and 93a: "Triangular fields pointing upward are considered fire triangles, whereas those facing downward are thought to be water triangles."] Next, a transversal line should be drawn through the midpoint of the sattva [-guṇa] triangle.

95. And likewise a line should be drawn across the tamas triangle at midelevation. Then two more equilateral triangles can be formed by diagonal lines between these transversals that intersect at the rajas bindu.

96. Thus this supreme yantra is composed of five triangles, [three facing] downward and [two facing] upward. Finally, two more triangles are drawn to converge at the rajas bindu from the sides.

97. Down the middle axis it is the the yoginī rekhā (line) that activates the entire yantra by penetrating all the bindus and triangles like a rod.

98. This is the auspicious Yoginī yantra, enjoined for Tantric establishments (pīṭhās). Wherever temples are thus undergirded by yoginīs, the acquisition of siddhis (supernatural powers) is a certainty.

99. Sixteen mother goddesses reside on [a corresponding number of] the yoginī-bindus (peripheral points of the yantra, including both ends of the center "rod"; four yoginīs are also to be assigned to each bindu, in sequential order).

100. This yantra has great power when established within a temple's inner sanctum (*garbha-gṛha*); the yantra should be made coterminus with dimensions of the Goddess-sanctum (*devī-pīṭha*).

101. The skilled practicioner should make sure that the yantra's coordinates are aligned in all directions with the sanctum floor.

102. By means of measuring cord and other instruments a priest should lay out the yantra, affixing it [and its attendent deities] with aloe wood and vermillion (*kuṅkum*) mixed with red sandal paste.

103. Then the yantra-nyāsa pūjā (the worship associated with the establishment of the yantra) should be performed with the king present, worshiping the yoginīs invoked at each of the yantra's [peripheral] bindu-points.

104. By depositing various jewels and other elements, including cakra diagrams engraved on metal discs, each bindu-point should be assiduously worshiped.

105. After completion of these oblations the sanctum floor should raised [to seal them in place]. This royal yantra ceremony assures victory, the destruction of all obstacles.

106. Thus the king's aspirations for victory are fulfilled and all siddhis are granted. Purification of the sanctum and the entire temple grounds is also achieved without a doubt.

Śilpa Prakāśa 2.498—539

THE TRUTH ABOUT EROTIC ART (KĀMAKALĀ TATTVA)

498. In this context [of the ornamentation of exterior temple walls], hear the rationale for erotic sculpture panels (*kāma-bandhas*). I will explain them according to the received tradition among sculptors (*śilpa-vidyā*).

499. Kāma is the root of the world's existence. All that is born originates from kāma. It is by kāma also that primordial matter and all beings eventually dissolve away.

500. Without [the passionate engagement of] Śiva and Śakti, creation would be nothing but a figment. Nothing from birth to death occurs without the activation of kāma (*kāma-kriyā*).

501. Śiva is manifest as the great liṅga, Śakti's essential form is the yoni. By their interaction, the entire world comes into being; this is called the activity of kāma.

502. Canonical erotic art (*kāmakalā vidyā*) is an extensive subject in authoritative scriptures (*Āgamas*). As they say, "a place devoid of erotic imagery is a place to be shunned."

503. By Tantric authority (*kaulācāra*) such places are considered inferior, and to be avoided always, as if tantamount to the lair of Death, or impenetrable darkness.

504. Without [first] performing pūjā to the Kāmakalā Yantra, any worship of the Goddess (*Śakti-pūjā*) or Tantric practiçe (*sādhana*) is as futile as an elephant's bath.

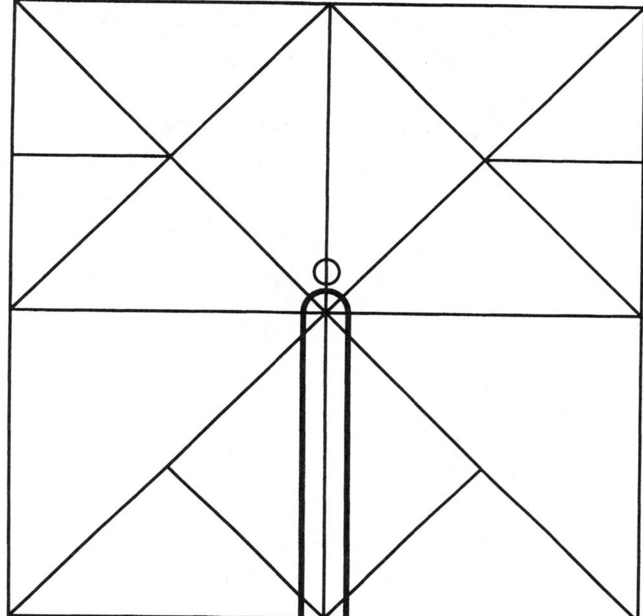

Figure 25.4. A Kāmakalā yantra

505. Where this yantra is consecrated, that building may be considered a Tantric temple (*vīra-mandira*). There all obstacles and fears, and so on, are sure to be destroyed.

506. From the mere sight of this yantra all manner of ghosts, demons, and other hideous creatures are sure to flee far away.

507. Listen, and I will carefully expound its secrets. [But remember,] this yantra must never be divulged to anyone who is not a Tantric practitioner.

THE KĀMAKALĀ YANTRA

508. The ground for this Tantric figure (*vīra-bhūmi*) must be four-sided, either square or rectangular. Across the total area of this four-square field two lines should be made.

509. One vertical and the other horizontal, these lines should intersect at the "jewel house" [center point]. Starting from the jewel-point, diagonals should be drawn to the corners, thus dividing the entire figure into triangular yonis.

510. Vertically extending from the lower baseline to the yantra's center, a nar-

row liṅga should be formed, with a jewel-like rounded top extending above the center point.

511. Above this jewel-top the kāma-bindu's very essence is marked by a bulbous drop, the bindu that bestows all supernatural powers.

512. After this, the sixteen mātrikas are consigned to [a like number of] triangle yonis, making sure that each is in captivating contact with the liṅga.

513. These sixteen facets (*kalās*) are all formally conceived as being yonis, only by virtue of linear conjunction with the liṅga, thus becoming [a complete set of sixteen] facets.

514. How, then, is the segmented field apportioned so as to constitute the fifteen [that is, sixteen] principal orifices that are conjoined with the liṅga?

515. By what means are those three-sided figures considered to represent yonis, the totality of which constitute this yantra?

516. In the upper half, two oblique lines should connect the top central bindu to the ends of the horizontal center line; similarly, draw lines from the lower center up to [but not beyond] the corner diagonals.

517. [The upper side triangles are then subdivided horizontally:] Kāmeśi is the first Śakti [assigned to the upper side triangle on the proper right]; Bhagamālikā is second [below her]; Nityaklinnā is third [to the proper left top triangle]; and fourth is Bherundā [below her].

518. [Below] on the proper left set of three fields Mahāvajreśvarī is assigned the bottom triangle, Śivadūtikā is beside her [to the liṅga's proper right].

519. Beside her, in the [other proper] left corner field, is the citśakti [named] Vahnivāsinī, joined with captivating lines.

520. To her left, and conjoined to the jewel-tip (*maṇi-kṣetra*) portion of the liṅga is placed the goddess Vajreśvarī.

521. Above, on the proper right [and horizontally extended from the liṅga] is Tvaritā, the steadfast essence of the Śakti facets (*kalātmikā*), and opposite [her, on the] left, Kulasundarī.

522. In this order are the beautiful fields occupied on the sides. In the great yantra of the vulva-altar (*bhaga-pīṭha*) only six more remain to be enumerated.

523. Against the liṅga's right side is Śakti Kīlapatākā, opposite her the lovely limbed Jvālamālinī.

524. Vijayā, the constant Companion [goes across the top left], Kāmakaleśvarī extends below her to the liṅga's jewel-tip.

525. On her side to the proper right, the divine Tripurāsundarī is placed, [and

above her], opposite Vijayā, [goes Bhairavī], the constant love of Bhairava, beloved of the powerless.

526. These are the sixteen Śaktis, goddesses who are the very essence of Love (*kāmakalātmikā*), together constituting the yantra's field; around its outer periphery a protective ring of [eight] yoginīs [is invoked].

527. Nirbharā at the upper centerpoint, Rahasyakā in the upper left corner, Kulotkīrṇa at the middle left, Atirahasyā in the lower corner.

528. At the lower center place Saṃpradāyā; in the next corner Guptataraṅgikā; Guptayoginī at the proper right center; and Nigarbhā at top right.

529. These are the yoginīs of the peripheral field, as distinguished from the [interior, sixteen-] faceted Love Field. [Finally], the Supreme Śakti, the great goddess of Love's Facets [or of the Art of Love], Parāśakti Mahā-Kāmakaleśvarī [is visualized at] the central drop.

MEDITATION ON MAHĀ-KĀMAKALEŚVARĪ

530–31. Wearing colorful garments, gracious, [yet] aroused like an elephant in rut, ever sex-crazed, radiant in a circle of light, with a snare of lotus-flowers, and making the auspicious yoni-mudrā [in right and left hands respectively], she holds a bow on her [upper] left hand and and in her upper left a spray of kiṃśuka (*Butea frondosa*) buds.

532. [In a third pair of hands] the Goddess holds a rudrākṣa rosary while confering boons and fearlessness (with the varadā and abhaya mudrās), though afflicted herself by Kāma's five sharp arrows.

MEDITATION ON KĀMAKALĀ'S LORD, ŚIVA

533–34. Just below her, from the jewel-tip [of the yantra's liṅga] appears Śiva, Kāmakalā's Lord, his complexion somewhat dark, profoundly still in a seated yogic pose, almighty, [yet] constantly absorbed in lovemaking to Kāmakaleśvarī, mounted in the ājña cakra, always delighting to partake of her sexual fluids (*rajaḥ-pāna-rataḥ*).

535. Wearing the ascetic's garb, [he is] the yogin Kāmakaleśvara, presiding lord of the great Kāmakalā Yantra, the dark Śaṅkara.

536. This most secret yantra is the ultimate means of protecting any place. It is a perceptible power aid, and manifestly the [ultimate] bestower of all siddhis.

537. In all the best Śākta and Śaiva temples this yantra must certainly be deployed; then their fame will remain unmoved, like mountains.

538. [But] this most secret of secret yantras must not be be seen by just anyone.

This is the reason that images of erotic play [should hide] the yantra's alignments.

539. The considered opinion among tāntrikas is that erotic images should adorn upper panels on pilasters of the exterior temple wall. There erotic sculpture panels should be mounted in order to delight the general public.

—26—

The Six Rites of Magic

Gudrun Bühnemann

References to magical practices are found throughout ancient Indian literature, especially the *Atharva Veda*. Rites of magic are a common topic in Tantric texts, where we often encounter them in a group called the "six rites." This group represents a systematization of magical practices. Although elements of folk traditions are certainly present, the dependence on brahmanical rituals is clearly evident.

The *Mantramahodadhi* (Great Ocean of Mantras), a Sanskrit text that prescribes the mantras of different deities and ritual practices connected with them, was composed by Mahīdhara at Varanasi, in 1588. Mahīdhara wrote the work with the intention of gathering all significant information on the topic in a single book. Because of the clarity of its presentation, the *Mantramahodadhi*—along with the *Naukā* (The Boat), the author's commentary written to enable practitioners to cross the "Great Ocean of Mantras"—has enjoyed great popularity in all parts of India up to the present day. Throughout the work, Mahīdhara enumerates various deities, the mantras of those deities, and the rites in which the mantras are employed and which may be performed, once the mantras have been mastered, for the attainment of specific objectives. Among the rites are those usually classified as "the six rites" (*ṣaṭkarmāṇi*).

Chapter 25, the final chapter of the text, comprises 132 verses. Verses 1–102 address broader issues connected with the six rites. Five of these fall under the category of abhicāra, sorcery or destructive magic, and one may be classified as an auspicious beneficial rite of white magic. The chapter bears some similarity to sections of the anonymous *Prapañcasāra* and Lakṣmaṇadeśika's *Śāradātilaka* (especially 23.121–45), both well-known Tantric compendiums of the tenth to eleventh centuries. The text is precise but highly condensed, and presupposes a thorough knowledge of Indian ritual practice on the part of the practitioner. Although the text does not give details about how to perform such rituals—such descriptions being scattered throughout the work—it provides general information about the times, materials, and so forth that were considered suitable for these rites.

Even though the six rites are often mentioned in Tantric literature, the names used for them vary. The six rites referred to in the *Mantramahodadhi* are appeasement (*śānti*), subjugation (*vaśya, vaśīkaraṇa*), immobilization (*stambha, stambhana*), enmity (*dveṣa, vidveṣa*), eradication (*uccāṭa, uccāṭana*), and liquidation (*māraṇa*).

Appeasement is defined as the curing of diseases; it is an auspicious, benevolent rite, whereas the other five rites are of a destructive nature. Subjugation entails bringing a person under the practitioner's control, especially seducing a woman against her will. Immobilization means stopping a person's activity. Enmity is defined as creating dissension or dislike between two persons who are attached to each other. Eradication means depriving a person of his place, usually with reference to such activities as breaking an object or removing someone from a location. Liquidation means taking life. Similar definitions appear earlier in *Śāradātilaka* 23.121–25. Magical rites performed for these and similar objectives are also described in Indian Buddhist Tantric texts, such as the *Guhyasamājatantra*, as well as in some texts contained in collections of sādhanas (texts describing methods of spiritual realization) like that published under the title *Sādhanamālā*.

After defining the rites, Mahīdhara states that the practitioner should know nineteen items before performing a rite. These items are listed in verses 4 and 5 and then explained one by one in verses 6 to 65ab of the chapter. They are: the deity, the deity's color, the season, the direction, the day, the posture/seat, the arrangement, the symbolic shape, the gesture, the letters, the rise of the element, the fire sticks, the rosary, the fire, the material for writing, the fire pit, the small wooden sacrificial ladle, the large ladle, and the stylus.

The Nineteen Items

To each rite a presiding goddess with a specific body color is assigned (verses 6–7ab; Table 26.1). Flowers of the respective colors are offered before undertaking a rite. Here the color white is considered suitable for appeasement, whereas the

TABLE 26.1
Rites by Goddess and Color

Rite	*Goddess*	*Color*
1. appeasement	Rati	white
2. subjugation	Vāṇī/Sarasvatī	red
3. immobilization	Ramā	yellow
4. enmity	Jyeṣṭhā	variegated
5. eradication	Durgā	dark
6. liquidation	Kālī	gray

dark and gray colors are appropriate for destructive rites. In the three-color scheme commonly found in Indian texts, white, red, and dark (black) are connected with the three qualities of the Sāṃkhya system of philosophy, namely, goodness/purity, passion, and inertness/darkness, or with the cosmic functions of creation, maintenance, and destruction.

The next section addresses suitable times of the day. The twenty-four hours of the day are considered a replica of the entire year (verses 7cd–9ab; Table 26.2). They are divided into the six seasons, with each, beginning at sunrise, lasting four hours. Each season is favorable to one of the six rites. Each rite is further connected with the direction (verses 9cd–10ab; Table 26.2) the practitioner faces during the performance. Omitting south and west, the two remaining cardinal and the four intermediate directions are of significance. The topic of directions is taken up again later (verses 60–61ab) in connection with the directions in which the fire pits face. Except for two of the rites, appeasement and liquidation, they agree with the above scheme.

Each rite should be performed on suitable days of the lunar month and the week (verses 10cd–15ab; Table 26.3). The lunar month is divided into two fortnights: the bright half, when the moon waxes, and the dark half, when it wanes. It is only to be expected that a rite such as liquidation should be mainly connected with the dark half, whereas the auspicious rite of appeasement should be performed during the bright half.

The practitioner is advised to maintain one of six postures in the rites while seated on one of six animal hides (15cd–17ab; Table 26.4) We do not know how far this classification was ever observed in practice, but we can perceive a connection between the characteristics of the animals and the nature of the rites performed. The hide of the sacred cow is suited for the auspicious appeasement rite, whereas the hide of the powerful and large elephant suits the act of immobilization.

Mahīdhara goes on to describe six special methods or arrangements for connecting the mantra or sacred spell to be uttered in each rite with the letters of the name of the person to be influenced (verses 17cd–23ab; Table 26.5). The sym-

TABLE 26.2
Rites by Season and Direction

Rite	*Season*	*Direction*
1. appeasement	winter	northeast
2. subjugation	spring	north
3. immobilization	cool season	east
4. enmity	summer	southwest
5. eradication	rainy season	northwest
6. liquidation	autumn	southeast

TABLE 26.3
Rites by Suitable Day

Rite	*Day*
1. appeasement	2nd, 3rd, 5th, and 7th of the bright half, coinciding with a Wednesday or Thursday
2. subjugation	4th, 6th, 9th, and 13th of the bright half, coinciding with a Monday or Thursday
3. immobilization and 6. liquidation	8th and 14th of the dark half, new moon day, and 1st day of the bright half, coinciding with a Sunday, Tuesday, or Saturday
4. enmity	8th, 9th, 10th, and 11th of (the bright half), coinciding with a Friday or Saturday
5. eradication	8th and 14th of the dark half, coinciding with a Saturday

Table 26.4
Rites by Posture and Animal Hide

Rite	*Posture*	*Animal Hide*
1. appeasement	lotus	cow
2. subjugation	svastika	rhinoceros
3. immobilization	vikaṭa	elephant
4. enmity	cock	jackal
5. eradication	diamond	sheep
6. liquidation	bhadra	buffalo

bolic shapes (*maṇḍalas*) of each of the five elements are also assigned to the six rites (verses 23cd–26ab; Table 26.6). Note that the fire shape is employed twice. This assignment of the elements to the six rites appears again in the discussion of the rise of the elements (verses 33cd–36), which is determined on the basis of that part of the nose which the breath touches.

Next, six ritual hand gestures (*mudrās*) are assigned to the six rites, and three special gestures are described for the fire ritual (verses 26–29). The letters inscribed in the geometrical figures, or yantras, used in the rites are said to be the letters governed by a particular element (verses 30–32ab). Details about which letters are related to which elements are discussed in an earlier chapter (chapter 24, verses 80–81) of the text. There are also six closing words of mantras (verses 32cd–33ab), each connected with one of the six rites (Table 26.7). *Svāhā, vaṣaṭ* and *vauṣaṭ* have long been employed as exclamations when making offerings in

TABLE 26.5
Rites by Arrangement

Rite	*Arrangement*	*Definition*
1. appeasement	granthana (for grathana)	one letter of the mantra alternates with one letter of the name
2. subjugation	vidarbha	two letters of the mantra alternate with one letter of the name
3. immobilization	saṃpuṭa	the mantra is repeated before and after the name
4. enmity	rodhana	the mantra is inserted at the beginning, middle, and end of the name
5. eradication	yoga	the mantra appears at the end of the name
6. liquidation	pallava	the mantra is followed by the name

TABLE 26.6
Rites by Element and Symbolic Shape of (Maṇḍala)

Rite	*Element*	*Shape*
1. appeasement	water	half moon marked with two lotuses on both sides
2. subjugation	fire	triangle with one or several svastikas
3. immobilization	earth	square with one or several thunderbolts
4. enmity	ether	circle
5. eradication	wind	circle marked with six dots
6. liquidation	fire	triangle with one or several svastikas

TABLE 26.7
Rites by Closing Word

Rite	*Closing Word*
1. appeasement	*namaḥ*
2. subjugation	*svāhā*
3. immobilization	*vaṣaṭ*
4. enmity	*vauṣaṭ*
5. eradication	*huṃ*
6. liquidation	*phaṭ*

the fire in a ritual. *Namaḥ* means "salutation," and is used for offering respect to a deity or person. *Phaṭ* imitates the sound of bursting or breaking. These six closing words also appear in nyāsa rites, that is, the imposition of syllables, deity names, and so forth, upon the practitioner's body. These rites are a part of the worship ritual.

An interesting topic briefly touched upon in verses 33cd–36 is that of the rise of elements, which is observed from the part of the nose where the breath touches. It was observed that the breath does not pass equally through both nostrils at all times, but touches certain parts of the nostrils over various intervals of time. Certain rites or actions can be performed successfully when a certain element is predominant (Table 26.8). This branch of knowledge is also known as "rise of breath" (*svarodaya*) and is addressed in independent treatises. It is a method often used for making predictions.

Rosaries are commonly used to count the number of repetitions of mantras. Mahīdhara gives some information about the material for the beads of rosaries, their number, and the method of rotation (verses 40–44). Instructions regarding the fire ritual (*homa*), which is an ancient Indian practice, follow. Fire sticks of different woods, smeared with different substances, are offered in the fire ritual, which constitutes a portion of the rites (verses 37–39). The offerings are made into different fires, which are produced by rubbing sticks of different types of wood together. The different flames of the fire are worshiped for each rite. They are called "tongues," because they consume the offerings. An almost identical list of the names of the tongues appears earlier in *Śāradātilaka* (5.23). To each of the rites a fire pit of a particular shape is assigned, which faces a particular direction (verses 60–61ab). The materials for the two ladles used in pouring libations into the fire are specified in verses 61cd–62ab.

After the fire ritual, brahmans, who represent deities, are fed. This ritual feeding of brahmans also figures in other rites. The number of brahmans fed varies with the rite (verses 49cd–55ab). Their blessing is said to destroy the sin that accrues from the performance of destructive magic.

Mahīdhara describes different substances used as ink substitutes in drawing a yantra as part of the rites, and suitable materials on which to draw the yantras

TABLE 26.8
Rites by Element and Movement of Breath

Rite	*Element*	*Movement of Breath*
1. appeasement	water	lower part of the nostrils
2. subjugation	fire	upper part of the nostrils
3. immobilization	earth	ridge of the nose
4. enmity	ether	middle of the nostrils
5. eradication	wind	sideways
6. liquidation	fire	upper part of the nostrils

(verses 55ab–59). Depending on the nature of the rite to be performed, different materials are used for the stylus, and certain days are recommended for making that instrument (verses 62cd–65ab).

Following his discussion of the nineteen topics, Mahīdhara addresses other issues, such as the appropriate diet for the practitioner (verses 65cd–67), substances and vessels used for pouring libations (verses 68–70), and the body posture that is to be maintained (verse 71).

In his concluding discussion of these ritual procedures, Mahīdhara declares that he has described the desire-oriented rites only for the sake of persons who are attracted to sense pleasures, based on instructions he has found in the works of earlier preceptors (verses 72–76ab). Mahīdhara extolls the superiority of the worship of deities without any desire for personal gain, as well as of the attainment of the highest knowledge, the realization of the unity of the individual self (*ātman*) with the universal principle (*brahman*; verses 76cd–81).

The text then continues with a discussion of a preliminary ritual, to be performed for determining the success of the rite (verses 82–87). Not every mantra is suitable for every individual. The practitioner prays to the god Śiva to reveal "the truth" in a dream. Auspicious and inauspicious dreams are listed in detail (verses 88–97ab). Finally, the signs by which one recognizes that the practitioner has attained mastery over the mantra are given. The practitioner is again advised to strive for the highest knowledge and emancipation (verses 97–101).

A critical edition of the *Mantramahodadhi* is not yet available. The translation is based on my new edition of chapter 25, published as appendix 2 of my study, *The Iconography of Hindu Tantric Deities. Vol. 1, The Pantheon of the Mantramahodadhi* (Groningen: Egbert Forsten, 2000), Gonda Indological Studies series, no. 9. This volume also provides detailed information on the *Mantramahodadhi* and its author. I have used the printed edition entitled *Mantramahodadhiḥ saṭīkaḥ* (Bombay: Srivenkatesvar Steam Press, 1910, 1962), as well as the manuscript reproduced in lithographic form in *Mantramahodadhi*, edited by Raghuvara Prasāda (Lucknow: Smarahimsakadatta Press, 1872), and the three following manuscripts: Manuscript 1008 of 1891–1895, and 1138 of 1881–1892 (dated 1789), both held in the Bhandarkar Oriental Research Institute, Poona, India; and Manuscript 0793 (dated 1757), held in the library of the Centre of Advanced Study in Sanskrit, University of Poona, India.

In the following translation of *Mantramahodadhi* 25.1–102, the text is divided into subsections, each with a separate heading. These headings are not part of the Sanskrit text, but were introduced to help orient the reader and facilitate understanding.

Further Reading

Data on the six rites, similar to those described in the *Mantramahodadhi*, may also be found in the *Śāradātilakatantra* (*Śāradā-Tilaka Tantra*), edited by Arthur Avalon (reprint Delhi: Motilal Banarsidass, 1982). Detailed information on Indian magic can be found in Teun Goudriaan, *Māyā Divine and Human* (Delhi: Motilal Banarsidass, 1978), and H.-G. Türstig, "The Indian Sorcery Called Abhicāra," *Wiener Zeitschrift für die Kunde Südasiens* 24 (1985): 69–117. Mantra-related practices are described in Gudrun Bühnemann, "Selecting and Perfecting Mantras in Hindu Tantrism," *Bulletin of the School of Oriental and African Studies* 54 (1991): 292–306. Tibetan magic is addressed in Stephan Beyer, *The Cult of Tārā: Magic and Ritual in Tibet* (Berkeley and Los Angeles: University of California Press, 1973), and its place within Tibetan Buddhism is considered in P. Schwieger, "Schwarze Magie im tibetischen Buddhismus," *Studies in Central & East Asian Religions. Journal of the Seminar for Buddhist Studies* (Copenhagen) 9 (1996): 18–36. Information on similar rituals in Jainism may be gleaned from M. B. Jhavery, *Comparative and Critical Study of Mantrashastra* (Ahmedabad: Sarabhai Manilal Nawab, 1944).

THE SIX RITES AND THEIR DEFINITIONS

I shall now explain the six rites, which grant success [if] the [correct] procedure [is followed]. The following are called the rites: 1. appeasement, 2. subjugation, 3. immobilization, 4. enmity, 5. eradication, and 6. liquidation. "Appeasement" is the destruction of diseases, and so on."Subjugation" is the state of one who executes a command. "Immobilization" is obstructing an activity. "Enmity" is the dislike between two affectionate people. "Eradication" is deprivation from a place. "Liquidation" is the taking of life. These are the definitions of the six rites. (Verses 1–3)

THE NINETEEN ITEMS A PRACTITIONER OF THE RITES SHOULD KNOW

One should practice the six rites after knowing the following [nineteen items] precisely: i. the deity, ii. the deity's color, iii. the season, iv. the direction, v. the day, vi. the posture/seat, vii. the arrangement, viii. the symbolic shape, ix. the gesture, x. the letters, xi. the rising of the element, xii. the fire sticks, xiii. the rosary, xiv. the fire, xv. the material for writing, xvi. the fire pit, xvii. the small wooden sacrificial ladle, xviii. the large ladle, and xix. the stylus. (Verses 4–5)

I–II. THE PRESIDING DEITIES OF THE SIX RITES AND THEIR COLORS

1. Rati, 2. Vāṇī, 3. Ramā, 4. Jyeṣṭhā, 5. Durgā, and 6. Kālī are the deities [of the rites]. They are 1. white, 2. red, 3. yellow, 4. variegated, 5. dark, and 6. gray. At the beginning of the rite [the practitioner] should worship them with flowers of the [deity's] respective color in sequence. (Verses 6–7ab)

III. THE SIX SEASONS AND THEIR CONNECTION WITH THE SIX RITES

The six seasons are spring, and so forth. Day and night come in sequence [as they are mentioned]. The duration of each season is considered to be ten times twenty-four minutes [four hours]. The wise man should connect 1. winter [November-January], 2. the [season] called spring [March-May], 3. the cool season [January-March], 4. summer [May-July], 5. the rainy season [July-September], [and] 6. autumn [September-November] with the six rites in sequence. (Verses 7cd–9ab)

IV. THE SIX DIRECTIONS THE PRACTITIONER FACES DURING THE RITES

The directions are, in sequence, 1. northeast, 2. north, 3. east, 4. southwest, 5. northwest, and 6. southeast. (Verses 9cd–10ab)

V. DAYS OF THE LUNAR MONTH AND OF THE WEEK SUITABLE FOR THE RITES

He should perform the respective rites while repeating the mantra [and] facing the respective direction. And the second [lunar day] and seventh as well as the fifth [and] the third [lunar day] in the bright half [of the month] coinciding with a Wednesday or Thursday is approved of in the 1. appeasement rite. Equally, the fourth, ninth, sixth, [or] thirteenth lunar day [of the bright half] coinciding with a Thursday or Monday is recommended in the 2. subjugation rite. And the eleventh, tenth, ninth, and again the eighth coinciding with a Saturday or Friday is prescribed in the 4. enmity rite. The rite called 5. eradication should be performed on the [following days] for attainment of success: the fourteenth or eighth in the dark [half of the month], when it coincides with a Saturday. When the fourteenth and eighth day occuring in the dark [half of the month], [and] when the new moon day [and] the [day] coming at the end of the [dark half, that is, the first day of the bright half] coincide with a Sunday, Saturday and Tuesday, [the time] is auspicious for 3. immobilization and 6. liquidation. (Verses 10cd–15ab)

VI. SIX SUITABLE POSTURES AND SEATS FOR MANTRA REPETITION

In appeasement and other [rites], he should maintain in sequence the most excellent posture: 1. the lotus, 2. svastika, 3. vikaṭa, 4. cock, 5. diamond, and 6. bhadra. Having sat on the hide of 1. a cow, 2. rhinoceros, 3. elephant, 4. jackal, as well as 5. a sheep or 6. buffalo, he should perform the repetition [of the mantra] in the rites of appeasement, and so forth. (Verses 15cd–17ab)

VII. SIX ARRANGEMENTS FOR THE LETTERS OF THE MANTRA AND THOSE OF THE VICTIM'S NAME

Having explained the seats in this way, the arrangement is now being explained. The following are considered the six arrangements in the rites: 1. granthana, the [arrangement] called 2. vidarbha, 3. saṃpuṭa, as well as 4. rodhana, 5. yoga, and 6. pallava. And now the definition of each of these six is stated:

1. There should be one syllable of the mantra, then a syllable of the [victim's] name; again a syllable of the mantra and a syllable of the name. In this way, granthana is described.

2. In the beginning, there are two letters of the mantra, then one letter of the name; in this way [it is done] again and again. [Thus] vidarbha is explained by the most excellent connoisseurs of mantras.

3. Having first uttered the mantra, he should then recite the complete name [and] at the end the mantra in inverted order. This is called saṃpuṭa.

4. The mantra [inserted] in the beginning, middle, and end of the name, however, is rodhana.

5. The mantra [inserted] at the end of the name, on the other hand, is yoga.

6. The name [appearing] at the end of the mantra is pallava. (Verses 17cd–23ab)

VIII. THE SYMBOLIC SHAPES OF THE ELEMENTS

The symbolic shape of water is said to resemble a half moon, marked with two lotuses on both sides; it is recommended in the 1. appeasement rite.

The symbolic shape of fire, however, for 2. subjugation is a triangle endowed with svastika[s].

A square connected with thunderbolt[s], however, is the symbolic shape of earth for 3. immobilization.

A circle is the [symbolic shape] of ether for 4. enmity.

A [circle] marked with six dots, on the other hand, is the symbolic shape of wind for 5. eradication; the fire shape [described before is the symbolic shape] for 6. liquidation. (Verses 23cd–26ab)

IX. SIX HAND GESTURES FOR THE SIX RITES; THREE HAND GESTURES FOR THE FIRE RITUAL AND THEIR DEFINITIONS

The 1. lotus, 2. noose, 3. mace, 4. pestle, 5. thunderbolt, and 6. sword should be the six hand gestures in the six rites. Now the [gestures] for the fire ritual are being told: "[female] deer," "goose," [and] "sow" are the three hand gestures approved of in the fire ritual.

When the middle finger, ring finger, and thumb are joined, the gesture is considered the "[female] deer."

When all except the little finger are joined [the gesture] is considered the "goose."

When the hand is contracted it is the "sow." The definitions of gestures have been stated. For appeasement and subjugation, the "[female] deer" and "goose" are employed; for immobilization and others, the "sow." (Verses 26–29)

X. THE LETTERS: LETTERS ASSIGNED TO THE MOON AND THE ELEMENTS EMPLOYED IN THE YANTRAS OF THE RITES; THE SIX "CLASSES" OR CLOSING WORDS OF MANTRAS

Practitioners of mantras state that, in the six rites, the seed syllables of a yantra consist of the letters of the moon, water, earth, ether, wind, and fire. The [sixteen] vowels [and] *sa* and *ṭha* are the letters of the moon. The letters of the [five] elements have been mentioned [in 24.80–83]. These [letters] without the letters of the moon, should be taken in rites, such as subjugation. Some specify 1. *sa*, 2. *va*, 3. *la*, 4. *ha*, 5. *ya*, [and] 6. *ra* [equivalent to water, earth, ether, wind, fire] as the letters of the moon, and so forth. (Verses 30–32ab)

In rites such as appeasement, the most excellent connoisseurs of mantras should know the following six as "classes" in sequence: 1. *namaḥ*, 2. *svāhā*, 3. *vaṣaṭ*, 4. *vauṣaṭ*, 5. *huṃ*, and 6. *phaṭ*. (Verses 32cd–33ab)

XI. THE RISE OF THE ELEMENTS DETERMINED BY OBSERVING THE TOUCH OF THE BREATH ON THE NOSTRILS

Should the breath move below both nostrils, then the rise of the water [element] is to be known, which grants success in the 1. appeasement rite.

When the movement of the breath resorts to the ridge of the nose, it is the rise of the earth, [the element suitable] for 3. immobilization.

When it moves in the middle of the nostrils, it is the rise of ether, which is auspicious for 4. enmity.

When the breath moves above the nostrils, it would be the rise of fire, [and] then there is success in two rites, for 6. liquidation and 2. subjugation.

When the breath moves sideways, the rise of wind should be recognized [as suitable] for 5. eradication. (Verses 33cd–36)

XII. THE FIRE STICKS SMEARED WITH DIFFERENT SUBSTANCES AND USED IN THE FIRE RITUAL FORMING PART OF THE SIX RITES

Dūrvā [used as] fire sticks, smeared with the clarified butter of a cow, [is used] for 1. appeasement. Pomegranate shoots smeared with the clarified butter of a goat [are offered] in a fire ritual for 2. subjugation. Fire sticks from the rāja tree smeared with clarified butter from a sheep [are used] for 3. immobilization. Fire sticks from the thorn apple [tree] smeared with atasī oil [are used] for 4. enmity. [Fire sticks] from the mango [tree] smeared with mustard oil are approved of in the 5. eradication rite. [Fire sticks] from the khadira [tree] smeared with mustard oil are recommended for 6. liquidation. (Verses 37–39)

XIII. ROSARIES: MATERIALS USED, FINGERS EMPLOYED IN ROTATION AND NUMBER OF BEADS

The [following] rosaries should be known in sequence in rites beginning with appeasement: those made from 1. conch shells, 2. lotus seeds, 3. the fruits of the nimba and ariṣṭa [trees], 4. the teeth of the deceased, 5. the teeth of a horse, [and] 6. the teeth of a donkey.

The wise man should rotate the rosary placed on the middle finger with the thumb in 1. appeasement, 2. subjugation and acquisition [-related rites, and] in mantra repetition whose aims are worldly enjoyment and liberation. The wise man should repeat the mantra [rotating the rosary] by joining the ring finger and thumb in the rite of 3. immobilization. However, the wise man should repeat the mantra by joining the index finger and thumb for 4. enmity and 5. eradication, [and] by joining the little finger and thumb for 6. liquidation.

The number of beads in an auspicious rite would be 108, half of it [54], or half of the [half, 27]. In destructive magic, the number [of beads] is 15. (Verses 40–44)

XIV. FIRE RITUAL: FIRE STICKS USED IN LIGHTING THE FIRE; THE TONGUES OF THE FIRE; AND THE RITUAL FEEDING OF BRAHMANS

1. Appeasement [and 2.] subjugation [are performed] in the ordinary fire, 3. immobilization in a fire lit by vaṭa [sticks], [and] 4. enmity [in a fire] lit by bibhītaka [sticks]; the remaining two [rites, that is, 5. eradication and 6. liquidation, are performed in a fire] located in the cremation grounds. In an auspicious rite, the connoisseur of the mantra should light the fire for the fire ritual with fire sticks from the bilva, arka, palāśa, or kṣīra trees; in an inauspicious [rite, with sticks] from the viṣa and bibhītaka, nimba, thorn apple, and śleṣmātaka.

In the rite of 1. appeasement, he should worship the tongue of the fire called Suprabhā; in 2. the subjugation rite, indeed, [the tongue] called Raktā; for 3. immobilization, the one called Kanakā; for 4. enmity, the tongue Gaganā; and for 5. eradication, Atiraktikā. For 6. liquidation, on the other hand, he should worship Kṛṣṇā. However, [he may worship] Bahurūpā in any case. (Verses 45–49ab)

In rites, such as appeasement, he should also know the special number [of brahmans] to be fed. For 1. appeasement [and] 2. subjugation, he should feed brahmans [numbering] one-tenth the [number of offerings in the] fire ritual. That would be the best rite; the mediocre one, on the other hand, is [performed] with [the feeding of brahmans numbering] one twenty-fifth [the number of fire offerings]. The feeding of brahmans, on the other hand, [numbering] one one-hundredth [the number of offerings] of the fire ritual, that is, indeed, the lowest [rite]. For 3. immobilization, the feeding of brahmans is held to be double [that is, one-fifth] the proportion [of offerings given] for appeasement; for 4. enmity [and] 5. eradication, three times [the number of offerings in the fire ritual, and] for 6. liquidation, [the prescribed number] equals the [number of offerings in the] fire ritual. Brahmans should be fed with pleasing foods, should have been born in a very pure family, should know the Veda and [its] supplements, and should be pure, [and] devoted to virtuous conduct. One should consider them deities [and] should worship them. They should be bowed to repeatedly. They should be gratified with sweet words [and] by offerings of gold, and so forth. [The practitioner] obtains his wish before long, once he has received their blessings. The sin that accrues from destructive magical rites vanishes by the [auspicious] utterance of brahmans. (Verses 49cd–55ab)

XV. MATERIALS AND SUBSTANCES FOR DRAWING YANTRAS

Sandalwood paste, yellow pigment, turmeric, domestic smoke [-soot], charcoal from the funeral pyre, [and] the eight poisonous substances [are employed] in drawing yantras for appeasement, and so on. He may certainly also take those previously described [in 20.22–118] writing materials. The eight poisonous substances are black pepper, pippalī [long pepper], dry ginger, excrement of vultures, citraka [wood], domestic smoke, juice of the thorn apple [tree], and salt. For 1. appeasement [and] 2. subjugation, the most excellent connoisseur of mantras should draw the yantra on birchbark; for 3. immobilization, on tiger skin; for 4. enmity, on donkey skin; for 5. eradication, on a banner cloth; [and] for 6. liquidation, on human bone. Whatever receptacles were mentioned in the yantra chapter [20.12–13], they are also approved of. (Verses 55cd–59)

XVI. THE SHAPES OF THE FIRE PITS AND AUSPICIOUS DIRECTIONS

In the rites beginning with appeasement, the fire pit has [the form] of (1) a circle, (2) lotus, (3) square, (4) triangle, (5) hexagon, or (6) half moon, in the directions (1) west, (2) north, (3) east, (4) southwest, (5) northwest, and (6) south, in sequence. (Verses 60–61ab)

XVII.–XVIII. MATERIAL FOR THE SMALL WOODEN SACRIFICIAL LADLE AND THE LARGE LADLE

In [rites of] appeasement and subjugation, the small wooden sacrifical ladle and the large ladle are golden and made from the fig tree. In rites such as the one for immobilization, both are indeed held to be of iron. (Verses 61cd–62ab)

XIX. THE STYLUS: DIFFERENT MATERIALS USED AND THE SUITABLE TIME FOR ITS MANUFACTURE

The stylus is made of gold, made of silver, [or] made from jātī [twig] for 1. appeasement; for 2. subjugation, [it is] made from dūrvā sprouts; for 3.

immobilization, from the agastya tree—or it could be made from the rāja tree; for 4. enmity, however, from the karañja [twig]. For an auspicious rite, the wise man should make the stylus on a pleasant day; for 5. eradication, from bibhītaka; for 6. liquidation, however, from human bone. For an inauspicious rite, on the other hand, [the wise man should make] it, on the riktā days [that is, the fourth, ninth, and fourteenth day of the lunar month], on Tuesday, or on viṣṭi [-karaṇa, that is, one of eleven divisions of the day]. (Verses 62cd–65ab)

THE PRACTITIONER'S DIET

Now food, material for pouring libations, and the vessel for the [libations] are described. For 1. appeasement [and] 2. subjugation, food fit for sacrifice [is recommended]; for 3. immobilization, rice pudding; for 4. enmity, māṣa and mudga beans; for 5. eradication from a place, wheat; for 6. liquidation, rice with red lentils, as well as śyāma(ka) [grain], [and] pudding from goat milk. [Thus] the foods of the practitioners of mantras who perform the rites have been stated. (Verses 65cd–67)

SUBSTANCES FOR POURING LIBATIONS

For 1. appeasement [and] 2. subjugation, water mixed with turmeric is prescribed for the pouring of libations, [and] slightly warm [water] with black pepper, and so on, for 3. immobilization as well as 6. liquidation. Water mixed with the blood of a sheep is recommended for 4. enmity and 5. eradication. (Verses 68–69ab)

VESSELS USED FOR POURING LIBATIONS

A golden vessel should be [used] for pouring libations in the 1. appeasement and 2. subjugation rites; for 3. immobilization, a clay vessel; for 4. enmity, one made of khadira [wood]; for 4. eradication, one of iron. For 6. liquidation, however, a fowl's egg [should be used]. (Verses 69cd–70)

BODY POSTURES MAINTAINED WHILE POURING LIBATIONS

For 1. appeasement [and] 2. subjugation, he should pour libations while seated on a soft seat; for 3. immobilization, while resting on both knees; for 4. enmity, and so on, while standing on one foot. (Verse 71)

DRAWBACKS OF DESIRE-ORIENTED RITES

Thus the procedure for the six rites has been stated for the satisfaction of the connoisseurs of mantras. After having properly performed the types of nyāsa, and having performed the self-protection, the desire-oriented rites should be performed; otherwise, there would be defeat. The mantra can become the enemy of the practitioner who has performed either auspicious or inauspicious desire-oriented rites; therefore, he should not become attached to it. The desire-oriented rite described by previous teachers was explained for the satisfaction of those whose minds are attached to [sense] objects; but it is not conducive to welfare. Those who are attached to desire-oriented rites can only [obtain] limited results. Those who worship God without desire attain all siddhis [supernatural powers]. (Verses 72–76ab)

SUPERIORITY OF WORSHIP WITHOUT SELFISH MOTIVES

[The practitioner] should avoid attachment to whatever performances were stated [prior to the discussion of the six rites as appropriate] for each mantra, for attaining happiness, and should worship the deity without desire. In the Veda, three sections have been given: ritual, worship, and knowledge. The means is described in two of these sections; in the third, the goal is stated. Therefore [the practitioner] should perform what is stated in the Veda and worship the deities, by means of which a pure-minded man obtains the highest knowledge. The individual soul, consisting of consciousness which has entered the body, is the complete *brahman* itself. Knowing this, he is liberated. And having obtained a human body, he should worship the deities. He who is not liberated from existence is a great sinner. Therefore the most excellent of men should strive to obtain knowledge of the self by rites and the worship of deities, [and] by eliminating the group of enemies, such as desire. (Verses 76cd–81)

RITUAL FOR DETERMINING FUTURE SUCCESS BEFORE ATTEMPTING THE PROCEDURE OF PERFECTING A MANTRA

[The practitioner] who wishes to perform the worship of a deity should first consider the future. Having taken a bath, performed the twilight [ritual], and so on, [and] having recollected the lotuslike foot of Hari, he should lie down on a bed of kuśa [grass and] pray to the bull-bannered [Śiva]: "O Lord, Lord of the God of gods, bearer of the trident, who rides on a bull! Announce, O eternal one, the good and bad, while I am asleep. Salutation to the unborn, three-eyed, tawny, great-souled one. Salutation to the handsome, omnipresent lord of dreams. Tell me the truth in the dream regarding all matters completely. O great lord, by your grace I will accomplish success in the ritual." Having prayed to Śiva with these mantras, he should sleep calmly. In the morning he should tell the preceptor the dream he had at night. The connoisseur of the mantra should himself reflect on the [significance of] the dream, without the [preceptor, if he is unavailable]. (Verses 82–87)

AUSPICIOUS DREAMS

The vision of the following in the dream is auspicious: a phallic symbol [of Śiva]; the disks of the moon and sun; [the goddess] Sarasvatī; the [river] Ganges; the preceptor; crossing the Ocean of Blood; victory in battle; worship of [the fire god] Agni; residing in a chariot [yoked with] peacocks, geese, and ruddy geese; sexual intercourse; mounting a crane and acquisition of land; a river; a palace; a chariot; a lotus; a parasol; a girl; a tree with fruits; an elephant; a lamp; a yak; a flower; a bull and horse; a mountain; a jar with liquor; heavenly bodies; stars; a woman; sunrise; heavenly nymphs; ascending palaces, or mountains and chariots; going through the sky; consuming liquor and meat; applying feces [to the body]; sprinkling with blood; eating rice with curd; coronation as a king; a cow, bull, and banners; a lion; a lion throne; a conch; a musical instrument; yellow pigment; curd; a sandalwood [tree], or a mirror. (Verses 88–93)

INAUSPICIOUS DREAMS

The following are not auspicious in a dream: [the sight of] a man anointed with oil; a dark-colored one; a naked one; a pit, a crow, and a dry thorny tree; an outcaste; a man with a long neck, and a palace without roof. In the case of a bad dream, he should perform an appeasement. He should repeat the mantra with concentration. For three years, obstacles may arise for him who performs mantra repetition. Should he be devoted to the mantra repetition regardless of the host of obstacles, having faith in success, he attains success in the fourth year. (Verses 94–97ab)

INDICATIONS OF THE PERFECTION OF THE MANTRA

Tranquillity of mind, contentment, hearing the sound of a drum, of a song, of the sound of beating time; the vision of heavenly musicians; seeing his luster as equal to that of the sun; the conquest of sleep and hunger; beauty, health, composure, [and] the absence of anger and greed—if the connoisseur of the mantra notices these and other signs, he should recognize the perfection of the mantra [and] the deity's grace. Then he should make additional effort in mantra repetition for attaining knowledge. One who has attained knowledge will have his purpose accomplished. He is liberated from existence, knowing that the self is the highest *brahman*, as explained by the Vedānta [texts]. (Verses 97cd–101)

CONCLUDING VERSE

I worship that Brahman, the all-pervading Lord who, in the form of various deities, grants man [fulfillment of his] desire. (Verse 102)

—27—

The Worship of Kālī According to the *Toḍala Tantra*

Sanjukta Gupta

To many Hindu Bengalis, Kālī is the most important divinity. Identified with the great Goddess, Devī Bhagavatī, she subsumes all other goddesses. She is held to be equal in status to Durgā and their annual festivals, which occur close to each other, are celebrated with the greatest grandeur: feasts are held, gifts are exchanged, and new clothes are worn in honor of the Goddess. Both Durgā and Kālī, facets of the same supreme Goddess, are fierce and aggressive. The Goddess is the embodiment of the divine power, potency, and dynamism. After the great dissolution of the worlds she regenerates the creation and sustains it until the time arrives when she must withdraw it into herself. She possesses both negative and positive elements in her divine personality. She is the nurturing Mother of created beings as well as the sovereign cosmic ruler who maintains cosmic law and order through her invincible power and irresistible energy. She punishes the evil and rewards the righteous. Above all, she protects all her creatures and is especially kind and sweet to her loyal devotees, like an indulgent mother to her devoted children.

The cult of Kālī has a long history of development in which her character has undergone many changes. In an essay on "Śaivism and the Tantric Tradition," Alexis Sanderson explains that in the ninth and tenth centuries C.E., the Kashmiri Tantric exegetes classified and systematized Tantric texts according to the various cults, mainly of goddesses and fearsome gods. The main emphasis was on specific mantras and esoteric practices associated with those mantras, one of which is called the Seat of Awareness *(vidyā-pīṭha)*. The texts dealing with the most esoteric Kālī cults are associated with the vidyā-pīṭha. The practices they prescribe include the so-called left-hand tradition (*vāma-mārga*), antinomian practices that involve alcohol, blood, and sex; these came to be called Kaula practices. The name *vidyā* here denotes esoteric mantras that are considered embodiments of the supreme knowledge or awareness that is indeed Kālī. Here she is called Kālī not because of her dark complexion but because she absorbs and transcends Time (*kāla*), and is thus the eternal transcendent reality (Kālasaṃkarṣiṇī). Kālī thus became the supreme godhead of this cult transcending even Śiva. This Kālī cult developed through various streams and survived in the cult of Guhyakālī, worshiped in Nepal as Guhyeśvarī and in Mithila (Bihar) even today (Sanderson 1990: 138–54). At the same period in Kashmir, there grew up a strong parallel Tantric cult known as the cult of the three goddesses, the Trika. They are Parā, transcendent; Parāparā, transcendent as well as material; and Aparā, material. The second and the third are related to the cosmic process of creation; the second is the state in which the transcendent unity of reality is disturbed and the goddess experiences the stir of polarized existence within herself, which heralds the next moment in the cosmic evolution of diverse creation.

As Sanderson points out, these two cults affected one another. "The cult of the three goddesses and that of Kālī were not sealed off from each other in the manner of rival sects. The *Jayadrathayāmala* shows that the devotees of Kālī had developed their own versions of the cult of the three goddesses. The Trika in its turn assimilated these and other new and more esoteric treatments from the left. Consequently we find a later Trika in which Kālasamkarṣiṇī has been introduced to be worshipped above the three goddesses of the trident" (Sanderson 1990: 146). This tendency continued throughout the history of the Kālī cult and is clearly noticeable in the *Śakti-saṃgama Tantra* (1.1.28–47), in which the three goddesses of the vidyās—Kālī, Tārā, and Chinnā, that is, Chinnamastā—form a kind of triad. Indeed, Sanderson has described how the adherents of the Kālī cult interpreted the name Kālī. "So, as Abhinavagupta tells us in his *Tantrāloka*, the autonomous consciousness which is the Absolute is called Kālī (i) because it throws, in the sense that it projects the universe, causing to appear as though beyond it . . . ; (ii) because through it the projection returns to ('goes to') its identity as cognition . . . ; (iii) because it knows the projected, in the sense that it represents it as identical with its own identity . . . ; (iv) because it enumerates the projection, in the sense that it distinguishes each element from all the others within its own unity . . . ; and (v) because it sounds, in the sense that when it has dissolved the projection it continues as the resonance of internal self-awareness" (Sanderson 1990: 164).

In the Mahāvidyā cult, the primary goddess-emanations from Kālī the supreme and absolute consciousness form a horizontal triad at the cosmic differentiated level, that is, Mahāmāyā, Sundarī and Bhairavī, to replace the Puranic triad of Brahmā, Viṣṇu, and Rudra/Śiva (Brown 1974: 118–80). Although Brahmā and so on were not totally removed from their cosmic functions, they moved to a subservient position.

The *Toḍala Tantra*, translated below, was probably composed relatively late, in the fourteenth century C.E. It is a small Tantra that contains ten chapters (*paṭalas*) with 398 verses. It became very popular in Bengal, especially in the early modern period, and has been quoted as a scriptural authority in many Bengali priestly handbooks such as the *Purohita-darpaṇa* on the ritual worship of Dakṣiṇā Kālī, also called Ādyā Kālī. Our text is mainly interested in the ritual worship of Kālī and other Mahāvidyās. It mentions all the Mahāvidyās, who are here more than ten in number, and also mentions their companions, who are different manifestations of Śiva. It succinctly gives all the ritual sequences needed for the worship of the first two Mahāvidyās, including the esoteric formulas (*mantras*) and the accompanying process of meditation (see Gupta 1977: 125–57). It also records a complete program of Śiva worship with mantras and so on, which seems to be the same for every manifestation. According to it, it is imperative to worship Śiva immediately after worshiping the relevant Mahāvidyā.

In the traditional way, the text is presented as a dialogue between Śiva and his divine spouse Pārvatī, who is the pupil and the interlocutor, whereas Śiva is the teacher of the sacred science (*śāstra*). Very little theological or ontological discussion is found in the text, though often it refers to the ultimacy of Kālī. The text gives important information about the esoteric meaning of the mantras of the first three Mahāvidyās and the practice of Tantric yoga; the esoteric kuṇḍalinī-yoga receives special treatment. Inheriting the Krama tradition of monistic power-theism (*śakti-advaya*), the *Toḍala Tantra* asserts that esoteric yoga is higher than esoteric rituals, as the latter involve differentiated awareness whereas yoga does not. This is elaborated by means of a description of kuṇḍalinī-yoga, giving a detailed parallel of the microcosm with the macrocosm. Kuṇḍalinī-yoga leads to release from saṃsāra as the yogin becomes one with the Goddess, having severed the veil of delusion, māyā, by means of vidyā. In connection with esoteric yoga practice, our text gives three important yogic postures: the yoni mudrā, svalpa yoni mudrā, and kākīcañcu mudrā. All are postures for practicing kuṇḍalinī yoga, where controlling the flow of air in the body by blocking all natural outlets of air is of the highest importance. Although it presents mantras and rituals concerning the Mahāvidyās, the treatment is so brief that the text needs to be supplemented by other handbooks, such as the *Tantrasāra* of Kṛṣṇānanda or *Kaulāvalīnirṇaya* of Jñānānandagiri (see Goudriaan and Gupta 1981: 139, 144).

In order to understand the theological background of our text, we have to turn to other scriptural sources from the medieval period (roughly 1200 to 1800 C.E.). They mainly belong to eastern India, and some may be from Bengal. By this time the Tārā-Ugratārā-Ekajaṭā cult of the Buddhist Tantric tradition merged into the Kālī and other Mahāvidyā cults presented in the *Toḍala Tantra*. To understand the history and nature of Kālī, the supreme Goddess, in eastern India in the medieval period (roughly 1200 C.E. to 1800 C.E.), three texts can be considered the most important. One is the *Śakti-saṃgama Tantra* (*ŚsT*), a large compendium of the rituals and mantras and other esoteric practices associated with Kālī and her other manifestations. This text, as well as the *Tantra-sāra* and the *Devīmāhātmya* (*DM*), which constitutes the final section of the *Mārkaṇḍeya Purāṇa*, have shaped the Tantric philosophy, theology, and practice of the Kālī cult in Bengal. There the *Devīmāhātmya* is simply called *Caṇḍī* (the fierce lady), and devout Tantrics recite it daily. In fact Kālī's iconography, as followed by the traditional image makers, shows traces of the description of the goddess Kālī in that text.

The *Devīmāhātmya* represents Kālī as a minor emanation of the Goddess, a demonic figure, fearsome and grotesque. Having emanated from the angry third eye of the supreme Goddess to help the Goddess in her battle against the demon host of Śumbha and Niśumbha, she was employed to lick up every drop of blood of Raktabīja, the demon general. Raktabīja's peculiarity was that even a drop of his blood shed on the earth produced countless clones. Kālī's lolling tongue symbolizes this blood-licking task. Her demonic nature is also symbolized by her fangs and by the countless severed heads and limbs dripping blood that cover her body. She is intoxicated by drinking blood, and in her frenzy she laughs loudly, baring her upper teeth.

The *Kālikā Purāṇa* (*KP*), on the other hand, describes Kālī as possessing a soothing dark complexion, as perfectly beautiful, riding a lion, four-armed, holding a sword and blue lotuses, her hair unrestrained, body firm and youthful (*KP* 5.52). A third view is found in such Tantric texts as the *Śakti-saṃgama Tantra*, where Kālī, naked, is seated on the supine body of Śiva, immersed in the pleasure of reverse sexual intercourse with him. These three separate views of the supreme goddess Kālī have influenced her modern iconography, although the third variety, the goddess seated on the inert body of Śiva, is rarely used outside esoteric worship. In the *Śakti-saṃgama Tantra*, though, we get two quite different descriptions of Kālī. In her supreme state, Kālī is, as Sanderson describes, just the light of pure consciousness, but in the creating state she is depicted in a form more awe-inspiring than charming.

The supreme Goddess is forever associated with the supreme god Śiva, the pair forming an indivisible unit. But in this late tradition, Kālī often supersedes Śiva and acts independently to initiate creation. Although creation is based on her aspect as Māyā, this often appears to be a biological activity. This point is emphasized in the iconography of Kālī and Tārā, both of whom appear to be having coitus with Śiva, who is lying like a corpse. Śiva's representation as a corpse emphasizes his total inertness and passivity in the act of creation; the initiative in creation belongs to the Goddess. Therefore Śiva is not a corpse but is only depicted as one. The *Toḍala Tantra* emphasizes this point. Kālī's association with Viṣṇu as Viṣṇu-māyā is also underscored in this tradition. In order to enhance the supremacy of the Goddess, the *Devīmāhātmya* took over the early Vaiṣṇava myth of the creation of the earth from the marrow and fat of two demons called Madhu and Kaiṭabha, and replaced Viṣṇu with Devī as the slayer of the demons. The *Kālikā Purāṇa*, in fact, calls the cult of the supreme Goddess Vaiṣṇavī Tantra, and the main mantra, which is a salutation to the supreme deity with some mystical syllables added, indeed addresses that deity: *Oṃ hrīṃ śrīṃ vaiṣṇavyai namaṃ*. This has been noted by Brown: "Thus does the Devī Bhagavatī, although eternal, manifest herself again and again for the protection of the world, O King" (*Devīmāhātmya* 12.36), clearly echoing the famous description of Viṣṇu/Kṛṣṇa's avatāras in the fourth chapter of the *Bhagavad Gītā* (Brown 1990: 133–34). Both the *Toḍala Tantra* and *Śakti-saṃgama Tantra* make some sort of equation between the ten avatāras of Viṣṇu and the ten great vidyā emanations of the Goddess. Her closeness to Viṣṇu/Kṛṣṇa is often mythicized when she is cast as Viṣṇu's sister or the embodiment of Viṣṇu's māyā. In late tradition the Goddess superseded all three cosmic gods—Brahmā, Viṣṇu, and Rudra.

The *Śakti-saṃgama Tantra* describes the creative activity of the goddess Kālī as follows: Dakṣiṇā (compassionate) Kālī, the primeval goddess, was dancing the dance of cosmic dissolution surrounded by howling jackals and other carrion-devouring beasts. The destroyed universe lay at her feet like a heap of corpses. Kālī is pure consciousness, totally transcendent, the unique Being. She subsumes both Śiva and the divine Power, Śakti. At a certain primordial moment, Kālī suddenly saw inside herself her own mirror image or shadow, which is indeed delusion, Māyā. In that Māyā, Kālī created the imagined form of Śiva, who became the primeval god and Kālī's spouse. Kālī then created empty space, and the chaos of the destroyed universe disappeared as she engaged in sexual intercourse with Śiva, taking the reverse position and the active role. After a long coitus, Kālī produced one fetus, which developed into a perfectly beautiful girl whom Kālī called Sundarī, the beautiful lady. Her beauty completely deluded Śiva, who wanted to put into words his agitation and longing. Śiva's longing and desire for self-expression produced Speech, which from its central unity developed into the system of sounds, letters, and language, and became all-pervasive. Śiva, however, on creating Speech, first addressed the goddess Sundarī as his heart's desire, the loveliest in the three worlds, the exquisite sovereign deity and the ocean of nectarlike compassion. Next Śiva addressed Kālī as most terrifying, howling like a jackal, cruel-fanged and fearfully ugly, with lolling tongue and frightening roar. As Śiva uttered these two sentences addressing the two goddesses, Kālī, as if offended, suddenly disappeared, leaving Śiva with Sundarī, the product of delusion, to get on with the task of creation. Kālī, who is transcendent and the essence of the creation, transformed herself into the abstract cosmic dynamic power. But Śiva became utterly despondent and confused without Kālī; therefore the compassionate Kālī removed Śiva's confusion and infused him with unimpeded cognitive knowledge and desire to procreate. Moreover, in order to infuse him with power she taught Śiva the method of Tantric kuṇḍalinī yoga and gave him as his partner the beautiful goddess who is indeed the mother of the universe, Ambikā, the cosmic Creatrix (*ŚsT* 1.1.22–45).

This myth neatly puts forward the idea that the transcendent supreme divinity is female; that she is the goddess Dakṣiṇā Kālī, who contains both the cosmic male and female polarity; that she is the sovereign cosmic ruler who regulates the system of creation; and that the creation is based on cosmic delusion, which is her mirror image. This divine delusion, named Māyā or Mahāmāyā, is Kālī's divine capacity, which ensures that in spite of the perfect oneness of Kālī and Śiva, the latter is separated in an imaginary form by means of Kālī's delusory power. Śiva is then deluded into thinking himself to be a separate divinity from Kālī and so feels the attraction of the delusory image of Sundarī. Thus the main idea of monism, which emphasizes the unity of a single universal essence, and establishes the illusoriness of the dualistic worldview, is put forward through a creation myth. The polarized male and female cosmic divinities are results of delusion. In reality, the supreme goddess Kālī is unique and immutable, yet she is the source and foundation of all creation. Kālī, the eternally existent Reality, transcends both creation and the dissolution of the creation. The appearance of her beautiful mirror image, Māyā, heralds creation as an evolutionary process, and at that point of primeval creation Kālī, the pure consciousness who exists beyond the reach of speech and phenomenal creation, disappears behind delusion and its influence—desire—and becomes the cosmic dynamic energy activating the ongoing process of creation. Śiva at the point of creation is the primordial conscious entity, Puruṣa. He possesses vidyā, omniscience, and icchā, sexual desire, to procreate; and he is called Sadāśiva who, together with Sundarī, becomes the primordial couple (*ŚsT* 1.1.103–6). In Tantric ontology, he is Śiva-tattva, the cosmic self. The evolving Śakti/Māyā, who is identical with the supreme Goddess, is known as Vidyā-tattva. Together with the individual self, Ātma-tattva, they constitute the cosmic realities who are ultimately one and same.

The nature of the supreme goddess, Mahādevī, and that of supreme delusion, Mahāmāyā, are expounded in the *Devīmāhātmya*. The Goddess is called Mahāmāyā, the great delusion when she is seen as responsible for the unsatisfactory and transient nature of this life. The real cause of this is human desire for possesion and procreation, and Mahāmāyā deludes individuals by making desire their innate quality. But paradoxically the Goddess is also identified as supreme knowledge, Vidyā, which releases individuals from their bondage of desire and the consequent endless succession of lives and deaths. This is one of the many paradoxes that constitute the mystery of the Goddess's divine nature.

Another important statement in *Devīmāhātmya* identifies Māyā with Prakṛti which, in the dualistic Sāṃkhya philosophy, is the primordial evolving matter. This identity was first recorded in the *Śvetāśvatara Upaniṣad* (4.9–10). Coburn (1996: 34) explains this as follows: "On the basis of such passages (*DM* 1.59 and 4.6) it seems safe to say that the *Devī Māhātmya* has shifted the focus of the Sāṃkhya school and the *Śvetāśvatara Upaniṣad* by understanding *prakṛti* not as the material shroud or possession of spirit but as itself supremely divine, as Devī herself." The *Śakti-saṃgama Tantra* (1.100) confirms this view by saying that the supreme Śakti, that is, the Goddess, is Prakṛti whereas her mirror image is the evolving power Mahāmāyā. Thus Prakṛti here refers to the supreme Goddess, who ultimately is the unique source and origin of all, there being nothing outside of her.

The *Toḍala Tantra* endorses this theological tradition in its accounts of the nature of the goddess Dakṣiṇākālī and her other Vidyā emanations. Other important texts for the development of Kālī and her Mahāvidyā cult are the *Cīnācāra-krama Tantra*, *Mātṛkā-bheda Tantra*, *Gupta-sādhana Tantra*, *Kālikā Purāṇa*, *Brahma-vaivarta Purāṇa*, *Brahmāṇḍa Purāṇa* and other Tantric records of that period. The salient feature of this tradition is the total supremacy of the goddess Kālī. In the words of Brown (1990: 217–18),

> of the two genders, the feminine represents the dominant power and the authoritative will in the universe. Yet both genders must be included in the ultimate if it is truly ultimate. The masculine and feminine are aspects of the divine, transcendent reality, which goes beyond but still encompasses them. The Devī, in her supreme

> form as consciousness thus transcends gender, but her transcendence is not apart from her immanence. Indeed this affirmation of the oneness of transcendence and immanence constitutes the very essence of the divine mother, as presented in the Purāṇa (*Devī-bhāgavata*). And here we see what may be called "the ultimate triumph" of the goddess in our text. It is not finally, that she is infinitely superior to the male gods—though she is that, according to the myths in the *Devī-bhāgavata*—but rather that she transcends her own feminine nature as Prakṛti without denying it.

The speciality of the *Śakti-saṃgama Tantra* myth is that it neatly puts forward just this point. Prakṛti or the feminine source of the universe is Mahāmāyā, who is not Kālī but her mirror image. Kālī transcends her own evolving mirror image. In the universe of Mahāmāyā, both delusion and cognition function. In the case of Śiva, his delusion is restricted to his sexual desire for Sundarī, whereas his cognitive knowledge is otherwise untrammeled. In this sense, it is possible to find a parallel between the three goddesses Kālī, Mahāmāyā, and Sundarī and the three goddesses Parā, Parāparā and Aparā of the Trika tradition. Sundarī corresponds to the third deity of the Trika triad, that is, Aparā (ŚsT 1.1.102). The *Toḍala Tantra* (1.7–8) confirms this with the statement that she is called the fivefold lady, Pañcamī, because she is differentiated as the five cosmic elements.

Kālī and the Cult of the Ten Mahāvidyās

The *Toḍala Tantra* describes the ritual worship of the ten sacred esoteric formulas, the Mahāvidyās. The word *vidyā* has various Tantric connotations. The great Goddess is Vidyā because she is perfect knowledge unimpeded by any differentiated or discursive cognition—cognition without any reference to anything cognized. This pure cognition brings about release. Vidyā also connotes an esoteric formula which, empowered by its Śakti deity, is capable of bestowing on its Tantric worshiper great powers (*bhukti*) and eventually salvation (*mukti*). These ten Mahāvidyās or great mystic formulas are those of Kālī, Tārā, Ṣoḍaśī (also known as Sundarī or Tripurasundarī, meaning the Beautiful One in the Three Worlds), Bhuvaneśvarī (Sovereign of the Three Worlds), Bhairavī or Tripurabhairavī (the Fierce Lady), Chinnamastā (the Beheaded Lady), Dhūmāvatī (the Gray Lady, who is depicted in iconography as a widow with a crow as her symbol), Bagalā (the goddess of battle), Mātaṅgī (the goddess of the hunter tribes), and Kamalā (Lakṣmī). It is obvious that originally the number of formulas was not fixed at ten. Early texts, such as the *Toḍala Tantra*, mention a few other formulas, including those of Durgā, Annapūrṇā, and Kullukā. The first two are universally popular goddesses, and the third became very important in the esoteric practices of the mantras and vidyās. The *Śakti-saṃgama Tantra*, being an encyclopaedic text, mentions both a group of ten Mahāvidyās and also other lists of Mahāvidyās not confined to ten members.

The importance of this group of great formulas and their power goddesses grew enormously in late Tantric, tradition and the goddess Kālī became foremost amongst them. She is considered the original power deity, designated Ādyā, the primeval lady. The *Toḍala Tantra* deals only with the mantras and ritual worship of Kālī and Tārā, whereas Sundarī is treated in a rather fragmentary fashion. But the full treatment of their mantras, especially the monosyllabic seed (*bīja*) mantras, to some extent covers the other Mahāvidyās too, except for Dhūmāvatī. This last is a somewhat problematic figure: it is difficult to understand why she is included in this group of power goddesses. Like other ordinary deities, such as Gaṇeśa, her seed mantra simply consists of the first syllable of her name, *dhūṃ*. Thus, although the formulas of each of these goddesses are different, their identities are not always easy to determine and differentiate. It is also difficult to date the beginning of their popularity or the crystallization of the group of ten. The *Bṛhad-dharma Purāṇa* (*BdhP*) presents the myth of how the ten Mahāvidyās appeared in the following manner:

Śiva's wife Satī heard that her father Dakṣa was arranging the performance of a huge sacrifice to which all the gods and other celestials were invited except herself and Śiva. Incensed, she told her husband that she was going to her father's sacrifice to teach him a lesson in sensible behaviour. Śiva knew Dakṣa's animosity toward himself and Satī, and feared that Satī would be insulted, with catastrophic results, and so tried to dissuade her from going. Satī became irritated, and changed into her true Kālī form, which she had suppressed when she had agreed to be born as the beautiful daughter of Dakṣa and Prasūti, in order to marry Śiva. Upon seeing her terrifying transformation, Śiva became completely confused and began to run away. Even her reassuring words failed to stop him. Then the Goddess appeared in one of her manifestations in each of the directions as Śiva tried to flee. Finally, at Śiva's request, the Goddess explained that she herself was the supreme reality Kālī, the source of all phenomena. At the request of Dakṣa and his wife, she had manifested herself as their exquisitely beautiful daughter Satī and then married Śiva. The ten manifestations who were blocking Śiva's way in every direction were her own vidyā-manifestations. Before him, that is, to the east, appeared the Mahāvidyā Kālī; above him, Tarā; on his right (south), Chinnamastā; to his rear, (west), Bagalā; on his left, (north), Bhuvaneśvarī; to his southeast, Dhūmāvatī; to his southwest, Sundarī; to his northwest, Mataṅgī; to his northeast, Ṣoḍaśī; and immersed in his self was Bhairavī. At this revelation of the real identity and powers of the Goddess, Śiva apologized to her for assuming spousal authority and stopped resisting her departure to her father's home. As a result, Dakṣa was ruined, but escaped with his life; Satī, however, lost her life out of the anger and shame caused by her father's actions (*BdhP* 2.6.65–89, 128–52).

Let us now attempt to find out who these ten Mahāvidyās are. There seems to be nearly no difference between Kālī and Tārā in the eastern tradition. The *Mahācīnācāra-krama Tantra* 2.37 explains that in the Mahācīna tradition, antinomian practices are essential for Tārā worship. The *Toḍala Tantra* agrees about these special features of Tārā. Although the *Toḍala Tantra* prescribes for Tārā's worship the use of the five esoteric ingredients (meat, fish, alcohol, woman, and sexual fluids) that signify vāmācāra practice, it appears to believe that these practices are not essential for Kālī worship. Perhaps this is why this text has been taken in Bengal to be the scriptural authority for the nonesoteric worship of Kālī, both in temples and in private homes. Other texts like *Bṛhat-nīla Tantra* and *Mahā-nirvāṇa Tantra* assert that these practices are essential for Kālī worship. However, the *Mahācīnācāra-krama Tantra*, having said that the four goddesses Dakṣiṇā Kālī, Tārā, Sundarī, and Bhairavī share the same style of worship, informs us in a later statement (2.38) that the latter two goddesses share another, presumably more orthodox, style of worship (that is, *dakṣiṇācāra*), but that the former two must be adored with antinomian practices (that is, *vāmācāra*). In the *Bṛhat-nīla Tantra*, Tārā is called Nīlasarasvatī and is described as resting on the corpse, that is, Śiva, in a fighting attitude with her left leg advanced and her right drawn back, young and smiling yet of awe-inspiring appearance, garlanded with severed heads, short, pot-bellied, powerful, and wearing a tigerskin. She has four arms and her tongue is lolling. She has flame-colored matted tresses held on the top of her head in a single mass on which the face of Akṣobhya is placed. She is also addressed as Ekajaṭā and Ugratārā. The popular iconography of Kālī, as already noted, is not very different from Tārā's, except for the hair: Kālī's hair is loose and disheveled. All these peculiar features of Tārā show her close affinity with the Buddhist goddess Tārā (Saviouress), who is very popular among the Buddhists of Tibet and other Himalayan regions. The *Toḍala Tantra* and *Śakti-saṃgama Tantra* also name Akṣobhya as Tārā's spouse, although a curious myth is offered in the *Toḍala Tantra* to explain how Śiva came to be known by that name. The *Toḍala Tantra* gives her seed mantra as *strīṃ*. Another source, namely, the Pāñcarātra *Lakṣmī Tantra*, equates Tārā with the supreme divine Power that is identical with Vāc, the goddess Speech (Gupta 1972: 177–83; 286–96).

Ṣoḍaśī and Bhuvaneśvarī are, it seems, variations of Sundarī and Bālā and belong to the cult of Tripurasundarī or Lalitā; on this, see the *Paraśurāma-kalpa Sūtra* (*PkS*). Bhairavī alias Tripurabhairavī also belongs to the same cult. Chinnamastā or the Beheaded Lady is depicted as a goddess standing in a fighting posture with her left leg forward and right leg drawn back. Her right hand holds a sword with which she has just severed her own head. Three streams of blood flow from her neck; that on her left is being drunk by a minor goddess called Ḍākinī, that on her right by Varṇinī, and the middle one spouts upward and is being drunk by the goddess's own severed head. She stands on a prone woman who is in coitus with a supine man lying under her. This couple is considered to be Madana, the god of sexual desire, and his wife Rati, sexual pleasure. The goddess is the embodiment of the powerful mantra *hūṃ*, and is addressed as Vajravairocanī, which again points to a Buddhist goddess (Kinsley 1997: 144–66). A curious myth is recounted in *Śakti-saṃgama Tantra* 4.5.152–73 to explain this gory iconography. The goddess suddenly left her spouse Śiva in the midst of their amorous play. When she reappeared, Śiva asked her why she had disappeared so suddenly and why now she looked so pale. The goddess explained that she had had to go to bathe together with her friends Ḍākinī and Varṇinī, who were hungry. After their bath, the goddess had provided meals for all three of them with her own blood as it gushed from her severed neck.

Bagalā or Bagalāmukhī is a golden-complexioned form of Tripurasundarī, the deity who presides over deadly weapons. It is difficult to identify Dhūmāvatī, who is tall, dark, rough, and sick-complexioned. Her hair is thin and matted, and her disposition is restless and bellicose. She wears soiled clothes and rides a chariot with a banner displaying a crow. She is seen as an incarnation of all that is sordid, antisocial, and inauspicious in women, an antithesis of the goddess Śrī. She is depicted as a widow, who has allegedly gobbled up her husband Śiva in a fit of hunger. She was born from the smoking fire of the destruction of Dakṣa's sacrifice and the death of Satī. Frowning, she howls desolately and carries a winnowing fan. Lakṣmaṇa Deśika, the commentator on the *Śāradātilaka Tantra* (24.9–14), states that Dhūmāvatī is the same goddess as Jyeṣṭhyā.

The last two Mahāvidyās are again familiar to the Lalitā cult. Mātaṅgī is the same as Śyāmalā in that cult. She is mainly considered to be the deity presiding over such fine arts as the power to compose poetry. She is exquisitely beautiful and is dark complexioned, but otherwise closely resembles Lalitā in appearance (*PkS* 6.1–39). The tenth Mahāvidyā is goddess Lakṣmī alias Śrī alias Kamalā, the spouse of Viṣṇu—although she too is closely related to the mantra of Tripurasundarī.

Tantric Esoteric Practice

The *Toḍala Tantra* belongs to the corpus of Tantric scriptures that make up the Mantra mārga or Mantra path. The term *Mantra mārga* means the entire Tantric paradigm of ritual worship and meditation. Every mantra possesses a paradigmatical ritual system of its own, a pattern that has become more or less fixed, with variations to fit the relevant mantra and its deity, as well as the performer's intended application (Gupta, Hoens, and Goudriaan 1979: 121–57). Mantramārga is followed by Tantric practitioners for two broadly defined purposes: liberation from the bondage of endless transmigration (*saṃsāra*), or rewards such as supernatural power and achievements—mukti and bhukti respectively. The *Toḍala Tantra* is more concerned with mukti and hence does not deal with the esoteric worship of any Mahāvidyās other than the first three: Kālī, Tārā, and Sundarī (or Bhuvaneśvarī). Seekers of mukti are more respected than seekers of power and achievement, although the latter are held in awe and are much sought after by lay devotees for personal gain, such as protection from disease and misfortune, and destroying enemies.

The four important constituents in such esoteric Tantric worship are the preliminaries, invocation, ritual service, and conclusion.

Preliminaries. First, the divine is represented by esoteric formulas, hand gestures (*mudrās*), symbols of the deity worshiped mainly on a diagram (*yantra*), and sometimes an image and a pitcher full of water. Second, the practitioner (*sādhaka*) must have been properly initiated by a competent sectarian guru. Third, the worshiper, the symbol of the deity, and the objects used for offering must be physically and mystically purified. Fourth is the ritual of security. Tantric esoteric practices are considered to be full of dangers. Often they are personified as harmful spirits that obstruct the worshiper's every movement. Therefore the worshiper must take measures to remove these spirits from the sacred area of the ritual worship, by making threatening sounds; by stamping one's foot, clapping, or snapping one's fingers; by frowning and looking angry, and scattering threatening objects such as white mustard seeds; by making threatening gestures imitating shooting, and so forth. The fifth, and perhaps the most important, preliminary rite is called nyāsa. This means the installation, limb by limb, of the sacred mantras, which are the sonic manifestation of the divine, onto the material body of the worshiper, thus replacing the mundane body of the worshiper with a sacred body. The same installation is performed onto the deity's symbol for the same purpose.

Invocation. The goddess is invoked, first into the center or heart of the worshiper, and thence onto the seat he has ritually prepared for her adoration.

Ritual Service. The deity is first adored in meditative imagination, in which all the objects of offering are of an abstract nature. Next, the Tantric practitioner worships the Goddess with various objects of material enjoyment. This is followed by the service of the Goddess's spouse, Śiva, and then her entourage, the minor gods and goddesses encircling her. This is followed by the offering (*bali*), which in the Mahavidyā cult almost always implies an animal sacrifice, that is, beheading an animal in front of the image. The animal offering is followed by a fire sacrifice. Then a short meditation is done by means of repeating the main mantra a certain number of times (*japa*). The ritual offerings culminate, for the followers of the vāmācāra, with the offerings of the five objects (meat, fish, etc.). Finally, the worshiper offers the deity all the merit he has accrued from performing the service. He also offers himself to the goddess. These last two ritual acts refer to two very important concepts: renunciation and loyal devotion. The first requires an utter annihilation of one's ego and greed. Even the greed for accumulating merit for the ego-person must be destroyed. The second is rooted in the concept of bhakti, which came to mean total surrender to one's adored deity. The devotee offers all that belongs to himself and then offers his individuality as well.

Conclusion. Having invoked a fierce manifestation of the Goddess and worshiped it with some parts of the already offered objects for his own success and that of his ritual service, the worshiper recites certain set formulas for his physical well-being, and then recites hymns to the Goddess. Having partaken of a little of the offered food as the Goddess's grace, the worshiper has fulfilled his daily obligatory ritual service of his Goddess and is free to follow his normal way of life.

Tantra Ritual Practice

The *Toḍala Tantra* does not discuss Tantric initiation, and indeed, it does not discuss any theological concepts at all. It starts by describing the procedure for the ritual worship of Kālī. The first ritual act is to worship one's guru mentally. The guru is identified with the supreme deity Kālī when she is united with Śiva immediately prior to creation. This text is meant for experienced Tantric practitioners who are versed in the Tantric meditation on the kuṇḍalinī, the contracted and inert form of the creatrix goddess Kālī as she remains immanent in every creature (Eliade 1969: 200–67). The aim of Tantric meditation is to arouse the kuṇḍalinī by means of breath control (*prāṇāyāma*) and one-pointed meditation (*dhyāna*) on the practitioner's deity, who when awakened longs to unite with Śiva and swiftly flies upward through the innermost passage of the practitioner's yogic body, which contains six spiritual centers. At the top of this passage, just above the practitioner's body, the creating Goddess is united with Śiva, and this divine area, transcending the creation at a point prior to creation, is imagined as a sphere or a lotus with countless petals (*sahasrāra cakra*). This united yet differentiated stance of the supreme Goddess and Śiva is what the Tantric practitioner endeavors to understand and identify with. This is liberation because it transcends creation. The practitioner's guru is already liberated and is thus one with this two-in-one divinity. Even before the practioner actually leaves his bed, he performs the kuṇḍalinī meditation on his guru while repeating his name, declaring his total submission to him. Only then does he start his daily obligatory ritual acts (Gupta 1979: 130–39).

Bhūtaśuddhi

The next important ritual is the purification of the practitioner's material body, which is composed of five cosmic elements (*bhūtaśuddhi*). This is again a form of meditation: the practitioner meditates on each of the five ontological elements, starting with the element of solidity/earth and ending with ether/undefined space. He eliminates each element by dissolving it into the element preceding it. Thus in his imagination he contracts the entire differentiated creation in its microcosmic form, arriving at the center of the countless-petaled lotus circle, where the energy of the Goddess burns away the impurities of his microcosm, eliminating any residual elements. Saturated and rejuvenated by the nectar produced by the coitus of the divine couple, the microcosm is recreated, pure and consubstantial with the divine. The import of such daily meditative rites as bhūtaśuddhi is to repeat the process of internalizing the theological explanation of salvation as a direct experience of one's true identity with vidyā, nondual pure awareness, which in turn is but the supreme goddess Kālī in her transcendental form.

Mantra and Nyāsa

After this renewed confirmation of his consubstantiality with Kālī, the practitioner can replace his purified mundane body with the divine personality, that is, vidyā, through the rite of nyāsa. In this rite the mantras and their sonic source (*mātṛkā*), the letters of the Sanskrit alphabet, are the most important concepts. Mantras are the sonic forms of their deities, just as the images are their visual forms. The mantras of Kālī and Tārā are therefore considered to be the mantra bodies of these two goddesses. The *Toḍala Tantra* explains the concept of the Goddess's mantra physique in its sixth chapter. It is a Tantric custom to analyze the mantra of a deity into several components. The most important part is the seed or bīja mantra. Mahāvidyās like Kālī or Tārā have several such seeds, one of which is considered to be chief. The seed is the essence of a mantra. After the seed(s) comes the name of the deity. As the complete mantra is a sentence, the name is either inflected as a vocative, or is declined in the dative when it is followed by the term *namas*, which means "obeisance." Conventionally, formulas known as *vidyās* are considered to be of feminine gender, which requires them to end in *svāhā*. But in the case of the mantras found in the *Toḍala Tantra*, several seed mantras are often inserted before the word *svāhā*. It is interesting to note that this word is used for offering Vedic oblations, and is mythologized as the name of the fire god Agni's spouse. However, a practitioner receives his personal esoteric mantra from his guru who, knowing the initiate's special disposition, chooses a specific variant of his chosen deity. This then becomes the initiated practitioner's main or mūla mantra. The main mantra, which is considered the full physical form of its deity, is divided into six main limbs (*aṅgas*). These are the heart, the head, the tuft of hair, the eyes, the weapon, and the armored torso. These six limbs symbolize the deity's entire body. In the rite of nyāsa the worshiper first invests his hands and fingers with sacred formulas and then invests his six limbs with the same parts of his main mantra. Because the supreme goddess is Vāc, Speech, the worshiper uses the mātṛkā mantra for some specific nyāsa, since that is the Goddess's primordial manifestation. In the worship of Kālī, mātṛkā nyāsa is performed in six different ways.

Mudrā

Mudrā has more than one meaning. Its primary meaning is "seal," but in Tantric terminology, mudrā means a hand gesture or a posture of seated meditation (usually called āsana), and in the context of the five esoteric ingredients of offerings to the Goddess, it may either mean a female partner for ritual practice or just a snack. There are many uses of mudrās or hand gestures as the practitioner proceeds mentally to encounter divine and spiritual beings in his rituals. All actions at this stage are accompanied by miming, and often they are so graphic that it is easy to understand their meaning. For instance, for the dhyāna or envisaging of the deity, the worshiper utters the deity's mantra of her iconography while acting out in gestures the deity's special attributes. Thus, while uttering Kālikā's dhyāna mantra—"*Oṃ*, you seated on a corpse, of fierce appearance with terrifying teeth, who bestows desired objects [on her devotees], who laughs [all the time], who has three eyes, holds in her hands a skull and a sword, whose hair is untied and tongue is lolling out incessantly drinking the blood [of the asuras]. One should envisage you, O Goddess, [as] having four arms whose other two hands gesture fulfilment of the devotee's wishes and who promises protection"—the adept gestures with his fingers, graphically symbolizing the attributes described in that mantra. These are called the yoni, bhutinī, vara, abhaya, khaḍga, and muṇḍa mudrās (see Figure 27.1).

The Devanagari edition of the *Toḍala Tantra* was published in 1970, in *Tantrasaṃgraha* part 2, edited by Gopinath Kaviraj from the Yoga-Tantra department of Benares Sankrit University, Varanasi. There are several Bengali published editions, as well. The edition I have used is *Toḍala Tantra*, edited, translated, and commented on in Bengali by Pancanana Sastri (Calcutta: Navabharata Publications, 1976).

Further Reading

For further study, my essay on Tantric rituals in *Hindu Tāntrism*, by Sanjukta Gupta, Dirk J. Hoens, and Teun Goudraan (Leiden: E. J. Brill, 1979), pp. xxiii–xxxiv; Introduction to *Lakṣmī Tantra* by Sanjukta Gupta (Leiden: E. J. Brill, 1972); and *Hindu Tantric and Śākta Literature* by Teun Goudriaan and Sunjukta Gupta (Weisbaden: Otto Harrassowitz, 1981) are useful. Alexis Sanderson's essay "Śaivism and the Tantric Traditions" in *The World's Religions: Religions of Asia*, edited by Friedhelm Hardy (reprint London: Routledge & Kegan Paul, 1990), pp. 128–72, is a good source for the history of Tantric traditions. Thomas B. Coburn's essay "Devī: The Great Goddess," in *Devī: Goddesses of India*, edited by John Stratton Hawley and Donna Wulff (Berkeley: University of California Press, 1996), pp. 31–48; and Coburn, *Encountering the Goddess: A Translation of the Devī-Māhātmya and a Study of Its Interpretation* (Albany: State University of New York Press, 1991), are indispensible. The same is true of two books by C. Mackenzie Brown, *God as Mother: A Feminine Theology of India—An Historical and Theological Study of the Brahmavaivarta Purana* (Hartford, Vt.: Claude Stark, 1974), and *The Triumph of the Goddess: The Canonical Models and Theological Visions of the Devī-Bhāgavata Purāṇa* (Albany: State University of New York Press, 1990). For an understanding of the concept of the ten Mahāvidyās one should read David Kinsley's two works, *Hindu Goddesses: Visions of the Divine Feminine in the Hindu Religious Tradition* (Delhi: Motilal Bararsidass, 1987), and *Tantric Vision of the Divine Feminine: The Ten Mahāvidyās* (Berkeley and Los Angeles: University of California Press, 1997).

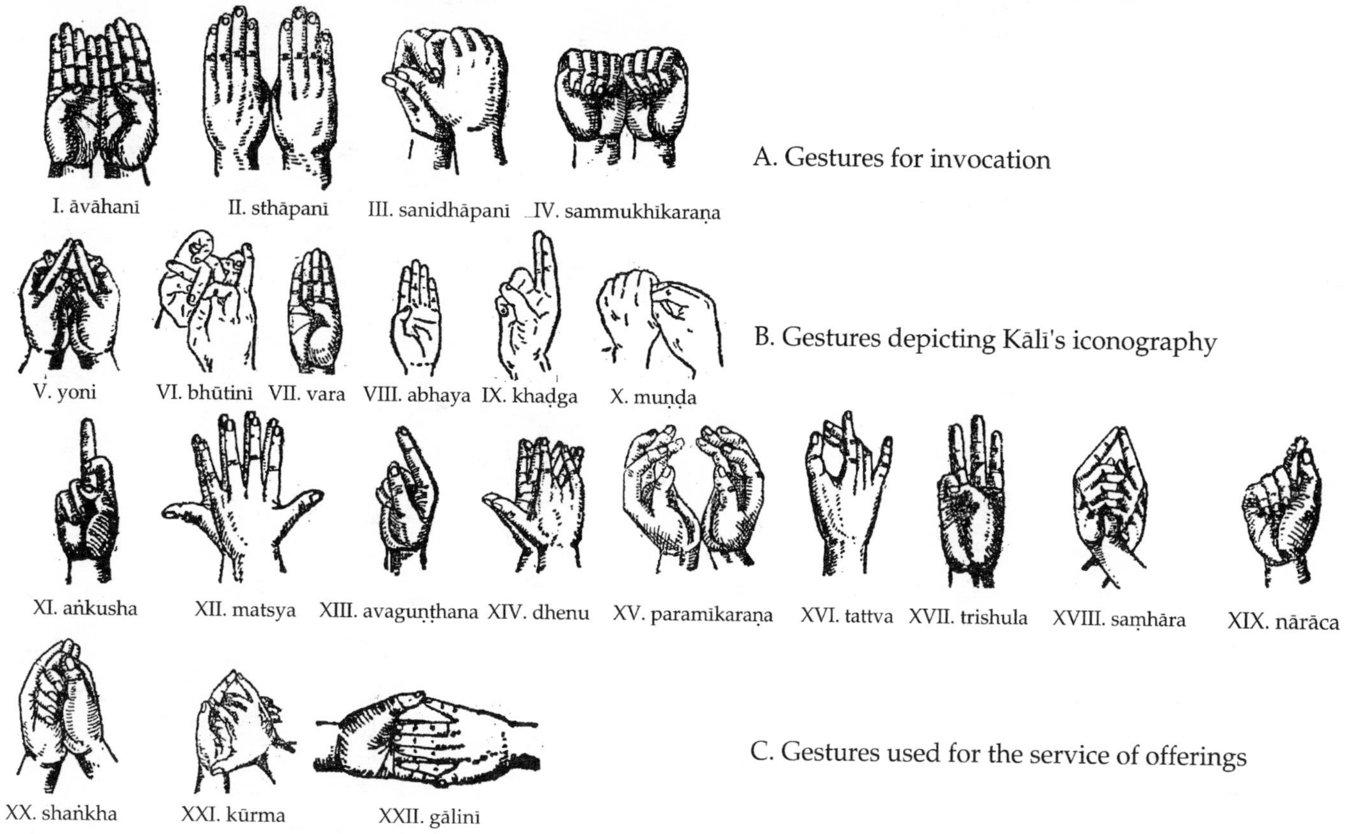

I. āvāhanī II. sthāpanī III. sanidhāpanī IV. sammukhīkaraṇa

A. Gestures for invocation

V. yoni VI. bhūtinī VII. vara VIII. abhaya IX. khaḍga X. muṇḍa

B. Gestures depicting Kālī's iconography

XI. aṅkusha XII. matsya XIII. avaguṇṭhana XIV. dhenu XV. paramīkaraṇa XVI. tattva XVII. trishula XVIII. saṃhāra XIX. nārāca

XX. shaṅkha XXI. kūrma XXII. gālinī

C. Gestures used for the service of offerings

Figure 27.1. Mudrās

On kuṇḍalinī yoga, I recommend Mircea Eliade, *Yoga: Immortality and Freedom*, 2d ed., translated by Willard R. Trask (London: Routledge & Kegan Paul, 1969).

Toḍala Tantra

CHAPTER ONE

The Names of Different Forms of the Great God Śiva as Spouse of the Deities of Great Sacred Formulas

The goddess spoke:
1–2. O Lord of the universe, my master, who are the embodiment of all the sacred formulas (*vidyās*), [please] tell me when all the great formulas (*mahāvidyās*) are venerated in the three worlds, [and] what are the specific forms of the trumpet-holding Mahādeva who is seated on the right side of each of these [mahāvidyās]; O Lord! please enumerate [these forms] to me.

Śrī Śiva spoke:

3–4. Listen O beautiful and blessed one! Bhairava Mahākāla [a form of Mahādeva] should be worshiped by the right side of the benevolent (*dakṣiṇā*) Kālī, [because] Dakṣiṇā is always engaged in love-play with Mahākāla. One should worship Akṣobhya by the right side of Tārā.

5–7ab. O goddess, at the time of the churning of the [cosmic] ocean there arose [the poison called] Kālakūṭa. Then all the gods, together with their wives, became greatly disturbed. Since [Śiva, even when he] drank that deadly poison, remained unaffected by any kind of agitation, therefore, O great sovereign lady, he is famous as Akṣobhya ("Unagitated"). With him [the goddess] Tāriṇī, the great goddess of delusion, is ever engaged in love-play.

7cd–9ab. O sovereign of the gods, one should worship the five-faced Śiva who has three eyes on each of his faces, on the right side of the great Tripurasundarī. Since the great Goddess is erotically excited [and is] ever [engaged in love-play] with him [who has five faces], therefore, O great Goddess, she is known as the fifth.

9cd–11ab. One should worship Tryambaka [Śiva] by the right side of the blessed Bhuvanasundarī [Bhuvaneśvarī]. [Śiva] is called Tryambaka [associated with three mothers] because he makes love to the primaeval sovereign Goddess of the creation, in heaven, earth, and the nether region (*pātāla*). Accordingly he [Śiva] is renowned for being always united with Śakti and is venerated in all the Tantras.

11cd–12ab. One should with great care worship [Śiva] called Dakṣiṇāmūrti by the right side of Bhairavī. He is indeed the same as the five-faced [Sadāśiva].

12cd–13cd. One should worship Śiva as a headless trunk (*kabandha*) by the right side of Chinnamastā [the Beheaded Goddess]. He who does tantric ritual worship of Kabandha [Śiva] certainly becomes the lord of all tantric perfection (*siddhi*). Dhūmāvatī, the great Vidyā, is manifest in the form of a widow [hence there is no form of Śiva by her side].

14. The one-faced great Rudra (the Fierce One) is worshiped by the right hand side of Bagalā. He is famed as the annihilator [performing the contraction] of the creation.

15. By Mātaṅgī's right side one should worship Mātaṅga Śiva. He indeed is the Dakṣiṇāmūrtī who is in the form of universal bliss.

16. [A worshiper (*sādhaka*)] should worship Sadāśiva in the form of Viṣṇu by Kamalā's right side. O great sovereign Goddess, there is no doubt that he would achieve perfection (*siddhi*).

17. By the right side of Annapūrṇā [a sādhaka] should worship the great sovereign god [Śiva], the bestower of great liberation (*mokṣa*), who is the manifest *brahman* and who possesses ten faces.

18–19ab. [He] should carefully worship [Śiva as] Nārada by the right side of Durgā. The syllable *nā* stands for the creator, and the syllable *da* always represents the protector. Because the syllable *ra* symbolizes the destroyer Nārada, it is held [to represent the great god Śiva who creates, sustains, and destroys the universe].

19cd–19ef. For all other Vidyās, the seer (*ṛṣi*) [of the vidyā] mentioned in the formula is indeed her [the vidyā-śakti's] husband and should be worshiped by her right side.

Explanation of Śiva's Transformation into a Corpse Who Nonetheless Has Sexual Union with the Goddess

The blessed Goddess asked:
20. The [great Śakti] who is the first great Vidyā and also the second supreme Bhairavī who is the mother of the three worlds and is eternal—how can she be mounted on a corpse?

The blessed Śiva answered:

21–23. O great Goddess! she who is the primordial [divine being], herself Death/Time, exists [identified] as the heart [essence] of the glorious Śiva in the form of the destroyer. Therefore the supreme Death/Time (Mahākāla) is the destroyer of the universe. But when Kālī as the embodiment of destruction manifests herself in her true form, immediately at that very moment, O Goddess, Sadāśiva appears in the form of a corpse and at that instant, O Lady with dancing eyes, she [Kālī] appears mounted on a corpse.

The blessed Goddess said:

24. The great god Sadāśiva as a corpse is a lifeless body. How could it then perform the sex act?

The blessed Śiva answered:

25. At the time that great Kālī [actively] manifests herself, Sadāśiva is devoid of active power. When, O Goddess, he is united with śakti, then he appears in the form of Śiva; [but though] when devoid of śakti he is virtually a corpse, he still does not lose his manliness [his phallus].

End of the first chapter, called a dialogue between Hara and Gaurī, of the most excellent of all Tantras, the *Toḍala-tantra*

CHAPTER TWO

Brief Enumeration of Kuṇḍalinī Yoga

The blessed Śiva said:

1–4. Listen O Goddess! I shall briefly recount the essence of yoga [meditation and Tantric mental adoration].

The [human] body is like a tree [in reverse form] whose roots are on top and branches hanging beneath. All the sacred places of the universe exist within this body. The very form of the macrocosm exists in the microcosm [of the human body]. There are thirty and a half million sacred places in the macrocosm, O You who are praised by the heroes [Tantric practitioners]! Out of all of these, only a hundred and forty thousand sacred places are visible. Out of these, only fourteen [are noteworthy], and out of these [fourteen], only three are auspicious. Amongst these [three again], O supreme sovereign Goddess, [the one called] Mahādhīrā bestows liberation (*mukti*).

5. Vāsukī [the divine serpent] is indeed Mahāmayā [the cosmic goddess of delusion], who is manifest in the form of a serpent, coiled three and a half times, and resides in the region under the nether region (*pātāla*).

6–8. O supreme sovereign Goddess, listen carefully while I recount the seven heavens [upper regions] in their proper order. [These are] the region of the earth, of the atmosphere, of the celestials, then the region of maha [of the great saints], the region of jana [generation], the region of tapa [austerity] and, O Lady with an elegant face, the region of satya [truth]. Here ends the list of seven regions. O eminent lady! now listen carefully to the enumeration of the nether regions. [These are the regions of] atala, vitala, sutala, talātala, mahātala, pātāla, and after that rasātala.

9–17ab. The liberating [yogic duct, called nāḍī] Mahādhīrā ranges from rasātala to the end of satya, which exists inside the central [channel, that is, the spinal column, meru]. Mahāviṣṇu Śiva resides in the satya region and Vāsukī is full of intense longing to meet him. When Vāsukī, having pierced the six regions (*cakras*), rises up [to that region of satya], all the other flowing rivers [that is, the ducts] become upward flowing. In the body [the microcosm], O sovereign Goddess, the ducts remain in the following order. If [the sādhaka] presses down air through both the iḍā and piṅgalā ducts, which have the suṣumṇā between them, O sovereign Goddess, while repeating the prāṇa mantra [*so'haṃ*], then the coiled one [Vāsukī] starts [moving upward through the suṣumṇā] following the order of the [six cakras], until she approaches the eternal and immutable lotus [the sahasrāra cakra]. With anxiety the coiled one enters that eternal abode. Simultaneously all other down-flowing [ducts] start flowing upstream. At that moment, O Goddess! [the sādhaka] should concentrate on the garland of letters. Then while repeating mentally 108 times his chief (*mūla*) mantra [received from his preceptor at the time of initiation] the intelligent [sādhaka] should bring the coiled one back to his mūlādhāra cakra [her original resting-place] in the same way, while refreshing the gods of the six *cakra*s with the nectar [from the thousand-petaled lotus].

Yogic Mudrās, or Special Physical Positions for Kuṇḍalinī Yoga

17cd–22ab. Now, my dear, I shall describe another yoga posture called the yonimudrā [the previous one was called śakti-cālanī].

The mantra practitioner first sits down on his seat facing the east or the north. With his arms he firmly holds his two knees and then, O Queen of the gods, he brings his nose near the knees while sitting upright [that is, keeping his back straight]. O Queen of the gods, [as before] he presses air down by inhaling (but, O great Goddess! does not let the air escape by exhaling), and simultaneously continues repeating the prāṇa mantra. At the same time, as described before, he should repeat [his chief mantra] 108 times in his upright pose, [only this time] he repeats [the mantra] in reverse order. While thus [repeating his mantra], O You of glorious face, he brings [the kuṇḍalinī] back to the basic root cakra [*mūlādhāra*] through the same path while refreshing the gods of the six cakras with nectar.

22cd–25. My dear, this yonimudrā removes all illness. O Goddess, without elaborating I can just say that it destroys great diseases and, O Goddess, without exaggerating I can say that this mudrā causes the realization of the mantra, brings about the direct perception of one's [true] self, and bestows on the practitioner the great liberation, mahāmokṣa. Had I possessed a hundred faces I would not have been able to exhaust all its details; but with only five faces how much can I enumerate? A Tantric practitioner practicing this mudrā becomes as beautiful as Cupid even if he began as a leper.

Here ends the second chapter of the Śiva-Pārvatī dialogue
in the *Toḍala Tantra* which is the best of all Tantras

CHAPTER THREE

The blessed goddess asked:

1. O God of gods, great God, the saver from the ocean of transient and recurring life [*saṃsāra*], O Ocean of compassion, please tell me the great mudrā called baddhayoni.

Śiva answered:

2–4ab. Listen, O Goddess, I shall briefly tell you the method of baddhayoni. O great Goddess, the mantra practitioner covers his anus with the tip of his penis. Then, O great Goddess, the intelligent practitioner gradually applies his fingers [to cover other apertures of his body] starting with the thumbs, to [cover] his ears, [and then in turn [covering his] eyes, nose, and mouth [with rest of the pairs of fingers of his hands].

4cd–7. [Thus covering all his bodily apertures] he should then inhale through his nose and fill his mouth with air and as before press it downward [through the iḍā and piṅgalā ducts]. When [the coiled goddess unites with Śiva] the practitioner should envisage the primaeval Sound (*śabda-brahman*) and then envisage the garland of syllables (*varṇamālā*) while repeating his main mantra. Then, repeating the mantra *so'ham*, he brings, O Goddess, [the kuṇḍalinī back to the mūlādhāra cakra] through the same central channel. On the way he refreshes all the cakra gods [with the nectar produced by the union of the goddess and Sadāśiva]. O great sovereign Goddess! O spotless One! I shall tell you [later] the achievements of one who peforms this [kuṇḍalinī yoga seated in baddhayoni posture].

Kālī's Mantra or Vidyā

The blessed Pārvatī asked:
8. O omniscient Īśāna! O most excellent of the erudite, who possesses all wisdom! O master of gods! please tell me the rare description of Kālikā's mantra system.

The Bīja [Seed] Mantra.

The blessed Śiva answered:

9–13. O ever-blissful Goddess, listen to my account of the excellent Kālikā mantra; even the mere discussion of its nature makes a man liberated in this life. For the first [seed mantra], cull the syllable *ka*, add to it *ī*, *r*, and the *bindunāda* [double nasalization, symbolized by a sickle shape topped by a point representing the normal nasalization]. O auspicious One! this is the very rare perfect vidyā, the queen of all vidyās.

The Vidyā

Now listen to me explaining the next one. First utter this seed [mantra *krīṃ*] three times. Then cull the syllable *ha* connected with the nasal *bindu* and the vowel *u* [*huṃ*], [and utter] it twice [after the first three]; and now I tell you the next one [that is the third seed mantra]. Then, O sovereign Goddess [utter the syllable *ha* joined with *r*, *ī*, and the nasal, and repeat it again [*hrīṃ hrīṃ*]; then add [Kālikā's] vocative, then again three of the first seed mantra, then twice the kūrca mantra [*hūṃ*] and twice the māyā mantra [*hrīṃ*] and finally *svāhā*. This mantra of twenty-five syllables is the queen of all vidyās and is very rare.

14. When this great vidyā is preceded by the vāgbhava mantra [*aiṃ*, the seed mantra of the supreme speech, Vāc], its inherent deity is Śrīkālī; when preceded by the praṇava mantra [*Oṃ*], its deity is known as Siddhikālikā.

15–16. When the mantra consists of two of the goddess's own mantras [*krīṃ*] followed by one kūrca mantra [*hūṃ*], O great Goddess, this trisyllabic supreme vidyā is known as Cāmuṇḍākālikā. There is no vidyā like this one for bringing about success. The six-syllabled vidyā [*krīṃ krīṃ krīṃ phaṭ svāhā*] and the three-syllabled vidyā [*krīṃ krīṃ hūṃ*] are of equal power.

17–18ab. O auspicious one! three of [Kālikā's] own seed mantra [*krīṃ krīṃ krīṃ*] followed by the [vocative] *śmaśānakālike*, then again the three seed mantras and finally *svāhā*, [together] constitute the fourteen-syllabled mantra that is worshiped in all the three worlds.

Eight Forms of the Kālī Vidyā

18cd–21ab. Dakṣiṇākālikā, Siddhikālikā, Guhyakālikā, Śrīkālikā, Bhadrakālī, Cāmuṇḍākālikā, and the supreme Śmaśānakālikā and Mahākālī, O Goddess! These are the eight [forms of goddess Kālī]. O sovereign Goddess! First utter Kālī's own seed mantra, then her name in the vocative followed by another Kālikā seed mantra, and finally add *svāhā* [*krīṃ kālike krīṃ svāhā*]. These eight forms of Kālikā's mantra are secretly expressed in all Tantras.

The blessed Goddess said:

21cd–23ab. I have [now] heard the very secret mantras of the great Kālikā. Now I wish to hear Tārā's royal mantra. O Īśāna! if you love me do tell me her mantra, whose mere mention prevents one from drowning in the ocean of [transitory] existence.

Tārā Bījas

Śrī Śiva answered:

Having uttered the moon seed [*saṃ*] add the syllable of fire [*r*] and *t* to it, together with the left eye [*ī*]. My beloved, this royal mantra, this single-syllabled vidyā [*strīṃ*] is venerated in three worlds. *Īśāna* [*h*] united with the nasal and the left ear [*ū*] [forms] the monosyllabic vidyā [*hūṃ*], which is [Tārā's] second royal mantra.

The Tārā Vidyā

23cd–32ab. Śiva [*h*] with the fire [*r*] and the left eye [*ī*] and the nasal added to it [*hrīṃ*] [should first be uttered]. Then the first seed [*strīṃ*] and then the second [*hūṃ*], then utter the weapon, astra mantra [*hrīṃ strīṃ hūṃ phaṭ*].

Different Forms and Efficacies of the Tārā Vidyā

When this vidyā is preceded by praṇava [*Oṃ*], then [the Goddess] is called Ugratārā. When without the praṇava this vidyā is called Ekajaṭā, the bestower of supreme liberation (*mokṣa*). With neither praṇava nor astra mantra [that is, *hrīṃ strīṃ hūṃ*], this trisyllabic vidyā is called Mahānīlasarasvatī. When the [trisyllabic] vidyā is preceded by the vāgbhava [seed mantra], it bestows [on the practitioner] the status of the god of speech. This supreme vidyā when preceded by the seed mantra *śrīṃ* bestows wealth and prosperity. When this great vidyā is preceded by the seed mantra māyā [*hrīṃ*], it bestows sure success and perfection (*siddhi*). When it is preceded by the kūrca [*hūṃ*], it reveals the entire system of speech. When this supreme vidyā is preceded by the seed of the sky [*haṃ*], it bestows the liberation of total resorption. When this geat vidyā starts with the prāsāda [seed mantra, *hauṃ*] it brings about the union of the practitioner with Śiva. When this mantra starts with the seed [mantra] of prāṇa [*prūṃ*] it bestows on the practitioner the fulfilment of whatever he wishes. When this supreme vidyā opens with the seed of Kālī [*krīṃ*] it bestows both liberation and prosperity.

Ritual Worship of the Deity

32cd–50abc. Now I shall describe the method of worshiping Kālī and Tārā. Arising in the morning, the practitioner who knows his mantra [and its method of meditation] first mentally worships his guru in the topmost cakra consisting of a thousand petals. Then, having pierced the six cakras, he should repeat his main mantra 108 times. Thereafter, having bowed down [to his preferred deity] he should perform his ritual bathing. He should start this bathing ritual with the following declaration of his intention (*saṃkalpa*): "Today [here he mentions the day and date and then] the solar month, [I bathe myself] for the pleasure of the deity." Then he bathes in the pure water.

Then he should utter *Oṃ* and then *gaṅge ca*, followed by *yamune*, then having uttered *godāvari, sarasvati, narmade* and *sindhu kāveri* he utters the words *asmin jale sannidhiṃ kuru* [*Oṃ* the rivers Ganges, Yamuna, Godavari, Sarasvati, Narmada, Sindhu, and Kaveri please abide in this water]. [While uttering this mantra the practitioner] with the hand gesture called the goad (*aṅkuśa*) should [in imagination] pull these sacred rivers from the orb of the sun and settle them [in the water in which he is bathing] by carefully showing four relevant hand gestures. Then having protected the water with the hand gesture called the fish [and scooping a palmful of water and covering it with the other palm], the worshiper repeats his [deity's seed] mantra [*krīṃ*] eleven times. Then, throwing this water toward the sun, he should repeat his main mantra twelve times while [in imagination] washing [Kālikā's] feet three times. Then [in imagination] he should three times bathe himself with that rinse water flowing from [Kālī's] feet while repeating the mantra. This is done by showing the gesture of the water pot (*kumbha*) while repeating his main mantra three times.

Then, O Queen of gods! he should decorate his forehead according to the custom of his sect. Then he performs ācamana [ritual cleansing of his mouth and hands] with water while uttering the mantras of the three tattvas—ātmatattva, vidyātattva, and śivatattva. The mantras consist of each tattva preceded by praṇava and ending with *svāhā* [this is the name of the wife of the god Agni, Fire].

[At this point he has left his bathing place, cleanly and decorously attired, and reached the actual place of worship, carrying a pitcher full of water brought from the water source. In this water pitcher] he invokes the sacred rivers with the same *gaṅge ca*, etc., mantra [following the aforesaid procedure]. Then he dips a bunch of kuśa grass into the sanctified water and with it sprinkles water on the ground [where he will hold his ritual worship]. Then in the same way he should sprinkle himself seven times. Then he performs his aṅganyāsa. Then, O Goddess of the celestials, he with his left hand [scoops up water] and repeats three times the [pañcabhūta] bīja mantras: *haṃ*, *vaṃ*, *yaṃ*, *laṃ* and *raṃ*. Having thus encapsulated that water with that pañcabhūta mantra, the practitioner should sprinkle himself seven times with his finger in the gesture of tattva [reality] while uttering his main mantra. This act at once removes all his sins.

Then, O great sovereign Queen, the adept transfers the rest of the water from his left hand to his right and in imagination inhales it through his iḍā duct [inside his left nostril], which water then cleanses his inner body. Thereafter, he should exhale that water through his piṅgalā duct [inside his right nostril]. Here he imagines that water to be black and the embodiment of sins; he immediately throws the water onto a slab of rock with the mantra *phaṭ*. Then he should wash his hands, perform ācamana and, having performed breath control, offer libation to his lineage god and then offer arghya [an offering of a few rice grains, tips of durvā grass and sanctified water] to the Sun god and arghya to his chosen deity.

50d–53. Thereafter he should repeat the great words of the [Kālikā] gāyatrī [the famous Vedic mantra with which brahmans worship the Sun every day, as follows]: first one should take the praṇava [*Oṃ*], then utter *kālikāyai*, then *vidmahe*; then *śmaśānavāsinyai dhīmahi*, then *tan no ghore pracodayāt*. While uttering this mantra, the worshiper should three times scatter the consecrated water upward.

54ab. Then, O great Goddess, having performed aṅganyāsa the worshiper again performs ācamana.

Tārā's Gāyatrī is Described with a Brief Mention of the Deity's Dhyāna as the Sun Deity

54cd–56ab. O great Goddess! Having envisaged in meditation one's chosen deity [here Tārā] in the orb of the sun, one should utter *Oṃ tārāyai vidmahe mahogrāyai dhīmahi tan no devī pracodayāt*. Then, having performed breath control, he should repeat this mantra 108 times.

Now, O Queen of gods, I offer in the form of aphorisms (*sūtrākāra*) an account of the system of worship

Preliminaries

56cd–58. First proclaim universal well-being (*svasti-vacana*), then the announcement of one's intention to worship (*saṃkalpa*). Next, one should carefully place the pitcher [full of consecrated water], followed by the act of ācamana with mantras; next comes the setting the pitcher of water for arghya for general purposes; then sprinkling the entrance [with consecrated water for purification], finishing that ritual by worshiping the entrance. Then, having removed the three categories of hindrances [concretized as evil spirits, belonging to the ground, atmosphere, and close to the body of the worshipper and the material objects around him gathered for the ritual] he removes [other evil] spirits [with mantras, sprinkling of water and threatening gestures].

Starting the Actual Worship

59–60ab. Having adored the seat, the intelligent worshiper first of all bows down to his guru. Then he purifies his hands, claps them three times, and then performs the rite of consolidating and safeguarding the area surrounding his person (*digbandhana*). Then he encompasses himself with fire. Then he performs bhūtaśuddhi.

Nyāsa

60cd–64ab. He should then first perform the nyāsa of the six limbs of the mātṛkā [the full Sanskrit alphabet], then the nyāsa of the mātṛkā on his inner body. Then he utters the dhyāna mantra [the mantra that gives the deity's iconography] of the mātṛkā. He should perform the same nyāsa on his external body. Then he performs the nyāsa of the seat of the deity (*pīṭha*) before completing his breath control. Then he performs the nyāsa of the sage, and so on [the sage poet, the meter, and the deity of his mantra]. Then he performs nyāsa of his hands and his limbs [identifying them with] the letters of the Sanskrit alphabet. Then he performs the six types of nyāsa [of his main mantra]. Then he performs vyāpaka [extended] nyāsa. With concentration he performs the nyāsa of the tattvas; then, O Goddess!, he performs the nyāsa of the seed mantra. He performs the vyāpaka nyāsa in seven different ways using his main mantra. Then in deep concentration he visualizes his deity, whereafter he worships that deity mentally [with imagined ingredients].

Adoration of the Deity

64cd–68ab. [The adept] prepares the consecrated special liquid for special argyha. Then he worships [the deity's] seat. Next he again performs the visualization of the deity in deep meditation (*dhyāna*) and this time he sees her with her eyes open. [All the time he utters specific mantras and appropriate gestures to accompany his ritual acts.] Then he in similar manner welcomes the deity. Then while purifying all objects of offering he shows the gestures of the cow's udder, and so on. [These are called the dhenu mudrā, the symbol for the celestial cow whose milk is nectar; the avagunṭhana mudrā, which symbolizes safety and cover; the gālinī mudrā which symbolizes the fusing of the sacred and the mundane water; and the nārāca mudrā, which symbolizes iron arrowheads to ward off any polluting evil spirits]. Then he performs the nyāsa of the deity's six limbs. Then he performs the rite of establishing life [in the image or other representation of the deity]. Then he worships [with offerings] his principal mantra and its deity, the Goddess. Then he requests the Goddess to authorize him [to exercise the power of the mantra]. Then he worships the deity's attendant deities like Kālī, and so on. [They are Kālī, Kapālinī, Kullā, Kurukullā, Virodhinī, Vipracittā, Ugrā, Ugraprabhā, and Dīptā. The second circle of her assistants consists of Nīlā, Ghanā, and Valakā, and the third circle consists of Mātrā, Mudrā, and Mitā]. Then he worships her attendant mother-goddesses Brāhmī, and so on, and their Bhairavas, Asitāṅga, and so on. [They are Brāhmī, Vaiṣṇavī, Māheśvarī, Cāmuṇḍā, Kaumārī, Aparājitā, Vārāhī, and Nārasiṃhī; and Asitāṅga, Ruru, Caṇḍa, Krodha, Unmatta, Kapāli, Bhīṣaṇa and Saṃhāra.]. Then he worships [the deity's consort] Mahākāla. Then he worships the Goddess's [weapons, that is,] her sword, and so on. Next he worships the lineage of his guru. Then the ritualist repeats the worship of Kālī. This is followed by the offering of bali [a sacrificial animal, or in some cases nonvegetarian food for the spirits]. This is followed by the fire sacrifice. Then, having performed prāṇāyāma [as a preparation for japa], he performs mantra repetition (*japa*) of his main mantra [which is a form of one-pointed meditation]. Finally, the intelligent worshiper dedicates the merit of his japa to the deity and then performs prāṇāyāma for a second time.

Esoteric Worship of the Goddess with Alcohol and Other Ingredients

68cd. At this moment the worshiper may, O Goddess, collect [esoteric ingredients such as] alcohol [meat, fish, fried food/a partner for intercourse, and the sexual fluids].

Concluding Section of the Worship

69–71. Afterward, the worshiper offers the deity arghya and also dedicates himself to the Goddess. Then he recites the Goddess's eulogy and then recites her protective kavaca ["armor," a special hymn used as a mantra, which guards every part of the worshiper's body]. Finally he prostrates himself. Afterward he mentally utters the formula, "I am Śiva," while making the gesture of bidding her farewell. He then draws a diagram on the southwestern corner and offers arghya and other offerings to the goddess Ucchiṣṭacaṇḍālī. He then himself puts a mark on his forehead with the sandal paste offered to the Goddess and partakes of some of the offered food. Thereafter he can do whatever he wishes.

Alternative Brief Ritual

Alternatively, the initiated Tantric ritualist who has composed and fixed his mind in devotion and meditation may perform a shortened version of the worship.

First he performs the nyāsa of the poet-sage, and so on, of his main mantra; then he purifies his hands [with nyāsa] followed by nyāsa of his fingers and the extensive nyāsa of his body. Then he performs the nyāsa of his six limbs. Then he claps his hands three times [to remove obstructing spirits], then encircles his surroundings with [a fiery barrier]. Then he performs breath control followed by dhyāna on his mantra deity and then mentally performs her worship. Then he prepares and places the pitcher of arghya water, and worships the seat [of the Goddess]. On that he invokes the Goddess after having meditated on her image. Then he performs her ritual welcome, and so forth, followed by establishing life in her symbol, jīvanyāsa or prāṇapratiṣṭhā, and finally worships the supreme Goddess. Then he worships the attendant deities Kālī, and so on, as well as the eight śaktis, Brāhmī, and so on, along with their bhairavas. Then having worshiped Mahākāla he worships his guru's lineage as well as the Goddess's attributes and weapons such as the sword. This is followed by a repeat of the worship of the Goddess. Then the foremost of all worshipers practices breath control before performing his japa. He dedicates the [merit of his] japa to the Goddess's hand. He performs the concluding breath control, prostrates himself, recites the Goddess's panegyric and kavaca and causes the special arghya to be offered. He then dedicates himself [to the Goddess] and bids her farewell with the gesture of resorption. He draws a diagram on his southwestern side and worships Ucchiṣṭacaṇḍālī. In conclusion, he partakes of some of the offered food and then he may do as he pleases.

—28—

Ritual Manual for the Protective Fire Offering Devoted to Mañjuśrī, Chuin Lineage

Richard K. Payne

Every Tantric tradition has its own version of the homa, a votive ritual in which offerings are made into a fire. In one form or another the homa is found from Mongolia to Bali, from south India to Japan. The homa is also a link to the Vedic ritual tradition and the broader Indo-European religious culture that includes Iranian, Greek, and Roman ritual traditions.

The homa ritual presented here is from the Shingon tradition of Japanese Buddhism, specifically the Chuin lineage, which predominates in contemporary Japan. The Shingon tradition was established in the ninth century by Kūkai, who is also known by his posthumously awarded title "Kōbō Daishi" and is sometimes simply referred to as "the Daishi" meaning "the Great Teacher." He traveled to China (804 to 806) with the specific goal of initiation into the Buddhist Tantra, and received authority for the dual lineage of the *Mahāvairocana* and *Tattvasaṃgraha Sūtras*.

The homa is one of the most important rituals that Kūkai brought to Japan, and it became the final of the four rituals practiced in the training of Shingon priests. The East Asian Tantric Buddhist tradition knows five kinds of homas, identified according to the purpose for which they are performed: protection (*śāntika*), increase (*pauṣṭika*), subjugation (*abhicāraka*), subordination (*vaśīkaraṇa*), and acquisition (*aṅkuśa*). Each is conducive to awakening in a dual sense. For example, the homa of subjugation both enables the practitioner to overcome enemies, either human or demonic, and to overcome the mental and emotional errors that obscure the naturally enlightened mind.

The ritual translated here is for protection, the kind most commonly performed in contemporary Japan. This homa takes as its chief deity Mañjuśrī, the bodhisattva of wisdom. Mañjuśrī is one of the best known of the Mahāyāna bodhisattvas, playing a central role in such popular sūtras as the *Vimalakīrti Nirdeśa Sūtra*.

In this homa five sets of offerings are made. The first is to Agni, the Vedic fire god who is almost invariably the first deity evoked in the homas of the Shingon tradition. This is followed by a set of offerings to the lord of the assembly, a figure that, like the chief deity, can vary from homa to homa. In this case the lord of the assembly is Hayagrīva, a horse-headed manifestation of Avalokiteśvara, the bodhisattva of compassion. Hayagrīva is also known to the Hindu tradition, where he is identified with Viṣṇu.

The central set of offerings is to Mañjuśrī, the chief deity of this ritual. This is followed by sets of offerings to the bodhisattvas accompanying Mañjuśrī, surrounding him in the maṇḍala, and to a set of Vedic deities and astral groupings.

These five sets of offerings are structured very similarly to one another—a fact that allows for the abridgment of the version of the ritual instructions given here. The basic pattern or syntax of each of the five sets of offerings is: 1. preparation of the altar-hearth, offerings, and practitioner; 2. visualization of the deity to be evoked within the practitioner's own body and in the altar-hearth; 3. evocation of the deity by inviting him to leave his original location in the cosmic maṇḍala (the totally of being as it actually is, that is, as experienced by an awakened one, a buddha) and to become identical with the deity as visualized in the hearth; 4. making of offerings to the deity; and 5. departure and leave-taking, in which the identification is dissolved and the deity returns to his original location. The model for this ritual structure is the feasting of an honored guest, and is rooted in the Indic origins of the homa. This systematic structure is also evidenced by the fact that the offerings prescribed here are to be embedded in a longer ritual, as indicated by the first line's reference to "the additional recitations," a particular point in the ritual into which these offerings are to be embedded. Often, however, the portion of the ritual preceeding the homa offerings is performed at some earlier time, perhaps the day before.

The efficacy of this ritual is understood to result from the three-way identification between the practitioner, the deity evoked, and the hearth. This identification is effected by the practitioner's visualization. Thus, the mouth of the hearth, into which offerings are made, is visualized as identical with both the mouth of the deity and the mouth of the practitioner. The physical offerings are identified with the practitioner's own self-frustrating emotional habits and intellectual misconceptions. Just as the fire burning on the hearth is understood as purifying the offerings, making them appropriate for the deity's consumption, the fire is also the fire of wisdom, purifying the emotional habits and intellectual misconceptions. The fire is both the deity's awakened mind and that of the practitioner. Thus, one is offering one's own emotional habits and intellectual misconceptions to oneself for purification in the fire of one's own awakened mind.

Like other ritual manuals, the present text assumes a great deal of knowledge on the part of the practitioner. Hence, the instructions at times only identify a well-known ritual action by name, such as "universal offering and three powers," which are a pair of brief recitations found together in nearly every Shingon ritual. It is expected that the trained practitioner will have these memorized, though individual practitioners often add the information to their own manuals. This assumption of prior knowledge makes for a "telegraphic" style in the ritual instructions, which I have preserved in my translation.

As with many esoteric systems, Shingon employs a set of associations between the body and mind of the practitioner and the alternate worldview that the tradition teaches. Each finger of the hands forming the mudrās is identified with one of the five elements: little finger with earth, ring finger (known as "nameless") with water, middle finger with fire, forefinger (known as "head") with wind, and thumb (known as "great") with empty space. This five-element system originates in India and is part of the Indian religious culture brought to China and Japan as part of the Buddhist tradition. This system of five elements was given particular importance in Shingon as a way for practitioners to experience themselves as identical with the cosmos as an awakened totality. The five elements also appear graphically as five cakras, though the term is used somewhat idiosyncratically here, since cakra is usually understood as a wheel. In the five-elements system, earth is a yellow square or cube, water a white circle or sphere, fire a red triangle or pyramid, wind a black half-circle or hemisphere, and empty space a blue raindrop. Other aspects of Indian religious culture found in this ritual include the repeated request that the deities perfect the practitioner's supernatural powers (*siddhis*), the use of phonemes (as written in the Siddhaṃ script) as part of visualizing the deity's presence, and the activation (called here "empowerment") of various elements of the ritual through the recitation of mantras.

Likewise, many of the implements employed in the ritual, such as the ladles, originate in Indian religious culture. The vajra, however, is even older, representing as it does the thunderbolt—the weapon of the high god across the entire Indo-European religious culture. In the esoteric Buddhist tradition it is explained as representing the qualities of awakened consciousness: like a thunderbolt, it suddenly illuminates the night of our confused and frustrating existence. It is also stronger than anything else, breaking the rock of our entrenched habits. The Shingon tradition makes use of three forms of the vajra: one-pointed, three-pointed, and five-pointed. At the start of the ritual, these are arranged on a plate (the "vajra plate") on the altar in front of the practitioner.

Not only is the altar itself the hearth upon which the fire is built, but it is also a maṇḍala. As the ritual enclosure in which the deities are evoked, it is enclosed by a rope of five strands, each strand the color of one of the five elements. In front of the practitioner the rope is raised to form a "gateway." Ritually identical with the deities, the practitioner is able to enter the maṇḍala through the gateway to make offerings and perform the other ritual actions.

The homa rite was appropriated by other Japanese religious traditions. For example, a homa using large logs and performed outdoors is found in the Shugendō tradition of mountain ascetics. Similarly, at least one of the nativist Shintō traditions initiated in the nineteenth century also incorporated a homa, despite a rhetoric of purifying Shintō of Buddhist influences.

In contemporary Japan, one can observe this Tantric rite or its variant forms quite easily. In some temples it is performed every day, in others on a monthly or annual basis. The performance of the homa throughout so much of Japan indicates the deep influence of Tantric Buddhism on Japanese religious culture.

The present translation of the homa to Mañjuśrī is based on Soeda Takatoshi, *Monju Soku Sai Goma Shiki Shidai*, Goma Zenshu, no. 35 (Osaka: Toho Shuppan, 1982).

Further Reading

Michel Strickmann, "Homa in East Asia," in Frits Staal, ed., *Agni* (Berkeley: Asian Humanities Press, 1983), Vol. 2, pp. 418–55; Richard K. Payne, *Tantric Ritual of Japan* (Delhi: Sata-Pitaka Series, 1991); Robert Hans van Gulik, *Hayagrīva: The Mantrayānic Aspect of Horse-Cult in China and Japan* (Leiden: E. J. Brill, 1935); E. Dale Saunders, *Mudrā: A Study of Symbolic Gestures in Japanese Buddhist Sculpture* (New York: Pantheon, 1960); Pierre Rambach, *The Secret Message of Tantric Buddhism* (New York: Rizzoli International, 1979); Taiko Yamasaki, *Shingon: Japanese Esoteric Buddhism* (Boston: Shambhala, 1988); Minoru Kiyota, *Shingon Buddhism: Theory and Practice* (Los Angeles: Buddhist Books International, 1978); Ryuichi Abe, *The Weaving of Mantra: Kūkai and the Construction of Esoteric Buddhist Discourse* (New York: Columbia University Press, 1999).

Ritual Manual for the Protective Fire Offering Devoted to Mañjuśrī, Chuin Lineage

Following the additional recitations, hang the rosary on the left wrist, throughout the homa.

First, empowerment of Mahāvairocana: form the wisdom fist mudrā, recite the mantra *Oṃ vajradhātu vaṃ.*

Next, empowerment of the lord of the assembly: form the Hayagrīva mudrā—make the empty bowl mudrā with both hands, the two head and two nameless fingers bent into the palm, their backs joined together; the two great fingers are aligned, but do not touch the two head together. Recite *Oṃ amṛtodbhava hūṃ phaṭ.*

Next, empowerment of the chief deity, Mañjuśrī: form the empty bowl mudrā—the two middle fingers touch the back of the two nameless fingers, the two great fingers are aligned, and the two head fingers bent—then the blue lotus mudrā. The preceding mudrā is turned up so that the two middle, two nameless, and two little fingers are placed above the two great fingers, and the two great fingers are shaped like a sword. Recite *Oṃ a ra pa ca na.*

Next, visualize the three identities using the dharmadhātu meditation mudrā. Contemplate the following: the heart of the Tathāgata is identical with what actually exists, what actually exists is identical with the fire of wisdom; the hearth is identical with the body of the Tathāgata; the fire is identical with the dharmakāya fire of wisdom; the mouth of the hearth is identical with the mouth of the Tathāgata; the fire is nothing other than the wisdom within the practitioner's body. Thus, the mouth of the Tathāgata's body, the mouth of the body of the hearth, and the mouth of the practitioner's body are all three the same.

Next, empower the poppy seeds: take the censer and place it in the left corner of the altar. Next, take the bowl of poppy seeds from the left table and place it where the censer had been; empower using the single-pronged vajra, reciting the mantra of the Fire Realm seven times [there is an oral instruction: recite the single-syllable chant twenty-one times]; at the end scatter the poppy seed to the four directions, to the four corners, above and below, with the right hand. Beginning from the northeast corner, recite the chant of the Fire Realm once for each of the directions, throwing a total of ten times. Then return the bowl to its original location.

1. FIRST, THE SECTION FOR AGNI

Start with Agni's mudrā and name: grasp the right wrist with the left hand; bend the thumb of the right hand, placing it in the middle of the palm; the remaining fingers extend straight out. Empower the four places; recite *Oṃ agnaye śāntika svāhā.*

Next, take the rosary and recite the short Agni mantra 108 times.

Next, take the ball incense, chip incense, and flowers, placing them in order beside the hearth. Next, take the vajra bell and place it where the ball incense had been on the left table. Next, take the three-pronged vajra and hold it in the left hand. Next, take the powdered incense and worship offerings from the right table and then place them beside the hearth. Next, untie the string around the twenty-one pieces of sapwood, turn the base toward the practitioner, and place it on the vajra plate. Throw the string into the hearth. Next, take the pincers and insert the offering wood, piling it up in the hearth in sequence. From the orientation of the practitioner, in sequence from left to right place six sticks in line; eleven sticks total. Next, with the pincers, insert a piece of pine into the flame of the lamp on the right and place it under the right corner of the firewood.

Next, take the fan and fan the flames: hold the fan partially open in the right hand, recite the mantra, and fan three times; imagine a syllable *hāṃ* on the surface of the fan; it changes, becoming a wind cakra, recite *Oṃ bhūḥ jvala hūṃ*, three times. Close it in the right hand and return to its original location.

Next, purification: sprinkle the wood in the hearth three times, sprinkle directly, recite the kili kili chant: *Oṃ kili kili vajra hūṃ phaṭ.*

Next, empower the firewood on the hearth: using the three-pronged vajra, empower by reciting the kili kili chant three times.

Next, invite Agni, form Amitābha's meditation mudrā.

First, visualize one's own body: visualize a syllable *raṃ* above your heart-moon cakra; this changes, becoming a triangular fire cakra. Your entire body becomes this fire cakra; the fire cakra changes, becoming the white body of the four-armed Agni, blazing flames completely surround his body; this is the great body of the vast dharmadhātu.

Next, empower oneself: form the mudrā of Agni, recite the short chant, adding the appropriate phrase: *śāntika svāhā*; empower the four actions.

Next, request Agni to enter into the hearth: take one flower, empower it by reciting the short chant of Agni three times, place it on top of the firewood in the hearth.

Next, visualize Agni in the middle of the hearth: form Amitābha's meditation mudrā, and visualize the flower going to the middle of the hearth, becoming a lotus-leaf seat, and visualize Agni on the lotus-leaf seat.

Next, invite Agni to arise from the *maṇḍala*: form Agni's mudrā and recite his mantra, beckon three times with the wind finger. Next, form the *mudrā* and recite the mantra of the four wisdoms: recite *Oṃ agnaye śāntika ehyehi jaḥ hūṃ baṃ hoḥ svāhā.*

Next, contemplation: form Amitābha's meditation mudrā, and imagine inviting Agni, located in his original place in the maṇḍala, to mysteriously unite with the Agni in the hearth, forming a single body, not two.

Next, declaration, ring the gong.

> "Only desiring that Agni descend to this seat
> and compassionately accept this marvelous homa offering."

Next, rinse the mouth: sprinkle directly three times, imagine washing the mouth of Agni, recite *Oṃ varada-vajra dhaṃ.*

Next, declaration, ring the gong.

> "Sincerely offering perfumed water for rinsing the mouth
> only requesting that Agni accept this homa
> protect his disciple, and perfect siddhi."

Next, powdered incense, three times; recite *Oṃ agnaye śāntika svāhā* each time.

Next, contemplation: form Amitābha's meditation mudrā, and imagine the incense entering Agni's mouth, going to the lotus blossom of his heart, becoming excellent offerings. Limitless, oceanlike clouds of powdered incense flow from his heart, through his body, and out his pores, offered to all the buddhas, bodhisattvas, pratyekabuddhas, śrāvakas, and worldly deities.

Next, declaration, ring the gong.

> "I now present the powdered incense offering
> only requesting that Agni accept this homa
> protect his disciple, and perfect *siddhi.*"

Next, ghee, large and small ladles three times each; chant, visualization and declaration as with the powdered incense, except contemplate "limitless ocean-like clouds of ghee flow out," and so on; change declaration to "ghee offering."

Next, repeat with appropriate changes for sapwood, three pieces; food, three ladles; five cereals, three ladles; flowers, three times; ball incense, three times; chip incense, three times; and ghee, large and small ladles one time each.

Next, recite the universal offering and the three powers, ring the gong.

Next, vows, ring the gong.

> "Sincerely requesting, only desiring that Agni
> compassionately accept this homa offering
> protect his disciple, and perfect siddhi."

Next, rinse the mouth: sprinkle directly three times, recite *Oṃ varada vajra dhaṃ*. Imagine washing Agni's mouth.

Next, declaration, ring the gong.

> "Sincerely offering perfumed water for rinsing the mouth
> only requesting that Agni accept this homa
> protect his disciple, and perfect siddhi."

Next, leave-taking: take one flower, recite the short Agni mantra and throw it to the original location in the maṇḍala: the northeast corner of the altar.

Next, contemplation: form Amitābha's meditation mudrā, and imagine that this flower, arriving at its original location, becomes a lotus leaf seat.

Next, form Agni's mudrā: press the empty finger against the back of the water finger, which is curled down; extend the wind finger sharply, recite *Oṃ agnaye śāntika gaccha gaccha muḥ*.

Next, contemplation: form Amitābha's meditation mudrā, and imagine that Agni returns to his original location in the maṇḍala from the middle of the hearth.

Next, declaration, ring the gong.

> "Solely requesting that Agni return to his original seat."

With the above the first section, the portion for Agni, is finished.

2. SECOND SECTION, FOR THE LORD OF THE ASSEMBLY, HAYAGRĪVA.

First, purify the offerings: repeat three times, wash clockwise, and recite the kili kili chant. Wash the various offerings.

Next, karma empowerment: empower the various offerings clockwise and counterclockwise three times each, recite *Oṃ vajra karma khaṃ*.

Next, rinse the mouth and empower, sprinkle clockwise three times; imagine washing the mouth of the hearth, recite *Oṃ varada vajra dhaṃ*.

Next, empower the hearth: three times, using the three-pronged vajra, recite the kili kili chant.

Next, pile the kindling: four pieces.

Next, take a flaming piece of pine and insert it.

Next, take the fan and fan the fire; imagine the syllable *haṃ* on the surface of the fan; it changes, becoming a wind cakra, recite *Oṃ bhūḥ jvala hūṃ* three times.

Next, purification: sprinkle the wood in the hearth three times, sprinkle directly, recite the kili kili chant.

Next, empower the kindling on the hearth: using the three-pronged vajra, empower by reciting the kili kili chant three times.

Next, invite the lord of the assembly.

First, visualize one's own body: form Amitābha's meditation mudrā, and visualize the syllable *haṃ* in the middle of the heart-moon cakra; this changes, becoming a horse's head; this changes, becoming Hayagrīva Avalokiteśvara Bodhisattva, his body flesh colored, and his head a white horse's head, with one face and four arms, his two front hands form a mudrā, his right hand holds a three-pronged vajra, and his left hand holds an unopened lotus blossom; the two hands joined together, the two head fingers and two nameless fingers bend into the palm, the others extend out touching at the tips, the two great fingers are aligned and extend straight out, pressing against the head fingers.

Next, empower oneself: form the root mudrā of Hayagrīva, recite *Oṃ amṛtodbhava hūṃ phaṭ śāntika svāhā.*

Next, request Hayagrīva to enter into the hearth: hold one flower cluster with both hands, insert it with the flower-holding mudrā; recite the mantra of the lord of the assembly three times, empower, offer on top of the kindling and make the request.

Next, visualization in the center of the hearth: form Amitābha's meditation mudrā and visualize the flower going to the center of the hearth, becoming a jeweled lotus flower bud, and visualize Hayagrīva on the flower bud.

Next, request the lord of the assembly to come out of the maṇḍala and into the hearth: make the mudrā and recite the mantra of Hayagrīva, at the end of the mantra, add the appropriate phrase, *śāntika,* together with the mantra of the four wisdoms and form the mudrā (beckon with the right head finger), recite *Oṃ amṛtodbhava hūṃ phaṭ śāntika ehyehi jaḥ hūṃ baṃ hoḥ svāhā.*

Next, request the entourage of the lord of the assembly to come out of the maṇḍala: form the great hook mudrā and recite the mantra; at the proper place form the mudrā and add the mantra of the four embracing deities; recite *namaḥ samanta-buddhānāṃ āḥ sarvatrā apratihata tathāgata aṅkuśa bodhicarya paripūraka śāntika ehyehi jaḥ hūṃ baṃ hoḥ svāhā.*

Next, contemplation: form Amitābha's meditation mudrā, and imagine inviting the lord of the assemby, located in his original place in the maṇḍala, to mysteriously unite with the lord of the assembly in the hearth, forming a single body, not two.

Next, declaration; ring the gong.

"Only desiring that the lord of the assembly descend to this seat
and compassionately accept this marvelous homa offering."

Next, rinse the mouth: sprinkle directly, three times; imagine washing the mouth of the lord of the assembly, recite *oṃ varada vajra dhaṃ*.

Next, declaration; ring the gong.

"Sincerely presenting perfumed water for washing the mouth
only requesting that the lord of the assembly accept this homa,
protect his disciple, and perfect siddhi."

Next, powdered incense: three times, recite *Oṃ amṛtodbhava hūṃ phaṭ śāntika svāhā.*

Next, contemplation: form Amitābha's meditation mudrā and imagine the incense entering the lord of the assembly's mouth, going to his heart's lotus flower bud, becoming excellent offerings. Limitless, oceanlike clouds of powdered incense flow from his heart, through his body, and out his pores, and are offered to all the buddhas, bodhisattvas, pratyekabuddhas, śrāvakas, and worldly deities.

Next, declaration; ring the gong.

"I now present the powdered incense offering
only requesting that the lord of the assembly accept this homa,
protect his disciple, and perfect siddhi."

Next, ghee: large and small ladles three times each; chant, visualization, and declaration as with the powdered incense, except contemplate "limitless oceanlike clouds of ghee flowing out," and change declaration to "ghee offering."

Next, repeat with appropriate changes for sapwood, three pieces; food offerings, three ladles; five cereals, three ladles; ball incense, three times; chip incense, three times; and ghee, large and small ladles one time each.

Next, recite the universal offering and the three powers, ring the gong.

Next, vows, ring the gong.

"Sincerely requesting and only desiring that the lord of the assembly
compassionately accept this homa offering,
protect his disciple, and perfect siddhi."

Next, rinse the mouth: sprinkle directly, and imagine washing the mouth of the lord of the asssembly, recite *Oṃ varada vajra dhaṃ.*

Next, declaration, ring the gong.

"Sincerely offering perfumed water for rinsing the mouth
only requesting that the lord of the assembly accept this homa,
protect his disciple, and perfect siddhi."

Next, leave-taking: take one flower cluster, recite the mantra of the lord of the assembly three times, and throw it to its original location in the maṇḍala, the northeast corner.

Next, contemplation: form Amitābha's meditation mudrā and imagine this flower arriving at its original location in the maṇḍala and becoming a jeweled lotus flower seat.

Next, leave-taking of the lord of the assembly: form the mudrā and recite the mantra *Oṃ amṛtodbhava hūṃ phaṭ śāntika gaccha gaccha muḥ.*

Next, send off the entourage of the lord of the assembly; form the great hook mudrā, and recite the mantra, adding the phrase of propitiation at the end; recite *namaḥ samanta buddhānāṃ āḥ sarvatrā apratihata tathāgata aṅkuśa bodhicarya paripuraka śāntika gaccha gaccha muḥ.*

Next, contemplation: form Amitābha's meditation mudrā, and imagine that the lord of the assembly returns to his original location in the maṇḍala from the middle of the hearth.

Next, declaration, ring the gong.

> "Solely requesting that the lord of the assembly return to his original seat."

With the above, the second section, the portion for the lord of the assembly, is finished.

3. THIRD SECTION, PORTION FOR THE CHIEF DEITY, MAÑJUŚRĪ

First, purify the offerings: repeat three times, wash clockwise, and recite the kili kili chant. Wash the various offerings.

Next, karma empowerment: empower the various offerings clockwise and counterclockwise three times each, recite *Oṃ vajra karma khaṃ.*

Next, rinse the mouth and empower: sprinkle clockwise three times; imagine washing the mouth of the hearth, recite *Oṃ varada vajra dhaṃ.*

Next, empower the hearth: three times using the three-pronged vajra, recite the kili kili chant.

Next, pile the kindling, six pieces: set six pieces as offering.

Next, take a flaming piece of pine and insert it.

Next, take the fan and fan the fire: imagine the syllable *haṃ* on the surface of the fan, it changes, becoming a wind cakra, recite *Oṃ bhūḥ jvala hūṃ* three times.

Next, purification: sprinkle the wood in the hearth three times, sprinkle directly, recite the kili kili chant.

Next, empower the kindling on the hearth: using the three-pronged vajra, empower by reciting the kili kili chant three times.

Next, invite the chief deity.

First, visualize one's own body: form Amitābha's meditation mudrā, and visualize the syllable *haṃ* in the heart-moon cakra; it changes, becoming a sūtra-box; this changes, becoming Mañjuśrī Bodhisattva, wearing a crown with five buddhas in front and a bright, full-moon cakra behind him, riding on the back of a lion, seated on a lotus blossom saddle, smiling joyously, manifesting the thought of compassion for all living beings. To his left is Nārāyaṇa with four distinctive features; on his right is Garuḍarāja, manifesting a fearful appearance, and respectfully attended by Akṣayamati Bodhisattva, Sudhana-dāraka, Subhūti, and so on.

Next, empower oneself: empty mudrā—touch the two middle fingers to the back of the two nameless fingers, the two great fingers are aligned, the two head fingers bent; place the two big fingers on top; the two middle, two nameless and two little fingers form a blue lotus, while the two big fingers are sword shaped. Recite *Oṃ arapacana śāntika svāhā.*

Next, request the chief deity to enter onto the kindling on the hearth: hold one flower cluster with the hands in the flower-holding mudrā, and empower by reciting the chief deity's mantra three times into the mudrā. Invite by placing the flower on top of the kindling.

Next, visualization in the center of the hearth: form Amitābha's meditation mudrā and visualize the flower going to the center of the hearth, becoming a jeweled lotus flower bud, and visualize Mañjuśrī on the flower bud.

Next, request the chief deity at the head of the maṇḍala-assembly into the hearth: great hook mudrā and the mantra of the chief deity; recite together with the appropriate phrase, *śāntika,* at the end; then form the four-wisdoms mudrā, summoning three times with the right head finger while adding the four wisdoms mantra: recite *Oṃ arapacana śāntika eihyehi jaḥ uṃ baṃ hoḥ svāhā.*

Next, contemplation: form Amitābha's meditation mudrā, and imagine inviting the chief deity, located in his original place in the maṇḍala, to mysteriously unite with the chief deity in the hearth, becoming one body, not two.

Next declaration, ring the gong.

> "Only desiring that the chief deity descend to this seat
> and compassionately accept this excellent homa offering."

Next, rinse the mouth: sprinkle directly three times, imagine washing the mouth of the chief deity, recite *Oṃ varada vajra dhaṃ.*

Next, declaration, ring the gong.

> "Sincerely presenting perfumed water for washing the mouth
> only requesting that the chief deity accept this homa,
> protect his disciple, and perfect siddhi."

Next, powdered incense: three times, recite *Oṃ arapacana śāntika svāhā.*

Next, contemplation: form Amitābha's meditation mudrā and imagine the incense entering the chief deity's mouth, going to the lotus flower bud of his heart, becoming exellent offerings; limitless, oceanlike clouds of powdered incense flow from his heart, through his body, and out his pores, offered to all buddhas, bodhisattvas, pratyekabuddhas, śrāvakas, and worldly deities.

Next, declaration, ring the gong.

> "I now present the powdered incense offering
> only requesting that the chief deity accept this homa,
> protect his disciple, and perfect siddhi."

Next, ghee, large and small ladles three times each; chant, visualization, and declaration as with the powdered incense, except contemplate "limitless, oceanlike clouds of ghee flowing out," and change declaration to "ghee offering."

Next, sapwood, 108 pieces: take three pieces at a time, put the ends into the ghee, turn the wood over and offer up and chant three times; burn thirty-six times for a total of 108 pieces. Throw the binding string into the middle of the hearth. In the contemplation, "limitless, oceanlike clouds of pieces of wood flow out," change to "pieces of wood for the homa" in the declaration portion.

Next, repeat with appropriate changes for food offerings, three ladles; five cereals, three ladles; flowers, three times; ball incense, three times; and chip incense, three times.

Next, mixed offerings: first, take the chip incense, put it into the flower cup; next, take the ball incense, put it into the same cup; next, take the ball incense cup and put it on top of the chip incense cup; next, take the flower cup and put it into the food offerings cup; next, put the flower cup on top of the ball incense and chip incense cup; next, take the five cereals cup and put it into the food offerings cup and mix thoroughly; next, separate the two cups and divide evenly; next, return each cup to its original place.

Next, ghee, large and small ladles one time each; "limitless, oceanlike clouds of ghee flow out," "excellent offering of ghee."

Next, mudrā and mantra of universal offering, one repetition, adding the appropriate phrase (śāntika) of course; the two head fingers are jewel-shaped.

Next, sapwood: take six pieces together from the bundle of twenty-one, offer together into the hearth; "limitless, oceanlike clouds of pieces of wood flow out," "excellent wood for the homa."

Next, medicinal herbs, seven times: take the cup and place it where the censer had been; the offering done, return the cup to its original place, "limitless, oceanlike clouds of medicinal herbs flow out," "excellent offerings of medicinal herbs."

Next, worship offerings: the appropriate offering is white sesame seed; take the cup and place it where the censer had been; holding the three-pronged vajra, take up the single-pronged vajra and use the Hayagrīva mantra, recite *Oṃ amṛtodbhava hūṃ phaṭ śāntika svāhā* twenty-one times.

Next, offer the mantra of the chief deity 108 times—holding the rosary on the left, count 108 times, recite *Oṃ arapacana śāntika svāhā.*

Next, contemplation: form Amitābha's meditation mudrā and imagine these worship offerings enter the mouth of the chief deity, going to the lotus blossom of his heart, becoming vast numbers of brightly shining cakras; then from each and every one of his pores these brightly shining cakras flow out through the entirety of empty space. Next, the various buddhas and bodhisattvas of the world having received the worship, these brightly shining cakras return, entering one's own and the donor's heads: the evil consequences of greed, hatred, and ignorance are completely erased from our bodies, the calamities and unhappiness caused by evil people and evil destinies are destroyed, vitality and lifespan increase, and peace and tranquillity are attained.

Next, declaration, ring the gong.

> "I now present worship offerings
> only requesting that the chief deity accept this homa,
> protect his disciple, and perfect siddhi."

The offering finished, return the cup to its original location.

Next, recite the universal offering and the three powers, ring the gong.

Next, vows; put down the three-pronged vajra, rub the rosary and when finished make the pledge; ring the gong.

> "Sincerely requesting and only asking that the chief deity
> compassionately accept this excellent homa offering,
> protect his disciple, and perfect siddhi."

Next, take up the three-pronged vajra.

Next, rinse the mouth: sprinkle three times directly, and imagine washing the mouth of the chief deity, recite *Oṃ varada vajra dhaṃ.*

Next, declaration, ring the gong.

> "Sincerely presenting perfumed water for washing the mouth
> only requesting that the chief deity accept this homa,
> protect his disciple, and perfect siddhi."

Next, leave-taking: holding one flower cluster, recite the mantra of the chief deity, to the northeast corner of the altar.

Next, contemplation: form Amitābha's meditation mudrā and imagine this flower arriving at its original position in the maṇḍala, becoming a jeweled lotus flower throne.

Next, leave-taking of the chief deity: form the mudrā and recite the mantra *Oṃ arapacana śāntika gaccha gaccha mūḥ.*

Next, contemplation: form Amitābha's meditation mudrā, and imagine the chief deity returns from the middle of the hearth to his original location in the maṇḍala.

Next, declaration, ring the gong.

> "Only requesting that the chief deity to return to his original seat."

With the above, the third section, the portion for the chief deity, is finished.

4. FOURTH SECTION, PORTION FOR THE VARIOUS DEITIES: THE THIRTY-SEVEN DEITIES.

First, purification: wash the various offerings three times, wash clockwise, recite the kili kili chant.

Next, karma empowerment: empower the various offerings, clockwise and counterclockwise three times each, recite *Oṃ vajra karma khaṃ.*

Next, rinse the mouth and empower: wash clockwise three times, and imagine washing the mouth of the hearth, recite *Oṃ varada vajra dhaṃ.*

Next, empower the hearth: three times, using the three-pronged vajra, and recite the kili kili chant.

Next, pile the kindling, ten pieces: on top of a square of four, set six pieces in order from the left. Next, order the offerings in place.

Next, take a flaming piece of pine and insert it.

Next, take the fan and fan the fire, imagine the syllable *haṃ* on the surface of the fan, it changes becoming a wind cakra, recite *Oṃ bhūḥ jvala hūṃ* three times.

Next, purification: sprinkle the wood in the hearth three times, sprinkle directly, recite the kili kili chant.

Next, empower the kindling on the hearth: using the three-pronged vajra, empower by reciting the kili kili chant three times.

Next, invite the various deities.

First, visualize one's own body: form Amitābha's meditation mudrā, and visualize above the heart-moon cakra the five syllables *vāṃ, hūṃ, trāḥ, hrīḥ, aḥ;* these change, becoming first like a stūpa, then the five wisdoms, a jewel, a lotus, and a karma-sign. These change into the five buddhas: Mahāvairocana, together with Akṣobhya, Ratnasambhava, Amitābha, and Śākya with perfected features; the four pāramitā bodhisattvas, and the sixteen great-, eight worship- and four embracing wisdom-bodhisattvas all surround them.

Next, empower oneself: inner five-pronged vajra mudrā; empower the four locations; and recite *Oṃ vajradhātu vāṃ hūṃ trāḥ hrīḥ aḥ śāntika svāhā.*

Next, invite the various deities onto the kindling in the hearth: invite by offering five flower clusters onto the kindling, reciting *Oṃ kamala śāntika svāhā* three times.

Next, visualize the various deities in the hearth: form Amitābha's meditation mudrā, and visualize these flowers going to the middle of the hearth, becoming unlimited lotus blossom seats, and visualize the various deities on the lotus blossom seats.

Next, invite the various deities from the maṇḍala assembly: form the outer five-pronged vajra mudrā. At the end of the mantra for the various deities, add the appropriate phrase and the beckoning phrase, beckon three times with the right head finger. Next, form the mudrā and recite the mantra of the four wisdoms, recite *Oṃ vajradhātu vāṃ hūṃ trāḥ hrīḥ aḥ śāntika eihyehi jaḥ uṃ baṃ hoḥ svāhā.*

Next, contemplation: form Amitābha's meditation mudrā and imagine inviting the various deities, located in their original places in the maṇḍala, to mysteriously unite with the various deities in the hearth, becoming one body, not two.

Next, declaration, ring the gong.

> "Only desiring that the various deities descend to this seat
> and compassionately accept this excellent homa offering."

Next, rinse the mouth: sprinkle directly three times, imagine washing the mouths of the various deities, recite *Oṃ varada vajra dhaṃ*.

Next, declaration, ring the gong.

> "Sincerely offering perfumed water for washing the mouth
> only requesting that the various deities accept this homa,
> protect their disciple, and perfect siddhi."

Next, powdered incense, three times: recite *Oṃ vajra dhātu vāṃ hūṃ trāḥ hrīḥ aḥ śāntika svāhā*.

Next, contemplation: form Amitābha's meditation mudrā and imagine the incense enters the mouths of the various deities, going to the lotus blossoms of their hearts, becoming vessels with offerings of delicacies; limitless, oceanlike clouds of powdered incense flow from their hearts, through their bodies and out their pores, offered to all the buddhas, bodhisattvas, pratyekabuddhas, śrāvakas, and worldly deities.

Next, declaration, ring the gong.

> "I now present the excellent offering of powdered incense
> only requesting that the various deities accept this homa,
> protect their disciple, and perfect siddhi."

Next, ghee, large and small ladles three times each; chant, visualization and declaration as with the powdered incense, except with the contemplation "limitless, oceanlike clouds of offerings of ghee flow out," change the declaration to "excellent offering of ghee."

Next, sapwood, three pieces, "limitless, oceanlike clouds of pieces of wood flow out," "pieces of wood for the homa."

Next, mixed offerings.

First, Mahāvairocana, three ladles, recite *Oṃ vajradhātu vaṃ śāntika svāhā*.

Next, Akṣobhya, one ladle, recite *Oṃ akṣobhyam hūṃ śāntika svāhā*.

Next, Ratnasambhava, one ladle, recite *Oṃ ratnasambhava trāḥ śāntika svāhā*.

Next, Amitābha, one ladle, recite *Oṃ lokeśvararāja hrīḥ śāntika svāhā*.

Next, Śākya, one ladle, recite *Oṃ amoghasiddhe aḥ śāntika svāhā*.

Next, the thirty-two deities, three ladles, recite the universal offering mantra.

Next, the deity who extinguishes evil destinies, three ladles, recite *namaḥ samanta buddhānāṃ dhvaṃsanaṃ abhud dhāraṇī sattva dhātuṃ śāntika svāhā*.

Next, for the chief deity of the temple, three ladles, add the appropriate phrase to the recitation.

Next, for the Great Teacher Kūkai, one ladle, same as above.

Next, for the clear light mantra which when practiced extinguishes sins, one repetition, same as above.

Offering to the sacred spirits of the site, three ladles, same as above.

Next, retinue of this group: recite the universal offering mantra, and at the end offer all of the remaining mixed offerings.

Next, declaration, ring the gong.

> "I respectfully offer these excellent mixed offerings
> only desiring that the various deities accept this homa,
> protect their disciple, and perfect siddhi."

Next, ghee, large and small ladles one time each, "limitless, oceanlike clouds of ghee flow out," "excellent offerings of ghee."

Next, recite the universal offering and the three powers, and ring the gong.

Next, vows, ring the gong.

> "Sincerely requesting and only desiring that the various deities
> compassionately accept this excellent homa offering,
> protect their disciple, and perfect siddhi."

Next, rinse the mouth: three times, sprinkle directly, and imagine washing the mouths of the various deities. Recite *Oṃ varada vajra dhaṃ.*

Next, declaration, ring the gong.

> "Sincerely offering perfumed water for rinsing the mouth
> only requesting that the various deities accept this homa,
> protect their disciple, and perfect siddhi."

Next, leave-taking: take five flower clusters and offer to the northeast corner of the altar, recite *Oṃ kamala śāntika svāhā.*

Next, contemplation: form Amitābha's meditation mudrā, and imagine these flowers arrive at their original location in the maṇḍala, becoming jeweled lotus-blossom thrones.

Next, form the outer five-pronged vajra mudrā, and recite the leave-taking mantra together with the mantra of the various deities, recite *Oṃ vajra dhātu vaṃ hūṃ trāḥ hrīḥ aḥ śāntika gaccha gaccha muḥ.*

Next, contemplation: form Amitābha's meditation mudrā, and imagine the various deities returning to their original locations in the maṇḍala from the middle of the hearth.

Next, declaration, ring the gong.

> "Solely requesting that the various deities return to their original seats."

With the above, the fourth section, the portion for the various deities is finished.

5. FIFTH SECTION, PORTION FOR THE WORLDLY DEITIES: ACALA AND THE TWELVE DEVAS.

First, purification: wash the various offerings three times, wash clockwise, recite the kili kili chant.

Next, karma empowerment: empower the various offerings clockwise and counterclockwise three times each, recite *Oṃ vajra karma khaṃ.*

Next, rinse the mouth, and empower: wash clockwise three times, imagine washing the mouth of the hearth, recite *Oṃ varada vajra dhaṃ.*

Next, empower the hearth: three times using the three-pronged vajra, recite the kili kili chant.

Next, pile the kindling: set five pieces in order from the left.

Next, take a flaming piece of pine and insert it.

Next, take the fan and fan the fire; imagine the syllable *haṃ* on the surface of the fan, this changes becoming a wind cakra, recite *Oṃ bhūḥ jvala hūṃ* three times.

Next, purification: sprinkle the wood in the hearth three times, sprinkle directly, recite the kili kili chant.

Next, empower the kindling on the hearth: using the three-pronged vajra, empower by reciting the kili kili chant three times.

Next, invite the worldly devas, using flower clusters: take three clusters, break the stems off by twisting; take one more leaf and wrap around the rest; recite the one-syllable mantra of Acala; and invite the worldly devas onto the kindling on the hearth.

Next, visualize the worldly devas in the hearth: form Amitābha's meditation mudrā, and visualize one's own body as the class of worldly devas; empowering oneself is usually omitted. Visualize these flowers arriving at the center of the hearth, becoming flower thrones for the Vidyārājas and lotus leaf thrones for the devas; above these flower thrones is the syllable *hāṃ* which changes, becoming Acala Vidyārāja complete with four arms; further, above each lotus-leaf throne is the syllable *hūṃ,* which changes, becoming the twelve devas, the seven celestial lights, and the twenty-eight lunar mansions. The dignified bearing and appearance of each and every one is clearly evident.

Next, invite the worldly devas from their assembly in the maṇḍala; at the end of the great hook mudrā and mantra say the appropriate phrase, together with forming and reciting the four embracing wisdoms mudrā and mantra. Recite *namaḥ samanta buddhānāṃ āḥ sarvatrā apratihata tathāgata aṅkuśa bodhicarya paripuraka śāntika eihyehi jaḥ uṃ baṃ hoḥ svāhā.*

Next, contemplation: form Amitābha's meditation mudrā, and imagine inviting the worldly devas, located in their original places in the maṇḍala, to mysteriously unite with the worldly devas in the hearth, forming one body not two.

Next, declaration, ring the gong.

"Only desiring that the worldly devas descend to this seat
and compassionately accept this excellent homa offering."

Next, rinse the mouth: sprinkle directly three times, imagine washing the mouths of the worldly devas, recite *Oṃ varada vajra dhaṃ.*

Next, declaration, ring the gong.

"Sincerely offering perfumed water for washing the mouth
only requesting that the worldly devas accept this homa,
protect their disciple, and perfect siddhi."

Next, powdered incense, three times, recite *namaḥ samanta vajrānāṃ hāṃ śāntika svāhā.*

Next, contemplation: form Amitābha's meditation mudrā, and imagine the incense enters the mouths of the worldly devas, going to the lotus blossoms of their hearts, becoming vessels with offerings of delicacies, limitless, oceanlike clouds of powdered incense flow from their hearts, through their bodies, and out their pores, being offered to all the buddhas, bodhisattvas, pratyekabuddhas, śrāvakas, and worldly deities.

Next, declaration, ring the gong.

"I now present the excellent offering of powdered incense
only requesting that the worldly devas accept this homa,
protect their disciple, and perfect siddhi."

Next, ghee, large and small ladles three times each; chant, visualization, and declaration as with powdered incense, except with the contemplation "limitless, oceanlike clouds of ghee flow out," change the declaration to "excellent offering of ghee."

First, Acala, three pieces with the one-syllable mantra; as above, but alter the contemplation to "limitless, oceanlike clouds of pieces of wood flow out," and so on.

Declare:

"I now present pieces of wood for the homa
only requesting that Acala accept this homa,
protect his disciple, and perfect siddhi."

Next, Agni, three pieces; recite the short Agni chant, the following as above—this is to be done as in the previous Agni section. Repeat declaration, change to Agni.

Next, mixed offerings.

First, Acala, three ladles, recite the compassion chant—with the appropriate phrase added.

Next, Īśāna, one ladle, recite *namaḥ samanta vajradhāṃ īśānāya śāntika svāhā.*

Next, Indra, one ladle, recite *namaḥ samanta vajradhāṃ indrāya śāntika svāhā.*

Next, Agni, three ladles, recite *namaḥ samanta vajradhāṃ agnaye śāntika svāhā.*

Next, Yama, one ladle, recite *namaḥ samanta vajradhāṃ yamāya śāntika svāhā.*

Next, Rākṣasa, one ladle, recite *namaḥ samanta vajradhāṃ nirṛtye śāntika svāhā.*

Next, Varuṇa, one ladle, recite *namaḥ samanta vajradhāṃ varuṇāya śāntika svāhā.*

Next, Vāyu, one ladle, recite *namaḥ samanta vajradhāṃ vāyave śāntika svāhā.*

Next, Vaiśravaṇa, one ladle, recite *namaḥ samanta vajradhāṃ vaiśravaṇāya śāntika svāhā.*

Next, Brahmā, one ladle, recite *namaḥ samanta vajradhāṃ brahmane śāntika svāhā.*

Next, Pṛthivī, one ladle, recite *namaḥ samanta vajradhāṃ pṛthiviye śāntika svāhā.*

Next, Āditya, one ladle, recite *namaḥ samanta vajradhāṃ ādhityāya śāntika svāhā.*

Next, Candra, one ladle, recite *namaḥ samanta vajradhāṃ candrāya śāntika svāhā.*

Next, the seven celestial lights, one ladle, recite *namaḥ samanta vajradhāṃ graheśvarya prāpata jyotirmaya śāntika svāhā.*

Next, the twenty-eight lunar mansions, one ladle, recite *namaḥ samanta vajradhāṃ nakṣatra nirṇādaniye śāntika svāhā.*

Next, for the practitioner or the donor, the four sets of constellations, one ladle each:

1. Birth star: that star of the seven stars that applies to the year of birth,
2. Birth celestial light: that star of the seven celestial lights that applies to the year of birth,
3. Birth lunar mansion: that star of the twenty-eight lunar mansions that applies to the day of birth; and
4. Birth constellation: that star of the twelve constellations that applies to the month of birth.

Next, the retinue of the worldly devas: recite the clear light mantra, at the end offering the entirety of the remaining offerings.

Next, ghee, large and small ladles, one time each: "limitless, oceanlike clouds of ghee flow out," "excellent offering of ghee."

Next, recite the universal offering and the three powers, ring the gong.

Next, vows, ring the gong.

> "Sincerely requesting and only desiring that the worldly devas
> compassionately accept this excellent homa offering,
> protect their disciple, and perfect siddhi.

Next, rinse the mouth: sprinkle directly three times, and imagine washing the mouths of the worldly devas. Recite *Oṃ varada vajra dhaṃ.*

Next, declaration, ring the gong.

> "Sincerely offering perfumed water for rinsing the mouth
> only requesting that the worldly devas accept this homa,
> protect their disciple, and perfect siddhi."

Next, leave-taking: take three flower clusters; break the stems off by twisting; take one more leaf and wrap around the rest; recite the one-syllable mantra of Acala—throw to the northwest corner of the altar.

Next, contemplation: form Amitābha's meditation mudrā, and imagine these flowers arriving at their original location, becoming a flower throne in line with lotus blossom seats.

Next, form Acala's single-pronged vajra mudrā. Next, reciting the mantra, open the wind fingers of the mudrā, extending them out three times, recite *namaḥ samanta vajradhāṃ hāṃ śāntika gaccha gaccha muḥ.*

Next, snap the fingers of the right hand three times, recite *Oṃ vajra mokṣa muḥ.*

Next, contemplation: form Amitābha's meditation mudrā, and imagine the worldly devas returning to their original location in the maṇḍala from the middle of the hearth.

Next, declaration, ring the gong.

> "Solely requesting that the worldly devas return to their original seats."

The above finishes the homa.

—29—

The Purification of the Body

Gavin Flood

The Tantric tradition's most elaborated source for the purification of the body and its ritual identification with the cosmos is the *Jayākhya Saṁhitā*, one of the three most important revealed texts of the Pāñcarātra, the tradition of Tantric Vaiṣṇavism, probably composed between the seventh and tenth centuries C.E. The Pañcarātra Saṁhitās are regarded by the tradition as revelation and are directly parallel to the Śaiva Tantras or Āgamas, though these were not recognized by the Pāñcarātrins. The status of the Saṁhitās within Vaiṣṇavism as a whole is ambiguous, though an early Śrī Vaiṣṇava teacher, Yāmunā, defended their status as revelation.

The chapter translated here, which takes the form of the Lord addressing teachings to the sage Nārada, concerns the purification of the body, or more specifically the purification of the elements (*bhūtaśuddhi*) within the body, as part of the description of a sequence of ritual acts. These rites are part of the practitioner's daily ritual activity (*nitya karma*) in order ultimately to attain liberation (*brahmasamāpatti*). The purification of the body is integral to Tantric ritual and prepares the practitioner to worship the deity; as the famous Tantric adage goes, "only a god can worship a god." The distinctively Tantric nature of the bhūtaśuddhi in the Pāñcarātra can be seen by its absence from worship in the related, orthoprax Vaikhānasa tradition, and its occurrence in the *Jayākhya* may be the earliest in Sanskrit literature. The general ritual sequence of Tantric worship is as follows: first, the purification of the body or bhūtaśuddhi "destroys" the gross or physical body in the imagination; second, a divine body is created through visualization and nyāsa or the imposition of mantras upon the body; third, there is internal or mental worship of the deity (*mānasayāga*); and finally, external worship (*bāhyayāga*) concludes with making offerings into the fire-pit (*kuṇḍa*).

The bhūtaśuddhi itself involves a complex process of visualization in which the practitioner or sādhaka identifies his body with the universe, particularly the five elements of earth, water, fire, air, and space, and visualizes phenomena associated with each of the elements. As in other Tantric systems, the Pāñcarātra hierarchical cosmology is recapitulated in the body. The *Jayākhya* divides the cosmos into the pure creation (*śuddhasarga*) and the material creation (*prādhānikasarga*). Within the pure creation the Lord, referred to as Vāsudeva, Nārāyaṇa, and Viṣṇu, manifests his six qualities of knowledge (*jñāna*), majesty (*aiśvarya*), power (*śakti*), strength (*bala*), energy (*vīrya*), and splendor (*tejas*) in his emanations (*vyūhas*). These emanations, Vāsudeva, Saṃkarṣaṇa, Pradyumna, and Aniruddha (the latter three being referred to in the *Jayākhya* by the names Acyuta, Satya, and Puruṣa), in turn produce further manifestations, the powers (*vibhavas*) and incarnations (*avatāras*), all of which are "contained" within the body (these various manifestations are referred to in verses 97–98).

Apart from the particular Pāñcarātra cosmology, the text also contains reference (at verse 82) to the six paths (*adhvans*). This is a well-known cosmological scheme from the Śaiva traditions and is divided into the three ways of sound (*vācaka*) (comprising varṇa, mantra, and pada) and the three ways of objects or referents (*vācya*) (comprising kalā, tattva, and bhuvana), also known as the ways of time (*kālādhvan*) and space (*deśādhvan*). These "paths" are mapped onto the body in the ritual systems of Śaivism and are simply assumed in the *Jayākhya*, though the text remains true to Pāñcarātra cosmology. The Pāñcarātra absolute is located at the crown of the head (called the dvādaśānta) above the aperture of the absolute (*brahmarandhra*). Space, air, fire, water, and earth are identified with the body from the head to the soles of the feet. During the rite described in our text, the sādhaka visualizes various segments of his body being pervaded by one of the elements: the earth from knees to feet, water from thighs to knees, fire from navel to anus, air from throat to navel, and space from the brahmarandhra to the ears. This pattern is the same for the Śaiva Siddhānta, and texts such as the *Somaśambhupaddhati*, a standard ritual manual, give roughly the same correspondences. In the *Jayākhya*, each element is visualized before the sādhaka, breathed into the body where it pervades its appropriate place, absorbed into its mantra, then into its subtle cause, and breathed out. Thus the element of air is visualized as a yellow square, which is then breathed in with the filling breath (*pūraka*) until it pervades the area from the knees to the feet. While the breath is retained (the kumbaka breath), it is absorbed into its mantra, then into its subtle cause, smell, and breathed out (the recaka breath). The same process occurs with each of the elements, water being absorbed into taste, fire into form, air into touch, and space into sound.

Fundamental to this system, and indeed to all Tantric ritual systems, is the cosmology of Sāṃkhya and the hierarchy of the categories (*tattvas*) in which the subtle elements (*tanmātras*) of sound and so on (here referred to as powers [*śaktis*]), give rise to the gross elements. On a cosmic scale, the gross elements are a manifestation of the subtle, so in ritual intended to return the sādhaka to the source of the cosmos, the process of manifestation is symbolically reversed. This process is accomplished through the repetition of sacred formulas or mantras, each element having its own mantra. Having absorbed each element into its mantra, into its subtle cause and emitted it through the breath, the sādhaka should lead his soul, located in his heart-center, up the subtle channel that runs through the center of the body, out through the aperture of the absolute—a mental act symbolic of liberation. There his soul is identified with the mantra of Viṣṇu, and the text (verse 62), echoing the Vedantic notion, describes this state as being beyond the sun, moon, and stars. He then imagines his body being burned from the feet upward, until it resembles a pile of ashes, which are swept away to the four directions by a flood of water arising from his meditation. Through this process, the gross, physical body is symbolically destroyed in order that a divine body can be created. Verse 72 describes this as the six coverings (*ṣaḍkośika*) being burned like grass. These "coverings" or "sheaths"—energy (*śakti*), magical illusion (*māyā*), "setting in motion" (*prasūti*), matter (*prakṛti*), the cosmic egg (*brahmāṇḍa*), and "the body of the soul" (*jīvadeha*)—surround both the purity of the soul and vast levels or regions of the hierarchical cosmos. These regions are described in chapter 6 of the *Lakṣmī Tantra* and correspond to the six sheaths of the Upaniṣads (the *annamayakośa* and so on). As in the Upaniṣads (e.g. *Chāndogya Upaniṣad* 8.1.3), the universe is here contained within the body. The sādhaka's divine body is made of light from the energy of mantra and contains the Pāñcarātra hierarchy of deities, which are emanations of Nārāyaṇa. This construction of the mantra body or body of light is identified with the subtle body, called the "city of eight" (*puryaṣṭaka*) (verse 94) because it comprises the five subtle elements along with the intellect (*buddhi*), ego (*ahaṃkāra*), and the mind (*manas*) of Sāṃkhya cosmology. As the subtle elements give rise to the gross elements, so the gross or physical body can be seen as an emanation of the subtle.

With the destruction of the physical body, the sādhaka then draws his soul, referred to in the text (verse 95) as an "image" (*bimba*), back down through the central channel (*suṣumṇā*) to the heart within the "new" body. He is then ready to perform the next stage of the rite described in the following chapter—the inner worship (*antarayāga*) or mental worship (*mānasayāga*), in which offerings are made to Nārāyaṇa in the imagination. Although the Pāñcarātra is a theistic tradition in which the Lord is the transcendent creator of the cosmos and the inner controller (*antaryāmin*) located in the heart of all beings, the present text presents a picture of the self as being both identical with him and distinct. Although the text does not use the term, this is a typical "difference-in-identity" (*bhedābheda*) kind of theology that resists any absolute distinction between the self and the Lord. Indeed, the self and Lord are identified in verse 70, though elsewhere there is a clear distinction: the Lord, for example, has the six qualities (listed above) in contrast to the devotee, whose body is bereft of these qualities (verse 15). Yet in spite of the ritual identification of self and Lord, many passages retain a sense of the Lord's distinction. Echoing the *Bhagavad Gītā* (18.65), where Kṛṣṇa tells Arjuna that "you are dear to me" (*priyo 'si me*), Bhagavān in this chapter of the *Jayākhya* (100b–101a) tells Nārada the same. Indeed, our source refers to a "mystical" text that is probably the *Gītā*.

Mantras are one of the key concerns of the *Jayākhya*, and the chapter on the purification of the body contains some details of their formation. The text assumes the general Tantric understanding and classification of mantras as comprising the seed (*bīja*) and the body (*piṇḍa*) of the mantra, and that mantras correspond to different levels of the Pāñcarātra cosmos. The "complete" (*niṣkala*) or "root" mantra (*mūla*) mantra is given to the sādhaka by the guru, here the famous six-syllabled Vaiṣṇava mantra, *Oṃ viṣṇave namaḥ*. Each of the elements purified in the rite has its own mantra, comprising the seeds and the name of the element in the dative case, and the text describes their formation (17b–19), with different syllables named as deities. Thus the syllable *śa* is called Śaṅkara, *ṣa* is called Agni, and so on, and these are combined to form the bījas of the mantra.

Accompanying the repetition of mantras is the practice of visualization. The verbs used in the *Jayākhya* for this process of ritual meditation or visualization are from the roots *smṛ* (to remember, recall), *dhyai* (to meditate), *bhū* (to exist, to come into being), and *cint* (to think), generally used in the third person optative case. I have generally rendered these terms as "visualize" because of the visual or imaginative practice referred to, though unlike the English word they do not have the implication of unreality in the ritual context. I have left the terms *mantra*, "sound formula," and *maṇḍala*, "ritual diagram" or "circle," untranslated, along with proper names.

This translation of chapter 10 of the *Jayākhya Saṁhitā* is taken from the printed edition of the text, although I have referred to two manuscript transcripts. For verse 95b I have followed the manuscript transcript R2195 and read *svamantra* rather than *svatantra*. The edition used is Embar Krishnamacharya, ed., *Jayākhyasaṁhitā*, Gaekwad's Oriental Series no. 54 (Baroda: Oriental Institute, 1931). The two manuscript transcripts are numbers R2195 and 2182 in the transcript library of the Centre d'Indologie, Pondicherry. I should like to acknowledge discussions that have greatly helped my understanding of the text, with the Śaivasiddhānta Tattvajñā, R. Subramanian, and Dr. T. Ganesan, both at the Centre d'Indologie, Pondicherry, and Dr. David Smith of Lancaster University.

Further Reading

Recommended sources and translations for Śaiva Siddhānta and Pāñcarātra ritual are Hélène Brunner-Lachaux, *Somaśambhupaddhati: Le rituel quotidien dans la tradition sivaite de l'Inde du Sud selon Somaśambhu*, vol. 1 (Pondichery: Institut Française d'Indologie, 1963); Richard Davis, *Ritual in an Oscillating Universe: Worshiping Śiva in Medieval India* (Princeton: Princeton University Press, 1991); Gavin Flood, "Ritual, Cosmos and the Divine Body in the *Jayākhya Saṁhitā*," in *Wiener Zeitschrift für die Kunde Sudasiens*, supplement (1992), pp. 167–77; Sanjukta Gupta, *The Lakṣmī Tantra* (Leiden: E. J. Brill, 1972); Gupta, "Yoga and Antaryāga in Pāñcarātra" in Teun Goudriaan, ed., *Ritual and Speculation in Early Tantrism: Studies in Honour of André Padoux* (Albany: State University of New York Press, 1992), pp. 175–208; and Otto Schrader, *Introduction to the Pāñcarātra and the*

Ahirbudhnya Saṁhitā (Madras: Adyar Library, 1916, 1973). For Pāñcarātra theology, see also M. Matsubara, *Pañcarātra Saṁhitās and Early Vaiṣṇava Theology* (Delhi: Motilal Banarsidass, 1994).

The Realization of Concentration

The Lord spoke:

1–2. O Nārada, placing a blade of panic grass, a flower, a leaf, or sesamum in the tuft of hair on his head, [reciting] the weapon mantra with holy water, and holding a pot filled with water, [the practitioner] should go to a lonely, unfrequented, but charming and clean place.

3. He should meditate upon the mantra situated in the middle of his heart, whose body is the fire of awakening, and not gazing into the distance, he should silently restrain the breath.

4–5a. When he reaches that place, he should emit his own mantra through the nose; then having fixed the weapon mantra outside of himself, he should strike the earth with his foot. He should meditate with mantra upon the complete (*sakala*) Viṣṇu seated upon Garuḍa.

5b–6a. Sitting in a special place, he should assume an agreeable posture on sacred grass, on a hide, or on a cloth over a wooden plank for the purpose of worship.

6b–7. O Brahman, praising the Lord with a devout mind and receiving a mental command from the lineage of teachers, with his head bowed to them, he should perform all action mentally, as has been established.

8. After consecrating the seat with holy water muttered over with the root mantra, [the practitioner] should offer the mantra again for its purification, snapping his fingers.

9. Hear this, O Nārada. He should then perform the purification of the hands, on both palms, on the backs of the hands and on all the fingers.

10. Purifying them with the weapon mantra, he should practice mantra repetition and meditation. Then, after purifying his hands, he should purify the place.

11–12. Meditating on the god whose form is flames, whose splendor is like a thousand suns, covered with millions of flames, vomiting flames from his mouth, [the practitioner] should fill the entire universe up to the World of Brahmā with that [visualization].

13. He should flood the directions, making them blaze with the splendor of

his mantra, and meditate upon the entire circle of the earth baked, like a clay pot, by the fire of his mantra, O Best of the Twice-Born.

14. This purification of the place of worship occurs due to the outpouring of the waves of nectar. Now hear, O Sage, about the purification of the elements [in the body] in exact order.

15. Know that the body, like Indra's net, comprises the five elements of earth, water, fire, air, and space, but is bereft of the six qualities of knowledge and so on.

16–17a. It is impure, without autonomy, arising from blood and semen, decaying. For as long as it is not purified correctly and continuously with concentration, it will be unfit for things such as mantra, imposition (*nyāsa*), and so on.

17b–19. [The practitioner] should join the five letters "Śaṅkara" [*śa*], "Agni" [*ṣa*], "Soma" [*sa*], "Sūrya" [*ha*], and "Antaka" [*kṣa*] in sequence together with "Dhareśa" [*la*], "Varāha" [*va*], "Anala" [*ra*], "Kambu" [*ya*], and "Pradhāna" [*ma*]. He should then use all these along with the primal deity possessing lordship of the three worlds, at the crown [the anusvāra, that is, the nasalized phoneme *ṃ*], O Twice-Born.

20. In sequence these are the seed syllables of earth, water, fire, air, and space. The syllables *huṃ* and *phaṭ* should be placed at the end of the names of the earth and so on, O Nārada.

21. [The practitioner] should utter [the mantras] three times for the purification of the elements, each preceded by the syllable *Oṃ*. They are established in sequence according to the superiority of the five Lords of the elements [that is, *Oṃ ślāṃ pṛthivyai huṃ phaṭ*; *Oṃ ṣvāṃ adbhyaḥ huṃ phaṭ*; *Oṃ srāṃ tejase huṃ phaṭ*; *Oṃ hyāṃ vāyave huṃ phaṭ*; *Oṃ kṣmāṃ ākāśāya huṃ phaṭ*].

22. The five [deities] Aniruddha, and so on, and Satya [are the Lords of the elements and] have been previously referred to. [The practitioner] should utter [their mantras] in sequence, accompanied by their powers.

THE PURIFICATION OF THE EARTH ELEMENT

23. Expelling the Lord through the right nostril, he is placed in the middle of a circular maṇḍala that has the appearance of a thousand suns and resembles the color of molten gold.

24. Then [the practitioner] should meditate upon his mantra-self seated in the highest place, twelve fingers above [at the crown of the head].

25. Below that circle of light, the lords of the cosmic principles (*tattvas*) are

added, and below them he should meditate upon the complete mantra-body in due sequence.

26–27a. [The practitioner] should then visualize a quadrangular, yellow earth, marked with the sign of thunder, connected with the five sounds and so on [that is, sound, touch, form, taste, and smell], filled with trees and mountains, and adorned with oceans, islands, good rivers, and walled towns.

27b–29. With an inhaled breath, he should visualize [that earth] entering his own body from outside, and uttering the mantra [*Oṃ ślāṃ pṛthivyai huṃ phaṭ*], he should imagine it as tranquilized, pervading in due order from the knees to the soles of the feet, by means of the retained breath. Then, O Twice-Born, [he should visualize the earth] gradually dissolved in its mantra-form, and this mantra-king dissolved in the energy of smell.

30a. After that he should emit the energy of smell with the exhaled breath.

THE PURIFICATION OF THE WATER ELEMENT

30b–31. Water is the power in the great substratum called water, comprising oceans, rivers, streams, and the six essences of herbs, and whatever water creatures there are, creatures in the other world.

32–34a. It has the same form as a half moon and is adorned with the sign of the lotus. After visualizing that aquatic power outside of himself, [the practitioner] fills his body with it by means of the inhaled breath, very gently, from the top of the thighs to the knees. O Twice-Born, he should meditate on his body as its own, complete maṇḍala, pervaded by the inhaled breath.

34b–35. After meditating on that water mantra [*Oṃ ṣvāṃ adbhyaḥ huṃ phaṭ*] called the substratum in the center of that [maṇḍala/body], the entire aquatic power dissolves in that [mantra]. Then that [mantra dissolves] in the energy of taste, [which in turn dissolves] in the maṇḍala of fire.

THE PURIFICATION OF THE FIRE ELEMENT

36–37a. With the exhaling breath, he should emit the effulgent power whose form is a triangular world, adorned with brilliance, containing lightning, the moon, the field of stars, gems, jewels, and minerals.

37b–39. It contains beings with self-luminous bodies and sky-goers without bodies, and svastikas and lights are established [within it]. Tiger of sages, once he has penetrated that great power he should then visualize the effulgent subtle element established within the maṇḍala. As before, uttering [the mantra *Oṃ srāṃ tejase huṃ phaṭ*] he should visualize [the fire element] entering him by that same method.

40. Holding it [in the mind] and making it pervade from the navel to the anus, he should meditate upon that total, effulgent power, O Brahman.

41. That [element] is pacified in the body of the mantra, and the mantra, whose nature is fire, dissolves in the energy of form, which is made of consciousness.

THE PURIFICATION OF THE WIND ELEMENT

42. The mantra-body itself is dissolved by its own energy. Exhaling, [the practitioner] emits the energy into the substratum of wind.

43–44a. He should then visualize that airy power outside of himself, accompanied by effulgent forms like a red stone, filled with many different smells and qualities.

44b. He should visualize it in this way with its own mantra [*Oṃ hyāṃ vāyave huṃ phaṭ*] called the Dharaṇa.

45. Having thus meditated upon this essence and uttered the mantra, he should destroy it, very softly through the nostril by the method previously described.

46–47. He should meditate upon [the wind element] pervading from throat to navel. Then, by the method previously described, he visualizes the wind power dissolved in its ruler, and, O Sage, that into the great energy called touch. That energy is indestructible.

THE PURIFICATION OF THE SPACE ELEMENT

48. He should project into the maṇḍala of space in the great substratum called sound, this energy itself, endowed with power, eternal and invisible, [by which he is] pervaded.

49–51. Then, O Twice-Born, he should visualize that total power called space outside this body. It is filled with various sounds, formless like collyrium, and filled with innumerable perfected beings who are without bodies and made of sound. He should meditate upon the support mantra called space [*Oṃ kṣmāṃ ākāśāya huṃ phaṭ*] in the middle of that. Always supporting itself by its own potency, the mantra of sound is formless and pervades the powers (*vibhavas*).

52. Establishing [the visualization] accurately with the imagination, and having infused [the power of space] into his body in the aforementioned way, [the practitioner] should become pervaded by it.

53. Space [pervades] from the ears to the orifice of the absolute. With that power, fixed by the inhaled breath, the yogin [restrains] time.

54. Afterwards, O Sage, he should meditate upon [space] transformed into its

own mantra. The support mantra called space is then dissolved in the power of sound.

55. He should experience that indestructible energy going forth through the orifice of the absolute, joining with the four energies of smell and so on.

56. He should keep in mind the untainted, complete mantra [*Oṃ viṣṇave namaḥ*] that is beyond space, and beyond the energies of truth and so on.

57. Know that sixfold, partless [mantra] previously mentioned. In stages, by means of mantra, he should bring each elemental power to its home.

THE STATE OF LIBERATION

58. Individualized consciousness, like a quivering star, is next to be meditated upon as at peace, departed from the cage of the elements [that is, the body].

59–60. Through the gradual process [just described], within his body comprising the five energies [of the elements], and within the supreme mantra devoid of extension, [the practitioner] sees his own self in the space of the heart by means of the self, like a mountain resplendent as the sun. This [self] is the Lord, supreme, pervading, and covered with vibrating light.

61–62. Then, established in the body of the mantra, he should practice the supreme concentration (*samādhi*). The supreme mantra body is manifested in the succession of letters. By means of the energies, the bounds of the sky, the sun, and so on are transcended, and having cognized that transcendence, [the practitioner] is established in that condition.

63. From worshiping the essence of mantra [the practitioner] becomes dissatisfied with worldly affairs and holding to the rope of knowledge, [he perceives] the truth of the self in the six syllables [of the mantra *Oṃ viṣṇave namaḥ*].

64–65. He should visualize his own self, by his own self, arising from the cave of the heart. That flame from the fire of mantra arises through the path of the subtle channel from the brilliant [heart]. [That channel] is the suṣumṇā, resembling the stalk of a lotus. Visualizing it going to the aperture of the absolute [at the crown of the head, he knows] this to be a good path, O Nārada.

66. Having emitted his own self, very gently, by the wind of consciousness, [the practitioner] should fix the particular sixfold mantra [*Oṃ viṣṇave namaḥ*] there.

67. Lord, may he attain this [supreme state] that arises from the supreme body. This is the unparalleled mass of splendor [previously] proclaimed, O tiger among the twice-born.

68a. [The self/Lord who] stands in the center of the circle of light is delighted by the joy of his own joy.

68b–69. The truth of the self is established in the [various] states of being, O Nārada. His nature is consciousness, alone, freed from the body, the real. The great joy that arises, that is the supreme power of Viṣṇu (Śaktivaiṣṇavī).

70–71a. Having made [himself] indistinguishable from him [the Lord], the soul is the agent of undiminished action. Wherever she [Śaktivaiṣṇavī] arises, there she yet remains. Know that, Nārada, to be the ineffable, the freedom from ideation.

BURNING THE BODY

71b–72. So, sitting down in his own place, having abandoned the elemental body, established there he should burn the body with the exception of the subtle elements of power. Then, the six worthless coverings of the self have the form of burned grass.

73–74a. With the fire arising from the birth of the mantra and due to his intention, [the practitioner] should fix the support of the entire universe, which is endowed with the four refuges [energy, knowledge, strength, and lordship], above the body in the space established above the Lords of the world.

74b–75. Starting with the seed syllable [the praṇava] and ending with the name expressing the fire of desire itself, [the practitioner] should visualize the body, blazing from the feet. After that, O Twice-Born, the fire is calmed and [the body] resembles a pile of ashes.

76–77. Meditating upon his reduction to ashes, [he should use the mantra] *tyaṃ* preceded by the syllable *Oṃ* and ending with *namaḥ*. Then he floods the ashes to the directions with the water, sprinkled with his own mantra, arising from his meditation and having the appearance of milk.

THE CREATION OF A RADIANT BODY

78–79a. He should meditate upon the universe, moving and unmoving, which has the appearance of a milky ocean, with [the mantra] *svaṃ*, with the lamp [mantra] as the second [term], understood as before.

79b–80a. The nectar of the twice-born, continuously meditated upon, is made to fall as a mass of streams from its elevated position, flowing out from the fourth state.

80b–81a. Having placed the energy of Viṣṇu there in the middle [of the ocean], which is his support [that is, Viṣṇu's throne] and is the seed of everything, he should visualize a lotus arising from it.

81b–82. [The practitioner] should visualize [himself as] Lord Nārāyaṇa in the middle of that [lotus], as the essence of mantra, the essence of the truth of the six paths, white, brilliant, beautiful, surrounded by a triadic maṇḍala [with three rings], and shining with vibrant rays.

83. O Twice-Born, he should meditate upon the complete, solitary, pure body of the five true mantras, bursting with the energies of the mantras.

84. He should visualize the five elements of space and so on, the Lord's fivefold mantra, and the power of space [and the other elements] flowing from that.

85. He should visualize this body born from the union [of the elements], from the cage of the powers, having the appearance of a thousand suns and a hundred brilliant moons.

86. In this way he has produced a body that is supreme in liberation and enjoyment, having the appearance of pure crystal, bereft of old age and death.

87–88a. O Tiger among Sages, having thus been [re]born by means of energy from that waveless place, [the practitioner] has gradually achieved the innate fulfillment of all living beings.

88b–90a. He should then rest in his own joy, from the great joy that is yet his own joy. His own form is from the solar, celestial circle. [This body] shines like millions of suns, glimmers with its own radiance, its form is like the colored balls of the kadamba tree and it is pure like the pollen of the blue niśāmbu flower.

90b–92. Having brought his self from its own place, by means of the self, O Twice-Born, let [the practitioner] enter his own mantra-body through the aperture of the absolute as before. [He thus goes] to the inner lotus of the subtle body by the path of the moonlight-channel. Then meditating on his own speech, which is the support of all the worlds, the complete word [the entire mantra] creates total satisfaction.

93–94. [The practitioner] should mark on himself the "deathless" mantra ending with *namaḥ*. This mantra to be known is the "savior," and it denotes the self. Then the whole mantra is the lustrous body, and [the practitioner] has attained a body of light [which comprises] the five [subtle elements] and the ego [that is, the subtle body].

95. He should sprinkle his body with the flood of nectar from his own mantra. Then pulling down the image [of his soul through the suṣumṇā], he fixes his own mantra in his heart.

96. The circle of light that is one's own shining form [created] from one's own bliss, is the supreme, waveless energy, comprising great bliss.

97–98. The path of the central channel is the complete body of the mantra (*piṇḍamantra*). [The practitioner] should visualize the energies, the group of mantras, the five Lords of Protection, and the assemblage of powers (*vibhavas*), as [within] the body. [He should visualize] that blazing totality as different yet nondifferent [from himself].

99. O Nārada, this complete, elemental purity arises due to three kinds of cause: gross, subtle, and supreme.

100. You are a devotee, unwearied, of firm intellect, and your soul is developed. You are dear to me, as declared by the mystic [text].

101. As you are in me, O Brahman, so he [the Lord] will be in you. This should not be made visible to another who is inferior.

102. This supreme, meritorious concentration gives the purification of the elements. Whosoever practices only this goes to the eternal abode.

103. What more is there, O Brahman? Having praised the one with consciousness joined to the [Lord's] body, [the practitioner] with a calm, cultivated soul should worship God.

Here ends the tenth chapter of the *Jayākhyasaṁhitā* of the Pāñcarātra, called the realization of concentration.

Yoga and Meditation

—30—

A Tantric Meditation on Emptiness

Donald S. Lopez, Jr.

From the origins of Tantric Buddhism in India, origins that remain in many ways mysterious, questions have been raised about the relation of Tantra to the pre-existing traditions of Buddhist thought and practice. These questions have been faced by scholars and practitioners throughout the Buddhist world over the course of centuries, and continue to intrigue modern scholars of Buddhism. One way of posing the questions has been: Does Tantra represent a complete and autonomous system that replaces and surpasses all that has come before, or is Tantra a supplement to be appended to the traditional path?

Such questions were debated at great length in Tibet, and the text translated below represents the views, offered in the form of a meditation manual, of one of the most influential Tibetan participants in the debate over the nature of Tantra. He is Tsong kha pa (1357–1419), whose followers would become the dGe lugs (Gelugpa) sect of Tibetan Buddhism, the largest and most powerful in Tibet. One of the hallmarks of Tsong kha pa's thought was his insistence on the harmony between the exoteric and esoteric teachings of the Buddha or, as Tsong kha pa put it, the compatibility of Sūtra and Tantra.

Tsong kha pa's most famous work, *The Stages of the Path to Enlightenment* (*Byang chub lam rim chen mo*), sets forth the practice of a single individual from the first sense of dissatisfaction with the sufferings of the world to the bodhisattva's insight into the nature of reality. Tsong kha pa describes an evolution: one moves from being a person who seeks only a better rebirth in the next life, to someone who seeks to escape entirely from the cycle of rebirth (the Hīnayāna motivation), to someone who seeks to become a buddha in order to provide the means for all beings in the universe to escape from the cycle of rebirth (the Mahāyāna motivation). Thus, for Tsong kha pa, there is a clear and intentional continuity between the Hīnayāna and Mahāyāna paths.

He finds a similar continuity between the exoteric and esoteric teachings of the Buddha. For Tsong kha pa, Tantra is a form of Mahāyāna Buddhism: like others, he divides the Mahāyāna into two parts, called the perfection vehicle (*pāramitā-*

yāna in Sanskrit, *phar phyin theg pa* in Tibetan) and the secret mantra vehicle (*guhyamantrayāna* in Sanskrit, *gsang sngags theg pa* in Tibetan). Both were taught by the Buddha himself for bodhisattvas, persons who have vowed to achieve buddhahood in order to free all beings in the universe from suffering. The secret mantra vehicle (also known as the Tantric vehicle and the Vajra vehicle) was set forth by the Buddha for "bodhisattvas of sharp faculties," that is, particularly intelligent bodhisattvas whose compassion is so great that they are in a great hurry to achieve buddhahood for the sake of others and have the capacity to use extraordinary means to do so. For these rare bodhisattvas, the Buddha revealed a more rapid path to enlightenment.

The next question that faced Tsong kha pa (and other Tantric exegetes) was precisely what it was about Tantra that made it a more rapid path; what were the extraordinary means that the Buddha provided to allow the path to buddhahood to be traversed more quickly than by the exoteric, or Sūtra, path. Tsong kha pa, following the lead of Indian scholars, approached the question in terms of method and wisdom, the two factors deemed essential for the attainment of buddhahood. Method encompasses the various ethical practices of the bodhisattva, practices such as giving gifts, maintaining patience in all circumstances, keeping vows, and developing deep states of concentration. Wisdom was the knowledge of the final nature of reality. If Tantra was superior to Sūtra, that superiority was to be found in one or both of these domains.

Tsong kha pa argued that there could be no wisdom more profound than that set forth by the Buddha in the Perfection of Wisdom Sūtras, and explicated by the great master Nāgārjuna. This wisdom was the knowledge of emptiness, the fact that everything in the universe is devoid of an independent or intrinsic nature, that everything in the universe, from physical forms to the omniscient consciousness of the Buddha, is contingent, depending for its existence on its causes, on its parts, or on a designating consciousness. Nothing exists in and of itself, nothing is able to stand alone. To believe that anything, whether it be a person, a material object, or an idea, exists autonomously, without depending on anything else, is ignorance, and this ignorance is the cause of all suffering in the universe. To understand that everything comes into being through other factors, that everything, in Buddhist terms, is "dependently arisen," to understand that everything is devoid of this falsely imagined independence—this is wisdom; and this wisdom is essential to the attainment of liberation from rebirth, whether one follows the Hīnayāna or the Mahāyāna, whether one follows the perfection vehicle or the secret mantra vehicle. Thus, for Tsong kha pa, there is no difference in the profundity of the highest wisdom in Sūtra and Tantra. The superiority of the Tantric vehicle must therefore be found in the domain of method.

Tsong kha pa argued that there was an important difference between the way that method and wisdom were practiced in the Sūtra vehicle. The purpose of wisdom was to create the mind of a buddha, a mind that was in constant and full awareness of the nature of reality, that is, of emptiness. In order to achieve such a state, the bodhisattva was to meditate on emptiness now. There was thus a similarity between the cause (meditation on emptiness) and the effect (realization of emptiness). But the method component of the path lacked such a similarity. Here, the goal was to achieve the magnificent form of a buddha, a body adorned with the major and minor marks of a superman and endowed with all varieties of supernormal powers. The exoteric technique was for the bodhisattva to engage in limitless compassionate deeds. Tsong kha pa thus discerned a disjunction between the cause (compassionate deeds) and the effect (the body of a buddha). He reasoned, therefore, that the Tantric vehicle offered a faster path to buddhahood because it had a special method that did not occur in the Sūtra system. He called this method "deity yoga," and it involved visualizing oneself as a buddha: one imagined oneself as having the magnificent body, speech, and mind of a buddha now. This method was superior to performing compassionate deeds (which Tantric bodhisattvas must also do) because of the similarity of the cause (imagining oneself to be a buddha) to the effect (being a buddha). This method, this deity yoga, was not only a superior method of achieving buddhahood; for Tsong kha pa it was the essential method. It was his position that all bodhisattvas must eventually enter the Tantric path to become buddhas, and that all bodhisattvas who have achieved buddhahood in the past have done so via the Tantric path.

The text translated below provides a striking example of Tsong kha pa's views on what is, and is not, unique to the Tantric path. It is an early example of what would become an important genre of dGe lugs literature, the "instructions on the view" (*lta khrid*), where "the view" is the correct view, that is, the correct understanding of emptiness. In contrast to philosophical texts that set forth elaborate proofs of emptiness, supported by quotations from the Indian masters, works in this genre are meant to serve as meditation manuals, providing specific and practical instructions on how to gain a deep understanding of emptiness. What is particularly interesting and unusual about the text translated here is that it provides such instructions for a Tantric practitioner.

It is a common tenet of Buddhist meditation theory that the ordinary human mind is too weak and distracted to be able to understand reality (in this case, emptiness) with sufficient depth and clarity to destroy the bonds of suffering and rebirth. It is therefore necessary to transform the mind into a suitable instrument for the understanding of reality, and this is achieved by developing a level of concentration superior to that of everyday experience. Buddhist texts provide elaborate descriptions of the levels of concentration that can be attained, and identify one, called "quiescence" (*śamatha* in Sanskrit, *zhi gnas* in Tibetan), as the minimum level of mental strength at which emptiness may be understood in a transformative way. Understanding emptiness at this level of concentration is called "insight" (*vipaśyanā* in Sanskrit, *lhag mthong* in Tibetan). Specific instructions are provided for developing this level of concentration; in the Tibetan tradition, these most commonly involve the sustained visualization of a golden image of the Buddha. But as will be recalled, for Tsong kha pa the superiority of Tantra lies in its extraordinary methods, and so here he offers a different set of instructions for developing quiescence, more complicated than that found in the exoteric instructions, but designed to bring the meditator to the level of quiescence more quickly.

It is also Tsong kha pa's conviction that the emptiness taught in the Sūtras is identical to that taught in the Tantras. Thus, it is not surprising that, after providing Tantric instructions for developing quiescence, he goes on to provide instructions for meditating on emptiness that are in no way Tantric. Whether one is following Sūtra or Tantra, he argued, the reality and the path to its understanding are the same. Tsong kha pa is emphatic here, as he is in all of his writings, that there is only one route to the vision of emptiness, and that route is reasoning. Emptiness is not self-evident. Indeed, to the unenlightened it is counterintuitive, because things appear to be real when in fact they are not. One must therefore seek diligently and dispassionately for the essence, for the self, that one falsely imagines to exist. Tsong kha pa thus provides detailed instructions for searching for the self among the places where is could possibly exist.

The text begins with a statement, in Sanskrit, of homage to the bodhisattva Mañjuśrī. It is appropriate that Tsong kha pa invoke Mañjuśrī here because he is the bodhisattva of wisdom, and the text is devoted to instructions for developing wisdom. But the bodhisattva is also invoked as the special protector of Tsong kha pa, who is said to have often met face-to-face with the bodhisattva. This homage is followed by a series of verses, with the remainder of the text presented as a commentary on those verses. Tsong kha pa declares that the statement, "I will set forth the mode of being just as it is, relying on the varieties of the dependently arisen," summarizes the entire practice. The mode of being is emptiness, but it is a central tenet of Madhyamaka (the Middle Way School of Buddhist philosophy) that emptiness cannot be understood without making skillful use of the various phenomena of the universe, the dependently arisen. Tsong kha pa will present in some detail which of these phenomena are to be utilized, and how one is to gain a vision of the nature of reality. After a cursory statement of standard Tantric preparatory practices (regarding one's guru as a buddha, offering simulacra of the universe to the buddhas and bodhisattvas, and reciting the purificatory mantra of the buddha Vajrasattva)—all designed to accumulate merit and remove obstacles and thus clearing the way for successful meditation—Tsong kha pa instructs the practitioner to meditate on dependent arising in "positive and negative order." Here dependent arising does not refer to the general Madhyamaka tenet of the mutual dependence of the phenomena of the universe, but rather to a specific sequence of dependence or cause and effect. This is the famous twelvefold dependent origination that some early texts identity as the content of the Buddha's enlightenment. In brief, it sets forth the sequence of ignorance, karmic condition, consciousness, name and form, sources, contact, feeling, attachment, grasping, birth, aging, and death. Although this list is widely interpreted, it is often seen as a description of how ignorance leads, over the course of one lifetime to the next, to aging and death—as Tsong kha pa explains. To meditate on these in the positive order is to examine the sequence, seeing how one leads to another. Such understanding induces a sense of revulsion toward saṃsāra. To meditate on the list in the negative order does not mean to go through the list backward but to negate each element. Thus, by stopping ignorance, one stops karmic conditions, by stopping karmic condition, one stops consciousness; and so on. The point is that by destroying ignorance, the first cause in the sequence, the edifice of saṃsāra will collapse.

Tsong kha pa then turns to detailed instructions on how to conduct a meditation retreat designed to result in the achievement of the state of concentration (or samādhi) called quiescence. After finding a place that is physically conducive to practice, the meditator sits down and visualizes himself or herself as the chosen buddha or bodhisattva, in this case the bodhisattva Mañjuśrī. The guru is visualized as a miniature buddha, seated on a lotus at one of three places: the top of the meditator's head, in the throat, or at the heart. With these Tantric visualizations in place, the meditator declares the Mahāyāna motivation to deliver all beings to buddhahood and undertakes the meditative session proper with that motivation.

The cultivation of quiescence takes place over three stages, focused on the body, speech, and mind of the meditator visualized as a buddha. In the first stage, the meditator is a white Mañjuśrī. On the crown of the head sits his or her teacher in the form of a miniature white buddha Vairocana. At the center of Vairocana's heart is a flat moon disk, upon which stands the syllable *Oṃ*. Directly in front of the meditator's eyes (or, if preferable, directly across from the heart) a small moon disk floats in space. Seated upon it is a miniature blue buddha Akṣobhya. Finally, the meditator visualizes a white drop the size of a pea on the ground directly in front of where he or she is seated. With this somewhat complicated visualization in place, the actual meditation begins. The meditator shifts his or her attention in sequence between three points: the blue buddha in front of the eyes, the *Oṃ* at the heart of the buddha seated on top of the head, and the drop on the ground. As mentioned above, the standard Sūtra version of quiescence meditation is much less complex; the meditator simply visualizes a golden buddha in space. Here, the meditator must maintain a clear visualization of himself or herself as the bodhisattva Mañjuśrī while shifting attention among three objects in sequence. Tsong kha pa specifies that the meditator should dwell on each object for between seven and one hundred "maṇis," that is, the length of time it takes to say the famous mantra *Oṃ maṇi padme hūṃ*. The process is then repeated, substituting a yellow buddha Ratnasambhava for the blue Akṣobhya in front. Next, the yellow buddha is replaced by a red Amitābha, a green Amoghasiddhi, and a white Vairocana. In this way, the buddhas of the five lineages are taken as the object of concentration in the space in front of the meditator, with the remainder of the visualization remaining the same. After this, the buddhas of the three lineages are used, followed by one lineage, where the buddha Vajradhara or Vajrasattva is visualized.

Tsong kha pa turns next to the instructions for meditation on the speech of a buddha. Here the meditator visualizes himself or herself as a red Mañjuśrī, with the lama taking the form of the red buddha Amitābha, residing not at the crown of the head but in the throat, the seat of speech. At his heart is the letter *āḥ*, symbolizing the purification of speech. In the space in front, the meditator visualizes not a moon disk with a buddha seated upon it but a moon disk with letters standing upright upon it. These letters are in nineteen groups: the three root mantras *Oṃ*, *āḥ*, and *hūṃ*, the vowels of the Sanskrit alphabet in eight groups, and the consonants of the Sanskrit alphabet in eight groups. The meditator is to focus on each of these eighteen groups in sequence as the third component in the rotation, focusing concentration in turn on the *āḥ* in the center of Amitābha's heart, the drop on the ground (now red in color), and letters or group of letters on the moon floating in space.

In the meditation on the mind of a buddha, the meditator visualizes himself or herself as a blue Mañjuśrī, with the lama in the form of the blue Akṣobhya at his heart, the seat of the mind. In the lama's heart is the blue letter *hūṃ*, representing the purification of the mind. In the space in front, a nine-pointed blue vajra stands upright on a moon disk. The meditator shifts focus among the *hūṃ* at Akṣobhya's heart, the drop on the ground (now blue), and the vajra. The vajra is what Akṣobhya holds in his hand. After focusing on the vajra, the meditator is to substitute what the other four buddhas of the five lineages hold in their hands: a jewel, a lotus, a sword, and a wheel.

Among the more interesting elements in Tsong kha pa's texts are his instructions on how to deal with experiences (*nyams*) that may occur as a result of meditation. This is a technical term that refers to the various apparitions, hallucinations, and visions (both visual and auditory) that may occur in the course of meditation, but that are not signs of authentic success in the practice. They are instead the side effects of concentration on the various energies or "winds" that course through the body. All manner of visions may occur, and it is important not to give them credence or let them distract attention from the meditation. Tsong kha pa does not deny that some of these experience may indeed be veridical; they are not necessarily all hallucinations. He therefore provides techniques for determining whether the various supernatural beings that materialize before the meditator are real or not. If what appears really is a buddha or bodhisattva, one should ask them to bestow magical powers (*siddhis*). If the meditator is simply overwhelmed by a multitude of apparitions, he or she should shift attention to the first of the apparitions to appear, until it disappears. Tsong kha pa also offers some fascinating remedies for dealing with the concentration of energies in the head that result from increased concentration.

Having provided the technique for turning the mind into a suitable instrument for the realization of emptiness, he turns next to instructions intended to bring about such realization. He approaches the topic in terms of the classic categories of the selflessness or lack of self, of persons and phenomena. It should be understood that self in this sense does not mean a soul but rather a quality of independence. In this sense, it can be said that everything in the universe, both persons and other phenomena, is devoid of self. He states at the end of the text that it is essential that one first have some idea of what this self is like before one sets out in search of it. In keeping with Tsong kha pa's dictum that the emptiness taught in the Tantras is identical to that taught in the Sūtras, there is nothing that one might identify as "Tantric" about his instructions for meditation on emptiness. He makes use of the classic Buddhist categories—such as the five aggregates, the six sources, the five elements—and subjects each to analytical scrutiny, breaking each down into its constituent parts, searching for a self, and finding none. This apparently tedious procedure is deemed necessary in order to come to the confident conclusion that the insidious self is not to be found anywhere. This "nonfinding" is the absence of self, or emptiness. He examines both the things of saṃsāra, such as the human body and a clay pot, and the things of nirvāṇa, such as the body, speech, and mind of a buddha, and finds them all to be devoid of self, all to be empty. This is what Tsong kha pa calls the equality of mundane existence and peace.

For reasons of length, the final portion of the text is not translated. Here Tsong kha pa provides a philosophical discussion, replete with quotations from the Madhyamaka masters Nāgārjuna, Āryadeva, and Candrakīrti, of precisely what emptiness means, dwelling at length on the classic Madhyamaka category of the two truths.

Tsong kha pa concludes with a declaration of his conviction that Nāgārjuna offers the authentic path to the knowledge of emptiness, whether one follows the path of Sūtra or Tantra. The text ends with Tsong kha pa's prayer, requesting blessings from the buddhas and bodhisattvas, for himself and for all beings in the universe.

The text, entitled *dBu ma lta ba'i khrid yig*, is translated from *The Collected Works (gsuṅ 'bum) of the Incomparable Lord Tsoṅ-kha-pa bLo-bzaṅ-grags-pa* (*Khams gsum chos kyis* [sic] *rgyal po shar tsong kha pa chen po'i gsung 'bum*), vol. *ba*, 1–24a (New Delhi: Mongolian Lama Guru Deva, 1978). MHTL no. 13943, P. no. 6140, Tohoku no. 5405.

Further Reading

For a general survey of Indian Buddhist Tantra, see David Snellgrove, *Indo-Tibetan Buddhism*, vol. 1 (Boston: Shambhala, 1987). On Tsong kha pa's exposition of emptiness, see Elizabeth Napper, *Dependent Arising and Emptiness* (Boston: Wisdom Publications, 1989). On Tsong kha pa's views of the difference between Sūtra and Tantra, see Jeffrey Hopkins, *Tantra in Tibet* (Ithaca, N. Y.: Snow Lion, 1987. For a discussion of the ancient and modern views on the nature of Tantra, with an analysis of a Tantric meditation, see Donald S. Lopez, Jr., *Elaborations on Emptiness: Use of the Heart Sūtra* (Princeton: Princeton University Press, 1996), pp. 78–140.

Written Instructions on the Madhyamaka View
by Tsong kha pa

Namo Guru Āryamañjuśriye

I will set forth the mode of being just as it is, relying on the varieties of the dependently arisen.

I go for refuge, amass the collections, clear away obstructions, and meditate on dependent arising in positive and negative order. Having the nature of the body, speech, and mind of a buddha and relying on advice on the profound, I—a fortunate practitioner of enlightenment—am absorbed in samādhi, knowing that all phenomena of saṃsāra and nirvāṇa, appearance and emptiness—whatever is dependently arisen—are without intrinsic nature.

Neither body, speech, and mind nor the collected aggregates is established as the self. There is also no self apart from them. Therefore, understand that this is the meaning of selflessness.

The aggregates and the sources, the elements, what arises from the elements, virtue and nonvirtue, appearance and emptiness, saṃsāra and nirvāṇa, all phenomena, whatever is dependently arisen is without intrinsic nature.

Free from production, cessation, and abiding, beyond expression as existent or nonexistent, as is or is not, free from elaboration, indivisible. Whoever understands this profound peace passes beyond sorrow. These are the virtuous vajra words of instruction on the view of the equality of mundane existence and peace.

Homage to the lama and the venerable protector Mañjughoṣa. Here, in order to set forth the instructions on the view of the equality of mundane existence and peace, there are three topics: the preparation, the basic practice, and subsequent identification of emptiness [not translated here]. The statement, "I will set forth the mode of being just as it is, relying on the varieties of the dependently arisen," summarizes everything.

First, the statement of the preparation, "I go for refuge, amass the collections, clear away obstructions." Cultivate guru yoga, which causes blessings to descend, draw maṇḍalas, which brings about the amassing of collections of merit, and meditate on and repeat the hundred-letter mantra, which causes obstructions to be cleared away. Most of this can be learned elsewhere.

Second, the actual practice has two parts, the ordinary and the special. First, "Dependent arising in positive and negative order." Meditate on dependent arising in positive and negative order in order to renounce saṃsāra and in order to understand that ignorance is the root of all faults. Meditate on dependent arising in positive and negative order so that you can understand that, in order to attain liberation and omniscience, you must abandon the view of self, the conception of "I," and realize the meaning of the mode of being.

The first of these is meditation on the positive order. Ignorance is the conception of self, holding that which arises in dependence on the coming together of the five aggregates to be a person and a sentient being. When one is under the power of the conception of self, you conceive yourself, which in fact is selfless, to be self, and you hold the impure to be pure and unhappiness to be happiness. Through being deceived by the four inverted views [seeing the impure as pure, the impermanent as permanent, unhappiness as happiness, and the selfless as self], you think, "This is my companion, my friend, my ally, and my blood relative, this person helped me, this person is on my side." You amass limitless karma produced entirely by desire. Also, you think, "This is my enemy, he is on the other side that does me harm." You amass limitless karma produced entirely by hatred. Similarly, there is the desire that wants nothing but happiness, fame, resources, riches, honor, and marvelous things for yourself and those who clearly believe in you and are on your side. And there is the hatred that wonders whether those who are clearly on the other side will bring nothing but insults, ill repute, poverty, destitution, a short life, many illnesses, bad luck, and masses of problems. Having come under the power of such desire and hatred, the afflictions rise like the current of a river: dissension, quarreling, covetousness, harmful intent, wrong view, killing, taking what is not given, sexual misconduct, senseless speech, harsh speech, divisive speech, and lying, and also jealousy, contentiousness, contempt, and pride. Having amassed limitless collections of sins, there arises a collection of karmic conditions that serves as the cause of experiences impossible to bear, the endless sufferings of the unfortunate realms. This occurs solely in dependence on the conception of self.

In dependence on that karmic condition, consciousness arises. In dependence on consciousness, there is name and form. Name is fourfold: feeling, discrimination, compositional factors, and consciousness. Form is the embryo that grows in stages from the mixing of the father's semen and mother's blood. In dependence on name and form, the sources arise and in dependence on the coming together of three—the sense organ, the consciousness, and the object—contact occurs. In dependence on that, feeling arises, which experiences things as pleasurable, painful, or neutral. In dependence on that, attachment arises: if the feeling is pleasant, there is attachment that desires not to separate from it; if the feeling is painful, there is attachment that desires to get rid of it; if the feeling is neutral, there is desire to remain equanimously. In dependence of that, there arises grasping, which experiences the object directly and appropriates it. In dependence on that, there arises existence, which brings about the experience of the sufferings of the unfortunate realms and of saṃsāra. In dependence on that, there arise the collections of the unfortunate realms and rebirth. In dependence on that, aging and death arise. Aging is the complete maturation of the body. Death is the complete abandonment of the body.

Furthermore, in dependence on the ignorance and karmic condition, and the consciousness from a former life, everything from the name and form through the existence of this life arise; in dependence on that the birth, aging, and death of the subsequent life arise. Furthermore, in dependence on the ignorance, karmic condition, and consciousness of this life, everything from the name and form through the existence of a future life arise. In dependence on that also the birth, aging, and death of a future life arise. Understand all past and future lives in that way. Thus, all sentient beings powerlessly undergo endless sufferings impossible to bear, like the water on the waterwheel of the twelvefold dependent arising.

Second, meditation on dependent arising in the negative order. In that way, all the sufferings of the unfortunate realms and saṃsāra have the nature of the conception of self. Therefore, by abandoning the conception of self, all the sufferings of the unfortunate realms and saṃsāra will be stopped. As long as one has not abandoned the conception of self, all sufferings will rise like the current of a river because the nature of all causes and conditions of all suffering is that conception of self. For example, as long as a great ocean exists, there will be drops of water.

Question: What abandons that conception of self? Answer: It is abandoned by the wisdom that understands selflessness. Question: Can't it be abandoned otherwise, by virtuous deeds? Answer: Even those, because they are branches of the conception of self, cause afflictions in some situations, particularly in cases of desire, hatred, jealousy. There are afflictions that arise in dependence on the qualities of scholarship, such as pride that thinks, "I have become a great scholar by virtue of study and contemplation," and "I am wise." There is jealousy and contention, contempt, and insulting others in every way. Also, some who have attained and abide in the sources of quiescence in an isolated place have good qualities to varying degrees. Because of their experience, they think that they are superior in all ways to other scholars who do not abide in an isolated place. They produce afflictions such as contempt for and jealousy of excellent beings like monks. Furthermore, whatever virtues might be performed—giving, maintaining ethics, cultivating patience, undertaking effort, being absorbed in concentration—serve merely as antidotes to the afflictions. Even though some temporary happy effects arise, it does not bring about the attainment of the final happiness of liberation and omniscience, nor does it abandon all the obstructions, because it lacks the wisdom that understands selflessness. Thus, virtuous deeds other than the wisdom that understands selflessness are not able to abandon the conception of self. As long as you conceive of "I" in dependence on aggregates that are conceived as a self, there is no opportunity to be liberated from the unfortunate realms and the sufferings of saṃsāra. The noble Nāgārjuna said, "As long as the conception of the aggregates exists, the conception of the I exists. When the conception of the I exists, there is action; from that comes birth." And the master Candrakīrti said, "Homage to the compassion for transmigrators who are powerless like a bucket traveling in a well through initially conceiving of a self, 'I,' and creating attachment to things, saying 'This is mine.'"

Therefore, yogins are not attached to body, life, acquisition, honor, poetry, or, in the end, even to food and drink. Like someone trying to put out a fire on his body or head, they make great effort and practice austerities . They rely on a teacher who has the signs of the Mahāyāna, they practice the profound instructions, they understand that the five aggregates lack intrinsic nature, and they put an end to the conception of self. By putting an end to the conception of self, they stop the coming together of karmic conditions. By stopping that, they stop the coming together of consciousness. By stopping that, they stop name and form. By stopping that, they stop the sources. By stopping that, contact; by stopping that, feeling; by stopping that, attachment; by stopping that, grasping; by stopping that, existence; by stopping that, they stop birth. By stopping that, they stop both aging and death. Thus, know that all suffering together with its causes arises from the conception of self and the source of all benefit and happiness is the wisdom that understands selflessness. These set forth the statement, "Meditate on dependent arising in positive and negative order."

The second, the special actual practice, has two parts, setting forth the initial training and setting forth the stages of practice. First, avoid staying in the low part of a house because lethargy increases there and the upper part of the house because excitement increases there. Make the place of meditation in the middle of the house, under a roof, where there is the right amount of heat and cold. Also have the right amount of food and drink. Get rid of all conditions contradictory to the practice of virtue, like bad friends. Make arrangements for all the concordant conditions like food and clothing. You must be able to abide only in the practice of virtue without needing to do anything other than abide in the practice and benefit beings.

The second has two parts: setting forth quiescence and setting forth insight. Regarding the first, it says, "Having the nature of the body, speech, and mind of a buddha and relying on advice on the profound, I—a fortunate practitioner of enlightenment—am absorbed in samādhi." This has two parts: setting forth the entity of quiescence and identifying the subsequent experiences. The first has three parts: cultivating samādhi in dependence on the nature of body, the nature of speech, and the nature of mind. Here, the three preparations for all practices are meditating on your body as the body of the tutelary deity (*yi dam*), meditating on the lama in any of the three places [the crown of the head, throat, or heart], and cultivating love, compassion, and the aspiration to enlightenment; cultivate the aspiration to enlightenment, thinking "I will definitely bring all sentient beings, equal to the limits of space, to the level of complete buddhahood. For that purpose I will practice these profound instructions."

The nature of body has three parts: meditation based on the five lineages, the three lineages, and the single lineage. The first: meditate on yourself as a white Mañjuśrī. On the crown of your head is [your lama in the form of] a white Vairocana. At his heart is a white *Oṃ* on top of a moon. In space in front of the point between your eyebrows, visualize on a moon a blue Akṣobhya a span or just an inch in size. All three have one face and two hands in the posture of equipoise. At the points where the fourth fingers and thumbs touch, they hold [the stems of] blue lotus flowers. On top of the blossoms next to their ears, there is a vajra and bell. They sit with their legs in the vajra posture. They are adorned with silk and precious ornaments. They are peaceful, and smiling, their bodies radiant and beautiful. Meditate on them as appearing but without intrinsic nature, like a reflection in a mirror.

Meditate on a white drop on the ground, on a straight line from the point at the tip of your nose; it is suitable for it to be just the size of a pea or a little bigger. You can draw it or imagine it. Sit with your two legs in the vajra posture and your two hands in equipoise. Place your body, straighten your spine, point your eyes at the tip of your nose, draw in your chin, put the tip of your tongue on your palate, and straighten your shoulders. As for your mind, without conceiving any activities in the three times—past, present, and future—to be good or bad, be in equipoise, shifting the visualization in turn from the deity either between the eyes or at the heart, the *Oṃ* at the heart of the teacher [on the crown of your head], and the drop [below] the tip of the nose. Also, whatever occurs, such as your legs hurting or your eyes burning and watering, do not break the posture. Don't touch anything; there is benefit in remaining just as you are. Although you remain focused in visualization for a long time on only one base of visualization, it is difficult to eliminate thought. Therefore, don't remain on any one base of visualization longer than the time of counting one hundred maṇis. But don't do it for a very short time; be in equipoise on each for just the time of counting seven or ten maṇis.

Next, the others are not different from before. In the place of the blue deity in front, visualize the others individually: a yellow deity, a red deity, a green deity, and a white deity. Do five cycles of visualization. Using these bases of visualization, you stop the conception of subject and object and wish to abide in the samādhi in which the mind is without thought, such that you do not lose focus on the base of visualization. Whatever other conceptions of subject and object are produced, totally eliminate diffusion and abide undistractedly in the state of mind of being without thought.

Second, based on the nature of the three lineages. The others are similar to the above. Meditate, doing cycles of visualization on the white, red, and blue deities, respectively, in front of you. No matter how short [a time] you do each of these cycles of visualization, do not do them less than five days each. Third, cultivate samādhi based on one lineage. Meditate on either Vajrasattva or Vajradhara in front of you; the other parts are like above. Thus, based on the nature of the body, there are nine objects of visualization.

At the time of cultivating samādhi based on those, if the mind still will not remain settled due to excessive excitement, meditate on the lama in your heart instead of on the top of your head. Meditate on the deity in front at a point across from your heart and hold the mind as before. If you meditate too much, the body and mind get too tense and problems will occur such as heart wind, and you will not want to remain in meditation. Therefore, don't lose the physical posture; remain relaxed. Relying on the mental base of visualization, having eliminated totally the diffusion and contraction that occurs from the dispersion and gathering of thought, remain in equipoise in the state of relaxation without distraction within the state of nonconception. Do not move even for a moment.

Put aside all activities of body, speech, and mind temporarily; do not analyze or investigate, have no hopes or doubts. If you have something virtuous to do physically or verbally that is very important, do it at noon or when you have finished eating and drinking. Otherwise at those times, go for refuge, meditate on the unpredictability of death, and on love, compassion, and the aspiration to enlightenment for just a bit. Apart from these [times], only meditate; meditate in the early evening and dawn because your awareness is clear at those times. If you become exhausted doing other things during the day, don't deprive yourself of sleep.

Second, the cultivation of samādhi based on the nature of speech. Meditate on yourself as a red deity and your lama in the form of a red Amitābha at your throat. Imagine a seed syllable in place of the deity in front and imagine a red *āḥ* in place of the *Oṃ* at the lama's heart. Everything else is the same as above. Also, in the space in front on a moon disc are three cycles of visualization of *Oṃ āḥ hūṃ*, eight cycles of visualization in eight sections—[1] *a ā* [2] *i ī* [3] *u ū* [4] *ṛi ṛī* [5] *ḷi ḷī* [6] *e ai* [7] *o au* [8] *aṃ aḥ*—and eight cycles of visualization in eight sections—[1] *ka kha ga gha nga* [2] *ca cha ja jha nya* [3] *ta tha da dha na* [4] *ṭa ṭha ḍa ḍha ṇa* [5] *pa pha ba bha ma* [6] *ya ra la va* [7] *śa ṣa sa ha kṣa* [8] *ya ra la va ḍa ḍa*—making nineteen cycles of visualization. Greatly condensed, there is one cycle of visualization of the three seed syllables and a cycle of visualization each for the vowels and consonants [making] three cycles of visualization. Thus, for all the visualizations, alternate, meditating on the letters in front, not one but in sequence, and alternate as before, remaining on the letter *āḥ* at the lama's heart and the letters.

Whatever experiences occur due to meditation—experiences of bliss, experiences of being empty, experiences of clarity, seeing things, hearing things—don't reject them or accept them, don't be discouraged or pleased; sustain the same samādhi. Act similarly regarding rough experiences, dangerous beasts, and vicious nonhumans that come during waking experience, in dreams, and in visions. Anything unpleasant that they do are experiences. In the same way, innumerable buddhas and bodhisattvas come. Whatever occurs—their teaching the dharma or making prophecies—are experiences. Whatever happens, like offerings made to you by sons and daughters of gods, are experiences. Therefore, sustain samādhi without rejecting or accepting them. If there are reasons and signs that it is not an experience, decide by means of dividing the various types into three categories: if it is your deity, ask for actual achievement (*siddhi*). If it is an experience, sustain what you were doing before. If it is a nonhuman, having analyzed the situation, instruct the kind who will become supportive of your practice and expel the kind that creates obstacles.

Regarding apparitions, if measureless apparitions occurs, take the first apparition that occurs as the base of visualization. Without letting others enter your awareness, remain in equipoise on the first. Then, when the apparition fades, be in equipoise on whatever occurs next. When that fades, take what arises newly as the base of visualization. In that way, sustain it as before as long as there are apparitions.

Whatever physical postures and glances have been explained to you, do not produce them. Without strongly tightening the mind, relax the entire body and the mind and don't lose hold of the essential parts of the posture, the unmistaken glance, and the mindfulness of the undistracted mind. This is most essential. If the body is sick, at midday and when the stomach is empty from not eating food, use whatever exercises that help. Furthermore, because sicknesses of cold, fever, and so forth occur, take the right kind of medicine.

Third, cultivating samādhi in dependence on the nature of the mind. You are the blue deity. At your heart is your lama in the form of a blue Akṣobhya. At his heart on a moon disc is a blue *hūṃ*. On the ground at the point of the tip of your nose is a blue drop. The way that all of them abide, their ornaments, hand implements, and so forth are as before. In the place of the deity between the eyebrows is a blue nine-pointed vajra on a moon disc. Meditate on it as appearing clearly but without intrinsic nature. As before, based on the visualization of the three—the *hūṃ* at the lama's heart, the drop on the ground, and the vajra—be in equipoise.

Whatever you do—getting up, moving about, speaking—do it skillfully and slowly; don't lose hold of undistracted mindfulness. This is extremely important. When you sleep, focus on the visualization of the lama at the heart and sleep without distraction. When you have completed this visualization cycle, in place of the vajra in front, base the visualization on a jewel, lotus, sword, and wheel. The rest is as before. Visualize the symbols: five visualizations based on the hand implements of the five lineages. If a definite certainty of being in quiescence does not arise, meditate on the implements of the five consorts, the four doorkeepers of the maṇḍala, and the thirty-two implements of [the wrathful buddha] Bhairava, respectively. If there is excessive lethargy on those occasions, meditate on the lama at the crown of your head. Visualize the implements in front and the drop and meditate as before.

When the mind has become very clear, the winds will increase upward. When there is a swelling at the Brahmā aperture [at the top of the skull], itching, or your head hurts, tie your belt around your head. Put a container of jewels such as *'gu rtse* on top of your head. Imagine that the Brahmā aperture is blocked with a golden crossed vajra. Put your two legs straight out with your two arms in line with your feet and imagine that on the soles of your two feet there is a white letter *a*. Focus on the visualization of that. If that doesn't help, transform your mind into a blue *hūṃ* on a thousand-petaled white lotus on a base of gold. Emerging from the anus, think that it comes gently to rest. Then, imagine a series of *hūṃs* from your own heart, [going] from your anus in that way and melting into the earlier *hūṃ*. Do that until it helps. Or, rise, imagining yourself as the deity, making vajra fists [index and little finger extended and middle and ring fingers held by thumb] crossed at the heart and crouch with your two heels together touching your thighs, hold your breath, and jump. If nothing comes from that, cover your head with your hand and put your heels together or separately and softly rub and hit your thighs. Furthermore, if you have pain, understand it having compared it with the needs and circumstances of any of the qualities of [the deity] Īśvara.

Second, identifying visions. Any experience that occurs based on the body—the body shaking or bliss—is physical experience. The utterance of Sanskrit language and the unintentional utterance of verses is verbal experience. Regarding the mind, producing the samādhis of happiness, bliss, and the nonconceptual, no matter how auspicious, is to be understood as experience as long as insight is not produced. As signs of conjunction with the earth wind, water wind, fire wind, wind wind, and space wind, there is, respectively, physical heaviness, cold, warmth, lightness, and becoming empty through the vision of having no body. Regarding apparitions, seeing smoke, fireflies, mirages, hooks, drops, the sky free from clouds, rainbows, sun and moon, stars, and golden earth, and so forth, fire, water, the body of the Tathāgata [the Buddha] the six abodes of rebirth, and the billion worlds—whatever apparitions appear are signs of the conjunction of wind and mind. Therefore, know that they are apparitions. Hearing sounds like a bee, poetic Sanskrit verses, heart mantras of the deity, whatever occurs, good or bad, pleasant or unpleasant, know to be experiences that are aural apparitions. By practicing without adopting or discarding, rejecting or accepting such visions, you will produce the samādhi of insight.

Second, the practice of insight has two parts, meditation on the selflessness of the person and meditation on the selflessness of phenomena. Regarding the first, it says, "Neither body, speech, and mind or the collected aggregates is established as the self. There is also no self apart from them. Therefore, understand that this is the meaning of selflessness." This has two parts, meditating on the body, speech, and mind as without self, and meditating on the five aggregates as without self. The first has three parts, meditating on body, speech, and mind as without self. First, adopt the physical posture and gaze as before. Remain like that and meditate, knowing through scripture and reasoning that this body of yours is not established. There are six objects of consciousness, such as form [sounds, odors, tastes, objects of touch, and phenomena]. Form includes the head, legs, arms, chest, intestines, flesh, blood, pus, marrow, the sense organs, winds, channels, warmth, impurities. None of these individually is established as the body. Therefore, the body is not established anywhere apart from them. By analyzing well in that way, you will not find any body anywhere. Eliminating dispersion and agitation by the conception of subject and object, be in equipoise on just that. If the mind becomes dispersed, decide that the body is not established anywhere as before and is not to be found. Be in equipoise on just that. By meditating in that way every day, decide that the body cannot be found and meditate on the fact that the parts of the body are not established when they are divided individually. Thus, regarding the head, the eyes, ears, nose, tongue, mouth, teeth, lips, hair, brain, flesh, blood, bone, pus, tears, mucous, saliva, the upper skull, the lower skull, and the body hairs individually are not the head. Therefore, having analyzed well that the head is not to be found anywhere, place yourself in equipoise on just that as before. Understand it in that way. Similarly, the ear is not established. The ear is not established anywhere in the ten directions; having divided each of the directions into minute parts, it not established anywhere. Understand everything in that way.

Know that the entity of speech is also not established. Second, understand that the speech of the past has ceased, the speech of the future has not been produced, and present speech is not established as "This is it." Speech cannot be found anywhere. Be in equipoise on the state of just that. Third, the mind does not abide from the crown of the head to the soles of the feet and does not exist elsewhere. It also does not exist anywhere between the head and feet. In that case, the mind is not found anywhere. Be in equipoise on the state of just that. Third, thus, because body, speech, and mind are not established anywhere, those three are not self, the self is not other than them and the self is also not established in between. Therefore, be in equipoise in the state that begins with that not finding of the self.

Second, meditation on the five aggregates as selfless. First, regarding the form aggregate, if you analyze individually color, shape, touch, smell, and taste, they are not the self. Similarly, if you analyze them individually in terms of parts—the cardinal directions and particles—they are not established as the entity of form. Be in equipoise in the state of just that. Second, the feeling aggregate: feeling is the experience of pleasure, pain, or neutrality. By analyzing whether they abide outside, inside, or between the body, they are not established as the entity of feeling. Thus, be in equipoise in the state of just that. Third, meditation on the nonestablishment of discrimination. Be in equipoise on the discrimination that discriminate objects individually, as in the case of feeling. Fourth, meditation on the conditioning factors aggregate as not established. Understand that conditioning factors, which have the nature of attachment and aversion, rejection and acceptance, are like feeling, and be in equipoise. Fifth, meditation on the entity of consciousness as not being established. The collections of consciousness that individually apprehend objects such as form do not abide in the top or bottom of the body or outside, inside, or in between; they do not abide in the cardinal directions of the body, or above or below; they do not abide someplace other than those. Therefore, be in equipoise in the state of not finding. Therefore, when the five aggregates are analyzed individually, they are not established anywhere. Therefore, the five aggregates are not the self. The self is also not the five aggregates; a self is not established apart from the five aggregates and the five aggregates also are not intrinsically established. Be in equipoise in the state beginning with the nonobservation of the self anywhere and understand that the self is dependently arisen in the sense of not being intrinsically established. Until you have generated a pure ascertaining consciousness, which decides that the self is dependently arisen, meditate repeatedly on the object of observation.

Second, meditation on the selflessness of phenomena. It says, "The aggregates and the sources, the elements, what arises from the elements, virtue and nonvirtue, appearance and emptiness, saṃsāra and nirvāṇa, all phenomena, whatever is dependently arisen is without intrinsic nature." This has two parts: meditation on the impure phenomena of saṃsāra as selfless and meditation on the pure phenomena of nirvāṇa as selfless. The first has two parts: meditation on objects as without intrinsic nature and meditation on subjects as without intrinsic nature. Regarding the first, meditate on everything, like the five elements, the five things that arise from the elements, the constituents, sources, as without intrinsic nature. First, meditation on the earth element as not intrinsically established. Observe something made of earth. By analyzing its shape, color, feel, and so forth individually, it is not established as earth. Through analyzing it in terms of its cardinal directions and particles, it is also not established as earth. Be in equipoise in the state of earth not existing intrinsically. Understand the same thing about water. Regarding fire, it arises in dependence on tinder, the effort of a person's hands, and so forth. If these are analyzed individually, it does not arise from any of them. Upon analyzing the shape, color, feel, and so forth, they are not fire. Be in equipoise as before. Observe wind. It does not arise from the cardinal directions or above and below. Upon analyzing its shape individually, it is not established, as before. Space does not first come from any direction; it does not then go back again. Because the present entity is not established anywhere, the five elements are not intrinsically established. Be in equipoise in that way.

Meditate on the five things arisen from the elements as not intrinsically established. Observe something like the visible form of a pot. Its shape, color, feel, mouth and neck, belly base, inside and outside are not established as the pot individually. Therefore, be in equipoise as before. In the same way, observe sounds, odors, tastes, and objects of touch individually. Upon analyzing the individual aspects of the cardinal directions, above and below, the three—inside, outside, and in between—the top and bottom, the shape, the color, sound, odor, taste, the feel do not arise from any of these. They are not inherently established. Therefore, be in equipoise in the state of that.

Thus, all conditioned phenomena, such as the aggregates illustrated with the five elements and the five things arisen from the elements, the constituents, and sources are naturally free from elaboration, and unconditioned phenomena, illustrated by space, are naturally free from elaboration. In general, understand that just as the two types of phenomena are free from elaboration, all phenomena are dependently arisen, in that they are without intrinsic nature, free from elaboration, profound, tranquil, not intrinsically established as the entity of anything whatsoever.

Second, meditation on subjects as not intrinsically existent. An eye consciousness arises in dependence on the conjunction of the eye sense organ, a form, and a prior substantial cause, and so forth. Upon analyzing that, the prior substantial cause is not the eye consciousness, the two—the eye sense organ [and] the object (that is, the form)—the color, the shape the feel, the outside, inside and in between, the cardinal directions, above and below, and the middle area: [these] are not the eye consciousness. It does not abide in any of those individually and it does not go to or come from any of those. The eye consciousness does not intrinsically exist. Be in equipoise in the state of that nonfinding. In the same way, the ear consciousness, the nose consciousness, the tongue consciousness, the body consciousness, and the mental consciousness arise respectively in dependence on the conjunction of their respective sense organ and substantial cause; that is, the sound, odor, taste, object of touch, or phenomenon that is its object. However, upon analyzing them individually, they do not intrinsically exist. Therefore, be in equipoise in that understanding, as above. Thus, all phenomena of saṃsāra comprised by objects and subject exist as entities in the analysis of dependent arising; they are not intrinsically established. Understand them to be like illusions, dreams, and mirages.

Second, the meditation on the phenomena of nirvāṇa as not intrinsically existent has three parts: meditation on the body, speech, and mind of a buddha as not intrinsically existent. First, meditation on the appearance of a form body lacks intrinsic existence. Take the body of the Tathāgata as the basis of visualization and consider the limbs of the body like the head and hands, the senses organs like the eyes, the thirty-two major marks like the crown protrusion, the eighty minor marks like copper-colored fingernails, and the hair pores. By analyzing them individually, none of them is established as the body of the Tathāgata. Similarly, it does not arise from the cardinal directions, above, below, the aggregates, constituents, sources, elements, what arises from the elements, the impermanent, the permanent, conditioned phenomena, unconditioned phenomena, the appearing or the empty, saṃsāra or nirvāṇa. Thus, it does not abide in the entity of any of those. It does not go into any of those. Therefore, be in equipoise on it being free from elaboration and without intrinsic nature.

Second, regarding speech, take the three seed syllables [*Oṃ āḥ hūṃ*] as the object of observation. The vowels and consonants are expressed as speech in accordance with thought, as well as the sixty branches of euphonious speech, are without intrinsic nature, like the sound of an echo. Where does sound come from? The throat, tongue, teeth, flesh, bones, bloods, the inside the body, outside the body, in between, above or below? Where is it now? Then, where does it go? Understand through analysis that it does not come from any of those; it does not abide, and it does not go. Be in equipoise.

Third, take any of the hand implements, like the vajra, as the object of observation. By analyzing their outside, inside, and in between, their big parts and small parts, their top and bottom, shape, and color individually, none of those is the vajra, and so forth. They are not naturally established by anything; they are free of all elaborations; they have become like space. Therefore, be in equipoise.

Thus, the body, speech, and mind of the Tathāgata are dependently arisen. They are established as real when they are not analyzed. As entities of meditative equipoise, which are analyzed with reasoning, they are not established as the nature of anything at all; they are free from elaboration, passed beyond being objects of speech or thought; they cannot be illustrated by anything; they are free from all extremes. Understand all phenomena of saṃsāra and nirvāṇa in the same way. The nature of everything is indivisible and of the same nature. Therefore, when you understand that it is beyond adopting and discarding, negation and proof, and all signs of apprehended and apprehender, subject and object, understand that you have attained peace with regard to the profound saṃsāra and nirvāṇa. Meditate until you have understood it in that way.

It is of great importance to search for the person prior to meditating on the selflessness of person; to search for something separate, such as form, prior to meditating on the selflessness of phenomena; to search for the body of the Tathāgata prior to meditating on nirvāṇa as without intrinsic nature; to inquire into each of the objects of observation, to study them and, indeed, on the occasion of observing with insight, to seek with scripture and reasoning to prove, for each of the objects of observation, that reality is dependent arising and the absence of intrinsic nature. Until you have the ascertainment that decides on dependent arising, there is no opportunity to create the experience of insight.

[The section on the identification of emptiness is not translated here.]

This instruction on the view of the equality of mundane existence and peace has been put into letters by dPa' bo rdo rje in accordance with the words of the venerable Mañjughoṣa, adorned slightly with scripture and reasoning of the pure Mādhyamika tradition of the noble Nāgārjuna and his son [Āryadeva] and the glorious Candrakīrti. All the scriptures of the Teacher are included in the two, Sūtra and Tantra. All the topics of Sūtra are included in two stages. All the topics of Tantra are included in two stages. In the system of Nāgārjuna and his son, the two—the ultimate explained from the perspective of the exoteric perfections and the clear light explained from the perspective of the esoteric secret mantra—are asserted to be the same. Therefore, I have faith only in the system of Nāgārjuna and his son and I follow Nāgārjuna and his son in their system of extracting the Buddha's intention from the Sūtras and Tantras as well. These instructions indeed set forth the very pure Mādhyamika view. However, the actual practice contains instructions on the clear light as described in the *Guhyasamāja Tantra*. Therefore, in the section on quiescence, the method of cultivating samādhi based on the five lineages and four consorts is unique to Tantra.

NAMO ŚRĪ GURU MAÑJUGHOṢAYA

I make supplication to the Conqueror Vajradhara, the protector of existence and peace, who does not abide in existence or peace, who, through wisdom, expels the bonds of existence and who, through compassion, casts the love of his own peace far away.

I supplicate the protector Mañjughoṣa, body of wisdom concentrating into one the limitless treasure of wisdom of the conquerors without number, exceeding the number of particles in a billion lands.

I supplicate the feet of dPa' bo rdo rje, all of whose webs of doubt were cleared away in direct perception by Mañjughoṣa himself through the power of great waves of prayers made long ago.

I pray to be able to create faith and devotion effortlessly at all times by merely calling to mind the kind lord, the root of all qualities of virtue and goodness, mundane and supramundane.

I pray to have little desire, to know satisfaction, to abide in peace and discipline, to seek liberation from my heart, to speak honestly, to act conscientiously, to rely on superior companions, to create pure appearances impartially.

I pray to remember that there is no time and that it is not just words to say that death is definite and the time of death indefinite, to turn away completely from attachment to fame and honor, to create a mind free of doubt.

I pray to create compassion effortlessly by knowing all embodied beings as kind mothers, to remember the sufferings of the weary, and turn away from the wish for my happiness alone.

I pray to understand, exactly as it is, the meaning of profound dependent arising free from extremes, the single medicine removing all sickness of extreme views, the intention of the supreme noble Nāgārjuna and his son.

With this virtue as an example, may all the roots of whatever virtue is created by myself and others in the three times become causes only of unsurpassed enlightenment and never fructify even for an instant as causes of what does not agree with supreme enlightenment: profit, fame, retinue, resources, wealth, and honor.

May this pure prayer be realized by the power of the blessings of the conquerors and their excellent children, by the incontrovertible truth of dependent arising, and by my own pure intentions.

This cluster of grain of achievements, a prayer to teachers of the dear lineage of blessings, was written by the glorious bLo bzang grags pa of rGyal khams, who has heard much, at O' de gung rgyal of Lha zhol, the king of snow mountains in the snowy range.

—31—

Japanese Tantra, the Tachikawa-ryū, and Ryōbu Shintō

Bernard Faure

Scholars have often tried to define Buddhism through its theory of causality. The Buddhist conception of karmic retribution, although derived from Brahmanic thought, is usually presented as the most significant advance, not only over Brahmanism but also over such other religious trends as Daoism and Confucianism, which emphasized a system of cosmological connections based on "correlative thinking." In this respect, it is significant that Tantric Buddhism also emphasized cosmological connections rather than linear causality, and seems to have returned to the Vedic conception of man as a microcosm. This macro-microcosmic conception of the universe as emanating from a first principle is a major departure from early Buddhism which, never overly concerned with cosmogony, instead focused on ontogeny; that is, on the series of causes forming the so-called twelve-linked chain—from ignorance to birth and death—leading to the emergence of the individual.

Tantra, an offshoot of the Vedic-Brahmanic and yogic traditions, is first of all a system of correspondences between microcosm and macrocosm, man and the universe. Whereas early Buddhism was defined by its ascetic world rejection and its conception of man as an ultimately otherworldly being, Tantra may be defined as its reintegration of the world into the soteriological path—since man and the world are now fundamentally identical. By reintegrating the world into its practice, Tantra also reintegrated sexuality, one of the world's main driving forces. Consequently, sexuality and fertility came to constitute basic elements of the Tantric worldview. If the return to primordial unity remains the distant horizon of this metaphysical teaching, Tantric practice is by contrast governed by a fundamental duality, usually defined in sexual terms. Thus, Tantra is in a true sense a nondual dualism: whereas the theory emphasizes nondualism, the practice is by and large characterized by dualism.

Tantric Buddhism is therefore not, as some still believe, a degeneration of Buddhism caused by the deleterious influence of popular Indian culture. It is rather a highly philosophical and ritual synthesis, a development of the notion of the Two Truths (that is, ultimate and conventional truths). This feature accounts for the fact that Tantric Buddhism was readily able to integrate another complex cosmological system, the Chinese theory of yin and yang and of the five agents. It is this synthesis, effected during the eighth and ninth centuries in China and Japan, that became the core of Japanese Tantra. Japanese Tantra—or at least its mainstream, redefined as "esoteric Buddhism" (*mikkyō*)—attempted to "purify" itself of the sexual elements that characterized Indian Tantra; that is, to elude sexuality and return to the strictly ascetic conception of early Buddhism. This attempt was not entirely successful, however. In any case, it is important to see that sexuality in Tantra is of an eminently cosmological and ritual nature. The union of the male and female principles is seen as the source of all things, expressed in Tantric mythology as the sexual union of the god or buddha with his female partner, who represents his energy (*śakti*).

By becoming the main discourse of medieval Japanese ideology, Tantric Buddhism contributed to the "Indianization" of Japan. Matters were, of course, more complex, since in the meantime Japan had already integrated the principles of Chinese cosmology. This integration took another step forward with the rise of the Tachikawa-ryū. This branch of Shingon has been traced back to a priest named Ninkan (fl. twelfth century). After being exiled to the town of Tachikawa (in Izu province), Ninkan studied yin-yang cosmology (*onmyōdō*) and incorporated cosmological elements into Shingon doctrine. His teaching soon flourished, and, according to tradition, was systematized by Raiyu (1126–1304). However, the Tachikawa-ryū was eventually declared to be "heretical." The reasons alleged were essentially doctrinal, having to do with the "immoral" elements in the Tachikawa teachings. This led to the interdiction of the Tachikawa-ryū and to the destructions of its scriptures, at the end of the Muromachi period. Nevertheless, Tachikawa ideas, which in some respects were a resurgence of Indian Tantra, continued to influence Buddhist discourse and even provided significant components for the late medieval and early modern worldview.

In India, Tantric Buddhism had already assimilated local Hindu gods into its pantheon. This synthesis was so successful that Buddhism, losing its sharp distinctive features, was eventually reabsorbed into the fold of Hinduism. On the contrary, in Japan, a similar synthesis triggered a reaction and led to the emergence of a distinctly "Japanese" religion named Shintō. This tradition, which emerged in centers like Ise Shrine, finds its origins in a particular brand of Japanese Tantra, the so-called Ryōbu Shintō. This new ideology, according to which Shinto deities were the local manifestations of "original" buddhas, led, for instance, to the identification of the sun goddess Amaterasu with the buddha Vairocana (Dainichi, "Great Sun" in Japanese), and of the two shrines of Ise with the two great maṇḍalas of Shingon (the Womb realm and Vajra realm maṇḍalas). These two maṇḍalas were used in the Tachikawa-ryū as symbols of sexual polarity, the Tachikawa influence being very strong in this Tantric Ise tradition.

This "nondual dualism" is illustrated in such works as the *Ise denki*, or, to give its full (and rather enigmatic) title, the *Ise shōsho Nihongi yūshiki honshō nin denki* (Transmitted Record of the *Nihongi*, of the Consciousness, Fundamental Nature, and Humanity, produced by I-Se). According to its colophon, this work was copied in 1537 at the Myōō-in, a temple near Ise, after being transmitted by the priest Sonkai (1472–1543) to his disciple Ryōkan. The *Ise denki* is divided into ten sections, which treat of various aspects of the esoteric Buddhist tradition with regard to Ise. Here we will present the first three sections, describing the main phases of the cosmic emanation process—which are also, in reverse order, those of the soteriological process. Even so, it will be difficult to provide a simple idea of the text's intricate symbolism, encoded in multple layers of meanings that appear at first blush to be mere repetitions of numerical symbols (sets of polarities, triads, and pentads). On closer examination, the text describes a maṇḍala, that is, in a dynamic form, the cosmogonic or psychogenic process of emanation (and resorption). The following is but a preliminary attempt to decode some of these meanings.

The name Ise is interpreted here in a very idiosyncratic fashion, typical of medieval exegesis. The two graphemes (Sino-Japanese characters) of this compound are used to symbolize the fundamental polarity out of which everything arises. Thus, "I" and "Se" become the Tantric and Shintō equivalents of the Chinese yin and yang. They are also symbols of (and symbolized by) the two great Shingon maṇḍalas. In other Ryōbu Shintō texts, the two principles of yin and yang (and the two maṇḍalas) are associated with the two primordial Shintō deities Izanami and Izanagi, whose lovemaking brought about a Genesis of sorts. This is why, in the following translation, I will read the term as I-Se, to emphasize that it is the cosmological polarity, more than the geographical toponym in the Kii peninsula, that is being referenced.

1. ON THE HARMONIOUS UNION OF HEAVEN AND EARTH OF I-SE

In the so-called harmonious union of Heaven and Earth of I-Se tradition, beings are the flower, earth is the tathāgata Vairocana of the two Womb and Vajra realms; and beings are the fundamentally unborn calyx of the letter *a*. Thus, it is written: "If your own mind is pure, all the buddhas dwell in it; when the mind with a single voice recollects the letter *a*, all the buddhas constantly preach the Law." The letter *a* in question is none other than the two characters I-Se, and it is the origin of man and woman. This is why it is said in the esoteric teaching: "All beings have in their chest a letter *a*, whose sequence is as follows: within the lotus appears the moon disk; and within the moon disk appears the letter *a*, which transforms into five colors: blue, red, yellow, white, and black." Under this letter *a* is a three-pronged vajra, representing the six sense faculties of beings. It is also said that the two buddhas and the four bodhisattvas dwell there, sharing the six kinds of ritual implements. . . . Thus, the one-pronged vajra is the stem of the lotus flower; it is the body of all beings. The five-pronged vajra is the root of the lotus flower; it is the right and left feet of beings. The three-pronged vajra is the petals of the lotus flower; it is the right and left arms of beings.

In I-Se, we find the gate of the letter *a*, the first of the forty-two letters. The five-pronged vajra is the great earth of the Dharma realm; it is called the "Palace of Suchness." The three-pronged vajra is the unborn principle and wisdom inside the mind; it is the retribution earth of the retribution body. The one-pronged vajra is the essence of the principle outside the body; it is the wonderful domain of ultimate reality.

It is also said: "The letter *a* is the bodily karma of the dharma body; the moon disk is the verbal karma of the retribution body; the lotus is the mental karma of the metamorphosis body." These three bodies of the fundamental essence of the three periods are also symbolized as follows: the one-pronged vajra is the bodily karma of dharma body; the three-pronged vajra is the verbal karma of the retribution body; the five-pronged vajra is the mental karma of the metamorphosis body. When above and below unite harmoniously, one speaks of the dharma body of the six great elements. All classes of beings without exception are endowed with this nature. Thus, in the interval of the unconditioned sound, the phoneme *a* arises and the fruits of buddhahood are perfected. If one knows and realizes this letter *a*, even the four serious offences and the five transgressions turn into the merits of the maṇḍala. If one cultivates this letter, the three poisons—ignorance, greed, and hatred—are transmuted into the secret practices of yoga.

The "harmonious union of heaven and earth" is the union of I-Se. "I" is the tathāgata Vairocana of the Womb realm; "Se" the tathāgata Vairocana of the Vajra realm. It is also said: "When one consider the origins of the letter *a*, it is the tathāgata Vairocana of the Womb realm; it is heaven. It is none other than I-Se. With the letter *ba* (*va* in Sanskrit), again: it is the tathāgata Vairocana of the Vajra realm, the earth; it is also I-Se. If one divides the human body into five sections, the top of the head corresponds to the realm of the buddhas; the right arm to that of the bodhisattvas; the left arm to that of the pratyekabuddhas; the right leg to that of the devas; the left leg to that of the śrāvakas. When one thus unites the heaven and earth of I-Se, the letter is on the tip of each of the fingers of the four hands and each of the toes of the four feet. These letters correspond to the bodhisattvas of the forty-two stages. The two highest stages are those of the two buddhas of I-Se, who are are man and woman. The man's stage is always that of a buddha body. Man is ruled by heaven, woman by the earth. This is what is called the union of heaven and earth. The seed-letters born from "I" are red; those born from "Se" are white. . . . This is called the harmonious union of heaven and earth, of the two Womb and Vajra realms.

Because Indian metaphysics takes the Word or Speech (*vāc*) to be the ultimate principle, we need first to explain briefly Indian conceptions regarding language.

Most significant in this respect are the forty-nine or fifty phonemes of the Sanskrit phonetic system, called mātṛkās or "little Mothers" because they are seen as the source of all sounds—hence of all things. Incidentally, these phonemes served as model for the Japanese kana syllabary, attributed to Kūkai (774–835), the founder of Shingon. There is another arrangement of forty-two phonemes, called *a-ra-pa-ca-na* after the sequence of its five first phonemes. It is this arrangement that is mentioned here in association with the forty-two stages of the bodhisattva's career. In both cases, the first of these phonemes is the syllable *a*, which came to take on mystical values, not only as the symbol of all beginnings but also as constitutive of all other syllables; and furthermore, as the marker of the negative (as in English and French, two other Indo-European languages). This phoneme thus came to express the ultimate principle, from which everything emanates. As a vowel, *a* is also the first of the sixteen vowels of the Sanskrit "garland of letters," which includes *ṃ* (the anusvāra or bindu) and *ḥ* (the visarga), two phonemes said to give birth to the series of consonants, from *ka* to *ha*. If this vocalic-consonantal sequence is perceived in cosmogonic terms as symbolizing the emanation process, the reverse sequence indicates the resorption process, which is that taken by the Tantric practitioner who is intent on returning to its source. This is why our text emphasizes the uttering of the single sound: this inarticulate sound is the nāda, the primal manifestation of the absolute, the knowledge of which is tantamount to deliverance. This is the sound that corresponds to the phoneme *ṃ*, the bindu ("dot" or "drop"), marked graphically by a dot above the syllable. This bindu is a "drop" of phonic but also photic, or luminous, energy, that is temporarily collected before again dividing itself to create the multiplicity of consonants and the totality of things. This nasal resonance is said to be born from the union of the god and his śakti, an idea expressed graphically by two bindus, red and white, fusing to form a "mixed bindu." The bindu, in short, is the point of convergence and expansion; it symbolizes, therefore it is, the Absolute; or rather, it represents the point of contact with the source of energy. Hence the importance of mantras, and their magical but also cosmogonic efficacy, uniting sound and breath, and the cosmic and human planes.

To summarize: from the phonetic standpoint, the energy of sound, born from the sexual union of the god and his consort, first creates the sixteen vowels, before concentrating into the bindu, and then disseminating, through the visarga (graphically represented as two bindus) into the consonants. In cosmogonic terms, the initial duality first expands, forming a first level; then concentrates into a drop, which subdivides into three or five elements to form a second level, before further engendering the multiplicity of things. From the standpoint of generic Tantric meditation, this may be visualized as the generation of three maṇḍalas: the practitioner first visualizes the god and his śakti in sexual union. This vision merges into a single point of pure light (the bindu), from which another maṇḍala arises, divided into five colored sectors. At the center is an eight-petaled lotus, which serves as a dais for the god, from whom emerge the four deities of the cardinal directions, who in turn produce the four subordinate deities of the four intermediate directions. The practitioner then visualizes another maṇḍala, the jewel palace, representing the human world, at the center of which the god and his consort are engaged in sexual union, surrounded by lesser deities.

This dynamic may also be expressed in terms of the mantra *Oṃ* (*a-hūṃ*, in Japanese *a-un*). Here again, the emanation process starts with a duality, or rather the union of two principles, and resorbs into unity with the "adornment" of the bindu. For reasons that have little to do with phonetics, the two phonemes and the bindu, *a-u-n*, are replaced in the *Ise denki* by the two ideograms I-Se. The "harmonious union" of these two principles is not only phonetic but also sexual, and indeed the sexual metaphor pervades our text, giving some credibility to the claim that Tachikawa rituals involved sexual intercourse between the priest and his female partner. Whatever the case, the phoneme *a* is said to change into five phases (and five colors), giving rise to a fivefold symbolism that is another leitmotiv of this text. These "five *as*" (called the "five turns" or the "five dots" of the *a*, because they are expressed graphically by dots) are: the short *a*, the long *a* (*ā*), the bindu (*aṃ*), the visarga (*aḥ*), and finally the synthesis of all these: *āḥṃ* (or *āḥ*).

The phoneme *a* is also said to be "the jade gate" of a woman; that is, her vulva, the source of all buddhas and human beings. As we will see, the female womb is assimilated to the ultimate principle, the primordial chaos, before the emergence of the buddhas and of the world. This image is reminiscent of Courbet's famous painting of a woman's vulva, entitled "The Origin of the World." In Japanese Tantra, this letter *a*, as ultimate principle, is also the cosmic buddha Vairocana, represented at the center of the maṇḍala (or cosmic realm) that emanates from him. In Indian Tantra, the deity is often represented in cosmic union with his śakti (or female energy), whereas in Japanese Tantra this element is often downplayed (it is implied, however, in the fact that Vairocana is androgynous). This conception of the deity as a polarized (and sexualized) couple, masculine and feminine, is the central characteristic of Tantra. Here, the reference to the "two buddhas of I-Se" in the context of sexual union is more in line with the Indian conception.

Whereas Indian culture favors orality, Chinese and Japanese cultures emphasize the written letter—as shown by this text. Thus, the grapheme *a* (together with its phoneme) comes to play an important role in the Shingon meditation known as "Aji-kan" (contemplation of the grapheme *a*). In this meditation, the practitioner is told to visualize the clear white disk of the full moon, and in this disk the letter *a* (written in a particular script known as Siddhaṃ) on a lotus. This visualization is a dynamic creation process, the creation of a mental maṇḍala from the central buddha Vairocana, through the four buddhas of the cardinal directions (in the sequence E, S, W, N) and the four bodhisattvas of the ordinal directions (SE, SW, NW, NE), down to the peripheral deities and the multiplicity of sentient beings. Our text merely alludes to the principal phases of this process, as they are visualized—that is, enacted—by the practitioner. But here, instead of the emanation process—from unity to multiplicity—we are dealing with a resorption process in three phases—from multiplicity (symbolized by the lotus and its petals), through oneness (symbolized by the moon disk), to the ultimate principle (the letter *a*). The basic schema—simply alluded to here, but more explicit in Indian sources—remains the same: the energy of the two principles is first resorbed into one point (*bindu*), before evolving into a pentad, from which multiplicity evolves. In the embryological terms of section 3, the drops (red and white) of mother and father unite to form a bindu, which evolves into a formed embryo possessed of five limbs; the subsequent birth of this pentadic being marks the emergence of another level of reality or consciousness: the creation of a new world, the "jeweled palace," which the *Ise denki* calls the "Palace [or Capital] of Suchness."

The phases of emanation are often described as being three or five in number. The three phases are here described in terms of the three most common types of vajras, a ritual instrument used in Shingon ritual. The number of prongs of the vajra (one, three, or five) lends itself to all kinds of symbolism. This is particularly true of the five-pronged vajra, called the "human-shaped vajra" owing to its vague resemblance to the human body. Our texts manipulate these numerical categories ad nauseam, in order to reinforce the equivalence between macrocosm (the universe) and microcosm (the human body). Here, the three types of vajras first correspond to the three parts of the lotus (the stem, the root, and the petals), as well as to the three sections of the human body (the head and torso, the legs, and the arms). They also represent the three types of karmic retribution caused by acts of the mouth, body, and mind. Thus, reaching the level of the letter *a* means returning to the source of everything, the stage before anything whatsoever arises; and it cancels all the evil karma one may have accumulated in the past. Likewise, the three symbols of the lotus, the moon, and the letter *a* correspond to the three bodies of the Buddha, from its most down-to-earth form, the metamorphosis body (*nirmāṇa-kāya*) to the most absolute, the dharma body (*dharma-kāya*)—with both relative and absolute being mediated by the retribution body (*saṃbhoga-kāya*), seen only by beings who have acquired merits through practice.

The text mentions six buddhas; that is, the two buddhas of I-Se and the four buddhas of the cardinal directions. Here, as in Indian Tantra, Vairocana is represented as a divine polarity. These six buddhas, symbolizing the six elements of Shingon Buddhism, are also represented by ritual instruments, namely, two sets of three vajras, symbolizing, respectively, the microcosm (the human body) and macrocosm. These three vajras also represent the three levels of reality, the three maṇḍalas: the five-pronged vajra symbolizes the pentadic human world (the "Palace of Suchness"); the three-pronged vajra the intermediary level of the duality of the two principles; and the one-pronged vajra the ultimate reality. Thus, the sequence from five-pronged to three-pronged to one-pronged vajra represents the cosmic resorption from pentadic reality to duality to unity, as experienced symbolically by the practitioner. Again, the two series of three bodies symbolized by the three symbols (the letter *a*, the moon disk, and the lotus on the one hand; and the three types of vajra on the other) represent the bodies of the buddha

Vairocana and of sentient beings, whose "harmonious fusion" constitutes the "dharma body made of the six elements"—that is, the body of the enlightened being, or of the embryo in the mother's womb.

Recall that the process of emanation begins with the sexual union of the two polar opposites, the male deity and his female śakti (energy) or, in Ryōbu Shintō terms, the "I" and "Se" of Ise (the character *se*, not so incidentally, happens to mean "energy"). This union is presented in Chinese cosmological terms as a union of heaven and earth, of yin and yang. In Tantric terms, the emanation process is first a phonetic one, from the first to the last of the forty-two phonemes of the *a-ra-pa-ca-na* sequence. In the translated passage, the first two letters *a* and *va* (or *vaṃ* with the bindu) symbolize the "two buddhas of I-Se," that is, Vairocana in his two aspects, in the Womb and Vajra realms. The remaining forty letters are associated (and written on) the twenty fingers and toes, realizing a microcosmic/phonetic body, as well as the soteriological path of the bodhisattva's career, with its forty-two stages. These letters are said to be either female or male, arising from the female principle ("I") or the male principle ("Se"). Their respective colors, red and white, refer to the Indian (and Sino-Japanese) belief that the human embryo is formed by the union of the blood of the mother and the semen of the father. The two letters *a* and *va* are also the first of the sequence *a/va/ra/ha/ka*, representing the syllables of the five elements (earth, water, fire, wind, space).

2. ON THE EIGHT-PETALED LOTUS OF I-SE

The "eight-petaled lotus" is the great earth of the dharma realm of the harmonious union of the two Womb and Vajra sections. The above-mentioned "harmonious union" of the two male and female bodies, with their four arms and four feet, is this "eight-petaled lotus." It is the source of all things. Thus, "capital of the suchness of innate awakening" refers to the gate of the letter *a*, the first of the forty-two letters. One also calls this the making of the Tathāgata. The two dharmas of consciousness and body are called "unborn." The Dharma gate of the two truths, conventional and ultimate, means that all things under heaven are the body of the Buddha; everything contains this lotus. You must inquire well into this and realize its truth. Without the ultimate reality of the suchness of ultimate and conventional truths, in which concentration and wisdom are harmoniously united, nothing could come to life. Like the forms of the seeds of the five wheels, the Buddha's mind sustains the sweet and wondrous practices of the Three Secrets. All the actions of sentient beings, without exception, are contained in the sound of the wisdom of ultimate reality. What a pity! Failing to realize this from lack of wisdom we are born in this world, and in the end we die, having forgotten the great merits of innate awakening. It is a shame not to have realized I-Se until now. The resonance of the voice at the moment of birth, all this is the suchness of I-Se. This is why it is said in the scripture: "The actions truly manifested by all beings, the awakening realized by the buddhas, the wondrous and subtle practices: all of these have to be like what the Buddha spoke." It is also said: "He explained that verbal characteristics, words and speech, are all mantras; corporeal characteristics, actions and movements, all are secret seals (*mudrās*); mental characteristics, thoughts, all are secret contemplation." This is why, when sentient beings are born, the eight-petaled lotus of the mind/heart is the great earth of the fundamentally unborn letter *a*. When one is born, one expresses through words the wondrous practice of I-Se; when one dies, too, one returns to the great earth of the suchness of innate awakening. "Fundamentally unborn" means that one must realize the principle, for a long time constantly playing on the terrace of the secret words; "to obtain the wondrous practice of Sha-na" simply means that one must become the mind described in this teaching. The eight petals are the letter *a*, and this letter *a* is the jade gate of woman.

In this second section, the symbolism of the lotus is brought to the forefront. The eight-petaled lotus in question is that found at the center of the Womb realm maṇḍala. It represents the emanation process of the world, but also, in human terms, sexual union—and the Tachikawa-ryū did in fact graphically represent a man and woman making love on a giant lotus as an expression of its ultimate secret. This lotus also represents the mother's womb, the source of all beings, whence the phoneme *a*. It finally expresses, in ontogenic terms, the mind/heart of the embryo, from which various types of consciousness arise. The sexual union is further expressed by various polarities such as consciousness and body, ultimate and conventional truth, or concentration and wisdom—the two main elements of Buddhist practice. One such polarity seems to imply a play on words on the expression *sha-na*, which is an abbreviation for Vairocana, but also a reference to the two Chinese demonstrative pronouns: the "this" and "that" that symbolize duality.

Here again, we have an emphasis on the identity between the microcosm and the macrocosm, between the various phenomena and the cosmic buddha Vairocana. This identity is expressed in terms of the five wheels (*cakras*) of the Indian tradition, or of the "three secrets" of the Shingon tradition. The primal cry of the child at birth is said to be the primordial name of I-Se. In other sources, the two phonemes *a-un* (or *a-a*, *ha-ha*) are the orgasmic sounds uttered at the peak of sexual union. Not only these sounds, but all others, are seen (or heard) as mantras; that is, as expressions of ultimate reality, as the voice of the cosmic Buddha. Likewise, all gestures are mudrās, symbolic gestures, gestures of Vairocana; and all thoughts are Vairocana's contemplation. In the Shingon tradition, these represent the "three mysteries" of speech, body, and mind. Thus, this section illustrates the reintegration of the world into the soteriological path.

3. METHOD OF INITIAL COMPLETION OF I-SE

The first stage is illustrated by a circle, in which are written two letter *a*'s in Siddhaṃ script, above two Sino-Japanese characters meaning red and white; and, at the center, Mind and Lewdness.
The essence and flesh of the mother, symbolizing the Womb realm (eastern direction), represent the mind of one suchness of the harmonious union of I-Se. The essence and bones of the father, symbolizing the Vajra realm, are the virtue of energy of the harmonious union of heaven and earth. This is the essence of the five limbs [according to the I-Se teaching]; it is the primordial body, the seed-syllable *ran*, the beginning of the passions of greed and love, when father and mother have intercourse, and the two drops, red and white, unite harmoniously. The red letter *a* is the efficiency of the mother's emission; it is the seed-letter that constitutes the flesh of beings. The white letter *a* is the breath of the father's emission; it is what constitutes the bones of beings. These two letter *a*'s, red and white, are the universal body of the Vairocana of the two Womb and Vajra realms; they constitute a buddha body in which causes and effects are constantly abiding. This is why the Vairocana of the two realms as well as the five hundred Worthies and the seven hundred Worthies are enshrined in the body of beings. This awakening of I-Se means to become a buddha in this very body.

The second stage is illustrated graphically by a kind of vessel with two horns, in which are inscribed the letters *a* and *ban*.

It corresponds to the tathāgata Ratnasambhava. It is called Wisdom of the Equal nature. It is the buddha of the south, the gate of practice. In two seven-day periods, the embryo's body become like this. It is called "three-pronged vajra." Its right and left extremities are the Vairocana of the two Womb and Vajra sections. Its seed is called abudon. The two red and white colors merge. It is the stage of the two moons.

The third stage is illustrated by a kind of trident, in which are inscribed the letters *a*, *ban*, *un*.

It corresponds to the buddha Akṣobhya of the western direction. It is called Wisdom of Wondrous Contemplation. It is the bodhisattva gate. It is the stage called peśī. After three seven-day periods, the body thus has the shape of a three-pronged vajra. The bones harden, and on each side two arms appear. The three-pronged vajra shape symbolizes the three secrets; it is also the three bodhisattvas, the three bodies, and the form of the three-petaled lotus. "Three seven-day periods" means that, in the matter of harmonious union, one spends three months in the womb; thus it is called "three sevens." The soul is now present and active: this is when the divine power of I-Se begins. This is the initial stage of awakening.

The fourth stage is symbolized by a five-wheel stūpa, inscribed with the five Siddhaṃ letters *a, ba, ra, ha, kha* in ascending order.

This shape represents the Buddha Śākyamuni of the northern direction. [As wisdom,] it is called Wisdom of the Perfection of Action. It is also what one calls the nirvāṇa gate. It is the stage called ghana. In the fourth seven-day period, the embryo already has a body like this. This shape is the tathāgata of innate awakening, the body which produces the wisdom of the buddhas of the five sections. The four Confucian virtues—humanity, righteousness, propriety, and wisdom—also correspond to this.

The fifth stage is illustrated by a small buddha, with two letter *a*'s in Siddhaṃ script, above two Sino-Japanese characters meaning red and white.

This stage is that of the buddha Vairocana at the center. It is the wisdom of the nature of the dharmadhātu body. It is the buddha with the ten thousand perfected merits. It is the stage called bano bonga. During the fifth seven-day period, such a body is formed. This form is the perfectly completed body of the effects of buddhahood. By focusing one's contemplation on the bodhisattva who aspires upward, one comes to dwell in the unconditioned, where one no longer knows even the beginningless self. However, as a result of the contemplation of the bodhisattva going downward to convert beings, one becomes a buddha endowed with the ten thousand practices, according to the right principle of I-Se.

The fifth seven-day period is the fifth month. It represents the totality of the nine months. The number of days now exceeds 38 days, and when 275 days have elapsed, birth takes place. In this, there are differences, based on the poverty or wealth of that person. When nine months have been spent in the womb, nine full moons disks have appeared, and one leaves the fundamental nature of I-Se.

"Becoming a buddha in this very body" (*sokushin jōbutsu*) is a fundamental conception of Tantric Buddhism, popularized in Japan by Kūkai. After describing in symbolic terms the sexual union that is the source of both the cosmogonic and the ontogenic processes, the text proceeds to describe the transition from duality to multiplicity as a process of embryonic gestation in five stages. The five gestation stages in Indian medicine are kalalaṃ (*gararan* in Japanese), arbudaṃ (*abudon* in Japanese), peśī (*heishi* in Japanese), ghana (*kennan* in Japanese), and praśākha (*harashakya* in Japanese): these correspond to five periods of seven days each, after which the embryo is said to be completely formed. According to Indian (as well as Chinese and Japanese) embryology, the flesh of the embryo comes from the mother, and the bones from the father. The two elements (blood and semen) are here represented graphically by two letter *a*'s, one red, the other white, symbolizing the two maṇḍalas, the two realms of reality. The Womb realm corresponds to the mother (blood, the flesh, the red letter *a*), the truth of Suchness; whereas the Vajra realm corresponds to the father (semen, bones, the white letter *a*), to energy. Note here the inversion from Indian Tantra, in which the male element—the god—is the unmoving principle, whereas the female element—the goddess, his śakti—symbolizes his energy.

This embryo is, literally, a "buddha in this very body"—and the five stages correspond to the five "wheels" (cakras) and the five elements that constitute the body of the cosmic buddha Vairocana, as well as of all beings. Childbirth was traditionally perceived negatively as a fall into the world of suffering, produced by karmic retribution—and the second part of the text will develop this notion. But in the first part, the gestation process and the birth that ensues are sanctified as a process of awakening, and they are those of the bodhisattva who, instead of wishing to rise toward nirvāṇa, decides in his compassion to be reborn in this world, in order to save sentient beings. To illustrate that this gestation process is also a process of awakening, the five embryonic stages are identified with the five gates of Buddhist practice (production of the thought of awakening, cultivation of practice, bodhi, nirvāṇa, and upāya or skillful means), the five directions (east, south, west, north, and the center), and the five buddhas.

Vairocana, endowed with the five buddha wisdoms, is the beginning and end of this process. As we saw earlier in the vajra symbolism of the human body, each stage is now symbolized by a different type of vajra. Thus, the human embryo is none other than Vairocana. But just as the five buddhas first emanate from Vairocana, so too, when this body becomes differentiated, the five buddhas first appear at each stage of its gestation. The gestation process is thus a sort of temporal maṇḍala. Out of these buddhas and their wisdoms, the entire world will appear, and this is tantamount to the birth of the child, the creation of another maṇḍala. These five stages are sometimes followed by others, but usually the remainder of the gestation process is implied. Sometimes the nine months are represented by the phases of the moon, illustrated by nine superimposed moon disks—an echo of the cakras of the subtle body of human beings.

Thus, the new human being is the perfect Vairocana, the coming together of the Womb and Vajra realms, of the two maṇḍalas. In this body reside all the gods—that is, all the energies—of the universe. It is a divine body, a perfect microcosm. The idea was already found in such Hindu texts as the Upaniṣads, according to which "the gods dwell in the body, like cows in a stable." This equivalence of the body of Vairocana with that of sentient beings is also achieved ritually through the practice of nyāsa, "imposition." Nyāsa is the cosmologization or divinization of the body (or of an object), which is effected by touching its various parts, depositing the corresponding deities or energies in them, and "sealing" them with appropriate mudrās (symbolic gestures). Through these macro- and microcosmic correlations, which allow for the superimposition of a cosmic diagram on the grid of the body, man is cosmicized, while the cosmos is divinized (and ultimately, humanized). Man becomes a universe in expansion (and resorption), that is, a living maṇḍala.

The five wheels (cakras) or elements (earth, water, fire, wind, space) are symbolized by the five seed-syllables (*bījas*): *a*, *va*, *ra*, *ha*, *kha*. The practitioner contemplates these five wheels and their bījas on his own body: the section below the hips corresponds to the earth wheel, and its seed-syllable is *a*; the navel corresponds to the water wheel (*va*); the heart to the fire wheel (*ra*); the space between the eyebrows to the wind wheel (*ha*); the top of the head—and the twelve-inch space above it—to the space wheel (*kha*). Thus he becomes Vairocana. These five wheels or elements evolved in ancient India as a combination of the five shapes of the Vedic fire altar (square, circle, triangle, half-moon, dumpling), the five colors (yellow, white, red, blue, black), and the five cakras and sections of the human body, according to the spiritual physiology of yoga.

Tantric Buddhism recognizes not only five elements, but six; the sixth element, represented by the seed-syllable *vaṃ*, is consciousness. Kūkai was apparently the first to assert that the six elements are the permanent, nonborn realities of the Dharma realm (and no longer simply the composite, impermanent elements of the phenomenal world). In the Vajra realm, the five wheels are formed by the turning of the letter *va*, whereas in the Womb realm they are formed by that of the letter *a*. In both realms, they are also formed or symbolized by the *a*, *va*, *ra*, *ha*, *kha* sequence. In the *Mahavairocanasūtra*, one of the principal scriptural authorities of East Asian Tantra, we already find the five great elements associated with the five shapes and the five seed-syllables (*a vaṃ*, *raṃ*, *haṃ*, *khaṃ*). This synthesis allowed for the development of the five-wheel stūpa (*gorintō* in Japanese). In this stūpa, which is unique to Japanese Tantra, the seed-syllables *a*, *va*, *ra*, *ha*, *kha* are inscribed on the front of each element (the five building blocks of different shapes of the stūpa), whereas *vaṃ* (consciousness), placed on the back, pervades all five elements.

The embryo, once fully formed with its five limbs, is an eminently pentadic being. Because, according to Buddhist notions of transmigration, its gestation takes place in the liminal phase between a previous life/death and a subsequent rebirth, it came to be assimilated to the early Buddhist notion of "intermediary being" (*antarābhava*), the paradoxical entity surviving after death to form a link with the next life—whence, perhaps, the association with such a prominent funerary symbol as the stūpa. Whereas the fivefold gestation process served to emphasize the temporal aspect of cosmogonic emanation, the five-wheel stūpa served as a convenient mnemonic device for summarizing the structural relationships betwen various elements of reality—at the pentadic stage of its emanation.

The five-wheel stūpa is described in the fourth section of the *Ise denki* in terms of the grapheme *a*, whose five constitutive elements (brush strokes) are used to illustrate various pentadic series (the five buddhas, the five directions, the five aggregates of personality, and so forth). This equivalence is also represented diagrammatically at the end of the text. Other sections elaborate specific points.

Section 5, which marks the beginning of the second part, discusses the impurity of the human body. Now described in more physiological terms, it is no longer the "subtle body" of yogic physiology but rather the mortal body, made of flesh and bones, bound for the cemetery. However, the microcosmic interpretation is not entirely absent, since its twelve great bones and 354 small bones are said to represent the twelve months and 354 days of the lunar year. But we are now in the realm of conventional truth, and the text itself emphasizes its use of the Two Truths theory when it refers to the twofold gate of purity and impurity. Section 7 discusses the ultimate principle of I-Se, the suchness to be realized by buddhas and sentient beings alike. It emphasizes the identity beween buddhas, kamis, and humans; or, in more Confucian terms, between buddhahood and "humanity." Section 8 is an explanation of ultimate awakening (*saṃbodhi*) in terms of the three Sino-Japanese characters that form the name of the buddha Amida. Its identification of these characters with the three bodies of the cosmic buddha Vairocana suggests an influence from the work of the Shingon reformer Kakuban (1095–1143), who identified Vairocana and Amitābha (Amida). Section 9 deals with the "eight sufferings" of the human body (birth, old age, and so on), and describes human life in rather grim terms. These sufferings, however, can be voided when one realizes the ultimate truth of the mantra of I-Se. Section 10 concerns "empowerment" (*adhiṣṭhāṇa* in Sanskrit; *kaji* in Japanese), the ritual through which humans are metamorphosed into buddhas, merging the two great maṇḍalas within their own body. Such mystical/sexual union of the androgynous practitioner is what one calls "becoming a buddha in this very body." Once this is achieved, nothing more needs to—or can—be said.

The *Ise shōsho Nihongi yūshiki honshō nin denki* passage translated above is taken from the following published edition: *Shintō taikei: Ronsetsu-hen 2, Shingon shintō* 2, edited by Shinto taikei hensankai (Tokyo: Shinto taikei hensankai, 1992), pp. 555–77.

Further Reading

Additional sources on Japanese Tantra and the Tachikawa-ryū include Bernard Faure, *The Red Thread: Buddhist Approaches to Sexuality* (Princeton: Princeton University Press, 1998); Michel Strickmann, *Mantras et mandarins: Le bouddhisme tantrique en Chine* (Paris: Gallimard, 1996); Susan Blakeley Klein, "Allegories of Desire: Poetry and Eroticism in *Ise Monogatari Zuinō*," *Monumenta Nipponica* 52.4 (1997): 441–65; James H. Sanford, "Wind, Waters, Stūpas, Maṇḍalas: Fetal Buddhahood in Shingon," *Japanese Journal of Religious Studies* 21.1–2 (1997): 1–38; and Sanford, "The Abominable Tachikawa Skull Ritual," *Monumenta Nipponica* 46.1 (Spring 1991), pp. 1–15.

—32—

Assorted Topics of the Great Completeness by Dodrupchen III

Anne Carolyn Klein

Oral commentary by Khetsun Sangpo Rinpoche

The Great Completeness tradition is considered the highest of the hierarchically arranged ninefold path described by the most ancient order of Tibetan Buddhism, known as Nyingma. Great Completeness, or Dzogchen (rDzogs chen) entails, above all, discovery of one's actual, and utterly natural, condition. This condition is also known as the base, and the process of coming to recognize it is the path. Through such recognition the fruit, one's own buddhahood, becomes manifest. All three—base, path, and fruit—are in important ways identical, not causally related or sequential. This text describes base, path, and fruit in terms of three delightful and spontaneous qualities: smoothness, splendor, and freshness.

Dzogchen is sometimes even called a path without meditation because once one fully realizes one's own mind-nature or base there is no need for effort of any kind. Until then however, practice is necessary for clearing away the internal obstructions that prevent one from clearly experiencing the profundity of one's own being. Nyingma is the only Buddhist tradition in which Dzogchen exists, though Dzogchen is also prominent in the Tibetan Bon tradition, where it is likewise regarded as the most exalted of the nine vehicles described there. Both Buddhism and Bon Dzogchen emphasize simplicity, purification, and the possibility of uncovering enlightenment in this lifetime. We will say more of this shortly; first, a bit of background.

Medieval and Modern Masters of the Great Expanse Practice

A variety of Buddhist textual traditions elaborate the practice of Dzogchen. One of the best-known bodies of literature, and the one from which the following selection is taken, is the *Essential Heart of the Great Expanse* (*kLong chen snying thig*). This lineage traces its spiritual roots to one of the most revered figures of Tibetan religious history, the fourteenth-century scholar and meditation master Longchen Rabjam (kLong-chen pa Dri-med-'od-zer, 1308–1363), said to be the author of 263 works, 25 of which are still extant. In the late 1700s, the renowned yogin-practitioner, Jigme Lingpa ('Jigs-med-gling-pa Rang-byung rdo-rje, 1729–1798) had three visions of Longchen Rabjam, as well as powerful visions and overwhelming awe with respect to Guru Rinpoche (Padmasambhava), whereby he was inspired to codify the Great Expanse liturgies into their present form. It was the power of his devotion and confidence in these two masters, rather than his intellect or scholarly endeavors, that gained him full realization of Dzogchen practice and philosophy. To this day, Longchen Rabjam's brilliant philosophical structuring of Dzogchen realization, his evocative verses, and the poetically expressed devotation of Jigme Lingpa remain hallmarks of the Heart Essence of the Great Expanse style of study and practice.

The Great Expanse relies significantly on a unique literary genre of special importance in the Ancient (Nyingma) school. These are works said to have been hidden either in the ground or, as in the case of Jigme Lingpa, in the minds of special persons who are prophesied to discover them, usually through visionary experience. Through such Treasures (*gTer ma*), which include major works of Great Expanse literature, Nyingma continually renews itself, while still maintaining allegience to the past.

In Tibet, each lineage, and even each monastic college, has textual and Treasure traditions unique to it. The historical background and monastic context of our text is therefore of interest. Its author is the third in a line of reincarnate lamas that began with the first lama in the Dodrupchen lineage, Jigme Thrinley Özer ('Jigs-med-sphrin-las-'od-zer, 1745–1821), who at the age of thirty-nine was named principal holder of the Essential Heart of the Great Expanse lineage by Jigme Lingpa himself, from whom he received the Great Expanse teachings in their entirety. Thus, he is referred to as the first Dodrupchen Rinpoche; Rinpoche is a title of honor that literally means "Precious One," and is used mainly in referring to recognized reincarnations and sometimes to persons regarded as very highly accomplished in this life. Subsequently, the first Dodrupchen Rinpoche founded Drodon Lundrup Monastery in the Do Valley and Pemakö Tsasum Khadriling Monastery in the Yarlung Valley. His successor, the second Dodrupchen Rinpoche, known as Jigme Phuntshog Jungnay, established Dodrupchen Monastery on the Tsangchen plain of the Do Valley.

This monastic college occupies a key place in the intellectual and intersectarian history of Tibetan Buddhism. By the time of the third Dodrupchen (rDo Grub chen 'Jigs-med-bstan-pa'i-nyi-ma), author of the text translated here, this monastery's curriculum incorporated Gelugpa authors of philosophical texts, in particular Jamyang Shayba, as preparation for its study and practice of the Great Completeness. As discussed by Tulku Thondup in *Masters of Meditation and Mystery*, this intersectarian tradition was continued in the nineteenth century by Shabgar Tshogdrug Rangdrol (1781–1850), a teacher of Alag Dongag Gyatso. Alag had also studied with the great Patrul Rinpoche (1808–1887), author of the recently translated *Words of My Perfect Teacher*, a richly storied discussion of the foundational practices of Dzogchen. Alag and his own student, our author, the third Dodrupchen, were both teachers of the four great abbots of Dodrupchen Monastery. Dodrupchen himself studied with three of the most famous Nyingma masters of the past century; in addition to Patrul Rinpoche, the prolific and brilliant philosopher Ju Mipham (1846–1912) and Mipham's extraordinary student, Jamyang Khyentse Wangpo (1820–1892), were his teachers.

In all these ways, the narrative of Dodrupchen intertwines with the illustrious history of Nyingma masters in eastern Tibet. Especially in the context of an esoteric and often philosophically abstract tradition like Dzogchen, it is important to remember that its most venerated examplars, like Tibetan practitioners in general, were deeply embedded in a familial and social context that grounded their endeavors.

The father of the third Dodrupchen was prophesied by Guru Rinpoche to be Dudjom Lingpa, the first Dudjom Rinpoche (1835–1903). In this way, his family position combined with his reincarnation lineage to allow him to be intimately connected with both the Great Expanse and the Dudjom traditions, this latter being another important Dzogchen lineage within Nyingma. The connection between these lineages is replicated in the person of Khetsun Sangpo Rinpoche, whose oral commentary expands on the text translated here. Khetsun Rinpoche teaches the Essential Heart tradition and constructed the Dudjom Temple in Baudha, outside Kathmandu, now the site of a sacred reliquiry containing remains of the second Dudjom Rinpoche, who died in 1987.

The third Dodrupchen incarnation, known as Jigme Denba Nyima ('Jigs-med-bstan-pa'i nyi-ma, 1865–1926), was especially renowned for his ability to make connections between the Tantric systems of Nyingma and the later schools of Tibetan Buddhism. In Tibet it was common for even great scholars to restrict their focus to works of their own orders, but Dodrupchen studied the writing of all four Buddhist orders; the present Dalai Lama has called him the best scholar of the commentarial literature in any of the Tibetan orders. The oral interpretative tradition that began with Jigme Lingpa is still alive today. The fourth Dodrupchen, Thubten Thrinley Palzang, is based in Gantok, Sikkhim, and visits the United States every two years to teach at his center in western Massachusetts; the great Dilgo Khentze Rinpoche was among the most prominent modern bearers of this tradition.

Other important recent and contemporary teachers in this tradition include Lama Gompo Tsayden (d. 1991) (himself a student of Dilgo Khentse Rinpoche) whose students, especially a number of nun retreatants, still practice at his monastery in Amdo; Tulku Thondup, considered a reincarnation of Konchog Dronme (one of the four great abbots of Dodrupchen Monastery), currently a close associate of the fourth Dodrupchen, and author/translator of the most authoritative English works on this tradition; and Khetsun Sangpo Rinpoche of Baudha, author of a thirteen-volume work on Tibetan history who has taught widely in Japan, France, and the United States, and has established a monastic training institute outside Kathmandu, where he supports and trains Nyingma monks. Trulzhig Rinpoche was invited by the Dalai Lama to represent the Nyingma school at the historic Year of Tibet program held in New York's Madison Square Garden in 1991. He is currently abbot of Thupten Chöling in Solo Kumbu, Nepal, the largest monastery and nunnery in Nepal. Khetsun Sangpo Rinpoche and Trulzhig Rinpoche are the only senior lineage holders of certain Soaring Path practices which originated with a former incarnation of Trulzhig Rinpoche known as Dongag Trulzhig Lingpa.

Another senior yogin whose repertoire importantly includes the Heart Essence tradition is Chatrul Rinpoche, now eighty-six and famous for, among many other accomplishments, having spent six years prostrating his way from eastern to central Tibet. He resides and teaches above the Kathmandu Valley, an area sacred to Nyingma since Padamsambhava meditated in its caves in the seventh century. His student Lama Tharchin Rinpoche founded a practice and study center near Santa Cruz, California. Lama Tharchin is tenth in a lineage begun by Palchen Namkha Jigme, who studied with the first Dodrupchen; he also teaches and maintains practices from the Dudjom lineage. Nyo Shul Khen Rinpoche is another contemporary figure whose main tradition is the Essential Heart; he belongs to a branch of the Kathog Monastery in East Tibet. Founded in 1109 by Kathogpa Tampa Desheg, this is the oldest of the four principal Nyingma monasteries of Kham; its main lineages are those associated with two great Treasure discoverers of the seventeenth century, Dudul Dorje and Longsel Nyingpo. Active in Tibet today are Khenbo Jigme Phuntsok Adzom Choktul Paylo Rinpoche, considered an incarnation of Jigme Lingpa as well as the son of the famous Adzom Drukpa (early twentieth century), who received visionary transmission of the *Heart Essence* from Jigme Lingpa. Essential Heart is also the lineage of Sogyal Rinpoche, founder of Rig pa Fellowship. In the West, groups centered on this lineage include the Dzogchen Foundation in Boston and Dawn Mountain in Houston; Tara Mandala near Pagosa Springs, Colorado, often hosts teachers from this tradition as well. The worldwide Dzogchen Community based in Conway, Massachusetts, founded by Chogyal Namkhai Norbu Rinpoche, also incorporates practices from this lineage into its diverse liturgies

Introduction to the Text

In the Tibetan context, religious texts are not treated, like much of Western literature today, as independent emissaries, carrying their information to anyone who takes them home and makes of them what she or he will. Rather, one is introduced to a text—such as the one translated here—by a lama trained in its traditions, whose oral commentary embroiders on the written words and whose person is understood to embody the text's essential meaning of compassion and wisdom. On the advice of the Dalai Lama, I studied the present text in 1980, and was fortunate to do so in conjunction with the oral instruction of Khetsun Sangpo Rinpoche.

Assorted Topics of the Great Completeness (rDzogs chen thor bu) is one of Dodrupchen's shorter works. It contains three essays, the first of which is translated here. In it, as the author himself states, he has "amply applied" what surfaced in his mind without the apparatus of sūtra quotations. In this way he crystallizes basic principles of Great Completeness. Most important among these is that this tradition, like Chan or Zen, understands the complete path to be already present in one's own mind. The actual nature of the mind is regarded as the womb (*garbha*) of one's own buddhahood, for a buddha is by definition one who has gone (*gatha*) through and to that very nature. Such enlightened beings are therefore known as "Ones [who have] Gone Thus" (*tathāgathas*), and one's own nature is known as the *tathāgathagarbha*. It is to be uncovered through meditating in accordance with a text like this one.

The Great Completeness is a path of discovery, not the cultivation of newly emerging qualities. It is a path that allows full openess to the mind-nature, or base. It also involves becoming free from all the tendencies, or predispositions, that are said to stain the mind-basis of all unenlightened beings. These predispositions are the residue of past mental, verbal, or physical actions. Above all, then, one seeks to discover one's own open awareness (*rig pa*). In this way, one becomes aware of the base, one's actual nature, which is described as a union of primordial purity, sometimes described as similar to the emptiness taught in Middle Way (Mādhyamika) philosophy, with the spontaneous occurence of whatever qualities display themselves within the base. To discover this is to allow the natural, but usually thwarted, process of self-settling to unfold, in the same way that the waves of a lake, which, if unstirred by winds or engines, will naturally subside.

This point is clear from the opening verses of the text. In accordance with time-honored Buddhist custom, Dodrupchen begins with a verse of refuge in Mañjuśrī (also known as Mañjughoṣa) usually described as the embodiment of all buddhas' wisdom. The author then immediately reframes this as a refuge not in an external figure but in one's own open awareness. The full manifestation of this open awareness, together with all its spontaneous good qualities, is tantamount to enlightenment. Because primordial wisdom (*ye shes* in Tibetan, *jñāna* in Sanskrit) is a full and natural settling into one's own deepest being, this open awareness is the source of enlightenment. Through practice, this naturally open awareness (*rig pa* in Tibetan, *vedanā* in Sanskrit) can be distinguished experientially from the ordinary contrived and conceptual mind. Dodrupchen therefore points out that recognizing rig pa is the true meaning of refuge in Mañjughoṣa.

Like other Buddhist schools, Dzogchen often presents its teachings under the three main headings of the base, path, and fruit. Our text focuses on the special meaning of these terms in this tradition. Dodrupchen explains each in terms of three adjectives associated with the name Mañjughoṣa ('Jam-dpal-ye-shes-sems-pa in Tibetan, Mañjughoṣa or Mañjuśrī-kumāra-bhūta in Sanskrit): smooth (*mañju*), splendid (*ghoṣa*), and fresh or youthful (*gzhon nu* in Tibetan, *kumāra* in Sanskrit). Like other Mahāyāna schools, Dzogchen recognizes that each buddha has three dimensions or bodies (*kāyas*). The emanation body, such as that displayed by Śākyamuni, the historical Buddha, is what ordinary persons like ourselves can see. Resplendent Dimension (*sambhogakāya*) buddhas manifest their own pure lands, and there teach bodhisattvas who are highly developed enough to see and hear them. Like the buddhas' own bodies, these lands and all they contain are made entirely of light, and are conjoined with the buddha's own mind-nature, the formless Actual Dimension (*dharmakāya*) buddha from which the other two emanate. All buddhas exist in all three dimensions.

The nature of the mind, also called the base, is the same whether one is enlightened or not: its natural freedom from conceptual dualistic appearance is its smoothness; its external luminous manifestations are its splendor; and its unification of primordial and spontaneous qualities are its freshness. To be fully present to this basic nature is to recognize the great completeness of one's own being. Such presence is always direct and experiential, never discursive or intellectual.

There are two methods for discovering and fully manifesting open awareness. The first is known as the primordially pure Setting Free path, meaning that the mind frees itself from its bonds of dualistic focusing on objects. This, according to Namkhai Norbu Rinpoche, is like cutting the rope around a stack of kindling—in one sense nothing changes, but the wood is no longer bound. This ease of being is the path's smoothness. The path's splendor has to do with the second of the Great Completeness practices, known as the Soaring path because, within the primordial purity that characterizes the Setting Free path, a variety of appearances spontaneously emerge, multicolored and moving. These are the light and splendor intrinsic to one's own being. They are most elaborately described in the more esoteric Dzogchen teachings of the Soaring path, and in descriptions of the various light visions, especially of peaceful and wrathful deities, which occur in the intermediate state (*bardo*) between death in one life and birth in another. *The Tibetan Book of the Dead* is the most famous exposition of these experiences in the West. (In Tibet, it is only one, relatively obscure, volume in a vast literature devoted to this topic). Indeed, the iconography of vision and a detailed concern with near-death, bardo, and rebirth experiences, is a special feature of the Dzogchen school, which was probably the first to introduce them in Tibet.

Dzogchen teaches that because these Soaring Path appearances are fundamentally the same in nature as ordinary sensory appearances, it is possible for a fully accomplished yogin to transform the physical body into a body of light, known as a rainbow body. The accomplishment of such a rainbow body is considered a unique effect of the Dzogchen path. The path's freshness refers to the vitality of meditative experiences that emerge through Setting Free and Soaring. The fruit or effect of the path is an open awareness in the continuum of one who has smoothed away the obstructions to enlightenment: that open awareness is splendid because it is now embodied in the form of enlightened beings, and it is fresh because it has a continuous clarity that never grows dull.

Our text combines language unique to the Great Completeness tradition with occasional references to classic Middle Way philosophy. It is addressed primarily to the yogin, rather than to the philosopher. It briefly indexes the types of meditative experience associated with the paths of Setting Free and Soaring. In addition to its descriptions of one's nature as smooth, splendid, and fresh, all of the important terms of this text—open awareness mind nature (*sems nyid*), the natural condition (*gnas lugs*), appearance of light (*'od*), dynamic display (*rtsal*)—refer to specific meditative experiences that have been known and described by practitioners for centuries. It is obvious, yet worth reiterating, that these experiences cannot be had by reading about them. Indeed, for most of us these special Dzogchen words have no actual referent, or at best only an imaginary one. For persons who have experientially identified their mind nature, the section describing the smoothness of the fruit is read as a set of explicit instructions for meditation.

These later sections of the text also touch on the physiology fundamental both to Tibetan esoteric practices and Tibetan medicine—descriptions of channels within the body that are associated with the process of meditation. How exactly does one gain open awareness, and what is its relationship to the ordinary mind? Our text does not tell us; it assumes that this knowledge will have been received already through other means, both oral and meditative. Thus, in a traditional Tibetan context, none but initiated meditation practitioners would read a text such as this. Nor would they read it on their own, left to construe it as they might. Rather, they would study it with a teacher accomplished in both scholarship and meditation, who would provide oral commentary, like the one included interlinearally here. And they would meditate. For such practitioners, the text helps clarify the relationship and significance of their own meditative experiences. In the altogether different academic context in which this text is now presented—through the generosity of several teachers of this tradition, especially Khetsun Sangpo Rinpoche—it serves the entirely different function of providing a glimpse into the vocabulary and structure of an ancient esoteric tradition that will be taking its place among the vital living traditions of the twenty-first century.

The text translated here can be found in *The Collected Works of rDo Grub chen 'Jigs-med-bstan-pa'i-nyi-ma*, 5 vols. (Gantok: Dodrupchen Rinpoche, 1975), vol. 5, pp. 179–87. In order to give some flavor of the interplay between written and oral traditions, small segments of Khetsun Sangpo Rinpoche's commentary on this work are included interlinearly. I have also included some remarks from Lama Tharchin, who in 1984 kindly entertained numerous questions arising from my work on this text, as well as insights provided by Tulku Thondup, author of numerous works on this lineage; and the Dzogchen master Namkhai Norbu Rinpoche.

Further Reading

For general background on the Nyingma tradition, see Khetsun Sangpo, *Tantric Practice in Nyingma*, translated by Jeffrey Hopkins (Ithaca: Snow Lion, 1982); and

Tulku Thondup, *Enlightened Journey: Buddhist Practice as Daily Life* (Boston and London: Shambala, 1995). For general background on the Dzogchen tradition, see David Germano, *Prophetic Histories of Buddhas, Ḍākinīs, and Saints in Tibet* (Princeton: Princeton University Press, 2000); Germano, "Architecture and Essence in the Secret Tantric History of the Great Perfection (*rdzogs chen*)," *Journal of the International Association of Buddhist Studies* 17.2, (1994): 203–335; and Namkhai Norbu, *Dzogchen, The Self-Perfected State*, edited by Adriano Clemente, with translation from Italian by John Shane (London: Arkana Books, 1989). For a detailed discussion of Dzogchen theory and practice based on Bon sources, see Tenzin Wayngyal, *Wonders of the Natural Mind* (Barrytown, N.Y.: Station Hill, 1993). A close reading of Jigme Lingpa's work and life is found in Janet Gyatso, *Apparitions of the Self: The Secret Biographies of a Tibetan Visionary, a Translation and Study of Jigme Lingpa's "Dancing Moon in the Water" and "Dakki's Grand Secret-Talk"* (Princeton: Princeton University Press, 1998). For the consummate narrative of the history of Nyingma (Ancient) Buddhsim in Tibet, see Dudjom Rinpoche, *The Nyingma School of Tibetan Buddhism*, translated by Gyurme Dorje (Boston: Wisdom Publications, 1991). For background on the leading female figure of the Longchen Nyingthig tradition and intersections of Geluk and Nyingma thought, see Anne Klein, *Meeting the Great Bliss Queen: Buddhists, Feminists and the Art of the Self* (Boston: Beacon, 1995). See also Steven D. Goodman, "'Rig'dzin 'Jigs-med gling-pa and the kLong-Chen sNying Thig," in *Tibetan Buddhism: Reason and Revelation*, edited by Steven Goodman and Ronald Davidson (Albany: State University of New York Press, 1992). The modern-day master Namkhai Norbu's autobiographical reflections may be found in *The Crystal and the Way of Light: Sutra, Tantra, and Dzogchen* (New York and London: Routledge & Kegan Paul, 1986). Other works on Dzogchen masters include Patrul Rinpoche, *Words of My Perfect Teacher* (*Kun bzang bla ma'i shel lung*), translated by Padmakara Translation Group (San Francisco: Harper Collins, 1994); and Tulku Thondup, *Masters of Meditation and Miracles* (Boston and London: Shambala, 1996). On the various oral genres in Tibet associated with textual readings, see Anne Klein, "Oral Genres and the Art of Reading in Tibet," *Oral Traditions* 9.2 (October 1994): 281–314; Klein, introduction to *Path to the Middle, Oral Madhyamika Scholarship in Tibet* (Albany: State University of New York Press, 1995).

Assorted Topics of the Great Completeness

Salutation

Acknowledging open awareness, I give homage to the primordially pure, stainless, and authentic (*nyug ma*) Mañjughoṣa who is endowed with the splendor of excellent, spontaneous appearance.

People like ourselves offer homage within a conventional perspective, bowing down in a conventional sense with body, speech, and mind. The author's homage is enacted within a recognition of the indivisibility of base and the fruit. These are actually one taste, indivisible. Thus, although the author here makes homage to Mañjughoṣa, if he were thinking of a conventional Mañjughoṣa, this would not be an homage concordant with the ultimate or actual view; it would be an homage made within a conventional perspective.

Promise to Compose

I will discuss the meaning of the name, *Mañju-śrī-ghoṣa-jñāna-manas-vīra*, "heroic glorious mind, the smooth and splendid primordial wisdom."

Main Text

Non-dualistic primordial wisdom, the enlightened mind of all Conquerors [buddhas] without exception, is known as heroic mind, a primordially fresh wisdom that is smooth and splendid. Because the buddhas' primordial wisdom is none other than the primordially free, spontaneously occurring, open awareness, taking it as the path from now on is the way of the natural Great Completeness.

This path does not function as a cause (of wisdom) in the sense of virtuous action leading to a positive effect, as in the theory of karma. In the Great Completeness, to take the effect (wisdom) as the path means to recognize that the natural condition of one's mind is obscured only by the adventitious obstructions that prevent liberation (*nyon sgrib*) and omniscience (*shes sgrib*). These obstructions, consisting of everything from gross nonvirtue to the most subtle tendency to perceive objects as real, are in no way intrinsic to the mind. Like the sky, which is without any obstructions whatever, the mind's actual nature is utterly clear. Because adventitious obstructions obscure our actual nature, practitioners seek to abandon them and accumulate the collections of merit and wisdom. However, from the viewpoint of its own way of being, the actual nature is beyond conventions of "something to be abandoned or achieved" and "someone who abandons or achieves." The topics to be understood regarding this state are the base, path, and fruit.

A. EXPLAINING THE MEANING OF THE BASE AND ITS DESCRIPTION AS SMOOTH, SPLENDID, AND FRESH

SMOOTH

Smoothness is the primordially pure essence (*ngo bo*), the actuality (*chos nyid*) of all phenomena. It is beginninglessly free from the eight elaborated extremes [described in detail in Mādhyamika] of production, cessation, permanence, annihilation, coming, going, being one, or being many because [the base and its primordial purity] impartially pervade, without any bias, all phenomena, from forms through to omniscient consciousnesses. There is no phenomenon, not even the merest atom, which is otherwise.

The base is the same for unenlightened sentient beings and for buddhas. The "time of the base" (*zhi dus*) occurs when one is neither in cyclic existence nor nirvāṇa; neither a buddha nor a sentient being. When primodial wisdom arises from this base, one is a buddha; when ignorance arises, a sentient being. (Lama Tharchin)

The difference between being enlightened or not lies with whether or not one realizes the natural state which is the actuality of one's base. However, even when we are born into cyclic existence, born into the mud of desire, hatred, and ignorance, the actuality of our own minds, like the lotus flower, is not covered by the defilement of mud. The mind's natural state is utterly without contrivance, and self-settled. It is [the ordinary consciousness] relaxed into its own nature. The emptiness that is the actuality of one's own mind (*rang gi sems gyi chos nyid stong ba nyid*) is the nature of all buddhas. It is not newly established but has existed all along, for it is the completely present base which is the tathāgatagarbha element in all living beings.

Since [the essence] has neither production nor true establishment, how would even lack of production be imputed in relation to it? In the view [of the Great Completeness], this essence is beyond conventions of understanding, expression, and use.

All worldly beings live within the conventions of knowing, expressing, and understanding. To say "the name of this is water" allows you to understand something as water; it is a correct convention. However conventions cannot express the ultimate, actual state.

This base is free from the various predispositions on the basis of all (*kun gzhi* in Tibetan, *ālayvijñāna* in Sanskrit), and from all that remains of those predispositions [that is, the body]. It is also free from the minds and mental evolutes (*sems las byung ba*) of the three realms, as well as from ignorance.

Even though errors arise as its dynamic display, [open awareness] is not covered by the stains of error, just as even when clouds arise in the sky, the sky is not covered by them. Because the internal sky (*dbyings* in Tibetan, *dhātu* in Sanskrit), having no foundation and no root, is free from the roughness of any sign [of conceptuality, therefore the base that is united with one's own aware presence] is called smooth.

SPLENDID

What is splendid? Your own spontaneous nature [is splendid]. The ocean of divine figures and the primordially fresh consciousness is neither sought elsewhere nor newly established, but is complete where it rests. Thus, even though, in terms of how [phenomena] appear [apparent] impurities do arise; in terms of how it is (*gnas tshul*), [open awareness] is established as a great primordial wisdom. [Therefore, the way the mind appears and its genuine state are different.] The mind's essence neither improves when errors are purified nor worsens when adventitious obstructions occur due to error.

In terms of its appearance, because [open awareness] dawns as outgoing energy (*thugs rje*), compassion (*snying rje*) emerges for all living beings. Because [open awareness] dawns as light, there shine rays having the nature of the five primordial wisdoms. Because [open awareness] dawns as primordially fresh consciousness, it dwells in an innate open awareness purified of mental stains. Because [open awareness] dawns as the figures of deities, space brims with deities of purest (*dangs ma*) clear light.

To say that open awareness "appears as light" refers to a meditative experience (*mnyam*) of light shining forth. This light is actually the radiance of the five primordial wisdoms that shine through the empty actuality of one's own mind. They are the glow of primordial wisdom.

Because open awareness dawns nondualistically, there is no holding onto sameness or difference. Because open awareness is free from extreme positions, the primordial wisdom which is the complete base appears in its own clarity. Because it dawns as primordially pure wisdom, the appearance of nirvāṇa is unceasing; because it dawns as impure cyclic existence, the six realms of rebirth appear like illusions.

The precious interiority—that is, the spontaneously occurring base—serves as a base for appearances through the eight doors. Because this becomes the base for the good qualities of liberation, it is known as "splendid."

FRESH

Internal karmic winds act as the root of the contaminated mind. Due to their movement, you are trapped in cyclic existence as if inside a vase. Yet, contamination does not enter one's actual nature (*chos nyid* in Tibetan, *dharmatā* in Sanskrit). Your actual nature has a freshness that is a deathless permanence, a stability without illness, freedom from aging and deterioration; a freshness that is utterly beyond momentary change. Because [the natural condition of mind is] an amalgamation of all unsurpassed good qualities, it has the meaning of heap or kāya, this is what it means to call [a buddha manifestation] a body. The word "fresh" in the [Dzogchen] phrase, "fresh and vaselike body" signifies the union of primordial purity and spontaneous occurrence.

It is called a "vase" in the sense of containing everything, with nothing lacking. (Chogyal Namkhai Norbu Rinpoche)

B. AN INDICATION OF PATHS AS SMOOTH, SPLENDID, AND FRESH

SMOOTH

The first of these, smoothness, has to do with the principle of the path of Setting Free (*khregs chod*). One gains certainty in the view that the mind of enlightenment itself—the open awareness in which there is no occurrence whatever of anything that goes under the rubric of either the afflicted or the purified—is a great expanse free from extremes. For one who relies on the essential precepts on meditation and behavior, all appearances (such as sights, sounds, and other knowable things) emerge as aids [to one's practice, rather than as distractions from it].

Once you have experienced your own open awareness, you seek to maintain unwaveringly the continuum of mindfulness and awareness of the natural state of your own mind, regardless of what types of conceptual thoughts arise. All these thoughts, like wood taken for fire, only help your awareness: they do not do it any harm.

When one relaxes freely in the great primordial spacious expanse of an authentic self-settling, [one is] unimpeded and without activity. Like a thief entering an empty house [which he neither harms nor helps], there is neither the establishment of good thoughts nor the elimination of bad ones; these are the dynamic display [of open awareness].

Therefore, like whirling a lance in empty space, [such thoughts] neither help nor harm [open awareness], nor does one have any grasping inclination either to be free of appearing objects or to engage with them or anything whatsoever that appears at the [sense] doors. Like a lion at whom a stone is thrown, one investigates the source [of conceptuality] itself. In this way, all thought accumulations are primordially liberated and smoothly vanish into the expanse of equality, so that appearances to the six collections [of consciousnesses, consisting of the five senses and the mind] become aids to the primordial wisdom.

If one throws a stone at a lion, he goes after the person who threw it, unlike a dog, who ignores the threatening person and just chases after the stone. In a similar fashion, if when thoughts arise one thinks "This is an excellent thought" or "This is a terrible thought" one is like the dog who observes where the stone has fallen. Correct meditation will not come at all. Like the lion, we should attend to the source, where the thoughts came from.

At that time, do not bind with [a beginner's] stringent mindfulness the pure meditative experiences which are the sapience of Samantabhadra, and do not provide causal conditions for ordinary error. Without placing yourself in chains of stubborn bondage, and without entering through the narrow aperture of a meditation focused on objects, maintain a continuity of great ease, looseness, self-settling, relaxation, and liberation. Because [the path-aware open awareness which maintains the mind-and-body continuum in this way] is free from the rough touch of a conception which adheres [to objects], it is called smooth.

When the eyes focus, you have valid cognition in the sense that the object you observe is valid. However, although such seeing is valid in terms of the world, when it comes to the view of Dzogchen, it is like a harmful poison. Whenever valid cognition focuses on an object, some conception of a self still remains. Even this valid cognizer is a grasping; therefore, it is necessary to eliminate completely all valid cognizers that focus on objects.

Conceptual thoughts are always arising. We cannot be free of them. You need to distinguish between the [ordinary] way of thinking and the instructions on mindfulness of the natural state.

SPLENDID

The meaning of "splendid" has to do with Soaring. When one takes up any of the postures—that of the lion, elephant, or sage—the very clear channels of light that are the [1] watery luminosity of expansiveness [that is, the eyes] are directed upward, downward, or straight ahead. Thereby the [2] pure-space-luminosity initially appears as a pervasive deep blue light. Then, from this, within a circle of five colored lights are arrayed the five groups of [3] empty orbs of luminosity. In between these are the [4] self-arisen-wisdom luminosities [a series of shapes appearing as] a vajra (diamond-like) chain, laid out like a string of pearls, or as a golden chain. These are the radiance of the innately clear, spontaneously perfected open awareness which is the primordial wisdom of open awareness in its own place.

These last three [namely, the pure-space-luminosity, the empty-drop luminosity, and the self-arisen wisdom luminosities that appear as the vajra chain] will become, respectively, causes for the pure land, palatial residence, and body of [yourself as] a buddha. In addition to these four luminosities there is the [5] heat-flesh luminosity and [6] the luminosity of the soft white channel, also called a "crystal piping." When one adds these two, which have clear hollow insides, there come to be six luminosities.

In addition to these six, there are three [additional luminosities], adding up to nine. These are: [7] the precious primordial wisdom that is a union of emptiness and clarity—this is renowned as the basic luminosity, the natural condition; [8] the intermediate state (*bardo*) luminosity, whose internal radiance, shining externally, is an appearance of the base during the intermediate state; and [9] the effect luminosity, which is the hollow interiority of the spontaneously occuring completion. However, the luminosities occasioned on the path are those explained above [as the nine luminosities].

In this way, through the hidden and manifest doors, and through the treasure comprised of the secret qualities of the Ones Gone Thus, you manifestly see the appearance of the body and land of a Conqueror, and hear the intrinsic sound of your actual nature. Therefore, [the open awareness that is the path] is called "splendid."

FRESH

"Freshness" is a meditative experience of union. The current open awareness is not illustrated by ordinary examples. Beyond verbal exprssion, it is free from the bondage of hope and fear, a union of open awareness and emptiness that dwells [in a manner] free from [the ordinary] mind.

The initial seeing of the vajra chain-continuum, which is the radiance of open awareness, is the actual nature [of open awareness] become manifest [and is the first of the four levels of the spontaneous Soaring path (*thod rgal*)]. When the appearances, which are light, become clearer, and appearances of orbs of light increase further, the vajra chain-continuum becomes steady. When, at the end [of this level], one sees the unaccompanied [Buddha] bodies, one has arrived at the second level of the spontaneous Soaring path known as the "increase of experience."

When there is only one figure appearing, this is like half of the increase of clear appearance. It is not the end. This has to do with the degree to which the mind is accustomed to this practice.

From the time when the bodies become joined in union until all appearances are perceived as clear light is the third level of the Soaring path called the "full measure of open awareness." [At that time] the external, the internal, as well as the secret (respectively, the material body, the mind's mass of thoughts, and the manner of appearance of the bodies and luminous orbs) are extinguished into the actual nature. This is an extinguishing into what is beyond mind [and the fourth level of the Soaring path known as] the extinguishing into the actual nature.

At this time, one's own material body becomes almost like a rainbow. Sunlight passes through it, leaving no shadow. Thoughts and predispositions for thoughts are extinguished, as are the appearances of deities' form, the drops, and primordial wisdom, and so forth. This is the extinguishing that is beyond mind.

If one who has gained power over birth [and death] wishes to effect the welfare of all beings through arising in the body of the Great Transformation (*'pho chen*), then at the time of gradually extinguishing appearances, one arises in a rainbow form. One does this by focusing open awareness on the five fingers of one's hand, which appear as light.

Nyingmas consider the body of Great Transformation to be the superior of three types of rainbow bodies; it is this that Padmasambhava and Vimalamitra are said to have attained. This rainbow form (*'ja' sku*) is not to be confused with *'ja' lus*, usually translated as "rainbow body." Those with rainbow bodies are said to disappear into another dimension, whereas the practitioner of the Great Transformation creates a unique body of light that can appear to others for their benefit, and even if, due to lack of suitable disciples, it does not manifestly appear for some time, it does not entirely disappear. (Tulku Thondup)

If one's body does not effect great waves [of activities] for others' benefit through gaining power with respect to engagement, one at that point disappears into the spacious expanse of the original sphere, just like mist evaporating. This is extinguishment into the natural state, the aware presence ready to unite with the final fruit. Because stainless and extraordinary meditative experiences open up at those times like a fresh young flower, open awareness, the path which is a union of primordial purity and spontaneous occurence is called "fresh," like a youthful person of great zest.

C. HOW THE FRUITS [OF THE PATH] ARE SMOOTH, SPLENDID, AND FRESH

SMOOTH

What is its smoothness? Abandonment of (1) desire and so forth that obstruct liberation and (2) adherence to uncontaminated phenomena and so forth that obstruct omniscience, together with the very subtle karmic inner winds [associated with them]. Smoothness is [also] the progressive pacification of all characteristics of [a grasping] mind, the clearing away of all adherence to dualistic conceptions right where they are.

Because one is free of that which obstructs the actual nature of the natural nirvāṇa [through which one attains buddhahood], the nirvāṇa purified of adventitious [obstructions] becomes manifest. The four demons are overcome. These are: (1) the demon that is the contaminated aggregates, (2) the demon that is the lord of death, cutting off one's lifetime; (3) the demon of the afflictions, that prevents liberation, and (4) the god-child demon that is the interferences [preventing] attainment of enlightenment. One is freed from all elaborations of existence, nonexistence, "is," "is not," and so forth, and is immersed in the total attainment of the great spacious sphere of neither production nor cessation. Being free from the rough feel of obstructions [to liberation and omniscience], the resulting open awareness is smooth.

SPLENDID

What is splendid? [A Buddha's omniscience that] simultaneously knows how and what things are and that manifests the twenty-one types of primordial wisdom knowing the stainless. In the Magnificently Ornamented Highest Pure Land [oneself, as a buddha] appears in great resplendence (*sambhoga*), possessed of the seven qualities of being (1) greatly enjoyable, (2) a conjoining [of method and wisdom], (3) great bliss, (4) without inherent existence, (5) fully compassionate, (6) an uninterrupted continuum, and (7) ceaseless.

In the Pure Land of Natural Emanations, the appearances of the teacher—the Form Conqueror, Feeling Conqueror, Compositional Factor Conqueror, Discrimination Conqueror, and Consciousness Conqueror—appear in their own way. Thereby, by acting for the sake of pure disciples who appear in other retinues, a Resplendent Buddha which is half an Emanation Buddha [appears]; and, for the sake of impure disciples, there are emanations such as art [trees, statues, images], rebirth and so forth, effecting the welfare of living beings.

The five Conquerors refer to the purification in their own place of the five ordinary aggregates—form, feeling, and so forth. The effect of this purification is that they now appear as buddhas. The last, the Consciousness Conqueror, refers to the purification of all thoughts, in their own place.

This Resplendent dimension is a great spontaneous activity; it is neither sporadic, biased, nor bound by effortful thought. Finding this very profound and extensive body is an unsurpassed treasure of good qualities, and for this reason [the aware presence which is the effect] is called splendid.

FRESH

The meaning of [the fruit's] freshness is this. The dissolution of all appearances of dynamic display into the spacious expanse free of extremes and center—into the actual nature—is the very secret, precious, spontaneously perfected interiority. It is also the great unchanging, unceasing, indestructible subtle wisdom. Moreover, one's great omniscience is completed as a clarity undarkened by the obscurations of sleep, fainting, lack of discriminatory capacity, or the two absorptions. One has abandoned even the most subtle production [of thoughts] in the manner of ordinary mentality as well as inconceivably subtle movements [of the winds]. Therefore, [the open awareness which is your own omniscient mind] is permanent and pure, possessing an unchangeability as extensive as space.

Consider this somewhat extreme example: if you meet a person who does not age, it is suitable to say that such a person remains perpetually youthful. The completed fresh and vaselike body is said to be like that.

Through these [explanations], I have indicated the Great Completeness which is smooth and splendid.

> The Great Completeness, open awareness and emptiness,
> Free from mind, smooth and splendid,
> Unspeakable, inconceivable, inexpressible,
> Is the actual profound and natural condition.
>
> In consonance with Words provided by my omnipresent Lama
> I have made a very brief clarification
> By which virtue may those with minds, extensive as space,
> Become Conquerors over all bonds of mental analysis
> And see, in the manner of sightless vision,
> Mañjuṣrī, in whose aware presence
> Cyclic existence and nirvāṇa are not separate.

Due to the injunctions that came my way from the mouth of the precious omnipresent Lama to do this I, Jigme, leaving aside elaborations such as the use of scriptural quotations, amply applied whatever I remembered.

—33—

On the Seal of Śambhu: A Poem by Abhinavagupta

Paul E. Muller-Ortega

The "Anubhava-nivedana-stotra" or the "Song of Praise Intended to Communicate the Direct Experience of the Absolute" is a poetic composition in Sanskrit attributed to the eleventh-century Kashmiri Tantric master, Abhinavagupta. It is one of but a handful of short poetic works or hymns of praise (*stotras*) attributed to this important Tantric philosopher and theologian. Probably written toward the end of his life as a kind of elegant summary of the author's vision of Śaiva mysticism, the poem is an evocation of the experience of the ultimate consciousness known as Śiva, the achievement of the highest goal of Śaiva Yoga.

In the religious and spiritual literature of Hinduism, stotra is a well-known compositional category that is quite varied in its form. It generally denotes a eulogistic hymn of praise directed at a particular object that the author wishes to praise. Any number of stotras of varying length, meter, and style were composed in praise of deities, religious teachers and reformers, and many diverse holy objects of veneration.

The "Anubhava-nivedana-stotra" is unusual in that it was written not so much in praise of a deity as in praise of this Tantric author's own state of achieved mystical illumination. It might be said that the poem forms a conceptual window through which the author, a great master of medieval Tantric Śaivism, allows the reader to peer into this state of mystical illumination. Although a complex philosophical theology lies in the background of all that the author says, nevertheless the poem evokes a simplicity beyond all of the philosophical and ritual complexity that encompass it: the Tantric master's direct adoration of the unity of the absolute consciousness called Śiva.

Abhinavagupta accomplishes this, in part, by centering his poem on the so-called śāmbhavī mudrā, here rendered as the "seal of Śambhu": a sophisticated formulation of the highest stance of the Śaivite yogin's achievement of mystical illumination (verse 1). Śambhu ("producing happiness") is a name for Śiva, also known as Mahādeva, the great god of medieval Tantric Śaivism. Although a personal theistic reference is not excluded, in this case Śiva primarily denotes the state of ultimate consciousness that lies beyond all limitation: the transcendent, ultimate consciousness. Through a consideration of this central idea, the poem unfolds to give expression to the brand of nonduality (*advaya*) that is fundamental to the Śaivite sādhaka or mystic's understanding of reality.

The Author of the Poem

Born sometime between 950 and 975 C.E to a rich and noble brahman family in the city of Srinagar, Abhinavagupta grew up and matured in an atmosphere supercharged with religious devotion and dedication to learning. Abhinavagupta's father, Narasiṁhagupta, claimed descent from one Atrigupta, who had been brought to Kashmir by King Lalitāditya (725–761 C.E.). Abhinavagupta's mother, Vimalā, died when Abhinavagupta was still young, and there is no doubt that her death affected him greatly.

The family were devout followers of Śiva, and Abhinavagupta began his early studies of Śaivism with his learned father but quickly began visiting teachers in Kashmir and elsewhere. While he was studying literature and poetry, he was spontaneously overcome with an intoxicating devotion to Śiva. In his own subsequent self-understanding, this event would be seen as the initial impulse of Śiva's śaktipāta or the descent of divine grace. Following this event, he seems to have studied very widely in all of the fields of philosophical, religious, and literary knowledge that were available to him. His love of learning and his spiritual search led him to travel to Jalandhara, where he encountered the Tantric master Śambhunātha, who initiated him into the practices of the left-handed Kaula tradition.

This early period of study and spiritual practice lead to a mature life dedicated to the absorption of knowledge in an atmosphere of extreme religious fervor. Abhinavagupta never married and spent his life living in the homes of his many teachers. At the height of his fame, he was revered as a charismatic Tantric master whose authority as a guru or teacher was enhanced by the fact that he was considered to be a Mahāsiddha, that is to say, a highly perfected and accomplished mystic. A prolific writer, he was the author of twenty-one still extant works (and there are references to titles of twenty-three others now apparently lost). We have no definitive information about Abhinavagupta's death. Local Kashmiri legend has it that the great master walked into a cave with 1,200 of his disciples and simply disappeared.

The intellectual context of Abhinavagupta's writings is very broad, in part due to his relatively late date in relation to the earlier traditions of Indian philosophy and religion. In addition to the revealed literature of the Āgamas and Tantras, and the texts produced by his predecessors in the Śaivism of Kashmir, Abhinavagupta's work resonates with practically all that precedes him in Indian thought, including the traditional Brahmanical or Vedic literature, the debates of the various philosophical traditions, the mysticism of the yogins, the various devotional (*bhakti*) traditions, as well as the varieties of Buddhist and Jaina philosophical discourse.

As a result, Abhinavagupta is considered to be one of the most sophisticated and definitive theoreticians of medieval Hindu Tantra. His work as an authoritative interpreter of the revealed scriptures of Śaivism was deeply intertwined with his life as a devotee of Śiva. His Tantric synthesis—termed the Trika-Kaula because of its skillful melding of doctrinal and ritual elements drawn from these two Śaivite preceptorial lineages—is so compellingly accomplished that it subsequently became the normative formulation of what is later known as Kashmir Śaivism.

Writing in a fluid and often difficult Sanskrit, Abhinavagupta composed a large number of influential works of philosophical theology including the *Īśvara-pratyabhijñā-vimarśinī* (Commentary on the Recognition of the Lord); the *Tantrāloka* (Light on the Tantras), and the *Parātriṃśikā-vivaraṇa* (The Long Commentary on the Thirty Verses on the Supreme). Although he must be counted among the first rank of India's greatest thinkers, outside Kashmir his name was practically forgotten until the early twentieth century.

Śāmbhavī-mudrā or the Seal of Śambhu

At the core of the "Anubhava-nivedana-stotra," Abhinavagupta focuses on the śāmbhavī mudrā, the seal of Śambhu. He does this in order to describe the paradoxical state of the yogin who does not close his eyes to the outer world (verse 1), yet who never loses sight of the innermost consciousness. This description of mystical attainment is characteristic of the Śaiva Tantra, and it differs greatly from the much more rigidly enclosed or purely introversive definitions of achieved mysticism found in earlier traditions of Indian thought.

From a doctrinal point of view, the articulation that Abhinavagupta gives in these longer works of the nondual Śaivism of Kashmir is to be distinguished philosophically by its assertion that what is termed "Śiva"—the absolute and primordial consciousness—is advaya or nondual. Moreover, this nondualism differs in important ways from the advaita taught in the various schools of the philosophical Vedānta. For the Kashmiri nondual Śaivites, the nondualism or advaya of Śiva does not in any way imply that the world and all who dwell in it are an illusion or not real. Instead, Abhinavagupta asserts that this world is real precisely because it is only Śiva—the absolute consciousness.

However, the assertion of the reality of the world does not fall into "naive" realism—asserting the ultimacy of the reality of the world *as* world. Instead, it seeks to articulate the enlightened and transformed vision of the mystic for whom the paradoxical omnipresence of Śiva has become a tangible experience; this is the abiding in the śāmbhavī mudrā. Thus, Śiva's nonduality encompasses without contradiction the arising of duality and diversity within it.

This stance or gesture of consciousness has often also been called the bhairavī mudrā, the seal of Bhairava (a name for a form of Śiva). An anonymous verse often quoted in the texts of the tradition describes the bhairavī mudrā as follows: "Even though gazing outside, the eyes neither opening nor closing, one should direct one's attention within. This is the seal (*mudrā*) of Bhairava, concealed as the best secret of all the Tantras." Curiously, this verse begins with the same term in Sanskrit that begins Abhinavagupta's poem: *antar-lakṣya*, literally, that which is to be perceived within, referring to the innermost object of perception. This is Śiva, the highest consciousness to be recognized or perceived inwardly by the yogin as the true and deepest nature of both the inner Self and the outer world.

Thus, whether it is called the śāmbhavī mudrā or the bhairavī-mudrā, this term describes a kind of bifocal mystical vision that involves the simultaneity of outer sensory perception and inner yogic vision. When this vision is achieved, the Śaivite yogin need never repudiate the outer "thisness" (*idantā*) of the objects of perception in an exclusively introversive, closed-eyed samādhi or meditative absorption. Instead, his outer vision is transformed so that it does not finally fall on the world's apparent "outwardness" or "manifestness" (verse 1). Rather, what is truly seen is the hidden interiority concealed within the world's apparent objectivity, an interiority in which the separateness and duality of the world have melted into the all-pervasiveness of the paradoxical and boundaryless consciousness known as Śiva.

This theme of the melting or dissolving (*vilīna*, *līnatā*, *galita*, mentioned in verses 1, 2, and 3) of the world into the unitary consciousness is widespread in Śaiva mysticism. Abhinavagupta tells us that it is achieved by the grace (*prasāda*) of the master, and this state is described as affording access to the highest consciousness beyond both the ordinary conditions of awareness, and the states of purely introversive meditative absorption (verse 1). In order to understand in more detail the play of meanings that combine in great richness around the notion of śāmbhavī mudrā, we now examine in more detail what Abhinavagupta means by a mudrā.

The Meanings of Mudrā

In Sanskrit, the term *mudrā* most commonly denotes a seal in the sense of any instrument used for sealing or stamping. In the ancient Indus valley civilization, there were carved stone seals engraved with a variety of designs and used to imprint this design into the wet clay of a pot or other object. In this same sense, ancient India knew of other seals such as metallic signet rings or other engraved implements that could be pressed into melted wax. The plot of a classical Sanskrit play, the *Mudrā-rākṣasa* or "Rakṣasa's Ring" (by the sixth-century C.E. author Viśakhadatta) revolves around just such a signet ring that belongs to the chief minister of a king, and the authority that the signature engraved on such a ring would bring to one who was not its rightful owner.

In the context of Indian dance, a mudrā is often understood as a stylized physical gesture of the hands, eyes, or body that carries or conveys symbolic meanings. Many of these same mudrās or symbolic gestures of the body are encountered in the textual descriptions of Indian deities, and in the artistic representation of these deities in sculpture and painting. Thus, for example, there is the famous cinmudrā or "seal of consciousness" displayed by the hands of many deities. In this sense as well, many varieties of Hindu religious ritual (including that of Śaivism) employ numerous hand mudrās as an essential element of their ritual performances.

In the traditions of haṭha yoga, a mudrā carries the meaning of a variety of physical gestures or poses, or esoteric techniques of a specific sort that often include some sort of lock (*bandha*) on the subtle energy of the body. In this sense, we encounter in the texts of yoga the famous khecarī mudrā, literally the "seal of flying through the void," which was interpreted as a difficult technique for swallowing the tongue and thus tasting the nectar of immortality that drips down inside the accomplished yogin's skull. Another example from haṭha yoga is the aśvinī-mudrā, the "equine seal," which involves locking the energy in the anal or perineal region. There are many more such mudrās in the traditions of haṭha yoga.

In a related though slightly different environment, there are the mudrās that involve techniques for Tantric sexual intercourse such as the vajrolī mudrā (dubbed in recent literature in the West the "reverse fountain-pen effect") for reabsorbing ejaculated semen back from the vulva into the male urethra, and thus, it was thought, absorbing as well the female ejaculatory fluids and orgasmic energies.

In the wider ambit of the Hindu Tantra, the term mudrā is encountered in the traditional list of the so-called pañcamakāra or five Ms, the listing of five "forbidden substances"—each of which begins with the letter M in Sanskrit—that were thought to constitute an integral part of the transgressive ritual of the Tantra. Here, the term mudrā referred to a parched grain that was thought to have an aphrodisiac effect (see Bharati, *Tantric Traditions*, p. 243). However, in Kashmiri Tantra, and especially in the works of Abhinavagupta, the term mudrā does not appear to have been used with this last connotation. For the Kashmiri traditions, the list of the five Ms appears to have been reduced to the three Ms: madya, consecrated wine; māṃsa, flesh or meat; and maithuna, ritual sexual intercourse (*Tantrāloka* 29.96). Mudrā does not appear on this list; instead, Abhinavagupta devotes an entire chapter of his summa of the Śaiva Tantras and Āgamas, the *Tantrāloka* (*TĀ*), to explaining the nature of mudrā in a different and quite subtle way (*TĀ* 32. 1–3). As we will see, Abhinavagupta presents a theory of mudrā that is intended to explain both its practice and its origins.

Abhinavagupta first offers a traditional, interpretive etymology of the term *mudrā*. He says—breaking the term apart into two constituent elements—that a mudrā is described in the traditional texts or śāstras as that which gives (*rā*) pleasure or happiness (*mud*). That is to say, Abhinavagupta continues, a mudrā is the name for that by means of which one attains the intrinsic nature of consciousness. Most importantly, he adds, a mudrā is that which presents the gift of the Self by means of the body (*TĀ* 32.3). Kṣemarāja, one of the disciples of Abhinavagupta and an important Tantric author in his own right, adds to these traditional interpretive etymologies of the term mudrā. In his comment on sūtra 19 of his *Pratyabhijñāhṛdayam*, Kṣemarāja says a mudrā is so called first, because it dispenses joy (*muda*) as a result of being of the nature of the highest bliss (*paramānanda*); second, because it dissolves or melts (*drāvaṇāt*) all spiritual bondage; and third, because it seals (*mudrāṇat*) the entire universe into the state of the transcendent consciousness (*turīya*). All of these interpretations convey different aspects of the tradition's understanding of mudrā.

Then Abhinavagupta becomes even more specific and technical. He tells us that a mudrā is a pratibimba, a counterpart form or reflected image, in contrast to the bimba or the original image or form. Abhinavagupta goes on to assert a double causal relationship between these two images or forms. He says that the counterpart image or form arises or is produced from the bimba, the original image or form, but that the original image or form can be produced or made to arise from the pratibimba, the counterpart form. In order to understand what Abhinavagupta means by all this, we can begin by adopting an additional terminology of translation and say that, in this definition, Abhinavagupta is telling us that a mudrā is a sign, and that the sign (*pratibimba*) is the counterpart of that which is signified (*bimba*).

To illustrate: even in English, the term "seal" carries two different meanings. It means either the engraved or otherwise carved or decorated implement or tool, or the imprint that is created by that tool or implement.

In the first case, the design on the imprinting tool might be called the bimba or original image, and the design left behind on the wax might be called the pratibimba or counterpart image or form. In this case, then, the bimba or engraved tool gives rise to the pratibimba or waxen seal. It is this pratibimba that Abhinavagupta wishes to call the mudrā.

We also recall Abhinavagupta's claim of a double causal directionality: pratibimba arises from bimba, but also bimba arises from pratibimba. In what sense can the original image be said to arise from the counterpart image? Or, in what sense can a sign give rise to that which it signifies? We here arrive at the first of two important uses of mudrā in Śaiva yogic mysticism: first, the practice of mudrā as strategic method that gives rise to yogic attainments, and second, the spontaneous mudrās that are born from the supreme consciousness. A mudrā is, first, considered to be a bodily "sign" of consciousness; by practicing it, the experience of that consciousness can be attained. In this first usage, the context is that of the not yet realized yogin who takes up the practice of mudrā as a method by means of which to attain yogic results or transformation. Specific poses, hand gestures, or sensory or mental techniques are practiced by the yogin in the attempt to precipitate the experience of some change or alteration in awareness. In this sense, the mudrā is a bodily technique consciously and strategically applied as part of a yogic methodology designed to achieve the goals of yoga.

As Abhinavagupta has told us, a mudrā is that which presents the gift of the Self by means of the body. In this sense, Abhinavagupta explains that there are at least four different kinds of mudrās: those that are made by the whole body (*kāya*); those that are made by the hands (*kara*); those that are made by speech (*vāk*) (or the mouth or tongue); and those that are made in the awareness or mind (*citta*) (*TĀ* 32.9b). Thus, by means of the bodily positions, hand poses, esoteric physical techniques of mouth, tongue, or sexual organ, or, indeed, by means of meditative techniques performed by the bodily senses and the mind—all of which are varieties of mudrās that are described in the traditions of Indian yoga—there can arise the experience of supreme consciousness.

It is in this sense that the śāmbhavī mudrā of the poem is first presented. It can be understood initially under this rubric of upāya or yogic method. The seal of Śambhu is a sign of the ultimate consciousness. By "practicing" that sign, that which it signifies can be experienced. Specifically, the śāmbhavī mudrā itself can be understood as a technique of the breath, mind, and senses for achieving the highest consciousness by means of the kind of "bifocal" vision described above. A good description of the technique is found in the *Vijñāna-bhairava-tantra*, which describes this form of meditative practice as follows (verse 80): "Fixing the gaze on some outer object and yet at the same time making his mind free of the prop of all thought constructs, the yogin acquires the state of Śiva without delay." In this mode of understanding, the various practices called mudrā are the counterpart images of the original consciousness, an experience of which they are meant to precipitate. Hence, returning to Abhinavagupta's analysis, in this sense, bimba is born of pratibimba. In the poem we can see that Abhinavagupta is alluding, particularly in verses 1 and 2, to the śāmbhavī mudrā as a technique or practice to be performed.

In verses 3 and 4 of the poem, however, we encounter a different idea of the śāmbhavī mudrā. Rather than being a technique, the śāmbhavī mudrā is understood as a description of the highest state of yogic achievement. Here Abhinavagupta seems to insist that he is now telling us about the true mudrā (and mantra and yoga), which is spontaneously produced as a result of the yogin's state of abiding in the supreme nondual consciousness. Indeed, this reversal is further emphasized in verse 4 by the verbal play (which verges on punning) in the Sanskrit words of the verse: he tells us about mantras that have no syllables, mudrās in which no physical gestures are performed, and a yoga in which no prāṇāyāma or deliberate breath control is practiced.

This reversal is significant, for here the poem speaks about the śāmbhavī mudrā as a spontaneous occurrence in the body, which is precipitated not as a practice engaged in order to attain liberation but rather as that very condition of liberation itself. In this second mode of understanding the nature of mudrā, the directional causality has reversed, and now bimba, original image, gives rise to pratibimba, counterpart form. This reversal signals an explanatory Tantric theory for the origin of mudrās (just as the previous analysis was an explanatory Tantric theory for their *use* in yogic practice).

Of the many mudrās mentioned in Abhinavagupta's works (and in the wider literature of Śaivism), there are at least four that seem especially to fall into this category of mudrā as denoting states of achieved mystical consciousness. In addition to the śāmbhavī mudrā, we find the bhairavī mudrā used to depict a state of liberation (as described above). In the *Tantrāloka*, Abhinavagupta praises another important mudrā as primary: the khecarī mudrā, the "stance of moving or flying through the void of the supreme consciousness." Abhinavagupta asserts that all the other mudrās of consciousness are derivations or variations of the khecarī mudrā (*TĀ* 32. 6). As we have seen above, the practice of this mudrā was understood in a very different sense from that interpreted by Abhinavagupta here. Nevertheless, it is here understood by Abhinavagupta as describing the stance of the accomplished yogin for whom all possible signs of duality or differentiation have completely vanished. Another important Śaiva mudrā relating to the condition of liberation (mentioned in several places, including in Kṣemarāja's *Pratyabhijñāhṛdayam*) is the krama mudrā, the "seal of sequentiality" in which there is the sequential movement (*krama*) of outer awareness into the innermost consciousness, and a countervailing (and sometimes simultaneous) movement of the inner consciousness into outer awareness.

In addition to these, we find mentioned (in *TĀ* 32.4–6a, as well as in the *Vijñānabhairava-tantra* verse 77, and many other places) mudrās with such names as the triśulinīm—relating to the trident; the karaṅkiṇīm—the skeletal; the krodhanām—the wrathful; the lelihānikām—the seal of tasting or licking, as well as many others. All of these appear to denote "stances" or "gestures" of consciousness of the Śaivite mystic in the ascending evolution toward the highest realization.

Thus, the śāmbhavī mudrā refers to stance of the yogin in which the absolute consciousness is realized in its completeness and totality. It is, therefore, a description of the state of liberation within the body (*jīvanmukti*) *and* of the impact of that state of absolute consciousness on the limited individuality of the practitioner.

Śāmbhavī-mudrā, the Great Seal of the Absolute

To understand this poem it is necessary to see that the metaphor of the seal as implement is here transposed to the impact (*śaktipāta*) of the Absolute. It is like an invisible and transcendent "implement" that emerges from within to "seal" its design on the person of the yogin. Like wax that has been melted, the mind and body of the yogin have been "melted" by dedicated yogic practice. The yogin must be responsive to the impact of this experience of the Absolute. He must not be rigid, contracted, or given over to tightly limiting and constricting activities of the body, the vital energy, and the mind. Such constricted "bodily" activities (representative of those of the ordinary person) would only serve to "harden," as it were, the being of the yogin and to make him unresponsive to the influx of the potency of the Absolute.

All the preliminary stages of yoga thus seem to be meant to prepare the yogin for this condition of responsiveness to the influx of the supreme power or śakti. What is sought, finally, is a kind of existential transparency to absolute consciousness. Upon reaching the summit of mystical consciousness, the being of the yogin then reveals the shape of the Great "Seal" of the Absolute, like the signet ring that is impressed into the warm and receptive surface of the wax. The resulting shapes and impressions are the mudrās of consciousness, even as the force of the impact of the Seal of the Absolute—the state of liberation—is also called a mudrā. Indeed, the body of the enlightened yogin is understood to be continuously forming mudrās, some overt, others subtle. Every activity of the enlightened yogin is a mudrā: a "gesture" or "sign" that reveals the shape and character of the absolute consciousness that is invisibly impressing itself into the receptive yogin's being.

The mudrā as pratibimba or counterpart image, then, refers to the responsive molding of the yogin's individuality: the mind, breath, body, and demeanor of the yogin are all shaped by the overwhelming impact of the potency of the Absolute. It, so to speak, molds the yogin into its own design; it "seals" its imprint on the being of the yogin. In this way, though transcendent, invisible, and beyond the reach of the senses, the Absolute nevertheless, by means of the force or śakti of its descent into the individuality of the practitioner, reveals its nature in the transformation of the state of the realized yogin. The state of the mystical experience of the absolute consciousness—the śāmbhavī mudrā as bimba or original image or form—can thus be understood to "seal" its effect or invisible design upon the outer assemblage (this is the sense of the term *saṃsthāna* in verse 3) of the body, breath, and mind of the yogin. This creates the many mudrās or physical gestures or responsive demonstrations in the sense of pratibimba or counterpart image or form of the absolute.

Such a double understanding of mudrā reflects what the Śaivite tradition will call anupāya or "no-practice" (discussed below). It seems to be implicit in Abhinavagupta's definition of mudrā that the sense of mudrā as yogic practice is subservient to and dependent upon the sense of mudrā as spontaneous existential gesture of the condition of liberation. Indeed, in the *Tantrāloka* Abhinavagupta explicitly singles out the spontaneously appearing mudrās of consciousness by insisting that "Whatever bodily configuration appears spontaneously in one who has ascended completely to the sphere of the absolute consciousness (*khecari cakra*), that alone is to be considered a mudrā. The rest, which are devoid of the impact of the absolute consciousness, are simply unnatural deformations of the body" (*TĀ* 32.65).

This understanding of spontaneously appearing mudrās provides us with what amounts to a Tantric theory of origin for mudrās. By implication, we can speculate that the strategic practice of mudrā appears to be the imitation of such gestures, stances, and poses. What had previously been observed in the posture and demeanor of the enlightened yogin as spontaneous manifestations of deep inner transformation are purposefully imitated by other yogins as a conscious stratagem for precipitating or reduplicating that very state of illuminated consciousness. Although the poem does not explicitly take up these themes, they hover in its conceptual background, particularly in the sharp contrast between the first two verses and the last two.

Śāmbhavī-mudrā and the Nonduality of Śiva

This poem sings about abiding in this space of deepest interiority. What is at stake for the Śaiva Tantric yogin here is not just a momentary breach or preliminary entry into the supreme consciousness. Rather, the poem extols the state of the most accomplished Śaivite mystic for whom the experience of the great Self has matured, stabilized, and become a continuous experience, a quotidian state of being (verse 2).

Such a state is not understood to exclude the dynamic, swirling, and abundant variety of the world. Rather, it is the full revelation of the intrinsic and unchanging source from which this kaleidoscopic drama of saṃsāra continuously emerges and manifests. Therefore, the nonduality of the ultimate consciousness of Śiva is understood to be continuous with, contiguous, and subjacent to the differentiated and variegated play of the world. It is the source of all differentiation (*sṛṣṭi*), it is that which underlies, supports, and inheres in the variety of differentiation (*sthiti*), and it is that into which the differentiation finally merges (*saṃhāra*).

In the final state of vision described by the śāmbhavī mudrā, the "world" reveals itself to be only consciousness. It is "sealed" with the stamp of Śiva's blissful nonduality. Such a yogin succeeds in tasting the unitary flavor of Śiva (*ekarasa*) in every moment of the apparently differentiated perception of a supposedly separate and objective world. Whether the accomplished yogin gazes within or without, what is perceived is the boundaryless consciousness of Śiva. As a result, for that yogin, the very distinction between inward and outwardly turned perception and, indeed, between self and other, between the supposedly only silent and tranquil absolute consciousness and the apparently only dynamic and active relative world—all of these distinctions collapse.

Because this poem was probably directly addressed to a small audience of initiated disciples, it unfolds against the background of a shared understanding of such philosophical argumentation about the nonduality of Śiva, as well as of the complex technicalities of Śaiva yoga and its understanding of an ascending path of mystical consciousness. But although the philosophical theology of Abhinavagupta's branch of Śaivism posits the notion of advaya or radical nonduality as a fundamental tenet, the Tantric sādhaka nevertheless seeks to actualize fully the experience of this philosophical formulation as the direct and unmediated realization of his daily practice. Indeed, the yogin seeks, finally, a stabilized condition of achieved mystical consciousness that both fulfills and in some significant sense brings to an end all explicit forms of practice.

In the yoga of Śaivism, central to such a practice are the forms of samāveśa or absorptive meditative merging, of which there are several varieties or degrees of intensity. For Abhinavagupta, the definitive classification of these is to be found in the *Mālinī-vijaya-tantra.* There, the yogic methods or means (*upāyas*) for attaining the supreme consciousness are arranged in terms of samāveśa. These range from the so-called āṇava or "minute," to the śākta or "empowered," to the śāmbhava or "supreme." Thus, the highest method or degree of yogic absorption is usually termed śāmbhava: that which relates to Śambhu or Śiva. Here, the effort and technique, the dedicated practice and discipline of the lesser modes of Śaiva yoga have been left behind. The śāmbhava upāya involves the highest states of mystical dissolution of individuality beyond the realm of the thought-constructs. Furthermore, although effort in any explicit sense has been left behind, such a "method" is understood to be empowered by the force and impact of the grace of the master (verse 1). By means of it, the practitioner is led to the ultimately effortless yogic merging into the englobing consciousness of Śiva, the absolute consciousness.

The accomplished Śaivite mystic is one who—even as his vision falls on the surface play of existence—is capable of penetrating its pulsating layers and continuously discovering, uncovering, and recognizing its ultimate, unitary, and silent source in the supreme consciousness. The seal of Śambhu, the śāmbhavī mudrā, then, is this paradoxical state of Tantric attainment that is neither exclusive nor repudiatory, nor does it in any way reject the variety of the world's astonishing play.

Abiding in the space that encompasses both inwardness and outwardness in one overarching and paradoxical consciousness, the yogin is capable of seeing that the world now reveals its deeper layers of being, finally laying bare its ultimate and secret source in the resplendent domain of Śiva: the silent, pulsating core essence of the supreme consciousness (verse 2).

Although what Abhinavagupta describes in this poem is certainly rooted in the technical practice of Śaiva yoga of a complex sort, it enters into the zone of what this and other Śaivite traditions characterize as the anupāya or the "method of no practice." Such a "no-practice method" consists of the summit of the mystical life where the "practice," so to speak, involves abiding in surrender to the Absolute, finally yielding the vestiges of limited individuality to the supreme consciousness. From this vantage point, we can understand this poem as giving expression to that most rarefied of mystical movements: the final transition from the highest practice or method of the Śaiva yoga—the śāmbhava upāya—to the anupāya or "no practice" as the state of liberation and enlightenment itself. Here, the need for yogic practice, method, technique, and effort with regard to mantra, mudrā, and breath have all been transcended in the stabilized condition of fully illuminated awareness. Such is the śāmbhavī mudrā.

In this poem Abhinavagupta, one of the definitive theologians of a branch of the later "high" Hindu Tantra, reveals himself as an ecstatic, mystical poet; Abhinavagupta, the masterly theoretician of Śaiva ritual, lays bare his own accomplishment as a yogin; Abhinavagupta, the sober philosopher and capable expositor of the most subtle forms of reasoned philosophical argumentation, allows himself to be seen as an intoxicated devotee of absolute consciousness. As a result, the poem is less stylistically rigid and formal than many comparable stotras directed toward deities. It is—within the constraints of the rich technical vocabulary that Abhinavagupta employs—quite descriptive and evocative. One senses the extreme familiarity with which Abhinavagupta addresses himself to his theme. As we have seen, in the poem, Abhinavagupta takes features of the technical yoga—in particular the idea of mudrā—and transposes them beyond their complexity as practice in order to reveal what he claims to be their true nature.

The poem exists against the background of an immense array of Tantric technicalities but finally settles down in the intimacy of the Tantric practitioner's inner state. It is itself an inspired mystical expression, a mudrā, if you will, for it attempts to speak in poetic terms of a state of mystical attainment in such a way that carries the weight of that attainment. Finally, the poem is not concerned with philosophical argumentation, nor does it engage in didactic teaching, nor is it instructive about the intricacies of the practice of Śaiva yoga—or, indeed, of its complex rituals. It is, in the end, a celebratory exclamation: a stotra or hymn in praise, a true poem in that it gives expression to the direct experience of the absolute with elegance and in a way that opens that experience to others. Hence, Abhinavagupta's title for this stotra: a song of praise intended to communicate (*nivedana*) the direct experience (*anubhava*) of the Absolute.

Though little known outside Kashmir, the short poetical compositions of Abhinavagupta appear to have been central to the lore of Kashmir for a millennium. They appeared in published form in 1935 in K. C. Pandey's massive study of Abhinavagupta: *Abhinavagupta: An Historical and Philosophical Study*, Chowkhamba Sanskrit Studies, vol. 1 (Varanasi: Chowkhamba Sanskrit Series Office, 1963). Pandey (p. 73) describes finding the Sanskrit text of this poem in a collection of Abhinavagupta's stotras in the possession of one Harabhatt Shastri of Kashmir. He warns us, however, that he finds no other authority for attributing the work to Abhinavagupta. He includes this stotra in Sanskrit (along with a number of other short works by Abhinavagupta) as an appendix to his book. The stotra does not appear in the listing of the Kashmir Series of Texts and Studies. Lilian Silburn tells us that she studied this and other such stotras of Abhinavagupta under the direction of Swami Lakshman Joo. In 1970 she published a translation of a number of them into French, along with a very useful thematic and interpretive introduction and commentary. I have translated the stotra as it appears in Appendix C of Pandey's book (p. 953).

Further Reading

See Mark Dyczkowski, *The Stanzas on Vibration* (Albany: State University of New York Press, 1992) for the Spanda lineages of Kashmiri Śaivism and for a useful discussion of upāya and mudrā. For an introduction to Abhinavagupta and the

Kaula mysticism of the Heart, see Paul E. Muller-Ortega, *The Triadic Heart of Śiva: Kaula Tantricism of Abhinavagupta in the Non-Dual Shaivism of Kashmir* (Albany: State University of New York Press, 1989). André Padoux, *Vāc: The Concept of the Word in Selected Hindu Tantras* (Albany: State University of New York Press, 1990), treats in detail the philosophy of language and the topic of mantra. The original publication of this stotra in the modern period seems to be in Pandey, *Abhinavagupta*, which is also the only existing in-depth study of Abhinavagupta's life and work. For detailed solutions to many historical and interpretive problems surrounding the Śaivism of Kashmir, see Alexis Sanderson, "Maṇḍala and Āgamic Identity in the Trika of Kashmir," in *Mantra et diagrammes rituels dans l'hindouisme*, edited by André Padoux (Paris: Centre National de la Recherche Scientifique, 1986) and "Purity and Power among the Brahmans of Kashmir," in *The Category of the Person: Anthropology, Philosophy, History*, edited by M. Carrithers, S. Collins, and S. Lukes (Cambridge: Cambridge University Press, 1986), pp. 190–216. See Lillian Silburn, *Hymnes de Abhinavagupta*, Publications de l'Institut de Civilisation Indienne, fasc. 31 (Paris: Institut de Civilisation Indienne with the Centre National de la Recherche Scientifique, 1970), in which Silburn presents a rendering and introduction to this stotra. See Agehananda Bharati, *Tantric Traditions* (Delhi: Hindustan Publishing Corporation, 1993), for useful discussion of the idea of mudrā. For a translation of one of Abhinavagupta's longer works see Jaideva Singh, *A Trident of Wisdom* (Albany: State University of New York Press, 1989.)

The Anubhava-nivedana-stotra of Abhinavagupta
The Song of Praise Intended to Communicate the Direct Experience of the Absolute

1. The accomplished Tantric yogin, whose mind and breath have been dissolved through complete immersion in the innermost object of perception, the supreme goal of yoga—such a yogin then abides with a silenced though open vision, the pupils of the eyes unmoving. Though he [is seen to] gaze still on the outer world, in truth his vision assuredly does not rest on its [apparent outwardness]. This is the seal of Śambhu—the śāmbhavī mudrā, the Śaiva "seal" of unitary consciousness, the performing of the ultimate "gesture" or "stance" of Śiva's illumination.

This state of true and ultimate mystical vision, O Divine Master, is produced only because of your potent and illuminating grace. This is the domain of Śambhu, the gracious Lord, the true state of reality which is beyond the experience of both the fullness [of the conditions of ordinary awareness], as well as lying beyond even the [extraordinary] void states [of advanced Tantric meditation].

2. Such a yogin abides with eyes half opened and yet with a mind that is motionless and serene, his gaze fixed steadily [at the secret portal that opens to the yogin's subtle perception found] at the tip of the nose. The sun and

moon [either the "sun" as the means of knowledge (*pramāṇa*) and the "moon" as the known objective universe (*prameya*), or the two breaths and the whole world of duality that they stir] have dissolved into the great interiority of awareness that pulsates naturally with the triple vibration [either the vibration of the energies of will, knowledge, and action or the vibration of the supreme śakti that constantly tends toward the manifestation of the visible reality, the counterbalancing reabsorptive pulsation of consciousness, and the supreme pulsation or ādya-spanda that abides beyond such polarizing movements].

Here, the yogin achieves the One reality, the domain whose nature is essentially the pure light of consciousness, devoid entirely of all externality, the supreme spirit, the true principle, the abode of the highest, the supreme essence. More than this, what is there to be said of it?

3. In that state, whatsoever words may emerge from the mouth of such a yogin are, indeed, transcendentally charged mantras. The aggregate form of the body—within which the experience of pleasure and pain are constantly arising—that very bodily form [of the illuminated yogin] is indeed nevertheless the mudrā or seal that reveals [the experience of the Absolute].

The spontaneous and natural flow of the breath [which produces the natural mantric sound *haṃsa* continuously]—that, indeed, is the extraordinary and highest yoga itself. Having directly experienced the unparalleled splendor, the illuminating glory of the divine śakti, in truth, what will then not reveal itself to me?

4. The [true and highest] mantra that then reveals itself in that state has no distinguishable arrangement of syllables or phonemes to be seen within it [for it is of the nature of the potency of the ultimate consciousness *ahaṃ* itself.] When the entirety of the [separative or contractive] bodily activities have dropped away or when the practice of all bodily techniques [engaged strategically by the yogin] has stopped, then the [true and highest] mudrā or seal of the absolute rises up to reveal itself. As soon as the [separative and dualizing] flow of the breath has ceased or when the [practice of the] flow of the breath [that is, prāṇāyāma techniques of yoga] have stopped being performed, that, indeed, is [the true] yoga which then appears.

In the magnificent festival of mystical illumination that leads to the attaining of your splendor, what, indeed, does not then reveal itself to the enlightened wise ones as completely extraordinary?

—34—

Vajrayoga in the Kālacakra Tantra

John Newman

The Vajrayāna tradition of Buddhism is the second of two modes of Mahāyāna Buddhist practice. In the first of these—the "system of the Perfections" (*pāramitā-naya*)—the bodhisattva strives to attain the supreme awakening of buddhahood by means of a lengthy and gradual training in generosity, morality, forbearance, perseverance, meditative concentration, and wisdom. In the "Mantra system" (*mantra-naya*), a synonym for Vajrayāna, the bodhisattva develops the same virtues and knowledge, but uses special magical ritual meditative techniques that greatly accelerate the process. Because the Vajrayāna is primarily a type of mystical praxis, its sacred scriptures and exegetical literature are mostly devoted to practical matters rather than to philosophical doctrine. This has sometimes led to the misconception that the Vajrayāna is merely a body of techniques, and that philosophy is marginal or irrelevant to its central concerns. In fact the opposite is true. Vajrayāna can only be correctly understood as a ritual-meditative implementation of insights developed within the common Mahāyāna philosophical tradition.

The principal philosophical view underlying Vajrayāna mysticism is Madhyamaka ("the Middle"), which was originally taught by the Buddha in the *Perfection of Wisdom Sūtras* and later elucidated by Nāgārjuna (ca. second century C.E.) in his *Madhyamaka-śāstra* ("Treatise on the Middle"). Madhyamaka steers a middle course between the two ontological extremes of a realism that ascribes inherent existence to phenomena and a nihilism that denies phenomena's causal efficacy. It does this by asserting that although phenomena are utterly devoid of inherent existence, they nevertheless originate in dependence on causes and conditions, and function in an entirely regular and predictable fashion. Thus any given phenomenon can be viewed from two perspectives. When one scrutinizes a phenomenon in search of its intrinsic, independent identity, no such identity is found. This absence of inherent existence, or "own-being" (*svabhāva*), is its "emptiness" (*śūnyatā*). On the other hand, when one observes a phenomenon as it ordinarily appears, without engaging in an investigation of its ultimate status, it is seen to arise within a specific matrix of causes, and it in turn serves to produce specific effects. This causal regularity of phenomena is called "dependent origination" (*pratītya-samutpāda*). According to the Madhyamaka view, emptiness and dependent origination mutually entail one another: things are empty of inherent existence because they originate in dependence on extrinsic factors, and things are able to originate and function in causal relationships because they are devoid of an absolute nature that would preclude such relationships.

The Madhyamaka ontology of emptiness and dependent origination is closely related to its epistemology of two truths, "conventional truth" (*saṃvṛti-satya*) and "ultimate truth" (*paramārtha-satya*). Conventional truth is the world of appearance. For ordinary people—that is, those who have not gained insight into emptiness and dependent origination—phenomena appear to possess inherent existence, and such people hold these appearances to be real, to exist as they appear. Buddhist adepts who have realized emptiness alternate between two modes of cognition: while absorbed in meditative concentration on emptiness they perceive only emptiness, and conventional appearances do not appear to them at all; when they arise from meditation conventional phenomena reappear and appear to exist inherently, but adepts understand that these appearances are illusory, and thus do not cling to them as real. Buddhas, finally, see conventional truth (appearance) and ultimate truth (emptiness), simultaneously.

In Vajrayāna practice, Madhyamaka doctrine is realized through yogic control of the mind. Whereas mind in its samsaric state generates and is infatuated by mundane illusory appearances, the first phase of the Vajrayāna path, the "generation stage" (*utpatti-krama*), harnesses the creative power of mind to produce a new divine vision of reality. This imaginative vision, called a maṇḍala, is a transformation of the practitioner's perception, so that ordinary appearances of self and environment are replaced by an ideal universe inhabited by deities. The elaborate symbolism of the maṇḍala is a divinization of basic Buddhist psychological and metaphysical categories: the deities of the maṇḍala are the phenomena that make up the practitioner's personality purified through recognition of their emptiness. During the generation stage, the practitioner first dissolves ordinary perception into perception of emptiness. Then within this perception of emptiness, the practitioner's mind manifests in the form of the maṇḍala. By conditioning him- or herself through the maṇḍala practice of the generation stage, the Vajrayāna practitioner gains a deeper understanding that phenomena are devoid of independent inherent existence, that they are instead the products of mental fabrication.

Whereas the generation stage uses imagination to produce an alternative vision of conventional reality, the second phase of the Vajrayāna path, the "completion stage" (*utpanna-krama*), cognizes the ultimate nature of mind itself. The Tantric yoga of the completion stage ceases sensory perception and ideation. When these coarse forms of mental activity have been shut down, the "connate luminosity" (*sahaja prabhāsvara*) of mind appears. Through yogic conditioning, this most subtle form of mind can be awakened so that it becomes aware of its own emptiness.

This special kind of direct realization of emptiness, unique to Vajrayāna, is called the "transcendental mahāmudrā siddhi." *Mahāmudrā* can be roughly glossed as the "Great Seal." It is gnosis realizing the mind's own emptiness in a nondual, nonconceptual fashion: mind is "sealed" by emptiness, and emptiness is "sealed" by mind. Mahāmudrā is likened to a divination in which a maiden perceives a hidden object in a mirror. The appearing object is a manifestation of the maiden's own mind; the maiden does not "think" of the object, yet she directly perceives it. Similarly, for the yogin or yoginī practicing mahāmudrā, the subjective aspect of mind (gnosis) and the objective aspect of mind (the appearance of the mind's own emptiness) are blended in a single essence so that it is impossible to distinguish knowledge from object of knowledge. This gnosis is called "the gnostic mind of imperishable bliss" (*akṣara-sukha jñāna-citta*).

The perfect integration of the conventional truth of the mentally fabricated maṇḍala and the ultimate truth of the connate luminosity realizing emptiness is called vajrayoga, "adamantine union," in the text translated below. Vajrayoga is the inseparable fusion of wisdom realizing emptiness and compassion spontaneously manifesting appearances in order to guide living beings to freedom from saṃsāra. Personal names for this transcendent reality include Ādibuddha (Primal Awakened One), Bhagavān Kālacakra (Lord Wheel of Time), and Vajrasattva (Adamantine Sentient Being). Because vajrayoga surpasses the limitations of dichotomizing, dualistic thought, language cannot fully encompass its true nature. Nevertheless, language can point toward the transcendent, and the second half of our text describes vajrayoga in terms designed to undermine reification of the categories that define ordinary conceptions of reality.

The transcendent vajrayoga is heterogeneous because it is the integration of purified conventional appearance and emptiness. Whereas appearance is a positive phenomenon that functions in accordance with the causal law of dependent origination, emptiness is a mere negation, the simple absence of inherent existence. Ordinary thought cannot grasp both aspects of reality simultaneously, yet "the conventional is embodied in emptiness, and emptiness is embodied in the conventional": vajrayoga confounds conceptual thought, which is based on the dichotomy existence/nonexistence. Our text quotes the *Aṣṭasāhasrikā Prajñāpāramitā* ("Perfection of Wisdom Sūtra in Eight Thousand Lines") to illustrate this point: "Mind that is non-mind exists." The perfection of wisdom—the compassionate wisdom realizing emptiness—is "non-mind" because it is free from conceptual elaboration and is fused with spacelike emptiness, mind's mere lack of intrinsic existence. Yet this non-mind "exists" because it is directly perceived by the awakened person, and it displays myriad forms that serve to awaken others.

Vajrayoga is "without relation" (*niranvaya*) because it pervades everything. It cannot be localized within mundane existence (the "desire," "form," and "formless" existences of Buddhist cosmology) or nirvāṇa (the cessation of the three realms of existence) because thought defines mundane existence and nirvāṇa as contraries, and vajrayoga transcends such reifying, dualistic thinking. Similarly, when fire is generated by spinning a fire-drill on its base, the fire is inseparable from the totality of the causes that produce it; it cannot be localized in any particular cause. Like that, vajrayoga pervades the entire universe of the outer world (*bāhya*), the self (*adhyātma*), and the transcendent (*para*).

As initial realization, vajrayoga is called "supreme, perfect awakening in one moment" (*ekakṣaṇābhisambodhi*). When the Vajrayāna practitioner first realizes vajrayoga he or she experiences a moment of "supreme imperishable great bliss" (*paramākṣara-mahāsukha*): blissful connate luminosity embraces its own naked emptiness. In the Vajrayāna system treated here, supreme imperishable great bliss is repeatedly developed in order to produce 21,600 moments of gnosis. This number—a conventional designation for the number of human respirations in a day and the number of years in a cosmic cycle—is a symbol of temporal totality, the embodiment and transcendence of time. Cultivation of supreme imperishable great bliss serves as a path that purifies the mind of contaminating stains, eventually culminating in the achievement of perfect buddhahood. From the point of view of perfect buddhahood, we cannot speak of the conventional momentary origination, duration, and disintegration of phenomena because awakened mind is free from erroneous discrimination that reifies cause and effect, one and many, being and nonbeing, and so forth. Such mind is said to be "devoid of own-being" (*niḥsvabhāva*) because it knows dependent origination and emptiness in a totally integrated, nondualistic way. This gnosis is also called "reality" (*tattva*).

The following translation is a dewdrop lifted from the ocean of the *Vimalaprabhā* (Stainless Light), the great commentary on the *Śrī Kālacakra* (Splendid Wheel of Time), the primary Tantra of the Kālacakra (Wheel of Time) system of Vajrayāna mysticism. The Kālacakra was the last major Tantra produced by the Indian Vajrayāna tradition, and the *Śrī Kālacakra* and *Vimalaprabhā* contain a date that enables us to determine that these texts were completed between 1025 and ca. 1040 C.E. The earliest masters of the Kālacakra included Piṇḍo, a brahman Buddhist monk born in Java, and Nāropā, the famous Vajrayāna guru of Naalandaa monastic university. During the eleventh to thirteenth centuries, the Kālacakra flourished among the Buddhist elite of northeastern India, whence it was transmitted to Tibet. In Tibet, the Kālacakra became an important item in the spiritual repertoire of most Buddhist lineages, and it continues to be studied and practiced today.

The translation, "A Summary of the Vajrayoga" (*Vimalaprabhā* 1.3.1 [commentary on *Śrī Kālacakra* 1.1d]), is based on my unpublished edition of this passage, which relies on Asiatic Society of Bengal manuscript G.10766 and on the printed edition of the *Vimalaprabhā*, which was edited by Jagannatha Upadhyaya and published in the Bibliotheca Indo-Tibetica Series, no. 11 (Sarnath, Varanasi: Central Institute of Higher Tibetan Studies, 1986), pp. 42.15–45.3. In the course of his discussion, the author of the *Vimalaprabhā* cites the following works, in some cases anonymously: the *Śrī Kālacakra*, which was edited and published together with the *Vimalaprabhā*, as cited above; the *Aṣṭasāhasrikā Prajñāpāramitā*, which was edited by P. L. Vaidya and published in the Buddhist Sanskrit Texts Series, no. 4 (Darbhanga: Mithila Institute of Post-Graduate Studies and Research in Sanskrit Learning, 1960); the *Abhisamayālaṅkārakārikā* of Maitreya, which was published in the volume just cited; the *Nāmasaṅgīti*, which was edited by Ronald M. Davidson and published in *Mélanges chinois et bouddhiques*, vol. 20 (Bruxelles: Institut Belge des Hautes Études Chinoises, 1981); and the *Paramādibuddha*, the Kālacakra mūlatantra ("basic Tantra"), which has come down to us only in fragmentary form.

Further Reading

Study of the Vajrayāna tradition is still in its infancy, and little has been written about the relationship between common Mahāyāna philosophical doctrine and Vajrayāna practice. For an overview of the Kālacakra system, see Geshe Lhundub Sopa, Roger Jackson, and John Newman, *The Wheel of Time* (Ithaca: Snow Lion, 1991). For a technical note on Buddhist philosophy in the *Vimalaprabhā* see John Newman, "Buddhist Siddhānta in the Kālacakra Tantra," *Wiener Zeitschrift für die Kunde Südasiens* 36 (1992): 227–34.

A Summary of the Vajrayoga

Now "yoga in the *Śrī Kālacakra*" [in *Śrī Kālacakra* 1.1d] summarizes the vajrayoga.

In the Mantra system, the Bhagavān Buddha, depending on worldly and transcendental truth, indicated two types of meaning in this and other Tantras: one with worldly convention, the second in accordance with the ultimate. Provisional meaning is indicated with worldly convention. Definitive meaning is indicated in accordance with the ultimate. Disciples should understand these two meanings from a guru's instructions.

Likewise, in all the other Tantras the subject matter is of two types: one in accordance with worldly convention, the second in accordance with the ultimate. That which is in accordance with worldly convention is characterized by the colors, arms, symbols, and shapes [of the deities in the maṇḍala]. That which is in accordance with ultimate truth is devoid of the colors, arms, symbols, and shapes [of the deities in the maṇḍala].

Of these two, that which is taught in accordance with worldly convention is [the maṇḍala of deities], a phenomenon of one's own mental fabrication that produces the worldly siddhis in order to achieve the worldly siddhis in the outer world and in the self. That which is taught in accordance with ultimate truth is free from the phenomena of one's mental fabrication in order to achieve the transcendental mahāmudrā siddhi that possesses the best of all aspects. It is directly perceived: an appearance of his own mind manifests in the sky for the yogin, just as a divination appears in a mirror for a maiden. It produces the result that is the desired aim. The result is the gnostic mind of imperishable bliss.

The unity of these two minds—the vajrayoga consisting of wisdom and method, the supreme imperishable great aim, the Ādibuddha without relation, Bhagavān Kālacakra—is renowned in all the other Tantras as Vajrasattva. That very Bhagavān is called the "Nature Body" in the Perfection of Wisdom—in the Perfection system that is designated as the cause. Thus, when determining the four functions [of buddhahood] in the *Abhisamayālaṅkārakārikā* [1.17], Maitreya says:

> [The buddha bodies] are said to be fourfold: the Natural [body], Dharma body, Enjoyment [body], and Emanation [body], with Activity as well.

That very Bhagavān is called "connate joy" and the "connate body" in the Mantra system that is designated as the effect. It has abandoned object and subject; it is beyond the phenomenality of limited consciousness; it is not fixated in existence or nirvāṇa; it is the assembly of the buddhas and the congregation of the goddesses. The definitive meaning of this is that it has the same essence as the gnosis body.

This vajrayoga is without relation. It has abandoned eternity and annihilation. It is beyond worldly examples. It has thoroughly forsaken ideas about existence and nonexistence. Like a divination in a maiden's mirror, it is not imagined by one's mind—it is directly seen, an object of experience. It is all aspects; it originates from the sky. It is completely good, the total cognitive faculty. It is the connate joy that dwells in the self of everyone. It has completely abandoned logical reasons and examples.

The heterogeneity of the unity of existence and nonexistence serves as an example for this vajrayoga for yogins so that they may destroy all grasping at positions. It is like the following worldly example: "Since it is heterogeneous with 'pot,' 'sky-flower' does not exist, because it is entirely nonexistent. Likewise, since it is heterogeneous with 'sky-flower,' 'pot' exists, because it is entirely existent." Because these two are mutually heterogeneous, they are an example.

Similarly, since it is heterogeneous with annihilation, existence exists, because it is entirely existent. Since it is heterogeneous with existence, annihilation does not exist, because it is entirely nonexistent. The word "annihilation" indicates nirvāṇa that is characterized by nonexistence.

Similarly, the unity of these two, pot and sky-flower, serves as an example for the transcendent because it is heterogeneous. These two, pot and sky-flower, are not unified from the point of view of worldly convention because they are mutually contradictory. For due to the nature of existence and nonexistence, that which exists does not not exist, and that which does not exist does not exist. Since it is contradictory, that which makes mind characterized by existence does not make it characterized by nonexistence; that which makes mind characterized by nonexistence does not make it characterized by existence.

Here too, the image that consists of emptiness and compassion—the purified mind that is like a maiden's divination—is not characterized by form because it is not made of atoms. It is not characterized by formlessness because it is present in the void.

Therefore, the conventional is embodied in emptiness, and emptiness is embodied in the conventional. Since it is beyond worldly examples, "mind that is non-mind exists" [*Aṣṭasāhasrikā Prajñāpāramitā* 3]: it is free from the characteristics of eternal and annihilated phenomena, it is indivisible emptiness and compassion. Because of the heterogeneity of both minds from the point of view of ultimate truth, nondual vajrayoga is beyond "is" and "is not", and it is the termination of existence and nonexistence, because the speech of the Tathāgata is without relation.

Here, the Bhagavān said in the *Basic Tantra* [the *Paramādibuddha*]

> Nondual vajrayoga, the great bliss, is beyond "is" and "is not". It is the termination of existence and nonexistence; it is indivisible emptiness and compassion. (1)
>
> The vajrayoga without relation is beyond the nature of atoms and it has abandoned void phenomena. It is free from eternity and annihilation. (2)

Thus, in other Tantras the Tathāgata has said that vajrayoga accomplishes the mahāmudrā.

That pure vajrayoga, being the supreme perfect buddhahood in one moment, is the great aim, the supreme imperishable, connate joy. It does not abide in the desire existence, it does not abide in the form existence, it does not abide in the formless existence, it does not abide in the desire nirvāṇa, it does not abide in the form nirvāṇa, and it does not abide in the formless nirvāṇa, because it is not fixated in existence or nirvāṇa. It does not abide in both because they are mutually contradictory; like sun and shadow, existence and nirvāṇa are not identical. Just as fire does not abide in the base of the fire-drill, in the fire-drill, or in the effort of the person's hand, a yogin should comprehend the vajrayoga everywhere in the outer world, in the self, and in the transcendent.

The so-called "supreme, perfect awakening in one moment" is a moment of supreme imperishable great bliss. That supreme buddhahood in one moment develops all the moments through to the end of the count of the breaths. Then the supreme, perfect buddhahood completed in that moment is the true, perfect buddha. After that moment of completion in which all tathāgatas obtain supreme, perfect buddhahood, all phenomena do not originate, do not abide, and do not disintegrate, because they are without relation.

During the moment all phenomena originate they do not abide and do not disintegrate. During the moment they abide they do not disintegrate and do not originate. During the moment all phenomena disintegrate they do not originate and do not abide. Also, all phenomena do not momentarily originate, momentarily abide, and momentarily disintegrate in sequence. And this does not happen simultaneously: at a single time when all phenomena exist, the moments of origination, abiding, and disintegration are not identical.

However, you might say: In sequence, the moment of abiding arises from the moment of origination, the moment of disintegration arises from the moment of abiding, and the moment of origination arises from the moment of disintegration. But that is irrelevant from the point of view of reasoning about the ultimate: here, another moment does not arise from a prior moment that has not ceased; likewise, it does not arise from a moment that has ceased. For example, a sprout does not arise from a seed that is destroyed, and a sprout does not arise from a seed that is not destroyed. Similarly, since ultimate being does not exist, there is no one moment, because one and many are contradictory.

With regard to "the supreme, perfect buddhahood in one moment that develops all the moments" [*Nāmasaṅgīti* 141cb]: Being first fully awakened in a moment of supreme imperishable bliss, one develops the 21,600 moments of supreme imperishable bliss. After that, when all moments are nonexistent, the supreme nondual yoga of the buddhas—separate from one and many—is ultimate because it is separate from being and nonbeing. As long as there is worldly being, phenomena are discriminated by means of one and many because of the appearance of momentary mind. When mind is separate from momentary phenomena, it is called "devoid of own-being."

Therefore, the Bhagavān said that the position devoid of own-being is a nonposition. So-called "positions" are: existent/nonexistent, being/nonbeing, is/is not, one/many, eternity/annihilation, existence/nirvāṇa, form/nonform, sound/nonsound, moment/nonmoment, desire/nondesire, hatred/nonhatred, delusion/nondelusion. These and others are positions because they are mutually dependent. The buddhas' nonfixated nirvāṇa that is separate from this position is devoid of own-being. Gnosis that is separate from one and many moments is called "reality" by the victorious buddhas.

—35—

Jain Tantra: Divinatory and Meditative Practices in the Twelfth-Century *Yogaśāstra* of Hemacandra

Olle Qvarnström

The study of Jain medieval Sanskrit texts reveals a Tantric influence on the two main traditions of Jainism—Digambara and Śvetāmbara—both in the sense of ideas and practices and in the sense of a literary class. This influence was restricted neither geographically nor confessionally, and manifested itself within different literary genres and contexts. Its impression is also visible in iconography and art.

The questions of the precise extent to which Tantra penetrated into Jainism, the historical development of Jain Tantra, and its indebtedness to Hindu and Buddhist Tantra are at the present stage of research not entirely clear, even though their outlines have been sketched by scholars such as John Cort and Paul Dundas. Many Tantric texts are still only available in manuscript form. Few have been critically edited. For various reasons Jain Tantra has not caught the attention of Indologists. This has in its turn made it difficult to integrate Jain Tantra into a broader religious, cultural, and historical framework, as well as to define its distinctive character.

Rather than attempting to give a historical survey of Jain Tantra, the following study is, therefore, based on a single text: the *Yogaśāstra* of Hemacandra (1089–1172 C.E.). This, the most comprehensive treatise on Śvetāmbara Jainism that has come down to us, was regarded as a normative account of that tradition even by non-Jains. Today it serves as a handbook for the Śvetāmbara community in Gujarat as well as among their coreligionists in East Africa, Great Britain, and North America.

Even though the *Yogaśāstra* is neither a Tantric text nor an historical work that might provide us with a description of the gradual infusion of Tantra into Śvetāmbara Jainism and its ideological provenance, it is the result of a historical process during which the incorporation of Tantric ideas and practices was natural and necessary. The *Yogaśāstra* is thus valuable for uncovering the Tantric influence on medieval and contemporary Śvetāmbara Jainism, since it informs us of the means and extent of Tantric influence on mainstream Śvetāmbara Jainism. At the same time, we have to be on our guard for doctrinal elements that do not necessarily reflect the view of either the Jain congregation or the leading circles within the exegetical tradition, but which are merely the predilections and hidden motives of the author himself. This is especially important with regard to the *Yogaśāstra,* since it was written at the request of the author's employer, King Kumārapāla, who reigned over Gujarat during this time and who was himself in the process of converting from Śaivism to Jainism. One may therefore assume that the motive behind the composition of the *Yogaśāstra* was in part apologetic and propagandistic, and that it was linguistically and doctrinally designed to serve the purpose of converting Gujarati Śaivites to Jainism, as well as to propagate a coherent creed among the Jains themselves. As an erudite writer of elegant verse, Hemacandra was well equipped for such a task. This is confirmed by posterity, even if, for political and religious reasons, the spread and development of Jainism during this time and in this part of India had its limitations.

In the first four chapters of the *Yogaśāstra,* Hemacandra, like many of his predecessors, structures what he perceives as Jain orthopraxy and orthodoxy into three main categories or "jewels" (*ratnatraya*): correct faith (*darśana*), knowledge (*jñāna*), and conduct (*cāritra*). These are also designated "yoga," a term that is therefore synonymous with Jainism, which explains the title of the work: *Yogaśāstra* or "Handbook on Jainism."

The division of Jainism into three jewels is a reformulation of the doctrine of a twofold dharma or teaching (*dvidharma*) that was known to Hemacandra and shared by all Jains. Jainism, according to this doctrine, is founded on two basic principles. The first consists of theoretical and practical instructions related to activity (*pravṛtti*), the second of similar instructions related to nonactivity (*nivṛtti*). Activity includes moral acts and rituals (*karma*), whereas nonactivity encompasses intellectual and experiential cognition (*jñāna*). Both posit faith (*darśana*) in the teaching and in its principal communicators.

The main components of Jainism—faith, knowledge, and conduct—complemented each other and applied to mendicants as well as to the laity. Both groups were subordinated to the same moral system, both were engaged in ritual activity, and both sought knowledge through intellectual and contemplative means. The difference between the doctrine and practice of these two main segments of the Jain congregation (*saṅgha*) and their views on morals and rituals (*karma*), on the one hand, and intellectual and experiential cognition (*jñāna*), on the other, can be analyzed in terms of emphasis, mode of expression, and purpose. They agreed that no ritual or moral activity by itself could result in liberation (*mokṣa*), even if the activity in question encompassed intellectual and meditative components. In accordance with the law of karma, any activity whatsoever, moral or ritual, resulted in rebirth, preceded at best by a heavenly existence. The ethical code separated mendicants and laity in terms of the extent to which the moral vows were to be observed. Yet the same ethics brought them together as a religious group by excluding certain rituals, not least of which were those of what is known as left-hand Tantra (*vāmācāra*). The most significant dividing line was, however, related to the purpose of moral and ritual activity or, differently expressed, the art of performing any act, moral or ritual. Whereas lay religion sought to improve activity mainly by performing rituals and observing moral vows, and was hence directed toward the first three objects of human activity (*puruṣārthas*)—duty (*dharma*), wealth (*artha*), and desire (*kāma*)—monastic religion sought to transcend activity largely through advanced intellectual, ascetic, and meditative practices, thereby bringing the performer of ritual and moral activity in contact with the agent of all activity, the Self (*jīva*). The monk or nun could then attain the same moral, ritual, and cognitive perfection as that of the preeminent communicators of the Jain faith, the tīrthaṅkaras or Jinas.

The above portrayal of Jainism in the form of three jewels (*ratnatraya*) or a double teaching (*dvidharma*) is based on the first four chapters of the *Yogaśāstra*, which in its turn draws on the Śvetāmbara canonical scriptures (*śrūta*) and the exegetical tradition (*sampradāya*) down to the time of Hemacandra. The remaining chapters of the *Yogaśāstra* contain information that gives a slightly different, or rather, supplementary picture of mendicant doctrine and practice. This latter part of the text reveals a Tantric influence of Trika Śaiva provenance, which by the time of Hemacandra had entered into mainstream Śvetāmbara Jainism, as mediated through the Digambara tradition. The relation between classical Jainism and Tantra is stated in *Yogaśāstra* 1.5:

> Yoga [or the three jewels of Jainism] is [like] a sharp-edged axe for the tangle of creepers of all calamities. It is a supernatural means for [attaining] the happiness of liberation without [the use of] medical herbs (*mūla*), spells (*mantra*) or Tantric [teachings] (*tantra*).

Accordingly, Tantra was regarded neither as an essential part of Jain theory nor as the principal means for attaining liberation. As we shall see, however, it did penetrate into mendicant divinatory and meditative practice, and promised mundane as well as soteriological results. Above all else, Tantric influence manifested itself in a general ritualization, using previously unknown methods and theories. This emphasis on certain forms of ritual activity may itself be viewed as constituting a Tantric influence. Furthermore, and in parallel with the development of Buddhist Tantra or Vajrayāna, the laity was not alone in performing Tantra. Members of the monastic community, including Hemacandra himself, embraced various forms of Tantric practice. These included elements of ritual as well as exercises of a more meditative, cognitive nature. As Paul Dundas has discussed, the adherence to a strict ethical code and the absence of a linguistic theory of sacred, mantric sound, combined with a pluralistic metaphysical philosophy, were factors that ultimately hampered the general influence of Tantra on Jainism as compared with the wide-ranging effects it had on Hinduism and Buddhism. As far as Śvetāmbara Jainism and its principal summa is concerned, the *Yogaśāstra*'s first four chapters, containing a description of classical Jain orthopraxy and orthodoxy, received considerably wider circulation among Jains in India and later abroad than did the remaining eight chapters, which were of a more Tantric bent. Whatever the overall extent of Tantric influence on Śvetāmbara Jainism may have been, the *Yogaśāstra* seems not to have contributed appreciably toward the inclusion of Tantra into that tradition.

In the following, I provide two sets of examples illustrating Śvetāmbara Jain Tantra as it manifested in divinatory and meditative practices, respectively. They consist of translated passages from the *Yogaśāstra* based on Jambūvijaya's critical edition and furnished with additional information in square brackets from the autocommentary, the *Svopajñavṛtti*.

The translated passages from the *Yogaśāstra* and the *Svopajñavṛtti* are based on Muni Jambuvijaya's critical edition, *Yogaśāstraṃ Svopajñavṛttivibhūṣitam*, 3 vols. (Bombay: Jaina Sahitya Vikasa Mandala, 1977–1986). An English translation of the *Yogaśāstra* will shortly be published by the present author under the title, *The Yogaśāstra of Hemacandra. A Twelfth-Century Handbook on Śvetāmbara Jainism.*

Further Reading

On Hemacandra and Kumārapāla, see Georg Bühler, The *Life of Hemacandrācārya*, translated from the German by Manilal Patel (Santiniketan: Singhi Jaina Jnanapitha, 1936), and John Cort, "Who Is a King? Jain Narratives of Kingship in Medieval Western India," in *Open Boundaries. Jain Communities and Cultures in Indian History*, edited by John Cort (Albany: State University of New York Press, 1998), pp. 85–110. The meditative and divinatory practices described in the *Yogaśāstra* are best understood in the light of the following two general introductions to Jainism: Padmanabh S. Jaini, *The Jaina Path of Purification* (Berkeley and Los Angeles: University of California Press, 1979), and Paul Dundas, *The Jains* (London: Routledge & Kegan Paul, 1992). In addition, one may consult specialized studies, such as John Cort, "Medieval Jaina Goddess Traditions," *Numen* 34.2 (1987): 235–55; Paul Dundas, "Becoming Gautama: Mantra and History in Śvetāmbara Jainism," in *Open Boundaries*, edited by John Cort, pp. 31–52; Kalipada Mitra, "Magic and Miracle in Jaina Literature," *Indian Historical Quarterly* 15.2 (1939): 175–82; Mitra, "Magic and Miracle in Jaina Literature," *Jaina Antiquary* 7.2 (1941): 81–88, and 8.1 (1942): 9–24; Umakant P. Shah, "A Peep into the Early History of Tantra in Jaina Literature," in *Bhāratakaumudī. Studies in Indology in Honour of Dr. Radha Kumud Mookerji*, part 2 (Allahabad, 1947), pp. 839–54. For more general context, see Agehananda Bharati, *The Tantric Tradition* (London: Rider, 1975), pp. 138–52, 161–62; and Sanjukta Gupta, Dirk J. Hoens, and Teun Goudriaan, *Hindu Tantrism* (Leiden: E. J. Brill, 1979). On the adoption of Tantric elements in Śvetāmbara Jainism, see Olle Qvarnström, "Stability and Adaptability: A Jain Strategy for Survival and Growth," *Indo-Iranian Journal* 41 (1998): 33–55; and on the doctrine of a double dharma (*dvidharma*), see Qvarnström, "Hari-bhadra and the Beginnings of Doxography in India," in *Approaches to Jaina Studies: Philosophy, Logic, Rituals and Symbols*, edited by Olle Qvarnström and Narain K. Wagle (Toronto: University of Toronto, Centre for South Asian Studies, 1999), pp. 169–210. Jain Tantric and Siddha traditions in Gujarat are treated by David Gordon White, *The Alchemical Body: Siddha Traditions in Medieval India* (Chicago: University of Chicago Press, 1996), pp. 114–18, 331–34. Tantric influence on Jain art is beautifully illustrated in Pratapaditya Pal, *The Peaceful Liberators: Jain Art from India* (Los Angeles: Los Angeles County Museum of Art, 1994), pp. 56, 79–80, 229; and Colette Caillat and Ravi Kumar, *The Jain Cosmology* (Basel, Paris, New Delhi: Ravi Kumar Publications, 1981), pp. 36, 193–94.

Selections from the *Yogaśāstra* and the *Svopajñavṛtti*

The first set of examples is drawn from the fifth chapter of the *Yogaśāstra*. This chapter contains a description of breath control (*prāṇāyāma*) along with an inventory of various divinatory practices.

The definition of prāṇāyāma basically agrees with that of the classical commentators on the *Yogasūtra*, the principal textbook on yoga with which Hemacandra was familiar and whose fundamental tenets most Indian religions acknowledged. The use of seed syllables (*bīja mantra*s) and the adoption of Tantric physiognomy, including the theory of cakras or lotuses (*padma*s) and channels (*nāḍī*s), clearly demonstrate, however, a Tantric influence on the kind of breath control used by Jain mendicants as an optional precondition to meditation. The main purpose of controlling the breath was to improve physical health (*kāyārogya*) and thereby the capacity for intellectual and meditative cognition.

The knowledge of the breath and its movement in the different parts of the body was also part of mendicant divinatory practice. The main purpose of this was to determine the time of death (*kālajñāna*) and foretell future (negative) events. The span of life could be prolonged thereby, its quality raised, and the necessary preparations for death carried out fully and properly. This concern was shared by all Indian religions and especially prevailed during the medieval period.

The different forms of divination described in the *Yogaśāstra* are also mostly of a pan-Indian character and include the observation of changes in the body (*aṅgavidyā*), palmistry (*sāmudra*), interpretation of dreams (*svapnaśāstra*), animal portents (*śakuna*), oracular voices (*upaśruti*), and interrogation with the help of astrology (*praśna*). Occasionally the divinatory methods are amalgated with Jain doctrine in combination with Tantric practice. These include the inspection of the month and number of days during which the breath blows in a certain channel (*nāḍī*), reading of shadows (*chāyā*) in combination with pictorial, geometric symbols (*yantra*s), potent words (*mantra*s or *vidyā*s) repeated in meditation and ritual, the mental installation of seed mantras and letters of the Sanskrit syllabary (*mātṛkā*s) on various parts of the body (*aṅga*s) through ritual touch (*nyāsa*), and interrogation with the help of Tantric physiognomy.

The first example of divination is drawn from *Yogaśāstra* 5.173–76. It illustrates how the time of death was determined by means of invoking a divinity (*devatā*) through muttering (*japa*) a spell (*vidyā*) on a given celestial occurence.

A [female] deity who has properly been made to descend into a mirror, a thumb, a wall, [or] a sword through [the repetition of] a magical spell (*vidyā*) will inform [a person] of her decision as to [the time of] death on being questioned. The [deity] is realized by muttering the spell *Auṃ naravīre ṭha ṭhā* 10,008 times at [the occasion of] a solar or lunar eclipse. If [that spell] is to be brought into play, one should once more mutter [it] 1,008 times. Then the deity becomes absorbed into the mirror, and so forth, [and] announces [her] decision [as to the time of death, in the form of] a virgin. Thus the deity herself, attracted by the [moral] character of the virtuous worshiper, announces her definite decision on the duration of life [of the questioner].

The next example is derived from *Yogaśāstra* 5.208–15 and illustrates the use of yantras, mantras, mātṛkās, aṅganyāsa, and shadow reading in measuring a person's longevity.

One should first prepare a [hexagonal] yantra that contains the sacred syllable *Auṃ* and place within [that *Auṃ*] the name of the person [whose lifetime is to be determined]. [Inside each] corner [of the yantra should be inscribed] the letter *ra,* which is filled with hundreds of flames related to the fire [element]. At the sides, [the yantra should be] surrounded by six vowels, beginning with *a,* together with an anusvāra [*i.e., aṃ, āṃ, iṃ, īṃ, uṃ,* and *ūṃ*]. On the outside of every corner should be a svastika mark drawn with one's own handwriting. [Finally], the four sides [of the square that frames the yantra] should be enveloped by a visarga [*ḥ*] preceded by ya [*yaḥ*]. [Then] one should [mentally] install [the yantra] on [one's own] feet, heart, head, and joints. After that, having turned [one's] back toward the sun at the time of sunrise, a wise man should observe his own shadow in order to determine his own and another person's lifetime. If he sees the whole shadow, then [there will be] no death within a year, but if the ears are absent, death will occur within twelve years. If the hands, fingers, shoulders, hair, flanks, and the nose are absent, it forebodes death in the course of ten, eight, seven, five, three, and one year[s], respectively. If the head or chin are missing, he will die in six months, whereas if the neck or eyes are absent, [death will occur] in one month [or] eleven days, [respectively]. If the thorax contains an aperture, death will occur in seven days, [and] if one were to see two shadows, then one moves close to Yama [or death].

The final example of divination demonstrates how a spell is mentally installed on the body (*aṅganyāsa*) in order to consecrate the body and its shadow. The shadow is then examined and the time of death ascertained. The spell urges the thunderbolt-handed (*vajrapāṇin*) Indra, who overcomes death, and the spear-handed (*śūlapāṇin*) Śiva, to show their [true] nature, as propagators of Jainism. According to Jain legend, a similar device was used by Hemacandra when he brought Kumārapāla to a Śaiva temple and had Śiva manifest himself in front of the king and proclaim the superiority of the Jain faith. *Yogaśāstra* 5.217–23 reads as follows.

First one should [mentally] install the syllable *svā* on the crown of the head (*cūḍā*) and *Auṃ* on the crest of the head (*mastaka*). Then [one should install] *kṣi* in the eyes, *pa* in the heart, and the syllable *hā* in the lotus of the navel. Having consecrated one's shadow and eyes by [repeating] the spell [*Auṃ juṃ saḥ auṃ mṛtyuṃ jayāya auṃ vajrapāṇine śūlapāṇine hara hara daha daha svarūpaṃ darśaya darśaya huṃ phaṭ*] 108 times, [and] having turned [one's] back toward the sun at sunrise, a competent person who has performed this [type of] worship (*pūjā*) in a proper way should take notice of the shadow of another when it concerns others' [length of life], and his own shadow when it comes to his own. If the entire shadow is seen, then death [will] not [occur] in a year. On the other hand, if the legs, shanks, or knees are missing, death [will occur] within three, two, and one year[s], [respectively]. If the thighs are absent, [death will occur] in ten months. If the waist [is missing] one will die within eight or nine months, whereas if the stomach is absent, [death occurs] in five months. Again, if the neck is lacking, one will die in four, three, two, or one month[s]. If the armpit is lacking, [death will occur] in fifteen days, whereas if the arm is nonexistent, [death will occur] in ten days. If the shoulder is absent, [death will occur] in eight days, but if the heart is removed, [death will occur] in twelve hours [or four yāmas, "watches"]. However, if the head is absent, [death will occur] in three hours [or one yāma]. If, finally, the entire [body] does not appear [in the shadow, death will occur] instantaneously.

The second set of examples of Tantric influence on Śvetāmbara Jainism concerns meditative practices and, more specifically, virtuous meditation or dharmadhyāna. According to canonical and traditional Śvetāmbara Jainism, this kind of meditation does not result in liberation (*mokṣa*), which requires the practice of the subsequent pure meditation (*śukladhyāna*). In the *Yogaśāstra*, however, dharmadhyāna is furnished with an additional variety unattested in prior Śvetāmbara texts. Whereas the canonical form of virtuous meditation does not present any Tantric influence, this new addition does reflect such an influence, which probably originated from Trika Śaivism, and stems either from a direct influence or—and this is more likely—indirectly from a Digambara work, entitled the *Jñānārṇava*, written by Śubhacandra in the tenth century C.E. This philosopher was then instrumental in introducing Tantric meditation into both Digambara and Śvetāmbara Jainism, and thereby also bringing Jain meditation into conformity with parallel developments in Hinduism and Buddhism.

Tantric virtuous meditation as presented in the *Yogaśāstra* consists of four main types. We focus on the second of these, called padastha-dhyāna, "meditation on sacred syllables." If not meditated upon as such, these syllables constituted different spells. Unlike common Tantric linguistic usage, these spells were synonymously labeled mantras or vidyās. Here, Hemacandra deviated from the distinction between mantras as letters presided over by male deities and mastered by mere repitition, and vidyās as combination of words invoking female divinities and mastered only through the practice of the prescribed rite (*sādhana*). The spells ranged in length from monosyllabic to multisyllabic formulae, and reproduced meaningless sounds, acronyms of central Jain concepts, and meaningful dogmas couched in Prakrit rather than in Sanskrit, which was the dominant language of Indian mantric science (*mantraśāstra*). The spells further show distinct syntactical features, as demonstrated by Agehananda Bharati. The application of spells in meditation as well as in divination was criticized by early Jainism, but was gradually incorporated into it, and had by the time of Hemacandra become one of the main components of Śvetāmbara Jain Tantra. Judging from the *Yogaśāstra,* it was even looked upon as paramount over the rest of the Jain teaching, which was reckoned as simply "textual details" (*granthavistara*). Hemacandra, however, urges meditators to use only Jain mantras and to avoid those of Hindu provenance, which were considered part of the "evil sciences" (*durvidyā*). From a historical point of view, however, Dundas has shown that many of the Jain mantras and vidyās indicate that Jain involvement in mantraśāstra often corresponded to that of the Hindus. The efficacy of the spells resulted in everything from knowledge of the scriptures to miraculous powers (*siddhi*s or *labdhi*s), heaven and liberation (*svargāpavarga*). The majority of spells found in the *Yogaśāstra* are variations of the pañcanamaskāra mantra or "the reverent salutation to the five [supreme beings (*parameṣṭhins*)]." This served as a Jain litany and was used at various ceremonial occasions. The mantra paid homage to the Jinas or the worthy ones (*arahantas*), the perfected beings (*siddhas*), the mendicant leaders (*āyariyas*), the mendicant preceptors (*uvajjhāyas*), and the mendicants (*sāhus*).

In the following, I attempt to give a few examples of how the various forms of the pañcanamaskāra mantra were used as part of virtuous meditation or dharmadhyāna. The first example illustrates how the eight syllables constituting the first sentence of the pañcanamaskāra mantra are envisioned as stationed on the eight petals of a lotus representing the Self (*jīva*). By intensive and prolonged meditation on these syllables, with or without *Auṃ*, worldly and spiritual goals are obtained. The mantra *Auṃ* is here used in a Jain fashion as an acronym denoting the five holy beings worshiped in the Jain litany. The letter *a* signifies the arahantas (the worthy ones), aśarīras (the Siddhas, "the perfected beings"), and āyariyas (the [mendicant] leaders); *u* the uvajjhāyas ([the mendicant] preceptors); and *m* the munis (that is, the sāhus, "the mendicants"). *Yogaśāstra* 8.66–71 says as follows:

One may [further] meditate on the luminous Self in an eight-petaled lotus which on its petals has [the eight] syllables of the mantra, [*na-mo a-ra-haṃ-tā-ṇaṃ*], beginning with *Auṃ* respectively. Having installed the first [syllable on the petal] facing east from the circle, one should repeat [this] eight-lettered mantra 1,100 times. In this manner, the other petals, pointing in due order from the east, [should be installed with *na-mo a-ra-haṃ-tā-ṇaṃ*, respectively]. The mendicant should [then] repeat [this mantra for] eight days in order to neutralize all obstacles. When eight days have elapsed, these [eight] syllables, installed successively on the petals, begin to look as if alive to him, and even such terrifying beings as lions, elephants, demons (*rākṣasas*), evil spirits (*vyantaras*) and others, which [all] cause resistance in meditation, are instantly pacified. Those who desire the fruits of this world should meditate on the mantra [*na-mo a-ra-haṃ-tā-ṇaṃ*] preceded by *Auṃ*, but those who are desirous of the state of liberation should meditate on [this mantra] without *Auṃ*.

The second passage constitutes yet another example of how an acronym is used as an object of Jain Tantric meditation. Analogous to *Auṃ*, this acronym is composed of the initial letters of the names of the five elevated beings celebrated in the pañcanamaskāra mantra. The acronym reads *a-si-ā-u-sā* and derives *a* from arahanta, *si* from siddha, *ā* from āyariya, *u* from uvajjhāya, and *sā* from sāhu. The different syllables are to be related to the cakras or lotuses positioned in the navel, head, mouth, heart, and throat. *Yogaśāstra* 8.76–77 reads as follows:

One should [also] meditate on the syllable *a* [from the mantra *a-si-ā-u-sā*], located in the lotus of the navel, the syllable *si* in the lotus of the head, the syllable *ā* in the lotus of the mouth, the syllable *u* in the lotus of the heart, [and] the syllable *sā* in the lotus of the throat. Similarly one should meditate on other seed [syllables] which are beneficial to all.

The final example of Jaina Tantric meditation concerns the most central of all spells based upon the pañcanamaskāra mantra, namely *arhaṃ*. This word is the Sanskrit equivalent of the Prakrit *arahanta*, denoting the first category of supreme beings. As the syllables constituting this mantra also are the first and last syllables of the Sanskrit syllabary, it was the object of considerable speculation in medieval Tantric texts. The autocommentary on *Yogaśāstra* 8.18–22 states, for example, that "[*arhaṃ*], which begins with *a* and ends with *ha* has the letter *r* in the middle together with a dot (that is, the character *ṃ*), that is, the ultimate reality. He who knows this is a knower of reality." The mantra *arhaṃ* was, however, primarily used as an object of meditation.

The following quote demonstrates how to meditate on the mantra *arhaṃ*. This act is preceded by envisioning an eight-petaled lotus situated below the center of the navel, comprising a pericarp with a line of vowels as well as petals with the different classes of letters in the Sanskrit syllabary. The pañcanamaskāra mantra is inscribed in all eight of the interstices between the petals, and the sacred syllables *Auṃ* and *hriṃ* appear on top of each of the petals. Having meditated on *arhaṃ*, one should imagine that one splits the various knots (*granthis*) or obstacles related to the different cakras by means of this very subtle sound as it moves through the middle path, the suṣumṇā channel. This and other additional practices finally result in one becoming all-seeing, free from attachment, aversion, and delusion, worshiped by gods, and merged into the state of the supreme Self (*paramātman*). *Yogaśāstra* 8.8–9 explains this as follows:

The first letter [of the syllabary, *a*], should be placed in front [of the lotus] and the final letter [*ha*], at its center accompanied by [the letter] *r*—which is spotless as snow—a pleasant crescent, and a dot (*ṃ*). This holy word, *arhaṃ*, which brings one in contact with the essence of life, [should first be uttered in the mind] with a short [sound], then with a long, [then with a] protracted, [then with a] subtle and [finally with an] excessively subtle sound.

—36—

Cheating Death

Michael Walter

Death and dying are significant topics for all religions, including Buddhism. When Tantra was the dominant form of Buddhism in both northern India and Tibet, Buddhists displayed a voracious curiosity about this topic. Ritual and meditational materials show a variety of methods for dealing with the process of decline and death.

Sometime before the year 1000, Tantric teachings that dealt with preparation for death, cremation, and so forth, had been organized into cycles. One group is a set of teachings by Atiśa, an eleventh-century Buddhist master from Bengal, on the goddess Tārā, called the "Thirteen Spells." These teachings provide instruction in recognizing and preparing for death, as well as in perpetuating the practice of merit making, a process that allows a Buddhist to accrue merit for spiritual improvement and then selflessly to transfer that merit to beings who are not in a position to obtain such merit. (Tārā and the bodhisattva Avalokiteśvara are Buddhist deities who model and display selfless compassion to suffering sentient beings, and thus are especially to be sought at times of physical danger and distress.) Six of these teachings, including one entitled "Cheating Death" (*mṛtyuvañcana* in Sanskrit, *'Chi bslu* in Tibetan) deal with the human lifespan, its lengthening, decline, and end. The first teaching is an introduction to the significance of the spells; the last is on the casting and distribution of tsha tshas, small, usually circular pressed sacred images made in part from the ashes of the dead, which are designed to generate merit continuously. By the fourteenth century, such ritual instructions had attained great size, as exemplified by Karma Gling-pa's gatherings in the *Bar do thos grol* cycles. The literal title of these texts, which teach people how to avoid an evil rebirth, is "Release from the Intermediate State by Merely Hearing These Teachings." Selections from this cycle have been studied and published as "The Tibetan Book of the Dead"; in fact, the cycles total many hundreds of pages in length. It is these cycles that include sections devoted to "cheating death."

In addition to eight texts on "cheating death" found in the Tantra commentary section of the Tibetan canon—all taught by or connected with Vāgīśvarakīrti, a predecessor of Atiśa as abbot at the Nālandā monastery and the author of the text studied here—various recipes, instructions, and rites, with accompanying anecdotal materials and fulsome praises, are also found embedded in medical, alchemical, and Tantric ritual materials. In addition, much supporting anecdotal and mythological material is also found in histories of Tibetan Buddhist traditions, biographies of yogins, and even general sketches of the development of Buddhism. This is because "cheating death" helps one to continue exercising the vows of a bodhisattva, a Buddhist who has taken a vow to aid suffering sentient beings to achieve enlightenment.

The goal of Mahāyāna Buddhism is enlightenment, with a view to universal enlightenment: that is, to become enlightened, but to do so in order to help fill the universe with other enlightened sentient beings who see existence as it is, and who act selflessly and with compassion because they share the realization of the Buddha about the nature of all things. The Mahāyāna view of the nature of things is that saṃsāra, the endless cycle of births that unenlightened sentients go through, and nirvāṇa, release from saṃsāra, are ultimately mere concepts of the unenlightened mind, and are empty of reality. They are, instead, of the nature of Voidness (*śūnyatā*). Insight into the true nature of Voidness is achievable because we have the Buddha nature within us, and there is a variety of ways in which Mahāyāna Buddhist traditions teach its realization. The present text comes from the Tantric tradition, which aims its followers at buddhahood itself, at realizing the fully developed Buddha nature within us.

Tantra, which has been practiced in Hinduism and Buddhism for centuries, is a set of practices based on two principles. The first is that of subtle physiology. The body exists on a series of vibrational levels, and our physical body is the lowest of those levels. We also contain what might be called a subtle body, which consists of channels through which flow our life energy and our consciousness, the latter in what are described as "winds." To understand our true nature—the goal of this yoga—we must gain control over the elements (water, air, fire, earth, and "ether," that is, space) of which we are made, and the winds just described. The cosmos is made up of these same elements, and the second principle states that the structure and function of our subtle body parallels the greater structures of the cosmos: the planets, stars, constellations, and so forth. This second principle, sometimes referred to as a system of macrocosmic and microcosmic correspondences, allows the yogin to escape human finitude by understanding how both his individual body and the cosmos are ruled by the same processes.

In terms of dying, a yogin must know how to overcome his internal "time" mechanism—what we call aging—by controlling it in the same way that Buddhism and Hinduism believe that external time can be stopped: by stopping the motion of the sun and moon. The yogin does this internally, in the present text, by meditating on deities who represent the reality behind the internal sun and moon, respectively: red Amitābha, the buddha of infinite light, and white Abhaya Lokeśvara, a form of Avalokiteśvara, the bodhisattva of compassion. (Of course, people also die from accidents, and so on; such deaths are explained in this text as death "coming from the gods.")

The sun dries, burns, and robs beings of their energy. Thus, the yogin's "internal sun" also causes the desiccation of his life force; at one point this text advises the yogin to shield his nutritive moisture, called "ambrosia," from that sun, since we are all born with this ambrosia and it has the potential to give us eternal life if we protect it from our internal sun and open the body up to its flow. Similarly, our ambrosia originates near the top of our skull, dripping from our internal moon. Thus, the way Tantra visualizes internalized universal processes is by orienting them around the body, especially in power centers aligned along the spinal cord.

Astrological correspondences are an important part of Tantra yoga. The spinal cord is a "cosmic pillar" as well, perhaps (from an astrological point of view), as the Milky Way, around which two "veins" representing the paths of the sun (heating and drying) and the moon (cooling and moist) twine themselves. These paths are actually the channels by which breath enters, in the yogin's practice, through either the left or right nostril, and exits through the opposite nostril. The breath thereby passes through both the solar and lunar paths, as well as through the constellations, which are conceived to be located on the twelve "petals" of that circle which, at the level of the heart, is usually conceived to be a lotus. When the yogin controls the powers of the sun and moon, and then unites them, he overcomes their grip on his life-breath and ambrosia, and takes in his grasp the very process of time in the universe. This also provides the yogin with the experience of ultimate transcendence ("enlightenment," in Buddhist terms). Tantric yogins with perfect practice do not, in fact, die, but pass into subtle bodies that are eternal; the Knowledge Holders in Part Three below are one such group of yogins.

The yogin must calculate the time at which the sun passes through the twelve houses of his zodiac; as the text shows, it has a set time for transiting, or crossing, each of these; variations can affect the power or length of life of the yogin. The yogin should also analyze both outer and inner astrological systems to understand propitious and nonpropitious times for meditations, and so on, as well as personal traits (such as susceptibility to illness, and preferred seasons and times of the day to do things) and changes in his internal states. The yogin's universe becomes divided into two-hour intervals (the six transits of both the sun and mooon through the signs of the zodiac in a twenty-four-hour day) as well as time intervals based on the control of the circulation of this breath. Through continual attention to these processes, he escapes the control of the sun and signs of the zodiac, and controls the winds that suppport his mind and consciousness.

In fact, the ultimate reason why the yogin engages in this yoga is to purify his consciousness; he uses his control over the heat of his inner sun to cleanse the impurities in the winds that shape that consciousness. Unenlightened consciousness is prevented from realizing its enlightened nature because of these impurities, whereas through these practices they are gradually removed, if the yogin controls each inhalation and exhalation in what Buddhism calls a mindfulness yoga centered on the observation and regulation of breathing.

Mention was made above of the Buddha nature within us; Buddhist Tantra develops this through spiritual cultivation (*sādhana*). A repetition of the "seed" syllable of a deity will actualize it and bring it clearly into the yogin's consciousness, so that the deity will merge with the yogin, and become the true "self" of the yogin. This process is accompanied by yogic postures (*āsanas*) and gestures (*mudrās*), and sometimes dance. This deity represents enlightened being, and the consciousness of the yogin also becomes enlightened, through two stages of practice: these are the development and perfection of the presence of the deity, followed by the dissolution of that deity, such that the yogin comes to realize the Voidness (*śūnyatā*) from which all things—even Buddhas—emerge and back into which they dissolve.

It is partly because of the refined state of a yogin's consciousness through this practice, and partly due to the homologous system described above, that dreams, omens, and such as presented in the text here provide insight into the yogin's physical and meditative states. Furthermore, Tantric "subtle physiology" provides the link between an individual's meditative and visionary experiences and the external signs that are meaningful for events transpiring in a yogin's practice.

Buddhism does not depend solely on Tantra and its yogic practices to lengthen life, or even to attain immortality. Elixirs based on organic ingredients, as well as mercury- and sulphur-based compounds, are also used, as in Western alchemy. Even Buddhist medical traditions contain compounds designed to lengthen life. The effectiveness of many of these preparations rests either on the meditative practices that accompany their creation or on the "empowering" of compounds through a blessing by a master, such as when he blows on it. Power over life is also attained by the yogin through sexual activity with an accomplished consort. By retaining his semen, the yogin reverses the normal bodily processes; and, here, as described in Part Three, special power comes from bodily fluids generated during sexual union. Acts of devotion also have a place here: we see that building and restoring stūpas, circular structures that are circumambulated to gain merit and show respect for the Buddha, are also means to achieve a longer life. (Stūpas have a central wooden pole, analogous to the spinal column and here called the "life-tree pole," which is an auspicious object when viewed in a dream). In Part Three, we see that simply contributing a robe to a monk creates sufficient merit to hold death at bay.

In addition, it is maintained in many sources that advanced yogins can create elixirs or obtain other powers (as mentioned here, an enchanted sword and medicine for the eyes afford the yogin the power to see through matter and the ability to travel long distances rapidly) as a routine benefit of advanced practices. These are known as "accomplishments" (*siddhis*), which the yogin is eventually to discard as he procedes to complete enlightenment, since to concentrate on them would be a sign of the yogin's clinging to his ego rather than eradicating it totally.

Much of what has been presented here applies to both Hindu and Buddhist

Tantra. The truly Buddhist elements in these teachings come out both in the visualization of Buddhist spiritual beings, such as Amitābha (buddha of infinite light), and Amṛtakuṇḍalin (who represents the process of uniting the sun and moon, and causing the ambrosia to flow), as well as in the centrality of śūnyatā and belief in the creation and transfer of merit.

The selections below come from the most extensive teaching in the Tibetan canon on "cheating" or "tricking" death. It was composed by Vāgīśvarakīrti, and must have been a standard Buddhist work on the subject—first in India, and later, through Atiśa, in Tibet—but one filled with uncertainties of interpretation, since a second translation of this text, also found in the canon, is supplemented with many interlinear notes. The material here is presented with some interpretation from those notes and other commentaries. These teachings mix divinatory practices, astrological guidance (most of the materials not included here were detailed astrological calculations), and Tantric practices, in a set of indications of death and how to avoid it, especially intended for yogins but also for lay Buddhists in their analysis of dreams, visions, internal changes, and so on.

The material presented here is a translation of excerpts from the *Teaching on Cheating Death* (*'Chi ba bslu ba'i man ngag* in Tibetan, *Mṛtyuvañcanopadeśa* in Sanskrit) by Vāgīśvarakīrti, as found in *The Tibetan Tripitaka, Bstan-hgyur*, vol. 59, pp. 103–110, and in the *Sde-dge Bstan 'Gyur, Rgyud 'Grel*, vol. 27, columns 236–66, along with a few elucidations from various commentaries. This work is divided into four parts: external signs of death; internal signs of death; instructions for cheating death by external means; and instructions for internal means for cheating death.

Further Reading

To gain some idea of the wealth of Buddhist practices and attitudes toward death, see some of the recent works by Gregory Schopen, including "Deaths, Funerals, and the Division of Property in a Monastic Code," in Donald S. Lopez, Jr., ed., *Buddhism in Practice* (Princeton: Princeton University Press, 1995), pp. 473–502, as well as Tadeusz Skorupski, *The Sarvadurgatipariśodhana Tantra: Elimination of All Evil Destinies* (Delhi: Motilal Banarsidass, 1983). Also of value are the numerous selections of and commentaries to the *Bar do thos grol* texts, such as Robert Thurman, *The Tibetan Book of the Dead* (New York: Bantam, 1993), and Chogyam Trungpa and Francesca Freemantle, *The Tibetan Book of the Dead* (London: Oxford University Press, 1975). Lati Rinbochay, *Death, Intermediate State, and Rebirth in Tibetan Buddhism* (Ithaca, N.Y.: Snow Lion, 1985) is a useful overview. A good source on the connections between astrology and Tantric yoga is Alex Wayman, "Tantric Teachings about the Inner Zodiac," in his *The Buddhist Tantras* (New York: Samuel Weiser, 1973), pp. 151–63.

Mṛtyuvañcana/'Chi bslu

PART ONE

[The work opens with an homage to Mañjuśrī, the bodhisattva who bequeaths wisdom, especially that connected with traditional sciences.]

The Lord of Death manifests all variety of illusion; the answer to this is to achieve power over old age and death. This teaching being difficult to grasp by those of inferior intellect—whose minds vacillate—attaining power over the Lord of Death and the signs of death, the texts on death, and their commentaries, will be explained here.

Total cheating of the Lord of Death is the realm of liberation itself; extending for some short time the lives of all sentients is not being liberated. The ceasing of life-duration, the senses, and the working of the mind is the characteristic of death. Living on for some time through various means has been explained to be "the cheating of death."

Disciplining the senses through practicing the Dharma, one will live as long as he wishes in saṃsāra; for that long, one accumulates merit, and so on. Acting so as to cultivate the thought of enlightenment, it will truly arise. So, not seeing anything more dear than life in saṃsāra, quickly and by many means one will act habitually to deceive death. Applying means in the right way to this end, it is not at all difficult to achieve. By the powers of precious stones, spells, and medicines, a person realizes anything he wishes.

Signs that death is approaching should be understood by any means necessary. Although some develop the desire to know the signs of death, there may also well be hesitation by others about such objects of knowledge, because these latter are then in a state of well-being. However, when those people who were well become controlled by painful states, passions, dimness of mind, and so on, and as a consequence of the fear, suffering, and so on that arise from those symptoms, signs of death will of course manifest themselves to those people, as well.

Through a division into outer and inner, it is intended that the signs of death are to be analyzed as twofold, the upsetting of the gods and the upsetting of the elements. Dying from the total upsetting of the gods is explained to be "coming from the gods"; famine and so on, and lightning, hail, and so on, are the signs of their being upset. Dying from the total upsetting of the elements is explained to be "coming from the elements." When the elements are upset, bile, and so on, and the fire and water elements, and so on, are damaged. When both are upset, death is explained as "coming from both." When both are upset, [there is] thunder, and so on, and bile, phlegm, and so on, are damaged.

Although one may see signs of death at any time, at some times they show that death is not coming; in an unerring way, they can be examined [by the yogin] for impediments that damage one's practice of the Dharma. Likewise, any time that one does not see signs of death, even at some of those times death will appear. At such times, in the lack of [appearance of] a fixed time for death, it is not that there is a lack of signification concerning a fixed time for one's death [that is, there are always signs, if one knows how to look for them].

When the yogin is permanently established in equanimity, with his mind accordingly placed in one-pointedness by that practice, he should first closely examine, briefly, the external signs.

[What follows here is an excursus on searching for external signs of death.]

The transiting of the sun, the fifteenth lunar day, and so on, may result in that illness, and so on, suddenly becoming one's master.

When the time of death is explained to be "certain," it is not certain only insofar as there is a mistaken understanding of the signs of death. [For example,] when the far side of one's left cheek shakes, that is a very strong indicator of death. When one's inner winds and a feeling of cold rush together, however, one must search elsewhere for any signs of death.

Signs of death appear in the house of Cancer, in the middle summer month, and in Capricorn, proceeding through the middle month of winter. On the day of the sun's transit, in the middle month of summer, the measure of its foot [that is, the angle of its rays] is at midday; when one looks to the north then, the shadow there is the true nature [of his lifespan]. On the exact day of transit in the middle winter month, there are seven measures to its foot; at noon of that day, if the sky is clear, one should examine his shadow.

For each month there is an increase of one foot, and [then] there is a decrease of one. If anything other than this is seen, the yogin should truly fear death. From the middle summer month until Capricorn, the sun's foot increases. From Capricorn until Cancer, the sun's foot diminishes. From the middle summer month they increase in degrees; likewise, from the middle winter month they decrease in stages. If one sees a change in his shadow [at those times], one will truly die in one month. If there is an increase of one's shadow when it should diminish, and a diminishing when it should increase, then, calculating from that time, one will truly die in one month. If there is too much increase [of one's shadow] at the time of increase, one will be harmed by various illnesses. Likewise, if there is too much diminishment at the time of diminishing, death will undoubtedly occur.

At the end of the middle summer and winter months, timely and untimely death are accurately calculated from the first six days each of Cancer and Pisces. The twenty-four-hour days of the middle and last summer months and the extra days of the middle and last winter months may be either good or bad for calculating death.

If someone feels a depression [in the flesh] somewhere between the innermost soles of the feet and the tip of the nose, then, truly, three days hence one will die at once. At the time of defecating and urinating, if one is simultaneously seized by [a fit of] sneezing, then, from the moment of being seized, one will age and die in one year. If one experiences a depression [in the flesh] at the nape of the neck, after five days he will die. If one cannot see the tip of his tongue, he will then die in three days.

If one feels that something is continuously stinging the tip of the nose, he will die in four months. If one imagines a depression in the spot between his eyebrows, death is truly imminent. Whenever there is pain simultaneously in both nostrils, one will die one month hence. For this reason, merit should be gathered [during that month], cheating death [that is, lengthening this period].

At night, while uniting the wind from both channels, if one sneezes during and at the end of the session, one will die five months after equanimity of meditation has been achieved.

If one feels pain at the same time in the joints of the little fingers and toes, death will come in one month's time. If pain occurs at the same time all the way from the heart to the throat, and if one is not grounded in Dharma practice, death will occur in half a month. If pain occurs at the same time on three of one's palms and soles, then, even if one is equal [in strength] to Indra, he will die in three days.

Whoever cannot see his left eye in a mirror, and doesn't act to correct this situation, he will truly die in seven days. When engaging in sex, if someone doesn't hear a bell when it is rung, even though he is equal to Brahmā, he will die three months from that time.

On the first day of the waxing moon, if one's semen is black, he will die in six months; if red, he will be struck with an illness. If pain occurs between the tip of the nose and the space between the eyes, or at the top of the head, death is imminent and cannot be averted.

If there is pain with fever, starting at the toes and going to the navel, one will certainly die in six months. If there is pain from the toes to the heart, throat, or even as far as the head, developing by degrees from half a month to three month's time, one will be dead within one day.

If one's heart suddenly sinks in the body, death will occur after two weeks. If the two veins on the sides of the neck are cut, death will also occur in two weeks.

If a black spot suddenly appears in the middle of the tongue, then, gritting one's teeth tightly, one will die in two days from that time.

If the veins behind, inside, and around the ears appear cut, if not on that day, then in five days, one will die. If the red color of one's nails suddenly disappears, and if one then doesn't practice mantra, and so on, he will die in six months.

If one is meditating and making a threatening gesture, and is suddenly disturbed by fear and anger, then, to the extent that he is not grounded in the Dharma, he will die in one or two years.

Fluid dripping constantly from the eyes, causing one to be mistaken in what one sees; not seeing one's shadow in water, or in a mirror; also, seeing rainbows at night or groups of stars in the daytime; seeing lightning in a clear sky in the south, or the Milky Way in the daytime; likewise, seeing a star fall in the daytime; and seeing geese, crows, and peacocks mixing together: after seeing these, death will come in two months and two days.

Likewise, seeing a glow around one's head; a gandharva city [gandharvas are spirits who dwell in the air and live on scents] at the top of a tree or at the base of a mountain, or seeing pretas (ghosts) and piśācas (ghouls) or other fearsome beings; shaking violently; falling down again and again; seeing gold and silver coloring in vomit, feces, and urine—one who sees each of these things will die within a month.

If semen, feces, and urine flow from the body at the same time, the person who suffers that will die in one year; however, he can be healed by medicines. Whoever has half his body hot while the other is cold, since death will come after seven days, that person should begin thinking about the world beyond.

That yogin who experiences himself as filled with the letter *ha*, and whose breath has become like fire, will see the Lord of Death after ten days. If one sees a black spot at the base of the ring finger, then, at the end of eighteen days, he will truly die. If a three-colored chameleon climbs onto someone's head and then runs away quickly, that person will truly die after five months.

If no sound comes from the yogin's body when he rubs it with his hands, and all his limbs feel cold, he will die in ten days. If someone's calves and hands suddenly twitch and move, and he lacks the thread of the twice-born [castes], he will die after one or two years.

When someone fills his mouth each day with water warmed while the sun is hot, and then blows out his breath, he will see various rainbows that persist in stages in the midst of that breath. Such people, who are generally very long-lived, will fail to see that they have only six months to live.

All these things are general knowledge; these particular points need to be made:

One will die in six months from a change in one's basic nature. If one cannot see the tip of his nose, he will die in five months. If one becomes deaf, one will die after four months. If the senses become dispersed and one falls off his seat, he will die in three months. If one sees light between his eyebrows, he will see Yama [the Hindu and Buddhist god of death, who gathers the spirits of the dead in his house] in two months. If one's testicles shrink, he will die after one month. If the yogin doesn't see his reflection in another's eyes, he will die in two weeks. If someone can't move his tongue, he will die after ten days. If one turns away from food, he will meet Yama after five days. If one feels a pulling at his sides, he will die after three days. If one's whole body becomes stiff, that person will die in one day.

During the waxing or waning of the moon, if one's semen becomes black and this isn't cured, he will die in six months. However, if someone completely avoids doing things in the dark half of the month, and turns to doing things in the bright half, then, when the breath exits from the left nostril and enters [the right nostril], he will be healed again.

Although one's body may be firm, if his shadow is crooked, he will die in four months.

Those learned in such things have taught the following:

If one sees his shadow going in the southern direction, he will die, it is said.

In such ways, one sees the signs of his perishability. Although such signs have been explained [by some] to be meaningless, misleading, perverse, and so on, even if *all* dreams were untrue, such a criticism would not apply to this path, which involves a mind strengthened in faith through practice of the repetition of spells. The gods [that is, the personal deities of yogins] teach in dreams, and yogins who see the truth in dreams will develop faith in them and then will look for signs of death in them.

Whenever lac, kovidāra (*Bauhinia*) or open karavīra (*Nerium indicum*) flowers appear at the end of a dream, that person will die in six months. When an offering-lamp to whatever god, or [when] sand or a pile of ashes arises in a dream, that person will also die in six months. If one heads off to the south, riding a donkey [in a dream], and does not return, one again has six months left [to live]. Whoever mounts a monkey and rides toward the south, if he awakens while he is still there, he will die as above. If one dreams of climbing up a long stick, the life-tree pole of a stūpa, an anthill, or a heap of dust, he will not live more than six months. Anyone bound [in a dream] by an angry, black girl will die; she is called "The Mark of Time" and causes death after seven days. The person who dreams of a woman wearing black clothing and enjoying a black man, or who dreams of a garland of karavīra, will go to the place of Yama.

If one dreams of a darkness, a wide-open place, or, likewise, being thrown into prison; or, if one dreams of falling from a tree, that person will reside with the Lord of Death. During sleep, if one sees a great tree, grass, or fruitless trees on his head and body, he will not live beyond six months.

A body rubbed with red aromatics, ornamented with a red rosary, or smeared with sesame is to be much feared. Likewise, cutting off of hair, wearing red, riding an ass, or a person heading quickly to the south—if someone sees such [visions] as these in a dream, he will die in six months. Incense with a red rosary, or red clothing—if these are [seen] in someone's dreams, he will die in eight months.

The externals of death are beyond number. Since these have been made known, a yogin should quickly strive to cheat death through spells, and so on, when he experiences these signs.

PART TWO

Now will be discussed clearly the internal signs of death, which are understood from the appearance of the vital wind. The mouth and the nose are the spheres of action of the wind.

To whatever extent one does not understand well and truly the internal signs, to that same extent the reality of death will not be truly comprehended in its external signs.

The certainty we can have about death is twofold: [Its time] having been established with certainty, [the signs] can then be explained completely.

If a person, upon reflection, makes an accurate analysis of one twenty-four-hour day in some appropriate way, then, calculating from that day, he will know how much time will elapse until he will die. [This is because] the life-force possessed by ordinary sentient beings wanders constantly and in all of them [in the form of] the vital wind that is based for each of them in their right and left nostrils. Those [paths] that we call "sun" and "moon" are that wind, [which] circulates every ninety minutes. The wise yogin will analyze the wind, since death, and so on, result from a deviation from this regularity.

When death is coming in six months, one should practice mindfulness of the Dharma. When the order of the wind is disturbed in the last month, friends and relatives will become troubled. In the last two weeks, because one's mind has become deranged, the illness will appear to be intolerable. When the motion of the wind has been disturbed during the last one, three, four, five, or six days, contention and quarreling will appear. When the natural state [of the wind's movements] has been lost, and it moves along the three paths to try to gain perception, there is no power to become healthy again, and one will die after half a day has passed.

[Using the movement of the vital wind to calculate death:]

Calculating from the time of the sun's transiting in the first month of winter, if the wind travels five days in the sun, one will die eighteen years after that time. Calculating from the time of the sun's transiting in the middle fall month, if the wind travels [in the sun's path] for a period of five days, one will die after fifteen years. Carrying out the same calculation from the last month of summer, one will die after twelve years; from the first summer month, one will die after nine years. Calculating from the time of the transiting of the middle spring month, if the wind travels [in the sun's path] for five days at that time, one will die after six years; from the middle winter month, after three years.

Perceptions about the inner wind and all the paths of the sun should be examined by learned ones for either timely or untimely death.

Whenever the wind, traveling [through] the body, suddenly enters another path and so, at that time, quickly exhausts one's life-force, there will no doubt be death at that time.

If the yogin perceives his wind to be in the sun [path, that is, the right nostril], and it travels for half a solar day at the time that the sun is at its maximum distance from the horizon, it should be understood that he will die fourteen years after that time. If, for one solar day, a day and night, two twenty-four-hour days, or three, or four [days], the wind travels on the sun path, one will die within twelve years. If it travels in such a way through five, ten, or fifteen twenty-four-hour days, then, one will die in three, two, or one years, respectively.

Likewise, if it travels there for twenty or twenty-five twenty-four-hour days, then one will die in six or three months. If it travels there for twenty-six, twenty-seven, twenty-eight, or twenty-nine such days, then one will die in two months, one month, one-half month, or ten days. If it travels there for thirty, thirty-one, or thirty-two such days, then one will die after three, or two, or one day(s), respectively. When the wind travels the sun path for thirty-three days, one will die that very day; even if one is Viṣṇu, without a doubt.

This is the appearance of the signification of death.

Developments regarding the vital wind are to be known through the senses. There are no indicators more important than the senses.

I have thus explained the inner signs of death, otherwise known as "omens of death." Having made those signs known to himself, the yogin should therefore strive to cheat death through meditative concentration, and so on, as quickly as possible.

PART THREE

Having made known to the yogin the collection of omens of death relating to both the outer and inner signs, I will now make known a condensed set of indications for cheating death that relates to both sets of signs.

Because of the workings of body and speech, internal cheating is accomplished through the action of meditative concentration. External cheating through wealth, spells, and medicines becomes internal as well through the power of yoga.

Faith makes possible one's efforts to cheat the Lord of Death, so one should make oneself firm in faith. Otherwise, even if a yogin tires himself from practice through body and speech [that is, postures and chanting], no benefit will result. Indeed, the faithless god Indra will not find any subtle Dharma with his hoards of wealth for his bodily sufferings. Faith is the most subtle Dharma; it is the release to Paradise [in the use of] ascetic practice, fire offerings, and wisdom. Faith is the basis for success in all these methods. One may have wealth, life, everything—such things mean nothing if one has no faith. Even though there seems to be some small result due to one's wealth and so on, nothing will ultimately be accomplished if one has no faith.

Acting to protect oneself from death by means of the Dharma [that is, by studying the teachings of the Buddha] has been explained to be "cheating death." By delighting in irreligiosity and by being heedless, a person behaves as if he would not remain in this life for even an instant. Even though one were Brahmā, when there is no Dharma practice there is no power to cheat the Lord of Death. The Dharma of the Holy Ones is true; they delight in giving, and in enduring ascetic practices. They have the highest love for all—what do they need from the many other teachings? When one's heart drips with compassion for sentients at all times (and because the Dharma is a liberating wisdom), what does one need from the many other teachings? Human life is asserted in all religious and philosophical systems to be the most excellent of the elements of existence; if one studies that constantly, he will gradually increase his distance from the Lord of Death.

If one eschews nonvirtuous acts, takes the Three Vows for refuge [that is, the vow to be a lay supporter of Buddhism, the vow of an ordained monk, and the vow of a Tantric yogin], and keeps the temporary vows or the vows of a layperson as his Buddhist practice, his distance from the Lord of Death will be lengthened.

People are afraid of such things as being thrown into prison or struck [down] by a great disease; if they are protected from such dangers, their lives are truly lengthened, and the Lord of Death is cheated. In the devotion that the lowly and the lordless have in accepting the wonderful moral teachings of the Buddha, they realize the goals of their desires, and their lifetimes truly increase. By understanding one's father, mother, and elder guru, one has reverence for the aged, and so on; when one bestows offerings and honor upon them, the Lord of Death will not approach them. One should likewise revere one's personal deity. The life[span] of the yogin is increased when, with equal devotion in undertaking ascetic practices for that being, he constantly and faithfully pays inward obeisance to it.

If one repairs cracked or broken stūpas with bricks, and so on, a short life will be lengthened, and this will create the same merit as that of giving alms to a monk. Life is perpetually extended by creating temples, images, stūpas, and so on, by establishing pleasure groves, and by offerings, and so on, at the eight great stūpas. If one offers feasts, with supplies collected by supplication, to the saṅgha, then, after seven days, one will acquire power over a long life equal to that of Dharmarāja Aśoka [a Buddhist "King of Dharma" who ruled India in the third century B.C.E.].

When one creates stūpas of sand, and casts tsha tshas in the same way, and then pays homage to those stūpas and tsha tshas, the length of one's life will truly be extended.

In reading the *Mahāsamaya* (the *Sūtra on the Teachings of the Great Bodhisattva Vow*) [and other sūtras], if someone intones them with reverence, long life will be achieved and the Lord of Death will be cheated. Likewise, if one reads all of the Yoga Tantras, and so on, taught by the Buddha, or through the rites taught in the five texts of protective spells known as the Pañcarakṣa, one will come to cheat the Lord of Death. Likewise, by making circumambulations of such a stūpa as that which is constructed with a top-knot, or causing the recitation of spells, one counters the efforts of the Lord of Death.

The wise ones who practice such methods cause death and the sun to dwell far from them. Likewise, drawing maṇḍalas and making fire offerings, mudrās, strewn offerings, and food offerings to yogins will also cheat the Lord of Death.

When one offers food, drink, and bedding, or even merely a robe, for the possession of the Ārya Saṅghas [the monks and nuns of the Buddhist community] of the four directions, one cheats the Lord of Death.

Undertaking such actions that should be done is the signifier of Dharma and merit. Through merit, life is extended and, accordingly, the Lord of Death is cheated. In the same way, even considering increasing the teaching of the Dharma by a small amount has been taught by the learned to cheat the Lord of Death.

Making efforts such as these at practicing the Dharma causes immediate confidence in spells of accomplishment, medicines, and other matters that completely clear away the Lord of Death. When one apprehends that the Lord of Death [can be] kept away from our world by the power of spells of wealth, medicines of accomplishment, and medical elixirs, one also realizes [the state of being of a] Knowledge Holder.

If a yogin understands all the texts there are on testing jewels, then that learned one will find himself in the possession of a jewel for realizing any wish, and will even be fit to hold the Jewel of Life of Vajradhara, which is just the same as the jewel for realizing all of one's wishes. Because these teachings can bring one precious sapphires as well as other great jewels, there is no doubt that all the Lords of Death will be repulsed. For these reasons, one should not raise doubts about the power of such jewels; everyone wishes to have a jewel with inconceivable powers.

If one makes offerings in a desolate place before a figure of one's personal god on cotton cloth, and so on, then, by merely reciting the proper spells, the cheating of death will come about.

[An example of this follows:]

If a yogin repeats this spell 100,000 times, with faith, to Lokeśvara, for that one to truly appear before him, [then] death will truly be cheated. First, say *vairocana*; after that, say *tāre* three times; then *tuttāre* and *ture* two times each; finishing with *svāhā*—death will be deceived. As it is said in the *Tārābhavatantra* [the "Tantra on the Arising of Tārā"]: "When one recites this spell 100,000 times before the eyes of Tārā, with curds and honey placed before her, and with a sprout of dūrva grass to the east and a fire offering showing its flames to the north, then the yogin will truly cause death, which has sprung from the totality of former actions, to be averted."

One would really do things just this way.

The spell that is the heart of the *Ārya Pratisāra* is the bestower of all magical powers. One should recite the ten letters of this secret spell, called "Victor over Death," 100,000 times in the presence of Lokeśvara. After that, offer 100,000 fire offerings with white flowers lifted up and cast into melted butter as a means of pacification for bringing down Avalokiteśvara. Following this, by the power of this spell, the deceiving of the Lord of Death will truly occur: First, say *oṃ*, then *aṃ*; after that, *oṃ* and *aṃ* again; then, *oṃ mṛtyuñ ja ya* ("victory over death"), and after that, again, *oṃ*—these are the ten syllables of that spell. This was taught by the tathāgatas [buddhas] for living a kalpa [the duration of a universe] or longer.

Along with the rites explained by those who know, and other preparations the yogin may wish to use, he should [also] combine medicines [derived from] *Sophora flavescens* and urine for regions with great hunger. *Sophora flavescens* should always be used either by itself or together with the three myrobalans. After that, one's body will become firm and he will not see the gate of Yama. Although there are other such medicines of realization, when one has true faith in any of them, one's life is extended and one does not see death, because the power that illness and old age hold over him has come to an end.

If one eats mercury with gold and silver in it, prepared according to the correct ritual, it will possess the nature of a medical elixir, and will cheat death. After a day, or about a month or so, when it has overcome the [mortal] condition of the body, then, one will, by the rite of administering it as a medicine through the nose, come to deceive death.

Some who have died in a number of ways can be seen to live again. One example [of a method for achieving this] would be that of a man, or of a woman having her menses: their blood and other bodily elements, which have become mixed when they emerge in the course of their mutual exchange, are not connected strongly together. Extract two drops of such blood immediately upon the death of someone. These two drops will be released via a small, hollow cylinder smeared with butter, so as to be injected into the nostrils. When one drop emerges from a nostril, it should be rolled into the other. This is done, in turn, for each nostril. It has been seen that people become alive again in this way, so this is a recommended procedure for stopping death in this life.

An indestructible [literally, vajra, "diamond"] body possesses a pleasing form. When one attains through it a lifetime matching the years in kalpa, such is truly a turning back of death.

Some urines protect the body when magically realized according to the relevant teachings. They will cheat death immediately when drunk or rubbed on [the body]. Someone who habituates himself to the constant practice of such teachings, along with the correct use of butter and honey, will cause both timely and untimely death to be averted.

It is not proper to cast doubt on the power of such medicines; their potency appears, in a manner that is inconceivable, everywhere. There is a direct relationship between the reverence one shows these teachings in his external religious actions and the extent to which one can cheat the Lord of Death in this life. There is a great degree of fear attached to death, which has great power; accordingly, there are inner religious actions given here for that fear.

PART FOUR

Now, with regard to cheating death:

Death is explained to be truly cheated when some learned one possessing inner greatness exerts himself. Such a person is fearless before a king, a thief, a great māra [there are four māras: these are beings who attempt to seduce bodhisattvas and yogins into attachment to the world], a tiger, and so on. He is a mountain, or something like that, free from human bustle, abiding by himself, wherever it pleases him. Eating moderately and speaking little, he finds no pleasure in a strong desire for things. Much of the time, he remains in meditation and sleeps little, exerting himself greatly in the repetition of spells. The action of making offerings to a personal deity, and so on, of reading holy texts, casting strewn offerings, and so on, are efforts he makes with a compassionate mind for sentient beings of the past, present, and future.

He realizes what he wishes for through his merit; to accumulate merit, he must avoid distractions. Because everything is realized through faith, he works to increase his faith. Through diligence, what one begins is finished; therefore, he makes diligence a preliminary practice. Because wished-for results can be assured through meditation, he makes one-pointed effort in that [meditation]. By avoiding distractions, he develops his practice; thus, he diligently avoids [distractions]. Since everything can be achieved by means of perfect knowledge, he possesses all knowledge through his great faith and diligence. Because he sees that suffering arises in the act of dying, he also sees that Dharma originates from the act of living. Free of all doubt, he practices at all times the cheating of death through veneration of Amṛtakuṇḍalin.

[Now follows the invocation of Amṛtakuṇḍalin, which opens thus:]

For that cheating, there are first 100,000 recitations of a spell that, performed through meditation, is an enemy of obstacles. When it is properly recited, and when one has made 10,000 fire offerings during this recitation, all obstacles are repelled.

These spells remove all māras and obstacles; the yogin who wishes to practice fearlessly in this way will meditate day and night while reciting them. Residing in the abode of Ghanavyūha [a Buddhist paradise], he acts as a buddha again and again through peaceful means. Atop a lotus-moon seat, in a squatting posture and with a mudrā that represents the highest thought of enlightenment, he emanates clusters of white light. While the yogin is meditating in this way on White Vairocana [a buddha who, although a solar deity, originates from the lunar center], it is not deserving that he should die and return to the cycle of birth and death.

Meditating on Akṣobhya [a buddha associated with winter and the sun] and the other tathāgatas, with their colors and mudrās, when the yogin bases himself in their divine pride, his body will truly become indestructible. When the yogin then resides in the union of the sun and moon, there is white Abhaya Lokeśvara, peaceful like the moon and decked out with all possible ornaments, and red-bodied Amitābha, holding all the marks of complete buddhahood, atop [his] two lotus feet in a squatting posture. When this lord of yogins centers his mind on ever more subtle forms of Lokeśvara, the Lord of Death himself will die, and illnesses born for the skandhas [the aggregates from which we construct our illusion of a self] will be destroyed.

Chant this spell of ten syllables with a mind unwearied by other practices: Having established first *Oṃ*, join *tāre* to it immediately; then, *tuttāre ture*; *svāhā* completes it. Brahmā, Śiva, Viṣṇu, the Sun, the Moon, the rudras [a group of spirits who represent storms and wind], dikpālas [the guardians of the directions], and even Kāmadeva [the god of sensual love]—will all conquer death in this way, [even] as the Lord of Death himself had [done], without so much as damaging the tips of one of their hairs. White hair, wrinkles, pernicious conditions, illness, and poverty—all will disappear. The eight great fearful things—such as fear of a lion, and so on—as well as entire aggregates of miseries, will be destroyed. Food and drink, clothing, and so on, will be obtained without the effort of gathering them. Magical powers, such as the enchanted sword, eye medicine, quick-foot salve, the good vessel for all wishes, and others; having a skillful mind; knowing how to speak in verse; immaculate, unique insight; and other desired magical powers as well—all will arise from this circle of magic syllables. This is taught in the *Cakrasaṃvaratantra* [a teaching on Heruka, a form of the buddha Akṣobhya]:

Meditate on the form of Heruka [a form of Akṣobhya who frightens away evil spirits and helps yogins]. Having accomplished this, when one has really become him, meditate on the form of a skull, on a skeleton, or on the form of an ascetic's staff. Since it is wrong to kill a yogin, death will not come to him.

All the parts of a yogin will be satiated by drops of ambrosia dripping, in the form of the moon, at the top of the head, which then appear from all the pores of his body.

Completely avoiding all distractions, the yogin should meditate in this manner for six months; having thereby conquered all illnesses, he will conquer death, even in the form of the Lord of Death.

Likewise, practicing mindfulness meditation on inhalation and exhalation of the breath itself, the yogin should direct his efforts toward other divisions of the respiratory process. Being certain about the increasing number of breaths, the yogin will become ageless and deathless. The breath of sentient beings travels [is breathed in and out] over 21,600 times in the course of a day and night: the number of these breaths should be called aloud. Because the syllable by which we bring the deity into our consciousness is the source of ambrosia, that syllable is repeated each time the wind enters the yogin. And, since ambrosia is the means by which we remain alive, when one is mindful of these breathings [in and out], death will not find a hold in his body.

One should number the breaths that enter the body. According to one method, [when one is] in one-pointed concentration one counts the breaths that enter the body up to 100,000 or another [higher] number, in increments. It is taught that this should be a silent recitation. When one finishes counting [by] using such a method, he will then certainly live another five years, even if his life span has been diminished [for some special reason]. If one repeats that recitation 200,000 times, and so on, the extension of his liftime will then be multiplied. Becoming learned in the means for doing this, the yogin should strive in the recitation of his breaths. [By] enumerating the breaths constantly and correctly 1,000 times in their inner rising, one is freed from all illness and will live as long as the sun and moon remain [in the sky].

Since the yogin enjoys nothing other than adhering to these teachings, he will strive not to sleep for even a moment until he has conquered sleep; then, he will do the same for food, drink, and so on. Because the yogin makes the travels of the wind manifest in his body, the yogin who strives, in an appropriate manner, to attend to its movements will truly conquer death. If he departs from this but once, for some pleasure, because his mind has become obscured, he will die because his means have become inappropriate. The yogin's own body shall become an appropriate means; if the yogin turns away from that means, his methods will not be appropriate [for realizing his goal].

One can obstruct the wind by binding it with the "Gesture of the Lion's Play" [the gesture used by the Buddha to show the fearlessness his teachings instill]. In other words, by conquering death through blocking the wind, the yogin creates "the cheating of death by obstruction." The yogin should fill up his body, in stages, with wind, all the way to the bottom of his feet, and then hold it; this is called "the pot" (*kumbhaka*). When breath-holding is divided into small and middling, and so on, it is to assert that there are three sorts of stoppage of the upper wind. What is called "stopping the upper wind" is explained as follows to make its meaning clear: The small [breath-holding] is thirty-six units in measure; the middling is two times that; the great, three times. Through such holdings, the yogin becomes victorious over death. When the yogin has filled himself with breath from this stoppage, he will then lightly rest his hands on his kneecaps and snap his hand six times, and then begin the practice again.

Further, if the yogin suspends his wind for a long period, and examines its nature constantly during that time, he will render himself victorious over death, māra, and other enemies. All evils being completely pacified, all virtues will then spring up in their place. A yogin who is victorious by such methods will realize his most fervently desired things.

When one does not meditate on meditation or the lack of meditation, śūnyatā is realized. The wise one, not meditating on existents, and not meditating on the absence of existents, completely abandons both. Such meditation is free of meditating. When a yogin meditates continually on "the śūnyatā that completely avoids grasping," he becomes invisible to the Lord of Death. The dying that comes from the merest discursive thought will also not see him; indeed, the many māras and their retinues, and others, will not see him.

As it has been taught, "This discursive perception known as 'dying,' which has no place in any existents, is overcome by the miraculously transformed perception of ordinary beings [that is, through yogic practice]. All the sufferings of discursive perception are explained as 'the māra of perception.' Overcoming mistaken perception by that understanding, the yogin acts in a state of nonperceptivity."

Meditating constantly [on the yogin's personal deity], with special emphasis on reverence based in faith, and so on, the yogin is comfortable in whatever arises [in meditation]—that this and that are becoming clear, and that, for example, desire and misery are manifestations of the mind. Treatises are hard to find wherein these practices are easy to achieve; it is not hard to find these practices, however, in the world of those who know them. Being skilled in such practices, and truly established in [the perfections of] patience and heroism, the yogin who knows how to strive in constructive meditation is a fit vessel for cheating death.

Using butter, the heart of a person who has died in old age, and other items, the yogin uses butter lamps and such for acts of destruction; again, by using materials such as grain and butter offerings, he will abide [in his body] for the duration of a kalpa. The same applies to dying from old age in this body: why shouldn't one live to the end of this kalpa if he has procured these teachings of realization? Old houses, for example, will stand a long time through maintenance, so why shouldn't the bodies of the elderly also endure for a long time through maintenance?

There is nothing difficult to achieve through effort; so, do not shirk in your effort for something that is precious. In time, even slabs of stone are perforated by the gentle, constant fall of water; fire comes from rubbing sticks together; water rises out of the earth when it is ploughed. If someone takes pains, there will certainly be realization. Realized through effort, and correctly, one will have all results he strives for.

Human beings in the mouth of the Lord of Death are like boats in the mouth of a sea monster; if their religious actions are not perfect, they will fall into the waves of his realm. In a like way, any means of cheating death is taught to be an enemy of the Lord of Death. A yogin should cultivate the work of meditation that is realized on the basis of benefiting oneself and others. He should put his effort into means that will free people from the fear of dying without being loved. For this reason, there is nothing more pleasing than life.

When the yogin will have endeavored [to gain understanding] in the texts on these teachings, and will have understood them, the complete deception of the Lord of Death will have been explained, with loving care, for future generations.

GLOSSARY OF FOREIGN TERMS

Except where indicated, all terms are in Sanskrit. Literal translations appear in quotation marks.

abhiṣeka (Chinese *guanding*; Japanese *kanjō*) — "Annointing"; a form of consecration, often involving sprinkling, that transforms an heir apparent into a royal sovereign, or a novice into a monk or member of a religious order. In Tantra, abhiṣeka qualifies a person to initiate or consecrate others.

ācārya — "Teacher, preceptor"; a guru or instructor of sacred or secret teachings.

adhikārin — "One who possesses authority"; a person authorized to undertake a given Tantric practice or give a Tantric teaching.

advaita — "Nondualism"; the philosophical position that all is one.

āgama — In Hindu Tantra, an early corpus of scripture, generally dualist in its metaphysics, revealed by Śiva to the Goddess.

ahiṃsa — "Noninjury"; doctrine of noninjury or nonviolence, common to Jainism, Buddhism, and some forms of Hinduism.

ājñā — Name of the sixth of the seven cakras in most Hindu and Jain mappings of the yogic body. It is at the level of the ājñā that the three principle subtle channels come together in a plait between the eyebrows. *See also* cakra; nāḍī.

amṛta — "Nondeath"; the nectar of immortality that is generated internally through yogic practice. In Hinduism, the sacred fluid in which the feet of a divine image or one's guru have been bathed.

Anuttarayoga Tantra — "Tantra of Supreme Yoga"; one of the four classes of Buddhist Tantric texts, sects, and teachings.

arghya — An offering of a few rice grains, tips of durvā grass, and sanctified water to a deity in Tantric worship.

āsana — "Seated position"; yogic posture in which a practitioner holds himself ịmmobile while practicing breath control and various types of meditation.

ātman — The individual self or soul. See also *brahman*.

avadhūtī — In Tantric Buddhist mapping of the yogic body, the female energy that rises up from the lower abdomen to the heart or cranial vault, where it "melts" or is merged with the subtle male principle. *See also* cāṇḍālī.

bardo (Tibetan) — "Liminal passage, intermediate state"; the state of consciousness in the course of migration between death and rebirth.

bdud (Tibetan) — "Demon"; in gcod yul, psychopathological mental or emotional states.

bhakti — "Partaking"; Hindu devotionalism, in which selfless loving devotion to a personal deity is reciprocated with that deity's grace.

bhāva — "Becoming, being"; in Hinduism, a religious disposition or emotional approach to the divine and to one's practice. *See also* rasa.

bhukti — "Enjoyment"; in Hindu Tantra, pleasure as a goal of one's practice. *See also* mukti.

bhūtaśuddhi — "Purification of the elements"; preliminary ritual process of self-purification in which the practitioner identifies his body with the five elements of the macrocosmic universe, and implodes these into their higher evolutes.

bīja — "Seed"; the seminal essence of a sacred utterance or formula, usually monosyllabic, which constitutes the energy of the deity it acoustically embodies. *See also* mantra *and* shingon.

bodhi — "Enlightenment"; perfect knowledge or wisdom by which a person becomes a buddha (in Buddhism) or a jina (in Jainism).

bodhicitta — "Thought of Enlightenment"; in Buddhism, the mental state in which an individual takes the decision to become an enlightened being. In Buddhist Tantra, the inner energy or fluid that flows through the practitioner's cakras following the internal union of female Wisdom and male Skill in Means. *See also* prajñā, upāya.

bodhisattva — "One Who Possesses the Essence of Enlightenment"; in Buddhism, a deified savior figure, a fully enlightened being who remains in the world in order to release other creatures from suffering existence.

brahmajñāna — "Knowledge of the absolute"; the infinite wisdom sought by the Hindu Tantric practitioner.

brahman — In Hindu metaphysics, absolute Being; the self-existent, eternal, universal soul; the infinite power of beginningless being and becoming. *See also* ātman.

buddha — "Enlightened being"; in Buddhism, a fully enlightened being. In the Mahāyāna and Vajrayāna systems, a number of celestial buddhas spread the Buddhist teachings of the way to enlightenment throughout a multiplicity of universes.

Buddha — "The Enlightened One"; Gautama Buddha, the historical founder of Buddhism, who lived in Nepal and India in the sixth to fifth centuries B.C.E.; the Absolute.

cakra — "Circle, wheel"; one of the usually seven energy centers aligned along the spinal column of the subtle or yogic body; in East Asian Tantric Buddhism, one of the five geometric forms representing the five elements.

cakravartin — "Wheel-turner"; in Buddhist polity, a universal monarch, a patron and protector of Buddhism.

cāṇḍālī — "Female outcaste"; in Buddhist Tantra, the idealized Tantric consort; in Buddhist Tantric mapping of the subtle body, the "red element," female energy that rises up from the lower abdomen to melt the male "white element" in the cranial vault. *See also* avadhūtī.

Caryā Tantra — "Tantra of Observance"; one of the four classes of Buddhist Tantric texts, sects, and teachings.

chi bslu (Tibetan) — "Cheating death, ransoming from death"; term employed for a number of rituals employed to postpone the time of death.

ḍākinī — One of a group of powerful female beings, possessed of the power of flight, who mediate between the worlds of the buddhas, the demonic, and the human in Tantric ritual and meditative practice. In Tantric Buddhism, a woman embodying enlightened wisdom.

ḍamaru — Hourglass-shaped two-headed "shaman's drum" carried and played by Tantric deities and practitioners.

dantian (Chinese) — "Cinnabar field"; in Daoism, one of the three centers of pure energy in the subtle body. Control of these centers enables the practitioner to achieve liberation from the coarse or gross body and become an "Immortal."

darśana — "Seeing"; in Hindu worship practice, the act of viewing a deity through its image (*mūrti*). Eye contact with the eyes of the icon effect a direct experience of the divine.

deva (Tibetan *lha*; Japanese *ten*) — "Shining one"; a celestial deity; one of the high gods of Hinduism, who also figure as "unliberated deities" in Buddhist and Jain pantheons.

dhāraṇī — In Buddhist Tantra, an esoteric formula, magical verse, or charm, employed against demons. *See also* shingon.

dharma — The teachings of the Buddha; the law, doctrine, or ethical precepts of Buddhism; an underlying cosmic principle taught by the Buddha; a constituent element of reality; a phenomenon. The complex of religious and social obligations that a devout Hindu is required to fulfill; right action, duty; morality; virtue.

dharmadhātu — In Buddhism, the absolute reality experienced in enlightenment.

dharmakāya — "Body of teaching"; in Mahāyāna and later forms of Buddhism, the third and most exalted of the three bodies of the Buddha, composed of the Buddha's teachings. Tantric Buddhism knows of a fourth, called the diamond body (*see also* vajrakāya) or the body of essential nature (*svabhāvikakāya*).

dhātu (Tibetan *dbyings*) — In Buddhism, the space or sphere of absolute reality itself.

dhyāna — Ritual visualization, inner vision, yogic meditation; instructions for visualizing a Tantric deity.

dīkṣā — Inititation; the ritual by which a person is rendered fit to undertake a given type of religious practice. *See also* abhiṣeka.

dorje, rdo rje (Tibetan) — *See* vajra.

garbha maṇḍala — "Womb circle"; in Shingon traditions, a meditation support that uses the imagery of womb and fetus to represent both the compassionate soteriological activity of the Buddha that permeates the entire universe and the principle of universal salvation. Like the vajra maṇḍala, this diagram is divided into sections centered on a specific buddha or bodhisattva representing various aspects of the enlightened cosmos.

gcod yul, chö yul (Tibetan) — "The object that is to be cut off"; system of dramatic shamanic practices that effect the severing or cutting off of demons as a means to annihilating the ego that otherwise keeps one trapped in suffering existence.

goma (Japanese) — *See* homa.

guru — A religious preceptor or teacher, often the person from whom one receives initiation or consecration.

gurupāraṃparya — "One guru after another"; a succession or lineage of teachers and disciples. *See also* kula.

haṭha yoga — Body of yogic practice that combines postures, breath control, seals, and locks as a means to bodily immortality and supernatural powers.

himitsu (Japanese) — Secret, esoteric.

homa (Chinese *humo*; Japanese *goma*) — Fire offering, fire invocation; ritual practice that involves offering an oblation of an animal, vegetable, or dairy substance into fire. In East Asian Tantric Buddhism, there are five types of homa rites, practiced for the goals of protection, increase, subjugation, subordination, and acquisition.

honji (Japanese) — Fundamental or universal basis; the universal, which is united with the particular through initiation. *See also* suijaku.

iḍā — In the Hindu mapping of the yogic body, the major subtle channel identified with the moon that runs the length of the spinal column, to the left of the medial channel. *See also* nāḍī.

'ja' lus (Tibetan) — "Rainbow body"; supernatural body attained through Tantric techniques, by means of which the practitioner is able to disappear into another dimension.

jamāt (Urdu) — "Meeting, assembly"; in the Nizārī Isma'ilism of India and Pakistan, the gatherings or meetings in which sacred songs are sung.

japa — "Muttering"; in Hinduism and Jainism, the muttered, chanted, or whispered repetition of prayers, spells, or charms. *See also* mantra.

jiachi (Chinese) — *See* kaji.

jina — "Conquerer"; title or epithet of a Jain tīrthaṅkara.

jīvanmukti — "Bodily liberation"; in Hindu Tantra, the goal of liberation in life, of immortality while still inhabiting one's physical human body.

jñāna (Tibetan *ye shes*) — "Gnosis"; supreme knowledge; the highest form of knowledge, which affords liberation from suffering existence.

jogī (Hindustani) — Member of an antinomian medieval Hindu Tantric order; a Nāth or Nāth Siddha. Although a vernacularization of the Sanskrit *yogin*, the term jogī has this more specialized meaning.

kaji (Japanese; Sanskrit *adhiṣṭhāna*) — In Buddhist Tantra, the empowerment ritual by means of which a practitioner's body is transformed into a buddha-body through his interaction with a buddha.

kalpa (Chinese *yigui*) — Sacred precept, law, ritual, or ordinance; a ritual handbook, compendium of ritual instructions; an eon, a fantastically long period of time.

kāma — In Tantra, desire and sexuality used as a means to liberation or transcendence of the human condition.

kami (Japanese) — A local, indigenous deity of Japan.

kāpālika — "Skull-bearer"; member of a medieval Hindu (and perhaps Buddhist) religious order or movement who carried the skull of a murdered brahman as his begging bowl, in imitation of the Tantric god Bhairava.

kaula, kaulika — Overarching term for a movement or period within early medieval Hindu Tantra, in which erotic ritual practice was highlighted. *See also* kula.

kechimyaku (Japanese) — "Blood line"; chart or genealogical table tracing a Zen Buddhist teacher-disciple lineage, in which master and disciple physically mix their blood together to produce ink for writing the chart.

kekkai (Japanese) — "Binding the realm"; boundary line, railing, or marker surrounding a monastery or shrine to demarcate sacred and profane space; the Japanese Tantric ritual by means of which the borders of a kingdom, a piece of land, or institutional structure are sealed off and protected from interference from outsiders or invasion by demons.

kenmitsu bukkyō (Japanese) — The combined exoteric and esoteric form of Buddhism that dominated medieval Japan.

kirikami (Japanese) — Documents on which secret initiations into the esoteric lore of Zen Buddhism were recorded.

kongō — *See* vajra.

kongō hō kai (Japanese) — "Vajra Jewel Precepts"; the intangible, wordless essence of the buddha wisdom.

Kriyā Tantra — "Action Tantra"; one of the four classes of Buddhist Tantric texts, sects, and teachings.

kula — "Famly, clan"; a Tantric lineage or family, extending back through a series of male and female teachers to a divine pantheon and the supreme god at the heart or summit of the pantheon itself.

kulācāra — "Clan practice"; in Hindu Tantra, the definitive body of ritual practice that differentiates the Tantric clan from other groups and practices.

kuṇḍalinī — "She who is coiled"; in Hindu haṭha yoga and Tantra, the female energy that lies coiled at the base of the yogic body. Through combined yogic techniques, the kuṇḍalinī is "awakened" and made to rise through the cakras to the cranial vault. *See also* śakti.

lama, bla ma (Tibetan) — A Tantric teacher or guru, in Tibetan Buddhism.

liṅga — The male sexual organ; the phallic image by which the Hindu god Śiva is repesented iconographically. *See also* yoni.

lta khrid (Tibetan) — "Instructions on the view"; dGe lugs teachings of the correct understanding of the Mahāyāna concept of emptiness (*śūnyatā*).

mahāmudrā — "Great seal"; gnosis realizing the mind's own emptiness in a nondual, nonconceptual fashion, with the mind "sealed" by emptiness, and emptiness "sealed" by mind. In Mahāyāna and Tantric Buddhism, the ultimate nature of mind; an instantaneous practice for purifying the mind.

mahāsiddha — "Great perfected being"; a highly perfected and accomplished mystic; one of a legendary class of demigods or superhuman Tantric practitioners who propagated Tantra throughout South Asia and Tibet.

maithuna — "Pairing, coupling"; sexual intercourse as a means to liberation, gnosis, and transcendence of the human condition; the fifth and ultimate Tantric "sacrament"; an iconic representation of a pair engaging in sexual intercourse. *See also* makāra; yab-yum.

makāra — "M-word"; one of the five Tantric "sacraments" beginning with the Sanskrit letter *ma-*. The five are *māṃsa* (meat), *matsya* (fish), *mudrā* (parched grain?), *madya* (alcohol), and *maithuna* (sexual intercourse).

maṇḍala (Japanese *mandara*) — "Circle"; an idealized circular model of the cosmos, with the source of cosmic or temporal power located at the center, and deities or beings representing lesser powers or energies radiating outward toward the periphery, the limits of the system. In Tantric practice, maṇḍalas are often employed as visual meditation supports.

mantra — "Mental device, instrument of thought"; an acoustic formula whose sound shape embodies the energy-level of a deity; a spell, incantation or charm employed in Tantric ritual or sorcery. Tantric practitioners use mantras more than any other meditative device to identify with the deity that is the object of their practice. *See also* shingon.

mantraśāstra — "Teaching on mantra"; a manual or compendium on the theory and practice of mantras; the science of mantra and yantra.

mantrasiddha — In Jain Tantra, a master of mantra; one of the legendary superhuman figures who were exemplars in the practice of mantra-based magic.

mārga — "Path"; way of practice. Certain classificatory systems divide Hindu Tantric practice into "left-handed" (*vāma-mārga*) and "right-handed" (*dakṣiṇa-mārga*).

mātṛkā — "Mother, matrix"; one of a class of mother goddesses, closely identified with the yoginīs. In Hindu Tantra, the mātṛkās are the phonemes of the Sanskrit language, acoustic matrices that are the ground for mantric utterances.

māyā — "That which is measured out; cosmic illusion"; in pure nondualist philosophy, māyā is the illusion that impedes human understanding of the unity underlying all apparent multiplicity. In Hindu Śākta Tantra, māyā is the generative, creative power of the Goddess.

mikkyō (Japanese; Chinese *mijiao*) — "Secret teaching"; pure Buddhist esotericism, stripped of the taint of transgressive, heterodox Tantric belief or practice.

mkha' 'gro ma (Tibetan) — "She who flies in space." *See* ḍākinī.

mokṣa — "Release, liberation"; liberation from rebirth into the cycle of suffering existence; the fourth aim of life and the ultimate goal of mainstream Hindus.

mudrā — "Seal"; a symbolic gesture of the body. In ritual practice, a mudrā is an intricate configuration of the fingers of one or both hands; in yogic practice, it is an inner "hydraulic" seal effected through breath control and other techniques. In Hindu Tantra, mudrā is one of the five makāras: in this context, the term is often translated as "parched grain." In Buddhist Tantra, mudrā is one of the terms used for a male practitioner's female consort. The thick hoop earrings of the Nāths are called mudrās. *See also* śāmbhavī-mudrā.

mūlādhāra — "Root support"; in Hindu and Jain yogic body mapping, the lowest of the seven cakras, located at the level of the anus.

mūrti — An image or icon of a deity, executed in wood, stone, paint, or other materials.

nāḍī — One of an elaborate network of 72,000 subtle ducts of the yogic body through which breath and energy are channeled.

nam mkha' sgo 'byed (Tibetan) — "Opening the door of the sky"; in Tibetan Buddhism, ascension to a state of transcendent consciousness, the projection of consciousness up through the fontanelle. This same expression is also found in popular Tibetan religion, where it designates ascent into the celestial sphere by means of a magic rainbow light cord.

nāth (Hindi; Sanskrit *nātha*) — "Master, lord"; member of a medieval Hindu Tantric order founded by Gorakhnāth. *See also* jogī.

nirmāṇakaya — "Form body"; in Mahāyāna and later forms of Buddhism, the first of the three bodies of the Buddha; the physical form in which the historical Buddha appeared to the world.

nirvāṇa — "Extinction"; the soteriological goal of Buddhism; the final cessation of rebirth into suffering existence.

nyāsa — "Laying down, superimposition"; the cosmologization or divinization of the body (or of an object), effected by touching its various parts and depositing corresponding deities or energies into them, usually through the use of bīja-mantras.

pañcamakāra — *See* makāra.

piṅgalā — In Hindu mapping of the yogic body, the major subtle channel identified with the sun that runs the length of the spinal column, to the right of the medial channel. *See also* nāḍī.

pīr (Persian, Hindi-Urdu) — "Venerable old man"; a South Asian Muslim saint, holy man, or wonder-worker, whose tomb (*dargah*) is generally associated with miracles and healing.

pīṭha — "Bench, footstool"; in South Asian Tantra, a pilgrimage site and power place identified with a goddess and her male consort.

prajnā — "Wisdom"; insight into the true nature of reality, a principal goal of Mahāyāna Buddhism; a Tantric practitioner's female consort. In Mahāyāna, Prajnā becomes deified as a Buddhist goddess whose bipolar relationship to male Upāya ("Skill in Means") closely resembles that between Śiva and Śakti in Hinduism. *See also* upāya.

prajñā-pāramitā — "Perfection of wisdom"; the female embodiment of wisdom. In Mahāyāna, Prajñā-pāramitā becomes deified as a Buddhist goddess, also considered to be the "mother of all buddhas."

prāṇa — "Breath"; the breath of life; one of the multiple breaths or energies that, flowing through the nāḍīs, vitalizes and is the active element in the transformation of the yogic body.

pratyekabuddha — A buddha who lives a solitary existence and realizes *nirvāṇa* for himself alone. *See also* buddha.

pūjā — "Honoring, veneration"; the body of practices that comprise the worship of a deity.

qi (Chinese) — In Daoism, the breath-energy residing inside the human body.

rasa — "Juice, flavor"; an essential fluid of yogic, alchemical, or Tantric practice. In the Sahajiyā school of Hindu Tantra, the elevated state of religious rapture in which one experiences the purified emotion of love for the divine.

sādhaka — A Tantric practitioner; a level of initiation among Hindu tāntrikas.

sādhana — Tantric practice.

sādhu (Prakrit *sāhu*) — A South Asian holy man; a level of initiation among Jain monks.

sahaja — "Simultaneously arisen; innate"; the original state of cosmic unity and bliss; a state that transcends the realm of phenomenal reality; the fourth in a succession of Buddhist Tantric initiations involving sexual intercourse. In the Hindu Sahajiyā tradition, sahaja is the state of liberation attained through a body of yogic, ritual, and sexual techniques.

śakti — "Energy"; the energy of a deity personified as his female consort; a name for the Hindu Goddess.

samādhi — Total yogic integration; enstatic consciousness; in the *Yoga Sūtras* of Patañjali, the culminating phase of the meditative process, in which the meditator's consciousness identifies with the object of his meditation.

śamatha (Tibetan *zhi gnas*) — "Tranquil abiding, quiescence"; a Buddhist form of meditation; in Tibetan systems, the minimum level of mental strength at which emptiness may be understood in a transformative way.

samaya — "Coming together [of a transcendent image and an immanent image]"; conventional rule or practice; sacrament; a specific body of Buddhist precepts. In Hindu Tantra, a level of initiation.

śāmbhavī-mudrā — "The seal of Śambhu, Śiva"; in Hindu Tantra, a type of "bifocal" mystical vision involving the simultaneity of outer sensory perception and inner yogic vision.

sambhogakāya — "Body of shared enjoyment"; in Mahāyāna and later forms of Buddhism, the second of the Buddha's three bodies, in which he preaches to the assembled bodhisattvas. This body is seen only by beings who have acquired merits through practice. In Vajrayāna Buddhism, the sambhogakāya is the plane of reality on which the Tantric deities operate.

sampradāya — "Tradition, transmission"; in Hinduism, an established doctrine, belief or usage, or sectarian tradition.

saṃsāra — "Flowing together"; the cycle of transmigration; suffering existence; phenomenal reality.

saṅgha — "Assembly"; Buddhist society, comprised of monks, nuns, laymen and laywomen.

sannyāsi — In classical Hinduism, a renouncer who has laid together (*sannyāsa*) and ritually internalized his sacrificial fires.

sanrinjin (Japanese) — "Three bodies with discs" theory, which divides the Buddha's appearances in the phenomenal world into three types, as an explicit means for incorporating the Indian deities of Hinduism into the Buddhist fold as "propagators of Buddhism," as well as for Buddhicizing indigenous Japanese kami deities

śāstra — Precept, rule, teaching, instruction; any book or treatise; a sacred book or composition of divine authority.

ṣaṭkarmāṇi — "Six acts"; a group of six Tantric rites, of which one (appeasement) is auspicious and five (subjugation, immobilization, enmity, eradication, and liquidation) are destructive forms of "black magic."

shingon — (Japanese; Chinese *zhenyan*). "True words"; general term for spells such as dhāraṇīs, mantras, and bījas; name for the school of Japanese Tantric Buddhism founded by Kūkai.

shugendō (Japanese) — Practice of mountain asceticism in which pilgrimage through designated peaks is visualized as a journey through a maṇḍala.

siddha — "Perfected Being"; a Tantric practitioner who has realized embodied liberation. In Hindu and Buddhist Tantra, the Siddhas are a group of itinerant and idiosyncratic culture heros who founded lineages and traditions of teaching and practice. The Siddhas also form a class of demigods who inhabit the atmospheric regions.

siddhaṃ — The hieratic script of East Asian Tantra; the Indic script used in East Asia for writting Sanskrit, especially dhāraṇīs, mantras, and bījas.

siddhi (Chinese *chengjiu*) — "Perfection"; one of the many supernatural powers possessed by Siddhas as a result of their practice, their sādhana. Included among the siddhis are the power of flight, invisibility, the power of attraction, and the power to realize one's every desire.

sokushin jōbutsu (Japanese) — "Becoming a buddha in this very body"; a fundamental concept of Tantric Buddhism, popularized in Japan by Kūkai.

śrāvaka — "Auditor"; a person who attains emancipation while listening to a buddha; a disciple of the historical Buddha. Mahāyāna Buddhists use this term to designate a follower of the Hīnayāna.

stūpa — A Buddhist funerary monument in the shape of a dome or pyramid, containing a relic of a buddha or some other object of veneration; a meditation support symbolizing the formless body of the Buddha and the essential structure of the cosmos.

suijaku (Japanese) — "Trace"; a particular or concrete appearance, which is united with the universal through initiation. *See also* honji.

śūnyatā — "Emptiness"; in Mahāyāna and later forms of Buddhism, the principle that all objects of the senses, mental concepts, and categories are void of self-existence.

sūrimantra — "Mantra transmitted by a Jain teacher"; a Prakrit-language formula transmitted privately by a senior Jain teacher or sūri of one of the Śvetāmbara image-worshiping sects to a pupil during the ceremony in which the latter is promoted to that same rank.

suṣumṇā — In Hindu mapping of the yogic body, the major subtle channel identified with fire, which runs down through the center of the spinal column. *See also* nāḍī.

tāntrika — A specialist of Hindu Tantra.

tapas — Internal heat generated through yogic practice; religious austerity.

tathāgata — "One who has come thus"; an epithet of the Buddha or of one of the five celestial buddhas.

terma, gter-ma (Tibetan) — "Treasure"; indigenous Tibetan Buddhist collections of works, mainly containing instructions for special forms of Tantric practice, concealed in the eighth- and ninth-century imperial period of Tibetan history for the express purpose of being revealed at the "right time" in the future, and brought to light by Treasure-Discoverer specialists, either in the form of hidden manuscripts or of visionary revelations with no physical substrate.

tīrthaṅkara — "Ford-Maker"; in Jainism, one of the twenty-four saviors of the present world age. Mahāvīra, the founder of Jainism is the last of this series.

torma, gtor ma (Tibetan) — In Tibetan Buddhism, conical flour and butter cones used as ritual offerings to a person's enlightened beings and protectors.

tsha tsha (Tibetan) — A small, usually circular, pressed sacred image made in part from the ashes of the dead, designed to generate merit continuously.

tulku, sprul sku (Tibetan) — "The form body of a Buddha" (*see also* nirmāṇakāya); in Tibetan Buddhism, a recognized reincarnation of a past Buddhist master, such as the Dalai Lama.

upāya (Japanese *hōben*) — "Skill in Means"; array of expedient devices employed by bodhisattvas to enlighten beings trapped in suffering existence. In Mahāyāna Buddhism, Upāya becomes deified as the male member of a bipolar relationship—with the female Prajnā ("Wisdom")—that closely resembles that between Śiva and Śakti in Hinduism.

utpanna-krama — "Completion stage"; the second phase of the Vajrayāna Buddhist path, in which sensory perception and ideation cease, and the practitioner cognizes the ultimate nature of mind itself.

utpatti-krama — "Generation stage"; the first phase of the Vajrayāna Buddhist path, in which the creative power of mind is harnessed, through the use of a maṇḍala, to produce a new divine vision of reality.

vajra (Tibetan *dorje*; Chinese *jingang*; Japanese *kongō*) — "Thunderbolt, diamond, penis"; adamantine symbol of the strength, immovability, and transcendent nature of the state aimed at by Tantric practitioners; name of an implement used in Tantric ritual.

vajra maṇḍala — "Diamond circle"; in Shingon traditions, a meditation support that represents the absolute wisdom attained by the enlightened practitioner. Like the garbha maṇḍala, this diagram is divided into sections centered on a specific buddha or bodhisattva that represents various aspects of the enlightened cosmos.

vajrakāya — "Diamond body"; the fourth and most exalted of the four bodies of the Buddha, in Vajrayāna Buddhism.

vajrayoga — "Adamantine union"; in Vajrayāna Buddhism, the fusion of wisdom realizing emptiness and compassion, which spontaneously manifests appearances in order to guide living beings to freedom from saṃsāra.

vidyā — "Esoteric knowledge, wisdom"; wisdom personified as a goddess in Hindu Tantra; a type of mantra directed to and identified with a goddess; a magical spell. In Buddhist Tantra, vidyā is one of the terms used for a male practitioner's female consort.

vidyārājā (Chinese *ming wang*; Japanese *myōō*) — "King of wisdom"; one of a class of supernatural beings, similar to the Siddhas (and Hindu vidyādharas), who inhabit the atmospheric regions.

vipassana (Pali; Sanskrit *vipaśyanā*; Tibetan *lhag mthong*) — "Penetrative insight"; a classical Buddhist form of meditation. In the Tibetan tradition this most commonly involves the sustained visualization of a golden image of the Buddha.

vīra — "Hero"; in Hindu and Jain Tantra, a male Tantric pracitioner; one of a class of powerful male deities who protect faithful Jains and defeat enemies of the Jain community.

vyūha — "Array"; in Vaiṣṇava theology, one of the four formations taken by the supreme deity Vasudeva to produce the cosmos and its creatures.

xianren (Chinese) — "Immortal being"; goal of Daoist practice, which follows on liberation from the coarse or gross body.

yab-yum (Tibetan) — "Father-mother"; term used in Tibetan Buddhism to describe deities in sexual union.

yakṣiṇī — One of a class of supernatural female beings, often in the form of voluptuous yet dangerous tree-spirits, who are closely related to the yoginīs. Yakṣiṇīs are sought after by Tantric practitioners for the supernatural powers and other boons they grant.

yantra — "Instrument of restraint; machine"; one of a group of instruments, including diagrams (*see also* maṇḍala), amulets, and alchemical apparatus, used by a Tantric practitioner to control or subdue his own mind, demonic beings, or elements of the phenomenal world.

yi-dam (Tibetan; Sanskrit *iṣṭadevatā*) — "Vow, oath, covenant"; in Tibetan Buddhism, a tutelary deity.

Yoga Tantra — "Tantra of yoga"; one of the four classes of Buddhist Tantric texts, sects, and teachings.

yogin — A male practitioner of yoga; a Tantric practitioner.

yoginī — One of a class of powerful, fierce and often sexually alluring female demigods, and the human sorceresses who imitate or are identified with them; a female Tantric practitioner.

yoni — The female sexual organ, womb; the setting or chasing into which the liṅga, the phallic representation of the Hindu god Śiva is inserted.

zhenyan (Chinese) — *See* mantra.

INDEX